S0-BAY-222

# Standard & Poor's 100 Best Growth Stocks

# Standard & Poor's 100 Best Growth Stocks

Standard & Poor's

**McGraw-Hill**

New York   San Francisco   Washington, D.C.   Auckland   Bogotá
Caracas   Lisbon   London   Madrid   Mexico City   Milan
Montreal   New Delhi   San Juan   Singapore
Sydney   Tokyo   Toronto

**FOR STANDARD & POOR'S**
Vice President, Publications, S&P Equity Services: Ron Oliver
Managing Editor: Joseph Spiers
Associate Publisher: Frank LoVaglio

## McGraw-Hill

*A Division of The McGraw·Hill Companies*

Copyright © 1998 by The McGraw-Hill Companies, Inc. All rights
reserved. Printed in the United States of America. Except as permitted
under the United States Copyright Act of 1976, no part of this publication may be reproduced or distributed in any form or by any means, or
stored in a data base or retrieval system, without the prior written permission of the publisher.

1 2 3 4 5 6 7 8 9 0  DOC/DOC  9 0 2 1 0 9 8 7

ISBN 0-07-052555-2

*The sponsoring editor for this book was Susan Barry, the editing supervisor
was Jim Halston, and the production supervisor was Claire B. Stanley. The
front matter was set by Priscilla Beer of McGraw-Hill's Professional Book
Group composition unit.*

*Printed and bound by R. R. Donnelley & Sons Company.*

McGraw-Hill books are available at special quantity discounts to use as
premiums and sales promotions, or for use in corporate training programs. For more information, please write to the Director of Special
Sales, McGraw-Hill, 11 West 19th Street, New York, NY 10011. Or contact your local bookstore.

This publication is designed to provide accurate and authoritative information
in regard to the subject matter covered. It is sold with the understanding that
the publisher is not engaged in rendering legal, accounting or other
professional service. If legal advice or other expert assistance is required, the
services of a competent professional person should be sought.
—*From a declaration of principles jointly adopted by a committee of the
American Bar Association and a committee of publishers*

This book is printed on recycled, acid-free paper containing a
minimum of 50% recycled, de-inked fiber.

# Contents

# ABOUT THE AUTHORS

Standard & Poor's, a division of The McGraw-Hill Companies, Inc., is the nation's leading securities information company. It provides a broad range of financial services, including the respected debt ratings and common stock rankings, advisory services, data guides, and the most closely watched and widely reported gauges of stock market activity—the S&P 500, S&P MidCap 400, S&P SmallCap 600, and the S&P SuperComposite 1500 stock price indexes. S&P products are marketed around the world and used extensively by financial professionals and individual investors.

Mark Arbeter, who authored the Introduction and oversaw the selection of the 100 stocks in the book, is an Investment Officer for Standard & Poor's MarketScope, a real-time market information and investment advisory service for stock brokers. Mark is also S&P's Chief Technical Analyst and a member of S&P's Investment Policy Committee. Mark is well known for his "Stock of the Week," which he has produced for MarketScope since 1991.

# Introduction

When the term "growth stock" is mentioned, two types usually come to mind: large-capitalization stocks that seem to have been around forever and still manage to grow faster than the economy, and small- to medium-capitalization stocks that are in their primary growth stage and setting the world on fire. In this book, we have drawn on both types to put together a well-rounded list of small, medium, and large stocks that would make any growth mutual fund manager proud. The list includes growth stock stalwarts like Microsoft, Intel, Merck, and Cisco Systems, as well as lesser known smaller stocks like Keane, Comverse Technology, and Innovex. These stocks have provided investors with well-above-average returns and they should continue to do so during the rest of the decade.

What we looked for when searching Standard & Poor's vast database of stock information were three defining features: consistent sales and earnings per share (EPS) growth in the past, sustainable sales and EPS growth into the future, and just plain old rapid growth in both EPS and sales. Our list is heavily weighted toward technology stocks since this sector has shown the most rapid growth during the '90s, and Standard & Poor's analysts project it will continue to lead the economy. The list is also well represented by the healthcare industry, another rapidly growing sector, and includes major pharmaceutical companies such as Pfizer and Johnson & Johnson as well as biotechnology issues like Amgen, Biogen, Centocor, and Biotechnology General. The list is also sprinkled with consumer nondurable stocks that have been around forever such as Coca-Cola, Campbell Soup, and Procter & Gamble.

What might be surprising to many investors is broad representation from the financial sector, including companies in the insurance, mortgage, mutual fund, and credit card businesses. This sector has provided investors huge gains during the decade due to consistent financial results that have provided stability in uncertain times. Names here include American International Group, Travelers, Conseco, Federal Home Loan Mortgage, SunAmerica, Franklin Resources, and MBNA Corp.

The greatest stock market winners in history have for the most part been companies whose EPS and sales growth have exceeded 20% a year on average. Hence in picking future winners, we like to see a close correlation between sales and EPS growth, because EPS gains are simply not sustainable over the long term without a concurrent increase in sales. Companies can make their EPS look better on a short-term basis by cutting costs and becoming more efficient, but such tactics cannot be repeated forever. Companies can also cut back on research and development, especially in cases where R&D is usually a large percentage of sales, as with technology and healthcare companies. This can lead to an apparent improvement in EPS, but it is short-sighted and will hurt results down the road. On the other hand, we do not like to see big jumps in sales without a matching gain in EPS. This suggests that the new business mix is not as profitable as the old mix and that results will eventually suffer.

To uncover the truly super growth stocks before they get too big, one must look not only for year-over-year jumps in sales and EPS on a 3- to 5-year horizon, but must also find those stocks that are growing on a sequential (quarter-to-quarter) basis. Such companies are doing very well on their own—but in addition, such growth implies that their industries too are experiencing explosive growth. Many of the larger-cap technology stocks on our list exhibited this feature when they were small- and medium-sized companies. Along with sequential gains in sales and EPS, we also like to see an *acceleration* in growth year-over-year.

Two more defining characteristics of our growth stocks are that they typically play leading roles in their industries, or they dominate niche markets. Some of these stocks were pioneers in their fields, defining whole new industries. Stocks that come to mind include Amgen (biotechnology), Cisco Systems (networking), American Power Conversion (uninterruptible power supplies), and Fair Isaac & Co. (credit-evaluation software). Many have improved on an idea or concept and have gone on to lead their industries. Cases in point: Home Depot, Dell Computer, Microsoft, Oracle, Intel, Watson Pharmaceuticals, Oxford Health Plans, Coca-Cola, and Green Tree Financial. Companies that have found special niches that provide good growth but are too small for big companies to bother with include Vesta Insurance, HCC Insurance, Avery Dennison, Callaway Golf, Viking Office Products, and Mutual Risk Management.

The next important factor in selecting growth stocks is strong industry growth. If an industry is growing rapidly, the leaders in that industry will grow even faster. Conversely, we would not pick a company that is dominating a dying industry. Industries that are prospering currently and should do so in the future include technology, healthcare, telecommunications, specialty retailing, some financial areas, consumer nondurable stocks that have a global presence, consulting companies dealing specifically with technology integration, specialty insurers, and staffing and outsourcing firms.

Profitability measures are also crucial in growth stock selection. Many companies on the list have very high margins both relative to the market as a whole and also relative to their respective industries. Once again, companies that can show expanding margins on both a year-over-year basis and on a sequential basis will tend to outperform. Sometimes the first sign of trouble does not appear on the sales or EPS line but shows up on the margin lines of the income statement. When costs start to get out of hand and rise faster than sales, that always raises a red flag, alerting the astute investor that trouble may lie ahead.

A stock might have great earnings and sales growth, yet scare away investors because of its high price as measured by valuation yardsticks such as the ratio of stock price to EPS (the P/E ratio). In general, a stock with a P/E ratio above, say, 25 is considered pricey. But the biggest and most common mistake investors make when looking at growth stocks, especially those growing over 30%, is to look at the P/E ratio in an absolute sense or versus the market as a whole. The key to valuing growth is to look at a company's P/E ratio relative to its growth rate. A stock growing 100% over a 3-year period should command a way-above-average P/E (which in mid-1997 was 18 for the S&P 500). Just because this stock sells at 30 times EPS does not mean it is overvalued or expensive—on the contrary, this stock is very attractive to our mind. For super growth stocks, P/E ratios are often irrelevant. Some issues on our list have never sold for less than 25 times earnings—investors ignoring such stocks would miss out on great growth opportunities.

Sustainable growth is also key when valuing growth stocks. Many companies show rapid growth in their early stages, but have little chance of keeping their track records intact. One industry that comes to mind is restaurants. A restaurant stock with a hot concept can grow rapidly for a few years, but it isn't sustainable. First, the restaurant industry is not growing rapidly. Second, the hot concept can be easily duplicated by competitors because barriers to entry are low. There really are no proprietary products or services in the restaurant industry with staying power. On the opposite end of the scale is pharmaceuticals, where barriers to entry are high: many proprietary products are protected by patents; scores of talented and highly intelligent personnel turn out new products; and high profitability leads to big R&D budgets. Demographics also make this industry attractive—aging baby boomers are hitting 50.

On the technical analysis side, the most important criterion for growth stock selection is a favorable chart pattern. You can buy the greatest stocks on our list, but if your timing is faulty, you will start out behind the eight ball. There are many favorable chart patterns to look for, but the best is when a stock consolidates (moves sideways in a narrow range) and then breaks out into all-time high territory on heavy volume. Many investors have a terrible misconception that buying stocks near their highs is wrong. To the contrary, this is the most rewarding time to buy because, in technical talk, there is little supply of stock—no one who owns the stock has a loss and might be looking to sell in order to cut losses or break even. Buying the stocks on our list every time they broke out to all-time highs during the '90s would have created a great deal of wealth.

Another important technical tool is relative strength. You will notice that many of the stocks on our list, and many of the industries they are in, have performed well on a relative basis versus the rest of the market. It is imperative that both a stock and its industry are performing well on a relative strength basis. The greatest stock moves come when the whole industry is moving as a group. This is simply due to the fact that money flows follow performance, and when a certain sector of the market is hot, many investors will be chasing it. A stock with a relative strength of 90 means that this issue is performing better than 90% of all other stocks. A baseball analogy is useful here: Do you want a player coming to the plate for your team who is batting .200 or a player who is batting .375. Easy answer. The same rationale can be applied to stocks.

For long-term investors, we believe a well-balanced portfolio of growth stocks can provide above-average returns. The list in this book contains stocks that should appeal to everyone—from aggressive investors looking for smaller rapid-growth companies whose stock prices may be volatile, to more conservative types who prefer proven large-cap companies that won't grow as quickly but will provide a smoother ride. The wisest strategy, however, is to combine both high-risk and low-risk growth stocks in a single portfolio, which—believe it or not—will be no more volatile than the overall market.

To aid your stock picking, we have sorted through our 100 issues in two different ways to zero in on some top candidates (see pages xvii and xviii). The first table shows the stocks with the highest three-year EPS growth rates. For the convenience of investors with well-defined strategies, we have divided the table into the top five performers by market capitalization. As you will notice, all stocks in the table have above-average EPS growth rates and most have very high expected EPS growth rates for 1997 and 1998. The second "sort" adds a valuation component. We compared each stock's P/E ratio, based on expected 1997 EPS, with its 3-year growth rate. The result: 15 stocks selling well below their growth rates, a strong sign that the stocks are undervalued. Both tables provide you with an excellent starting point for making investment decisions.

Following this introduction are detailed descriptions of what S&P believes are the 100 best growth stocks. The descriptions include a number of valuation and ranking measures that provide different perspectives on a stock. Definitions of these measures are presented on pages xv and xvi.

When selecting growth stocks, you may find that candidates cannot always meet all the key criteria outlined above. However, if the majority of criteria are fulfilled, the probability of success is high. The Standard & Poor's Stock Reports in the remainder of this book provide you with the information you need to make those determinations. This information, obviously, is not static. So as you re-evaluate your portfolio in coming months in light of changing conditions, you can obtain current data and analysis on any stock in this book by ordering the latest version of the company's Stock Report. Touch-tone phone users may receive reports by fax or mail, by calling 800-292-0808. A basic two-page Stock Report is $6; quantity discounts are available. Stock Reports are also sold via Standard & Poor's website: http://www.stockinfo.standardpoor.com.

# NOTES

## STARS RANKINGS:

> \*\*\*\*\*Buy—Expected to be among the best performers over the next 12 months.
>
> \*\*\*\*Accumulate—Expected to be an above-average performer.
>
> \*\*\*Hold—Expected to be an average performer.
>
> \*\*Avoid—Likely to be a below-average performer.
>
> \*Sell—Expected to be a well-below-average performer and fall in price.

## QUANTITATIVE EVALUATIONS:

> **Outlook**—Using S&Ps exclusive prorietary quantitative model, stocks are ranked in one of five groups—ranging from Group 5, listing the most undervalued stocks, to Group 1, the most overvalued issues. Group 5 stocks are expected to generally outperform all others. To identify a stock that is in a strengthening or weakening position, a positive (+) or negative (-) Timing Index is placed next to the ranking.
>
> **Fair Value**—The price at which a stock should sell today as calculated by S&P's computers using our quantitative model based on the company's earnings, growth potential, return on equity relative to the S&P 500 and its industry group, price to book ratio history, current yield relative to the S&P 500, and other factors. The current fair price is shown given today's S&P 500 level. Each stock's Fair Value is calculated weekly.
>
> **Risk**—Rates the volatility of the stock's price over the past year.
>
> **Earnings and Dividend Ranking (Quality ranking)**—S&P's appraisal of a stock's growth and stability of earnings and dividends over the past 10 years. The highest letter ranking is A+ and the lowest is C. Stocks of companies with less than 10 years of earnings history and those in industries not included in the ranking system are not ranked (NR). Quality rankings are not intended to predict stock price movements.

**Technical Evaluation**—In researching the past market history of prices and trading volume for each company, S&P's computer models apply special technical methods and formulas to identify and project price trends for the stock. They analyze how the price of the stock is moving and evaluate the interrelationships between the moving averages to ultimately determine buy or sell signals—and to decide whether they're bullish, neutral, or bearish for the stock. The date the signals were initiated is also provided so you can take advantage of a recent or ongoing uptrend in price, or see how a stock has performed over time since our last technical signal was generated.

**Relative Strength Rank**—Shows, on a scale of 1 to 99, how the stock has performed compared with all other companies in S&P's universe of companies on a rolling 13-week basis.

**Insider Activity**—Gives an insight as to insider sentiment by showing whether directors, officers, and key employees—who may have proprietary information not available to the general public—are buying or selling the company's stock during the most recent six months.

# STOCKS WITH HIGHEST THREE–YEAR GROWTH RATES

The issues below were selected from the 100 stocks in our book. They are ranked in order of their annual growth rates in earnings per share from 1993 to 1996. They are also classified by market capitalization to help you pick stocks to meet your portfolio strategy.

| Company (Ticker) | Business | 3-Year EPS Growth Rate (%) | Fiscal Year End | 1996 Actual EPS | 1997 Est. EPS | 1998 Est. EPS | Recent Price | 1997 P/E | Sales $ Mil. |
|---|---|---|---|---|---|---|---|---|---|
| **LARGE–CAP** | | | | | | | | | |
| Ascend Communications (ASND) | Network access products | 331 | Dc | 0.89 | 1.57 | 2.05 | 44.93 | 28.6 | 549 |
| Applied Materials (AMAT) | Reactors to manufacture thin films | 79 | Oc | 3.27 | 2.13 | 3.28 | 63.85 | 30.0 | 4145 |
| Oracle Corp (ORCL) | Database management software | 62 | My | 0.90 | 1.27 | 1.67 | 44.31 | 34.9 | 4223 |
| PeopleSoft Inc (PSFT) | Human resource management software | 59 | Dc | 0.30 | 0.71 | 1.05 | 46.87 | 66.0 | 450 |
| Cisco Systems (CSCO) | Computer network products | 57 | Jl | 1.37 | 2.08 | 2.67 | 62.00 | 29.8 | 4096 |
| **MID–CAP** | | | | | | | | | |
| McAfee Associates (MCAF) | Network, security software | 92 | Dc | 0.73 | 1.50 | 2.24 | 59.06 | 39.4 | 181 |
| Altera Corp (ALTR) | Integrated circuits | 90 | Dc | 1.19 | 1.55 | 2.03 | 49.50 | 31.9 | 497 |
| Oxford Health Plans (OXHP) | Managed care in N.Y. area | 77 | Dc | 1.24 | 1.77 | 2.38 | 63.87 | 36.1 | 3075 |
| Newpark Resources (NR) | Oil & gas environmental services | 76 | Dc | 1.46 | 2.10 | 2.75 | 46.62 | 22.2 | 122 |
| Corrections Corp Amer (CXC) | Prison management services | 66 | Dc | 0.38 | 0.69 | 1.03 | 34.87 | 50.5 | 293 |
| **SMALL–CAP** | | | | | | | | | |
| Technitrol Inc (TNL) | Electronic/mechanical products | 61 | Dc | 1.27 | 1.58 | 1.86 | 22.12 | 14.0 | 274 |
| Robbins & Myers (ROBN) | Electric motors, fans, pumps | 49 | Au | 1.84 | 2.10 | 2.41 | 29.00 | 13.8 | 351 |
| Fair Isaac & Co (FIC) | Credit evaluation systems | 42 | Sp | 1.27 | 1.59 | 1.97 | 36.75 | 23.1 | 149 |
| Respironics Inc (RESP) | Home medical respiratory products | 35 | Je | 0.84 | 0.99 | 1.25 | 19.25 | 19.4 | 126 |
| Vitalink Pharmacy (VTK) | Institutional pharmacies | 24 | My | 0.99 | 1.11 | 1.35 | 18.62 | 16.8 | 141 |

# STOCKS WITH MOST ATTRACTIVE P/E RATIOS

The issues on this page were selected from the 100 stocks in our book. They are sorted by their price/earnings ratio as a percent of their 3-year growth rate in earnings per share. The important point here is that a high P/E ratio should not necessarily turn you away from a stock—a high P/E may be well justified by an even higher growth rate. The lower the P/E ratio relative to growth, the less you are paying for that growth.

| Company (Ticker) | Business | '97 P/E as % of 3 Yr. Growth Rate | 3 Year EPS Growth Rate | 1997 P/E EPS | 1996 Actual EPS | 1997 Est. EPS | 1998 Est. EPS | Recent Price |
|---|---|---|---|---|---|---|---|---|
| **LARGE-CAP** | | | | | | | | |
| Ascend Communications (ASND) | Network access products | 8.7 | 330.63 | 28.6 | 0.89 | 1.57 | 2.05 | 44.93 |
| Sun Microsystems (SUNW) | Networked workstations | 34.5 | 51.32 | 17.7 | 1.21 | 1.80 | 2.16 | 31.87 |
| Applied Materials (AMAT) | Reactors to manufacture thin films | 38.1 | 78.67 | 30.0 | 3.27 | 2.13 | 3.28 | 63.85 |
| HFS Inc (HFS) | Hotel franchiser/services | 40.5 | 54.25 | 22.0 | 1.29 | 2.63 | 3.41 | 57.75 |
| Compaq Computer (CPQ) | Personal computers | 48.3 | 31.58 | 15.3 | 4.72 | 6.13 | 7.26 | 93.50 |
| **MID-CAP** | | | | | | | | |
| Newpark Resources (NR) | Oil & gas environmental services | 29.1 | 76.30 | 22.2 | 1.46 | 2.10 | 2.75 | 46.62 |
| Money Store (MONE) | Consumer & commercial loans | 30.0 | 45.10 | 13.5 | 1.44 | 1.80 | 2.16 | 24.37 |
| Vesta Insurance Group (VTA) | Property & casualty insurance | 30.9 | 43.80 | 13.5 | 2.66 | 3.11 | 3.93 | 42.12 |
| Green Tree Finl (GNT) | Consumer loans for mfrd housing | 30.6 | 35.15 | 10.8 | 2.20 | 3.00 | 3.58 | 32.25 |
| Innovex Inc (INVX) | Thin-film disk drive products | 32.7 | 58.44 | 19.1 | 0.90 | 1.97 | 2.20 | 37.62 |
| **SMALL-CAP** | | | | | | | | |
| Technitrol Inc (TNL) | Electronic/mechanical prod | 23.0 | 60.89 | 14.0 | 1.27 | 1.58 | 1.86 | 22.12 |
| Robbins & Myers (ROBN) | Electric motors, fans, pumps | 28.0 | 49.32 | 13.8 | 1.84 | 2.10 | 2.41 | 29.00 |
| Respironics Inc (RESP) | Home medical respiratory prod | 55.8 | 34.83 | 19.4 | 0.84 | 0.99 | 1.25 | 19.25 |
| Fair Isaac & Co (FIC) | Credit evaluation systems | 55.7 | 41.51 | 23.1 | 1.27 | 1.59 | 1.97 | 36.75 |
| Benchmark Electronics (BHE) | Circuit boards | 66.9 | 18.92 | 12.7 | 1.92 | 2.42 | 2.94 | 30.62 |

# Standard & Poor's
## 100 Best
## Growth
## Stocks

**17-MAY-97**

**Industry:**
Computers (Peripherals)

**Summary:** Adaptec is the leading provider of Small Computer System Interface (SCSI) technology, which manages the input and output of data between a computer and its peripherals.

| S&P Opinion: Buy (★★★★) | Recent Price • 35⅝ | Yield • Nil |
| | 52 Wk Range • 46⅞-17½ | 12-Mo. P/E • 38.3 |

**Quantitative Evaluations**

**Outlook**
(1 Lowest—5 Highest)
• **5**

**Fair Value**
• **48**

**Risk**
• **High**

**Earn./Div. Rank**
• **B**

**Technical Eval.**
• **Bearish** since 1/97

**Rel. Strength Rank**
(1 Lowest—99 Highest)
• **29**

**Insider Activity**
• **Neutral**

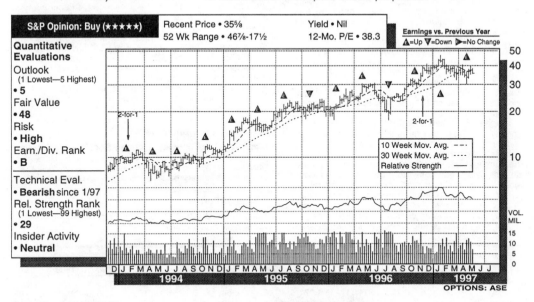

Earnings vs. Previous Year
▲=Up ▼=Down ▶=No Change

10 Week Mov. Avg. – – –
30 Week Mov. Avg. · · · ·
Relative Strength —

2-for-1

2-for-1

1994 1995 1996 1997

VOL. MIL.

OPTIONS: ASE

## Overview - 12-MAY-97

Net sales are projected to advance more than 25% in FY 98 (Mar.), as strong market demand for servers and high-end desktop systems is fueling higher sales of the company's input/output (I/O) products. High performance systems require advanced I/O devices like ADPT's SCSI adapter cards to alleviate performance bottlenecks. In addition, a continuing transition to Microsoft's Windows 95 and Windows NT operating systems, both of which are 32-bit, multi-tasking operating systems, should further boost demand for the company's products. ADPT's acquisition strategy, bolstering its prospects in networking, should also help top-line prospects. Gross margins are likely to remain steady in the 57% to 58% range, while operating costs equal 30% to 31% of sales. We are projecting EPS of $2.20 in FY 98, versus FY 97's $1.72 (excluding one-time charges). The shares were split two for one in late 1996.

## Valuation - 12-MAY-97

This dominant provider of SCSI I/O solutions is well positioned to benefit from secular growth trends in servers and high-performance desktops, which are increasingly utilizing SCSI technology to alleviate performance bottlenecks. ADPT has a strong penetration rate in the server market, which is growing 20% to 30% per year, and, as it offers more desktop solutions, its penetration on the desktop (currently near double digits) should continue to increase as well. Recent acquisitions, and efforts to expand its product line and extend its customer relationships, also add to the company's revenue prospects. As a result, we see strong sales and EPS momentum through FY 98, and expect the shares to outperform the market.

## Key Stock Statistics

| | | | |
|---|---|---|---|
| S&P EPS Est. 1998 | 2.20 | Tang. Bk. Value/Share | 5.11 |
| P/E on S&P Est. 1998 | 16.2 | Beta | 1.70 |
| Dividend Rate/Share | Nil | Shareholders | 700 |
| Shs. outstg. (M) | 111.1 | Market cap. (B) | $ 4.0 |
| Avg. daily vol. (M) | 2.052 | Inst. holdings | 84% |

Value of $10,000 invested 5 years ago: $ 171,140

### Fiscal Year Ending Mar. 31

| | 1998 | 1997 | 1996 | 1995 | 1994 | 1993 |
|---|---|---|---|---|---|---|
| **Revenues (Million $)** | | | | | | |
| 1Q | — | 202.0 | 138.0 | 106.1 | 86.51 | 69.40 |
| 2Q | — | 215.0 | 149.1 | 106.6 | 87.92 | 75.00 |
| 3Q | — | 251.7 | 176.2 | 123.4 | 96.07 | 82.00 |
| 4Q | — | 265.1 | 196.0 | 130.2 | 101.8 | 84.94 |
| Yr. | — | 933.9 | 659.3 | 466.2 | 372.3 | 311.3 |
| **Earnings Per Share ($)** | | | | | | |
| 1Q | — | 0.16 | 0.29 | 0.17 | 0.13 | 0.11 |
| 2Q | — | 0.01 | Nil | 0.17 | 0.11 | 0.12 |
| 3Q | — | 0.36 | 0.28 | 0.26 | 0.15 | 0.13 |
| 4Q | — | 0.40 | 0.38 | 0.28 | 0.16 | 0.13 |
| Yr. | E2.20 | 0.93 | 0.95 | 0.88 | 0.55 | 0.47 |

**Next earnings report expected: mid July**

### Dividend Data

| Amount ($) | Date Decl. | Ex-Div. Date | Stock of Record | Payment Date |
|---|---|---|---|---|
| 2-for-1 | Oct. 17 | Nov. 18 | Nov. 01 | Nov. 15 '96 |

This report is for information purposes and should not be considered a solicitation to buy or sell any security. Neither S&P nor any other party guarantee its accuracy or make warranties regarding results from its usage. Redistribution is prohibited without written permission. Copyright © 1997

*A Division of The McGraw-Hill Companies*

STANDARD
&POOR'S
STOCK REPORTS

# Adaptec, Inc.

## 3016

### 17-MAY-97

## Business Summary - 12-MAY-97

Adaptec is a leading supplier of input/output hardware and software used to eliminate performance bottlenecks between a microcomputer's central processing unit (CPU) and its peripherals, such as storage devices and network file servers. Products, mostly based on Small Computer System Interface (SCSI) technology, include host adapters, proprietary VLSI circuits and software-based development systems.

With the increased power of microprocessors and the emergence of high-performance peripherals, there has been significant growth in multi-user and multi-tasking computing environments and in the development of increasingly sophisticated applications software. These trends have increased the need for substantially greater and faster data transmission, or improved input/output (I/O) performance, between CPUs and peripherals. The company addresses this need through products that significantly enhance and optimize overall microcomputer system performance.

The company has developed a broad array of integrated hardware and software products that support major IBM-compatible microcomputer architectures and interface with leading operating environments. Subsystem products, including SCSI host adapters and related software, support diverse customer requirements. Adaptec has introduced host adapter kits targeted to support specific applications such as multimedia and data backup. SCSI host adapters are sold to major computer manufacturers.

In April 1996, ADPT purchased certain assets and the ongoing business of Western Digital's Connectivity Solutions Group. As part of the agreement, the company will serve as Western Digital's sole source for certain advanced storage control solutions. ADPT made several other acquisitions during 1996, including Sigmax Technologies, Inc., a developer of CD-ROM controllers, for $14 million in cash; Data Kinesis, Inc., a software developer for better system performance in file management and RAID applications, for $32 million in cash and $15 million in stock; and Corel Corp.'s CD creator software program and PD optical recording technology, for $12 million in cash.

## Important Developments

**Mar. '97**—The company acquired Skipstone, Inc., a privately held company, for $7.5 million in cash. The purchase added to Adaptec's technology in FireWire, a complex serial bus protocol used in video applications.

## Capitalization

**Long Term Debt:** $230,850,000, incl. $230,000,000 in conv. sub. notes (03/31/97).

### Per Share Data ($)

| (Year Ended Mar. 31) | 1997 | 1996 | 1995 | 1994 | 1993 | 1992 | 1991 | 1990 | 1989 | 1988 |
|---|---|---|---|---|---|---|---|---|---|---|
| Tangible Bk. Val. | NA | 4.83 | 3.59 | 2.84 | 2.22 | 1.41 | 1.21 | 1.05 | 0.63 | 0.60 |
| Cash Flow | NA | 1.11 | 1.02 | 0.65 | 0.54 | 0.23 | 0.19 | 0.23 | 0.06 | 0.08 |
| Earnings | 0.93 | 0.95 | 0.88 | 0.55 | 0.48 | 0.17 | 0.15 | 0.19 | 0.03 | 0.06 |
| Dividends | Nil | Nil | Nil | Nil | Nil | Nil | Nil | Nil | Nil | Nil |
| Payout Ratio | Nil | Nil | Nil | Nil | Nil | Nil | Nil | Nil | Nil | Nil |
| Cal. Yrs. | 1996 | 1995 | 1994 | 1993 | 1992 | 1991 | 1990 | 1989 | 1988 | 1987 |
| Prices - High | 41⅛ | 24¼ | 12¼ | 10 | 7¾ | 2⁷⁄₁₆ | 3 | 2½ | ¹⁵⁄₁₆ | 2⁵⁄₈ |
|      - Low | 17½ | 10⅞ | 7 | 4⅝ | 2⅛ | 1¹⁄₁₆ | 1⅛ | ⁹⁄₁₆ | ⁹⁄₁₆ | ⁹⁄₁₆ |
| P/E Ratio - High | 44 | 26 | 14 | 18 | 16 | 14 | 20 | 14 | 39 | 42 |
|      - Low | 19 | 12 | 8 | 8 | 4 | 6 | 7 | 3 | 23 | 9 |

### Income Statement Analysis (Million $)

| | 1997 | 1996 | 1995 | 1994 | 1993 | 1992 | 1991 | 1990 | 1989 | 1988 |
|---|---|---|---|---|---|---|---|---|---|---|
| Revs. | NA | 659 | 466 | 372 | 311 | 150 | 129 | 109 | 65.0 | 59.0 |
| Oper. Inc. | NA | 196 | 133 | 88.6 | 69.7 | 21.1 | 17.2 | 19.4 | 2.8 | 5.6 |
| Depr. | NA | 17.6 | 15.7 | 11.4 | 7.0 | 4.7 | 3.8 | 3.0 | 2.1 | 1.2 |
| Int. Exp. | NA | 0.8 | 1.2 | 1.3 | 1.0 | 0.2 | 0.2 | 0.3 | 0.1 | Nil |
| Pretax Inc. | NA | 138 | 125 | 78.6 | 65.9 | 19.5 | 17.1 | 18.1 | 1.6 | 5.6 |
| Eff. Tax Rate | NA | 25% | 25% | 25% | 25% | 25% | 29% | 27% | 11% | 32% |
| Net Inc. | NA | 103 | 93.4 | 59.0 | 49.4 | 14.6 | 12.2 | 13.2 | 1.5 | 3.8 |

### Balance Sheet & Other Fin. Data (Million $)

| | 1997 | 1996 | 1995 | 1994 | 1993 | 1992 | 1991 | 1990 | 1989 | 1988 |
|---|---|---|---|---|---|---|---|---|---|---|
| Cash | NA | 295 | 247 | 183 | 147 | 66.8 | 59.8 | 51.5 | 13.7 | 18.7 |
| Curr. Assets | NA | 465 | 350 | 293 | 235 | 123 | 96.0 | 90.0 | 41.0 | 36.0 |
| Total Assets | NA | 646 | 436 | 358 | 283 | 139 | 109 | 98.0 | 48.0 | 41.0 |
| Curr. Liab. | NA | 130 | 56.4 | 38.5 | 35.7 | 17.2 | 10.2 | 14.2 | 7.6 | 4.6 |
| LT Debt | NA | 4.3 | 7.7 | 11.1 | 14.5 | 0.4 | 1.0 | 1.5 | 2.0 | Nil |
| Common Eqty. | NA | 512 | 372 | 298 | 225 | 116 | 95.0 | 82.0 | 38.0 | 36.0 |
| Total Cap. | NA | 516 | 379 | 309 | 247 | 121 | 99 | 84.0 | 40.0 | 37.0 |
| Cap. Exp. | NA | 39.7 | 31.6 | 17.3 | 36.8 | 5.9 | 7.1 | 4.0 | 4.2 | 3.0 |
| Cash Flow | NA | 121 | 109 | 70.4 | 56.4 | 19.4 | 16.0 | 16.2 | 3.5 | 5.0 |
| Curr. Ratio | NA | 3.6 | 6.2 | 7.6 | 6.6 | 7.2 | 9.4 | 6.3 | 5.4 | 7.9 |
| % LT Debt of Cap. | NA | 0.8 | 2.0 | 3.6 | 5.8 | 0.3 | 1.0 | 1.8 | 4.9 | Nil |
| % Net Inc.of Revs. | NA | 15.6 | 20.0 | 15.8 | 15.9 | 9.7 | 9.5 | 12.0 | 2.2 | 6.4 |
| % Ret. on Assets | NA | 19.4 | 23.5 | 18.1 | 21.8 | 11.5 | 11.8 | 16.5 | 3.3 | 9.5 |
| % Ret. on Equity | NA | 23.3 | 27.9 | 22.3 | 26.8 | 13.5 | 13.8 | 20.2 | 3.9 | 11.2 |

Data as orig. reptd.; bef. results of disc. opers. and/or spec. items. Per share data adj. for stk. divs. as of ex-div. date. E-Estimated. NA-Not Available. NM-Not Meaningful. NR-Not Ranked.

**Office**—691 S. Milpitas Blvd., Milpitas, CA 95035. **Tel**—(408) 945-8600. **Website**—http://www.adaptec.com **Chrmn**—J. G. Adler. **Pres & CEO**—F. G. Saviers. **VP-Fin, CFO & Investor Contact**—Paul G. Hansen. **Secy**—H. P. Massey Jr. **Dirs**—J. G. Adler, L. B. Boucher, J. East, R. J. Loarie, B. J. Moore, W. F. Sanders, F. G. Saviers, P. E. White. **Transfer Agent**—Chase Trust Co. of California, SF. **Incorporated**—in California in 1981. **Empl**— 1,800. **S&P Analyst:** Megan Graham Hackett

# Altera Corp.

## 3071S

Nasdaq Symbol **ALTR**

In S&P MidCap 400

**17-MAY-97**

**Industry:** Electronics (Semiconductors)

**Summary:** Altera is a leader in high-performance, high-density programmable logic devices (HPLDs) and associated computer-aided engineering logic development tools.

| S&P Opinion: Hold (★★★) | Recent Price • 50¼ | Yield • Nil |
| --- | --- | --- |
| | 52 Wk Range • 54⅜-13⅛ | 12-Mo. P/E • 41.2 |

### Quantitative Evaluations

**Outlook**
(1 Lowest—5 Highest)
• **2**

**Fair Value**
• **49¼**

**Risk**
• **High**

**Earn./Div. Rank**
• **B**

**Technical Eval.**
• **Bullish** since 9/96

**Rel. Strength Rank**
(1 Lowest—99 Highest)
• **80**

**Insider Activity**
• **Unfavorable**

**Earnings vs. Previous Year**
▲=Up ▼=Down ▶=No Change

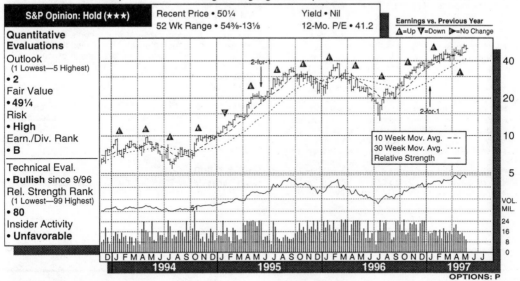

10 Week Mov. Avg. - - - -
30 Week Mov. Avg. ·······
Relative Strength ——

OPTIONS: P

## Overview - 15-APR-97

Due to better than expected first quarter results and favorable business conditions, we have raised our 1997 revenues and EPS projections for Altera. The company has indicated that booking patterns are so strong that it is turning away orders from customers to guard against another build-up of excess inventories which hurt results in the second half of 1996. Revenues should gain about 30% in 1997, as significant design wins in recent years will translate into higher sales. Demand for the company's complex programmable logic devices (CPLDs) will be especially brisk for communication and computer applications. Despite late 1996 price cuts in the Flex 10K, Flex 8000 and Max 9000 families of CPLDs, the company has achieved its targeted goal of 62% gross margins, which we feel it will be able to maintain for the remainder of the year. The higher volume should allow ALTR to leverage operating and interest expenses, which will lift operating margins. We are projecting EPS (primary) of $1.65 for 1997. The shares were split two for one in January 1997.

## Valuation - 15-APR-97

Despite our second 1997 EPS estimate increase in as many quarters, we are maintaining our hold recommendation on the shares. We think that the stock is fairly valued at the current level of 28X our 1997 EPS estimate, and expect significant near-term gains to be difficult, in light of the sharp rally in the shares since July 1996. However, ALTR remains a good long-term holding for aggressive investors. The market for CPLDs, although cyclical, is expected to grow rapidly through the end of the decade. ALTR should be able to maintain its position as an industry leader for these rapidly growing devices. Geographic and end market diversity may lessen the negative impact of any future downturn in a specific region or user application.

## Key Stock Statistics

| | | | |
| --- | --- | --- | --- |
| S&P EPS Est. 1997 | 1.65 | Tang. Bk. Value/Share | 4.13 |
| P/E on S&P Est. 1997 | 30.5 | Beta | 2.45 |
| Dividend Rate/Share | Nil | Shareholders | 20,000 |
| Shs. outstg. (M) | 87.6 | Market cap. (B) | $ 4.4 |
| Avg. daily vol. (M) | 2.503 | Inst. holdings | 79% |

Value of $10,000 invested 5 years ago: $ 74,867

### Fiscal Year Ending Dec. 31

| | 1997 | 1996 | 1995 | 1994 | 1993 | 1992 |
| --- | --- | --- | --- | --- | --- | --- |
| **Revenues (Million $)** | | | | | | |
| 1Q | 142.4 | 137.1 | 75.04 | 43.51 | 29.10 | 29.80 |
| 2Q | — | 116.3 | 92.16 | 47.06 | 33.07 | 23.00 |
| 3Q | — | 116.7 | 109.1 | 49.05 | 37.07 | 22.60 |
| 4Q | — | 127.2 | 125.3 | 59.17 | 41.08 | 26.00 |
| Yr. | — | 497.3 | 401.6 | 198.8 | 140.3 | 101.5 |
| **Earnings Per Share ($)** | | | | | | |
| 1Q | 0.37 | 0.34 | 0.17 | 0.09 | 0.04 | 0.06 |
| 2Q | E0.40 | 0.26 | 0.22 | 0.10 | 0.06 | 0.04 |
| 3Q | E0.43 | 0.26 | 0.26 | 0.10 | 0.08 | 0.02 |
| 4Q | E0.45 | 0.32 | 0.31 | -0.11 | 0.08 | 0.03 |
| Yr. | E1.65 | 1.19 | 0.96 | 0.17 | 0.25 | 0.14 |

**Next earnings report expected: mid July**

### Dividend Data

| Amount ($) | Date Decl. | Ex-Div. Date | Stock of Record | Payment Date |
| --- | --- | --- | --- | --- |
| 2-for-1 | Dec. 04 | Jan. 07 | Dec. 18 | Jan. 06 '97 |

This report is for information purposes and should not be considered a solicitation to buy or sell any security. Neither S&P nor any other party guarantee its accuracy or make warranties regarding results from its usage. Redistribution is prohibited without written permission. Copyright © 1997 | A Division of The McGraw-Hill Companies

## Business Summary - 15-APR-97

Altera (ALTR) is a world leader in one of the semiconductor industry's fastest growing segments: high density programmable logic devices (PLDs) and associated software for logic development. This growth is being driven by competitive advantages provided by Altera's products to electronic system manufacturers, including improved performance and lower production costs, and the ability to get end-products to market faster.

The company's PLDs are standard products, that is, they are shipped blank for programming by the user. They are programmed at the customer's PC or workstation through the use of ALTR's proprietary software. Since ALTR's chips are programmed at a desktop, and not at a foundry, a product's time to market is dramatically shortened. In addition, since ALTR's integrated circuits are standard products, inventory risks for both the company and its customers are minimized.

ALTR seeks to induce system designers to incorporate its PLDs into the early stage of their design cycles. Such "design wins" can lead to use of the company's PLDs in prototyping and, ultimately, in volume production of the customer's products, potentially for the life cycle of the product. In addition, system designers who have become familiar with the company's PLDs may be more inclined to use them in future designs, potentially resulting in additional sales for the company. As part of its strategy to achieve design wins, ALTR offers its development software systems at relatively modest prices.

ALTR is a "fabless" semiconductor company. It does not operate its own production facilities, but obtains its silicon chips through supply arrangements with leading semiconductor manufacturers. This allows the company to concentrate its resources on the design process and avoids the capital commitment and overhead burden associated with owning a fabrication facility.

Primary applications for the company's PLDs include communications, computer, and industrial, which accounted for 58%, 19% and 14% of 1996 revenues, respectively. International sales are significant, accounting for 49% of the 1996 total. ALTR has the second highest market share for PLDs, trailing only Silicon Valley arch-rival Xilinx, Inc.

### Capitalization

**Long Term Debt:** $230,000,000 of sub. debs. due 2002, conv. into com. at $51.17 a sh. (3/97).

### Per Share Data ($)

| (Year Ended Dec. 31) | 1996 | 1995 | 1994 | 1993 | 1992 | 1991 | 1990 | 1989 | 1988 | 1987 |
|---|---|---|---|---|---|---|---|---|---|---|
| Tangible Bk. Val. | 4.13 | 2.80 | 1.84 | 1.49 | 1.19 | 1.03 | 0.79 | 0.62 | 0.47 | 0.32 |
| Cash Flow | 1.42 | 1.08 | 0.25 | 0.35 | 0.23 | 0.29 | 0.22 | 0.18 | 0.13 | 0.04 |
| Earnings | 1.19 | 0.96 | 0.17 | 0.25 | 0.14 | 0.22 | 0.17 | 0.14 | 0.09 | 0.02 |
| Dividends | Nil | Nil | Nil | Nil | Nil | Nil | Nil | Nil | Nil | Nil |
| Payout Ratio | Nil | Nil | Nil | Nil | Nil | Nil | Nil | Nil | Nil | Nil |
| Prices - High | 40 | 35½ | 10¾ | 8⅜ | 9 | 7⅛ | 3¾ | 2⅜ | 1¹³/₁₆ | NA |
|    - Low | 13⅛ | 9⅞ | 5⅜ | 3 | 2¹/₁₆ | 2⁵/₁₆ | 1¹¹/₁₆ | 1³/₁₆ | 1 | NA |
| P/E Ratio - High | 34 | 37 | 63 | 33 | 64 | 33 | 22 | 17 | 19 | NA |
|    - Low | 11 | 10 | 32 | 12 | 15 | 10 | 10 | 9 | 10 | NA |

### Income Statement Analysis (Million $)

| | 1996 | 1995 | 1994 | 1993 | 1992 | 1991 | 1990 | 1989 | 1988 | 1987 |
|---|---|---|---|---|---|---|---|---|---|---|
| Revs. | 497 | 402 | 199 | 140 | 101 | 107 | 78.0 | 59.0 | 38.0 | 21.0 |
| Oper. Inc. | 189 | 146 | 60.1 | 39.7 | 23.9 | 32.0 | 23.6 | 16.9 | 9.3 | 3.3 |
| Depr. | 20.9 | 9.3 | 7.0 | 7.8 | 7.3 | 5.8 | 4.6 | 3.4 | 2.5 | 1.4 |
| Int. Exp. | 12.3 | 7.4 | Nil | Nil | Nil | Nil | Nil | 0.0 | 0.2 | 0.5 |
| Pretax Inc. | 169 | 138 | 31.5 | 31.4 | 18.0 | 27.8 | 20.7 | 15.4 | 8.2 | 2.2 |
| Eff. Tax Rate | 36% | 37% | 54% | 33% | 36% | 36% | 35% | 30% | 14% | 44% |
| Net Inc. | 109 | 86.9 | 14.6 | 21.2 | 11.5 | 17.8 | 13.4 | 10.8 | 7.1 | 1.2 |

### Balance Sheet & Other Fin. Data (Million $)

| | 1996 | 1995 | 1994 | 1993 | 1992 | 1991 | 1990 | 1989 | 1988 | 1987 |
|---|---|---|---|---|---|---|---|---|---|---|
| Cash | 281 | 365 | 92.6 | 81.6 | 50.6 | 40.1 | 23.3 | 26.0 | 21.9 | 8.7 |
| Curr. Assets | 473 | 518 | 177 | 129 | 85.6 | 72.2 | 51.9 | 45.8 | 35.5 | 14.6 |
| Total Assets | 778 | 716 | 214 | 156 | 115 | 102 | 75.0 | 56.0 | 43.0 | 22.0 |
| Curr. Liab. | 178 | 172 | 559 | 34.1 | 19.1 | 20.8 | 13.9 | 8.8 | 7.8 | 6.1 |
| LT Debt | 230 | 289 | Nil | Nil | Nil | Nil | Nil | Nil | Nil | 2.4 |
| Common Eqty. | 370 | 255 | 158 | 122 | 95.6 | 81.5 | 61.0 | 46.6 | 35.3 | 13.5 |
| Total Cap. | 600 | 544 | 158 | 122 | 95.6 | 81.5 | 61.0 | 46.6 | 35.3 | 15.8 |
| Cap. Exp. | 45.2 | 46.0 | 10.5 | 5.5 | 6.0 | 7.8 | 8.1 | 5.6 | 5.2 | 1.7 |
| Cash Flow | 130 | 99 | 21.6 | 29.0 | 18.9 | 23.6 | 18.0 | 14.2 | 9.5 | 2.6 |
| Curr. Ratio | 2.7 | 3.0 | 3.2 | 3.8 | 4.5 | 3.5 | 3.7 | 5.2 | 4.6 | 2.4 |
| % LT Debt of Cap. | 38.3 | 53.2 | Nil | Nil | Nil | Nil | Nil | Nil | Nil | 14.9 |
| % Net Inc.of Revs. | 21.9 | 21.7 | 7.3 | 15.1 | 11.4 | 16.7 | 17.1 | 18.3 | 18.7 | 5.8 |
| % Ret. on Assets | 14.6 | 18.7 | 7.7 | 15.6 | 10.6 | 19.9 | 20.3 | 21.2 | 21.8 | 6.1 |
| % Ret. on Equity | 34.9 | 42.1 | 10.2 | 19.4 | 12.9 | 24.8 | 24.6 | 27.2 | 29.0 | 9.6 |

Data as orig. reptd.; bef. results of disc. opers. and/or spec. items. Per share data adj. for stk. divs. as of ex-div. date. E-Estimated. NA-Not Available. NM-Not Meaningful. NR-Not Ranked.

**Office**—2610 Orchard Pkwy., San Jose, CA 95134-2020. **Tel**—(408) 894-7000. **Chrmn, Pres & CEO**—R. Smith. **VP-Fin & CFO**—N. Sarkisian. **VP & Investor Contact**—Thomas J. Nicoletti. **Secy**—C. W. Bergere. **Dirs**—M. A. Ellison, P. Newhagen, R. W. Reed, R. Smith, W. Terry. **Transfer Agent & Registrar**—Boston EquiServe L.P. **Incorporated**—in California in 1984. **Empl**— 918. **S&P Analyst:** Stephen T. Madonna, CFA

# American Int'l Group    130

NYSE Symbol **AIG**

In S&P 500

**19-MAY-97**

**Industry:** Insurance (Multi-Line)

**Summary:** One of the world's leading insurance organizations, AIG provides property, casualty and life insurance, and other financial services, in over 100 countries.

| S&P Opinion: Accumulate (★★★★) | Recent Price • 130⅜ | Yield • 0.3% |
| --- | --- | --- |
| | 52 Wk Range • 136⅞-90⅛ | 12-Mo. P/E • 20.4 |

**Earnings vs. Previous Year**
▲=Up ▼=Down ▷=No Change

**Quantitative Evaluations**

**Outlook**
(1 Lowest—5 Highest)
• **2**

**Fair Value**
• **120**

**Risk**
• **Low**

**Earn./Div. Rank**
• **A+**

**Technical Eval.**
• **Bullish** since 5/97

**Rel. Strength Rank**
(1 Lowest—99 Highest)
• **74**

**Insider Activity**
• **Favorable**

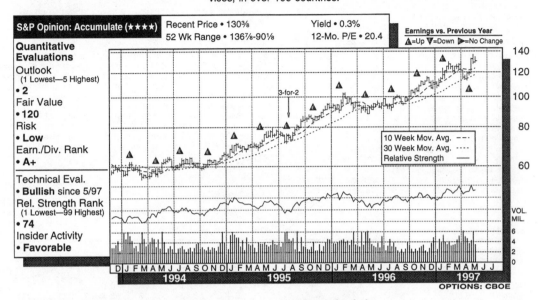

- 10 Week Mov. Avg. —·—
- 30 Week Mov. Avg. ----
- Relative Strength ——

OPTIONS: CBOE

## Overview - 17-MAY-97

Property-casualty written premiums will likely rise 7%-10% in 1997 as the effect of a strong U.S. dollar masks otherwise double digit premium growth. U.S. market conditions remain competitive, but AIG's expansion into selected personal lines, middle market commercial lines, and specialty coverages should limit the downside from weak commercial lines pricing. Overseas, the London insurance market is also competitive, but growth opportunities in various emerging markets where AIG is well positioned (like Latin America and Southeast Asia) will more than offset this. Assuming a "normal" level of catastrophe losses, underwriting results should remain profitable, thanks in part to stringent cost controls. Earnings growth will also be aided by continued profit contributions from life insurance and financial services operations. Stock repurchases (including the 5.4 million shares reacquired in 1996 for a total cost of $492.5 million) will aid per share results.

## Valuation - 19-MAY-97

The shares have generally trended upward since 1994, thanks to a favorable interest rate environment for financial stocks. Despite renewed concerns over higher interest rates and extremely competitive conditions in the U.S. property-casualty market, investors have continued to bid up the shares, choosing instead to focus on AIG's solid long term underwriting and earnings growth track record and dominant market position. As a result of their recent strength, we lowered our opinion on the shares to accumulate from strong buy. We view any near term pullback from current share price levels as an opportunity to add to positions.

## Key Stock Statistics

| | | | |
| --- | --- | --- | --- |
| S&P EPS Est. 1997 | 6.70 | Tang. Bk. Value/Share | 46.96 |
| P/E on S&P Est. 1997 | 19.5 | Beta | 1.09 |
| S&P EPS Est. 1998 | 7.70 | Shareholders | 18,000 |
| Dividend Rate/Share | 0.40 | Market cap. (B) | $ 61.2 |
| Shs. outstg. (M) | 469.4 | Inst. holdings | 50% |
| Avg. daily vol. (M) | 0.863 | | |

Value of $10,000 invested 5 years ago: $ 30,475

### Fiscal Year Ending Dec. 31

| | 1997 | 1996 | 1995 | 1994 | 1993 | 1992 |
| --- | --- | --- | --- | --- | --- | --- |
| **Revenues (Million $)** | | | | | | |
| 1Q | — | 6,645 | 6,007 | 5,226 | 4,311 | 4,363 |
| 2Q | — | 6,956 | 6,458 | 5,626 | 5,339 | 4,530 |
| 3Q | — | 7,182 | 6,547 | 5,675 | 5,120 | 4,636 |
| 4Q | — | 7,422 | 6,863 | 5,915 | 5,360 | 4,859 |
| Yr. | — | 28,205 | 25,875 | 22,442 | 20,130 | 18,389 |
| **Earnings Per Share ($)** | | | | | | |
| 1Q | 1.66 | 1.42 | 1.21 | 1.06 | 0.99 | 0.85 |
| 2Q | — | 1.53 | 1.34 | 1.16 | 1.01 | 0.88 |
| 3Q | — | 1.56 | 1.33 | 1.14 | 0.95 | 0.71 |
| 4Q | — | 1.64 | 1.43 | 1.22 | 1.07 | 0.96 |
| Yr. | E6.70 | 6.15 | 5.30 | 4.58 | 4.03 | 3.40 |

**Next earnings report expected: late July**

**Dividend Data** (Dividends have been paid since 1969.)

| Amount ($) | Date Decl. | Ex-Div. Date | Stock of Record | Payment Date |
| --- | --- | --- | --- | --- |
| 0.100 | May. 20 | Sep. 04 | Sep. 06 | Sep. 20 '96 |
| 0.100 | Sep. 16 | Dec. 04 | Dec. 06 | Dec. 20 '96 |
| 0.100 | Nov. 11 | Mar. 05 | Mar. 07 | Mar. 21 '97 |
| 0.100 | Mar. 17 | Jun. 04 | Jun. 06 | Jun. 20 '97 |

This report is for information purposes and should not be considered a solicitation to buy or sell any security. Neither S&P nor any other party guarantee its accuracy or make warranties regarding results from its usage. Redistribution is prohibited without written permission. Copyright © 1997

*A Division of The McGraw-Hill Companies*

STANDARD
&POOR'S
STOCK REPORTS

# American International Group, Inc.

**130**

**19-MAY-97**

## Business Summary - 19-MAY-97

AIG is a holding company whose subsidiaries engage in property, casualty, marine and life insurance underwriting throughout the U.S. and in approximately 129 other countries. It also offers various financial services, including airline leasing and currency trading. Contributions to revenues in recent years were:

|  | 1996 | 1995 | 1994 |
|---|---|---|---|
| General insurance | 48% | 50% | 53% |
| Life insurance | 42% | 40% | 38% |
| Agency operations | 1% | 1% | 1% |
| Financial services | 9% | 9% | 8% |

International operations accounted for 53% of revenues and pretax profits in 1996.

General insurance written premiums totaling $12.7 billion in 1996 were derived: commercial casualty 50%, international 34%, personal lines 6%, commercial property 4%, pools and associations 3%, and mortgage guaranty 2%. AIG's general insurance operations are multiline property-casualty companies. The Domestic General-Brokerage division deals principally with insurance brokers representing major industrial and commercial clients. The Agency division provides coverage to small and medium-size businesses and writes selected personal lines. Financial service operations include interest rate and currency swaps, cash management, pre-

mium financing, airline leasing and private banking. AIG also owns 48% of Transatlantic Holdings, Inc., a reinsurer.

Life insurance subsidiaries offer individual and group life, annuity and accident and health policies. Foreign operations accounted for 92% of the segment's operating income in 1996.

## Important Developments

**Apr. '97**—AIG's premium and earnings growth in 1997's first quarter continued to be masked by the effects of a strong U.S. dollar. Property-casualty written premiums rose 6.0%, year to year (8.1% before the impact of a strengthening U.S. dollar). Underwriting results remained profitable, evidenced by a combined loss and expense ratio of 96.25%, versus 96.79%. Life insurance premiums rose 12.7%, year to year (16.3% before currency exchange), and operating income rose more than 22%. Financial services operating profits rose more than 23%. Aggregate operating earnings rose 16%, to $1.60 a share in the 1997 period, from $1.38 in the 1996 interim.

## Capitalization

**Total Debt:** $23,520,514,000, incl. $5.7 billion of GIC obligations (12/96).

**Minority Interest:** $400,000,000.

### Per Share Data ($)

| (Year Ended Dec. 31) | 1996 | 1995 | 1994 | 1993 | 1992 | 1991 | 1990 | 1989 | 1988 | 1987 |
|---|---|---|---|---|---|---|---|---|---|---|
| Tangible Bk. Val. | 46.96 | 41.81 | 34.66 | 31.95 | 26.53 | 23.41 | 20.15 | 17.65 | 13.91 | 11.93 |
| Oper. Earnings | 6.03 | 5.20 | 4.46 | 3.88 | 3.27 | 3.11 | 2.95 | 2.79 | 2.54 | 2.04 |
| Earnings | 6.15 | 5.30 | 4.58 | 4.03 | 3.40 | 3.23 | 3.07 | 2.95 | 2.63 | 2.25 |
| Dividends | 0.37 | 0.33 | 0.29 | 0.26 | 0.23 | 0.21 | 0.18 | 0.16 | 0.12 | 0.09 |
| Relative Payout | 6% | 6% | 6% | 6% | 7% | 6% | 6% | 5% | 5% | 4% |
| Prices - High | 116⅜ | 95½ | 67⅛ | 66⅞ | 54 | 45⅜ | 37⅝ | 39⅞ | 24½ | 29¾ |
|    - Low | 88⅛ | 64⅛ | 54½ | 49 | 36½ | 32 | 25⅜ | 23½ | 17⅜ | 19 |
| P/E Ratio - High | 19 | 18 | 15 | 17 | 16 | 14 | 12 | 14 | 10 | 15 |
|    - Low | 14 | 12 | 12 | 12 | 11 | 10 | 8 | 8 | 7 | 9 |

### Income Statement Analysis (Million $)

| | 1996 | 1995 | 1994 | 1993 | 1992 | 1991 | 1990 | 1989 | 1988 | 1987 |
|---|---|---|---|---|---|---|---|---|---|---|
| Life Ins. In Force | 421,983 | 376,097 | 333,379 | 257,162 | 210,606 | 193,226 | 160,373 | 131,983 | 118,431 | 108,445 |
| Prem. Inc.: Life A & H | 8,978 | 8,038 | 6,724 | 5,746 | 4,853 | 4,059 | 3,478 | 2,995 | 3,459 | 2,772 |
| Prem. Inc.: Cas./Prop. | 11,855 | 11,406 | 10,287 | 9,567 | 9,209 | 9,104 | 9,149 | 8,529 | 4,933 | 4,423 |
| Net Invest. Inc. | 4,365 | 3,811 | 3,184 | 2,840 | 2,566 | 2,303 | 2,037 | 1,760 | 1,435 | 1,159 |
| Oth. Revs. | 591 | 2,620 | 2,247 | 1,982 | 1,761 | 1,418 | 1,038 | 866 | 3,786 | 2,924 |
| Total Revs. | 25,877 | 25,875 | 22,442 | 20,135 | 18,389 | 16,884 | 15,702 | 14,150 | 13,613 | 11,278 |
| Pretax Inc. | 4,013 | 3,466 | 2,952 | 2,601 | 2,137 | 2,023 | 1,812 | 1,706 | 1,398 | 1,098 |
| Net Oper. Inc. | NA | 2,463 | 2,119 | 1,848 | 1,561 | 1,492 | 1,372 | 1,284 | 1,175 | 945 |
| Net Inc. | 2,897 | 2,510 | 2,176 | 1,918 | 1,625 | 1,553 | 1,442 | 1,367 | 1,217 | 1,042 |

### Balance Sheet & Other Fin. Data (Million $)

| | 1996 | 1995 | 1994 | 1993 | 1992 | 1991 | 1990 | 1989 | 1988 | 1987 |
|---|---|---|---|---|---|---|---|---|---|---|
| Cash & Equiv. | 3,265 | 3,574 | 3,402 | 6,039 | 5,568 | 7,880 | 7,262 | 5,008 | 4,687 | 3,167 |
| Premiums Due | 9,617 | 9,410 | 8,802 | 8,364 | 9,010 | 9,027 | 8,793 | 7,734 | 6,219 | 5,387 |
| Invest. Assets: Bonds | 48,625 | 42,901 | 35,431 | 30,067 | 23,613 | 23,613 | 20,639 | 18,049 | 15,900 | 12,692 |
| Invest. Assets: Stocks | 6,006 | 5,369 | 5,099 | 4,488 | 2,705 | 2,291 | 1,987 | 2,230 | 1,627 | 1,281 |
| Invest. Assets: Loans | 7,877 | 7,861 | 5,353 | 3,577 | 3,080 | 2,999 | 2,629 | 1,612 | 1,230 | 895 |
| Invest. Assets: Total | 104 | 91,627 | 73,388 | 60,947 | 56,977 | 44,404 | 34,826 | 26,593 | 21,284 | 15,245 |
| Deferred Policy Costs | 6,471 | 5,768 | 5,132 | 4,249 | 3,658 | 3,243 | 2,777 | 2,350 | 2,027 | 1,730 |
| Total Assets | 148,431 | 134,136 | 114,346 | 101,015 | 79,835 | 69,389 | 58,143 | 46,143 | 37,409 | 27,908 |
| Debt | 23,521 | 17,990 | 17,519 | 15,689 | 13,464 | 11,922 | 10,385 | 5,860 | 3,952 | 1,384 |
| Common Eqty. | 22,044 | 19,827 | 16,422 | 15,224 | 12,632 | 11,313 | 9,754 | 8,255 | 6,852 | 5,610 |
| Comb. Loss-Exp. Ratio | 96.9 | 97.0 | 98.8 | 100.1 | 102.4 | 100.4 | 99.6 | 100.0 | 99.4 | 99.5 |
| % Return On Revs. | 11.2 | 9.7 | 9.7 | 9.5 | 8.8 | 9.2 | 9.2 | 9.7 | 8.6 | 8.4 |
| % Ret. on Equity | 13.8 | 13.9 | 13.7 | 13.8 | 12.6 | 14.7 | 15.9 | 18.0 | 18.7 | 18.2 |
| % Invest. Yield | 4.5 | 4.6 | 4.7 | 4.8 | 4.9 | 5.8 | 6.6 | 7.4 | 7.8 | 8.7 |

Data as orig. reptd.; bef. results of disc. opers. and/or spec. items. Per share data adj. for stk. divs. as of ex-div. date. E-Estimate. NA-Not Available. NM-Not Meaningful. NR-Not Ranked.

**Office**—70 Pine St., New York, NY 10270. **Tel**—(212) 770-7000. **Chrmn & CEO**—M. R. Greenberg. **Pres**—T. R. Tizzio. **Treas**—W. N. Dooley. **VP & Secy**—K. E. Shannon. **Investor Contact**—Charlene M. Hamrah. **Dirs**—M. B. Aidinoff, L. M. Bentsen, P. Chia, M. A. Cohen, B. B. Conable, Jr., M. Feldstein, L. L. Gonda, E. R. Greenberg, M. R. Greenberg, C. A. Hills, F. J. Hoenemeyer, E. E. Matthews, D. P. Phypers, J. J. Roberts, T. R. Tizzio, E. S. W. Tse.. **Transfer Agent & Registrar**—Bank of New York, NYC. **Incorporated**—in Delaware in 1967. **Empl**— 36,600. **S&P Analyst:** Catherine A. Seifert

# American Power Conversion    3109

Nasdaq Symbol **APCC**

In S&P MidCap 400

**17-MAY-97**

**Industry:**
Electrical Equipment

**Summary:** APCC manufactures uninterruptible power supply (UPS) products that protect data in personal computers and other electronic devices from disruptions or surges in electric power.

| S&P Opinion: Accumulate (★★★★) | Recent Price • 19⅞ | Yield • Nil |
| --- | --- | --- |
| | 52 Wk Range • 31½-8½ | 12-Mo. P/E • 19.1 |

**Quantitative Evaluations**

Outlook
(1 Lowest—5 Highest)
• **5**

Fair Value
• **28¼**

Risk
• **High**

Earn./Div. Rank
• **B+**

Technical Eval.
• **Bullish** since 8/96

Rel. Strength Rank
(1 Lowest—99 Highest)
• **19**

Insider Activity
• **NA**

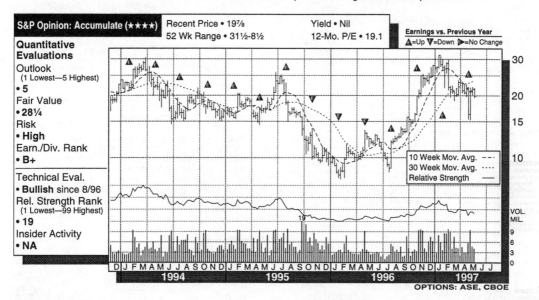

Earnings vs. Previous Year
▲=Up ▼=Down ▷=No Change

10 Week Mov. Avg. ---
30 Week Mov. Avg. ·····
Relative Strength ——

OPTIONS: ASE, CBOE

## Overview - 06-MAY-97

Demand for APCC's products continues to be driven by the proliferation of local area networks (LANs) and the rise of the Internet/Intranet. This trend is expected to continue, supplemented by expansion into international markets. We estimate sales growth of approximately 20%-25% in 1997, as the company targets the server market and international and emerging markets with rapidly growing PC penetration rates. Gross margins have been in a downtrend, as a result of higher inventory reserves related to a product transition and a shift in the product mix toward lower margin equipment. Operating expenses in 1997 should grow at a slightly faster rate than revenues as the company expands capacity, but with cost cutting initiatives and manufacturing efficiencies, operating margins should stay stable at 18% of revenues. In February 1997, APCC acquired software developer Systems Enhancement for 480,144 shares of common stock valued at about $12.6 million.

## Valuation - 06-MAY-97

We recently raised our rating on the stock to accumulate from hold on a price basis. The shares were unfairly punished with the release of first quarter earnings that just about made estimates. Revenue growth in the period was 22% and gross margins rose sharply on a more favorable product mix and cost reduction efforts. North American sales were up 29% and international sales growth slowed to 10%, curtailed by a strengthening dollar. We estimate 1997 EPS at $1.20, a 20% gain from 1996 earnings of $0.98. The stock is trading at 13 times 1997 estimates and represents a significant discount to long-run earnings growth of 17%-20%. Long-term, patient investors will find current prices as an attractive entry point.

## Key Stock Statistics

| | | | |
| --- | --- | --- | --- |
| S&P EPS Est. 1997 | 1.20 | Tang. Bk. Value/Share | 4.16 |
| P/E on S&P Est. 1997 | 16.6 | Beta | 0.85 |
| S&P EPS Est. 1998 | 1.45 | Shareholders | 2,800 |
| Dividend Rate/Share | Nil | Market cap. (B) | $ 1.9 |
| Shs. outstg. (M) | 94.9 | Inst. holdings | 49% |
| Avg. daily vol. (M) | 1.755 | | |

Value of $10,000 invested 5 years ago: $ 32,149

## Fiscal Year Ending Dec. 31

| | 1998 | 1997 | 1996 | 1995 | 1994 | 1993 |
| --- | --- | --- | --- | --- | --- | --- |
| **Revenues (Million $)** | | | | | | |
| 1Q | — | 172.0 | 141.6 | 109.2 | 74.62 | 48.13 |
| 2Q | — | — | 161.4 | 122.6 | 86.36 | 56.99 |
| 3Q | — | — | 193.8 | 142.0 | 103.8 | 70.11 |
| 4Q | — | — | 210.1 | 141.5 | 113.5 | 75.06 |
| Yr. | — | — | 706.9 | 515.3 | 378.3 | 250.3 |
| **Earnings Per Share ($)** | | | | | | |
| 1Q | — | 0.22 | 0.16 | 0.20 | 0.15 | 0.09 |
| 2Q | — | E0.26 | 0.20 | 0.19 | 0.17 | 0.11 |
| 3Q | — | E0.34 | 0.30 | 0.18 | 0.21 | 0.15 |
| 4Q | — | E0.38 | 0.32 | 0.18 | 0.25 | 0.18 |
| Yr. | E1.45 | E1.20 | 0.98 | 0.74 | 0.77 | 0.53 |

**Next earnings report expected: late July**

### Dividend Data

No cash dividends have been paid on the public shares. A two-for-one stock split was effected September 24, 1993. The shares were split two-for-one in December 1992 and December 1991, three-for-one in October 1990, five-for-four in 1989, and five-for-one in 1988.

This report is for information purposes and should not be considered a solicitation to buy or sell any security. Neither S&P nor any other party guarantee its accuracy or make warranties regarding results from its usage. Redistribution is prohibited without written permission. Copyright © 1997

*A Division of The McGraw-Hill Companies*

## Business Summary - 06-MAY-97

American Power Conversion Corp. designs, develops, manufactures and markets a line of uninterruptible power supply (UPS) products, electrical surge protection devices, power conditioning products and associated software and interface cables that are used with personal computers, engineering workstations, file servers, communications and internetworking equipment and other sensitive electronic devices that rely on electric utility power.

As microcomputers have become increasingly important to the business strategy of many organizations, it has become necessary to ensure that data stored in, and operating instructions for, microcomputers are protected from fluctuations in utility power. A UPS protects against these disturbances by providing continuous power automatically and virtually instantaneously after the electric power supply is interrupted or sags, as well as line filtering and protection against surges while the electric utility is operating.

APCC's strategy has been to expand market share by designing products that incorporate high performance and quality at competitive prices and to defend its position by providing excellent customer service and support. The company is also mindful of costs and has developed overseas manufacturing where labor costs are cheap. In addition, its products are designed to be aesthetically pleasing and appropriate for use in an office environment. Products are engineered and extensively tested for compatibility with nearly all common microcomputers and small minicomputers. Over 140 standard domestic and international UPS models are offered, ranging in capacity from 200 to 5,000 volt-amps and in end-user list price from $119 to $6,767.

During 1995, the company introduced 155 new products, including a major transition of its flagship product line, the Smart-UPS, from its five year old design to a new third generation product feature set including automatic voltage regulation and adjustment, an user-replaceable battery replacement system and an internal accessory option slot. APCC also introduced its Back-UPS Pro product for departmental server applications. In 1996's second quarter, this line was expanded with the successful launch of Back-UPS Office designed for Internet users. During 1997, the company plans to introduce the Symmetra Power Array, a redundant modular system designed for use with legacy systems.

APCC markets its products through a domestic and international network of computer distributors, computer dealers and catalog merchandisers. It also sells directly to some large value-added resellers, which integrate the company's products into specialized microcomputer systems and then market turnkey systems to selected vertical markets, and to manufacturers. Sales outside of North America accounted for 38% of the company's net sales in 1996, up from 36% in 1995.

### Capitalization

**Long Term Debt:** None (3/97).

### Per Share Data ($)

| (Year Ended Dec. 31) | 1996 | 1995 | 1994 | 1993 | 1992 | 1991 | 1990 | 1989 | 1988 | 1987 |
|---|---|---|---|---|---|---|---|---|---|---|
| Tangible Bk. Val. | 4.16 | 3.11 | 2.29 | 1.45 | 0.87 | 0.51 | 0.31 | 0.19 | 0.11 | 0.03 |
| Cash Flow | 1.12 | 0.85 | 0.83 | 0.56 | 0.32 | 0.19 | 0.11 | 0.08 | 0.05 | 0.02 |
| Earnings | 0.98 | 0.74 | 0.77 | 0.53 | 0.31 | 0.17 | 0.11 | 0.08 | 0.04 | 0.02 |
| Dividends | Nil | Nil | Nil | Nil | Nil | Nil | Nil | Nil | Nil | Nil |
| Payout Ratio | Nil | Nil | Nil | Nil | Nil | Nil | Nil | Nil | Nil | Nil |
| Prices - High | 28$^{1}/_{8}$ | 25$^{7}/_{8}$ | 30$^{1}/_{2}$ | 24$^{3}/_{4}$ | 14$^{3}/_{8}$ | 7$^{1}/_{8}$ | 2$^{7}/_{16}$ | 1$^{1}/_{16}$ | $^{5}/_{16}$ | NA |
| - Low | 7$^{7}/_{8}$ | 9$^{1}/_{8}$ | 14$^{1}/_{2}$ | 10$^{1}/_{2}$ | 5$^{1}/_{4}$ | 1$^{13}/_{16}$ | $^{5}/_{8}$ | $^{5}/_{16}$ | $^{1}/_{4}$ | NA |
| P/E Ratio - High | 29 | 35 | 40 | 47 | 47 | 41 | 23 | 15 | 8 | NA |
| - Low | 8 | 12 | 19 | 20 | 17 | 10 | 6 | 4 | 6 | NA |

### Income Statement Analysis (Million $)

| | 1996 | 1995 | 1994 | 1993 | 1992 | 1991 | 1990 | 1989 | 1988 | 1987 |
|---|---|---|---|---|---|---|---|---|---|---|
| Revs. | 707 | 515 | 378 | 250 | 157 | 93.6 | 59.2 | 35.4 | 17.4 | 8.1 |
| Oper. Inc. | 147 | 114 | 112 | 77.9 | 44.7 | 25.1 | 15.4 | 9.9 | 4.6 | 1.8 |
| Depr. | 13.5 | 10.1 | 6.1 | 3.0 | 1.8 | 0.9 | 0.7 | 0.5 | 0.3 | 0.1 |
| Int. Exp. | Nil | 0.3 | Nil | Nil | 0.1 | 0.4 | 0.3 | 0.1 | 0.1 | 0.0 |
| Pretax Inc. | 139 | 105 | 109 | 75.9 | 43.1 | 24.2 | 14.7 | 9.5 | 4.4 | 1.7 |
| Eff. Tax Rate | 34% | 34% | 35% | 36% | 36% | 36% | 37% | 37% | 36% | 41% |
| Net Inc. | 92.4 | 69.5 | 71.3 | 48.6 | 27.8 | 15.6 | 9.3 | 6.0 | 2.8 | 1.0 |

### Balance Sheet & Other Fin. Data (Million $)

| | 1996 | 1995 | 1994 | 1993 | 1992 | 1991 | 1990 | 1989 | 1988 | 1987 |
|---|---|---|---|---|---|---|---|---|---|---|
| Cash | 153 | 39.0 | 41.5 | 47.8 | 21.0 | 12.1 | 3.0 | 6.1 | 5.2 | 0.4 |
| Curr. Assets | 424 | 278 | 211 | 135 | 82.7 | 46.9 | 29.5 | 20.7 | 11.9 | 3.7 |
| Total Assets | 504 | 347 | 265 | 159 | 99 | 58.2 | 35.9 | 24.7 | 13.4 | 4.2 |
| Curr. Liab. | 106 | 51.9 | 50.3 | 25.4 | 21.5 | 14.0 | 7.1 | 6.0 | 4.6 | 2.3 |
| LT Debt | Nil | Nil | Nil | Nil | Nil | Nil | 3.0 | 3.5 | 0.1 | 0.2 |
| Common Eqty. | 392 | 290 | 212 | 132 | 76.0 | 43.7 | 25.6 | 15.1 | 8.7 | 1.7 |
| Total Cap. | 398 | 295 | 215 | 134 | 77.0 | 44.2 | 28.7 | 18.6 | 8.8 | 1.9 |
| Cap. Exp. | 25.0 | 24.0 | 35.9 | 10.9 | 6.4 | 5.9 | 3.2 | 2.9 | 1.1 | 0.5 |
| Cash Flow | 106 | 79.6 | 77.4 | 51.5 | 29.6 | 16.5 | 10.0 | 6.5 | 3.1 | 1.1 |
| Curr. Ratio | 4.0 | 5.4 | 4.2 | 5.3 | 3.9 | 3.3 | 4.1 | 3.4 | 2.6 | 1.6 |
| % LT Debt of Cap. | Nil | Nil | Nil | Nil | Nil | Nil | 10.6 | 18.9 | 1.6 | 11.0 |
| % Net Inc.of Revs. | 13.1 | 13.5 | 18.8 | 19.4 | 17.6 | 16.6 | 15.8 | 17.0 | 16.0 | 12.2 |
| % Ret. on Assets | 21.7 | 22.8 | 33.4 | 37.2 | 35.2 | 32.9 | 30.7 | 31.3 | 28.9 | NA |
| % Ret. on Equity | 27.1 | 27.8 | 41.2 | 46.1 | 46.1 | 44.7 | 45.7 | 50.2 | 50.6 | NA |

Data as orig. reptd.; bef. results of disc. opers. and/or spec. items. Per share data adj. for stk. divs. as of ex-div. date. E-Estimated. NA-Not Available. NM-Not Meaningful. NR-Not Ranked.

**Office**—132 Fairgrounds Rd., West Kingston, RI 02892. **Tel**—(401) 789-5735.**E-mail**—investorrelationa@apcc.com **Website**—http://www.apcc.com **Chrmn, Pres & Secy**—R. B. Dowdell, Jr. **CFO**—D. M. Muir. **VP & Secy**—E. E. Landsman.**Investor Contact**—Debbie Grey. **Dirs**—R. B. Dowdell, Jr., J. D. Gerson, E. E. Landsman, E. F. Lyon, N. E. Rasmussen. **Transfer Agent & Registrar**—The First National Bank of Boston. **Incorporated**—in Massachusetts in 1981. **Empl**— 2,650. **S&P Analyst:** Ted Groesbeck

# Amgen

**3123K**

Nasdaq Symbol **AMGN**

In S&P 500

**22-MAY-97**  Industry: Biotechnology

**Summary:** This leading biotechnology concern's key products are Epogen and Neupogen, genetically engineered versions of natural hormones that stimulate production of blood components.

| | |
|---|---|
| **S&P Opinion: Accumulate (★★★★)** | Recent Price • 64⅛ |
| | 52 Wk Range • 65⅛-51⅜ |

Yield • Nil

12-Mo. P/E • 25.0

**Quantitative Evaluations**

Outlook (1 Lowest—5 Highest)
• **3**

Fair Value
• **60¼**

Risk
• **Low**

Earn./Div. Rank
• **B**

Technical Eval.
• **Bullish** since 5/97

Rel. Strength Rank (1 Lowest—99 Highest)
• **81**

Insider Activity
• **Neutral**

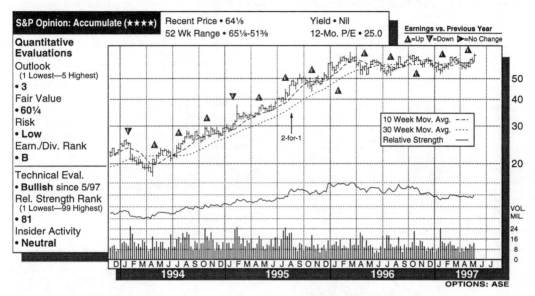

Earnings vs. Previous Year
▲=Up ▼=Down ▶=No Change

10 Week Mov. Avg. - - -
30 Week Mov. Avg. ·····
Relative Strength ——

2-for-1

OPTIONS: ASE

## Overview - 13-MAY-97

Total revenues should post another good double-digit advance in 1997, but the gain will probably fall somewhat short of the 15.5% rise of 1996. Sales of Epogen red blood cell stimulant should remain strong, reflecting growth in the U.S. dialysis population, higher per patient dosing regimens, and better Medicare reimbursement. Although gains for Neupogen are not expected to match those of Epogen, sales of this white blood cell stimulant should improve over the coming quarters, aided by further expansion in the chemotherapy market, greater marketing efforts abroad, and new therapeutic indications. Off-label sales to AIDS patients should also help Neupogen sales. Although R&D will remain at a high level, profitability should benefit from higher volume, good control over operating costs and a lower tax rate.

## Valuation - 13-MAY-97

The shares traded in a relatively narrow range over the past 12 months, reflecting sluggish sales of Neupogen overseas, a possible competitive threat to Epogen, and certain unfavorable clinical developments. During 1996, Amgen disclosed disappointing clinical results on experimental drugs BDNF for Lou Gehrig's disease and MGDF for patients with acute myeloid leukemia. However, studies on MGDF for boosting platelet growth in blood donors were encouraging. The R&D pipeline also includes new indications for Epogen and Neupogen, Leptin anti-obesity agent, Infergen to treat hepatitis C, TNF-bp growth factor for arthritis, GDNF for Parkinson's disease, NESP for anemia, and other drugs. Despite their high multiple, Amgen's shares merit accumulation for long-term appreciation in the volatile biotechnology sector.

## Key Stock Statistics

| | | | |
|---|---|---|---|
| S&P EPS Est. 1997 | 2.80 | Tang. Bk. Value/Share | 7.20 |
| P/E on S&P Est. 1997 | 22.9 | Beta | 1.09 |
| S&P EPS Est. 1998 | 3.15 | Shareholders | 14,000 |
| Dividend Rate/Share | Nil | Market cap. (B) | $ 18.1 |
| Shs. outstg. (M) | 265.4 | Inst. holdings | 57% |
| Avg. daily vol. (M) | 2.387 | | |

Value of $10,000 invested 5 years ago: $ 16,932

### Fiscal Year Ending Dec. 31

| | 1997 | 1996 | 1995 | 1994 | 1993 | 1992 |
|---|---|---|---|---|---|---|
| **Revenues (Million $)** | | | | | | |
| 1Q | 575.5 | 507.9 | 439.4 | 364.0 | 310.2 | 220.0 |
| 2Q | — | 571.4 | 493.7 | 414.7 | 343.1 | 261.0 |
| 3Q | — | 567.0 | 493.3 | 426.4 | 354.9 | 303.0 |
| 4Q | — | 593.5 | 513.5 | 442.9 | 365.6 | 308.0 |
| Yr. | — | 2,240 | 1,940 | 1,648 | 1,374 | 1,093 |
| **Earnings Per Share ($)** | | | | | | |
| 1Q | 0.65 | 0.51 | 0.39 | 0.33 | 0.28 | 0.22 |
| 2Q | E0.70 | 0.64 | 0.50 | 0.39 | 0.35 | 0.24 |
| 3Q | E0.72 | 0.64 | 0.52 | 0.41 | 0.36 | 0.30 |
| 4Q | E0.73 | 0.64 | 0.52 | 0.02 | 0.32 | 0.46 |
| Yr. | E2.80 | 2.42 | 1.92 | 1.14 | 1.30 | 1.21 |

**Next earnings report expected: mid July**

### Dividend Data (Dividends have been paid since 1997.)

| Amount ($) | Date Decl. | Ex-Div. Date | Stock of Record | Payment Date |
|---|---|---|---|---|
| 0.008 | Feb. 19 | Mar. 24 | Mar. 21 | Mar. 21 '97 |

This report is for information purposes and should not be considered a solicitation to buy or sell any security. Neither S&P nor any other party guarantee its accuracy or make warranties regarding results from its usage. Redistribution is prohibited without written permission. Copyright © 1997

A Division of The **McGraw·Hill** Companies

## Business Summary - 13-MAY-97

The world's largest independent biotechnology company, Amgen was founded in Thousand Oaks, CA, in 1980 as AMGen (Applied Molecular Genetics). Using the tools of recombinant DNA and molecular biology, the company has developed two of the industry's leading commercial products -- Epogen, which had worldwide sales of $1.1 billion in 1996 ($883 million in 1995), and Neupogen, which had sales of $1 billion in 1996 ($936 million in 1995). Foreign operations represented 19% of 1996 sales and 4% of operating profits.

Epogen is a genetically engineered version of human erythropoietin (EPO), a natural hormone that stimulates the production of red blood cells in bone marrow. The drug's primary market is dialysis patients suffering from severe chronic anemia as a result of their failure to produce adequate amounts of natural EPO. Epogen supplements low levels of EPO, eliminating severe and chronic anemia. Amgen has EPO rights to the U.S. dialysis market and has licensed Johnson & Johnson U.S. rights to all other indications.

Neupogen is a recombinant version of human granulocyte colony stimulating factor (G-CSF), a protein that stimulates the production of neutrophils (a type of white blood cell that defends the body against bacterial infection). Its principal use is to build neutrophil levels in cancer patients whose natural neutrophils were destroyed by chemotherapy. Neupogen has an estimated 30% of the U.S. myelosuppressive chemotherapy market. The drug is also being explored as a potential support therapy for pneumonia. An FDA filing is also pending to use Neupogen to treat acute myelogenous leukemia. Amgen has marketing rights to Neupogen in the U.S., Canada and Australia and markets the drug jointly in Europe with F. Hoffmann-La Roche. The latter has rights to the drug in most other areas (rights in Japan are held by Kirin Brewery).

Amgen is committed to investing heavily in R&D to fund future biotech products, with 1996 R&D outlays of $528 million equaling 23.6% of revenues. The company currently has 12 potential therapeutics in more than 220 clinical trials. Important new products awaiting FDA review or under development include Infergen, a new treatment of hepatitic C; Stemgen, a hematopoietic growth factor used in chemotherapy support programs; GDNF, a treatment for Parkinson's and Lou Gehrig's diseases; Neurotrophin for use in patients with diabetic peripheral neuropathy; IL-1ra and TNF-bp for rheumatoid arthritis; MGDF, a platelet growth factor; KGF, a treatment for mucositis in cancer patients; NESP, a treatment for anemia associated with chronic renal failure; and Leptin, an anti-obesity treatment.

## Capitalization

**Long Term Liabilities:** $216,400,000 (3/97).

### Per Share Data ($)

| (Year Ended Dec. 31) | 1996 | 1995 | 1994 | 1993 | 1992 | 1991 | 1990 | 1989 | 1988 | 1987 |
|---|---|---|---|---|---|---|---|---|---|---|
| Tangible Bk. Val. | 7.20 | 6.29 | 4.81 | 4.36 | 3.42 | 2.02 | 1.57 | 0.90 | 0.79 | 0.82 |
| Cash Flow | 2.78 | 2.22 | 1.41 | 1.48 | 1.33 | 0.42 | 0.21 | 0.16 | 0.00 | 0.04 |
| Earnings | 2.42 | 1.92 | 1.14 | 1.30 | 1.21 | 0.33 | 0.13 | 0.09 | -0.04 | 0.01 |
| Dividends | Nil | Nil | Nil | Nil | Nil | Nil | Nil | Nil | Nil | Nil |
| Payout Ratio | Nil | Nil | Nil | Nil | Nil | Nil | Nil | Nil | Nil | Nil |
| Prices - High | 66½ | 59¾ | 30⅛ | 35⅞ | 39⅛ | 38 | 10⅝ | 5 | 3 | 3¾ |
|     - Low | 51⅜ | 28⅛ | 17⅜ | 15½ | 24⅝ | 9½ | 3⅝ | 2⅝ | 2⅛ | 1⅜ |
| P/E Ratio - High | 27 | 31 | 26 | 27 | 32 | NM | 81 | 54 | NM | NM |
|     - Low | 21 | 15 | 15 | 12 | 20 | NM | 27 | 28 | NM | NM |

### Income Statement Analysis (Million $)

| | 1996 | 1995 | 1994 | 1993 | 1992 | 1991 | 1990 | 1989 | 1988 | 1987 |
|---|---|---|---|---|---|---|---|---|---|---|
| Revs. | 2,240 | 1,940 | 1,648 | 1,374 | 1,093 | 682 | 381 | 190 | 70.0 | 44.0 |
| Oper. Inc. | 1,058 | 881 | 801 | 619 | 466 | 276 | 123 | 41.0 | 3.0 | -2.0 |
| Depr. | 100 | 84.2 | 74.5 | 48.9 | 32.5 | 21.5 | 17.4 | 11.9 | 8.0 | 4.1 |
| Int. Exp. | 10.4 | 20.0 | 15.8 | 10.1 | 6.2 | 3.4 | 4.3 | 5.3 | 1.4 | 0.7 |
| Pretax Inc. | 962 | 794 | 588 | 592 | 563 | 158 | 72.0 | 29.0 | -7.0 | 2.0 |
| Eff. Tax Rate | 29% | 32% | 46% | 37% | 37% | 38% | 53% | 35% | NM | 17% |
| Net Inc. | 680 | 538 | 320 | 375 | 358 | 97.9 | 34.3 | 19.1 | -8.2 | 1.7 |

### Balance Sheet & Other Fin. Data (Million $)

| | 1996 | 1995 | 1994 | 1993 | 1992 | 1991 | 1990 | 1989 | 1988 | 1987 |
|---|---|---|---|---|---|---|---|---|---|---|
| Cash | 1,077 | 1,050 | 697 | 723 | 555 | 378 | 157 | 80.0 | 66.0 | 106 |
| Curr. Assets | 1,503 | 1,454 | 1,116 | 1,055 | 873 | 590 | 327 | 182 | 98.0 | 119 |
| Total Assets | 2,766 | 2,433 | 1,994 | 1,766 | 1,374 | 866 | 514 | 308 | 207 | 193 |
| Curr. Liab. | 643 | 584 | 536 | 412 | 311 | 295 | 103 | 55.0 | 15.0 | 13.0 |
| LT Debt | 59.0 | 177 | 183 | 181 | 130 | 39.7 | 12.8 | 64.7 | 30.1 | 16.5 |
| Common Eqty. | 1,906 | 1,672 | 1,274 | 1,172 | 934 | 531 | 398 | 188 | 162 | 164 |
| Total Cap. | 2,122 | 1,849 | 1,458 | 1,353 | 1,064 | 571 | 411 | 253 | 192 | 180 |
| Cap. Exp. | 267 | 163 | 131 | 210 | 219 | 117 | 65.0 | 44.0 | 44.0 | 36.0 |
| Cash Flow | 780 | 622 | 394 | 424 | 390 | 119 | 52.0 | 31.0 | Nil | 6.0 |
| Curr. Ratio | 2.3 | 2.5 | 2.1 | 2.6 | 2.8 | 2.0 | 3.2 | 3.3 | 6.5 | 9.3 |
| % LT Debt of Cap. | 2.8 | 9.6 | 12.6 | 13.4 | 12.2 | 7.0 | 3.1 | 25.6 | 15.7 | 9.2 |
| % Net Inc.of Revs. | 30.4 | 27.7 | 19.4 | 27.3 | 32.7 | 14.3 | 9.0 | 10.0 | NM | 3.9 |
| % Ret. on Assets | 26.2 | 24.3 | 17.1 | 24.0 | 31.5 | 14.0 | 7.7 | 7.3 | NM | 1.1 |
| % Ret. on Equity | 38.0 | 34.5 | 26.3 | 35.8 | 48.2 | 20.7 | 11.0 | 10.8 | NM | 1.3 |

Data as orig. reptd.; bef. results of disc. opers. and/or spec. items. Per share data adj. for stk. divs. as of ex-div. date. E-Estimated. NA-Not Available. NM-Not Meaningful. NR-Not Ranked.

**Office**—1840 Dehavilland Dr., Thousand Oaks, CA 91320-1789. **Tel**—(805) 447-1000. **Website**—http://www.amgen.com **Chrmn & CEO**—G. M. Binder. **Pres & COO**—K. W. Sharer. **VP & Secy**—G. A. Vandeman. **SVP-Fin & CFO**—R. S. Attiyeh. **Investor Contact**—Denise Powell. **Dirs**—G. M. Binder, W. K. Bowes Jr., F. P. Johnson Jr., S. Lazarus, E. Ledder, G. S. Omenn, J. Pelham, K. W. Sharer. **Transfer Agent & Registrar**—American Stock Transfer & Trust Co., NYC. **Incorporated**—in California in 1980; reincorporated in Delaware in 1987. **Empl**— 4,646. **S&P Analyst:** H. B. Saftlas

STANDARD
&POOR'S
STOCK REPORTS

# Analysts International — 3129

NASDAQ Symbol **ANLY**

**17-MAY-97**

**Industry:** Computer (Software & Services)

**Summary:** This company provides contract programming and related software services through its branch and field offices to users and manufacturers of computers.

**Quantitative Evaluations**

Outlook
(1 Lowest—5 Highest)
• **3⁻**

Fair Value
• **37⅛**

Risk
• **Average**

Earn./Div. Rank
• **A-**

Technical Eval.
• **Bullish** since 10/94

Rel. Strength Rank
(1 Lowest—99 Highest)
• **96**

Insider Activity
• **Neutral**

Recent Price • 33
52 Wk Range • 36⅝-17½

Yield • 1.1%
12-Mo. P/E • 32.0

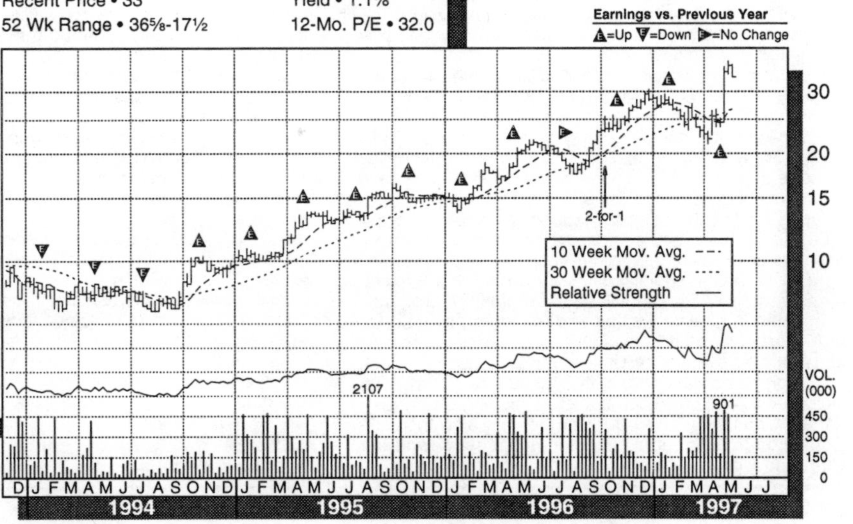

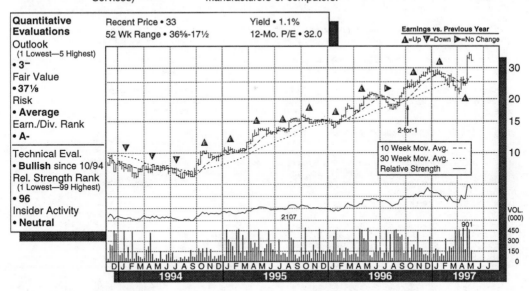

Earnings vs. Previous Year
E=Up E=Down E=No Change
30
20
15
10
2-for-1
10 Week Mov. Avg.
30 Week Mov. Avg.
Relative Strength
VOL. (000)
2107
901
450
300
150
0
D J F M A M J J A S O N D J F M A M J J A S O N D J F M A M J J A S O N D J F M A M J J
1994
1995
1996
1997


## Business Profile - 22-APR-97

The dramatic proliferation of computers and networking, along with the need for specialized technical expertise for certain projects and the trend of businesses eliminating non-essential computer support staff by outsourcing, led to record revenue and income levels in FY 95 (Jun.) and FY 96. Further gains were achieved in the first nine months of FY 97. Near-term prospects have been enhanced by the company's formation in August 1996 of a business unit to assist customers in solving the problem of preparing computer systems for the Year 2000 date conversion. In February 1997, the company was awarded a contract to assist NYSE-listed 3M Company for Year 2000 software compliance. In April 1997, it formed a strategic alliance with Viasoft, Inc. under which the company is licensed to use Viasoft's Year 2000 technology and services to better serve its clients.

## Operational Review - 22-APR-97

Revenues in the first nine months of FY 97 increased 32%, year to year, reflecting strong demand for technical personnel. Salaries, contracted services and direct charges rose 33%, but with well controlled SG&A expense (up 23%), operating income climbed 36%. Following lower non-operating income and taxes at 40.2%, versus 39.7%, net income was up 26%, to $11,934,000 ($0.80 a share), from $9,029,000 ($0.61, as adjusted).

## Stock Performance - 16-MAY-97

In the past 30 trading days, ANLY's shares have increased 50%, compared to a 9% rise in the S&P 500. Average trading volume for the past five days was 30,680 shares, compared with the 40-day moving average of 98,923 shares.

## Key Stock Statistics

| | | | |
|---|---|---|---|
| Dividend Rate/Share | 0.36 | Shareholders | NA |
| Shs. outstg. (M) | 14.8 | Market cap. (B) | $0.487 |
| Avg. daily vol. (M) | 0.087 | Inst. holdings | 59% |
| Tang. Bk. Value/Share | 3.66 | | |
| Beta | 1.24 | | |

Value of $10,000 invested 5 years ago: $ 72,648

## Fiscal Year Ending Jun. 30

| | 1997 | 1996 | 1995 | 1994 | 1993 | 1992 |
|---|---|---|---|---|---|---|
| **Revenues (Million $)** | | | | | | |
| 1Q | 98.02 | 73.07 | 48.40 | 41.74 | 37.00 | 29.50 |
| 2Q | 101.8 | 78.79 | 50.72 | 42.86 | 40.17 | 30.40 |
| 3Q | 113.7 | 85.98 | 55.22 | 45.05 | 41.55 | 33.80 |
| 4Q | — | 91.71 | 64.09 | 46.33 | 40.98 | 35.90 |
| Yr. | — | 329.5 | 218.4 | 176.0 | 159.7 | 129.6 |
| **Earnings Per Share ($)** | | | | | | |
| 1Q | 0.26 | 0.19 | 0.17 | 0.13 | 0.13 | 0.09 |
| 2Q | 0.26 | 0.19 | 0.18 | 0.14 | 0.15 | 0.08 |
| 3Q | 0.28 | 0.22 | 0.19 | 0.12 | 0.13 | 0.09 |
| 4Q | — | 0.23 | 0.23 | 0.15 | 0.17 | 0.12 |
| Yr. | — | 0.84 | 0.77 | 0.55 | 0.58 | 0.38 |

## Next earnings report expected: mid August

**Dividend Data** (Dividends have been paid since 1988.)

| Amount ($) | Date Decl. | Ex-Div. Date | Stock of Record | Payment Date |
|---|---|---|---|---|
| 2-for-1 | Aug. 15 | Oct. 01 | Sep. 09 | Sep. 30 '96 |
| 0.090 | Aug. 15 | Oct. 29 | Oct. 31 | Nov. 15 '96 |
| 0.090 | Dec. 19 | Jan. 29 | Jan. 31 | Feb. 14 '97 |
| 0.090 | Feb. 20 | Apr. 28 | Apr. 30 | May. 15 '97 |

This report is for information purposes and should not be considered a solicitation to buy or sell any security. Neither S&P nor any other party guarantee its accuracy or make warranties regarding results from its usage. Redistribution is prohibited without written permission. Copyright © 1997

*A Division of The McGraw-Hill Companies*

## Business Summary - 22-APR-97

Analysts International Corporation (AIC) primarily provides contract programming and related software services through its branch and field offices to users and manufacturers of computers. Software services offered include custom programming, systems analysis and design, software-related consulting and specialized software-related educational courses for computer programmers and analysts.

Revenues from software services accounted for the majority of total revenues in recent years. In FY 96 (Jun.), customers in the telecommunications, electronics, services and manufacturing sectors provided 24%, 30%, 10% and 9% of total revenues, respectively. Services rendered to IBM accounted for over 10% of revenues in each year since FY 93.

During FY 96, the company supported approximately 5,800 projects for 840 customers, of which 320 were new. Major projects during the year included the development of design specifications for updating a Project Management Information System for BASF Corp., implementation of a new sales and marketing system for M.A. Hanna Co., and development of a new international pricing system for United Van LInes.

AIC competes nationally with software consulting divisions of several large companies, including DEC, Andersen Consulting and IBM. Competitors also include Computer Task Group, Computer Horizons, Keane Inc., CGA and Computer Data Systems, Inc.

Out of the company's 3,770 employees at June 30, 1996, more than 3,200 were systems analysts, computer programmers and other technical personnel whose services are billable to clients.

In April 1995, AIC received a national service provider contract from IBM to provide technical services to IBM and its customers. Although rates on the contract were very competitive, the lower margins that may result were expected to be offset by the benefits of increased volume.

In June 1995, the company entered into a three-year contract with US West, under which ANLY will be the principal vendor to provide technical personnel to US West's data processing operations. ANLY formed a new division, AiC TechWest, to manage the US West business. ANLY has committed about 175 people to the project, which is expected to add $50 million in revenues.

In August 1996, the company announced the formation of a business unit to assist companies in solving the Year 2000 problem. The unit consists of a team of consultants with expertise in the problem that acts as a central resource to other consultants in the field. In April 1997, ANLY formed a strategic alliance with Viasoft, Inc. under which the company is licensed to use Viasoft's year 2000 technology and services in helping its clients manage the century date change.

## Capitalization

**Long Term Liabilities:** $6,398,000 (3/97).

### Per Share Data ($)

| (Year Ended Jun. 30) | 1996 | 1995 | 1994 | 1993 | 1992 | 1991 | 1990 | 1989 | 1988 | 1987 |
|---|---|---|---|---|---|---|---|---|---|---|
| Tangible Bk. Val. | 3.66 | 3.11 | 2.57 | 2.24 | 1.84 | 1.64 | 1.42 | 1.13 | 0.93 | 0.73 |
| Cash Flow | 0.99 | 0.90 | 0.66 | 0.68 | 0.46 | 0.45 | 0.47 | 0.39 | 0.26 | 0.14 |
| Earnings | 0.84 | 0.77 | 0.55 | 0.58 | 0.38 | 0.40 | 0.43 | 0.36 | 0.23 | 0.11 |
| Dividends | 0.36 | 0.25 | 0.23 | 0.20 | 0.19 | 0.18 | 0.16 | 0.17 | 0.04 | Nil |
| Payout Ratio | 43% | 33% | 41% | 29% | 49% | 45% | 31% | 46% | 17% | Nil |
| Prices - High | 30½ | 16½ | 10⅜ | 12 | 8⅝ | 6⅛ | 7⅞ | 6¾ | 3 | 2½ |
| - Low | 13⅝ | 9⅞ | 7¼ | 7½ | 5⅛ | 4 | 3⅜ | 2⅞ | 1¹³⁄₁₆ | 1⅛ |
| P/E Ratio - High | 26 | 21 | 19 | 21 | 23 | 15 | 18 | 19 | 13 | 23 |
| - Low | 16 | 13 | 13 | 13 | 14 | 10 | 8 | 8 | 8 | 10 |

### Income Statement Analysis (Million $)

| | 1996 | 1995 | 1994 | 1993 | 1992 | 1991 | 1990 | 1989 | 1988 | 1987 |
|---|---|---|---|---|---|---|---|---|---|---|
| Revs. | 330 | 218 | 176 | 160 | 130 | 117 | 108 | 90.0 | 70.0 | 57.0 |
| Oper. Inc. | 21.9 | 19.6 | 14.2 | 14.4 | 9.3 | 9.0 | 9.7 | 8.3 | 5.1 | 2.5 |
| Depr. | 2.2 | 1.8 | 1.7 | 1.4 | 1.1 | 0.7 | 0.5 | 0.4 | 0.4 | 0.4 |
| Int. Exp. | Nil | Nil | Nil | Nil | Nil | Nil | Nil | Nil | Nil | Nil |
| Pretax Inc. | 20.7 | 18.5 | 12.8 | 13.5 | 8.7 | 8.9 | 9.9 | 8.4 | 5.1 | 1.7 |
| Eff. Tax Rate | 40% | 39% | 38% | 39% | 38% | 38% | 39% | 41% | 40% | 16% |
| Net Inc. | 12.4 | 11.3 | 7.9 | 8.3 | 5.4 | 5.6 | 6.0 | 4.9 | 3.1 | 1.4 |

### Balance Sheet & Other Fin. Data (Million $)

| | 1996 | 1995 | 1994 | 1993 | 1992 | 1991 | 1990 | 1989 | 1988 | 1987 |
|---|---|---|---|---|---|---|---|---|---|---|
| Cash | 17.0 | 12.6 | 10.7 | 9.9 | 7.4 | 7.0 | 5.3 | 6.6 | 7.4 | 5.9 |
| Curr. Assets | 69.0 | 56.8 | 41.3 | 35.0 | 29.1 | 23.8 | 23.1 | 20.7 | 18.1 | 14.6 |
| Total Assets | 81.4 | 67.5 | 51.2 | 44.9 | 38.1 | 32.1 | 29.3 | 25.3 | 22.0 | 17.8 |
| Curr. Liab. | 22.0 | 17.0 | 9.9 | 8.9 | 8.6 | 6.8 | 7.4 | 8.3 | 8.4 | 7.3 |
| LT Debt | Nil | Nil | Nil | Nil | Nil | Nil | Nil | Nil | Nil | Nil |
| Common Eqty. | 53.7 | 45.1 | 36.6 | 31.7 | 25.8 | 22.7 | 19.6 | 15.3 | 12.5 | 9.8 |
| Total Cap. | 53.7 | 45.1 | 36.6 | 31.7 | 25.8 | 22.7 | 19.6 | 15.3 | 12.5 | 9.8 |
| Cap. Exp. | 2.9 | 1.9 | 1.3 | 1.5 | 2.2 | 2.1 | 1.6 | 0.6 | 0.5 | 0.1 |
| Cash Flow | 14.6 | 13.0 | 9.6 | 9.7 | 6.5 | 6.3 | 6.5 | 5.4 | 3.5 | 1.9 |
| Curr. Ratio | 3.1 | 3.3 | 4.2 | 3.9 | 3.4 | 3.5 | 3.1 | 2.5 | 2.2 | 2.0 |
| % LT Debt of Cap. | Nil | Nil | Nil | Nil | Nil | Nil | Nil | Nil | Nil | Nil |
| % Net Inc.of Revs. | 3.8 | 5.1 | 4.5 | 5.2 | 4.1 | 4.8 | 5.6 | 5.5 | 4.4 | 2.5 |
| % Ret. on Assets | 16.7 | 18.9 | 16.5 | 19.8 | 15.2 | 18.1 | 21.7 | 20.9 | 15.5 | 9.0 |
| % Ret. on Equity | 25.1 | 27.5 | 23.2 | 28.6 | 22.1 | 26.3 | 34.0 | 35.5 | 27.6 | 16.0 |

Data as orig. reptd.; bef. results of disc. opers. and/or spec. items. Per share data adj. for stk. divs. as of ex-div. date. E-Estimated. NA-Not Available. NM-Not Meaningful. NR-Not Ranked.

**Office**—7615 Metro Blvd., Minneapolis, MN 55439-3050. **Tel**—(612) 835-5900. **Chrmn & CEO**—F. W. Lang. **Pres & COO**—V. C. Benda. **VP-Fin, Treas & Investor Contact**—Gerald M. McGrath. **Secy**—T. R. Mahler. **Dirs**—V. C. Benda, W. K. Drake, F. W. Lang, M. A. Loftus, E. M. Mahoney, R. L. Prince. **Transfer Agent**—State Street Bank & Trust Co., Boston. **Incorporated**—in Minnesota in 1966. **Empl**— 4,400. **S&P Analyst:** Adam Penn

# STANDARD &POOR'S
STOCK REPORTS

# Applied Materials
## 3142
Nasdaq Symbol **AMAT**
### In S&P 500

**19-MAY-97** | Industry: Equipment (Semiconductor)

**Summary:** This company, the world's largest manufacturer of wafer fabrication equipment for the semiconductor industry, produces deposition, etching and ion implantation systems.

| S&P Opinion: Hold (★★★) | Recent Price • 65¾ | Yield • Nil |
| --- | --- | --- |
| | 52 Wk Range • 67¾-21¾ | 12-Mo. P/E • 32.2 |

**Quantitative Evaluations**

Outlook (1 Lowest—5 Highest)
• **2⁻**

Fair Value
• **62½**

Risk
• **High**

Earn./Div. Rank
• **B**

Technical Eval.
• **Bullish** since 11/96

Rel. Strength Rank (1 Lowest—99 Highest)
• **98**

Insider Activity
• **Neutral**

**Earnings vs. Previous Year**
▲=Up ▼=Down ▶=No Change

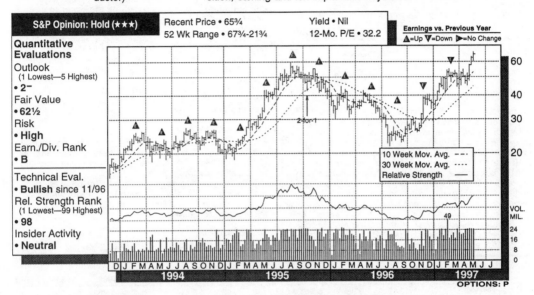

10 Week Mov. Avg. - - -
30 Week Mov. Avg. ·····
Relative Strength ——

## Overview - 16-MAY-97

We have once again raised our sales and earnings outlook for FY 97 (Oct.), as AMAT is distinguishing itself by recovering very quickly from the current slump in the semiconductor equipment industry. Revenues are likely to decline a little more than 5% in FY 97. The company is faring much better than its industry peers largely due to the strength of its products, which enable the production of semiconductors with linewidths (transistor size) of 0.25 micron or below. Longer-term, AMAT is also well positioned in equipment that will produce semiconductors from silicon wafers with 12 inch (300 millimeter) diameters. Margins will be hurt by the lower volume, although a recent restructuring and other cost-saving measures have had a positive effect thus far in FY 97. We look for the company to earn $2.45 a share in FY 97, excluding a $0.32 charge related to acquisitions recorded in the first quarter. Given the strong momentum AMAT is currently experiencing through all of its businesses, we look for EPS to jump to $3.70 in FY 98.

## Valuation - 16-MAY-97

Although the earnings outlook for AMAT continues to improve, we have lowered our ranking on the shares to "hold". The shares have nearly tripled in price since their 1996 bottom, and we think the stock may need some time to digest the gains. This is especially true in light of the overcapacity that remains for DRAM (dynamic random access memory) chips. Trading at approximately 17 times our estimate for FY 98 EPS, the shares are fairly valued. AMAT remains a solid holding for long-term investors willing to assume an above-average degree of risk. The company is the market leader in a growing industry, which should allow it to post solid long term earnings gains, although results will remain cyclical.

## Key Stock Statistics

| | | | |
| --- | --- | --- | --- |
| S&P EPS Est. 1997 | 2.13 | Tang. Bk. Value/Share | 13.13 |
| P/E on S&P Est. 1997 | 30.9 | Beta | 2.72 |
| S&P EPS Est. 1998 | 3.70 | Shareholders | 3,800 |
| Dividend Rate/Share | Nil | Market cap. (B) | $ 11.9 |
| Shs. outstg. (M) | 181.1 | Inst. holdings | 62% |
| Avg. daily vol. (M) | 5.697 | | |

Value of $10,000 invested 5 years ago: $ 149,219

### Fiscal Year Ending Oct. 31

| | 1997 | 1996 | 1995 | 1994 | 1993 | 1992 |
| --- | --- | --- | --- | --- | --- | --- |
| **Revenues (Million $)** | | | | | | |
| 1Q | 835.8 | 1,041 | 506.1 | 340.5 | 216.0 | 167.0 |
| 2Q | 900.9 | 1,128 | 675.4 | 411.3 | 256.0 | 180.0 |
| 3Q | — | 1,115 | 897.7 | 440.2 | 281.4 | 194.0 |
| 4Q | — | 861.0 | 982.7 | 467.8 | 327.4 | 210.0 |
| Yr. | — | 4,145 | 3,062 | 1,660 | 1,080 | 751.0 |
| **Earnings Per Share ($)** | | | | | | |
| 1Q | 0.16 | 0.93 | 0.38 | 0.22 | 0.09 | 0.05 |
| 2Q | 0.54 | 1.01 | 0.54 | 0.32 | 0.13 | 0.07 |
| 3Q | E0.67 | 0.92 | 0.79 | 0.34 | 0.17 | 0.08 |
| 4Q | E0.76 | 0.40 | 0.84 | 0.36 | 0.21 | 0.08 |
| Yr. | E2.13 | 3.27 | 2.56 | 1.25 | 0.60 | 0.27 |

**Next earnings report expected: mid August**

### Dividend Data

No cash has been paid. Two-for-one stock splits were effected in 1995, 1993, 1992 and 1986. A "poison pill" stock purchase rights plan was adopted in 1989.

This report is for information purposes and should not be considered a solicitation to buy or sell any security. Neither S&P nor any other party guarantee its accuracy or make warranties regarding results from its usage. Redistribution is prohibited without written permission. Copyright © 1997

*A Division of The McGraw·Hill Companies*

## Business Summary - 16-MAY-97

Applied Materials is the leading producer of wafer fabrication systems for the worldwide semiconductor industry. The company also sells related spare parts and services.
Contributions by geographic area in FY 96 (Oct.) were:

|  | Sales | Profits |
|---|---|---|
| North America | 31% | 32% |
| Japan | 24% | 27% |
| Korea | 14% | 12% |
| Europe | 17% | 11% |
| Asia/Pacific | 15% | 18% |

A fundamental step in fabricating a semiconductor is deposition, a process of layering either electrically insulating (dielectric) or electrically conductive material on the wafer. The company currently participates in chemical vapor deposition (CVD), physical vapor deposition (PVD) and epitaxial and polysilicon deposition.

AMAT is also a leader in etch systems. Before etch processing begins, a wafer is patterned with photoresist during photolithography. Etching then selectively removes material from areas which are not covered by the photoresist.

In February 1996, AMAT launched the Metal Etch DPS (Decoupled Plasma Source) Centura and Centura HDP-CVD, a new generation of Etch and CVD products aimed at producing critical interconnect device structures for advanced logic and memory chips.

The company also manufactures ion implantation equipment. During ion implantation, silicon wafers are bombarded by a high-velocity beam of electrically charged ions. These ions penetrate the wafer at selected sites and change the electrical properties of the implanted area.

In December 1995, AMAT unveiled a new family of products to address the rapidly growing CMP (Chemical Mechanical Polishing) market, a process increasingly being used in the manufacture of semiconductors.

The company is also a 50% stockholder in Applied Komatsu Technology, Inc., which produces thin film transistor (TFT) manufacturing systems for active-matrix liquid crystal displays.

### Important Developments

**May '97**—The company said that orders in the second quarter of FY 97 improved 10.5% from the first quarter of FY 97. The higher orders reflect customers accelerating their investment plans, especially for equipment which offers cutting-edge semiconductor production technology. AMAT also indicated that orders were particularly strong for the North American logic and microprocessor markets.

### Capitalization

**Long Term Debt:** $227,808,000 (4/27/97).

### Per Share Data ($)

| (Year Ended Oct. 31) | 1996 | 1995 | 1994 | 1993 | 1992 | 1991 | 1990 | 1989 | 1988 | 1987 |
|---|---|---|---|---|---|---|---|---|---|---|
| Tangible Bk. Val. | 13.15 | 9.95 | 5.74 | 3.72 | 3.03 | 2.41 | 2.26 | 1.96 | 1.58 | 1.24 |
| Cash Flow | 4.07 | 3.09 | 1.60 | 0.84 | 0.46 | 0.37 | 0.37 | 0.47 | 0.39 | 0.08 |
| Earnings | 3.27 | 2.56 | 1.26 | 0.60 | 0.27 | 0.19 | 0.25 | 0.39 | 0.30 | 0.00 |
| Dividends | Nil | Nil | Nil | Nil | Nil | Nil | Nil | Nil | Nil | Nil |
| Payout Ratio | Nil | Nil | Nil | Nil | Nil | Nil | Nil | Nil | Nil | Nil |
| Prices - High | 44¾ | 59⅞ | 27¼ | 20 | 9¾ | 4¾ | 5⅛ | 4⅛ | 4½ | 4¼ |
|     - Low | 21¾ | 18½ | 18⅛ | 8 | 4 | 2⁷⁄₁₆ | 2¹⁄₁₆ | 2¾ | 2⅛ | 1³⁄₁₆ |
| P/E Ratio - High | 14 | 23 | 22 | 33 | 36 | 25 | 20 | 11 | 15 | NM |
|     - Low | 7 | 7 | 14 | 13 | 15 | 13 | 8 | 7 | 7 | NM |

### Income Statement Analysis (Million $)

|  | 1996 | 1995 | 1994 | 1993 | 1992 | 1991 | 1990 | 1989 | 1988 | 1987 |
|---|---|---|---|---|---|---|---|---|---|---|
| Revs. | 4,145 | 3,062 | 1,660 | 1,080 | 751 | 639 | 567 | 502 | 363 | 174 |
| Oper. Inc. | 1,078 | 777 | 396 | 199 | 96.1 | 76.5 | 74.7 | 93.6 | 79.4 | 10.5 |
| Depr. | 149 | 83.2 | 58.5 | 37.8 | 27.7 | 24.5 | 16.4 | 11.7 | 11.4 | 9.3 |
| Int. Exp. | 20.7 | 21.4 | 16.0 | 14.2 | 15.2 | 14.0 | 6.7 | 2.8 | 3.2 | 3.3 |
| Pretax Inc. | 922 | 699 | 331 | 150 | 58.9 | 40.4 | 54.1 | 84.4 | 66.7 | 0.6 |
| Eff. Tax Rate | 35% | 35% | 35% | 34% | 33% | 35% | 37% | 39% | 40% | 42% |
| Net Inc. | 600 | 454 | 214 | 100 | 39.5 | 26.2 | 34.1 | 51.5 | 40.0 | 0.3 |

### Balance Sheet & Other Fin. Data (Million $)

|  | 1996 | 1995 | 1994 | 1993 | 1992 | 1991 | 1990 | 1989 | 1988 | 1987 |
|---|---|---|---|---|---|---|---|---|---|---|
| Cash | 404 | 769 | 422 | 266 | 223 | 140 | 72.0 | 107 | 101 | 71.0 |
| Curr. Assets | 2,693 | 2,312 | 1,231 | 776 | 582 | 434 | 367 | 343 | 276 | 179 |
| Total Assets | 3,638 | 2,965 | 1,703 | 1,120 | 854 | 661 | 558 | 434 | 339 | 233 |
| Curr. Liab. | 935 | 862 | 496 | 381 | 248 | 200 | 195 | 143 | 117 | 48.0 |
| LT Debt | 275 | 280 | 209 | 121 | 118 | 124 | 54.0 | 29.0 | 11.0 | 21.0 |
| Common Eqty. | 2,370 | 1,784 | 966 | 599 | 474 | 325 | 300 | 254 | 201 | 154 |
| Total Cap. | 2,658 | 2,075 | 1,187 | 727 | 599 | 456 | 362 | 290 | 219 | 183 |
| Cap. Exp. | 453 | 266 | 186 | 99 | 67.0 | 67.0 | 111 | 43.0 | 20.0 | 12.0 |
| Cash Flow | 748 | 547 | 272 | 137 | 67.2 | 50.7 | 50.5 | 63.6 | 52.0 | 9.1 |
| Curr. Ratio | 2.9 | 2.7 | 2.5 | 2.0 | 2.3 | 2.2 | 1.9 | 2.4 | 2.4 | 3.7 |
| % LT Debt of Cap. | 10.3 | 13.5 | 17.6 | 16.7 | 19.8 | 27.2 | 14.8 | 10.2 | 5.2 | 11.5 |
| % Net Inc.of Revs. | 14.4 | 14.8 | 12.9 | 9.2 | 5.3 | 4.1 | 6.0 | 10.3 | 11.0 | 0.2 |
| % Ret. on Assets | 18.1 | 19.5 | 14.9 | 10.0 | 4.9 | 4.3 | 6.8 | 13.2 | 13.9 | 0.2 |
| % Ret. on Equity | 28.9 | 33.0 | 26.8 | 18.4 | 9.3 | 8.3 | 12.1 | 22.4 | 22.3 | 0.3 |

Data as orig. reptd.; bef. results of disc. opers. and/or spec. items. Per share data adj. for stk. divs. as of ex-div. date. E-Estimated. NA-Not Available. NM-Not Meaningful. NR-Not Ranked.

**Office**—3050 Bowers Ave., Santa Clara, CA 95054-3299. **Tel**—(408) 727-5555. **Fax**—(408) 986-8352. **Website**—http://www.AppliedMaterials.com **Chrmn & CEO**—J. C. Morgan. **Pres**—D. Maydan. **SVP & CFO**—Gerald F. Taylor. **Secy**—D. A. Slichter. **Treas**—Nancy H. Handel. **Investor Contact**—Susan Overstreet. **Dirs**—M. Armacost, H. M. Dwight Jr., G. B. Farnsworth, P. V. Gerdine, T. Kawanishi, P. R. Low, D. Maydan, J. C. Morgan, A. J. Stein. **Transfer Agent**—Harris Trust Co. of California, LA. **Incorporated**—in California in 1967; reincorporated in Delaware in 1987. **Empl**— 9,700. **S&P Analyst:** Stephen T. Madonna, CFA

# Ascend Communications    3155

Nasdaq Symbol **ASND**

**17-MAY-97**

**Industry:** Computers (Network-ing)

**Summary:** Ascend develops, manufactures, markets, sells and sup-ports a broad range of high-speed digital wide area network access products.

---

**S&P Opinion: Buy (★★★★)**

**Quantitative Evaluations**

Outlook
(1 Lowest—5 Highest)
• **NA**

Fair Value
• **NA**

Risk
• **High**

Earn./Div. Rank
• **NR**

Technical Eval.
• **Bearish** since 2/97

Rel. Strength Rank
(1 Lowest—99 Highest)
• **24**

Insider Activity
• **Unfavorable**

| Recent Price • 47½ | Yield • Nil |
| 52 Wk Range • 80¼-36⅛ | 12-Mo. P/E • 47.0 |

Earnings vs. Previous Year
▲=Up ▼=Down ▶=No Change

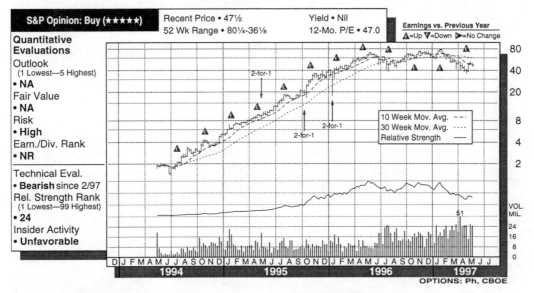

10 Week Mov. Avg. - - -
30 Week Mov. Avg. · · · ·
Relative Strength —

OPTIONS: Ph, CBOE

---

## Overview - 14-MAY-97

ASND agreed to acquire Cascade Communications for stock in March 1997, with ASND shareholders to retain 65% of the combined company. We expect the combi-nation of ASND's expertise in remote access servers and CSCC's specialization in ATM and Frame Relay switching technologies to offer substantial synergies. Revenues should continue their strong growth in 1997, reflecting exceptionally strong demand for all of the company's products. Ascend's MAX line of WAN ac-cess switches and Pipeline family of remote LAN ac-cess servers have become the products of choice for Internet service providers (ISPs), telecommuters and in-dividuals who need remote access to their networks. The company continues to innovate and to introduce new products to broaden its product lines. Customers have shown very strong interest in two of the com-pany's newest products, the MAX TNT and the GRF 400, which should bolster revenue growth in 1997.

## Valuation - 14-MAY-97

In our view, Ascend and Cascade have complementary products that will enable the combined company to offer end-to-end solutions to telephone carriers and ISPs. ASND's remote access products will reach the public carrier market through CSCC's strong distribution chan-nel and CSCC's Frame Relay products will be opened up to international markets through ASND's interna-tional channels. Moreover, the new Ascend will be much better positioned to challenge Cisco and the com-bined 3Com-U.S. Robotics. The company expects the acquisition to be mildly dilutive for 1997 and accretive to share earnings in 1998. Given a blended growth rate of 35-40% for the combined companies, we recommend purchase of ASND shares, which were recently trading at 20X our 1998 EPS estimate of $2.35.

## Key Stock Statistics

| | | | |
|---|---|---|---|
| S&P EPS Est. 1997 | 1.50 | Tang. Bk. Value/Share | 4.58 |
| P/E on S&P Est. 1997 | 31.7 | Beta | NA |
| S&P EPS Est. 1998 | 2.35 | Shareholders | 1,100 |
| Dividend Rate/Share | Nil | Market cap. (B) | $ 5.7 |
| Shs. outstg. (M) | 120.5 | Inst. holdings | 85% |
| Avg. daily vol. (M) | 6.007 | | |

Value of $10,000 invested 5 years ago: NA

### Fiscal Year Ending Dec. 31

| | 1998 | 1997 | 1996 | 1995 | 1994 | 1993 |
|---|---|---|---|---|---|---|
| **Revenues (Million $)** | | | | | | |
| 1Q | — | 202.4 | 92.03 | 20.36 | 6.80 | 3.10 |
| 2Q | — | — | 125.2 | 125.2 | 8.20 | 3.80 |
| 3Q | — | — | 154.6 | 40.04 | 10.29 | 4.00 |
| 4Q | — | — | 177.5 | 60.61 | 14.00 | 5.30 |
| Yr. | — | — | 549.3 | 149.6 | 39.34 | 16.20 |
| **Earnings Per Share ($)** | | | | | | |
| 1Q | — | 0.27 | 0.15 | 0.03 | 0.02 | NM |
| 2Q | — | E0.38 | 0.22 | 0.05 | 0.02 | 0.00 |
| 3Q | — | E0.40 | 0.20 | 0.07 | 0.03 | 0.00 |
| 4Q | — | E0.45 | 0.32 | 0.13 | 0.03 | 0.01 |
| Yr. | E2.35 | E1.50 | 0.89 | 0.28 | 0.09 | 0.02 |

**Next earnings report expected: early July**

**Dividend Data**

No cash dividends have been paid.

---

This report is for information purposes and should not be considered a solicitation to buy or sell any security. Neither S&P nor any other party guarantee its accuracy or make warranties regarding results from its usage. Redistribution is prohibited without written permission. Copyright © 1997

A Division of The McGraw-Hill Companies

## Business Summary - 14-MAY-97

Ascend Communications develops and manufactures high-speed digital remote networking access products that enable its customers to build Internet access systems, extensions and enhancements to corporate backbone networks, and videoconferencing and multimedia access facilities. These systems establish high-speed switched digital connections whose bandwidth, duration and destination can be adjusted to suit user application needs.

ASND's Multiband family of controllers is used for videoconferencing and multimedia networks and provides global bandwidth-on-demand at speeds from 56 kbit/s to 4 Mbit/s using switched digital services. The Multiband Plus product supports four simultaneous high-speed digital connections; it also incorporates inverse multiplexing, dynamic bandwidth allocation, global connectivity and comprehensive management capabilities. Sales of Multiband products accounted for 5% and 15% of net sales in 1996 and 1995, respectively.

The MAX family of integrated access servers provides bandwidth-on-demand for wide area network (WAN), Internet and multimedia access over a common set of digital access lines. The MAX can be configured with Multiband cards, providing up to 38 high-speed inverse multiplexing ports, or with Pipeline Ethernet cards and digital modem cards to act as a central-site remote LAN access server, allowing up to 672 remote users. In late 1996, ASND introduced the MAX TNT, a carrier class

WAN access switch. MAX sales accounted for about 82% and 63% of net sales in 1995 and 1994, respectively.

The GRF family of high performance IP switches, introduced in September 1996, enable carriers and ISPs to handle the high-bandwidth requirements of demanding network environments such as the Internet. GRF switches are able to deliver scaleable performance up to 10 million packets per second with 16 gigabits per seconds of bandwidth.

The Pipeline product family provides access equipment for remote office, telecommuting and small office/home office (SOHO) and Internet access. Pipeline sales accounted for about 12% and 20% of net sales in 1996 and 1995, respectively.

## Important Developments

**Mar. '97**—ASND agreed to acquire Cascade Communications (CSCC), a provider of ATM, Frame Relay and IP switching products. Under the terms of the agreement, each CSCC share will be exchanged for 0.70 ASND shares. Based on the closing price of Ascend shares on March 27, 1997 (52), the deal was valued at approximately $3.7 billion. The transaction is expected to close in the third quarter.

## Capitalization

**Long Term Debt:** None (3/97).

### Per Share Data ($)

| (Year Ended Dec. 31) | 1996 | 1995 | 1994 | 1993 | 1992 | 1991 | 1990 | 1989 | 1988 | 1987 |
|---|---|---|---|---|---|---|---|---|---|---|
| Tangible Bk. Val. | 9.58 | 2.69 | 0.46 | 0.36 | NA | NA | NA | NA | NA | NA |
| Cash Flow | 0.95 | 0.30 | 0.10 | 0.02 | -0.29 | -0.19 | NA | NA | NA | NA |
| Earnings | 0.89 | 0.28 | 0.09 | 0.02 | -0.33 | -0.21 | -0.27 | NA | NA | NA |
| Dividends | Nil | Nil | Nil | Nil | Nil | Nil | Nil | NA | NA | NA |
| Payout Ratio | Nil | Nil | Nil | Nil | Nil | Nil | Nil | NA | NA | NA |
| Prices - High | 75¼ | 40⅝ | 5⅝ | NA | NA | NA | NA | NA | NA | NA |
| - Low | 17½ | 5 | 1⁷⁄₁₆ | NA | NA | NA | NA | NA | NA | NA |
| P/E Ratio - High | 85 | NM | 60 | NA | NA | NA | NA | NA | NA | NA |
| - Low | 20 | NM | 15 | NA | NA | NA | NA | NA | NA | NA |

### Income Statement Analysis (Million $)

| | 1996 | 1995 | 1994 | 1993 | 1992 | 1991 | 1990 | 1989 | 1988 | 1987 |
|---|---|---|---|---|---|---|---|---|---|---|
| Revs. | 549 | 150 | 39.3 | 16.2 | 7.2 | 3.2 | 0.1 | NA | NA | NA |
| Oper. Inc. | 197 | 49.0 | 9.6 | 1.7 | -3.5 | -2.4 | NA | NA | NA | NA |
| Depr. | 8.8 | 2.1 | 0.6 | 0.4 | 0.4 | 0.2 | NA | NA | NA | NA |
| Int. Exp. | Nil | 0.0 | 0.1 | 0.1 | 0.1 | 0.1 | NA | NA | NA | NA |
| Pretax Inc. | 186 | 49.3 | 9.9 | 1.4 | -3.8 | -2.4 | -3.1 | NA | NA | NA |
| Eff. Tax Rate | 39% | 38% | 12% | Nil | Nil | Nil | Nil | NA | NA | NA |
| Net Inc. | 113 | 30.6 | 8.7 | 1.4 | -3.8 | -2.4 | -3.1 | NA | NA | NA |

### Balance Sheet & Other Fin. Data (Million $)

| | 1996 | 1995 | 1994 | 1993 | 1992 | 1991 | 1990 | 1989 | 1988 | 1987 |
|---|---|---|---|---|---|---|---|---|---|---|
| Cash | 373 | 211 | 35.5 | 6.3 | 6.6 | NA | NA | NA | NA | NA |
| Curr. Assets | 572 | 275 | 50.9 | 11.3 | 9.1 | NA | NA | NA | NA | NA |
| Total Assets | 652 | 335 | 53.3 | 12.4 | 10.0 | 5.8 | 2.2 | NA | NA | NA |
| Curr. Liab. | 104 | 39.3 | 9.6 | 2.5 | 1.5 | NA | NA | NA | NA | NA |
| LT Debt | Nil | Nil | 0.1 | 0.3 | 0.4 | 0.3 | 0.3 | NA | NA | NA |
| Common Eqty. | 547 | 296 | 43.7 | 9.6 | 8.1 | 4.3 | 1.4 | NA | NA | NA |
| Total Cap. | 547 | 296 | 43.8 | 9.9 | 8.5 | 4.7 | 1.8 | NA | NA | NA |
| Cap. Exp. | 58.7 | 8.9 | 1.9 | 0.3 | 0.4 | Nil | NA | NA | NA | NA |
| Cash Flow | 122 | 32.7 | 9.3 | 1.8 | -3.4 | -2.2 | NA | NA | NA | NA |
| Curr. Ratio | 5.5 | 7.0 | 5.3 | 4.5 | 6.0 | NA | NA | NA | NA | NA |
| % LT Debt of Cap. | Nil | NM | 0.2 | 3.2 | 4.6 | 7.4 | 17.6 | NA | NA | NA |
| % Net Inc.of Revs. | 20.6 | 20.4 | 22.1 | 8.3 | NM | NM | NM | NA | NA | NA |
| % Ret. on Assets | 22.1 | 15.7 | 10.4 | 12.1 | NM | NM | NM | NA | NA | NA |
| % Ret. on Equity | 25.9 | 18.0 | NM | 15.2 | NM | NM | NM | NA | NA | NA |

Data as orig. reptd.; bef. results of disc. opers. and/or spec. items. Per share data adj. for stk. divs. as of ex-div. date. E-Estimated. NA-Not Available. NM-Not Meaningful. NR-Not Ranked.

**Office**—1275 Harbor Bay Parkway, Alameda, CA 94502. **Tel**—(510) 769-6001. **Fax**—(510) 814-2345. **Website**—http://www.ascend.com **Pres & CEO**—M. Ejabat. **VP-Fin & CFO**—R. K. Dahl. **Investor Contact**—Paula Cook. **Dirs**—B. Atkins, R. K. Dahl, M. Ejabat, R. L. Evans, C. R. Kramlich, J. P. Lally, M. Schoffstall. **Transfer Agent & Registrar**—Bank of Boston, Canton, MA. **Incorporated**—in California in 1989; reincorporated in Delaware in 1994. **Empl**—721. **S&P Analyst:** Aydin Tuncer

**17-MAY-97**

**Industry:**
Manufacturing (Specialized)

**Summary:** This company is a leading worldwide manufacturer of pressure sensitive adhesives and materials, office products, labels, retail systems and specialty chemicals.

| S&P Opinion: Accumulate (★★★★) | Recent Price • 38½ | Yield • 1.8% |
| --- | --- | --- |
| | 52 Wk Range • 44½-24¾ | 12-Mo. P/E • 21.8 |

**Quantitative Evaluations**

**Outlook**
(1 Lowest—5 Highest)
• **3⁺**

**Fair Value**
• **39⅛**

**Risk**
• **Low**

**Earn./Div. Rank**
• **A-**

**Technical Eval.**
• **Bullish** since 4/97

**Rel. Strength Rank**
(1 Lowest—99 Highest)
• **47**

**Insider Activity**
• **Neutral**

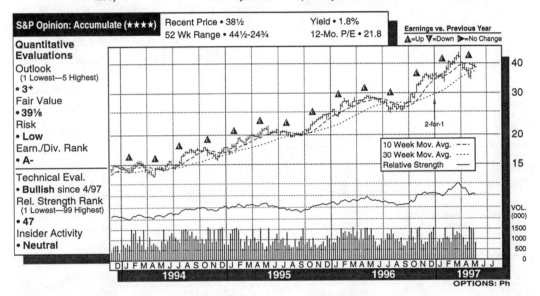

Earnings vs. Previous Year
▲=Up ▼=Down ▷=No Change

2-for-1

10 Week Mov. Avg. ---
30 Week Mov. Avg. ····
Relative Strength —

1994 1995 1996 1997

OPTIONS: Ph

## Overview - 10-APR-97

Sales of this manufacturer of pressure sensitive adhesives and materials are expected to advance 5% to 10% in 1997, as all business segments continue to benefit from growing global economies and strong packaging, durable goods, office and retail markets. Growth of newer products, such as battery labels and postal stamps, will also aid sales, boosted by capacity expansions in Germany, China, and Latin America. Currency exchange rates will remain unfavorable through the first half of 1997. Profitability should continue to improve, on the higher volumes and continuing productivity gains, while raw material costs are expected to be remain relatively stable. AVY will see the full benefit of restructuring actions taken in late 1995. The pace of stock buybacks may be slower than in 1996, which saw the use of proceeds from the sale of assets near the end of 1995. Capital spending is expected to be nearly $200 million, up from $188 million in 1996.

## Valuation - 10-APR-97

The company intends to focus on its core adhesives and office products businesses and grow through internal as well as geographic expansion. Long-term growth is being driven by the widening use of non-impact printing systems for computers and for product tracking and information needs. The proliferation of high quality graphics on packaging and consumer products is also spurring sales of pressure sensitive labels. The shares performed well since 1995, reflecting continued good gains in sales and earnings. A two-for-one split was effected at the end of 1996, and dividends have been increased for 21 consecutive years. The shares are still attractive, in view of the positive earnings outlook for the company.

## Key Stock Statistics

| | | | |
| --- | --- | --- | --- |
| S&P EPS Est. 1997 | 1.95 | Tang. Bk. Value/Share | 6.62 |
| P/E on S&P Est. 1997 | 19.7 | Beta | 0.73 |
| S&P EPS Est. 1998 | 2.20 | Shareholders | 10,900 |
| Dividend Rate/Share | 0.68 | Market cap. (B) | $ 4.0 |
| Shs. outstg. (M) | 104.2 | Inst. holdings | 58% |
| Avg. daily vol. (M) | 0.297 | | |

Value of $10,000 invested 5 years ago: $ 35,026

## Fiscal Year Ending Dec. 31

| | 1998 | 1997 | 1996 | 1995 | 1994 | 1993 |
| --- | --- | --- | --- | --- | --- | --- |
| **Revenues (Million $)** | | | | | | |
| 1Q | — | 828.9 | 796.6 | 773.2 | 667.7 | 666.5 |
| 2Q | — | — | 797.7 | 780.5 | 718.6 | 662.2 |
| 3Q | — | — | 819.3 | 783.5 | 733.7 | 638.1 |
| 4Q | — | — | 808.9 | 776.7 | 736.7 | 641.9 |
| Yr. | — | — | 3,223 | 3,134 | 2,857 | 2,609 |
| **Earnings Per Share ($)** | | | | | | |
| 1Q | — | 0.47 | 0.38 | 0.32 | 0.22 | 0.19 |
| 2Q | — | E0.47 | 0.39 | 0.33 | 0.25 | 0.19 |
| 3Q | — | E0.49 | 0.44 | 0.33 | 0.25 | 0.17 |
| 4Q | — | E0.52 | 0.46 | 0.36 | 0.26 | 0.17 |
| Yr. | E2.20 | E1.95 | 1.68 | 1.35 | 0.99 | 0.72 |

**Next earnings report expected: late July**

**Dividend Data** (Dividends have been paid since 1964.)

| Amount ($) | Date Decl. | Ex-Div. Date | Stock of Record | Payment Date |
| --- | --- | --- | --- | --- |
| 0.170 | Oct. 24 | Dec. 04 | Dec. 06 | Dec. 20 '96 |
| 2-for-1 | Oct. 24 | Dec. 23 | Dec. 06 | Dec. 20 '96 |
| 0.170 | Jan. 31 | Mar. 03 | Mar. 05 | Mar. 19 '97 |
| 0.170 | Apr. 24 | Jun. 02 | Jun. 04 | Jun. 18 '97 |

This report is for information purposes and should not be considered a solicitation to buy or sell any security. Neither S&P nor any other party guarantee its accuracy or make warranties regarding results from its usage. Redistribution is prohibited without written permission. Copyright © 1997

A Division of The McGraw-Hill Companies

## Business Summary - 10-APR-97

Avery Dennison Corp. is a leading global manufacturer of pressure sensitive technology and self-adhesive solutions for consumer products and label systems, including office products, product identification and control systems, and specialty tapes and chemicals. It is benefiting from the increasing demand for more informative labels on products, the expanding use of personal computers and printers, proliferation of bar codes, and the growth of consumer spending in developing countries. AVY achieved record net sales and earnings in 1996, despite costs of investments in new businesses and products. The company realized a 21.4% return on equity. Excluding divested units and currency, sales increased 6.4%. AVY was formed through the 1990 merger of Avery International Corp. and Dennison Manufacturing Corp. Industry segment contributions in 1996 were:

|                                  | Sales | Profits |
|----------------------------------|-------|---------|
| Adhesives and materials          | 50%   | 50%     |
| Consumer and converted products  | 50%   | 50%     |

Foreign operations, primarily in Europe, accounted for 36% of sales and 27% of profits in 1995. AVY is investing to build a business base in Asia Pacific, Latin America and Eastern Europe.

The adhesives and materials group includes pressure sensitive, self-adhesive coated papers, plastic films and metal foils in roll and sheet form, graphic and decoration films and labels, specialty fastening and bonding tapes, and adhesives, protective coatings and electroconductive resins for industrial, automotive, aerospace, appliance, electronic, medical and consumer markets.

Consumer and office products consist of pressure sensitive labels, laser and ink-jet print labels and software, notebooks, binders, presentation and organizing systems, marking devices and numerous other products for office, home and school uses.

Converted products include custom labels and application and imprinting machines for the industrial, durable goods, cosmetic, battery, consumer packaged goods and electronic data processing markets; self-adhesive postal stamps; automotive decoration films; and Soabar brand tags, labels, printers, marking and coding systems, application devices, plastic fasteners and cable ties for apparel, retail and industrial markets for use in identification, tracking and control applications.

About 3.8 million common shares were repurchased in 1996, at a cost of $109 million. AVY has bought back about 20% of its common stock since 1991, for $430 million. About 5 million shares remained authorized for purchase at the end of 1996. AVY plans to keep its total debt to capital ratio in the 35% to 40% range. The ratio was 35.9% at the end of 1996.

### Capitalization

**Long Term Debt:** $370,700,000 (12/96).

### Per Share Data ($)

| (Year Ended Dec. 31) | 1996 | 1995 | 1994 | 1993 | 1992 | 1991 | 1990 | 1989 | 1988 | 1987 |
|---|---|---|---|---|---|---|---|---|---|---|
| Tangible Bk. Val. | 5.73 | 6.52 | 5.54 | 5.17 | 5.65 | 5.54 | 5.60 | 4.55 | 4.22 | 3.95 |
| Cash Flow | 2.76 | 2.36 | 1.90 | 1.54 | 1.44 | 1.26 | 0.77 | 1.55 | 1.39 | 0.84 |
| Earnings | 1.68 | 1.35 | 0.99 | 0.72 | 0.66 | 0.51 | 0.05 | 0.98 | 0.88 | 0.40 |
| Dividends | 0.62 | 0.55 | 0.50 | 0.45 | 0.41 | 0.38 | 0.32 | 0.27 | 0.23 | 0.21 |
| Payout Ratio | 37% | 41% | 50% | 62% | 60% | 74% | 672% | 28% | 26% | 52% |
| Prices - High | 36½ | 25⅛ | 18 | 15¾ | 14⅝ | 12⅞ | 16½ | 16⅝ | 13 | 14⅝ |
| - Low | 23¾ | 16⅝ | 13¼ | 12⅝ | 11⅝ | 9½ | 7¾ | 10½ | 9⅝ | 7⅝ |
| P/E Ratio - High | 22 | 19 | 18 | 22 | 22 | 25 | NM | 17 | 15 | 36 |
| - Low | 14 | 12 | 13 | 17 | 17 | 19 | NM | 11 | 11 | 19 |

### Income Statement Analysis (Million $)

| | 1996 | 1995 | 1994 | 1993 | 1992 | 1991 | 1990 | 1989 | 1988 | 1987 |
|---|---|---|---|---|---|---|---|---|---|---|
| Revs. | 2,223 | 3,114 | 2,857 | 2,609 | 2,623 | 2,545 | 2,590 | 1,732 | 1,582 | 1,466 |
| Oper. Inc. | 419 | 375 | 318 | 271 | 266 | 235 | 245 | 195 | 197 | 161 |
| Depr. | 113 | 108 | 103 | 95.4 | 93.9 | 92.3 | 90.1 | 50.3 | 45.1 | 36.3 |
| Int. Exp. | 40.9 | 47.5 | 45.7 | 45.5 | 44.9 | 42.6 | 43.3 | 24.3 | 26.3 | 23.9 |
| Pretax Inc. | 271 | 225 | 173 | 132 | 130 | 105 | 16.0 | 139 | 128 | 78.0 |
| Eff. Tax Rate | 35% | 36% | 37% | 37% | 39% | 40% | 62% | 38% | 39% | 55% |
| Net Inc. | 176 | 144 | 109 | 83.3 | 80.1 | 63.0 | 5.9 | 86.5 | 77.7 | 34.7 |

### Balance Sheet & Other Fin. Data (Million $)

| | 1996 | 1995 | 1994 | 1993 | 1992 | 1991 | 1990 | 1989 | 1988 | 1987 |
|---|---|---|---|---|---|---|---|---|---|---|
| Cash | 3.8 | 27.0 | 3.1 | 5.8 | 3.9 | 5.3 | 6.5 | 3.1 | 5.9 | 8.0 |
| Curr. Assets | 805 | 800 | 677 | 615 | 661 | 701 | 847 | 506 | 503 | 489 |
| Total Assets | 2,037 | 1,964 | 1,763 | 1,639 | 1,684 | 1,740 | 1,890 | 1,142 | 1,119 | 1,051 |
| Curr. Liab. | 694 | 673 | 554 | 473 | 439 | 475 | 548 | 324 | 330 | 324 |
| LT Debt | 371 | 334 | 347 | 311 | 335 | 330 | 376 | 213 | 215 | 204 |
| Common Eqty. | 832 | 816 | 729 | 719 | 803 | 825 | 846 | 539 | 509 | 466 |
| Total Cap. | 1,247 | 1,191 | 1,116 | 1,075 | 1,205 | 1,235 | 1,310 | 818 | 790 | 727 |
| Cap. Exp. | 188 | 190 | 163 | 101 | 88.0 | 123 | 149 | 83.0 | 90.0 | 103 |
| Cash Flow | 289 | 252 | 212 | 179 | 174 | 155 | 96.0 | 137 | 123 | 71.0 |
| Curr. Ratio | 1.2 | 1.2 | 1.2 | 1.3 | 1.5 | 1.5 | 1.5 | 1.6 | 1.5 | 1.5 |
| % LT Debt of Cap. | 29.8 | 28.0 | 31.1 | 28.9 | 27.8 | 26.7 | 28.7 | 26.1 | 27.2 | 28.0 |
| % Net Inc.of Revs. | 5.5 | 4.6 | 3.8 | 3.2 | 3.1 | 2.5 | 0.2 | 5.0 | 4.9 | 2.4 |
| % Ret. on Assets | 8.8 | 7.7 | 6.6 | 5.1 | 4.8 | 3.5 | 0.3 | 7.6 | 7.1 | 3.5 |
| % Ret. on Equity | 21.4 | 18.2 | 15.5 | 11.2 | 10.0 | 7.6 | 0.7 | 16.5 | 15.9 | 8.2 |

Data as orig. reptd.; bef. results of disc. opers. and/or spec. items. Per share data adj. for stk. divs. as of ex-div. date. E-Estimated. NA-Not Available. NM-Not Meaningful. NR-Not Ranked.

**Office**—150 North Orange Grove Blvd., Pasadena, CA 91103. **Tel**—(818) 304-2000. **E-mail**—investorcom@averydennison.com **Website**—http:// www.averydennison.com**Chrmn & CEO**—C. D. Miller. **Pres & COO**—P. M. Neal. **SVP-Fin & CFO**—R. G. Jenkins. **VP & Secy**—R. G. van Schoonenberg. **VP, Treas & Investor Contact**—Wayne H. Smith. **Dirs**—D. L. Allison Jr., J. C. Argue, J. T. Bok, F. V. Cahouet, R. M. Ferry, C. D. Miller, P. W. Mullin, P. M. Neal, S. R. Petersen, J. B. Slaughter. **Transfer Agent & Registrar**—First Interstate Bank, LA. **Incorporated**—in California in 1946; reincorporated in Delaware in 1977. **Empl**— 15,850. **S&P Analyst:** Richard O'Reilly, CFA

# Benchmark Electronics  7299

NYSE Symbol **BHE**

**In S&P SmallCap 600**

**17-MAY-97**

**Industry:** Electrical Equipment

**Summary:** This company provides contract manufacturing and engineering services to OEMs in various industries.

## Quantitative Evaluations

**Outlook** (1 Lowest—5 Highest)
• **5**

**Fair Value**
• **57¾**

**Risk**
• **Average**

**Earn./Div. Rank**
• **B+**

**Technical Eval.**
• **Bearish** since 4/97

**Rel. Strength Rank** (1 Lowest—99 Highest)
• **77**

**Insider Activity**
• **NA**

Recent Price • 31¼
52 Wk Range • 34⅜-24¼

Yield • Nil
12-Mo. P/E • 15.4

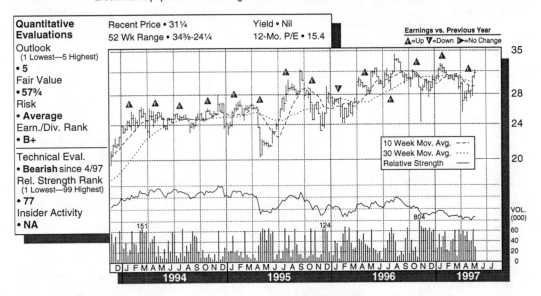

Earnings vs. Previous Year
▲=Up ▼=Down ▶=No Change

10 Week Mov. Avg. — -
30 Week Mov. Avg. ·····
Relative Strength —

## Business Profile - 06-MAY-97

BHE provides contract manufacturing services to original equipment manufacturers in various industries. Customers include manufacturers of medical devices, telecommunications equipment, computer systems, tests and instrumentation, and industrial controls. In July 1996, BHE acquired EMD Technologies, Inc., a provider of engineering services and contract manufacturing for the electronics industry. The acquisition provided the company with access to markets in the Midwest and Northeast, without any overlap of customers. It also provided additional production capacity and a broader base of technical resources. Continued outsourcing of products by OEMs has kept bookings and earnings strong.

## Operational Review - 06-MAY-97

Based on a brief report, net sales in the three months ended March 31, 1997, spurted 149%, year to year, largely reflecting the mid-1996 acquisition of EMD Technologies. Gross profit was up nearly as much (141%), but after much higher selling, general and administrative expenses, and goodwill amortization ($417,435) and interest expense ($613,656) in 1997 only, the advance in pretax income was trimmed to 78%. After taxes at 38.0%, versus 38.3%, net income was up 79%, to $3,290,930 ($0.56 a share, on 42% more shares), from $1,838,969 ($0.45).

## Stock Performance - 16-MAY-97

In the past 30 trading days, BHE's shares have increased 16%, compared to a 9% rise in the S&P 500. Average trading volume for the past five days was 5,600 shares, compared with the 40-day moving average of 10,303 shares.

## Key Stock Statistics

| | | | |
|---|---|---|---|
| Dividend Rate/Share | Nil | Shareholders | 100 |
| Shs. outstg. (M) | 5.7 | Market cap. (B) | $0.179 |
| Avg. daily vol. (M) | 0.009 | Inst. holdings | 53% |
| Tang. Bk. Value/Share | 14.05 | | |
| Beta | 0.15 | | |

Value of $10,000 invested 5 years ago: $ 25,520

### Fiscal Year Ending Dec. 31

| | 1997 | 1996 | 1995 | 1994 | 1993 | 1992 |
|---|---|---|---|---|---|---|
| **Revenues (Million $)** | | | | | | |
| 1Q | 75.72 | 30.38 | 23.12 | 24.28 | 15.20 | 10.00 |
| 2Q | — | 33.50 | 23.65 | 25.05 | 17.06 | 11.60 |
| 3Q | — | 62.30 | 24.39 | 25.10 | 19.57 | 15.10 |
| 4Q | — | 75.11 | 26.20 | 23.75 | 24.03 | 14.00 |
| Yr. | — | 201.3 | 97.35 | 98.17 | 75.86 | 50.60 |
| **Earnings Per Share ($)** | | | | | | |
| 1Q | 0.56 | 0.45 | 0.38 | 0.33 | 0.21 | 0.20 |
| 2Q | — | 0.49 | 0.39 | 0.34 | 0.25 | 0.19 |
| 3Q | — | 0.51 | 0.38 | 0.36 | 0.30 | 0.22 |
| 4Q | — | 0.48 | 0.35 | 0.39 | 0.34 | 0.22 |
| Yr. | — | 1.92 | 1.50 | 1.41 | 1.10 | 0.83 |

**Next earnings report expected: mid July**

### Dividend Data

No cash dividends have been paid. Benchmark expects to retain earnings for operation and expansion of its business.

This report is for information purposes and should not be considered a solicitation to buy or sell any security. Neither S&P nor any other party guarantee its accuracy or make warranties regarding results from its usage. Redistribution is prohibited without written permission. Copyright © 1997

*A Division of The McGraw·Hill Companies*

STANDARD
&POOR'S
STOCK REPORTS

**Benchmark Electronics, Inc.**

**7299**

**17-MAY-97**

## Business Summary - 06-MAY-97

Benchmark Electronics, Inc. provides contract electronicsmanufacturing and design services to original equipment manufacturers in select industries, including medical devices, communications equipment, industrial and business computers, testing instrumentation and industrial controls. The company specializes in manufacturing high quality, technologically complex printed circuit board assemblies with computer-automated equipment using surface mount and pin-through-hole interconnection technologies for customers requiring low to medium volume production runs. The company frequently works with customers from product design and prototype stages through ongoing production and, in some cases, final assembly of the customers' products andprovides manufacturing services for successive product generations. As a result, the company is often an integral part of its customers' operations.

Substantially all of the company's manufacturing services are provided on a turnkey basis, whereby the company purchases customer-specified components from its extensive network of suppliers, assembles the components on finished printed circuit boards, performs post-production testing and provides thecustomer with production process and testing documentation. The company offers its customers flexible, "just-in-time" delivery programs allowing product shipments to be closely coordinated with the customers' inventory requirements. In certain instances, the company completes the assembly of its customers' products at the company's facilities by integrating printed circuit board assemblies into other elements of the customers' products. The company alsoprovides manufacturing services on a consignment basis, whereby the company, utilizing components provided by the customer, provides only assembly and post-production testing services. The company operates a total of 29 surface mount production lines at its facilities in Angleton, Texas, Beaverton, Oregon and Winona, Minnesota.

On July 30, 1996, the company completed its acquisition of EMD Technologies, Inc., an independent provider of contract manufacturing and product design services for OEMs in industriescomparable to those targeted by the company. EMD's manufacturing services focus on manufacturing complex printed circuit board assemblies, operating 15 surface mount production lines at its Winona, Minnesota facilities. EMD's product design services include the complete design and development of electronic products andmechanical packages, from conceptual design of circuit boards to configuring subsystems and enclosures.

## Capitalization

**Long Term Debt:** $30,485,333 (12/96).
**Options:** To buy 678,830 shs. at an average of $23.99 a share.

### Per Share Data ($)

| (Year Ended Dec. 31) | 1996 | 1995 | 1994 | 1993 | 1992 | 1991 | 1990 | 1989 | 1988 | 1987 |
|---|---|---|---|---|---|---|---|---|---|---|
| Tangible Bk. Val. | 14.05 | 11.60 | 10.01 | 8.59 | 7.42 | 5.10 | 4.44 | 1.69 | 1.14 | NA |
| Cash Flow | 3.31 | 2.00 | 1.87 | 1.45 | 1.14 | 0.92 | 0.92 | 0.73 | NA | NA |
| Earnings | 1.92 | 1.50 | 1.41 | 1.10 | 0.83 | 0.66 | 0.76 | 0.65 | 0.34 | 0.22 |
| Dividends | Nil | Nil | Nil | Nil | Nil | Nil | Nil | Nil | Nil | Nil |
| Payout Ratio | Nil | Nil | Nil | Nil | Nil | Nil | Nil | Nil | Nil | Nil |
| Prices - High | 34⅜ | 31⅞ | 28 | 23⅞ | 17¾ | 12¼ | 8¾ | NA | NA | NA |
|      - Low | 24⅛ | 20¼ | 22½ | 15 | 10⅜ | 4⅝ | 3⅝ | NA | NA | NA |
| P/E Ratio - High | 18 | 21 | 20 | 22 | 21 | 19 | 12 | NA | NA | NA |
|      - Low | 13 | 13 | 16 | 14 | 13 | 7 | 5 | NA | NA | NA |

### Income Statement Analysis (Million $)

| | 1996 | 1995 | 1994 | 1993 | 1992 | 1991 | 1990 | 1989 | 1988 | 1987 |
|---|---|---|---|---|---|---|---|---|---|---|
| Revs. | 201 | 97.4 | 98.2 | 75.9 | 50.6 | 33.3 | 21.3 | 18.1 | 8.1 | 6.8 |
| Oper. Inc. | 21.8 | 11.3 | 10.7 | 7.9 | 5.4 | 3.8 | 3.0 | 2.0 | 0.8 | 0.4 |
| Depr. | 6.4 | 2.1 | 1.9 | 1.4 | 1.1 | 0.8 | 0.4 | 0.2 | 0.0 | 0.0 |
| Int. Exp. | 1.4 | Nil | Nil | Nil | Nil | Nil | 0.1 | 0.1 | 0.0 | 0.1 |
| Pretax Inc. | 14.4 | 9.5 | 9.0 | 6.9 | 4.8 | 3.3 | 3.1 | 1.9 | 0.8 | 0.5 |
| Eff. Tax Rate | 39% | 36% | 36% | 36% | 34% | 36% | 35% | 29% | 14% | Nil |
| Net Inc. | 8.9 | 6.2 | 5.8 | 4.5 | 3.1 | 2.1 | 2.0 | 1.4 | 0.7 | 0.5 |

### Balance Sheet & Other Fin. Data (Million $)

| | 1996 | 1995 | 1994 | 1993 | 1992 | 1991 | 1990 | 1989 | 1988 | 1987 |
|---|---|---|---|---|---|---|---|---|---|---|
| Cash | 13.8 | 2.8 | 8.4 | 10.1 | 13.3 | 3.1 | 7.1 | 0.1 | 0.1 | NA |
| Curr. Assets | 103 | 47.0 | 38.5 | 42.0 | 30.3 | 15.6 | 15.7 | 5.1 | 3.5 | NA |
| Total Assets | 168 | 57.0 | 48.2 | 47.4 | 34.4 | 20.0 | 17.4 | 6.6 | 3.9 | NA |
| Curr. Liab. | 30.7 | 9.7 | 7.6 | 12.9 | 4.5 | 3.3 | 2.8 | 2.3 | 1.4 | NA |
| LT Debt | 30.4 | Nil | Nil | Nil | Nil | Nil | Nil | 0.1 | 0.1 | NA |
| Common Eqty. | 105 | 46.6 | 40.1 | 34.2 | 29.6 | 16.3 | 14.2 | 3.5 | 1.9 | NA |
| Total Cap. | 137 | 47.4 | 40.7 | 34.6 | 29.8 | 16.5 | 14.3 | 3.7 | 2.0 | NA |
| Cap. Exp. | 8.7 | 2.3 | 6.3 | 2.8 | 0.9 | 7.2 | 0.5 | 1.3 | 0.3 | 0.1 |
| Cash Flow | 15.2 | 8.2 | 7.7 | 5.9 | 4.3 | 2.9 | 2.4 | 1.5 | NA | NA |
| Curr. Ratio | 3.4 | 4.9 | 5.1 | 3.3 | 6.8 | 4.7 | 5.6 | 2.2 | 2.6 | NA |
| % LT Debt of Cap. | 22.2 | Nil | Nil | Nil | Nil | Nil | Nil | 2.4 | 5.2 | NA |
| % Net Inc.of Revs. | 4.4 | 6.4 | 5.9 | 5.9 | 6.2 | 6.3 | 9.4 | 7.6 | 8.8 | 6.8 |
| % Ret. on Assets | 7.9 | 11.7 | 12.0 | 10.9 | 10.6 | 11.3 | 14.6 | 26.1 | 22.5 | NA |
| % Ret. on Equity | 11.7 | 14.2 | 15.5 | 14.0 | 12.5 | 13.8 | 20.6 | 50.3 | 59.9 | NA |

Data as orig. reptd.; bef. results of disc. opers. and/or spec. items. Per share data adj. for stk. divs. as of ex-div. date. E-Estimated. NA-Not Available. NM-Not Meaningful. NR-Not Ranked.

**Office**—3000 Technology Drive, Angleton, TX 77515. **Tel**—(409) 849-6550. **Fax**—(409) 848-5271. **Chrmn**—J. C. Custer. **Pres & CEO**—D. E. Nigbor. **EVP-Fin & CFO**—Cary T. Fu. **Dirs**—S. A. Barton, G. W. Bodzy, J. C. Custer, P. G. Dorflinger, C. T. Fu, D. E. Nigbor. **Transfer Agent & Registrar**—Harris Trust & Savings Bank, c/o Harris Trust Co. of New York, NYC. **Incorporated**—in Texas in 1981. **Empl**— 1,445. **S&P Analyst:** C.F.B.

# BioChem Pharma    3273F
### Nasdaq Symbol **BCHXF**

**17-MAY-97**

**Industry:**
Health Care (Drugs - Generic & Other)

**Summary:** This Quebec-based company is involved in the research and manufacture of therapeutics, vaccines and diagnostics.

| S&P Opinion: Accumulate (★★★★) | Recent Price • 22 | Yield • Nil |
| --- | --- | --- |
| | 52 Wk Range • 30¾-13 | 12-Mo. P/E • NM |

**Quantitative Evaluations**

**Outlook**
(1 Lowest—5 Highest)
• **NA**

**Fair Value**
• **NA**

**Risk**
• **High**

**Earn./Div. Rank**
• **B-**

**Technical Eval.**
• **Bearish** since 3/97

**Rel. Strength Rank**
(1 Lowest—99 Highest)
• **69**

**Insider Activity**
• **Neutral**

**Earnings vs. Previous Year**
▲=Up ▼=Down ▶=No Change

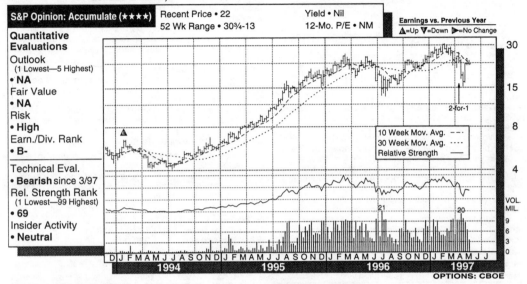

10 Week Mov. Avg. - - -
30 Week Mov. Avg. · · · ·
Relative Strength ——

2-for-1

VOL. MIL.

OPTIONS: CBOE

## Overview - 24-APR-97

This Canada-based biotechnology company operates through three subsidiaries: BioChem Therapeutic, IAF BioVac and BioChem ImmunoSystems. This maker of therapeutics, vaccines and diagnostics is a leader in viral, cancer, and pain research. Its 3TC AIDS drug, commercially known as Epivir, is being marketed together with Glaxo Wellcome's AZT as a first-line dual therapy for HIV positive patients. In the first quarter of 1997, BioChem received C$24.6 million in royalties from Glaxo, as worldwide sales of Epivir surged to C$187.4 million. Epivir and AZT are viewed as the cornerstones of HIV therapy, which may also include protease inhibitors as part of an anti-HIV cocktail. Positive Phase III results were recently announced for the company's other lead drug, lamivudine, for treating hepatitis B. BioChem expects to file for marketing approval for lamivudine in Asia in the summer of 1997, followed by filings in Europe and North America in the first half of 1998.

## Valuation - 24-APR-97

BioChem Pharma's operational cash flow has been bolstered significantly by the issuance of common shares and the rapid growth in royalties from 3TC/Epivir. As a result, the company has approximately C$319.2 million in cash and short-term investments, providing strength for its R&D activities, and also leaving the company well positioned for future acquisitions. The combination therapy with AZT and a protease inhibitor promises to expand the market for long-term AIDS management as the drug cocktail can frustrate the ability of the virus to develop immunity. On the basis of expected strong growth in Epivir, the company's R&D pipeline, and strong management, we recommend that investors accumulate BCHXF shares as part of a diversified portfolio.

## Key Stock Statistics

| | | | |
| --- | --- | --- | --- |
| S&P EPS Est. 1997 | 0.60 | Tang. Bk. Value/Share | 2.65 |
| P/E on S&P Est. 1997 | NA | Beta | 1.60 |
| S&P EPS Est. 1998 | 0.90 | Shareholders | 300 |
| Dividend Rate/Share | Nil | Market cap. (B) | $ 1.2 |
| Shs. outstg. (M) | 53.2 | Inst. holdings | 92% |
| Avg. daily vol. (M) | 1.753 | | |

Value of $10,000 invested 5 years ago: $ 22,675

## Fiscal Year Ending Dec. 31

| | 1998 | 1997 | 1996 | 1995 | 1994 | 1993 |
| --- | --- | --- | --- | --- | --- | --- |
| **Revenues (Million Can. $)** | | | | | | |
| 1Q | — | 63.34 | 50.91 | 48.80 | — | 3.60 |
| 2Q | — | — | 56.94 | 44.98 | — | 10.40 |
| 3Q | — | — | 60.81 | 41.74 | — | 13.60 |
| 4Q | — | — | 64.96 | 51.87 | — | 9.60 |
| Yr. | — | — | 233.6 | 187.4 | 109.6 | 42.20 |

| | 1998 | 1997 | 1996 | 1995 | 1994 | 1993 |
| --- | --- | --- | --- | --- | --- | --- |
| **Earnings Per Share (Can. $)** | | | | | | |
| 1Q | — | 0.12 | 0.02 | -0.01 | — | -0.03 |
| 2Q | — | E0.14 | 0.04 | -0.03 | — | -0.03 |
| 3Q | — | E0.16 | 0.07 | -0.06 | — | -0.01 |
| 4Q | — | E0.17 | 0.19 | 0.04 | — | -0.04 |
| Yr. | E0.90 | E0.60 | 0.31 | -0.05 | -0.15 | -0.10 |

**Next earnings report expected: late July**

## Dividend Data

| Amount (U.S. $) | Date Decl. | Ex-Div. Date | Stock of Record | Payment Date |
| --- | --- | --- | --- | --- |
| 2-for-1 | Mar. 12 | Apr. 08 | Apr. 07 | Apr. 07 '97 |

This report is for information purposes and should not be considered a solicitation to buy or sell any security. Neither S&P nor any other party guarantee its accuracy or make warranties regarding results from its usage. Redistribution is prohibited without written permission. Copyright © 1997

*A Division of The McGraw·Hill Companies*

## Business Summary - 24-APR-97

BioChem Pharma Inc., headquartered in Quebec, Canada, is engaged in the research and development, manufacture and marketing of pharmaceutical, diagnostic and vaccine products. BCHXF conducts business through three subsidiaries: BioChem Therapeutic, IAF BioVac and BioChem ImmunoSystems.

R&D efforts in therapeutics are the responsibility of wholly owned BioChem Therapeutic Inc. (formed in February 1993) and are focused mainly on novel therapeutic products to treat serious diseases, including AIDS and hepatitis B, cancer and pain. The most significant product is 3TC (generically known as lamivudine), a nucleoside analog developed in collaboration with Glaxo-Wellcome as a treatment for AIDS. In November 1995, BioChem received FDA approval to sell 3TC under the name Epivir as a dual therapy with Glaxo-Wellcome's AZT in AIDS treatment. In July 1996, BCHXF presented data that showed a triple combination of Epivir, AZT, and a protease inhibitor reduced viral loads in HIV infected patients to undetectable levels. The company is also developing lamivudine to treat hepatitis B.

IAF BioVac Inc. produces and markets classical vaccines for sale principally to the Canadian market. Vaccine products include influenza, diphtheria, tetanus and tuberculosis, among others. BioVac is currently proceeding with the construction of a $36.0 million manufacturing facility being funded through the sale of BioVac stock and loans/grants from government agencies.

BioChem ImmunoSystems makes and markets diagnostic products and a fully automated laboratory analyzer for the detection of various infectious and other diseases. Most of BCHXF revenues are derived from the sale of diagnostic products. Diagnostic product sales were C$119 million in the first nine months of 1996. ImmunoSystems plans to aggressively grow its diagnostic offerings through internal research and development.

In July 1995, BioChem entered into a long-term agreement with Warner-Lambert Co. to develop orally active, small-molecule compounds for the treatment and prevention of thrombosis. BCHXF estimated that it will receive nearly U.S.$30 million in up-front and milestone payments.

### Important Developments

**Apr. '97**—BCHXF announced positive results from a Phase III clinical study of lamiduvine in patients with chronic hepatitis B. The company intends to file for regulatory approval of lamiduvine worldwide beginning with filings in Asia in summer 1997.

### Capitalization

**Long Term Debt:** C$60,803,000 (3/97).
**Minority Interest:** C$11,920,000.

### Per Share Data (U.S. $)

| (Year Ended Dec. 31) | 1996 | 1995 | 1994 | 1993 | 1992 | 1991 | 1990 | 1989 | 1988 | 1987 |
|---|---|---|---|---|---|---|---|---|---|---|
| Tangible Bk. Val. | 2.65 | 0.81 | 0.57 | 0.74 | 0.85 | 0.76 | 0.50 | 0.36 | NA | NA |
| Cash Flow | 0.31 | 0.06 | -0.06 | -0.06 | -0.10 | 0.17 | 0.00 | 0.01 | NA | NA |
| Earnings | 0.23 | -0.03 | -0.05 | -0.08 | -0.13 | 0.15 | -0.02 | 0.00 | NA | NA |
| Dividends | Nil | Nil | -0.11 | Nil | Nil | Nil | Nil | Nil | NA | NA |
| Payout Ratio | Nil | Nil | Nil | Nil | Nil | Nil | Nil | Nil | NA | NA |
| Prices - High | 26¼ | 20⅝ | 6⅞ | 8½ | 15 | 11¾ | NA | NA | NA | NA |
| - Low | 13 | 6⅛ | 4⅛ | 4¼ | 5⅜ | 3⅞ | NA | NA | NA | NA |
| P/E Ratio - High | NM | NM | NM | NM | NM | 76 | NA | NA | NA | NA |
| - Low | NM | NM | NM | NM | NM | 25 | NA | NA | NA | NA |

### Income Statement Analysis (Million U.S. $)

| | 1996 | 1995 | 1994 | 1993 | 1992 | 1991 | 1990 | 1989 | 1988 | 1987 |
|---|---|---|---|---|---|---|---|---|---|---|
| Revs. | 171 | 137 | 77.9 | 29.4 | 26.9 | 23.0 | 12.2 | 3.6 | NA | NA |
| Oper. Inc. | 92.3 | 22.5 | 3.7 | -1.1 | -2.8 | -1.2 | -0.8 | -0.8 | NA | NA |
| Depr. | 8.4 | 9.5 | 4.4 | 2.2 | 2.2 | 1.3 | 0.5 | 0.3 | NA | NA |
| Int. Exp. | 5.5 | 6.3 | 3.2 | 1.0 | 0.9 | 0.7 | 0.4 | 0.2 | NA | NA |
| Pretax Inc. | 28.6 | 6.6 | -2.6 | -6.1 | -9.7 | 10.9 | -0.7 | 0.4 | NA | NA |
| Eff. Tax Rate | 3.70% | 60% | NM | NM | NM | 0.60% | NM | 55% | NA | NA |
| Net Inc. | 24.4 | -3.6 | -10.2 | -7.3 | -10.4 | 10.8 | -0.8 | 0.2 | NA | NA |

### Balance Sheet & Other Fin. Data (Million U.S. $)

| | 1996 | 1995 | 1994 | 1993 | 1992 | 1991 | 1990 | 1989 | 1988 | 1987 |
|---|---|---|---|---|---|---|---|---|---|---|
| Cash | 230 | 46.3 | 23.0 | 42.6 | 47.4 | 31.8 | 23.2 | 15.4 | NA | NA |
| Curr. Assets | 322 | 126 | 95.2 | 62.0 | 64.8 | 49.5 | 29.5 | 19.4 | NA | NA |
| Total Assets | 418 | 208 | 177 | 109 | 109 | 93.0 | 45.0 | 24.0 | NA | NA |
| Curr. Liab. | 56.9 | 50.7 | 41.9 | 16.1 | 14.0 | 16.4 | 5.9 | 1.0 | NA | NA |
| LT Debt | 42.1 | 50.9 | 57.7 | 10.6 | 2.3 | 3.3 | 4.5 | 1.4 | NA | NA |
| Common Eqty. | 304 | 98.3 | 71.5 | 79.6 | 89.9 | 71.4 | 34.2 | 21.7 | NA | NA |
| Total Cap. | 356 | 154 | 132 | 92.6 | 94.5 | 75.9 | 38.8 | 23.2 | NA | NA |
| Cap. Exp. | 13.4 | NA | 7.9 | 13.0 | 7.1 | 3.7 | 4.2 | 1.5 | NA | NA |
| Cash Flow | 32.7 | 5.9 | -5.8 | -5.2 | -8.2 | 12.1 | -0.3 | 0.5 | NA | NA |
| Curr. Ratio | 5.7 | 2.5 | 2.3 | 3.8 | 4.6 | 3.0 | 5.0 | 19.1 | NA | NA |
| % LT Debt of Cap. | 11.8 | 33.1 | 43.7 | 11.4 | 2.4 | 4.4 | 11.6 | 6.0 | NA | NA |
| % Net Inc.of Revs. | 14.3 | NM | NM | NM | NM | 46.8 | NM | 5.3 | NA | NA |
| % Ret. on Assets | 7.8 | NM | NM | NM | NM | 14.8 | NM | NA | NA | NA |
| % Ret. on Equity | 12.1 | NM | NM | NM | NM | 19.3 | NM | NA | NA | NA |

Data as orig. reptd.; bef. results of disc. opers. and/or spec. items. 1994 data is presented as 11 mos. ended Dec. 31, 1994. Yrs. ended Jan. 31 of foll. cal. yr. prior to 1994. Per share data adj. for stk. divs. as of ex-div. date. E-Estimated. NA-Not Available. NM-Not Meaningful. NR-Not Ranked.

**Office**—275 Armand-Frappier Blvd., Laval, Quebec, Canada H7V 4A7. **Tel**—(514) 681-1744. **Website**—http://www.biochem-pharma.com **Fax**—(514) 978-7755. **Chrmn**—J.-L. Fontaine. **Pres & CEO**—F. Bellini. **Vice Chrmn**—G. Lord. **SVP-Fin & Treas**—F. Legault. **Secy**—L. R. Wilson. **Dirs**—F. Bellini, J. de Clerk, G. Dionne, J.-L. Fontaine, M. Gagnon, J. A. Grant, R. L. Henry, L. P. Lacasse, P. Lucas, G. Lord, M. Perron, G. Savard. **Transfer Agent & Registrar**—General Trust of Canada, Montreal. **Incorporated**—in Quebec in 1972. **Empl**— 828. **S&P Analyst:** Richard Joy

# Biogen, Inc.
## 3276
### Nasdaq Symbol **BGEN**
**In S&P MidCap 400**

**17-MAY-97**

**Industry:** Biotechnology

**Summary:** This biotechnology company derives its revenues principally from royalties paid by licensees that sell products based on Biogen technology.

**S&P Opinion: Accumulate (★★★★)**

| | |
|---|---|
| Recent Price • 35 | Yield • Nil |
| 52 Wk Range • 52¾-25½ | 12-Mo. P/E • 40.2 |

**Earnings vs. Previous Year**
▲=Up ▼=Down ▶=No Change

### Quantitative Evaluations

**Outlook**
(1 Lowest—5 Highest)
• **4**⁻

**Fair Value**
• **39⅝**

**Risk**
• **Average**

**Earn./Div. Rank**
• **B-**

**Technical Eval.**
• **Bearish** since 2/97

**Rel. Strength Rank**
(1 Lowest—99 Highest)
• **18**

**Insider Activity**
• **Neutral**

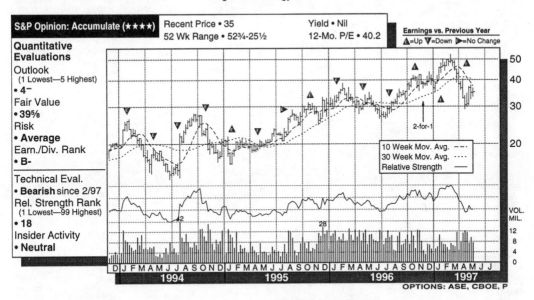

10 Week Mov. Avg. — · —
30 Week Mov. Avg. - - - -
Relative Strength ———

2-for-1

**OPTIONS: ASE, CBOE, P**

## Overview - 02-MAY-97

Total revenues are expected to post another substantial advance in 1997, primarily reflecting a full year of sales of Avonex and the recent launch of the drug in Europe. Avonex, a new breakthrough treatment for multiple sclerosis, was approved by the FDA in May 1996. Avonex sales totaled $76.5 million in 1996 and could reach $275 million in 1997. Biogen's royalties from alpha interferon should benefit from expansion in the drug's label, while royalties from hepatitis B vaccines could be helped by new government vaccination programs in Europe. Despite heavy R&D costs and expenses related to marketing Avonex both in the U.S. and abroad, EPS should reach $1.30 a share, up from 1996's $0.55 (which was reduced by $0.11 in the fourth quarter due to expenses related to a venture with Creative Biomolecules Inc.).

## Valuation - 02-MAY-97

The shares fell precipitously in recent weeks, reflecting profit taking after a strong runup, competition from a rival multiple sclerosis drug from Teva Pharmaceutical Industries, and a decision by the European Patent Office in April 1997 revoking Biogen's patent on its Avonex multiple sclerosis drug. However, the decision will not affect Biogen's ability to sell Avonex in Europe, where it was approved in March 1997. Shown to be effective in reducing relapsing MS exacerbations and in slowing the overall progression of the disease, Avonex is expected to become a lead therapeutic for MS, which afflicts more than 500,000 people worldwide. Biogen's R&D pipeline also includes experimental compounds for inflammatory and autoimmune diseases, renal failure, cystic fibrosis and other conditions. The shares have speculative appeal for recovery.

## Key Stock Statistics

| | | | |
|---|---|---|---|
| S&P EPS Est. 1997 | 1.30 | Tang. Bk. Value/Share | 6.53 |
| P/E on S&P Est. 1997 | 26.9 | Beta | 2.01 |
| S&P EPS Est. 1998 | 2.00 | Shareholders | 2,800 |
| Dividend Rate/Share | Nil | Market cap. (B) | $ 2.6 |
| Shs. outstg. (M) | 73.1 | Inst. holdings | 63% |
| Avg. daily vol. (M) | 1.773 | | |

Value of $10,000 invested 5 years ago: $ 17,375

### Fiscal Year Ending Dec. 31

| | 1998 | 1997 | 1996 | 1995 | 1994 | 1993 |
|---|---|---|---|---|---|---|
| **Revenues (Million $)** | | | | | | |
| 1Q | — | 99.7 | 34.38 | 35.97 | 44.78 | 35.42 |
| 2Q | — | — | 41.16 | 36.90 | 36.78 | 37.85 |
| 3Q | — | — | 96.75 | 38.18 | 31.81 | 37.31 |
| 4Q | — | — | 87.42 | 40.65 | 42.97 | 38.71 |
| Yr. | — | 259.7 | 151.7 | 156.3 | 149.3 | |

| | 1998 | 1997 | 1996 | 1995 | 1994 | 1993 |
|---|---|---|---|---|---|---|
| **Earnings Per Share ($)** | | | | | | |
| 1Q | — | 0.22 | -0.05 | 0.04 | 0.15 | 0.16 |
| 2Q | — | E0.29 | -0.13 | 0.01 | 0.01 | 0.08 |
| 3Q | — | E0.36 | 0.60 | 0.02 | -0.40 | 0.17 |
| 4Q | — | E0.43 | 0.11 | 0.02 | 0.13 | 0.06 |
| Yr. | E2.00 | E1.30 | 0.54 | 0.08 | -0.08 | 0.46 |

**Next earnings report expected: late July**

### Dividend Data

| Amount ($) | Date Decl. | Ex-Div. Date | Stock of Record | Payment Date |
|---|---|---|---|---|
| 2-for-1 | Oct. 22 | Nov. 18 | Nov. 04 | Nov. 15 '96 |

This report is for information purposes and should not be considered a solicitation to buy or sell any security. Neither S&P nor any other party guarantee its accuracy or make warranties regarding results from its usage. Redistribution is prohibited without written permission. Copyright © 1997

*A Division of The McGraw·Hill Companies*

## Business Summary - 02-MAY-97

Founded in 1978 by an international group of scientists, Biogen now ranks among leading U.S. biotechnology companies. Revenues are derived from royalties on products sold by licensees or affiliates in various countries, as well as from the sale of Avonex, a new proprietary drug for the treatment of multiple sclerosis. Foreign operations are very important, accounting for about 49% of royalties and product sales in 1996 (including Europe 24%, Japan 19%, and other areas 6%). Revenues in recent years were derived as follows:

| | 1996 | 1995 | 1994 |
|---|---|---|---|
| Product sales | 28% | --- | --- |
| Royalties | 66% | 89% | 90% |
| Interest | 6% | 11% | 10% |

Royalties are derived primarily from licensee sales of hepatitis B vaccines, alpha interferon and diagnostics. Biogen's licensees generated sales of over $2 billion in 1996 from products covered under license with Biogen. As part of its early commercial strategy, Biogen licensed its first generation of R&D discoveries to major drug companies. Schering-Plough developed its recombinant alpha interferon product, Intron A, based on Biogen's technology. Schering-Plough sells Intron A to treat hairy cell leukemia, hepatitis B & C, genital warts, Kaposi's sarcoma and other conditions. Royalties from Schering-Plough's sales of Intron A represented 27% of 1996 revenues (excluding interest).

The company also has patents related to hepatitis B antigens produced by genetic engineering. These antigens are used in recombinant hepatitis B vaccines sold primarily by licensees SmithKline Beecham and Merck. Royalties from these licensee sales accounted for 23% of revenues (excluding interest) in 1996. The company also licensed Abbott Laboratories and others to market hepatitis B diagnostic kits.

Royalties from the sale of products based on Biogen research are providing a stable revenue stream, which Biogen is using to develop new biopharmaceuticals that the company will marketitself. The company's first proprietary product, Avonex beta interferon for the treatment of multiple sclerosis, was launched following FDA approval in May 1996. Avonex is the first and only therapy shown in a pivotal clinical trial to both slow the accumulation of physical disability and reduce the frequency of neurological attacks in patients with relapsing forms of multiple sclerosis. Avonex sales totaled $76.5 million in 1996.

Ongoing R&D programs include new therapeutics for inflammatory and autoimmune diseases, pulmonary conditions, cancer, and other conditions. Collaborative R&D ventures include one with Genovo in the field of gene therapy and another with Creative BioMolecules in the area of new therapies for kidney diseases.

## Capitalization

**Long Term Debt:** $66,008,000 (3/97).

| Per Share Data ($) (Year Ended Dec. 31) | 1996 | 1995 | 1994 | 1993 | 1992 | 1991 | 1990 | 1989 | 1988 | 1987 |
|---|---|---|---|---|---|---|---|---|---|---|
| Tangible Bk. Val. | 6.53 | 5.28 | 4.85 | 4.93 | 4.39 | 3.77 | 1.53 | 1.45 | 1.44 | 1.45 |
| Cash Flow | 0.76 | 0.23 | 0.05 | 0.57 | 0.66 | 0.16 | 0.11 | 0.08 | 0.05 | -0.43 |
| Earnings | 0.55 | 0.08 | -0.08 | 0.46 | 0.56 | 0.08 | 0.03 | 0.00 | -0.03 | -0.51 |
| Dividends | Nil | Nil | Nil | Nil | Nil | Nil | Nil | Nil | Nil | Nil |
| Payout Ratio | Nil | Nil | Nil | Nil | Nil | Nil | Nil | Nil | Nil | Nil |
| Prices - High | 43 3/4 | 33 1/4 | 27 7/8 | 23 7/8 | 24 7/8 | 24 1/2 | 14 3/4 | 9 1/8 | 4 3/8 | 8 |
| - Low | 25 1/2 | 16 | 13 5/8 | 12 1/8 | 9 1/8 | 12 1/8 | 7 1/4 | 3 5/8 | 2 3/8 | 1 7/8 |
| P/E Ratio - High | 80 | NM | NM | 51 | 44 | NM | NM | NM | NM | NM |
| - Low | 46 | NM | NM | 26 | 16 | NM | NA | NA | NA | NA |
| **Income Statement Analysis (Million $)** | | | | | | | | | | |
| Revs. | 260 | 135 | 140 | 136 | 124 | 61.4 | 50.1 | 28.5 | 20.6 | 8.6 |
| Oper. Inc. | 40.4 | 1.3 | 22.6 | 34.4 | 44.1 | 3.9 | 4.6 | -5.5 | -8.7 | -20.4 |
| Depr. | 15.3 | 10.9 | 8.1 | 6.7 | 7.1 | 5.1 | 3.8 | 3.3 | 3.1 | 3.8 |
| Int. Exp. | Nil | Nil | Nil | Nil | Nil | Nil | Nil | Nil | Nil | Nil |
| Pretax Inc. | 40.8 | 7.4 | -1.9 | 34.6 | 39.9 | 7.4 | 8.0 | 3.4 | -0.9 | -22.4 |
| Eff. Tax Rate | 0.70% | 24% | NM | 6.40% | 4.10% | 3.50% | 3.60% | 5.80% | NM | NM |
| Net Inc. | 40.5 | 5.7 | -4.9 | 32.4 | 38.3 | 7.2 | 7.7 | 3.2 | -1.2 | -22.6 |
| **Balance Sheet & Other Fin. Data (Million $)** | | | | | | | | | | |
| Cash | 321 | 308 | 268 | 270 | 228 | 186 | 104 | 110 | 53.0 | 54.0 |
| Curr. Assets | 436 | 340 | 295 | 309 | 268 | 209 | 121 | 120 | 58.0 | 58.0 |
| Total Assets | 635 | 469 | 378 | 357 | 311 | 253 | 158 | 145 | 81.0 | 81.0 |
| Curr. Liab. | 87.9 | 53.4 | 47.9 | 31.8 | 26.2 | 14.1 | 12.7 | 6.0 | 8.0 | 7.6 |
| LT Debt | 62.3 | 32.8 | Nil | Nil | Nil | Nil | Nil | Nil | 4.8 | 5.2 |
| Common Eqty. | 484 | 383 | 330 | 325 | 285 | 239 | 76.0 | 70.0 | 68.0 | 68.0 |
| Total Cap. | 546 | 416 | 330 | 325 | 285 | 239 | 146 | 139 | 73.0 | 73.0 |
| Cap. Exp. | 62.0 | 48.0 | 40.5 | 10.8 | 9.4 | 8.4 | 11.1 | 3.1 | 2.7 | 1.3 |
| Cash Flow | 55.8 | 16.6 | 3.2 | 39.1 | 45.5 | 9.6 | 5.6 | 3.6 | 1.9 | -18.8 |
| Curr. Ratio | 5.0 | 6.4 | 6.2 | 9.7 | 10.2 | 14.9 | 9.5 | 19.9 | 7.2 | 7.6 |
| % LT Debt of Cap. | 11.4 | 7.9 | Nil | Nil | Nil | Nil | Nil | Nil | 6.6 | 7.1 |
| % Net Inc.of Revs. | 15.6 | 4.2 | NM | 23.8 | 31.0 | 11.7 | 15.4 | 11.3 | NM | NM |
| % Ret. on Assets | 7.3 | 1.3 | NM | 9.6 | 13.4 | 3.1 | 5.0 | 2.8 | NM | NM |
| % Ret. on Equity | 9.3 | 1.6 | NM | 10.5 | 14.4 | 2.6 | 2.5 | 0.3 | NM | NM |

Data as orig. reptd.; bef. results of disc. opers. and/or spec. items. Per share data adj. for stk. divs. as of ex-div. date. E-Estimated. NA-Not Available. NM-Not Meaningful. NR-Not Ranked.

**Office**—14 Cambridge Center, Cambridge, MA 02142. **Tel**—(617) 679-2000. **Fax**—(617) 679-2617. **Website**—http://www. biogen.com **Chrmn**—J. L. Vincent. **Pres & CEO**—J. R. Tobin. **VP-Fin, CFO & Treas**—T. M. Kish. **VP-Secy**—M. J. Astrue. **Investor Contact**—R. E. N. Lundberg. **Dirs**—A. G. Bearn, A. Belzer, H. W. Buirkle, R. H. Morley, K. Murray, P. A. Sharp, J. W. Stevens, J. R. Tobin, J. L. Vincent. **Transfer Agent & Registrar**—State Street Bank & Trust Co., Boston. **Incorporated**—in Massachusetts in 1988; predecessor company incorporated in Netherlands Antilles in 1979. **Empl**— 675. **S&P Analyst:** H.B. Saftlas

# Bio-Technology General 3277K
Nasdaq Symbol **BTGC**

**19-MAY-97**

**Industry:** Biotechnology

**Summary:** This company develops, manufactures and markets pharmaceuticals and biotechnology products for human health care, with a focus on treatments for growth and weight disorders.

| S&P Opinion: Buy (★★★★) | Recent Price • 15¾ | Yield • Nil |
|---|---|---|
| | 52 Wk Range • 17¾-6¼ | 12-Mo. P/E • 30.3 |

**Earnings vs. Previous Year**
▲=Up ▼=Down ▶=No Change

**Quantitative Evaluations**

Outlook (1 Lowest—5 Highest)
• **NA**

Fair Value
• **NA**

Risk
• **High**

Earn./Div. Rank
• **B-**

Technical Eval.
• **Bullish** since 5/95

Rel. Strength Rank (1 Lowest—99 Highest)
• **84**

Insider Activity
• **Neutral**

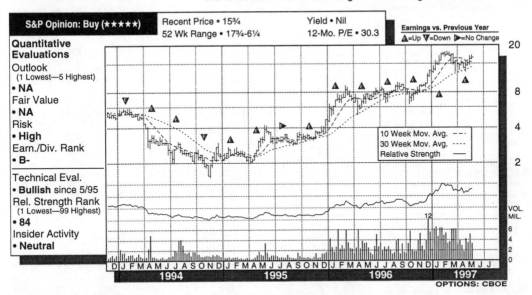

- 10 Week Mov. Avg. — - -
- 30 Week Mov. Avg. · · · · ·
- Relative Strength ——

VOL. MIL.

OPTIONS: CBOE

## Overview - 19-MAY-97

BTGC is one of only a handful of profitable biotechnology concerns. While revenues are derived from five commercialized products, the majority of near-term growth is expected to come from Oxandrin, the only FDA approved oral anabolic agent indicated for weight gain. We are extremely optimistic about this drug due to its broad indication, which will allow usage by a large patient population. We see Oxandrin sales advancing to $35 million in 1997, from 1996's $15 million. We are also sanguine about Androtest-SL, currently under FDA review for the treatment of hypogonadism, which affects nearly 5% of the male population. If approved, we expect commercialization in the U.S. in early 1998, with potential annual sales of $60 million by 2000. We believe that EPS in 1998 will surge to $0.65, from 1997's estimated $0.40 and 1996's $0.26 (excludes one-time charges and tax benefits).

## Valuation - 19-MAY-97

The shares have performed well in the past 12 months, reflecting explosive earnings growth and new product filings. We view the shares as deserving of a premium valuation, given the company's predictable earnings stream and blockbuster potential for OxSODrol, currently in Phase III clinical trials for bronchopulmonary dysplasia in premature infants. We forecast free cash flow to rise to approximately $70 million by 2000, up from $8.3 million in 1996. We believe that BTGC is one of the more conservative ways for investors to participate in the high-risk biotechnology sector, because of its profitability, clean balance sheet, sound management and rich product pipeline. Given our expectation of strong earnings growth, we recommend purchase of the shares for long-term capital appreciation, while urging investors to ignore the short-term price volatility.

## Key Stock Statistics

| | | | |
|---|---|---|---|
| S&P EPS Est. 1997 | 0.40 | Tang. Bk. Value/Share | 1.24 |
| P/E on S&P Est. 1997 | 39.4 | Beta | 1.68 |
| S&P EPS Est. 1998 | 0.65 | Shareholders | 1,600 |
| Dividend Rate/Share | Nil | Market cap. (B) | $0.735 |
| Shs. outstg. (M) | 46.6 | Inst. holdings | 25% |
| Avg. daily vol. (M) | 0.790 | | |

Value of $10,000 invested 5 years ago: $ 18,260

## Fiscal Year Ending Dec. 31

| | 1997 | 1996 | 1995 | 1994 | 1993 | 1992 |
|---|---|---|---|---|---|---|
| **Revenues (Million $)** | | | | | | |
| 1Q | 14.77 | 10.71 | 5.75 | 5.68 | 1.23 | 1.92 |
| 2Q | — | 12.19 | 7.29 | 7.76 | 3.00 | 1.23 |
| 3Q | — | 12.13 | 5.06 | 1.90 | 4.35 | 1.35 |
| 4Q | — | 12.67 | 9.86 | 2.10 | 5.29 | 1.53 |
| Yr. | — | 47.74 | 27.96 | 17.44 | 13.87 | 6.02 |
| **Earnings Per Share ($)** | | | | | | |
| 1Q | 0.07 | 0.02 | 0.01 | -0.02 | -0.10 | -0.09 |
| 2Q | E0.09 | 0.06 | 0.01 | 0.01 | -0.07 | -0.10 |
| 3Q | E0.11 | 0.07 | -0.02 | -0.12 | -0.09 | -0.10 |
| 4Q | E0.13 | 0.32 | 0.08 | -0.10 | -0.38 | -0.09 |
| Yr. | E0.40 | 0.47 | 0.08 | -0.23 | -0.63 | -0.38 |

**Next earnings report expected: late July**

## Dividend Data

The company has never paid a cash dividend.

This report is for information purposes and should not be considered a solicitation to buy or sell any security. Neither S&P nor any other party guarantee its accuracy or make warranties regarding results from its usage. Redistribution is prohibited without written permission. Copyright © 1997    *A Division of The McGraw·Hill Companies*

## Business Summary - 19-MAY-97

With strong demand for its human growth hormone and weight gain products bulking up its bottom line, Bio-Technology General (BTGC) is one of only a handful of profitable biotechnology concerns. Incorporated in 1980, BTGC's genetically engineered products address conditions such as endocrinology and metabolic disorders, cardio/pulmonary diseases, and ophthalmic and skin disorders.

The company's biggest seller, Bio-Tropin, an authentic human growth hormone (hGh), is used in the treatment of short stature and growth disorders. Bio-Tropin is marketed in Western Europe through licensee the Ferring Group and in Japan through JCR Pharmaceuticals. After receiving U.S. FDA approval to market Bio-Tropin, the company was issued a preliminary injunction prohibiting sale of the drug in the U.S. The action resulted from a motion filed by Genentech claiming patent infringement on one of its own growth hormone drugs. Bio-Tropin accounted for approximately 45% of BTGC's product revenues in 1996.

Bio-Technology's other lead drug, Oxandrin, was launched in late 1995 for the treatment of involuntary weight loss. Oxandrin is an oral anabolic agent used to promote weight gain after weight loss following extensive surgery, chronic infections and severe trauma. The company is currently conducting Phase IV (post ap-

proval) clinical studies to further support the role of Oxandrin in the treatment of many of these conditions. BTGC is also pursuing expanded use of Oxandrin in severe AIDS wasting patients and alcoholic hepatitis through Phase III studies. The drug accounted for 37% of 1996 product sales.

The company also markets BioLon (sodium hyaluronate) for the protection of the corneal endothelium during intraocular surgery. In 1996, this product comprised 12% of revenues. Other products include Bio-Hep-B, a vaccine against the hepatitis B virus; Silkis, a vitamin D derivative for the topical treatment of recalcitrant psoriasis, contact dermatitis and other skin disorders; and porcine growth hormone.

The research pipeline includes OxSODrol (recombinant superoxide dismutase), currently in phase III clinical trials for the prevention of bronchopulmonary dysplasia (BPD), a chronic lung disease that develops in premature infants. OxSODrol has been designated an Orphan Drug by the FDA, providing seven years of market exclusivity post approval.

The company's sublingual testosterone product for the treatment of hypogonadism and constitutional delay of growth and puberty, Androtest-SL, is currently undergoing FDA review.

### Capitalization

**Long Term Debt:** $282,000 (12/96).

## Per Share Data ($)

| (Year Ended Dec. 31) | 1996 | 1995 | 1994 | 1993 | 1992 | 1991 | 1990 | 1989 | 1988 | 1987 |
|---|---|---|---|---|---|---|---|---|---|---|
| Tangible Bk. Val. | 1.31 | 0.47 | 0.41 | 0.38 | 0.65 | 1.05 | 0.42 | -0.01 | -1.17 | -0.10 |
| Cash Flow | 0.53 | 0.14 | -0.16 | -0.53 | -0.30 | -0.30 | -0.30 | -0.93 | -0.97 | -0.89 |
| Earnings | 0.47 | 0.08 | -0.23 | -0.63 | -0.38 | -0.38 | -0.40 | -1.17 | -1.17 | -1.00 |
| Dividends | Nil | Nil | Nil | Nil | Nil | Nil | Nil | Nil | Nil | Nil |
| Payout Ratio | Nil | Nil | Nil | Nil | Nil | Nil | Nil | Nil | Nil | Nil |
| Prices - High | 13¼ | 5 | 5⅞ | 6¾ | 11⅝ | 10½ | 4⅜ | 3 | 7⅛ | 18½ |
|    - Low | 4½ | 2 | 1½ | 4½ | 4⅜ | 1⁵⁄₁₆ | 1 | 1 | 2¼ | 3 |
| P/E Ratio - High | 28 | 62 | NM | NM | NM | NM | NM | NM | NM | NM |
|    - Low | 10 | 25 | NM | NM | NM | NM | NA | NA | NA | NA |

## Income Statement Analysis (Million $)

| | 1996 | 1995 | 1994 | 1993 | 1992 | 1991 | 1990 | 1989 | 1988 | 1987 |
|---|---|---|---|---|---|---|---|---|---|---|
| Revs. | 46.6 | 27.2 | 16.9 | 13.3 | 4.9 | 4.7 | 2.6 | 3.2 | 4.6 | 3.6 |
| Oper. Inc. | 14.1 | 6.2 | -6.3 | -7.8 | -8.4 | -6.6 | -6.4 | -5.2 | -4.7 | -3.8 |
| Depr. | 2.8 | 2.6 | 2.8 | 3.6 | 2.0 | 1.6 | 1.6 | 1.6 | 1.2 | 0.6 |
| Int. Exp. | 0.2 | 0.2 | 0.3 | 0.4 | 0.4 | 0.2 | 0.1 | 2.0 | 2.8 | 2.2 |
| Pretax Inc. | 10.9 | 3.4 | -8.9 | 22.8 | -9.8 | -7.9 | -6.2 | -8.0 | -6.8 | -5.4 |
| Eff. Tax Rate | NM | NM | NM | NM | NM | Nil | Nil | Nil | Nil | Nil |
| Net Inc. | 22.9 | 3.4 | -8.9 | -22.8 | -9.8 | -7.9 | -6.2 | -8.0 | -6.8 | -5.4 |

## Balance Sheet & Other Fin. Data (Million $)

| | 1996 | 1995 | 1994 | 1993 | 1992 | 1991 | 1990 | 1989 | 1988 | 1987 |
|---|---|---|---|---|---|---|---|---|---|---|
| Cash | 19.8 | 6.9 | 16.9 | 16.1 | 18.4 | 24.0 | 8.1 | 5.2 | 11.6 | 20.5 |
| Curr. Assets | 49.7 | 20.6 | 21.4 | 19.6 | 20.4 | 26.2 | 9.4 | 6.2 | 13.2 | 22.5 |
| Total Assets | 73.6 | 31.7 | 32.3 | 31.1 | 32.9 | 36.1 | 16.7 | 14.6 | 26.3 | 33.1 |
| Curr. Liab. | 9.1 | 5.4 | 7.8 | 7.4 | 2.9 | 2.1 | 1.5 | 1.7 | 2.6 | 2.9 |
| LT Debt | 0.3 | 0.7 | 1.3 | 3.5 | 5.8 | 3.6 | 4.8 | 8.1 | 30.2 | 30.6 |
| Common Eqty. | 60.6 | 25.7 | 23.2 | 20.1 | 24.1 | 29.9 | 8.2 | 0.3 | -6.4 | -0.3 |
| Total Cap. | 60.8 | 26.4 | 24.5 | 23.6 | 29.8 | 33.5 | 13.0 | 8.4 | 23.7 | 30.2 |
| Cap. Exp. | 3.0 | 1.6 | 1.8 | 1.6 | 1.5 | 0.6 | 0.3 | 0.3 | 4.3 | 5.2 |
| Cash Flow | 25.7 | 6.0 | -6.1 | -19.2 | -7.7 | -6.3 | -4.6 | -6.4 | -5.6 | -4.8 |
| Curr. Ratio | 5.5 | 3.8 | 2.8 | 2.7 | 7.0 | 12.4 | 6.4 | 3.6 | 5.1 | 7.8 |
| % LT Debt of Cap. | 0.5 | 2.5 | 5.2 | 14.8 | 19.4 | 10.8 | 37.1 | 96.1 | 127.2 | 101.0 |
| % Net Inc.of Revs. | 49.1 | 12.2 | NM | NM | NM | NM | NM | NM | NM | NM |
| % Ret. on Assets | 42.7 | 10.7 | NM | NM | NM | NM | NM | NM | NM | NM |
| % Ret. on Equity | 53.1 | 14.0 | NM | NM | NM | NM | NM | NM | NM | NM |

Data as orig. reptd.; bef. results of disc. opers. and/or spec. items. Per share data adj. for stk. divs. as of ex-div. date. E-Estimated. NA-Not Available. NM-Not Meaningful. NR-Not Ranked.

**Office**—70 Wood Ave. South, Iselin, NJ 08830. **Tel**—(908) 632-8800. **Chrmn, Pres, CEO & Treas**—S. Fass. **SVP & COO**—D. Haselkorn. **VP-Fin & CFO**—Y. Sternlicht. **Dirs**—H. J. Conrad, S. Fass, H. Kaback, C. K. MacDonald, M. Marx, D. Tendler, Y. Sternlicht, V. Thompson, D. Tolkowsky. **Transfer Agent & Registrar**—American Stock Transfer & Trust Co., NYC. **Incorporated**—in Delaware in 1980. **Empl**— 235. **S&P Analyst:** Richard Joy

# Boston Scientific    355

NYSE Symbol **BSX**

**In S&P 500**

**19-MAY-97**

**Industry:**
Health Care (Medical Products & Supplies)

**Summary:** This maker of minimally-invasive medical devices for cardiology, radiology and other fields has significantly expanded its sales base through acquisitions and new products.

| S&P Opinion: Buy (★★★★★) | Recent Price • 49 | Yield • Nil |
|---|---|---|
| | 52 Wk Range • 71½-37¾ | 12-Mo. P/E • 36.8 |

**Quantitative Evaluations**

Outlook
(1 Lowest—5 Highest)
• 5

Fair Value
• 71⅝

Risk
• Average

Earn./Div. Rank
• NR

Technical Eval.
• **Bearish** since 4/97

Rel. Strength Rank
(1 Lowest—99 Highest)
• 13

Insider Activity
• NA

**Earnings vs. Previous Year**
▲=Up ▼=Down ▶=No Change

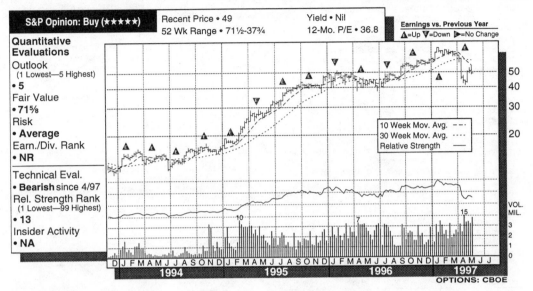

10 Week Mov. Avg. – – –
30 Week Mov. Avg. ·····
Relative Strength —

OPTIONS: CBOE

## Overview - 19-MAY-97

Sales are projected to exceed $1.9 billion in 1997, up from 1996's $1.5 billion. Despite the impact of foreign exchange, sales growth should be spurred by continued strong demand for the company's established vascular and non-vascular products. Volume should also be augmented by new medical devices (such as the Nir coronary stent), greater penetration of foreign markets and acquisitions. Despite managed care pricing constraints, ongoing costs related to past acquisitions and some dilution from the recent acquistion of Target Therapeutics, margins should benefit from the better volume and cost containment measures. Profitability should also be helped by the conversion to direct sales from independent distributors in many foreign markets. EPS are estimated at $1.90, up from 1996's $0.92 (before merger-related and nonrecurring charges of $0.63).

## Valuation - 19-MAY-97

The shares fell sharply in mid-April following BSX's disclosure that sales growth for the first quarter was below the pace of previous quarters and that EPS would be about $0.07 below consensus. First quarter results were hurt by negative foreign exchange and heavy costs associated with building a marketing infrastructure in Europe and the Far East. However, BSX's sales growth (24% in Q1) was still well in excess of its competitors and earnings expansion continues to be above average. The company maintains lead positions in its major minimally-invasive device markets, bolstered by the completion of ten major acquisitions over the past few years. BSX also leads in emerging technologies such as abdominal aortic aneurysms and atrial fibrillation. We view recent weakness in the stock as a good opportunity to build long-term positions in this rapidly expanding medical device concern.

## Key Stock Statistics

| | | | |
|---|---|---|---|
| S&P EPS Est. 1997 | 1.90 | Tang. Bk. Value/Share | 3.41 |
| P/E on S&P Est. 1997 | 25.8 | Beta | NA |
| Dividend Rate/Share | Nil | Shareholders | 7,200 |
| Shs. outstg. (M) | 194.5 | Market cap. (B) | $ 9.5 |
| Avg. daily vol. (M) | 1.576 | Inst. holdings | 46% |

Value of $10,000 invested 5 years ago: NA

### Fiscal Year Ending Dec. 31

| | 1997 | 1996 | 1995 | 1994 | 1993 | 1992 |
|---|---|---|---|---|---|---|
| **Revenues (Million $)** | | | | | | |
| 1Q | 399.2 | 322.4 | 257.6 | 105.3 | 88.94 | 72.60 |
| 2Q | — | 357.2 | 272.1 | 109.9 | 94.44 | 76.30 |
| 3Q | — | 373.7 | 277.7 | 112.2 | 95.60 | 81.90 |
| 4Q | — | 408.7 | 299.2 | 121.6 | 101.1 | 84.35 |
| Yr. | — | 1,462 | 1,107 | 449.0 | 380.1 | 315.2 |
| **Earnings Per Share ($)** | | | | | | |
| 1Q | 0.40 | -0.01 | -0.37 | 0.18 | 0.15 | 0.13 |
| 2Q | E0.43 | 0.13 | 0.28 | 0.19 | 0.17 | 0.14 |
| 3Q | E0.50 | 0.37 | 0.28 | 0.20 | 0.17 | 0.15 |
| 4Q | E0.57 | 0.42 | -0.16 | 0.24 | 0.21 | 0.15 |
| Yr. | E1.90 | 0.92 | 0.05 | 0.81 | 0.70 | 0.57 |

Next earnings report expected: late July

**Dividend Data**

Dividends have never been paid.

This report is for information purposes and should not be considered a solicitation to buy or sell any security. Neither S&P nor any other party guarantee its accuracy or make warranties regarding results from its usage. Redistribution is prohibited without written permission. Copyright © 1997

A Division of The **McGraw·Hill** Companies

## Business Summary - 19-MAY-97

Boston Scientific is a leading global maker of medical devices geared for minimally-invasive surgical procedures. The company's history began in the late 1960s when its co-founder, John Abele, acquired an equity interest in Medi-Tech, a maker of steerable catheters. In 1979, John Abele joined Pete Nicholas to form Boston Scientific Corporation, which acquired Medi-Tech. Since then, BSX has expanded significantly through an aggressive acquisition program and internal growth.

The company's products encompass over 7,500 separate catalog items in over 50 categories. Products include devices used in cardiology, gastroenterology, pulmonology, radiology, urology and vascular surgery. Generally inserted into the body through natural openings or small skin incisions, these products are then guided to various areas of the anatomy for the diagnosis and treatment of medical problems. Minimally-invasive procedures involve less trauma, risk to the patient, cost and recovery time than conventional surgical methods. Operations outside of North America accounted for 35% of sales and 51% of operating profits in 1996.

BSX sells a broad line of products designed to treat patients with peripheral vascular disease. These include catheters and other items used in coronary and vascular percutaneous transluminal angioplasty, a procedure to enlarge a blocked artery by means of a balloon-tipped catheter; coronary stents used after angioplasty procedures; the Greenfield Vena Cava Filter

System, a filter permanently implanted in high risk patients to reduce their incidence of pulmonary embolism; a line of surgical and endovascular grafts used to replace impaired arteries; a family of intravascular catheter-directed ultrasound imaging systems for diagnostic use in the blood vessels, heart chambers and coronary arteries; the Rotoblator plaque-removing artherectomy device; and electrophysiology (EP) diagnostic systems. In April 1997, BSX acquired Target Therapeutics, a maker of catheter-based disposable and implantable medical devices used to treat neurovascular diseases and disorders.

Non-vascular intervention products consist of catheters and accessories to drain fluid collections from the body, various forms of biopsy products and other accessory devices. The line includes hemostatic catheters and related products used to treat or diagnose gastrointestinal (GI) disorders; biliary intervention products used in endoscopic procedures in the gall bladder and bile ducts; devices used to diagnose and treat polyps and other ailments in the lower GI tract; products designed to treat patients with urinary stone disease; the Dowd Prostate Balloon Dilatation Catheter used to treat benign prostatic hypertrophy; a line of minimally-invasive devices to treat female urinary incontinence; and devices used to diagnose and treat chronic bronchitis and lung cancer.

## Capitalization

**Long Term Liabilities:** $47,193,000 (3/97).

### Per Share Data ($)

| (Year Ended Dec. 31) | 1996 | 1995 | 1994 | 1993 | 1992 | 1991 | 1990 | 1989 | 1988 | 1987 |
|---|---|---|---|---|---|---|---|---|---|---|
| Tangible Bk. Val. | 3.41 | 3.55 | 3.14 | 2.37 | 2.35 | 1.48 | 0.41 | NA | NA | NA |
| Cash Flow | 1.26 | 0.28 | 0.91 | 0.76 | 0.62 | 0.48 | 0.28 | 0.08 | NA | NA |
| Earnings | 0.92 | 0.05 | 0.81 | 0.70 | 0.57 | 0.44 | 0.25 | 0.06 | -0.01 | 0.04 |
| Dividends | Nil | Nil | Nil | Nil | Nil | NA | NA | NA | NA | NA |
| Payout Ratio | Nil | Nil | Nil | Nil | Nil | NA | NA | NA | NA | NA |
| Prices - High | 61½ | 49⅜ | 17⅞ | 23⅝ | 20⅞ | NA | NA | NA | NA | NA |
|    - Low | 37¾ | 16⅝ | 11⅞ | 9⅜ | 14 | NA | NA | NA | NA | NA |
| P/E Ratio - High | 67 | NM | 22 | 34 | 37 | NA | NA | NA | NA | NA |
|    - Low | 41 | NM | 15 | 13 | 25 | NA | NA | NA | NA | NA |

### Income Statement Analysis (Million $)

| | 1996 | 1995 | 1994 | 1993 | 1992 | 1991 | 1990 | 1989 | 1988 | 1987 |
|---|---|---|---|---|---|---|---|---|---|---|
| Revs. | 1,462 | 1,107 | 449 | 380 | 315 | 230 | 159 | 116 | 98.0 | 70.0 |
| Oper. Inc. | 403 | 781 | 139 | 115 | 97.2 | 73.9 | 42.0 | 16.0 | NA | NA |
| Depr. | 61.4 | 39.5 | 9.1 | 6.4 | 4.4 | 3.4 | 2.4 | 2.2 | NA | NA |
| Int. Exp. | 11.2 | 8.2 | 2.0 | 2.1 | 2.8 | 2.9 | 4.6 | 5.8 | NA | NA |
| Pretax Inc. | 297 | 85.8 | 129 | 109 | 91.6 | 68.8 | 35.5 | 8.0 | NA | NA |
| Eff. Tax Rate | 44% | 90% | 38% | 36% | 38% | 39% | 34% | 34% | NA | NA |
| Net Inc. | 167 | 8.4 | 79.7 | 69.7 | 56.6 | 41.5 | 23.5 | 5.3 | -0.9 | 3.9 |

### Balance Sheet & Other Fin. Data (Million $)

| | 1996 | 1995 | 1994 | 1993 | 1992 | 1991 | 1990 | 1989 | 1988 | 1987 |
|---|---|---|---|---|---|---|---|---|---|---|
| Cash | 75.5 | 115 | 118 | 103 | 137 | 66.1 | 0.3 | NA | NA | NA |
| Curr. Assets | 749 | 537 | 264 | 216 | 236 | 149 | 58.0 | NA | NA | NA |
| Total Assets | 1,512 | 1,075 | 432 | 323 | 299 | 208 | 102 | 86.0 | 77.0 | 55.0 |
| Curr. Liab. | 464 | 271 | 73.7 | 57.1 | 42.6 | 29.2 | 34.1 | NA | NA | NA |
| LT Debt | Nil | 13.2 | 8.9 | 6.0 | 6.1 | 23.2 | 19.1 | 31.6 | 8.8 | 17.6 |
| Common Eqty. | 916 | 752 | 340 | 247 | 249 | 156 | 48.0 | 24.0 | 18.0 | 19.0 |
| Total Cap. | 976 | 765 | 355 | 266 | 257 | 179 | 67.0 | 56.0 | 27.0 | 36.0 |
| Cap. Exp. | 135 | 68.6 | 35.8 | 35.8 | 17.6 | 7.3 | 3.5 | 7.3 | NA | NA |
| Cash Flow | 229 | 47.9 | 88.8 | 76.1 | 61.0 | 44.9 | 25.9 | 7.5 | NA | NA |
| Curr. Ratio | 1.6 | 2.0 | 3.6 | 3.8 | 5.6 | 5.1 | 1.7 | NA | NA | NA |
| % LT Debt of Cap. | Nil | 1.7 | 2.5 | 22.0 | 2.4 | 13.0 | 28.3 | 56.7 | 33.1 | 48.5 |
| % Net Inc.of Revs. | 11.4 | 1.0 | 17.8 | 18.3 | 18.0 | 18.0 | 14.8 | 4.5 | NM | 5.5 |
| % Ret. on Assets | 12.7 | 1.0 | 21.1 | 22.9 | 25.3 | NA | NA | 6.5 | NM | NA |
| % Ret. on Equity | 19.8 | 1.1 | 27.2 | 28.8 | 32.7 | NA | NA | 25.1 | NM | NA |

Data as orig. reptd.; bef. results of disc. opers. and/or spec. items. Per share data adj. for stk. divs. as of ex-div. date. E-Estimated. NA-Not Available. NM-Not Meaningful. NR-Not Ranked.

**Office**—One Boston Scientific Place, Natick, MA 01760-1537. **Tel**—(508) 650-8000. **Website**—http://www.bsci.com **Chrmn & CEO**—P. M. Nicholas. **SVP-Fin, CFO & Investor Contact**—L. C. Best (508) 650-8450. **SVP & Secy**—P. W. Sandman. **Dirs**—J. E. Abele, C. J. Aschauer, Jr., R. F. Bellows, J. A. Ciffolillo, J. L. Fleishman, L. L. Horsch, N. J. Nicholas, Jr., P. M. Nicholas, D. A. Spencer. **Transfer Agent & Registrar**—First National Bank of Boston. **Incorporated**—in Delaware in 1979. **Empl**—9,580.**S&P Analyst:** Herman Saftlas

# Cabletron Systems

**417X**

NYSE Symbol **CS**

In S&P 500

**17-MAY-97**

**Industry:**
Computers (Networking)

**Summary:** CS is a leading provider of intelligent hubs, switching products and management software for Ethernet, Token Ring, FDDI and ATM networking environments.

**S&P Opinion: Accumulate (★★★★)**

| Recent Price • 37¾ | Yield • Nil |
| 52 Wk Range • 43⅝-26½ | 12-Mo. P/E • 26.4 |

**Earnings vs. Previous Year**
▲=Up ▼=Down ▷=No Change

## Quantitative Evaluations

Outlook
(1 Lowest—5 Highest)
• 5

Fair Value
• 58¾

Risk
• Average

Earn./Div. Rank
• B+

Technical Eval.
• **Bullish** since 5/97

Rel. Strength Rank
(1 Lowest—99 Highest)
• 93

Insider Activity
• Neutral

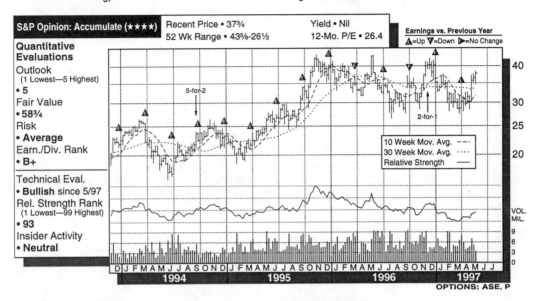

5-for-2

2-for-1

10 Week Mov. Avg. ---
30 Week Mov. Avg. ......
Relative Strength —

40
30
25
20

VOL.
MIL.
9
6
3
0

| D J F M A M J J A S O N D | J F M A M J J A S O N D | J F M A M J J A S O N D | J F M A M J J |
| 1994 | 1995 | 1996 | 1997 |

OPTIONS: ASE, P

## Overview - 23-APR-97

The company's consistent revenue and EPS growth is expected to continue over at least the next 18 months, as demand for networking products remains strong. We are projecting revenue growth of approximately 25% in FY 98 (Feb.), on continued strong demand for high-speed switching products. CS is beginning to see greater demand for its MMAC-Plus switching hub, which is now more than 25% of revenues, and has rolled out new switching modules resulting from its acquisition of the Standard Microsystems switching unit. Furthermore, new Token Ring and ATM products should find greater acceptance as end-users increasingly implement these technologies across their networks. Despite continuing competitive pressures, we believe that gross margins will remain in the 59% range, and operating costs should remain well controlled. We estimate FY 98 EPS at $2.15.

## Valuation - 23-APR-97

The company continues to be one of the networking industry's most consistent performers, despite criticism that it has been slow to adjust to new technologies. Recent product announcements in the fast-growing switching area and four acquisitions during 1996 are proof that CS is well equipped to offer these critical new technologies. The company has sported an impressive revenue and EPS record since the late 1980s, and recent actions should allow for continued above-average growth in coming years. These solid fundamentals, coupled with a valuation on earnings below that of leading competitors, should lead to continued above-average capital gains for shareholders in the years ahead.

## Key Stock Statistics

| | | | |
|---|---|---|---|
| S&P EPS Est. 1998 | 2.15 | Tang. Bk. Value/Share | 6.56 |
| P/E on S&P Est. 1998 | 17.6 | Beta | 1.63 |
| Dividend Rate/Share | Nil | Shareholders | 1,800 |
| Shs. outstg. (M) | 155.8 | Market cap. (B) | $ 5.9 |
| Avg. daily vol. (M) | 0.989 | Inst. holdings | 63% |

Value of $10,000 invested 5 years ago: $ 33,953

### Fiscal Year Ending Feb. 28

| | 1998 | 1997 | 1996 | 1995 | 1994 | 1993 |
|---|---|---|---|---|---|---|
| **Revenues (Million $)** | | | | | | |
| 1Q | — | 315.1 | 240.8 | 180.7 | 131.5 | 88.00 |
| 2Q | — | 338.6 | 257.3 | 194.0 | 141.9 | 96.70 |
| 3Q | — | 359.0 | 275.5 | 210.0 | 156.5 | 110.4 |
| 4Q | — | 380.6 | 296.2 | 226.0 | 168.2 | 123.0 |
| Yr. | — | 1,407 | 1,070 | 810.7 | 598.1 | 418.2 |
| **Earnings Per Share ($)** | | | | | | |
| 1Q | E0.49 | 0.43 | 0.33 | 0.25 | 0.19 | 0.13 |
| 2Q | E0.52 | 0.25 | 0.37 | 0.27 | 0.20 | 0.14 |
| 3Q | E0.55 | 0.46 | 0.39 | 0.29 | 0.22 | 0.16 |
| 4Q | E0.59 | 0.39 | 0.05 | 0.32 | 0.24 | 0.17 |
| Yr. | E2.15 | 1.43 | 1.14 | 1.14 | 0.84 | 0.59 |

**Next earnings report expected: mid June**

### Dividend Data

| Amount ($) | Date Decl. | Ex-Div. Date | Stock of Record | Payment Date |
|---|---|---|---|---|
| 2-for-1 | Oct. 29 | Nov. 27 | Nov. 07 | Nov. 26 '96 |

This report is for information purposes and should not be considered a solicitation to buy or sell any security. Neither S&P nor any other party guarantee its accuracy or make warranties regarding results from its usage. Redistribution is prohibited without written permission. Copyright © 1997

*A Division of The McGraw-Hill Companies*

STANDARD
&POOR'S
STOCK REPORTS

# Cabletron Systems, Inc.

**417X**

**17-MAY-97**

## Business Summary - 23-APR-97

Cabletron Systems is a leading vendor of internetworking products, most notably hardware and software connectivity solutions for local area and wide area networks (LANs and WANs). The company primarily distributes its products through a direct sales force. Sales contributions in recent fiscal years (Feb.) were:

| | FY 96 | FY 95 | FY 94 |
|---|---|---|---|
| Interconnection | 90.2% | 91.4% | 92.7% |
| Cables | 0.6% | 1.2% | 1.6% |
| Test equipment & services | 9.1% | 7.4% | 5.7% |

Customers outside the U.S. accounted for 29.2% of sales in FY 96, up from 28.8% in FY 95.

CS's networking approach is based on a strategy called Synthesis, a blueprint for transitioning end-users from traditional router-based internetworks to switch-based virtual networks. Synthesis incorporates the company's hub and management technologies with emerging switching technologies. A key component of Synthesis is CS's MMAC-Plus, an intelligent switching hub that, among other things, provides high-speed switching capabilities for shared-access, packet-based LANs. This product is complemented by CS's Multi Media Access Center (MMAC), an intelligent hub that allows the integration of multiple network standards such as Ethernet, Token Ring and FDDI. These products are

managed by SPECTRUM, the company's network management software product.

Interconnection products also include multiport repeaters designed to increase the reach of a geographically dispersed LAN; bridges, which perform high-speed filtering and data transmission; stand-alone transceivers that attach to PCs in a network, letting users communicate with other users in the LAN; and network interface cards (NICs) that provide a high-speed data connection for PC platforms.

In January 1996, CS acquired the Enterprise Networks Switching Group of Standard Microsystems Corp. In August, it acquired Network Express (NETK), a provider of Integrated Services Digital Network (ISDN) solutions for high-speed LAN access. In July, CS completed the acquisition of ZeitNet, Inc., a leader in connecting existing networks to ATM networks.

## Important Developments

**Feb. '97**—CS acquired privately held OASys Group, Inc., a supplier of management software for telecommunications devices and connections used in fiber-optic networks, in exchange for 240,000 CS shares. In November 1996, CS acquired privately held Netlink, a provider of frame relay access solutions, in exchange for about 4.5 million common shares.

## Capitalization

**Long Term Debt:** None (2/97).

## Per Share Data ($)

| (Year Ended Feb. 28) | 1997 | 1996 | 1995 | 1994 | 1993 | 1992 | 1991 | 1990 | 1989 | 1988 |
|---|---|---|---|---|---|---|---|---|---|---|
| Tangible Bk. Val. | NA | 5.39 | 4.11 | 2.97 | 2.04 | 1.45 | 1.01 | 0.51 | 0.15 | 0.02 |
| Cash Flow | NA | 1.36 | 1.32 | 0.96 | 0.68 | 0.47 | 0.30 | 0.19 | 0.10 | 0.04 |
| Earnings | 1.43 | 1.14 | 1.14 | 0.84 | 0.59 | 0.42 | 0.27 | 0.17 | 0.10 | 0.03 |
| Dividends | Nil | Nil | Nil | Nil | Nil | Nil | Nil | Nil | Nil | Nil |
| Payout Ratio | Nil | Nil | Nil | Nil | Nil | Nil | Nil | Nil | Nil | Nil |
| Cal. Yrs. | 1996 | 1995 | 1994 | 1993 | 1992 | 1991 | 1990 | 1989 | 1988 | 1987 |
| Prices - High | 43⅝ | 43⅞ | 26½ | 23¾ | 17 | 11 | 5⅞ | 3⅜ | NA | NA |
|    - Low | 26½ | 18¾ | 16½ | 14⅞ | 8⅜ | 5⅛ | 1⅜ | 1⅞ | NA | NA |
| P/E Ratio - High | 30 | 38 | 23 | 28 | 29 | 27 | 22 | 19 | NA | NA |
|    - Low | 19 | 16 | 15 | 18 | 14 | 12 | 5 | 11 | NA | NA |

## Income Statement Analysis (Million $)

| | | | | | | | | | | |
|---|---|---|---|---|---|---|---|---|---|---|
| Revs. | NA | 1,070 | 811 | 598 | 418 | 291 | 181 | 105 | 55.0 | 25.0 |
| Oper. Inc. | NA | 345 | 265 | 194 | 137 | 95.0 | 59.3 | 36.0 | 19.8 | 7.4 |
| Depr. | NA | 32.1 | 26.4 | 16.9 | 11.7 | 7.1 | 3.6 | 1.5 | 0.6 | 0.3 |
| Int. Exp. | NA | Nil | Nil | Nil | Nil | Nil | 0.0 | 0.4 | 0.1 | 0.2 |
| Pretax Inc. | NA | 245 | 248 | 183 | 130 | 91.8 | 57.3 | 33.0 | 19.1 | 6.9 |
| Eff. Tax Rate | NA | 33% | 35% | 35% | 36% | 37% | 37% | 32% | 39% | 42% |
| Net Inc. | NA | 164 | 162 | 119 | 83.5 | 58.0 | 35.9 | 22.5 | 11.8 | 4.0 |

## Balance Sheet & Other Fin. Data (Million $)

| | | | | | | | | | | |
|---|---|---|---|---|---|---|---|---|---|---|
| Cash | NA | 254 | 245 | 164 | 154 | 90.9 | 60.5 | 15.8 | 2.3 | 0.1 |
| Curr. Assets | NA | 624 | 471 | 326 | 285 | 193 | 129 | 73.0 | 35.0 | 11.0 |
| Total Assets | NA | 951 | 690 | 499 | 343 | 236 | 154 | 87.0 | 40.0 | 12.0 |
| Curr. Liab. | NA | 164 | 96.3 | 70.7 | 51.3 | 30.7 | 13.5 | 19.7 | 22.0 | 7.4 |
| LT Debt | NA | Nil | Nil | Nil | Nil | Nil | Nil | Nil | 0.1 | 1.9 |
| Common Eqty. | NA | 778 | 588 | 424 | 289 | 204 | 140 | 67.0 | 18.0 | 3.0 |
| Total Cap. | NA | 787 | 594 | 428 | 292 | 206 | 140 | 68.0 | 18.0 | 4.0 |
| Cap. Exp. | NA | 65.0 | 63.1 | 39.4 | 28.3 | 25.5 | 14.5 | 10.8 | 4.9 | 0.7 |
| Cash Flow | NA | 196 | 188 | 136 | 95.2 | 65.1 | 39.5 | 24.0 | 12.4 | 4.4 |
| Curr. Ratio | NA | 3.8 | 4.9 | 4.6 | 5.5 | 6.3 | 9.5 | 3.7 | 1.6 | 1.5 |
| % LT Debt of Cap. | NA | Nil | Nil | Nil | Nil | Nil | Nil | Nil | 0.5 | 42.6 |
| % Net Inc.of Revs. | NA | 15.4 | 20.0 | 19.9 | 20.0 | 20.0 | 19.9 | 21.5 | 21.5 | 16.2 |
| % Ret. on Assets | NA | 20.0 | 27.2 | 28.2 | 28.7 | 29.7 | 29.2 | 34.5 | 45.3 | 45.7 |
| % Ret. on Equity | NA | 24.1 | 32.0 | 33.3 | 33.8 | 33.6 | 34.0 | 51.8 | 113.8 | 235.2 |

Data as orig. reptd.; bef. results of disc. opers. and/or spec. items. Per share data adj. for stk. divs. as of ex-div. date. E-Estimated. NA-Not Available. NM-Not Meaningful. NR-Not Ranked.

**Office**—35 Industrial Way, Rochester, NH 03867-0505. **Tel**—(603) 332-9400. **Website**—http://www.cabletron.com **Chrmn, COO & Treas**—C. R. Benson. **Pres & CEO**—S. R. Levine. **CFO**—D. J. Kirkpatrick. **Secy**—M. D. Myerow. **Investor Contact**—Jim Caldwell (603) 337-4225. **Dirs**—C. R. Benson, P. R. Duncan, S. R. Levine, D. F. McGuinness, M. D. Myerow. **Transfer Agent & Registrar**—State Street Bank & Trust Co., Boston. **Incorporated**—in Delaware in 1988. **Empl**— 6,600. **S&P Analyst:** Megan Graham Hackett

# Callaway Golf 421

NYSE Symbol **ELY**

**In S&P MidCap 400**

**17-MAY-97**

**Industry:**
Leisure Time (Products)

**Summary:** This company designs, makes and markets premium, innovative golf clubs primarily under the "Big Bertha" brand name.

| | |
|---|---|
| **S&P Opinion: Accumulate (★★★★)** | |

Recent Price • 30½
52 Wk Range • 36⅝-26⅝

Yield • 0.9%
12-Mo. P/E • 17.0

**Earnings vs. Previous Year**
▲=Up ▼=Down ▶=No Change

**Quantitative Evaluations**

Outlook
(1 Lowest—5 Highest)
• **5**

Fair Value
• **43%**

Risk
• **Average**

Earn./Div. Rank
• **B**

Technical Eval.
• **Bullish** since 10/95

Rel. Strength Rank
(1 Lowest—99 Highest)
• **35**

Insider Activity
• **Neutral**

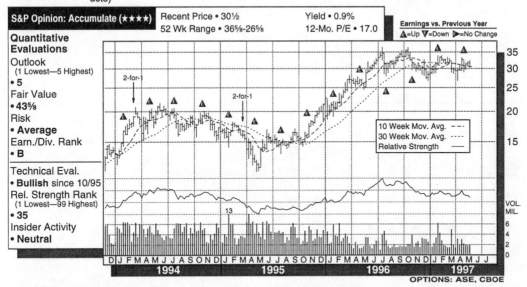

10 Week Mov. Avg. – – –
30 Week Mov. Avg. ·······
Relative Strength ———

OPTIONS: ASE, CBOE

## Overview - 24-APR-97

Net sales in 1997 are projected to rise 15% to 20%, reflecting continued strong growth for Great Big Bertha titanium metal drivers and fairway woods and initial sales of the new Biggest Big Bertha titanium driver, which was introduced in January. Sales of irons will benefit from further growth seen for Big Bertha irons and contributions from the new Great Big Bertha Tungsten Titanium irons, also introduced in January. However, Big Bertha metal woods are expected to continue to decline, due primarily to cannibalization by titanium products. Margins will probably be stable, as component cost reductions and further labor and overhead efficiencies will be offset by investments in the new golf ball unit. Long-term prospects are enhanced by favorable demographic trends, but Callaway's future success will depend on its ability to continue developing innovative golf clubs.

## Valuation - 24-APR-97

Through successful new product introductions, Callaway has seen its share of the premium golf club market grow to the 35%-40% range, which has been achieved despite the lackluster growth of the golf equipment industry in the past few years. ELY also benefits from significant brand identity, which it hopes to extend to other products, including the possible introduction of a premium golf ball in 1999. Attaining only a small share of the over-$1 billion domestic golf ball market could result in earnings accelerating above the 15% to 20% growth rate seen for the next few years. With demographics becoming more favorable, largely reflecting the aging of baby boomers, and the possibility of earnings growth accelerating on contributions from golf balls, we recommend accumulating the shares. Callaway is also financially strong, with no long-term debt and a return on equity of 42% in 1996.

## Key Stock Statistics

| | | | |
|---|---|---|---|
| S&P EPS Est. 1997 | 2.05 | Tang. Bk. Value/Share | 4.97 |
| P/E on S&P Est. 1997 | 14.9 | Beta | 1.70 |
| Dividend Rate/Share | 0.28 | Shareholders | 6,700 |
| Shs. outstg. (M) | 72.9 | Market cap. (B) | $ 2.2 |
| Avg. daily vol. (M) | 0.381 | Inst. holdings | 55% |

Value of $10,000 invested 5 years ago: NA

## Fiscal Year Ending Dec. 31

| | 1997 | 1996 | 1995 | 1994 | 1993 | 1992 |
|---|---|---|---|---|---|---|
| **Revenues (Million $)** | | | | | | |
| 1Q | 169.1 | 135.1 | 119.0 | 76.07 | 48.07 | 22.91 |
| 2Q | — | 210.0 | 155.7 | 126.3 | 66.57 | 36.53 |
| 3Q | — | 194.6 | 155.9 | 131.2 | 71.76 | 35.90 |
| 4Q | — | 138.8 | 122.6 | 115.2 | 68.25 | 36.73 |
| Yr. | — | 678.5 | 553.3 | 448.7 | 254.6 | 132.1 |
| **Earnings Per Share ($)** | | | | | | |
| 1Q | 0.34 | 0.28 | 0.23 | 0.15 | 0.10 | 0.05 |
| 2Q | E0.66 | 0.55 | 0.39 | 0.30 | 0.16 | 0.10 |
| 3Q | E0.64 | 0.54 | 0.44 | 0.35 | 0.18 | 0.09 |
| 4Q | E0.41 | 0.36 | 0.34 | 0.26 | 0.15 | 0.08 |
| Yr. | E2.05 | 1.73 | 1.40 | 1.07 | 0.59 | 0.32 |

**Next earnings report expected: mid July**

## Dividend Data (Dividends have been paid since 1993.)

| Amount ($) | Date Decl. | Ex-Div. Date | Stock of Record | Payment Date |
|---|---|---|---|---|
| 0.060 | Jul. 17 | Jul. 26 | Jul. 30 | Aug. 20 '96 |
| 0.060 | Oct. 16 | Oct. 25 | Oct. 29 | Nov. 19 '96 |
| 0.070 | Jan. 23 | Jan. 31 | Feb. 04 | Feb. 25 '97 |
| 0.070 | Apr. 17 | Apr. 25 | Apr. 29 | May. 20 '97 |

This report is for information purposes and should not be considered a solicitation to buy or sell any security. Neither S&P nor any other party guarantee its accuracy or make warranties regarding results from its usage. Redistribution is prohibited without written permission. Copyright © 1997

*A Division of The McGraw·Hill Companies*

## Business Summary - 24-APR-97

Callaway Golf Company, a leading designer and manufacturer of high-quality, innovative golf clubs, is best known for its Great Big Bertha and Big Bertha lines of oversized clubs. Callaway's golf clubs are sold at premium prices and have received unprecedented acceptance from both professional and weekend golfers on the basis of performance, ease of use and appearance. Superior product performance and effective marketing have helped to establish Callaway as a worldwide leader in the golf club industry in a relatively short time. The following table shows the breakdown of sales by product line in recent years.

| | 1996 | 1995 | 1994 | 1993 |
|---|---|---|---|---|
| Metal woods | 71% | 69% | 73% | 82% |
| Irons | 25% | 25% | 22% | 12% |
| Putters, wedges & other | 4% | 6% | 5% | 6% |

Metal woods consist of the current hot-selling Great Big Bertha titanium drivers and fairway woods, and Big Bertha stainless steel drivers and fairway woods. The original Big Bertha driver, named after a World War I cannon, was introduced in 1991 and quickly became the most popular driver in golf history, while the Great Big Bertha driver was added in early 1995. Big Bertha irons were introduced in early 1994. The company has continually upgraded and expanded its product offerings, most recently introducing the Biggest Big Bertha Titanium Driver and Great Big Bertha Tungsten Titanium irons in January 1997. Callaway also offers a line of putters, as well as golf-related equipment and supplies manufactured by others, including golf bags, travel bags, head covers, hats, umbrellas and other accessories.

Following the record results achieved in 1996, sales and earnings continued to advance strongly in 1997's first quarter, rising 25% and 26%, respectively, aided by strong growth for titanium metal woods (including initial contributions from the new Biggest Big Bertha line), which accounted for 48% of net sales. Product innovation has been the driving force behind the company's enviable record of consistently strong growth since going public in 1992. This performance has also been achieved despite only modest growth in the golf equipment industry in the U.S. in the last several years. Callaway's future performance will depend on its ability to create products that are both innovative and pleasingly different from competitors' offerings. To help round out its product line, ELY formed a golf ball company in May 1996 that will develop a premium-priced golf ball, which could hit the market by 1999. Callaway's major competitors in the premium end of the golf club market include Taylor Made, a unit of French-based Salomon, privately-owned Ping, and Cobra Golf, an American Brands subsidiary.

## Capitalization

**Long Term Debt:** None (3/97).

| Per Share Data ($) (Year Ended Dec. 31) | 1996 | 1995 | 1994 | 1993 | 1992 | 1991 | 1990 | 1989 | 1988 | 1987 |
|---|---|---|---|---|---|---|---|---|---|---|
| Tangible Bk. Val. | 4.97 | 3.17 | 2.74 | 1.73 | 0.87 | 1.18 | 0.63 | NA | NA | NA |
| Cash Flow | 1.91 | 1.55 | 1.15 | 0.64 | 0.34 | 0.13 | 0.04 | 0.01 | NA | NA |
| Earnings | 1.73 | 1.40 | 1.07 | 0.60 | 0.32 | 0.12 | 0.04 | 0.01 | -0.02 | -0.04 |
| Dividends | 0.24 | 0.25 | 0.10 | 0.03 | Nil | NA | NA | NA | NA | NA |
| Payout Ratio | 14% | 18% | 9% | 4% | Nil | NA | NA | NA | NA | NA |
| Prices - High | 36 5/8 | 22 5/8 | 21 3/4 | 16 3/8 | 4 5/8 | NA | NA | NA | NA | NA |
| - Low | 18 1/2 | 11 1/4 | 12 1/8 | 4 1/4 | 2 1/4 | NA | NA | NA | NA | NA |
| P/E Ratio - High | 21 | 16 | 20 | 27 | 14 | NA | NA | NA | NA | NA |
| - Low | 11 | 8 | 11 | 7 | 7 | NA | NA | NA | NA | NA |
| **Income Statement Analysis (Million $)** | | | | | | | | | | |
| Revs. | 679 | 553 | 449 | 255 | 132 | 55.0 | 22.0 | 10.0 | 5.0 | 3.0 |
| Oper. Inc. | 203 | 165 | 133 | 71.4 | 34.0 | 11.4 | 2.2 | 0.1 | NA | NA |
| Depr. | 12.7 | 10.8 | 6.2 | 3.0 | 1.3 | 0.6 | 0.3 | 0.1 | NA | NA |
| Int. Exp. | Nil | Nil | NA | NM | NM | 0.2 | NM | NM | 0.1 | 0.0 |
| Pretax Inc. | 196 | 158 | 129 | 69.6 | 33.2 | 10.8 | 2.2 | 0.3 | -0.5 | -0.9 |
| Eff. Tax Rate | 38% | 38% | 40% | 41% | 42% | 40% | 16% | Nil | Nil | Nil |
| Net Inc. | 122 | 98.0 | 78.0 | 41.2 | 19.3 | 6.4 | 1.8 | 0.3 | -0.5 | -0.9 |
| **Balance Sheet & Other Fin. Data (Million $)** | | | | | | | | | | |
| Cash | 109 | 59.2 | 54.4 | 49.0 | 20.0 | 5.2 | 1.3 | NA | NA | NA |
| Curr. Assets | 312 | 210 | 187 | 112 | 55.2 | 25.4 | 12.6 | NA | NA | NA |
| Total Assets | 428 | 290 | 244 | 144 | 68.9 | 28.8 | 14.7 | NA | NA | NA |
| Curr. Liab. | 61.1 | 62.8 | 56.6 | 27.8 | 15.8 | 9.2 | 3.9 | NA | NA | NA |
| LT Debt | Nil | Nil | Nil | Nil | 3.4 | 4.4 | 2.1 | Nil | Nil | Nil |
| Common Eqty. | 362 | 225 | 186 | 117 | 49.8 | 15.2 | 8.7 | 6.4 | 5.6 | 1.3 |
| Total Cap. | 362 | 225 | 186 | 117 | 53.1 | 19.7 | 10.8 | 6.4 | 5.6 | 1.3 |
| Cap. Exp. | 35.4 | 29.5 | 26.1 | 20.9 | 11.4 | 1.5 | 1.3 | 0.4 | NA | NA |
| Cash Flow | 135 | 109 | 84.2 | 44.2 | 20.6 | 7.0 | 2.1 | 0.5 | NA | NA |
| Curr. Ratio | 5.1 | 3.3 | 3.3 | 4.0 | 3.5 | 2.8 | 3.2 | NA | NA | NA |
| % LT Debt of Cap. | Nil | Nil | Nil | Nil | 6.3 | 22.6 | 19.3 | Nil | Nil | Nil |
| % Net Inc.of Revs. | 18.0 | 17.7 | 17.4 | 16.2 | 14.6 | 11.7 | 8.6 | 3.2 | NM | NM |
| % Ret. on Assets | 34.0 | 36.7 | 40.1 | 36.3 | 20.3 | 29.5 | 16.2 | 4.6 | NM | NA |
| % Ret. on Equity | 41.6 | 47.6 | 51.4 | 46.8 | 48.3 | 53.7 | 24.3 | 5.5 | NM | NA |

Data as orig. reptd.; bef. results of disc. opers. and/or spec. items. Per share data adj. for stk. divs. as of ex-div. date. E-Estimated. NA-Not Available. NM-Not Meaningful. NR-Not Ranked.

**Office**—2285 Rutherford Rd., Carlsbad, CA 92008-8815. **Tel**—(619) 931-1771. **E-mail**—CallawayGC@aol.com **Website**—http://www.callawaygolf.com **Chrmn**—Ely Callaway. **Pres & CEO**—D. H. Dye. **EVP & CFO**—D. Rane. **EVP & Secy**—S. C. McCracken. **Investor Contact**—Krista Mallory. **Dirs**—W. C. Baker, E. Callaway, D. H. Dye, B. A. Parker, A. L. Peters, F. R. Port, R. Rosenfield, W. A. Schreyer, M. Sherwin, E. L. Ward Jr., C. J. Yash. **Transfer Agent & Registrar**—Chase Mellon Shareholder Services, South Hackensack, NJ. **Incorporated**—in California in 1982. **Empl**— 2,152. **S&P Analyst:** Michael V. Pizzi

# STANDARD &POOR'S
STOCK REPORTS

B/O **Campbell Soup**

**428**

NYSE Symbol **CPB**

In S&P 500

**17-MAY-97**

Industry: Foods

**Summary:** Campbell Soup is a major producer of branded soups and other grocery food products. The Dorrance family controls more than 50% of the common stock.

| S&P Opinion: Accumulate (★★★★) | Recent Price • 46 | Yield • 1.7% |
|---|---|---|
| | 52 Wk Range • 52½-30¾ | 12-Mo. P/E • 31.7 |

**Earnings vs. Previous Year**
▲=Up ▼=Down ▶=No Change

**Quantitative Evaluations**

Outlook
(1 Lowest—5 Highest)
• **1⁻**

Fair Value
• **37⅛**

Risk
• **Low**

Earn./Div. Rank
• **B+**

Technical Eval.
• **Bullish** since 4/96

Rel. Strength Rank
(1 Lowest—99 Highest)
• **32**

Insider Activity
• **Neutral**

10 Week Mov. Avg. —--
30 Week Mov. Avg. ·····
Relative Strength —

2-for-1

VOL. MIL.

## Overview - 27-MAR-97

Net sales are projected to rise at a middle single-digit rate in FY 97 (Jul.), as unit volume gains for core soup and grocery products, contributions from acquisitions, and higher average selling prices more than offset the impact of recent business divestments. The company's relatively high operating profitability is expected to be further enhanced by the increased volumes, improvements in product mix, and productivity gains derived from the organizational and strategic actions announced in September 1996. Net interest expense in FY 97 may nearly double from prior year levels, reflecting an increased amount of debt to aggressively repurchase shares, holding net income growth in FY 97 to approximately 10%. However, assuming a 3% to 5% reduction in outstanding shares, EPS should advance by 15% in FY 97, to $1.85 (before a $0.32 charge).

## Valuation - 27-MAR-97

Given the company's reliable double-digit EPS gains and high relative returns on shareholder equity, we view Campbell Soup Co. as among the premier U.S. consumer growth companies. As such, we believe that this equity warrants its current premium valuation relative to its peers and to the S&P 500, and is attractive for purchase. In the near-term, earnings growth should be driven by steady volume growth, additional synergistic contributions from the integration of Pace Foods (acquired in January 1995), and aggressive cost cutting measures, which will allow for healthy EPS comparisons in FY 97 and beyond. In addition, the company's current aggressive stock repurchase stance should help support the stock's ascent over the next 12 months. Future earnings growth should also benefit from a more aggressive push abroad.

## Key Stock Statistics

| | | | |
|---|---|---|---|
| S&P EPS Est. 1997 | 1.53 | Tang. Bk. Value/Share | 1.89 |
| P/E on S&P Est. 1997 | 30.1 | Beta | 0.89 |
| S&P EPS Est. 1998 | 2.10 | Shareholders | 43,000 |
| Dividend Rate/Share | 0.77 | Market cap. (B) | $ 21.4 |
| Shs. outstg. (M) | 465.0 | Inst. holdings | 30% |
| Avg. daily vol. (M) | 0.693 | | |

Value of $10,000 invested 5 years ago: $ 26,150

### Fiscal Year Ending Jul. 31

| | 1998 | 1997 | 1996 | 1995 | 1994 | 1993 |
|---|---|---|---|---|---|---|
| **Revenues (Million $)** | | | | | | |
| 1Q | — | 2,052 | 1,990 | 1,864 | 1,763 | 1,696 |
| 2Q | — | 2,317 | 2,217 | 2,040 | 1,894 | 1,789 |
| 3Q | — | 1,870 | 1,831 | 1,744 | 1,568 | 1,632 |
| 4Q | — | — | 1,640 | 1,630 | 1,465 | 1,470 |
| Yr. | — | — | 7,678 | 7,278 | 6,690 | 6,586 |
| **Earnings Per Share ($)** | | | | | | |
| 1Q | — | 0.18 | 0.44 | 0.39 | 0.33 | 0.31 |
| 2Q | — | 0.59 | 0.51 | 0.46 | 0.40 | -0.23 |
| 3Q | — | 0.34 | 0.29 | 0.25 | 0.24 | 0.22 |
| 4Q | — | E0.42 | 0.36 | 0.29 | 0.29 | 0.24 |
| Yr. | E2.10 | E1.53 | 1.61 | 1.40 | 1.26 | 0.51 |

**Next earnings report expected: mid May**

**Dividend Data** (Dividends have been paid since 1902.)

| Amount ($) | Date Decl. | Ex-Div. Date | Stock of Record | Payment Date |
|---|---|---|---|---|
| 0.345 | Sep. 26 | Oct. 07 | Oct. 09 | Oct. 31 '96 |
| 0.385 | Nov. 20 | Jan. 06 | Jan. 08 | Jan. 31 '97 |
| 2-for-1 | Feb. 12 | Mar. 18 | Feb. 24 | Mar. 17 '97 |
| 0.193 | Mar. 27 | Apr. 08 | Apr. 10 | Apr. 30 '97 |

This report is for information purposes and should not be considered a solicitation to buy or sell any security. Neither S&P nor any other party guarantee its accuracy or make warranties regarding results from its usage. Redistribution is prohibited without written permission. Copyright © 1997

*A Division of The McGraw·Hill Companies*

STANDARD
&POOR'S
STOCK REPORTS

# Campbell Soup Company

**428**

**17-MAY-97**

## Business Summary - 27-MAR-97

Campbell Soup Co., through its subsidiaries, manufactures and markets branded convenience food products worldwide. Operations outside the United States accounted for 31% of net sales and 18% of pretax earnings in FY 96 (Jul.), mostly in Europe (14% and 5%) and Australia (8% and 6%). Contributions to sales and operating profits by division in FY 96 were:

| | Sales | Profits |
|---|---|---|
| U.S.A. | 59% | 76% |
| Bakery & Confectionery | 22% | 14% |
| International Grocery | 19% | 10% |

Major U.S. products include both condensed and ready to serve soups (Campbell's, Home Cookin', Chunky, Healthy Request); convenience meals (Swanson, Hungry Man); beans (Homestyle Pork and Beans); juices (Campbell's Tomato, V8); canned spaghetti and gravies (Franco-American); spaghetti sauce (Prego); pickles (Vlasic); refrigerated salad dressings (Marie's); and Mexican sauces (Pace). Foodservice operations serve the away-from-home eating market.

Bakery and Confectionery division products include Pepperidge Farm, Inc. in the U.S., a producer of bread, cakes and related products; Belgium-based Biscuits De-lacre, a maker of biscuit and chocolate products; and Arnotts Biscuits Ltd. of Australia, a maker of biscuit and bakery products. Godiva Chocolatier (worldwide) and Lamy-Lutti (Europe) serve the candy market.

The International Grocery division consists of soup, grocery and frozen foods businesses in Canada, Mexico, Argentina, Europe, Australia and Asia. Major brands include Fray Bentos, Betis, Pleybin, Freshbake and Groko.

## Important Developments

**Nov. '96**—Excluding restructuring charges amounting to $216.3 million ($160 million after tax, or $0.32 a share) incurred during the first quarter of FY 96, operating earnings during the first half rose 12%, to $868 million, from $777 million. Earnings growth in the U.S.A. division (up 16%) and Bakery & Confectionery (9%) more than offset a decline for International Grocery (down 9%). During the first half of FY 97, the company purchased 30.8 million common shares (as adjusted), pursuant to a three-year program to buy up to $2.5 billion of common stock.

## Capitalization

**Long Term Debt:** $938,000,000 (1/97).

### Per Share Data ($)

| (Year Ended Jul. 31) | 1996 | 1995 | 1994 | 1993 | 1992 | 1991 | 1990 | 1989 | 1988 | 1987 |
|---|---|---|---|---|---|---|---|---|---|---|
| Tangible Bk. Val. | 1.89 | 1.51 | 2.84 | 2.20 | 3.16 | 2.67 | 2.53 | 2.53 | 2.71 | 3.09 |
| Cash Flow | 2.27 | 1.99 | 1.80 | 0.96 | 1.37 | 1.17 | 0.36 | 0.36 | 0.78 | 0.74 |
| Earnings | 1.61 | 1.40 | 1.26 | 0.51 | 0.98 | 0.79 | 0.01 | 0.03 | 0.47 | 0.48 |
| Dividends | 0.67 | 0.60 | 0.54 | 0.46 | 0.36 | 0.28 | 0.24 | 0.22 | 0.20 | 0.18 |
| Payout Ratio | 42% | 43% | 43% | 90% | 36% | 35% | 879% | 890% | 43% | 37% |
| Prices - High | 35⅜ | 30⅝ | 23 | 22¾ | 22⅝ | 22 | 15½ | 15⅛ | 8⅞ | 8⅞ |
| - Low | 28 | 20½ | 17⅛ | 17⅝ | 15¾ | 13½ | 11 | 7⅝ | 6 | 5¾ |
| P/E Ratio - High | 22 | 22 | 18 | 44 | 23 | 28 | NM | NM | 19 | 19 |
| - Low | 17 | 15 | 14 | 35 | 16 | 17 | NM | NM | 13 | 12 |

### Income Statement Analysis (Million $)

| | | | | | | | | | | |
|---|---|---|---|---|---|---|---|---|---|---|
| Revs. | 7,678 | 7,278 | 6,690 | 6,586 | 6,263 | 6,204 | 6,206 | 5,672 | 4,869 | 4,490 |
| Oper. Inc. | 1,715 | 1,504 | 1,323 | 1,178 | 1,093 | 970 | 790 | 711 | 616 | 558 |
| Depr. | 326 | 294 | 273 | 223 | 200 | 195 | 184 | 176 | 162 | 139 |
| Int. Exp. | 137 | 123 | 85.0 | 96.0 | 120 | 137 | 122 | 98.0 | 61.0 | 59.0 |
| Pretax Inc. | 1,197 | 1,042 | 963 | 529 | 799 | 675 | 185 | 112 | 395 | 423 |
| Eff. Tax Rate | 33% | 33% | 36% | 50% | 39% | 39% | 95% | 84% | 37% | 40% |
| Net Inc. | 802 | 698 | 630 | 257 | 491 | 402 | 4.0 | 13.0 | 242 | 247 |

### Balance Sheet & Other Fin. Data (Million $)

| | | | | | | | | | | |
|---|---|---|---|---|---|---|---|---|---|---|
| Cash | 34.0 | 53.0 | 96.0 | 70.0 | 118 | 192 | 103 | 147 | 121 | 425 |
| Curr. Assets | 1,618 | 1,581 | 1,601 | 1,686 | 1,502 | 1,519 | 1,666 | 1,602 | 1,363 | 1,431 |
| Total Assets | 6,632 | 6,315 | 4,992 | 4,898 | 4,354 | 4,149 | 4,116 | 3,932 | 3,610 | 3,090 |
| Curr. Liab. | 2,229 | 2,164 | 1,665 | 1,851 | 1,300 | 1,278 | 1,298 | 1,232 | 863 | 686 |
| LT Debt | 744 | 857 | 560 | 462 | 693 | 773 | 806 | 629 | 526 | 380 |
| Common Eqty. | 2,742 | 2,468 | 1,989 | 1,704 | 2,028 | 1,793 | 1,692 | 1,778 | 1,895 | 1,736 |
| Total Cap. | 4,028 | 3,865 | 2,951 | 2,435 | 3,032 | 2,848 | 2,789 | 2,680 | 2,731 | 2,388 |
| Cap. Exp. | 416 | 391 | 421 | 644 | 374 | 361 | 422 | 284 | 387 | 334 |
| Cash Flow | 1,128 | 992 | 903 | 480 | 691 | 596 | 189 | 189 | 404 | 386 |
| Curr. Ratio | 0.7 | 0.7 | 1.0 | 0.9 | 1.2 | 1.2 | 1.3 | 1.3 | 1.6 | 2.1 |
| % LT Debt of Cap. | 18.5 | 22.2 | 19.0 | 19.0 | 22.9 | 27.1 | 28.9 | 23.5 | 19.3 | 15.9 |
| % Net Inc.of Revs. | 10.5 | 9.6 | 9.4 | 3.9 | 7.8 | 6.5 | 0.1 | 0.2 | 5.0 | 5.5 |
| % Ret. on Assets | 12.4 | 11.1 | 12.7 | 5.6 | 11.6 | 9.8 | 0.1 | 0.3 | 7.2 | 8.4 |
| % Ret. on Equity | 30.8 | 31.3 | 34.1 | 13.8 | 25.8 | 23.2 | 0.3 | 0.7 | 13.4 | 15.1 |

Data as orig. reptd.; bef. results of disc. opers. and/or spec. items. Per share data adj. for stk. divs. as of ex-div. date. E-Estimated. NA-Not Available. NM-Not Meaningful. NR-Not Ranked.

**Office**—Campbell Place, Camden, NJ 08103-1799. **Tel**—(609) 342-4800. **Website**—http://www.campbellsoups.com **Chrmn, Pres & CEO**—D. W. Johnson. **CFO & Treas**—B. L. Anderson. **Secy**—J. J. Furey. **Investor Contact**—Leonard F. Griehs. **Dirs**—A. A. App, E. M. Carpenter, B. Dorrance, T. W. Field Jr., K. B. Foster, H. Golub, D. W. Johnson, D. K. P. Li, P. E. Lippincott, M. A. Malone, C. H. Mott, G. M. Sherman, D. M. Stewart, G. Strawbridge Jr., C. C. Weber. **Transfer Agent & Registrar**—First Chicago Trust Co. of New York, Jersey City, NJ. **Incorporated**—in New Jersey in 1922. **Empl**— 40,650. **S&P Analyst:** Kenneth A. Shea

**17-MAY-97**  Industry: Biotechnology

**Summary:** This biotechnology company is developing therapeutic and diagnostic products for cardiovascular, inflammatory and infectious diseases.

| S&P Opinion: Accumulate (★★★★) | Recent Price • 32⅛ | Yield • Nil |
| --- | --- | --- |
| | 52 Wk Range • 41¼-23 | 12-Mo. P/E • NM |

**Quantitative Evaluations**

Outlook (1 Lowest—5 Highest)
• 1⁻

Fair Value
• 26⅛

Risk
• High

Earn./Div. Rank
• C

Technical Eval.
• Bullish since 3/97

Rel. Strength Rank (1 Lowest—99 Highest)
• 42

Insider Activity
• Neutral

**Earnings vs. Previous Year**
▲=Up ▼=Down ▶=No Change

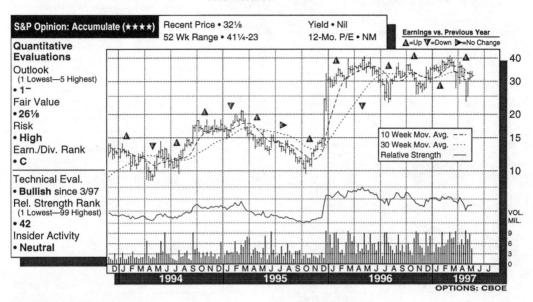

10 Week Mov. Avg. ---
30 Week Mov. Avg. ·····
Relative Strength —

OPTIONS: CBOE

## Overview - 08-MAY-97

Revenue gains should exceed 50% in 1997, driven primarily by continued solid growth in Centocor's lead drug ReoPro. Revenue from ReoPro sales grew more than fivefold in 1996, advancing to $88.7 million, from $15.5 million in 1995. We see 1997 revenue increasing to $156 million, as ReoPro is fast becoming the therapeutic choice during and after high-risk coronary angioplasty. Regulatory label expansion filings have been submitted in the U.S. and Europe, which will give ReoPro blockbuster potential once additional indications are cleared for marketing. Operating margins are expected to widen, aided by increased manufacturing efficiencies. We anticipate that EPS will improve to $0.50 in 1997 and $1.10 in 1998, from 1996's $0.19 loss, which included a $0.01 special credit.

## Valuation - 08-MAY-97

Given our forecast of solid earnings per share growth in 1997 and beyond, the shares are attractive for accumulation for above average near- and long-term appreciation. Positive data from ongoing studies of ReoPro have fundamentally changed the way the medical community views the drug, and market acceptance continues to build. It has also changed the way investors are valuing Centocor. Additionally, we believe that the recent positive Phase II trial data shows that CenTNF will prove to be one of the more significant breakthroughs in the treatment of inflammatory diseases. We feel this drug has the potential to contribute $150 to $200 million in sales by 2000. Based on the company's research pipeline, its strong balance sheet, and ReoPro's blockbuster potential, we view this stock as an attractive long-term biotechnology issue.

## Key Stock Statistics

| | | | |
| --- | --- | --- | --- |
| S&P EPS Est. 1997 | 0.50 | Tang. Bk. Value/Share | 3.25 |
| P/E on S&P Est. 1997 | 64.3 | Beta | 0.86 |
| S&P EPS Est. 1998 | 1.10 | Shareholders | 3,500 |
| Dividend Rate/Share | Nil | Market cap. (B) | $ 2.2 |
| Shs. outstg. (M) | 69.6 | Inst. holdings | 68% |
| Avg. daily vol. (M) | 1.867 | | |

Value of $10,000 invested 5 years ago: $ 5,887

### Fiscal Year Ending Dec. 31

| | 1998 | 1997 | 1996 | 1995 | 1994 | 1993 |
| --- | --- | --- | --- | --- | --- | --- |
| **Revenues (Million $)** | | | | | | |
| 1Q | — | 45.04 | 21.88 | 24.00 | 15.27 | 15.00 |
| 2Q | — | — | 30.59 | 20.75 | 16.38 | 13.80 |
| 3Q | — | — | 39.18 | 19.16 | 12.93 | 16.73 |
| 4Q | — | — | 43.84 | 15.01 | 22.64 | 30.47 |
| Yr. | — | — | 135.5 | 78.92 | 67.23 | 75.93 |
| **Earnings Per Share ($)** | | | | | | |
| 1Q | — | 0.05 | -0.16 | -0.14 | -1.13 | -0.62 |
| 2Q | — | E0.07 | -0.07 | -0.30 | -0.30 | -0.63 |
| 3Q | — | E0.08 | -0.02 | -0.21 | -0.34 | -0.38 |
| 4Q | — | E0.30 | 0.04 | -0.33 | -0.83 | -0.17 |
| Yr. | E1.10 | E0.50 | -0.20 | -0.98 | -2.55 | -1.79 |

Next earnings report expected: late July

## Dividend Data

No cash has been paid.

This report is for information purposes and should not be considered a solicitation to buy or sell any security. Neither S&P nor any other party guarantee its accuracy or make warranties regarding results from its usage. Redistribution is prohibited without written permission. Copyright © 1997 | *A Division of The* **McGraw-Hill** *Companies*

STANDARD
&POOR'S
STOCK REPORTS

# Centocor, Inc.

**3458N**

**17-MAY-97**

## Business Summary - 08-MAY-97

Centocor, Inc. is a biopharmaceutical company that develops and commercializes monoclonal antibody and DNA-based products for human health care. The company focuses on four major disease areas: infectious, cardiovascular, autoimmune and cancer. Centocor's clinical development and regulatory strategy for its therapeutic products is to pursue initial approval for a narrowly defined indication. The company then seeks to expand the indications for which the products may be marketed by conducting additional clinical trials.

Centocor has two therapeutic products approved for sale and several product candidates in various stages of development. The company's flagship therapeutic, ReoPro, a monoclonal antibody designed to inhibit clotting in the blood during and after high-risk coronary angioplasty, was launched for commercial sale in January 1995. The product has been shown to reduce the incidence of blood clot-related complications associated with coronary angioplasty. Other studies have shown beneficial results in long-term high and low risk angioplasty patients as well as unstable angina patients. Clinical trials are currently ongoing, testing ReoPro for treatment of acute myocardial infarction. Eli Lilly holds global marketing rights, excluding Japan. Fujisawa Pharmaceutical Co. Ltd. holds the exclusive distribution rights for ReoPro in Japan.

In February 1995, Centocor launched Panorex, used in the treatment of post-operative colorectal cancer, in Germany. Long term Phase III trials are proceeding in the U.S. and Europe. Glaxo-Wellcome holds marketing rights. In the area of autoimmune disease therapy, cA2 (CenTNF) completed Phase II trials for the treatment of rheumatoid arthritis and Crohn's disease with positive results. A Phase III trial has begun for rheumatoid arthritis, and the company expects to file for marketing approval for Crohn's disease late in 1997.

Centocor's in-vivo diagnostic, Myoscint, a cardiac imaging agent, is used in the detection of damage to heart tissue caused by transplantation, myocardial infarction, chemotherapy and viral infection. The company has received marketing approvals for Myoscint in the U.S., several European countries and Japan. Revenues from the sale of Myoscint have not yet proved significant on a worldwide basis.

In-vitro diagnostic products are used to test patient blood samples outside the body to detect or monitor disease. In this area, Centocor has focused primarily on developing cancer diagnostic assays, and other in-vitro diagnostic products for infectious disease. The company produces in-vitro cancer blood tests for ovarian cancer, pancreatic cancer, breast cancer, non-small cell lung cancer and gastric cancer. CNTO also sells infectious disease serology tests used in blood bank testing laboratories, and a multidrug resistance test used to detect resistance to chemotherapeutic drugs.

### Capitalization

**Long Term Debt:** $54,765,000 (12/96).
**Minority Interest:** $3,839,000.

### Per Share Data ($)

| (Year Ended Dec. 31) | 1996 | 1995 | 1994 | 1993 | 1992 | 1991 | 1990 | 1989 | 1988 | 1987 |
|---|---|---|---|---|---|---|---|---|---|---|
| Tangible Bk. Val. | 3.25 | NM | -0.08 | -0.65 | 0.31 | 3.67 | 5.78 | 5.31 | 5.27 | 5.11 |
| Cash Flow | 0.01 | -0.70 | -2.19 | -1.42 | -4.48 | -5.36 | -4.47 | 0.24 | 0.38 | 0.42 |
| Earnings | -0.20 | -0.98 | -2.55 | -1.79 | -4.90 | -5.72 | -5.10 | 0.01 | 0.18 | 0.31 |
| Dividends | Nil | Nil | Nil | Nil | Nil | Nil | Nil | Nil | Nil | Nil |
| Payout Ratio | Nil | Nil | Nil | Nil | Nil | Nil | Nil | Nil | Nil | Nil |
| Prices - High | 40⅞ | 33⅛ | 18¾ | 19½ | 60¼ | 56¼ | 24⅛ | 13½ | 15 | 24¼ |
|    - Low | 23 | 9⅝ | 8⅞ | 5¼ | 9½ | 19⅜ | 11⅞ | 7½ | 6¾ | 8½ |
| P/E Ratio - High | NM | NM | NM | NM | NM | NM | NM | NM | 83 | 80 |
|    - Low | NM | NM | NM | NM | NM | NM | NM | NM | 37 | 28 |

### Income Statement Analysis (Million $)

| | 1996 | 1995 | 1994 | 1993 | 1992 | 1991 | 1990 | 1989 | 1988 | 1987 |
|---|---|---|---|---|---|---|---|---|---|---|
| Revs. | 136 | 78.9 | 67.2 | 75.9 | 76.2 | 53.2 | 64.6 | 72.0 | 55.2 | 51.6 |
| Oper. Inc. | -1.3 | -29.3 | -26.0 | -31.0 | -122 | -110 | -15.0 | 3.0 | 4.0 | 11.0 |
| Depr. | 14.0 | 16.4 | 18.2 | 15.6 | 16.7 | 12.4 | 16.3 | 5.3 | 4.5 | 3.4 |
| Int. Exp. | 8.4 | 17.0 | 19.8 | 20.1 | 19.8 | 11.4 | 1.9 | 1.6 | 1.1 | 0.5 |
| Pretax Inc. | -13.5 | -57.1 | -126 | -74.0 | -193 | -195 | -133 | NM | 7.0 | 13.0 |
| Eff. Tax Rate | NM | NM | NM | NM | NM | NM | NM | 43% | 40% | 43% |
| Net Inc. | -13.5 | -57.1 | -126 | -74.0 | -193 | -195 | -131 | NM | 4.0 | 7.0 |

### Balance Sheet & Other Fin. Data (Million $)

| | 1996 | 1995 | 1994 | 1993 | 1992 | 1991 | 1990 | 1989 | 1988 | 1987 |
|---|---|---|---|---|---|---|---|---|---|---|
| Cash | 176 | 131 | 182 | 123 | 150 | 181 | 96.0 | 64.0 | 45.0 | 40.0 |
| Curr. Assets | 235 | 169 | 215 | 153 | 187 | 284 | 158 | 88.0 | 72.0 | 57.0 |
| Total Assets | 341 | 260 | 306 | 281 | 349 | 473 | 273 | 180 | 153 | 149 |
| Curr. Liab. | 45.0 | 56.0 | 67.2 | 59.6 | 77.1 | 63.6 | 43.6 | 17.9 | 12.4 | 16.0 |
| LT Debt | 54.8 | 232 | 232 | 238 | 238 | 259 | 42.0 | 23.0 | 13.0 | 7.0 |
| Common Eqty. | 236 | -29.4 | 5.0 | -19.0 | 31.0 | 144 | 169 | 133 | 122 | 115 |
| Total Cap. | 295 | 203 | 237 | 219 | 269 | 405 | 215 | 160 | 137 | 127 |
| Cap. Exp. | 4.7 | 4.8 | 4.6 | 2.0 | 23.3 | 32.5 | 47.8 | 15.4 | 19.4 | 8.2 |
| Cash Flow | 0.5 | -40.7 | -107 | -59.0 | -176 | -182 | -115 | 5.0 | 9.0 | 10.0 |
| Curr. Ratio | 5.2 | 3.0 | 3.2 | 2.6 | 2.4 | 4.5 | 3.6 | 4.9 | 5.8 | 3.6 |
| % LT Debt of Cap. | 18.6 | 114.3 | 92.6 | 108.5 | 88.4 | 64.0 | 19.6 | 14.0 | 9.5 | 5.6 |
| % Net Inc.of Revs. | NM | NM | NM | NM | NM | NM | NM | 0.2 | 7.5 | 13.4 |
| % Ret. on Assets | NM | NM | NM | NM | NM | NM | NM | 0.1 | 2.7 | 5.1 |
| % Ret. on Equity | NM | NM | NM | NM | NM | NM | NM | 0.1 | 3.4 | 6.4 |

Data as orig. reptd.; bef. results of disc. opers. and/or spec. items. Per share data adj. for stk. divs. as of ex-div. date. E-Estimated. NA-Not Available. NM-Not Meaningful. NR-Not Ranked.

**Office**—200 Great Valley Parkway, Malvern, PA 19355.**Tel**—(610) 651-6000. **Website**—http://www.centocor.com **Chrmn**—H.J.P. Schoemaker. **Pres & CEO**—D.P. Holveck. **VP-Fin & CFO**—D.J. Caruso. **VP-Secy**—G. D. Hobbs. **Dirs**—A. B. Evnin, W. F. Hamilton, D. P. Holveck, A. T. Knoppers, R. A. Matricaria, H. J. P. Schoemaker, R. D. Spizzirri, L. Steinman, J.C. Tempel. **Transfer Agent & Registrar**—First National Bank of Boston, Canton. **Incorporated**—in Pennsylvania in 1979. **Empl**— 545. **S&P Analyst:** Richard Joy

# STANDARD &POOR'S
STOCK REPORTS

✓ **Cisco Systems**

**3536C**

Nasdaq Symbol **CSCO**

In S&P 500

**17-MAY-97**

**Industry:** Computers (Network-ing)

**Summary:** Cisco offers a complete line of routers and switching products that connect and manage communications among local and wide area computer networks employing a variety of protocols.

| S&P Opinion: Buy (★★★★) | Recent Price • 61½ | Yield • Nil |
| --- | --- | --- |
| | 52 Wk Range • 75¾-44¾ | 12-Mo. P/E • 35.8 |

**Quantitative Evaluations**

Outlook (1 Lowest—5 Highest)
• **5**

Fair Value
• **91¼**

Risk
• **Average**

Earn./Div. Rank
• **B**

Technical Eval.
• **Bearish** since 2/97

Rel. Strength Rank (1 Lowest—99 Highest)
• **87**

Insider Activity
• **NA**

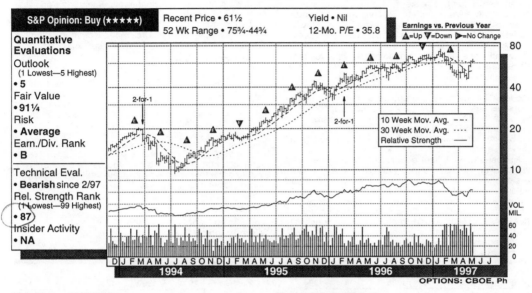

Earnings vs. Previous Year
▲=Up ▼=Down ▶=No Change

2-for-1

2-for-1

10 Week Mov. Avg. - - -
30 Week Mov. Avg. ......
Relative Strength ——

D J F M A M J J A S O N D J F M A M J J A S O N D J F M A M J J A S O N D J F M A M J J
**1994** **1995** **1996** **1997**

VOL. MIL.

OPTIONS: CBOE, Ph

## Overview - 12-MAY-97

Sales should grow nearly 60% in FY 97 (Jul.). CSCO is benefiting from its position of offering the industry's most comprehensive line of switching products, and of being chosen increasingly by customers looking for a single vendor able to provide complete end-to-end networking solutions. Demand for switches is being led by the need for increased bandwidth among corporate users. In addition, Cisco's acquisition strategy has given it a strong, broad-based product line, including its July 1996 acquisition of StrataCom (STRM), providing exposure to Frame Relay and ATM technologies used in WANs. Gross margin pressures are expected to continue, as the product mix shifts to less profitable low-end routers, switching and access products. STRM's products also carry lower margins than CSCO's. Operating expenses will continue to increase sharply, as CSCO builds its sales and marketing infrastructure and invests heavily in R&D. EPS of $2.10 are projected for FY 97, excluding non-recurring items.

## Valuation - 12-MAY-97

We recently raised our opinion to buy from accumulate in light of increasing evidence that Cisco's strong market position remains intact. Red flags of caution were raised earlier this year when management announced plans to slow its rate of hiring during the third quarter, indicating that sales growth was also expected to slow. Further concerns have been raised over greater competition coming from recent merger proposals to combine 3COM and U.S. Robotics, and Ascend Communications and Cascade. Nevertheless, CSCO remains the dominant vendor in the still growing data networking industry, and with its shares trading at a price/earnings multiple that represents a significant discount from its long term earnings growth rate, we recommend purchase.

## Key Stock Statistics

| | | | |
| --- | --- | --- | --- |
| S&P EPS Est. 1997 | 1.85 | Tang. Bk. Value/Share | 4.34 |
| P/E on S&P Est. 1997 | 33.2 | Beta | 1.45 |
| S&P EPS Est. 1998 | 2.80 | Shareholders | 8,300 |
| Dividend Rate/Share | Nil | Market cap. (B) | $ 40.8 |
| Shs. outstg. (M) | 663.6 | Inst. holdings | 67% |
| Avg. daily vol. (M) | 13.899 | | |

Value of $10,000 invested 5 years ago: $ 148,830

### Fiscal Year Ending Jul. 31

| | 1998 | 1997 | 1996 | 1995 | 1994 | 1993 |
| --- | --- | --- | --- | --- | --- | --- |
| **Revenues (Million $)** | | | | | | |
| 1Q | — | 1,435 | 710.2 | 392.9 | 248.5 | 126.4 |
| 2Q | — | 1,592 | 826.5 | 454.9 | 302.2 | 145.1 |
| 3Q | — | 1,648 | 985.2 | 509.9 | 331.2 | 172.4 |
| 4Q | — | — | 1,292 | 621.2 | 361.2 | 205.2 |
| Yr. | — | — | 4,096 | 1,979 | 1,243 | 649.0 |
| **Earnings Per Share ($)** | | | | | | |
| 1Q | — | 0.26 | 0.29 | 0.19 | 0.12 | 0.07 |
| 2Q | — | 0.49 | 0.33 | 0.09 | 0.15 | 0.08 |
| 3Q | — | 0.55 | 0.39 | 0.22 | 0.16 | 0.09 |
| 4Q | — | E0.57 | 0.41 | 0.25 | 0.17 | 0.10 |
| Yr. | E2.80 | E1.85 | 1.37 | 0.76 | 0.60 | 0.33 |

**Next earnings report expected: mid August**

### Dividend Data

No cash dividends have been paid. Five two-for-one stock splits were effected between 1991 and 1996.

This report is for information purposes and should not be considered a solicitation to buy or sell any security. Neither S&P nor any other party guarantee its accuracy or make warranties regarding results from its usage. Redistribution is prohibited without written permission. Copyright © 1997

*A Division of The McGraw·Hill Companies*

## Business Summary - 12-MAY-97

Cisco Systems develops, makes, markets and supports high-performance, multiprotocol internetworking products that enable customers to build large-scale integrated networks of computer networks. Its products connect and manage communications among local and wide area networks (LANs and WANs) that employ a variety of protocols, media interfaces, network topologies and cabling systems.

International sales accounted for 48% of the total in FY 96 (Jul.) versus 42% in FY 95 and FY 94.

The company's product family includes backbone and remote access routers, LAN and asynchronous transfer mode (ATM) switches, dial-up access servers and network management software. All products support multiprotocol multiple media connectivity in multivendor environments. CSCO's Internetwork Operating System (IOS) provides a common software platform across all network environments.

High-performance, intelligent routers interconnect networks using different protocols and media. Access routers extend the network to regional sales groups, small satellite offices and individual telecommuters.

The company has made many acquisitions in recent years. In July 1996, CSCO acquired StrataCom Inc. (NASDAQ: STRM), a leading maker of high speed ATM and Frame Relay switching technologies. During 1995, CSCO purchased Grand Junction Networks Inc., a leading provider of Fast Ethernet and Ethernet desktop switching products; Combinet Inc., a leading maker of ISDN remote-access networking products; Internet Junction, Inc., a developer of software that connects desktop users to the Internet; and Lightstream Corp., a developer of enterprise-class ATM switching technology. In 1994, it purchased Kalpana Inc., a leading worldwide supplier of Ethernet switches; and Newport Systems Solutions, a supplier of software-based routers. In September 1993, it acquired Crescendo Communications, a provider of high-performance workgroup solutions.

### Important Developments

**May '97**—CSCO said it planned to unveil its new Gigabit Switch Router (GSR) at an industry trade show. The high-end router is targeted at the Internet Service Provider market, and will compete against Ascend Communications' high-speed router, called the GRF. CSCO's GSR is expected to enter field trials during the summer, and be available in the fall. Cisco also announced the introduction of its 3800 multiservice access concentrator, which integrates switched voice, multiprotocol data and routing over Frame Relay and ATM. During a conference call with investors, the company said it planned to make 8 to 12 acquisitions during the year.

### Capitalization

**Long Term Debt:** None (4/97).
**Minority Interest:** $41,230,000.
**Options:** To purchase 69,089,000 shs. at $0.01 to $55.88 ea. (7/96).

### Per Share Data ($)

| (Year Ended Jul. 31) | 1996 | 1995 | 1994 | 1993 | 1992 | 1991 | 1990 | 1989 | 1988 | 1987 |
|---|---|---|---|---|---|---|---|---|---|---|
| Tangible Bk. Val. | 4.34 | 2.53 | 1.64 | 0.96 | 0.51 | 0.28 | 0.16 | 0.03 | 0.01 | 0.00 |
| Cash Flow | 1.61 | 0.87 | 0.65 | 0.36 | 0.18 | 0.09 | 0.03 | 0.01 | 0.00 | 0.00 |
| Earnings | 1.37 | 0.76 | 0.60 | 0.33 | 0.17 | 0.09 | 0.03 | 0.01 | 0.00 | 0.00 |
| Dividends | Nil | Nil | Nil | Nil | Nil | Nil | Nil | Nil | Nil | Nil |
| Payout Ratio | Nil | Nil | Nil | Nil | Nil | Nil | Nil | Nil | Nil | Nil |
| Prices - High | 69⅛ | 44⅝ | 20⅜ | 14⅞ | 10⅛ | 4¼ | 1⁷⁄₁₆ | NA | NA | NA |
| - Low | 32 | 16¼ | 9⅜ | 8¼ | 4 | 1¼ | ⁹⁄₁₆ | NA | NA | NA |
| P/E Ratio - High | 50 | 60 | 34 | 45 | 58 | 40 | 45 | NA | NA | NA |
| - Low | 23 | 21 | 16 | 25 | 24 | 14 | 18 | NA | NA | NA |

### Income Statement Analysis (Million $)

| | 1996 | 1995 | 1994 | 1993 | 1992 | 1991 | 1990 | 1989 | 1988 | 1987 |
|---|---|---|---|---|---|---|---|---|---|---|
| Revs. | 4,096 | 1,979 | 1,243 | 649 | 340 | 183 | 70.0 | 28.0 | 6.0 | 2.0 |
| Oper. Inc. | 1,533 | 701 | 519 | 277 | 136 | 69.0 | 22.0 | 7.0 | 1.0 | Nil |
| Depr. | 133 | 58.5 | 30.8 | 13.3 | 6.5 | 3.0 | 0.8 | 0.1 | 0.1 | 0.0 |
| Int. Exp. | NM | NA | NA | NA | NA | NA | 0.0 | NA | NA | NA |
| Pretax Inc. | 1,465 | 679 | 509 | 275 | 136 | 71.0 | 23.0 | 7.0 | 1.0 | Nil |
| Eff. Tax Rate | 38% | 38% | 38% | 38% | 38% | 39% | 41% | 40% | 40% | 34% |
| Net Inc. | 913 | 421 | 315 | 172 | 84.4 | 43.2 | 13.9 | 4.2 | 0.4 | 0.1 |

### Balance Sheet & Other Fin. Data (Million $)

| | 1996 | 1995 | 1994 | 1993 | 1992 | 1991 | 1990 | 1989 | 1988 | 1987 |
|---|---|---|---|---|---|---|---|---|---|---|
| Cash | 1,038 | 440 | 183 | 89.0 | 156 | 91.0 | 57.0 | 4.0 | 2.0 | NA |
| Curr. Assets | 2,160 | 996 | 508 | 268 | 247 | 141 | 78.0 | 16.0 | 5.0 | NA |
| Total Assets | 3,630 | 1,757 | 1,054 | 595 | 324 | 154 | 83.0 | 17.0 | 5.0 | 1.0 |
| Curr. Liab. | 769 | 338 | 206 | 120 | 78.3 | 26.3 | 13.2 | 8.8 | 1.7 | NA |
| LT Debt | NM | Nil | Nil | Nil | Nil | Nil | 0.1 | 0.2 | Nil | Nil |
| Common Eqty. | 2,820 | 1,379 | 848 | 475 | 246 | 128 | 69.0 | 8.0 | 3.0 | Nil |
| Total Cap. | 2,852 | 1,420 | 848 | 475 | 246 | 128 | 69.0 | 8.0 | 3.0 | Nil |
| Cap. Exp. | 283 | 112 | 59.6 | 33.9 | 21.6 | 11.3 | 4.1 | 0.3 | 0.3 | 0.1 |
| Cash Flow | 1,046 | 480 | 346 | 185 | 90.8 | 46.2 | 14.7 | 4.3 | 0.5 | 0.1 |
| Curr. Ratio | 2.8 | 2.9 | 2.5 | 2.2 | 3.2 | 5.4 | 5.9 | 1.8 | 2.6 | NA |
| % LT Debt of Cap. | NM | Nil | Nil | Nil | Nil | Nil | 0.2 | 2.7 | Nil | Nil |
| % Net Inc.of Revs. | 22.3 | 21.3 | 25.3 | 26.5 | 24.8 | 23.6 | 19.9 | 15.1 | 7.1 | 5.6 |
| % Ret. on Assets | 32.5 | 30.0 | 38.2 | 37.0 | 34.7 | 36.5 | 23.2 | 39.2 | 14.0 | 19.1 |
| % Ret. on Equity | 41.7 | 37.8 | 47.6 | 47.2 | 44.4 | 43.9 | 34.8 | 78.9 | 23.8 | 86.5 |

Data as orig. reptd.; bef. results of disc. opers. and/or spec. items. Per share data adj. for stk. divs. as of ex-div. date. E-Estimated. NA-Not Available. NM-Not Meaningful. NR-Not Ranked.

**Office**—170 W. Tasman Drive, San Jose, CA 95134-1706. **Tel**—(408) 526-4000. **Website**—http://www.cisco.com **Chrmn**—J. P. Morgridge. **Vice Chrmn**—D. T. Valentine. **Pres & CEO**—J. Chambers. **CFO, VP-Fin, Secy & Investor Contact**—L. R. Carter. **Dirs**— J. T. Chambers, M. S. Frankel, J. F. Gibbons, E. R. Kozer, R. M. Moley, J. P. Morgridge, R. L. Puette, M. Son, D. T. Valentine, S. West. **Transfer Agent & Registrar**—First National Bank of Boston. **Incorporated**—in California in 1984. **Empl**— 10,451. **S&P Analyst:** Megan Graham Hackett

**17-MAY-97**

**Industry:**
Insurance (Property-Casualty)

**Summary:** This company provides private mortgage insurance to residential mortgage lenders, including mortgage bankers, mortgage brokers, commercial banks and savings institutions.

## Quantitative Evaluations

**Outlook**
(1 Lowest—5 Highest)
• **2**

**Fair Value**
• **37¾**

**Risk**
• **Low**

**Earn./Div. Rank**
• **B**

**Technical Eval.**
• **Bullish** since 12/94

**Rel. Strength Rank**
(1 Lowest—99 Highest)
• **84**

**Insider Activity**
• **NA**

Recent Price • 37⅞
52 Wk Range • 37⅞-26¼

Yield • 0.3%
12-Mo. P/E • 14.9

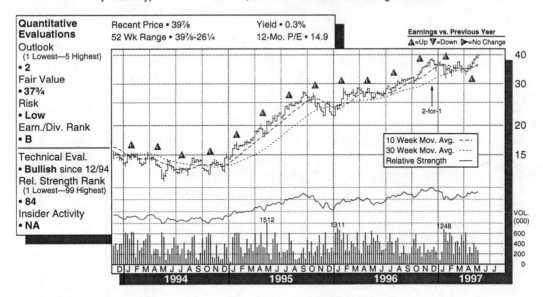

Earnings vs. Previous Year
▲=Up ▼=Down ▶=No Change

10 Week Mov. Avg. - - -
30 Week Mov. Avg. ·····
Relative Strength —

2-for-1

## Business Profile - 28-APR-97

CMAC Investment Corp. is the sixth largest of eight active private mortgage insurers in the U.S., with a market share of new primary insurance written of 9.6% in 1996. During the first quarter of 1997, the company experienced a 20% year to year increase in primary insurance-in-force, enabling CMAC to augment its competitive position. The company expects further growth in insurance-in-force, as government initiatives on affordable housing boost lending to low- and moderate-income borrowers, expanding the private mortgage insurance market. CMAC employs strict underwriting discipline, aided by the use of automated risk evaluation models. At March 31, 1997, the delinquency rate on primary insurance was 2.30% compared to 2.22% a year earlier.

## Operational Review - 28-APR-97

Total revenues in the three months ended March 31, 1997, rose 26%, year to year, reflecting a 30% gain in premiums earned and 14% higher net investment income. Revenue growth benefited from a 20% increase in primary insurance-in-force. Total expenses were up 28%, on a 34% rise in the provision for losses. Pretax income advanced 23%. After taxes at 26.3%, versus 24.3%, net income expanded 20%, to $17,284,000 ($0.71 a share), from $14,427,000 ($0.59).

## Stock Performance - 16-MAY-97

In the past 30 trading days, CMT's shares have increased 18%, compared to a 9% rise in the S&P 500. Average trading volume for the past five days was 52,900 shares, compared with the 40-day moving average of 73,523 shares.

## Key Stock Statistics

| | | | |
|---|---|---|---|
| Dividend Rate/Share | 0.12 | Shareholders | 4,500 |
| Shs. outstg. (M) | 22.4 | Market cap. (B) | $0.893 |
| Avg. daily vol. (M) | 0.060 | Inst. holdings | 91% |
| Tang. Bk. Value/Share | 15.91 | | |
| Beta | NA | | |

Value of $10,000 invested 5 years ago: NA

### Fiscal Year Ending Dec. 31

| | 1997 | 1996 | 1995 | 1994 | 1993 | 1992 |
|---|---|---|---|---|---|---|
| **Revenues (Million $)** | | | | | | |
| 1Q | 63.60 | 50.53 | 36.93 | 30.10 | 23.83 | 17.12 |
| 2Q | — | 54.48 | 39.69 | 32.33 | 27.94 | 22.38 |
| 3Q | — | 57.22 | 43.04 | 33.24 | 27.94 | 22.25 |
| 4Q | — | 60.36 | 45.98 | 34.87 | 30.18 | 21.78 |
| Yr. | — | 222.6 | 165.6 | 130.5 | 107.2 | 83.53 |
| **Earnings Per Share ($)** | | | | | | |
| 1Q | 0.71 | 0.59 | 0.46 | 0.38 | 0.28 | 0.33 |
| 2Q | — | 0.63 | 0.51 | 0.42 | 0.33 | 0.43 |
| 3Q | — | 0.65 | 0.54 | 0.44 | 0.37 | 0.38 |
| 4Q | — | 0.68 | 0.57 | 0.46 | 0.42 | 0.28 |
| Yr. | — | 2.55 | 2.09 | 1.70 | 1.39 | 1.39 |

**Next earnings report expected: mid July**

**Dividend Data** (Dividends have been paid since 1993.)

| Amount ($) | Date Decl. | Ex-Div. Date | Stock of Record | Payment Date |
|---|---|---|---|---|
| 0.060 | Oct. 17 | Nov. 05 | Nov. 07 | Dec. 02 '96 |
| 2-for-1 | Oct. 17 | Dec. 03 | Nov. 07 | Dec. 02 '96 |
| 0.030 | Jan. 21 | Feb. 05 | Feb. 07 | Mar. 03 '97 |
| 0.030 | Apr. 15 | May. 02 | May. 06 | Jun. 03 '97 |

This report is for information purposes and should not be considered a solicitation to buy or sell any security. Neither S&P nor any other party guarantee its accuracy or make warranties regarding results from its usage. Redistribution is prohibited without written permission. Copyright © 1997    *A Division of The McGraw·Hill Companies*

## Business Summary - 28-APR-97

CMAC Investment Corp. is the parent company of Commonwealth Mortgage Assurance Company, which provides private mortgage insurance to residential mortgage lenders, including mortgage bankers, mortgage brokers, commercial banks and savings institutions. Private mortgage insurance (also called mortgage guarantee insurance) protects lenders from default-related losses on residential first mortgage loans made to home buyers who make down payments of less than 20% of a home's purchase price. Private mortgage insurance also facilitates the sale of mortgage loans in the secondary mortgage market.

During 1996, CMAC's market share of new primary mortgage insurance written was flat from the prior year, at 9.6%. The company intends to expand its sales efforts to larger national accounts in 1997 in an effort to improve its competitive position. At the end of 1996, the company had $8.35 billion of direct primary risk in force, compared to $6.67 billion a year earlier.

The company generates a substantial portion of income from earnings on its investment portfolio, at least 95% of which, according to its investment policy, must consist of cash, cash equivalents and investment-grade securities. CMAC is considering altering these guidelines to permit the inclusion of a small percentage (5% to 10% of the total portfolio) of equity securities. At December 31, 1996, the entire investment portfolio was rated investment-grade.

CMAC also offers to primary lenders pool insurance that serves as a credit enhancement for certain mortgage-backed securities, in addition to primary insurance. Primary insurance covers defaults and certain expenses related to defaults and subsequent foreclosure on individual loans, which sum to the "claim amount." CMAC intends to limit pool risk in force to approximately 5% of CMAC's total risk in force.

In the event of a homeowner default, the company generally covers 7% to 30% of the claim amount, which is itself typically about 114% of the outstanding principal on the mortgage insured. The lender selects the amount of coverage based on the level needed to bring the loan into compliance with requirements for sale to FHLMC and FNMA.

## Important Developments

**Apr. '97**—CMAC reported that primary insurance-in-force at the end of 1997's first quarter grew by 20% from the year-earlier period and nearly 6% from year-end 1996. In addition, delinquency rates on primary insurance decreased to 2.30% from 2.38% at December 31, 1996. The level, however, is higher than the 2.22% default rate reported at the end of 1996's first quarter.

## Capitalization

**Long Term Debt:** None (3/97).
**Preferred Stock:** $40,000,000.

### Per Share Data ($)

| (Year Ended Dec. 31) | 1996 | 1995 | 1994 | 1993 | 1992 | 1991 | 1990 | 1989 | 1988 | 1987 |
|---|---|---|---|---|---|---|---|---|---|---|
| Tangible Bk. Val. | 15.91 | 13.42 | 10.91 | 9.71 | 8.25 | 7.76 | NA | NA | NA | NA |
| Oper. Earnings | NA | NA | NA | NA | NA | NA | NA | NA | NA | NA |
| Earnings | 2.55 | 2.09 | 1.70 | 1.39 | 1.39 | 0.90 | 0.65 | -0.16 | -0.17 | -0.18 |
| Dividends | 0.21 | 0.10 | 0.10 | 0.10 | Nil | NA | NA | NA | NA | NA |
| Payout Ratio | 8% | 5% | 6% | 7% | Nil | NA | NA | NA | NA | NA |
| Prices - High | 38¾ | 27⅞ | 15½ | 17⅝ | 13¼ | NA | NA | NA | NA | NA |
|    - Low | 22 | 14⅜ | 11⅝ | 11½ | 9 | NA | NA | NA | NA | NA |
| P/E Ratio - High | 15 | 13 | 9 | 13 | 9 | NA | NA | NA | NA | NA |
|    - Low | 9 | 7 | 7 | 8 | 6 | NA | NA | NA | NA | NA |

### Income Statement Analysis (Million $)

| | 1996 | 1995 | 1994 | 1993 | 1992 | 1991 | 1990 | 1989 | 1988 | 1987 |
|---|---|---|---|---|---|---|---|---|---|---|
| Premium Inc. | 188 | 137 | 106 | 81.6 | 67.1 | 61.7 | 53.2 | 54.7 | 52.8 | 56.2 |
| Net Invest. Inc. | 30.0 | 25.9 | 22.6 | 20.9 | 13.9 | 12.3 | 12.0 | 11.9 | 12.1 | 12.2 |
| Oth. Revs. | 4.7 | 2.6 | 1.8 | 4.6 | 2.5 | -2.6 | 0.2 | 0.2 | 0.9 | -0.4 |
| Total Revs. | 223 | 166 | 131 | 107 | 83.5 | 71.4 | 65.4 | 66.8 | 65.8 | 68.0 |
| Pretax Inc. | 82.6 | 68.2 | 56.4 | 48.2 | 32.4 | 17.8 | 14.4 | 1.4 | -3.2 | -4.0 |
| Net Oper. Inc. | NA | NA | NA | NA | 20.8 | 13.9 | 9.5 | -0.1 | 2.1 | 1.3 |
| Net Inc. | 62.2 | 50.8 | 41.1 | 34.1 | 21.8 | 12.7 | 9.1 | -2.2 | -2.5 | -2.5 |

### Balance Sheet & Other Fin. Data (Million $)

| | 1996 | 1995 | 1994 | 1993 | 1992 | 1991 | 1990 | 1989 | 1988 | 1987 |
|---|---|---|---|---|---|---|---|---|---|---|
| Cash & Equiv. | 3.2 | 3.7 | 3.9 | 7.6 | 2.3 | NA | NA | NA | NA | NA |
| Premiums Due | NA | NA | NA | NA | NA | NA | NA | NA | NA | NA |
| Invest. Assets: Bonds | 508 | 433 | 359 | 327 | 304 | NA | NA | NA | NA | NA |
| Invest. Assets: Stocks | Nil | Nil | Nil | Nil | Nil | NA | NA | NA | NA | NA |
| Invest. Assets: Loans | Nil | Nil | Nil | Nil | Nil | NA | NA | NA | NA | NA |
| Invest. Assets: Total | 513 | 438 | 359 | 327 | 304 | NA | NA | NA | NA | NA |
| Deferred Policy Costs | 23.9 | 21.4 | 16.9 | 16.2 | NA | NA | NA | NA | NA | NA |
| Total Assets | 593 | 499 | 410 | 375 | 335 | NA | NA | NA | NA | NA |
| Debt | Nil | Nil | Nil | Nil | Nil | Nil | NA | NA | NA | NA |
| Common Eqty. | 356 | 299 | 240 | 213 | 181 | 170 | NA | NA | NA | NA |
| Prop. & Cas. Loss Ratio | 50.6 | 44.3 | 37.7 | 38.6 | 47.0 | 59.8 | 65.3 | NA | NA | NA |
| Prop. & Cas. Expense Ratio | 23.2 | 28.5 | 27.6 | 27.6 | 27.6 | 30.6 | 32.8 | NA | NA | NA |
| Prop. & Cas. Combined Ratio | 73.8 | 72.8 | 65.3 | 66.2 | 74.6 | 90.4 | 98.1 | NA | NA | NA |
| % Return On Revs. | 27.9 | 30.6 | 31.5 | 31.8 | 26.0 | 17.8 | 14.0 | NM | NM | NM |
| % Ret. on Equity | 18.9 | 18.9 | 18.2 | 15.7 | 15.9 | NM | NM | NM | NM | NM |

Data as orig. reptd.; bef. results of disc. opers. and/or spec. items. Per share data adj. for stk. divs. as of ex-div. date. E-Estimated. NA-Not Available. NM-Not Meaningful. NR-Not Ranked.

**Office**—1601 Market St., Philadelphia, PA 19103.**Tel**—(215) 564-6600. **Chrmn**—H. Wender. **Pres & CEO**—F. P. Filipps. **VP & Secy**—T. J. Shelley Jr. **SVP & CFO**—C. R. Quint. **Dirs**—D. C. Carney, C. M. Fagin, F. P. Filipps, J. W. Jennings, J. C. Miller, R. W. Moore, R. W. Richards, A. W. Schweiger, H. Wender. **Transfer Agent & Registrar**—Bank of New York, NYC. **Incorporated**—in Delaware in 1991. **Empl**— 420. **S&P Analyst:** Brendan McGovern

# STANDARD &POOR'S
STOCK REPORTS

# Coca-Cola

**562**

NYSE Symbol **KO**

In S&P 500

**17-MAY-97**

Industry:
Beverages
(Non-Alcoholic)

**Summary:** Coca-Cola is the world's largest soft-drink company and has a sizable fruit juice business. Its bottling interests include a 45% stake in NYSE-listed Coca-Cola Enterprises.

| S&P Opinion: Hold (★★★) | Recent Price • 66⅞ | Yield • 0.8% |
| --- | --- | --- |
| | 52 Wk Range • 68⅜-44¼ | 12-Mo. P/E • 44.0 |

**Quantitative Evaluations**

Outlook
(1 Lowest—5 Highest)
• **1⁺**

Fair Value
• **58¼**

Risk
• **Low**

Earn./Div. Rank
• **A⁺**

Technical Eval.
• **Bullish** since 7/94

Rel. Strength Rank
(1 Lowest—99 Highest)
• **86**

Insider Activity
• **Neutral**

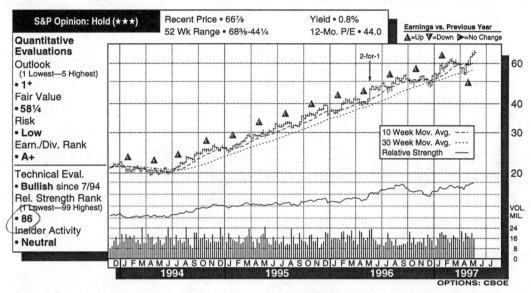

Earnings vs. Previous Year
▲=Up ▼=Down ▶=No Change

2-for-1

10 Week Mov. Avg. – – –
30 Week Mov. Avg. ·····
Relative Strength —

OPTIONS: CBOE

## Overview - 15-APR-97

Revenues are expected to rise at a 5% to 8% rate in 1997, as an approximate 8% increase in gallon shipments and higher prices are offset in part by unfavorable currency exchange translations (principally Eurpean currencies and the Japanese yen). Operating income is expected to advance at a faster pace than sales, reflecting the recent sale of certain low-margin bottling operations, and operating efficiencies realized from recent restructuring actions. Including the net proceeds realized from the early 1997 sale of the company's 49% interest in its Cadbury Schweppes bottling joint venture, and a stable effective tax rate, we look for net income to advance by 14% in 1997, to nearly $4 billion. With a modest reduction (1% to 2%) in the number of shares outstanding, we look for EPS growth of 16%, to $1.63 (includes $0.08 gain from the bottling sale), from $1.40 in 1996.

## Valuation - 15-APR-97

The shares have been stellar performers in recent years, reflecting investor preference for dependable growers like KO. As a consequence, the stock trades at a sizable P/E premium to that of its peers and to the S&P 500, leaving little room for possible earnings disappointments. Although Coca-Cola actively utilizes financial currency hedging instruments to help minimize the financial impact of adverse currency exchange movements, the rapid appreciation since 1995 of the U.S. dollar versus key foreign currencies could pressure near-term sales and earnings. We thus downgraded the shares in mid-April to hold from accumulate, and expect the shares to be market performers over the next 12 months. Longer term, KO's rising earnings and dividends should continue to make the stock attractive for virtually all accounts.

## Key Stock Statistics

| | | | |
| --- | --- | --- | --- |
| S&P EPS Est. 1997 | 1.63 | Tang. Bk. Value/Share | 2.18 |
| P/E on S&P Est. 1997 | 41.0 | Beta | 0.78 |
| S&P EPS Est. 1998 | 1.85 | Shareholders | 22,600 |
| Dividend Rate/Share | 0.56 | Market cap. (B) | $166.4 |
| Shs. outstg. (M) | 2488.2 | Inst. holdings | 47% |
| Avg. daily vol. (M) | 3.439 | | |

Value of $10,000 invested 5 years ago: $ 34,911

### Fiscal Year Ending Dec. 31

| | 1998 | 1997 | 1996 | 1995 | 1994 | 1993 |
| --- | --- | --- | --- | --- | --- | --- |
| **Revenues (Million $)** | | | | | | |
| 1Q | — | 4,138 | 4,194 | 3,854 | 3,352 | 3,060 |
| 2Q | — | — | 5,253 | 4,936 | 4,342 | 3,899 |
| 3Q | — | — | 4,656 | 4,895 | 4,461 | 3,629 |
| 4Q | — | — | 4,443 | 4,333 | 4,017 | 3,373 |
| Yr. | — | — | 18,546 | 18,018 | 16,172 | 13,957 |
| **Earnings Per Share ($)** | | | | | | |
| 1Q | — | 0.40 | 0.28 | 0.25 | 0.20 | 0.17 |
| 2Q | — | E0.45 | 0.42 | 0.36 | 0.29 | 0.26 |
| 3Q | — | E0.44 | 0.39 | 0.32 | 0.28 | 0.22 |
| 4Q | — | E0.34 | 0.31 | 0.26 | 0.22 | 0.18 |
| Yr. | E1.85 | E1.63 | 1.40 | 1.18 | 0.99 | 0.84 |

**Next earnings report expected: mid July**

**Dividend Data** (Dividends have been paid since 1893.)

| Amount ($) | Date Decl. | Ex-Div. Date | Stock of Record | Payment Date |
| --- | --- | --- | --- | --- |
| 0.125 | Jul. 18 | Sep. 11 | Sep. 15 | Oct. 01 '96 |
| 0.125 | Oct. 18 | Nov. 26 | Dec. 01 | Dec. 15 '96 |
| 0.140 | Feb. 20 | Mar. 12 | Mar. 15 | Apr. 01 '97 |
| 0.140 | Apr. 17 | Jun. 11 | Jun. 15 | Jul. 01 '97 |

This report is for information purposes and should not be considered a solicitation to buy or sell any security. Neither S&P nor any other party guarantee its accuracy or make warranties regarding results from its usage. Redistribution is prohibited without written permission. Copyright © 1997

*A Division of The McGraw·Hill Companies*

STANDARD
&POOR'S
STOCK REPORTS

**The Coca-Cola Company**

**562**

17-MAY-97

## Business Summary - 15-APR-97

The Coca-Cola Company is the world's largest producer of soft drink concentrates and syrups, as well as the world's largest producer of juice and juice-related products. Finished soft drink products bearing the company's trademarks have been sold in the United States since 1886, and are now sold in nearly 200 countries. The company's sales and operating profit breakdown in 1996 was as follows:

|  | Sales | Profits |
|---|---|---|
| North America | 33% | 21% |
| Greater Europe | 32% | 28% |
| Middle & Far East | 22% | 30% |
| Latin America | 11% | 18% |
| Africa | 2% | 3% |

The company's business may be the most focused and efficient of any in the world, and is, quite simply, the production and sale of soft drink and non-carbonated beverage concentrates and syrups. These products are sold to the company's authorized independent and company-owned bottling/canning operations, and fountain wholesalers. These customers then either combine the syrup with carbonated water, or combine the concentrate with sweetener, water and carbonated water to produce finished soft drinks. The finished soft drinks are packaged in authorized containers bearing the company's well-known trademarks, which include Coca-Cola (best-selling soft drink in the world, including Coca-Cola classic), caffeine free Coca-Cola (classic), diet Coke (sold as Coke light in many markets outside the U.S.), Cherry Coke, diet Cherry Coke, Fanta, Sprite, diet Sprite, Barq's, Mr. PiBB, Mello Yello, TAB, Fresca, PowerAde, Minute Maid, Hi-C, Fruitopia, and other products developed for specific markets, including Georgia ready to drink coffees. KO has equity positions in approximately 43 unconsolidated bottling, canning and distribution operations for its products worldwide, including bottlers representing about 51% of the company's U.S. unit case volume in 1996.

The company enters into forward exchange contracts, and purchases currency options (principally European currencies and Japanese yen) to reduce the risk that the company's eventual dollar net cash inflows resulting from sales outside the U.S. will be adversely affected by changes in exchange rates.

## Capitalization

**Long Term Debt:** $1,116,000,000 (12/96).

## Per Share Data ($)

| (Year Ended Dec. 31) | 1996 | 1995 | 1994 | 1993 | 1992 | 1991 | 1990 | 1989 | 1988 | 1987 |
|---|---|---|---|---|---|---|---|---|---|---|
| Tangible Bk. Val. | 2.18 | 1.77 | 1.80 | 1.55 | 1.34 | 1.55 | 1.31 | 1.10 | 1.05 | 1.06 |
| Cash Flow | 1.59 | 1.36 | 1.14 | 0.97 | 0.84 | 0.71 | 0.60 | 0.49 | 0.42 | 0.36 |
| Earnings | 1.40 | 1.18 | 0.99 | 0.84 | 0.71 | 0.60 | 0.51 | 0.43 | 0.36 | 0.31 |
| Dividends | 0.50 | 0.44 | 0.39 | 0.34 | 0.28 | 0.24 | 0.20 | 0.17 | 0.15 | 0.14 |
| Payout Ratio | 36% | 37% | 39% | 40% | 39% | 39% | 39% | 39% | 41% | 46% |
| Prices - High | 54¼ | 40¼ | 26¾ | 22⅝ | 22¾ | 20½ | 12¼ | 10⅛ | 5⅝ | 6⅝ |
| - Low | 36⅛ | 24⅜ | 19½ | 18¾ | 17¾ | 10¾ | 8⅛ | 5⅜ | 4⅜ | 3½ |
| P/E Ratio - High | 39 | 34 | 27 | 27 | 32 | 34 | 24 | 24 | 16 | 22 |
| - Low | 26 | 21 | 20 | 22 | 25 | 18 | 16 | 13 | 12 | 12 |

## Income Statement Analysis (Million $)

|  | 1996 | 1995 | 1994 | 1993 | 1992 | 1991 | 1990 | 1989 | 1988 | 1987 |
|---|---|---|---|---|---|---|---|---|---|---|
| Revs. | 18,546 | 18,018 | 16,172 | 13,957 | 13,074 | 11,572 | 10,236 | 8,966 | 8,338 | 7,658 |
| Oper. Inc. | 4,394 | 4,546 | 4,090 | 3,485 | 3,080 | 2,586 | 2,237 | 1,910 | 1,768 | 1,514 |
| Depr. | 479 | 454 | 382 | 333 | 310 | 254 | 236 | 184 | 170 | 153 |
| Int. Exp. | 286 | 272 | 199 | 178 | 171 | 185 | 231 | 315 | 239 | 285 |
| Pretax Inc. | 4,596 | 4,328 | 3,728 | 3,185 | 2,746 | 2,383 | 2,014 | 1,764 | 1,582 | 1,410 |
| Eff. Tax Rate | 24% | 31% | 32% | 31% | 31% | 32% | 31% | 32% | 34% | 35% |
| Net Inc. | 3,492 | 2,986 | 2,554 | 2,188 | 1,884 | 1,618 | 1,382 | 1,193 | 1,045 | 916 |

## Balance Sheet & Other Fin. Data (Million $)

|  | 1996 | 1995 | 1994 | 1993 | 1992 | 1991 | 1990 | 1989 | 1988 | 1987 |
|---|---|---|---|---|---|---|---|---|---|---|
| Cash | 1,658 | 1,315 | 1,531 | 1,078 | 1,063 | 1,117 | 1,492 | 1,182 | 1,231 | 1,468 |
| Curr. Assets | 5,910 | 5,450 | 5,205 | 4,434 | 4,248 | 4,144 | 4,143 | 3,604 | 3,245 | 4,136 |
| Total Assets | 16,161 | 15,041 | 13,873 | 12,021 | 11,052 | 10,222 | 9,278 | 8,283 | 7,451 | 8,356 |
| Curr. Liab. | 7,416 | 7,348 | 6,177 | 5,171 | 5,303 | 4,118 | 4,296 | 3,658 | 2,869 | 4,119 |
| LT Debt | 1,116 | 1,141 | 1,426 | 1,428 | 1,120 | 985 | 536 | 549 | 761 | 803 |
| Common Eqty. | 6,156 | 5,392 | 5,235 | 4,584 | 3,888 | 4,426 | 3,774 | 3,185 | 3,045 | 3,224 |
| Total Cap. | 7,573 | 6,727 | 6,841 | 6,125 | 5,090 | 5,611 | 4,650 | 4,330 | 4,376 | 4,237 |
| Cap. Exp. | 990 | 937 | 878 | 808 | 1,083 | 792 | 642 | 462 | 387 | 300 |
| Cash Flow | 3,971 | 3,440 | 2,936 | 2,521 | 2,194 | 1,872 | 1,600 | 1,355 | 1,208 | 1,069 |
| Curr. Ratio | 0.8 | 0.7 | 0.8 | 0.9 | 0.8 | 1.0 | 1.0 | 1.0 | 1.1 | 1.0 |
| % LT Debt of Cap. | 14.7 | 17.0 | 20.8 | 23.3 | 22.0 | 17.6 | 11.5 | 12.7 | 17.4 | 19.0 |
| % Net Inc.of Revs. | 18.8 | 16.6 | 15.8 | 15.7 | 14.4 | 14.0 | 13.5 | 13.3 | 12.5 | 12.0 |
| % Ret. on Assets | 22.4 | 20.7 | 19.9 | 19.0 | 17.9 | 16.6 | 15.8 | 15.5 | 13.6 | 11.1 |
| % Ret. on Equity | 60.5 | 56.2 | 52.4 | 51.8 | 45.7 | 39.6 | 39.3 | 38.5 | 33.9 | 27.7 |

Data as orig. reptd.; bef. results of disc. opers. and/or spec. items. Per share data adj. for stk. divs. as of ex-div. date. E-Estimated. NA-Not Available. NM-Not Meaningful. NR-Not Ranked.

**Office**—1 Coca-Cola Plaza, N.W., Atlanta, GA 30313. **Tel**—(404) 676-2121. **Website**—http://www.cocacola.com **Chrmn & CEO**—R. C. Goizueta. **Pres & COO**—M. D. Ivester. **CFO**—J. E. Chesnut. **Secy**—Susan E. Shaw. **Investor Contact**—Nancy W. Ford. **Dirs**—H. A. Allen, R. W. Allen, C. P. Black, W. E. Buffett, C. W. Duncan, Jr., R. C. Goizueta, M. D. Ivester, S. B. King, D. F. McHenry, S. Nunn, P. F. Oreffice, J. D. Robinson III, P. V. Ueberroth, J. B. Williams. **Transfer Agent & Registrar**—First Chicago Trust Co. of New York, Jersey City, NJ. **Incorporated**—in Delaware in 1919. **Empl**— 26,000. **S&P Analyst:** Kenneth A. Shea

**17-MAY-97**

**Industry:**
Beverages
(Non-Alcoholic)

**Summary:** This company is the world's largest bottler of Coca-Cola beverage products, distributing to about 58% of the population of the U.S. Coca-Cola Co. holds 45% of CCE's common stock.

---

**S&P Opinion: Accumulate (★★★★)**

| Recent Price • 19⅛ | Yield • 0.5% |
|---|---|
| 52 Wk Range • 22-10¼ | 12-Mo. P/E • NM |

**Quantitative Evaluations**

Outlook
(1 Lowest—5 Highest)
• **1+**

Fair Value
• **13⅜**

Risk
• **Average**

Earn./Div. Rank
• **B-**

---

Technical Eval.
• **Bullish** since 8/94

Rel. Strength Rank
(1 Lowest—99 Highest)
• **33**

Insider Activity
• **NA**

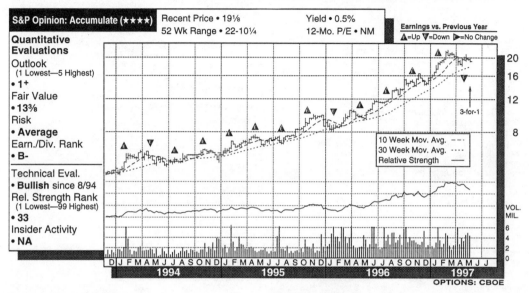

Earnings vs. Previous Year
▲=Up ▼=Down ▶=No Change

3-for-1

10 Week Mov. Avg. – – –
30 Week Mov. Avg. · · · ·
Relative Strength —

VOL. MIL.

1994 1995 1996 1997

OPTIONS: CBOE

---

## Overview - 17-APR-97

Including the early 1997 integration of the Cadbury Schweppes bottling operations, net operating revenues are projected to climb by approximately 30% in 1997. More than half of this projected growth is likely to come from contributions from the Cadbury operations, with the remainder from increased case volume from existing territories. Profit margins may narrow slightly, as acquisition expenses are absorbed, but cash operating profits (operating income plus depreciation and amortization charges) are seen advancing at an approximate 10% pace, to nearly $1.3 billion. For the longer term, cash operating profit growth (on a comparable basis) of 8% to 10% annually is anticipated. Although acquisition-related net interest expense will be sharply higher in coming quarters, earnings per share for 1997 are estimated at $0.95, up 12% from the prior year. Assuming most of the acquisition expenses are absorbed in 1997, EPS could rise significantly in 1998.

## Valuation - 17-APR-97

Given our bullish outlook for both cash operating profit and EPS growth through 1998, the shares are attractive at current levels, at only about 5.7 times our 1997 cash operating profit per share estimate of $10.25. This equity has been a strong performer over the past three years, driven by an improving, more stable reported earnings stream from prior years. Long-term prospects are enhanced by the company's unique position as the world's largest bottler of Coca-Cola products. As such, CCE enjoys many competitive advantages over its rivals, including sizable cost efficiencies. Despite a high debt load, finances are sound, reflecting CCE's strong cash generation capability and implicit credit backing by The Coca-Cola Co.

## Key Stock Statistics

| | | | |
|---|---|---|---|
| S&P EPS Est. 1997 | 0.32 | Tang. Bk. Value/Share | 3.75 |
| P/E on S&P Est. 1997 | 60.4 | Beta | 0.95 |
| S&P EPS Est. 1998 | 0.47 | Shareholders | 9,500 |
| Dividend Rate/Share | 0.10 | Market cap. (B) | $ 7.2 |
| Shs. outstg. (M) | 376.0 | Inst. holdings | 35% |
| Avg. daily vol. (M) | 0.851 | | |

Value of $10,000 invested 5 years ago: $ 38,735

## Fiscal Year Ending Dec. 31

| | 1998 | 1997 | 1996 | 1995 | 1994 | 1993 |
|---|---|---|---|---|---|---|
| **Revenues (Million $)** | | | | | | |
| 1Q | — | 2,141 | 1,600 | 1,462 | 1,320 | 1,208 |
| 2Q | — | — | 2,016 | 1,827 | 1,610 | 1,448 |
| 3Q | — | — | 2,187 | 1,841 | 1,595 | 1,487 |
| 4Q | — | — | 2,118 | 1,643 | 1,486 | 1,322 |
| Yr. | — | — | 7,921 | 6,773 | 6,011 | 5,465 |
| **Earnings Per Share ($)** | | | | | | |
| 1Q | — | -0.09 | 0.01 | 0.01 | -0.02 | -0.01 |
| 2Q | — | E0.26 | 0.15 | 0.12 | 0.10 | 0.04 |
| 3Q | — | E0.18 | 0.10 | 0.09 | 0.06 | -0.08 |
| 4Q | — | E-0.03 | 0.02 | -0.01 | 0.03 | 0.01 |
| Yr. | E0.47 | E0.32 | 0.28 | 0.21 | 0.17 | -0.04 |

**Next earnings report expected: mid July**

**Dividend Data** (Dividends have been paid since 1986.)

| Amount ($) | Date Decl. | Ex-Div. Date | Stock of Record | Payment Date |
|---|---|---|---|---|
| 0.025 | Oct. 15 | Nov. 27 | Dec. 02 | Dec. 16 '96 |
| 0.025 | Feb. 18 | Mar. 19 | Mar. 21 | Apr. 01 '97 |
| 3-for-1 | Feb. 18 | May. 13 | May. 01 | May. 12 '97 |
| 0.025 | Apr. 21 | Jun. 18 | Jun. 20 | Jul. 01 '97 |

---

This report is for information purposes and should not be considered a solicitation to buy or sell any security. Neither S&P nor any other party guarantee its accuracy or make warranties regarding results from its usage. Redistribution is prohibited without written permission. Copyright © 1997

*A Division of The McGraw·Hill Companies*

STANDARD
&POOR'S
STOCK REPORTS

**Coca-Cola Enterprises Inc.**

562E

17-MAY-97

## Business Summary - 17-APR-97

Coca-Cola Enterprises is the world's largest bottler of Coca-Cola beverage products, distributing approximately 58% of all bottle/can volume of carbonated soft-drink products of The Coca-Cola Co. (KO) in the U.S. KO owns approximately 45% of the company's common stock. The company's product line also includes other nonalcoholic beverages such as still and sparkling waters, juices, isotonics, and teas. In 1996, the company distributed approximately 2.1 billion unit cases (24 eight-ounce servings, or 192 ounces per case) of products in bottle, can and fountain containers. CCE distributes Dr Pepper and several other beverage brands.

In February 1997, CCE acquired for approximately $2 billion Coca Cola & Schweppes Beverages Limited, a British-based producer and distributor of Coca Cola and Cadbury Schweppes products in England, Scotland, Wales and the Isle of Man. The acquisition, together with CCE's July 1996 purchase of certain bottling operations in Belgium and France (for about $915 million), dramatically increased the company's geographic presence outside the U.S. In fact, management estimated that in 1997, CCE's European operations will generate more than 25% of the company's total unit case volume, up from only 9% in 1996. In the U.S., CCE's bot-

tling territories include portions of 41 states, the District of Columbia, the U.S. Virgin Islands, and the islands of Tortola and Grand Cayman. These territories contain approximately 145 million people, and represented about 54% of the population of the U.S. CCE also serves the Netherlands, whose population is about 15 million.

The company conducts its business primarily under bottle contracts with KO, whereby CCE receives the exclusive right to produce and market Coca-Cola soft drinks in authorized containers in specified territories and provide KO with the ability, in its sole discretion, to set prices for concentrates and syrups. CCE operates 310 facilities, 32,300 vehicles, and over one million vending machines, beverage dispensers, and coolers used to market, distribute, and produce the company's products.

In February 1997, the company's directors declared a three-for-one split of the company's common stock, to be paid May 12, 1997, to CCE holders of record May 1, 1997. CCE shareholders were to vote on the split April 21, 1997.

### Capitalization

**Long Term Debt:** $5,123,000,000 (3/97).
**Preferred Stock:** $115,000,000.

### Per Share Data ($)

| (Year Ended Dec. 31) | 1996 | 1995 | 1994 | 1993 | 1992 | 1991 | 1990 | 1989 | 1988 | 1987 |
|---|---|---|---|---|---|---|---|---|---|---|
| Tangible Bk. Val. | 3.75 | 3.64 | 3.38 | 3.18 | 3.23 | -7.14 | -4.85 | -3.92 | -3.45 | -2.78 |
| Cash Flow | 1.98 | 1.58 | 1.35 | 1.04 | 0.97 | 0.46 | 0.87 | 0.73 | 0.88 | 0.67 |
| Earnings | 0.28 | 0.21 | 0.17 | -0.04 | -0.04 | -0.26 | 0.22 | 0.14 | 0.34 | 0.21 |
| Dividends | 0.03 | 0.02 | 0.02 | 0.02 | 0.02 | 0.02 | 0.02 | 0.02 | 0.02 | 0.02 |
| Payout Ratio | 12% | 8% | 10% | NM | NM | NM | 7% | 11% | 5% | 8% |
| Prices - High | 16⅜ | 10 | 6½ | 5¼ | 5⅜ | 6¾ | 5⅝ | 6¼ | 5⅝ | 7⅛ |
| - Low | 8 | 5⅞ | 4⅝ | 3⅞ | 3¾ | 3⅞ | 4⅛ | 4⅞ | 4¼ | 3½ |
| P/E Ratio - High | 58 | 48 | 37 | NM | NM | NM | 26 | 46 | 16 | 34 |
| - Low | 28 | 29 | 27 | NM | NM | NM | 19 | 36 | 12 | 17 |

### Income Statement Analysis (Million $)

| | 1996 | 1995 | 1994 | 1993 | 1992 | 1991 | 1990 | 1989 | 1988 | 1987 |
|---|---|---|---|---|---|---|---|---|---|---|
| Revs. | 7,921 | 6,773 | 6,011 | 5,465 | 5,127 | 4,051 | 4,034 | 3,882 | 3,874 | 3,329 |
| Oper. Inc. | 1,172 | 997 | 901 | 804 | 695 | 538 | 582 | 539 | 606 | 531 |
| Depr. | 627 | 529 | 461 | 419 | 389 | 251 | 236 | 229 | 225 | 194 |
| Int. Exp. | 353 | 333 | 310 | 328 | 312 | 215 | 207 | 200 | 211 | 171 |
| Pretax Inc. | 194 | 145 | 127 | 55.0 | -12.0 | -91.0 | 184 | 138 | 268 | 173 |
| Eff. Tax Rate | 41% | 43% | 46% | 127% | NM | NM | 49% | 48% | 43% | 49% |
| Net Inc. | 114 | 82.0 | 69.0 | -15.0 | -15.0 | -82.0 | 93.0 | 72.0 | 153 | 88.0 |

### Balance Sheet & Other Fin. Data (Million $)

| | 1996 | 1995 | 1994 | 1993 | 1992 | 1991 | 1990 | 1989 | 1988 | 1987 |
|---|---|---|---|---|---|---|---|---|---|---|
| Cash | 47.0 | 8.0 | 22.0 | 11.0 | 6.0 | 64.1 | 0.5 | 9.7 | 0.2 | 11.3 |
| Curr. Assets | 1,319 | 982 | 810 | 746 | 701 | 706 | 495 | 493 | 488 | 452 |
| Total Assets | 11,234 | 9,064 | 8,738 | 8,682 | 8,805 | 6,677 | 5,021 | 4,732 | 4,669 | 4,250 |
| Curr. Liab. | 1,690 | 859 | 1,089 | 1,007 | 1,304 | 1,385 | 1,055 | 996 | 550 | 474 |
| LT Debt | 4,814 | 4,138 | 3,896 | 4,083 | 3,509 | 3,407 | 1,960 | 1,756 | 2,062 | 2,091 |
| Common Eqty. | 1,416 | 1,405 | 1,310 | 1,231 | 1,254 | 1,443 | 1,376 | 1,430 | 1,558 | 1,526 |
| Total Cap. | 6,230 | 7,605 | 7,119 | 7,174 | 6,330 | 5,141 | 3,922 | 3,702 | 4,092 | 3,770 |
| Cap. Exp. | 622 | 501 | 366 | 353 | 291 | 238 | 259 | 273 | 273 | 206 |
| Cash Flow | 741 | 611 | 528 | 404 | 374 | 160 | 313 | 283 | 368 | 282 |
| Curr. Ratio | 0.8 | 1.1 | 0.7 | 0.7 | 0.5 | 0.5 | 0.5 | 0.5 | 0.9 | 1.0 |
| % LT Debt of Cap. | 77.2 | 54.4 | 54.7 | 56.9 | 55.4 | 66.3 | 50.0 | 47.4 | 50.4 | 55.5 |
| % Net Inc.of Revs. | 1.4 | 1.2 | 1.1 | NM | NM | NM | 2.3 | 1.8 | 3.9 | 2.7 |
| % Ret. on Assets | 1.1 | 0.9 | 0.8 | NM | NM | NM | 2.0 | 1.6 | 3.5 | 2.2 |
| % Ret. on Equity | 8.1 | 5.9 | 5.3 | NM | NM | NM | 5.7 | 3.7 | 9.5 | 5.9 |

Data as orig. reptd.; bef. results of disc. opers. and/or spec. items. Per share data adj. for stk. divs. as of ex-div. date. E-Estimated. NA-Not Available. NM-Not Meaningful. NR-Not Ranked.

**Office**—One Coca-Cola Plaza, N.W., Atlanta, GA 30313. **Tel**—(404) 676-2100. **Website**—http://www.cokecce.com **Chrmn**—M. D. Ivester. **Vice Chrmn & CEO**—S. K. Johnston Jr. **Pres**—H. A. Schimberg. **SVP & CFO**—J. R. Alm. **Secy**—J. G. Beatty Jr. **Investor Contact**—Margaret Carton. **Dirs**—H. Buffett, J. L. Clendenin, J. B. Cole, T. M. Hahn Jr., C. M. Halle, L. P. Humann, E. N. Isdell, M. D. Ivester, J. E. Jacob, S. K. Johnston Jr., R. A. Keller, J. C. Killy, W. D. Looney, S. L. Probasco Jr., H. A. Schimberg, F. A. Tarkenton. **Transfer Agent & Registrar**—First Chicago Trust Co. of New York, NYC. **Incorporated**—in Delaware in 1944. **Empl**—43,200. **S&P Analyst:** Kenneth A. Shea

# Compaq Computer  596C

NYSE Symbol **CPQ**

In S&P 500

**17-MAY-97**

**Industry:** Computers (Hardware)

**Summary:** Compaq is the leading worldwide manufacturer of desktop and portable computers and PC servers. Products are sold in more than 100 countries through some 38,000 marketing locations.

**S&P Opinion: Buy (★★★★★)**

| | | |
|---|---|---|
| Recent Price • 94 | Yield • Nil | |
| 52 Wk Range • 96¾-40½ | 12-Mo. P/E • 18.0 | |

**Quantitative Evaluations**

**Outlook**
(1 Lowest—5 Highest)
• **4-**

**Fair Value**
• **118**

**Risk**
• **Average**

**Earn./Div. Rank**
• **B**

**Technical Eval.**
• **Bullish** since 5/96

**Rel. Strength Rank**
(1 Lowest—99 Highest)
• **92**

**Insider Activity**
• **Neutral**

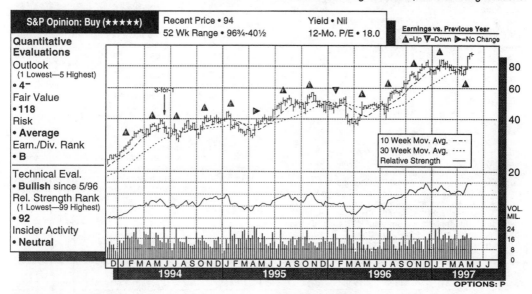

Earnings vs. Previous Year
△=Up ▽=Down ▷=No Change

10 Week Mov. Avg. – – –
30 Week Mov. Avg. · · · ·
Relative Strength —

VOL. MIL.

OPTIONS: P

## Overview - 16-MAY-97

Revenues are expected to grow 20% in 1997, as CPQ benefits from pent-up corporate desktop demand, a completely revamped product line, and growing revenue contributions from new workstation and networking products. The strong corporate upgrade cycle should be propelled by falling price points for Intel's sixth generation Pentium Pro microprocessor family and a new desktop version of Microsoft's Windows NT operating system. Server demand is expected to remain robust, as corporations continue to off-load data and applications from larger systems. Gross margins, which trended higher in 1996, are expected to improve further. This reflects the strength of new products, lower manufacturing costs, and a greater mix of more profitable workstation and networking products. Expenses are expected to remain tightly controlled. Earnings are forecast to reach $6.30 a share, up from $4.72 in 1996.

## Valuation - 16-MAY-97

We recently raised our recommendation on the shares to buy from accumulate as CPQ's positive revenue and cash growth prospects have been enhanced by early signs of excellent execution on the company's strategic goals.  Not only is CPQ one of the best positioned companies to capitalize on the industry's 17% projected growth, but cash management initiatives have resulted in higher cash balances, and its commitment to make further strides encourage us that CPQ will deliver in this area. Compaq is also experiencing strong gross profit margins, which should continue as the CPQ repositions itself as a systems company, lead a richer sales mix of servers and networking equipment. As a result of these strong fundamentals, we recommend purchasing the shares for above-average long-term capital appreciation.

## Key Stock Statistics

| | | | |
|---|---|---|---|
| S&P EPS Est. 1997 | 6.30 | Tang. Bk. Value/Share | 22.46 |
| P/E on S&P Est. 1997 | 14.9 | Beta | 1.26 |
| S&P EPS Est. 1998 | 7.70 | Shareholders | 8,700 |
| Dividend Rate/Share | Nil | Market cap. (B) | $ 25.8 |
| Shs. outstg. (M) | 274.0 | Inst. holdings | 75% |
| Avg. daily vol. (M) | 3.541 | | |

Value of $10,000 invested 5 years ago: $ 107,914

### Fiscal Year Ending Dec. 31

| | 1998 | 1997 | 1996 | 1995 | 1994 | 1993 |
|---|---|---|---|---|---|---|
| **Revenues (Million $)** | | | | | | |
| 1Q | — | 4,805 | 4,205 | 2,959 | 2,278 | 1,611 |
| 2Q | — | — | 4,001 | 3,501 | 2,499 | 1,632 |
| 3Q | — | — | 4,481 | 3,594 | 2,838 | 1,746 |
| 4Q | — | — | 5,422 | 4,701 | 3,251 | 2,202 |
| Yr. | — | — | 18,109 | 14,755 | 10,866 | 7,191 |
| **Earnings Per Share ($)** | | | | | | |
| 1Q | — | 1.36 | 0.85 | 0.80 | 0.80 | 0.41 |
| 2Q | — | E1.45 | 0.97 | 0.90 | 0.78 | 0.40 |
| 3Q | — | E1.58 | 1.26 | 0.89 | 0.75 | 0.42 |
| 4Q | — | E1.91 | 1.64 | 0.30 | 0.90 | 0.58 |
| Yr. | E7.70 | E6.30 | 4.72 | 2.88 | 3.23 | 1.82 |

**Next earnings report expected: late July**

### Dividend Data

No cash dividends have been paid on the common stock, and future earnings are expected to be retained for use in operations. A three-for-one stock split was effected in 1994. Poison pill stock purchase rights were issued in 1989.

This report is for information purposes and should not be considered a solicitation to buy or sell any security. Neither S&P nor any other party guarantee its accuracy or make warranties regarding results from its usage. Redistribution is prohibited without written permission. Copyright © 1997

*A Division of The McGraw-Hill Companies*

## Business Summary - 16-MAY-97

Compaq holds the leading share in the worldwide market for personal computers and servers. CPQ products are sold in more than 100 countries by more than 38,000 organizations, including authorized retailers, value-added resellers (VARs), system integrators, distributors and third-party maintainers. Sales contributions by product line in 1996 were:

|  | 1996 |
|---|---|
| Desktops & portable PCs | 56% |
| PC systems & options | 26% |
| Consumer PCs & options | 16% |

Operations outside the U.S. and Canada contributed 47% of revenues in 1996, down from 52% in 1995.

During 1996, Compaq redesigned and consolidated its commercial desktop PC line under a single brand, Deskpro. Compaq did the same to its new line of portables, which are sold under the Armada name. The company promises to offer a new product family in 1997 that reflects advances in sound quality, telephone and communications capabilities.

Targeting the enterprise market for computers, Compaq has introduced new clustering and internetworking solutions in its PC systems products group. In October 1996, CPQ entered the workstation market with its Professional Workstation line. This product family features Intel's Pentium Pro processor, Windows NT operating system, and hundreds of specialized applications. Compaq expects to maintain its strong position in the file server market and plans to expand its presence in the distributed enterprise market for complex enterprise-class networks. CPQ's Internetworking Products Group includes NetWorth Inc. (acquired in December 1995), a provider of Fast Ethernet networking products, and Thomas-Conrad Corp. (November), a maker of network interface cards and hubs.

For consumers and home office users, Compaq introduced a new family of products under its Presario line during 1996. A new lineup of home multimedia PCs included the first combination of a scanner/keyboard offered in the industry, as well as "rewriteable" CD-ROM drives and Pentium processors. Compaq is also looking at adding arcade-level graphics, videophone communications as well as colorful new PC designs to its product line.

During 1997 Compaq plans to center efforts in its Netelligent product line in developing switches, repeaters and options that lower the cost and complexity of migrating from Ethernet to Fast Ethernet. CPQ has targeted its networking products at smaller businesses and workgroups/departments in larger corporations.

In April 1997, Compaq announced it would acquire up to 25 million of its shares, to offset the dilutive impact of its stock issued under equity incentive pans, and it will be timed accordingly.

### Capitalization

**Long Term Debt:** $300,000,000 (3/97).

**Options:** To buy 27,961,000 shs. (12/96).

### Per Share Data ($)

| (Year Ended Dec. 31) | 1996 | 1995 | 1994 | 1993 | 1992 | 1991 | 1990 | 1989 | 1988 | 1987 |
|---|---|---|---|---|---|---|---|---|---|---|
| Tangible Bk. Val. | 22.46 | 17.28 | 14.07 | 10.49 | 8.38 | 7.64 | 7.20 | 4.97 | 3.52 | 1.95 |
| Cash Flow | 5.74 | 3.66 | 3.85 | 2.43 | 1.50 | 1.12 | 2.20 | 1.58 | 1.21 | 0.67 |
| Earnings | 4.72 | 2.88 | 3.23 | 1.82 | 0.86 | 0.50 | 1.71 | 1.30 | 1.05 | 0.60 |
| Dividends | Nil | Nil | Nil | Nil | Nil | Nil | Nil | Nil | Nil | Nil |
| Payout Ratio | Nil | Nil | Nil | Nil | Nil | Nil | Nil | Nil | Nil | Nil |
| Prices - High | 87⅛ | 56¾ | 42⅛ | 25¼ | 16⅝ | 24¾ | 22⅝ | 18¾ | 11 | 13⅛ |
| - Low | 35⅞ | 31⅛ | 24⅛ | 13⅞ | 7⅜ | 7⅜ | 11⅞ | 9⅞ | 7 | 3¼ |
| P/E Ratio - High | 18 | 20 | 13 | 14 | 19 | 50 | 13 | 14 | 12 | 22 |
| - Low | 8 | 11 | 7 | 8 | 9 | 15 | 7 | 8 | 7 | 5 |

### Income Statement Analysis (Million $)

| | 1996 | 1995 | 1994 | 1993 | 1992 | 1991 | 1990 | 1989 | 1988 | 1987 |
|---|---|---|---|---|---|---|---|---|---|---|
| Revs. | 18,109 | 14,755 | 10,866 | 7,191 | 4,100 | 3,271 | 3,599 | 2,876 | 2,066 | 1,224 |
| Oper. Inc. | 2,162 | 1,738 | 1,434 | 847 | 482 | 469 | 784 | 573 | 408 | 255 |
| Depr. | 285 | 214 | 168 | 155 | 159 | 164 | 135 | 84.0 | 48.0 | 22.0 |
| Int. Exp. | 91.0 | 106 | 74.0 | 63.0 | 47.5 | 43.9 | 54.9 | 46.8 | 27.7 | 14.2 |
| Pretax Inc. | 1,876 | 1,188 | 1,172 | 616 | 311 | 174 | 671 | 498 | 375 | 229 |
| Eff. Tax Rate | 30% | 34% | 26% | 25% | 31% | 25% | 32% | 33% | 32% | 41% |
| Net Inc. | 1,313 | 789 | 867 | 462 | 213 | 131 | 455 | 333 | 255 | 136 |

### Balance Sheet & Other Fin. Data (Million $)

| | 1996 | 1995 | 1994 | 1993 | 1992 | 1991 | 1990 | 1989 | 1988 | 1987 |
|---|---|---|---|---|---|---|---|---|---|---|
| Cash | 3,993 | 745 | 471 | 627 | 357 | 452 | 435 | 161 | 281 | 132 |
| Curr. Assets | 9,169 | 6,527 | 5,158 | 3,291 | 2,319 | 1,783 | 1,688 | 1,312 | 1,115 | 681 |
| Total Assets | 10,526 | 7,818 | 6,166 | 4,084 | 3,142 | 2,826 | 2,718 | 2,090 | 1,590 | 901 |
| Curr. Liab. | 3,852 | 2,680 | 2,013 | 1,244 | 960 | 639 | 644 | 564 | 480 | 343 |
| LT Debt | 300 | 300 | 300 | Nil | Nil | 73.0 | 73.0 | 274 | 275 | 149 |
| Common Eqty. | 6,144 | 4,614 | 3,674 | 2,654 | 2,007 | 1,931 | 1,859 | 1,172 | 815 | 400 |
| Total Cap. | 6,674 | 5,138 | 4,153 | 2,840 | 2,183 | 2,188 | 2,074 | 1,526 | 1,110 | 558 |
| Cap. Exp. | 342 | 391 | 357 | 145 | 159 | 160 | 325 | 362 | 286 | 113 |
| Cash Flow | 1,598 | 1,003 | 1,035 | 617 | 372 | 295 | 590 | 417 | 304 | 158 |
| Curr. Ratio | 2.4 | 2.4 | 2.6 | 2.6 | 2.4 | 2.8 | 2.6 | 2.3 | 2.3 | 2.0 |
| % LT Debt of Cap. | 4.5 | 5.8 | 7.2 | Nil | Nil | 3.3 | 3.5 | 17.9 | 24.8 | 26.7 |
| % Net Inc.of Revs. | 7.3 | 5.3 | 8.0 | 6.4 | 5.2 | 4.0 | 12.6 | 11.6 | 12.4 | 11.1 |
| % Ret. on Assets | 14.5 | 11.3 | 16.7 | 12.5 | 7.3 | 4.8 | 18.2 | 18.0 | 19.6 | 19.8 |
| % Ret. on Equity | 24.4 | 19.0 | 27.0 | 19.4 | 11.1 | 7.0 | 28.9 | 33.3 | 40.3 | 43.2 |

Data as orig. reptd.; bef. results of disc. opers. and/or spec. items. Per share data adj. for stk. divs. as of ex-div. date. E-Estimated. NA-Not Available. NM-Not Meaningful. NR-Not Ranked.

**Office**—20555 SH 249, Houston, TX 77070. **Tel**—(713) 370-0670. **Website**— http://www.compaq.com **Pres & CEO**—E. Pfeiffer. **SVP-Fin & CFO**—E. Mason. **SVP & Secy**—W. D. Fargo. **Dirs**—B. M. Rosen (Chrmn), R. T. Enloe III, G. H. Heilmeier, G. E. R. Kinnear II, P. N. Larson, K. L. Lay, E. Pfeiffer, K. Roman, L. Salhany. **Co-Transfer Agents & Registrars**—Co. itself; BancBoston Trust Co. of New York. **Incorporated**—in Delaware in 1982. **Empl**— 18,863. **S&P Analyst:** Megan Graham Hackett

**17-MAY-97**

**Industry:** Computer (Software & Services)

**Summary:** This company develops, markets and supports standard-ized software products, including systems software, database man-agement systems and applications software.

---

**S&P Opinion: Buy (★★★★)**

| Recent Price • 54⅛ | Yield • 0.2% |
|---|---|
| 52 Wk Range • 67⅞-37¼ | 12-Mo. P/E • 66.0 |

**Quantitative Evaluations**

**Outlook**
(1 Lowest—5 Highest)
• **3**

**Fair Value**
• **56**

**Risk**
• **Average**

**Earn./Div. Rank**
• **B+**

**Technical Eval.**
• **Bearish** since 1/97

**Rel. Strength Rank**
(1 Lowest—99 Highest)
• **92**

**Insider Activity**
• **NA**

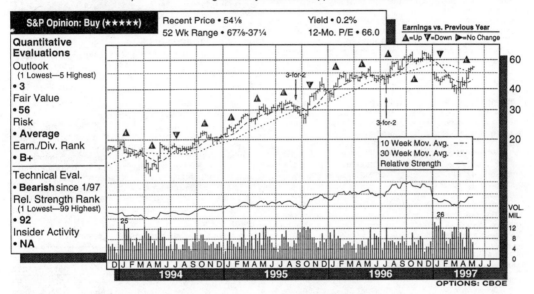

Earnings vs. Previous Year
▲=Up ▼=Down ▶=No Change

10 Week Mov. Avg. – – –
30 Week Mov. Avg. - - - -
Relative Strength —

OPTIONS: CBOE

---

## Overview - 27-JAN-97

Revenue growth is expected to remain sluggish in the fourth quarter of FY 97 (Mar.), on weak European sales, stemming in part from product transition problems from the slower growth mainframe software market to faster growing client/server software products, notably CA-Unicenter, the company's popular systems management offering. However, the pipeline of new business is full, and revenue growth is expected to reaccelerate in FY 98. Operating margins are expected to widen, aided by stringent cost controls in the final quarter of FY 97 as well as the higher revenues in FY 98. Operating share earnings should benefit from the higher revenues, wider margins, and a stock repur-chase program. Comparisons should benefit from the strong operating profits, and from the absence of the FY 96 second quarter $2.14 charge associated with the acquisition of Legent Corp., but will be penalized by FY 97's third quarter charge of $598 million ($1.61 a share) related to the acquisition of Cheyenne Software.

## Valuation - 27-JAN-97

The shares dropped sharply in late December 1996 on a projection of lower than expected FY 97 third quarter revenues; however, tight cost controls resulted in earn-ings coming in on target. CA commands a leading po-sition in the mainframe systems software market and is making the transition to the faster growing markets serving the enterprise-wide environment of networked computers. Earnings in FY 97 are expected to grow over 20% from those of FY 96, excluding nonrecurring charges, with a further 20% gain projected for FY 98. The stock should outperform the market during the next 12 months, reflecting faster-than-average earnings growth combined with potential expansion of the multi-ple attached to those earnings.

## Key Stock Statistics

| | | | |
|---|---|---|---|
| S&P EPS Est. 1997 | 0.90 | Tang. Bk. Value/Share | 0.93 |
| P/E on S&P Est. 1997 | 60.1 | Beta | 1.77 |
| S&P EPS Est. 1998 | 3.00 | Shareholders | 9,000 |
| Dividend Rate/Share | 0.10 | Market cap. (B) | $ 19.7 |
| Shs. outstg. (M) | 363.1 | Inst. holdings | 58% |
| Avg. daily vol. (M) | 1.968 | | |

Value of $10,000 invested 5 years ago: $ 106,838

### Fiscal Year Ending Mar. 31

| | 1998 | 1997 | 1996 | 1995 | 1994 | 1993 |
|---|---|---|---|---|---|---|
| **Revenues (Million $)** | | | | | | |
| 1Q | — | 792.1 | 577.5 | 476.6 | 423.4 | 367.0 |
| 2Q | — | 990.1 | 812.3 | 623.3 | 517.0 | 432.0 |
| 3Q | — | 1,053 | 1,004 | 721.0 | 574.4 | 501.5 |
| 4Q | — | — | 1,110 | 802.0 | 633.7 | 540.1 |
| Yr. | — | — | 3,505 | 2,623 | 2,148 | 1,841 |
| **Earnings Per Share ($)** | | | | | | |
| 1Q | — | 0.32 | 0.23 | -0.24 | 0.08 | 0.05 |
| 2Q | — | 0.59 | -1.76 | 0.35 | 0.23 | 0.12 |
| 3Q | — | -0.86 | 0.60 | 0.46 | 0.32 | 0.21 |
| 4Q | — | E0.85 | 0.70 | 0.56 | 0.41 | 0.25 |
| Yr. | E3.00 | E0.90 | -0.15 | 1.14 | 1.04 | 0.64 |

**Next earnings report expected: late May**

**Dividend Data** (Dividends have been paid since 1990.)

| Amount ($) | Date Decl. | Ex-Div. Date | Stock of Record | Payment Date |
|---|---|---|---|---|
| 0.070 | May. 30 | Jun. 06 | Jun. 10 | Jul. 09 '96 |
| 3-for-2 | May. 30 | Jul. 16 | Jun. 19 | Jul. 15 '96 |
| 0.050 | Dec. 05 | Dec. 13 | Jan. 07 | Jan. 07 '97 |

---

This report is for information purposes and should not be considered a solicitation to buy or sell any security. Neither S&P nor any other party guarantee its accuracy or make warranties regarding results from its usage. Redistribution is prohibited without written permission. Copyright © 1997

*A Division of The McGraw-Hill Companies*

## Business Summary - 27-DEC-96

Computer Associates International designs, develops, markets and supports standardized computer software products for use with a broad range of mainframe, midrange and desktop computers from many different hardware manufacturers.

Until 1982, the company was primarily a supplier of systems software for IBM mainframe computers using the VSE operating system. Since then, it has broadened its product line through new software development and a series of acquisitions and currently offers an extensive portfolio of systems management, information management, business management and consumer software products.

Systems management software enables a customer to more efficiently utilize its data processing hardware, software and personnel resources by providing tools to measure and improve a computer's performance and programmer productivity. Information management products include database management systems (used to store, retrieve and manipulate data) and applications generators, including front-end computer-aided software engineering (CASE) tools.

Business management applications are used in financial, human resource, manufacturing, distribution and banking applications systems. The company also sells consumer software through its 4Home products division.

CA's products primarily operate on mainframe computers utilizing the VSE, VM and MVS operating system, as well as minicomputers running the VMS operating system. However, the company has enhanced many of its software programs to operate in a networked environment of powerful desktop computers.

During the first quarter of FY 95 (Mar.), CA recorded a charge of $249,300,000 ($0.42 a share, as adjusted) related to the acquisition of The ASK Group.

## Important Developments

**Jan. '97**—The company attributed lower than expected revenue growth in the FY 97 (Mar.) third quarter to softer business in Europe, stemming from transition problems from the slower growth mainframe software market to the faster growing client/server software products. However, strict cost controls enabled the company to achieve its earnings expectations.

**Jan. '97**—In the third quarter of FY 97 (Mar.) the company recorded a $598 million ($1.61 a share) charge for expenses related to the acquisition of Cheyenne Software, a leading vendor of storage management software and provider of antivirus and communications software products. In the FY 96 second quarter, CA recorded an $808 million after tax charge ($2.14 a share, as adjusted) to reflect expenses associated with its acquisition of Legent Corp.

## Capitalization

**Long Term Debt:** $1,666,000,000 (12/96).

### Per Share Data ($)

| (Year Ended Mar. 31) | 1996 | 1995 | 1994 | 1993 | 1992 | 1991 | 1990 | 1989 | 1988 | 1987 |
|---|---|---|---|---|---|---|---|---|---|---|
| Tangible Bk. Val. | 1.91 | 3.55 | 2.84 | 2.15 | 1.97 | 2.51 | 2.22 | 1.82 | 1.32 | 0.98 |
| Cash Flow | 0.96 | 1.76 | 1.54 | 1.14 | 0.77 | 0.64 | 0.64 | 0.68 | 0.45 | 0.28 |
| Earnings | -0.15 | 1.14 | 1.04 | 0.64 | 0.41 | 0.38 | 0.38 | 0.45 | 0.29 | 0.16 |
| Dividends | 0.11 | 0.09 | 0.06 | 0.04 | 0.04 | 0.04 | Nil | Nil | Nil | Nil |
| Payout Ratio | NM | 8% | 6% | 7% | 11% | 12% | Nil | Nil | Nil | Nil |
| Cal. Yrs. | 1995 | 1994 | 1993 | 1992 | 1991 | 1990 | 1989 | 1988 | 1987 | 1986 |
| Prices - High | 47 | 22⅝ | 19⅝ | 9¼ | 5¼ | 7½ | 9⅞ | 7⅜ | 8¼ | 3½ |
| - Low | 20⅞ | 12⅛ | 9 | 4⅞ | 2¾ | 1¹⁵/₁₆ | 4⅝ | 5⅜ | 3 | 1¾ |
| P/E Ratio - High | NM | 20 | 19 | 14 | 13 | 20 | 26 | 16 | 29 | 21 |
| - Low | NM | 11 | 9 | 8 | 7 | 5 | 12 | 12 | 11 | 11 |

### Income Statement Analysis (Million $)

| | 1996 | 1995 | 1994 | 1993 | 1992 | 1991 | 1990 | 1989 | 1988 | 1987 |
|---|---|---|---|---|---|---|---|---|---|---|
| Revs. | 3,505 | 2,623 | 2,148 | 1,841 | 1,509 | 1,348 | 1,296 | 1,030 | 709 | 309 |
| Oper. Inc. | 1,678 | 1,190 | 821 | 579 | 405 | 364 | 369 | 345 | 226 | 94.0 |
| Depr. | 404 | 236 | 192 | 191 | 144 | 109 | 107 | 79.0 | 58.0 | 27.0 |
| Int. Exp. | 81.0 | 23.6 | 13.1 | 16.9 | 9.8 | 6.2 | 8.0 | 10.2 | 9.1 | 2.9 |
| Pretax Inc. | -100 | 697 | 627 | 384 | 267 | 261 | 236 | 268 | 170 | 67.0 |
| Eff. Tax Rate | NM | 38% | 36% | 36% | 39% | 39% | 33% | 39% | 40% | 46% |
| Net Inc. | -56.0 | 432 | 401 | 246 | 163 | 159 | 158 | 164 | 102 | 36.0 |

### Balance Sheet & Other Fin. Data (Million $)

| | 1996 | 1995 | 1994 | 1993 | 1992 | 1991 | 1990 | 1989 | 1988 | 1987 |
|---|---|---|---|---|---|---|---|---|---|---|
| Cash | 201 | 301 | 368 | 229 | 282 | 248 | 110 | 53.0 | 151 | 92.0 |
| Curr. Assets | 1,448 | 1,148 | 999 | 869 | 904 | 888 | 725 | 528 | 465 | 250 |
| Total Assets | 5,016 | 3,269 | 2,492 | 2,349 | 2,169 | 1,599 | 1,453 | 1,167 | 839 | 439 |
| Curr. Liab. | 1,501 | 848 | 549 | 528 | 593 | 361 | 329 | 285 | 176 | 86.0 |
| LT Debt | 945 | 50.0 | 71.0 | 167 | 41.0 | 25.0 | 26.0 | 44.0 | 117 | 105 |
| Common Eqty. | 1,682 | 1,578 | 1,243 | 1,055 | 988 | 1,090 | 990 | 748 | 500 | 220 |
| Total Cap. | 3,148 | 2,089 | 1,613 | 1,478 | 1,255 | 1,238 | 1,124 | 882 | 663 | 353 |
| Cap. Exp. | 21.0 | 35.0 | 29.0 | 22.2 | 15.1 | 19.2 | 22.8 | 22.4 | 18.9 | 10.4 |
| Cash Flow | 348 | 668 | 593 | 437 | 307 | 268 | 265 | 243 | 160 | 64.0 |
| Curr. Ratio | 1.0 | 1.4 | 1.8 | 1.6 | 1.5 | 2.5 | 2.2 | 1.9 | 2.6 | 2.9 |
| % LT Debt of Cap. | 30.0 | 2.4 | 4.4 | 11.3 | 3.3 | 2.0 | 2.3 | 5.0 | 17.6 | 29.7 |
| % Net Inc.of Revs. | NM | 16.5 | 18.7 | 13.3 | 10.8 | 11.8 | 12.2 | 15.9 | 14.4 | 11.8 |
| % Ret. on Assets | NM | 15.1 | 16.8 | 11.2 | 8.7 | 10.6 | 11.5 | 15.9 | 13.2 | 10.7 |
| % Ret. on Equity | NM | 30.9 | 35.4 | 24.7 | 15.9 | 15.5 | 17.3 | 25.6 | 23.9 | 18.4 |

Data as orig. reptd.; bef. results of disc. opers. and/or spec. items. Per share data adj. for stk. divs. as of ex-div. date. E-Estimated. NA-Not Available. NM-Not Meaningful. NR-Not Ranked.

**Office**—One Computer Associates Plaza, Islandia, NY 11788. **Tel**—(516) 342-5224. **Website**—http://www.cai.com **Chrmn & CEO**—C. B. Wang. **Pres**—S. Kumar. **SVP & CFO**—P. A. Schwartz. **SVP & Secy**—B. A. Frease. **SVP & Treas**—I. Zar. **Investor Contact**—Douglas Robinson. **Dirs**—R. M. Artzt, I. Goldstein, R. A. Grasso, S. S. Kenny, S. Kumar, E. C. Lord III, G. E. Martinelli, W. F. P. de Vogel, C. B. Wang. **Transfer Agent**—Mellon Securities Trust Co., Ridgefield Park, NJ. **Incorporated**—in Delaware in 1974. **Empl**—8,800. **S&P Analyst:** Peter C. Wood, CFA

STANDARD
&POOR'S
STOCK REPORTS

**Comverse Technology** **3592**

NASDAQ Symbol **CMVT**

In S&P SmallCap 600

**19-MAY-97**

**Industry:**
Communications
Equipment

**Summary:** CMVT designs, manufactures, and markets computer and telecommunications systems and software for communications and information processing applications.

| Quantitative Evaluations | |
|---|---|
| Outlook (1 Lowest—5 Highest) | • **4−** |
| Fair Value | • 55⅜ |
| Risk | • **Average** |
| Earn./Div. Rank | • **B-** |
| Technical Eval. | • **Bullish** since 5/97 |
| Rel. Strength Rank (1 Lowest—99 Highest) | • **88** |
| Insider Activity | • **NA** |

Recent Price • 45¾
52 Wk Range • 47⅝-22¾

Yield • Nil
12-Mo. P/E • 35.7

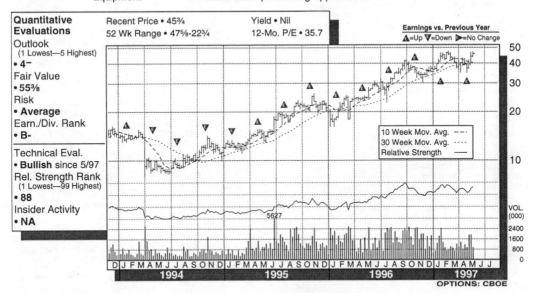

Earnings vs. Previous Year
△=Up ▽=Down ▷=No Change

10 Week Mov. Avg. - - -
30 Week Mov. Avg. ----
Relative Strength ——

OPTIONS: CBOE

## Business Profile - 19-MAY-97

Comverse Technology received new and repeat orders for its Trilogue Infinity multimedia enhanced services platform from wireless and wireline telecommunications network operators during the first quarter of 1997. About 130 phone companies worldwide, including around 80 wireless network operators, have selected Trilogue for revenue-generating enhanced services such as messaging. In addition, the ongoing global transition from analog to digital monitoring and recording technology by customers--such as law enforcement and security agencies, call centers, and others--has been benefiting sales of CMVT's Audiodisk and Ultra product families. After bottoming at $8 a share in 1994, the stock price has been in an uptrend. Officers and directors own about 5% of the shares.

## Operational Review - 19-MAY-97

Based on a brief report, sales (excluding interest and other income) for the first quarter of 1997 advanced 57%, year to year, reflecting sales gains for the Trilogue, Audiodisk, and Ultra product lines. Aided by the higher sales and a 126% gain in interest and other income, net income was up 74%, to $5.5 million, from $9.6 million. The smaller gain in share earnings, to $0.24 from $0.36, was due to dilution from the late 1996 conversion of $58 million of debentures into 3.1 million common shares.

## Stock Performance - 16-MAY-97

In the past 30 trading days, CMVT's shares have increased 14%, compared to a 9% rise in the S&P 500. Average trading volume for the past five days was 181,680 shares, compared with the 40-day moving average of 253,364 shares.

## Key Stock Statistics

| | | | |
|---|---|---|---|
| Dividend Rate/Share | Nil | Shareholders | 1,700 |
| Shs. outstg. (M) | 24.8 | Market cap. (B) | $ 1.1 |
| Avg. daily vol. (M) | 0.282 | Inst. holdings | 79% |
| Tang. Bk. Value/Share | 8.11 | | |
| Beta | 1.28 | | |

Value of $10,000 invested 5 years ago: $ 81,333

### Fiscal Year Ending Dec. 31

| | 1997 | 1996 | 1995 | 1994 | 1993 | 1992 |
|---|---|---|---|---|---|---|
| **Revenues (Million $)** | | | | | | |
| 1Q | 67.52 | 42.20 | 31.52 | 21.47 | 14.54 | 6.80 |
| 2Q | — | 48.71 | 35.81 | 24.36 | 17.49 | 7.78 |
| 3Q | — | 54.11 | 38.33 | 26.08 | 18.60 | 9.74 |
| 4Q | — | 62.30 | 40.24 | 20.76 | 19.80 | 14.10 |
| Yr. | — | 207.3 | 145.9 | 92.67 | 70.44 | 38.42 |
| **Earnings Per Share ($)** | | | | | | |
| 1Q | 0.36 | 0.24 | 0.13 | 0.12 | 0.14 | — |
| 2Q | — | 0.29 | 0.19 | 0.14 | 0.15 | — |
| 3Q | — | 0.31 | 0.21 | 0.15 | 0.17 | — |
| 4Q | — | 0.33 | 0.23 | 0.16 | 0.18 | 0.12 |
| Yr. | — | 1.16 | 0.75 | 0.57 | 0.65 | 0.32 |

**Next earnings report expected: early August**

### Dividend Data

The company has not paid any cash dividends and has said it does not expect to pay dividends in the foreseeable future.

This report is for information purposes and should not be considered a solicitation to buy or sell any security. Neither S&P nor any other party guarantee its accuracy or make warranties regarding results from its usage. Redistribution is prohibited without written permission. Copyright © 1997

*A Division of The McGraw-Hill Companies*

## Business Summary - 19-MAY-97

Comverse Technology, Inc., designs, develops, manufactures and markets computer and telecommunications systems and software for communications and information processing applications, including multimedia messaging and information processing systems. CMVT's systems are used in a broad range of applications by fixed and wireless telephone network operators, government agencies, call centers, and financial institutions. Revenue breakdown by product line--Ultra was introduced in April 1996--in recent years:

|  | 1996 | 1995 |
|---|---|---|
| Trilogue | 72% | 66% |
| Audiodisk and Ultra | 28% | 34% |

International business accounted for 66% of total sales in 1996.

Trilogue systems are designed to enable many simultaneous users to access a broad range of enhanced services, such as call answering, voice and fax messaging and information services, and personal number services. Trilogue's principal market consists of subscriber service provider organizations that use the systems to provide services to the public, usually on a subscription basis, and includes both fixed and wireless telephone network operators and other telecommunications services organizations. Trilogue is marketed throughout the world, with its own direct sales force and

in cooperation with international vendors of telecommunications equipment. CMVT believes it is a market-share leader in providing large capacity messaging systems for international telephone network operators.

Audiodisk systems are designed to enable many simultaneous users to monitor, record and process voice, image (facsimile) and data communications from multiple channels in a variety of analog and digital formats; provide facilities for archiving large volumes of recorded information; and allow the use of computer database processing techniques for analysis, management and retrieval operations.

The Ultra product line is a family of digital recording systems designed to address the need for recording and playback operations in a variety of public and private markets including inbound and outbound call centers, 911 emergency service providers, correctional facilities, and public health and safety organizations.

Research and development expenses amounted to $36.6 million, or 18% of total revenues, in 1996.

In October 1996, CMVT placed privately $115 million of 5.75% debentures due 2006, convertible at $45.75 a share. In November 1996, CMVT called for redemption the remaining $58,000,000 of its 5.25% convertible debentures due 2003; all of the debentures were converted into 3,096,768 common shares.

### Capitalization

**Long Term Debt:** $115,000,000 (12/96) of 5.75% sub. debs due 2006, conv. into com. at $45.75 a sh.

### Per Share Data ($)

| (Year Ended Dec. 31) | 1996 | 1995 | 1994 | 1993 | 1992 | 1991 | 1990 | 1989 | 1988 | 1987 |
|---|---|---|---|---|---|---|---|---|---|---|
| Tangible Bk. Val. | 8.51 | 5.57 | 4.99 | 4.41 | 1.71 | NA | NA | NA | NA | NA |
| Cash Flow | 1.33 | 1.01 | 0.77 | 0.78 | 0.41 | 0.25 | NA | NA | NA | NA |
| Earnings | 1.16 | 0.75 | 0.57 | 0.65 | 0.32 | 0.02 | NA | NA | NA | NA |
| Dividends | Nil | Nil | Nil | Nil | Nil | Nil | NA | NA | NA | NA |
| Payout Ratio | Nil | Nil | Nil | Nil | Nil | Nil | NA | NA | NA | NA |
| Prices - High | 41⅞ | 26 | 15⅝ | 21¾ | 18¾ | 7¾ | NA | NA | NA | NA |
| - Low | 16⅛ | 11 | 8 | 10⅜ | 5⅝ | 1⅞ | NA | NA | NA | NA |
| P/E Ratio - High | 36 | 35 | 27 | 34 | 59 | Nil | NA | NA | NA | NA |
| - Low | 14 | 15 | 14 | 16 | 18 | Nil | NA | NA | NA | NA |

### Income Statement Analysis (Million $)

| | 1996 | 1995 | 1994 | 1993 | 1992 | 1991 | 1990 | 1989 | 1988 | 1987 |
|---|---|---|---|---|---|---|---|---|---|---|
| Revs. | 207 | 137 | 93.0 | 68.0 | 37.0 | 21.1 | NA | NA | NA | NA |
| Oper. Inc. | 34.8 | 20.5 | 15.5 | 14.8 | 7.4 | 2.9 | NA | NA | NA | NA |
| Depr. | 7.1 | 5.9 | 4.2 | 2.6 | 1.4 | 0.7 | NA | NA | NA | NA |
| Int. Exp. | 7.1 | 4.4 | 3.8 | 0.8 | 1.4 | NA | NA | NA | NA | NA |
| Pretax Inc. | 31.3 | 19.1 | 13.5 | 13.7 | 6.7 | 2.8 | NA | NA | NA | NA |
| Eff. Tax Rate | 11% | 11% | 13% | 7.50% | 27% | 14% | NA | NA | NA | NA |
| Net Inc. | 28.0 | 17.1 | 11.8 | 12.7 | 4.9 | 2.5 | NA | NA | NA | NA |

### Balance Sheet & Other Fin. Data (Million $)

| | 1996 | 1995 | 1994 | 1993 | 1992 | 1991 | 1990 | 1989 | 1988 | 1987 |
|---|---|---|---|---|---|---|---|---|---|---|
| Cash | 236 | 123 | 128 | 126 | NA | NA | NA | NA | NA | NA |
| Curr. Assets | 351 | 190 | 167 | 154 | NA | NA | NA | NA | NA | NA |
| Total Assets | 391 | 221 | 188 | 169 | NA | NA | NA | NA | NA | NA |
| Curr. Liab. | 58.7 | 35.2 | 22.7 | 16.7 | NA | NA | NA | NA | NA | NA |
| LT Debt | 115 | 60.0 | 60.0 | 60.0 | NA | NA | NA | NA | NA | NA |
| Common Eqty. | 212 | 122 | 103 | 90.0 | NA | NA | NA | NA | NA | NA |
| Total Cap. | 327 | 182 | 163 | 150 | NA | NA | NA | NA | NA | NA |
| Cap. Exp. | 4.8 | 5.6 | 4.2 | 3.3 | NA | NA | NA | NA | NA | NA |
| Cash Flow | 35.1 | 22.9 | 16.0 | 15.3 | 6.3 | 3.1 | NA | NA | NA | NA |
| Curr. Ratio | 6.0 | 5.4 | 7.4 | 9.2 | NA | NA | NA | NA | NA | NA |
| % LT Debt of Cap. | 35.1 | 33.0 | 36.8 | 40.0 | NA | NA | NA | NA | NA | NA |
| % Net Inc.of Revs. | 25.9 | 12.4 | 12.6 | 18.7 | 13.0 | 11.6 | NA | NA | NA | NA |
| % Ret. on Assets | 9.2 | 8.2 | 6.6 | 7.5 | NA | NA | NA | NA | NA | NA |
| % Ret. on Equity | 16.8 | 15.3 | 12.2 | 14.1 | NA | NA | NA | NA | NA | NA |

Data as orig. reptd.; bef. results of disc. opers. and/or spec. items. Per share data adj. for stk. divs. as of ex-div. date. E-Estimated. NA-Not Available. NM-Not Meaningful. NR-Not Ranked.

**Office**—170 Crossways Park Dr., Woodbury, NY 11797. **Tel.**—(516) 677-7200. **Chrmn & Pres & Investor Contact**—Kobi Alexander. **VP-CFO**—I. Nissim. **Secy**—W. F. Sorin. **Dirs**—K. Alexander, Z. Alexander, J. H. Friedman, S. Oolie, W. F. Sorin, Y. Yemini. **Transfer Agent & Registrar**—American Stock Transfer & Trust Co., NYC. **Incorporated**—in New York in 1984. **Empl**—1,243. **S&P Analyst:** N.J. DeVita

# STANDARD &POOR'S
## STOCK REPORTS

# Conseco, Inc.

**609**

NYSE Symbol **CNC**

In S&P 500

**20-MAY-97**

**Industry:**
Insurance (Life & Health)

**Summary:** This holding company engages in the acquisition, ownership and management of annuity, life, and supplemental health insurance companies.

| S&P Opinion: Buy (★★★★) | Recent Price • 37⅞ | Yield • 0.3% |
|---|---|---|
| | 52 Wk Range • 43⅞-17½ | 12-Mo. P/E • 19.0 |

**Earnings vs. Previous Year**
▲=Up ▼=Down ▶=No Change

### Quantitative Evaluations

**Outlook**
(1 Lowest—5 Highest)
• **1⁻**

**Fair Value**
• **34⅞**

**Risk**
• **Average**

**Earn./Div. Rank**
• **B+**

**Technical Eval.**
• **Bullish** since 6/95

**Rel. Strength Rank**
(1 Lowest—99 Highest)
• **57**

**Insider Activity**
• **NA**

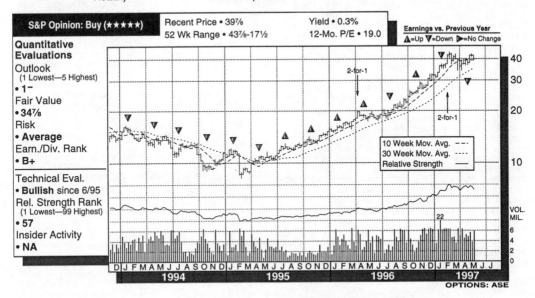

10 Week Mov. Avg. - - -
30 Week Mov. Avg. ⋯⋯⋯
Relative Strength ——

OPTIONS: ASE

## Overview - 19-MAY-97

Operating earnings growth in coming periods will be aided by contributions from an ongoing acquisition plan, assuming CNC continues to successfully choose acquisition candidates with complementary products and distribution systems. and is able to continue to smoothly integrate them into its fold. That aside, operating profit gains from internal sources are predicated on strong deposit growth and favorable interest rate spreads in the life insurance and annuity areas, and on continued favorable claim trends in the Medicare supplemental insurance line. Cross selling opportunities and further expense savings expected from the integration of recent and upcoming acquisitions also enhance the profit outlook. Stock repurchases, including the 4.1 million shares reacquired (as of 4/30/97) under a 5 million share authorization, will aid per share results. A two-for-one stock split was effected February 11, 1997.

## Valuation - 19-MAY-97

After a sharp correction in late 1994 when the company was unsuccessful at acquiring NYSE-listed Kemper Corp. (mainly because of its inability to secure adequate financing); CNC shares have since rebounded sharply. Some of the recent strength is attributable to a favorable interest rate environment in 1995 for financial stocks. But, investors have also reacted favorably to the company's very well defined strategic focus and to its accretive acquisitions. Because CNC actively buys and sells operating subsidiaries, year to year EPS comparisons are often not extremely meaningful. Despite their recent strength, the shares, which were recently trading at 14X our 1998 operating EPS estimate of $3.10 a share, have some additional upside, in view of CNC's superior long-term growth prospects.

## Key Stock Statistics

| | | | |
|---|---|---|---|
| S&P EPS Est. 1997 | 2.65 | Tang. Bk. Value/Share | 3.69 |
| P/E on S&P Est. 1997 | 15.0 | Beta | 1.42 |
| S&P EPS Est. 1998 | 3.10 | Shareholders | 13,000 |
| Dividend Rate/Share | 0.13 | Market cap. (B) | $ 7.1 |
| Shs. outstg. (M) | 183.2 | Inst. holdings | 52% |
| Avg. daily vol. (M) | 0.986 | | |

Value of $10,000 invested 5 years ago: $ 52,888

### Fiscal Year Ending Dec. 31

| | 1996 | 1995 | 1994 | 1993 | 1992 | 1991 |
|---|---|---|---|---|---|---|
| **Revenues (Million $)** | | | | | | |
| 1Q | 691.8 | 652.3 | 490.2 | 751.6 | — | — |
| 2Q | 672.5 | 737.1 | 413.9 | 619.0 | — | — |
| 3Q | 834.3 | 676.7 | 423.9 | 628.7 | 296.8 | — |
| 4Q | 866.5 | 789.2 | 534.0 | 636.7 | 490.8 | — |
| Yr. | 3,067 | 2,855 | 1,862 | 2,636 | 1,526 | — |
| **Earnings Per Share ($)** | | | | | | |
| 1Q | 0.60 | 0.23 | 0.69 | 1.17 | 0.28 | 0.19 |
| 2Q | 0.43 | 1.12 | 0.28 | 0.39 | 0.27 | 0.23 |
| 3Q | 0.55 | 0.46 | 0.30 | 0.40 | 0.35 | 0.24 |
| 4Q | 0.54 | 0.58 | -0.03 | 0.50 | 0.50 | 0.41 |
| Yr. | 2.12 | 2.37 | 1.29 | 2.47 | 1.40 | 1.08 |

**Next earnings report expected: late July**

### Dividend Data (Dividends have been paid since 1988.)

| Amount ($) | Date Decl. | Ex-Div. Date | Stock of Record | Payment Date |
|---|---|---|---|---|
| 0.063 | Nov. 06 | Dec. 18 | Dec. 20 | Jan. 02 '97 |
| 2-for-1 | Jan. 15 | Feb. 12 | Jan. 27 | Feb. 11 '97 |
| 0.031 | Feb. 19 | Mar. 18 | Mar. 20 | Apr. 01 '97 |
| 0.031 | May. 14 | Jun. 18 | Jun. 20 | Jul. 01 '97 |

This report is for information purposes and should not be considered a solicitation to buy or sell any security. Neither S&P nor any other party guarantee its accuracy or make warranties regarding results from its usage. Redistribution is prohibited without written permission. Copyright © 1997

*A Division of The McGraw·Hill Companies*

## Business Summary - 19-MAY-97

Conseco, Inc. is a holding company engaged in the acquisition, ownership and operation of annuity, life and health insurance companies. Its strategy has been to acquire companies with profitable product niches and strong distribution systems; to consolidate and streamline the management and administrative functions; to realize superior investment returns through active asset management; to eliminate any unprofitable products and distribution channels; and to expand the profitable distribution channels and products.

Premiums collected during 1996 equaled $3.2 billion, of which annuities accounted for 48%, supplemental health insurance 26%, life insurance 14%, and other 12%.

During 1996, CNC completed the following acquisitions: Life Partners Group, Inc. for $850 million (August); the 62% of American Life Holdings it did not already own for $165 million in cash (September); American Tavellers Corp. for $793 million in stock (December); Transport Holdings, Inc. for $311 million in stock (December); and the 10% of Bankers Life Holding it did not already own for $117 million in cash (December). From 1982 through year-end 1995, CNC completed 12 acquisitions, with the first seven as wholly owned subsidiaries and the last five through acquisition partnerships. In September 1996, CNC dissolved its acquisition partnership, Conseco Capital Partners II, because of regulatory changes.

## Important Developments

**Apr. '97**—CNC said it agreed to acquire Colonial Penn Life Insurance from Leucadia National Corp. (NYSE: LUK) for $460 million in cash and notes. CNC expects to complete the acquisition of this leading marketer of whole life insurance to senior citizens by the third quarter of 1997. Separately, CNC reported operating earnings (before the impact of restructurings and investment gains or losses) for the three months ended March 31, 1997 of $0.59 a share, up from $0.44 a share in the year ago interim. The increase reflected contributions from CNC's ongoing acquisition program, coupled with internal growth.
**Mar. '97**—CNC completed its acquisition of Capitol American Financial Corp. (NYSE: CAF) for $650 million in cash and stock. CAF is a supplemental health insurer. Separately, the acquisition of Pioneer Financial Services, for $477 million in stock, announced in late 1996, is set to close in the second quarter of 1997.

## Capitalization

**Notes Payable:** $1,094,900,000.
**Minority Interest:** $697,700,000.
**Preferred Stock:** $267,100,000

| Per Share Data ($) (Year Ended Dec. 31) | 1996 | 1995 | 1994 | 1993 | 1992 | 1991 | 1990 | 1989 | 1988 | 1987 |
|---|---|---|---|---|---|---|---|---|---|---|
| Tangible Bk. Val. | 3.69 | NM | -2.52 | 5.28 | 3.96 | 2.57 | NM | 0.52 | 0.03 | 0.01 |
| Oper. Earnings | 1.89 | 1.26 | 1.48 | 2.41 | 1.30 | 0.72 | 0.31 | 0.20 | 0.14 | NA |
| Earnings | 2.12 | 2.37 | 1.29 | 2.47 | 1.40 | 1.08 | 0.34 | 0.44 | 0.26 | 0.19 |
| Dividends | 0.08 | 0.02 | 0.13 | 0.08 | 0.02 | 0.02 | 0.01 | 0.01 | 0.01 | Nil |
| Payout Ratio | 4% | 1% | 10% | 3% | 2% | 2% | 4% | 3% | 2% | Nil |
| Prices - High | 33 1/8 | 15 3/4 | 16 5/8 | 19 | 11 7/8 | 8 1/2 | 1 7/8 | 1 3/4 | 15/16 | 1 3/16 |
| - Low | 14 7/8 | 8 1/8 | 9 | 11 1/8 | 5 1/8 | 1 1/2 | 1 1/16 | 11/16 | 9/16 | 7/16 |
| P/E Ratio - High | 16 | 7 | 13 | 8 | 8 | 8 | 5 | 4 | 3 | 6 |
| - Low | 7 | 3 | 7 | 5 | 4 | 1 | 3 | 2 | 2 | 2 |
| **Income Statement Analysis (Million $)** | | | | | | | | | | |
| Life Ins. In Force | NA | NA | NA | NA | 23,025 | 24,216 | 29,025 | 14,370 | 12,941 | 14,370 |
| Prem. Inc.: Life | 1,654 | 1,465 | 1,286 | 1,294 | 379 | 281 | 153 | 197 | 240 | NA |
| Prem. Inc.: A & H | Nil | Nil | NA | NA | NA | NA | NA | NA | NA | NA |
| Prem. Inc.: Other | 80.2 | 59.0 | 191 | 446 | 258 | 139 | 12.0 | 32.0 | 3.0 | NA |
| Net Invest. Inc. | 1,303 | 1,143 | 386 | 896 | 889 | 972 | 588 | 430 | 345 | 167 |
| Total Revs. | 3,067 | 2,855 | 1,862 | 2,636 | 1,526 | 1,392 | 753 | 659 | 588 | 278 |
| Pretax Inc. | 494 | 419 | 324 | 610 | 330 | 223 | 65.0 | 70.0 | 46.0 | 28.0 |
| Net Oper. Inc. | 268 | 131 | 175 | 302 | 163 | 84.0 | 39.0 | 32.0 | 26.0 | NA |
| Net Inc. | 252 | 223 | 154 | 309 | 175 | 121 | 42.0 | 47.0 | 30.0 | 20.0 |
| **Balance Sheet & Other Fin. Data (Million $)** | | | | | | | | | | |
| Cash & Equiv. | 297 | 208 | 126 | 168 | 157 | 172 | 575 | 408 | 143 | 216 |
| Premiums Due | 504 | 84.8 | 46.0 | 511 | 892 | NA | NA | NA | NA | NA |
| Invest. Assets: Bonds | 17,589 | 13,153 | 7,067 | 9,822 | 8,331 | 8,174 | 5,703 | 3,716 | 2,916 | 2,301 |
| Invest. Assets: Stocks | 100 | 36.6 | 39.6 | 30.3 | 71.6 | 48.2 | 43.8 | 34.5 | 29.7 | 37.7 |
| Invest. Assets: Loans | 1,346 | 907 | 387 | 675 | 362 | 1,107 | 735 | 418 | 446 | 455 |
| Invest. Assets: Total | 19,631 | 14,415 | 8,159 | 11,689 | 9,450 | 10,427 | 6,900 | 4,379 | 3,553 | 2,794 |
| Deferred Policy Costs | 2,559 | 1,427 | 1,322 | 862 | 934 | 768 | 613 | 278 | 248 | 228 |
| Total Assets | 25,613 | 17,298 | 10,812 | 13,749 | 11,773 | 11,596 | 8,284 | 5,176 | 4,031 | 3,383 |
| Debt | 1,095 | 871 | 192 | 703 | 555 | 497 | 527 | 308 | 331 | 353 |
| Common Eqty. | 2,818 | 828 | 463 | 855 | 544 | 382 | 120 | 108 | 41.0 | 39.0 |
| % Return On Revs. | 9.1 | 7.8 | 8.3 | 11.7 | 11.5 | 8.7 | 5.5 | 7.2 | 5.2 | 7.1 |
| % Ret. on Assets | 1.3 | 1.6 | 1.3 | 2.2 | 1.5 | 1.2 | 0.6 | 1.0 | 0.8 | 1.0 |
| % Ret. on Equity | 12.0 | 34.1 | 20.6 | 36.1 | 36.6 | 45.5 | 31.6 | 52.0 | 53.2 | 51.5 |
| % Invest. Yield | 7.7 | 11.8 | 4.0 | 8.5 | 8.9 | 10.9 | 10.4 | 10.8 | 10.8 | 10.1 |

Data as orig. reptd.; bef. results of disc. opers. and/or spec. items. Per share data adj. for stk. divs. as of ex-div. date. E-Estimated. NA-Not Available. NM-Not Meaningful. NR-Not Ranked.

**Office**—11825 North Pennsylvania St., Carmel, IN 46032. **Tel**—(317) 817-6100. **Website**—http://www.conseco.com **Chrmn, CEO & Pres**—S. C. Hilbert. **EVP & CFO**—R. M. Dick. **EVP & Secy**—L. W. Inlow. **VP & Investor Contact**—James W. Rosensteele (317-817-2893). **Dirs**—N. E. Cuneo, D. R. Decatur, R. M. Dick, D. F. Gongaware, M. P. Hathaway, S. C. Hilbert, J. D. Massey, D. E. Murray Sr., J. M. Mutz. **Transfer Agent & Registrar**—Bank One, Indianapolis. **Incorporated**—in Indiana in 1979. **Empl**— 3,700. **S&P Analyst:** Catherine A. Seifert

# Corrections Corp. of America  672R

NYSE Symbol **CXC**

In S&P SmallCap 600

**17-MAY-97**

**Industry:**
Services (Facilities & Environmental)

**Summary:** This company is the leading private sector provider of detention and corrections services to federal, state and local governments.

## Quantitative Evaluations

**Outlook**
(1 Lowest—5 Highest)
• **4⁻**

**Fair Value**
• **45⅞**

**Risk**
• **High**

**Earn./Div. Rank**
• **B**

**Technical Eval.**
• **Bullish** since 5/97

**Rel. Strength Rank**
(1 Lowest—99 Highest)
• **94**

**Insider Activity**
• **Neutral**

Recent Price • 35⅜
52 Wk Range • 45-20⅞

Yield • Nil
12-Mo. P/E • 78.6

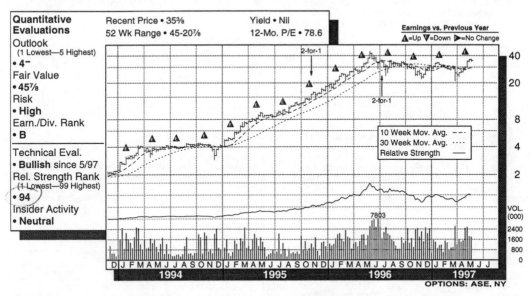

Earnings vs. Previous Year
▲=Up ▼=Down ▷=No Change

10 Week Mov. Avg. ----
30 Week Mov. Avg. ·······
Relative Strength ——

OPTIONS: ASE, NY

## Business Profile - 09-MAY-97

CXC's future growth is dependent upon its ability to obtain contracts to manage new facilities and to retain existing management contracts. The company is currently developing 12 facilities and expanding four others, representing a total of 14,475 beds. Management expects that all of the beds under development and expansion will be in operation by the third quarter of 1998. Recently, Corrections Corp. said it had proposed to sell several facilities to CCA Prison Realty Trust, a newly formed REIT, with the intention of managing the REIT-owned facilities under operating leases.

## Operational Review - 09-MAY-97

Revenues in the three months ended March 31, 1997, rose 45%, year to year, stemming from an increase in the number of beds in operation. Margins widened, reflecting the higher volume and well controlled G&A expense; operating income grew 85%. Following a significant reduction in interest expense, and 72% higher depreciation and amortization charges, pretax income jumped 109%. After taxes at 39.7%, versus 40.2%, net income advanced 110% to $11,995,000 ($0.14 a share, on 4.3% more shares), from $5,706,000 ($0.07, as adjusted for a 2-for-1 split in July 1996).

## Stock Performance - 16-MAY-97

In the past 30 trading days, CXC's shares have increased 37%, compared to a 9% rise in the S&P 500. Average trading volume for the past five days was 355,520 shares, compared with the 40-day moving average of 413,315 shares.

## Key Stock Statistics

| | | | |
|---|---|---|---|
| Dividend Rate/Share | Nil | Shareholders | 20,000 |
| Shs. outstg. (M) | 75.0 | Market cap. (B) | $ 2.7 |
| Avg. daily vol. (M) | 0.525 | Inst. holdings | 48% |
| Tang. Bk. Value/Share | 3.72 | | |
| Beta | 1.66 | | |

Value of $10,000 invested 5 years ago: $ 215,555

### Fiscal Year Ending Dec. 31

| | 1997 | 1996 | 1995 | 1994 | 1993 | 1992 |
|---|---|---|---|---|---|---|
| **Revenues (Million $)** | | | | | | |
| 1Q | 91.84 | 63.28 | 44.15 | 27.40 | 25.78 | 18.10 |
| 2Q | — | 67.45 | 51.25 | 29.33 | 26.29 | 22.30 |
| 3Q | — | 75.20 | 49.51 | 30.84 | 26.78 | 24.20 |
| 4Q | — | 86.58 | 62.33 | 33.14 | 27.36 | 25.70 |
| Yr. | — | 292.5 | 207.2 | 120.7 | 106.2 | 90.20 |
| **Earnings Per Share ($)** | | | | | | |
| 1Q | 0.14 | 0.07 | 0.03 | 0.03 | 0.02 | 0.01 |
| 2Q | — | 0.09 | 0.03 | 0.03 | 0.02 | 0.02 |
| 3Q | — | 0.10 | 0.06 | 0.04 | 0.02 | 0.02 |
| 4Q | — | 0.12 | 0.07 | 0.04 | 0.02 | 0.02 |
| Yr. | — | 0.38 | 0.19 | 0.13 | 0.08 | 0.07 |

**Next earnings report expected: late July**

### Dividend Data

| Amount ($) | Date Decl. | Ex-Div. Date | Stock of Record | Payment Date |
|---|---|---|---|---|
| 2-for-1 | Jun. 05 | Jul. 03 | Jun. 19 | Jul. 02 '96 |

This report is for information purposes and should not be considered a solicitation to buy or sell any security. Neither S&P nor any other party guarantee its accuracy or make warranties regarding results from its usage. Redistribution is prohibited without written permission. Copyright © 1997

A Division of The **McGraw·Hill** Companies

## Business Summary - 09-MAY-97

Corrections Corporation of America manages prisons and other correctional and detention facilities for governmental agencies. Since beginning operations in 1983, CXC has been the leader in privatizing such facilities. At April 24, 1997, 43,049 beds in 60 facilities were under contract in 17 states, Washington, D.C., Puerto Rico, Australia and the U.K.

Management services provided by CXC include the integrated design, construction and management of new correctional and detention facilities, and the redesign, renovation and management of older facilities. In addition to providing fundamental residential services relating to adult and juvenile inmates, the company's facilities offer a wide variety of rehabilitation and education programs, including basic education, employment training and substance abuse treatment. CXC also provides health care, institutional food services, transportational requirements, and work and recreational programs.

In addition to the opening of new facilities, over the past few years, CXC has expanded its service capabilities and broadened its geographic presence in the U.S. through a series of strategic acquisitions of prison management companies and individual facilities, as well as the acquisition of an inmate transportation company. The company intends to continue to pursue strategic acquisitions of prison management companies and facilities.

Compensation to CXC is based on the number of inmates held in each facility. Contracts may provide fixed per diem or monthly rates; some also provide for minimum guarantees. In 1996, the average occupancy rate was 94.1%, up from 93.9% in 1995.

In 1996, the U.S. Marshal Service and the State of Texas accounted for 9% and 16% of revenues, respectively.

### Important Developments

**Apr. '97**—The company proposed to sell nine facilities housing 6,687 beds, for $308 million, to CCA Prison Realty Trust, a newly formed real estate investment trust (REIT). The proceeds will be used to finance new projects. The company has also offered the REIT the option to purchase any or all of an additional five properties with 5,638 beds for an estimated $193 million. CXC will continue to manage the REIT-owned facilities under operating leases.

**Mar. '97**—CXC said that its pending contract to house 1,500 inmates for the District of Columbia in a facility it has built in Youngstown, Ohio, is being set aside in lieu of an expedited formal solicitation process. However, the company believes that the delay will not have a material effect on its operating performance in the first half of 1997.

### Capitalization

**Long Term Debt:** $189,191,000 (3/97).

### Per Share Data ($)

| (Year Ended Dec. 31) | 1996 | 1995 | 1994 | 1993 | 1992 | 1991 | 1990 | 1989 | 1988 | 1987 |
|---|---|---|---|---|---|---|---|---|---|---|
| Tangible Bk. Val. | 3.72 | 1.48 | 1.14 | 0.84 | 0.76 | 0.69 | 0.70 | 0.71 | 0.64 | 0.66 |
| Cash Flow | 0.52 | 0.28 | 0.21 | 0.16 | 0.14 | 0.02 | 0.05 | 0.08 | 0.03 | -0.03 |
| Earnings | 0.38 | 0.19 | 0.13 | 0.09 | 0.07 | -0.05 | 0.00 | 0.04 | 0.00 | -0.06 |
| Dividends | Nil | Nil | Nil | Nil | Nil | Nil | Nil | Nil | Nil | Nil |
| Payout Ratio | Nil | Nil | Nil | Nil | Nil | Nil | Nil | Nil | Nil | Nil |
| Prices - High | 45 | 19½ | 4½ | 2⅝ | 2 | 2⅝ | 4⅛ | 3⅞ | 2 | 3½ |
| - Low | 17¼ | 4 | 2¼ | 1⁹⁄₁₆ | 1³⁄₁₆ | 1⅛ | 1¾ | 1⅞ | 1 | ¾ |
| P/E Ratio - High | NM | NM | 33 | 28 | 31 | NM | NM | 90 | NM | NM |
| - Low | NM | NM | 17 | 17 | 18 | NM | NM | 43 | NM | NM |

### Income Statement Analysis (Million $)

| | 1996 | 1995 | 1994 | 1993 | 1992 | 1991 | 1990 | 1989 | 1988 | 1987 |
|---|---|---|---|---|---|---|---|---|---|---|
| Revs. | 293 | 207 | 121 | 100 | 90.2 | 67.9 | 55.5 | 36.8 | 24.8 | 17.0 |
| Oper. Inc. | 106 | 34.1 | 16.6 | 11.0 | 9.7 | 6.2 | 3.2 | 4.3 | 1.9 | -0.6 |
| Depr. | 11.3 | 6.5 | 4.1 | 2.8 | 2.9 | 2.4 | 1.6 | 1.2 | 1.2 | 1.0 |
| Int. Exp. | 8.7 | 6.3 | 5.0 | 5.6 | 6.1 | 6.4 | 4.6 | 3.2 | 1.3 | 1.0 |
| Pretax Inc. | 50.3 | 23.7 | 9.3 | 4.0 | 2.6 | -1.9 | 0.2 | 1.6 | -0.1 | -1.9 |
| Eff. Tax Rate | 39% | 39% | 20% | 2.00% | 1.60% | NM | 2.50% | 2.40% | Nil | Nil |
| Net Inc. | 30.9 | 14.3 | 7.4 | 4.0 | 2.5 | -1.9 | 0.0 | 1.6 | -0.1 | -1.9 |

### Balance Sheet & Other Fin. Data (Million $)

| | 1996 | 1995 | 1994 | 1993 | 1992 | 1991 | 1990 | 1989 | 1988 | 1987 |
|---|---|---|---|---|---|---|---|---|---|---|
| Cash | 8.3 | 2.7 | 4.1 | 6.3 | 5.2 | 5.2 | 5.7 | 1.5 | 0.8 | 0.3 |
| Curr. Assets | 114 | 46.6 | 32.0 | 24.7 | 24.3 | 16.8 | 18.1 | 12.5 | 6.1 | 3.3 |
| Total Assets | 469 | 213 | 130 | 100 | 102 | 96.7 | 94.1 | 67.6 | 44.2 | 34.6 |
| Curr. Liab. | 64.0 | 35.5 | 17.9 | 12.5 | 13.4 | 8.8 | 7.3 | 5.0 | 3.7 | 3.3 |
| LT Debt | 118 | 74.9 | 46.5 | 48.7 | 55.4 | 57.8 | 61.8 | 37.0 | 18.6 | 8.4 |
| Common Eqty. | 282 | 96.7 | 58.3 | 32.0 | 28.5 | 25.2 | 25.0 | 25.6 | 21.9 | 22.9 |
| Total Cap. | 404 | 176 | 108 | 87.3 | 88.9 | 88.0 | 86.9 | 62.6 | 40.5 | 31.3 |
| Cap. Exp. | 166 | 25.9 | 23.2 | 1.9 | 11.2 | 8.3 | 25.7 | 18.0 | 5.9 | 1.1 |
| Cash Flow | 42.2 | 20.9 | 11.3 | 6.3 | 5.4 | 0.6 | 1.8 | 2.8 | 1.1 | -0.9 |
| Curr. Ratio | 1.8 | 1.3 | 1.8 | 2.0 | 1.8 | 1.9 | 2.5 | 2.5 | 1.7 | 1.0 |
| % LT Debt of Cap. | 29.1 | 42.6 | 42.9 | 55.8 | 62.3 | 65.7 | 71.2 | 59.1 | 45.9 | 26.9 |
| % Net Inc.of Revs. | 10.6 | 6.9 | 6.1 | 3.9 | 2.8 | NM | 0.4 | 4.4 | NM | NM |
| % Ret. on Assets | 9.1 | 8.1 | 5.6 | 3.9 | 2.5 | NM | 0.2 | 2.8 | NM | NM |
| % Ret. on Equity | 16.3 | 18.1 | 14.2 | 11.5 | 9.0 | NM | 0.8 | 6.6 | NM | NM |

Data as orig. reptd.; bef. results of disc. opers. and/or spec. items. Per share data adj. for stk. divs. as of ex-div. date. E-Estimated. NA-Not Available. NM-Not Meaningful. NR-Not Ranked.

**Office**—102 Woodmont Blvd., Nashville, TN 37205. **Registrar & Transfer Agent**—First Union National Bank, Charlotte, NC. **Tel**—(615) 292-3100. **Chrmn & CEO**—D. R. Crants. **Pres**—D. L. Myers. **VP-Fin, Secy & Treas**—D. K. Massengale. **VP & Investor Contact**—Peggy W. Lawrence. **Dirs**—W. F. Andrews, S. W. Bartholomew Jr., T. W. Beasley, D. R. Crants, J. P. Cuny, J. F. Johnson, R. C. McWhorter. **Transfer Agent & Registrar**—First Union National Bank, Charlotte, NC. **Incorporated**—in Delaware in 1986; reincorporated in Tennessee in 1997. **Empl**— 7,235. **S&P Analyst:** Stephen J. Tekirian

# Dell Computer

## 3665T
Nasdaq Symbol **DELL**

**In S&P 500**

**16-MAY-97**

**Industry:** Computers (Hardware)

**Summary:** Dell is the leading direct marketer and one of the world's top 10 manufacturers of personal computers compatible with industry standards established by IBM.

| S&P Opinion: Hold (★★★) | | |
|---|---|---|
| Recent Price • 92¾ | Yield • Nil | |
| 52 Wk Range • 94½-20¼ | 12-Mo. P/E • 33.5 | |

**Quantitative Evaluations**

**Outlook** (1 Lowest—5 Highest)
• **3+**

**Fair Value**
• **94¾**

**Risk**
• **Average**

**Earn./Div. Rank**
• **B**

**Technical Eval.**
• **Bearish** since 10/96

**Rel. Strength Rank** (1 Lowest—99 Highest)
• **98**

**Insider Activity**
• **Unfavorable**

**Earnings vs. Previous Year**
▲=Up ▼=Down ▶=No Change

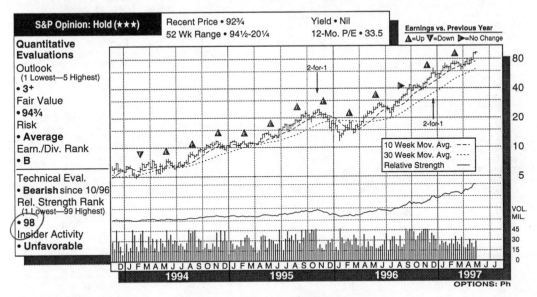

10 Week Mov. Avg. ---
30 Week Mov. Avg. ·····
Relative Strength ——

2-for-1

OPTIONS: Ph

## Overview - 14-MAY-97

Revenues are expected to grow some 40% in FY 98 (Jan.). DELL is well positioned to benefit from the corporate upgrade cycle over the next 12 to 18 months to Pentium and Pentium-Pro class machines featuring Microsoft's Windows NT operating system. The company is already seeing early returns from this upgrade cycle, as Pentium Pro systems now account for a growing percentage of its sales. In addition, Dell has strong momentum in the fast growing notebook and server segments. Dell is also benefiting from its direct selling model, which allows it to deliver the latest system features at aggressive price points. Gross margins are likely to stabilize in the 21%-22% range, which is up from recent quarters, reflecting benefits of lower component costs and a greater proportion of higher-margin notebook and server products.

## Valuation - 14-MAY-97

We recommend that investors "hold" the shares, in light of Dell's excellent long-term prospects. After nearly tripling in 1996, Dell's shares have continued their ascent during 1997, as the company consistently reports revenue and EPS growth that exceeds the rate of the overall industry. This reflects the strength of its direct sales model and strong brand name. In addition, we see further revenue and EPS momentum on the strength of the Pentium Pro upgrade cycle and a new line of aggressively priced server products. Nevertheless, Dell's stock price appreciation has resulted in a valuation that exceeds the high end of the range for PC vendors, based on our calendar 1998 estimate. Given Dell's current lofty valuation, we remain cautious for the near term, and would not recommend adding to positions at these levels.

## Key Stock Statistics

| | | | |
|---|---|---|---|
| S&P EPS Est. 1998 | 4.00 | Tang. Bk. Value/Share | 4.66 |
| P/E on S&P Est. 1998 | 23.2 | Beta | 1.34 |
| Dividend Rate/Share | Nil | Shareholders | 3,700 |
| Shs. outstg. (M) | 167.5 | Market cap. (B) | $ 16.9 |
| Avg. daily vol. (M) | 4.996 | Inst. holdings | 64% |

Value of $10,000 invested 5 years ago: $ 217,315

### Fiscal Year Ending Jan. 31

| | 1997 | 1996 | 1995 | 1994 | 1993 | 1992 |
|---|---|---|---|---|---|---|
| **Revenues (Million $)** | | | | | | |
| 1Q | 1,638 | 1,136 | 767.0 | 672.4 | 366.0 | 175.0 |
| 2Q | 1,690 | 1,206 | 791.5 | 700.6 | 458.0 | 200.0 |
| 3Q | 2,019 | 1,416 | 884.5 | 757.3 | 570.0 | 229.0 |
| 4Q | 2,412 | 1,539 | 1,033 | 743.0 | 620.3 | 286.0 |
| Yr. | 7,759 | 5,296 | 3,475 | 2,873 | 2,014 | 890.0 |
| **Earnings Per Share ($)** | | | | | | |
| 1Q | 0.42 | 0.28 | 0.10 | 0.06 | 0.13 | 0.08 |
| 2Q | 0.57 | 0.57 | 0.16 | -0.51 | 0.14 | 0.08 |
| 3Q | 0.78 | 0.38 | 0.23 | 0.07 | 0.18 | 0.09 |
| 4Q | 1.01 | 0.35 | 0.34 | 0.10 | 0.19 | 0.10 |
| Yr. | 2.77 | 1.33 | 0.85 | -0.26 | 0.65 | 0.35 |

**Next earnings report expected: mid May**

### Dividend Data

| Amount ($) | Date Decl. | Ex-Div. Date | Stock of Record | Payment Date |
|---|---|---|---|---|
| 2-for-1 | Nov. 12 | Dec. 09 | Nov. 25 | Dec. 06 '96 |

This report is for information purposes and should not be considered a solicitation to buy or sell any security. Neither S&P nor any other party guarantee its accuracy or make warranties regarding results from its usage. Redistribution is prohibited without written permission. Copyright © 1997

*A Division of The* **McGraw·Hill** *Companies*

## Business Summary - 14-MAY-97

Dell Computer Corporation is a direct marketer of personal computers, including desktops, notebooks and servers. International sales accounted for 32% of the total in FY 97 (Jan.), down from 34% in FY 96.

Dell's line of servers (4% of FY 97 system revenue), sold under the PowerEdge name, is used in a networked environment to distribute files, database information, applications and communication products. Dell's desktop computer systems (78%) include the OptiPlex line, which are targeted at corporate and other major account customers, and offer advanced features and high reliability; Dell Dimension XPS, a line targeted at technologically sophisticated business and individual users; and Dell Dimension, which is targeted at small-to-medium-sized businesses and individual users. Notebooks, or portables, (18%) include the Latitude XPi product lines, and the Latitude LM line, which is available with MMX multimedia technology.

In addition to its own branded products, Dell offers thousands of software packages and peripheral products through its DellWare program. The company also offers a number of specialized services, including custom hardware and software integration and network installation and support.

Manufacturing operations are conducted at facilities in Austin, Tex.; Limerick, Ireland; and Penang, Malaysia. During fiscal 1997, Dell began construction of an additional 285,000 sq. ft. manufacturing facility in Austin.

In July 1994, Dell discontinued retail channel sales to focus exclusively on its direct business.

### Important Developments

**Mar. '97**—According to International Data Corp., a Framingham, MA-based research firm, Dell held the number four marketshare position worldwide in the fourth quarter of 1996 for network servers. During 1996, server units grew by 310% year to year and by 76% sequentially, while revenue grew by 226% and 89%, respectively. Separately, the company said that sales from its Internet site are increasing 20% per month and generating revenues in excess of $1 million a day. At Dell's Internet site, customers can electronically design, price and purchase computer systems and obtain online support.

### Capitalization

**Long Term Debt:** $18,000,000 (2/2/97).
**Options:** To buy 11,183,046 shs. at $0.01 to $23.31 ea.

### Per Share Data ($)

| (Year Ended Jan. 31) | 1997 | 1996 | 1995 | 1994 | 1993 | 1992 | 1991 | 1990 | 1989 | 1988 |
|---|---|---|---|---|---|---|---|---|---|---|
| Tangible Bk. Val. | 4.66 | 5.18 | 3.32 | 2.27 | 2.51 | 1.92 | 0.96 | 0.71 | 0.67 | 0.14 |
| Cash Flow | 3.01 | 1.60 | 1.05 | -0.06 | 0.77 | 0.44 | 0.29 | 0.09 | 0.15 | 0.13 |
| Earnings | 2.77 | 1.33 | 0.85 | -0.26 | 0.65 | 0.35 | 0.23 | 0.05 | 0.13 | 0.12 |
| Dividends | Nil | Nil | Nil | Nil | Nil | Nil | Nil | Nil | Nil | Nil |
| Payout Ratio | Nil | Nil | Nil | Nil | Nil | Nil | Nil | Nil | Nil | Nil |
| Cal. Yrs. | 1996 | 1995 | 1994 | 1993 | 1992 | 1991 | 1990 | 1989 | 1988 | 1987 |
| Prices - High | 64³/₈ | 24³/₄ | 11⁷/₈ | 12¹/₂ | 12 | 6 | 3¹/₈ | 1¹³/₁₆ | 2¹/₈ | NA |
| - Low | 11¹/₂ | 9⁷/₈ | 4³/₄ | 3¹/₂ | 3³/₄ | 2⁵/₈ | ¹³/₁₆ | ⁷/₈ | 1⁵/₁₆ | NA |
| P/E Ratio - High | 23 | 18 | 14 | NM | 19 | 17 | 14 | 39 | 16 | NA |
| - Low | 4 | 7 | 6 | NM | 6 | 8 | 3 | 19 | 10 | NA |

### Income Statement Analysis (Million $)

| | 1997 | 1996 | 1995 | 1994 | 1993 | 1992 | 1991 | 1990 | 1989 | 1988 |
|---|---|---|---|---|---|---|---|---|---|---|
| Revs. | 7,759 | 5,296 | 3,475 | 2,873 | 2,014 | 890 | 546 | 389 | 258 | 159 |
| Oper. Inc. | 761 | 415 | 282 | 83.0 | 159 | 82.5 | 53.3 | 18.4 | 24.9 | 18.2 |
| Depr. | 47.0 | 38.0 | 33.1 | 30.6 | 19.6 | 13.8 | 7.9 | 5.4 | 2.1 | 1.0 |
| Int. Exp. | 7.0 | 15.0 | 12.2 | 8.4 | 7.9 | 1.8 | 1.5 | 3.4 | 1.3 | 0.9 |
| Pretax Inc. | 747 | 383 | 213 | -39.0 | 143 | 73.4 | 43.6 | 8.3 | 21.2 | 15.1 |
| Eff. Tax Rate | 29% | 29% | 30% | NM | 29% | 31% | 38% | 38% | 32% | 38% |
| Net Inc. | 531 | 272 | 149 | -36.0 | 102 | 50.9 | 27.2 | 5.1 | 14.4 | 9.4 |

### Balance Sheet & Other Fin. Data (Million $)

| | 1997 | 1996 | 1995 | 1994 | 1993 | 1992 | 1991 | 1990 | 1989 | 1988 |
|---|---|---|---|---|---|---|---|---|---|---|
| Cash | 1,352 | 646 | 527 | 337 | 95.0 | 155 | 37.0 | Nil | 36.0 | 85.0 |
| Curr. Assets | 2,747 | 1,957 | 1,470 | 1,048 | 853 | 512 | 236 | 143 | 149 | 52.0 |
| Total Assets | 2,993 | 2,148 | 1,594 | 1,140 | 927 | 560 | 264 | 172 | 167 | 56.0 |
| Curr. Liab. | 1,658 | 939 | 751 | 538 | 494 | 230 | 141 | 85.0 | 86.0 | 25.0 |
| LT Debt | 18.0 | 113 | 113 | 100 | 48.4 | 41.5 | 4.2 | 6.0 | 5.5 | 1.0 |
| Common Eqty. | 806 | 967 | 527 | 344 | 369 | 274 | 112 | 80.0 | 75.0 | 10.0 |
| Total Cap. | 824 | 1,080 | 765 | 571 | 418 | 316 | 116 | 86.0 | 81.0 | 31.0 |
| Cap. Exp. | 114 | 101 | 63.7 | 48.1 | 47.3 | 32.6 | 9.5 | 13.6 | 6.6 | 2.2 |
| Cash Flow | 578 | 310 | 174 | -9.0 | 121 | 64.7 | 35.1 | 10.6 | 16.6 | 10.3 |
| Curr. Ratio | 1.7 | 2.1 | 2.0 | 1.9 | 1.7 | 2.2 | 1.7 | 1.7 | 1.7 | 2.1 |
| % LT Debt of Cap. | 2.2 | 10.5 | 14.8 | 17.5 | 11.6 | 13.1 | 3.6 | 7.0 | 6.8 | 3.3 |
| % Net Inc.of Revs. | 6.8 | 5.1 | 4.3 | NM | 5.0 | 5.7 | 5.0 | 1.3 | 5.6 | 5.9 |
| % Ret. on Assets | 20.7 | 14.5 | 10.9 | NM | 13.5 | 11.5 | 12.3 | 3.0 | 11.0 | 23.4 |
| % Ret. on Equity | 59.9 | 36.3 | 32.2 | NM | 31.2 | 24.7 | 28.1 | 6.6 | 32.4 | 57.4 |

Data as orig. reptd.; bef. results of disc. opers. and/or spec. items. Per share data adj. for stk. divs. as of ex-div. date. E-Estimated. NA-Not Available. NM-Not Meaningful. NR-Not Ranked.

**Office**—2214 W. Braker Lane, Suite D, Austin, TX 78758-4053. **Tel**—(512) 338-4400. **Website**—http://www.dell.com **Chrmn & CEO**—M. S. Dell. **Vice-Chrmn**—M. L. Topher. **SVP-Fin & CFO**—T. J. Meredith. **VP-Treas**—A. Smith. **Secy**—T. B. Green. **Dirs**—D. J. Carty, M. S. Dell, P. O. Hirschbiel, Jr., M. H. Jordan, G. Kozmetsky, T. W. Luce III, K. Luft, C. B. Malone, M. A. Miles. **Transfer Agent & Registrar**—American Stock Transfer & Trust Co., NYC. **Incorporated**—in Delaware in 1987. **Empl**— 10,350. **S&P Analyst:** Megan Graham Hackett

STANDARD
&POOR'S
STOCK REPORTS

# Diamond Offshore Drilling

**751G**

NYSE Symbol **DO**

**17-MAY-97**

**Industry:**
Oil & Gas (Drilling & Equipment)

**Summary:** This company owns one of the world's largest fleets of offshore drilling rigs, providing specialized drilling services to the energy industry.

**S&P Opinion: Buy (★★★★★)**

Recent Price • 69
52 Wk Range • 73¼-46⅝
Yield • Nil
12-Mo. P/E • 24.9

**Quantitative Evaluations**

Outlook
(1 Lowest—5 Highest)
• **NA**

Fair Value
• **NA**

Risk
• **Average**

Earn./Div. Rank
• **NR**

Technical Eval.
• **Bullish** since 5/97

Rel. Strength Rank
(1 Lowest—99 Highest)
• **73**

Insider Activity
• **NA**

**Earnings vs. Previous Year**
▲=Up ▼=Down ▶=No Change

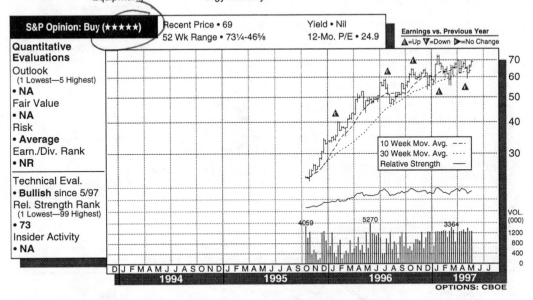

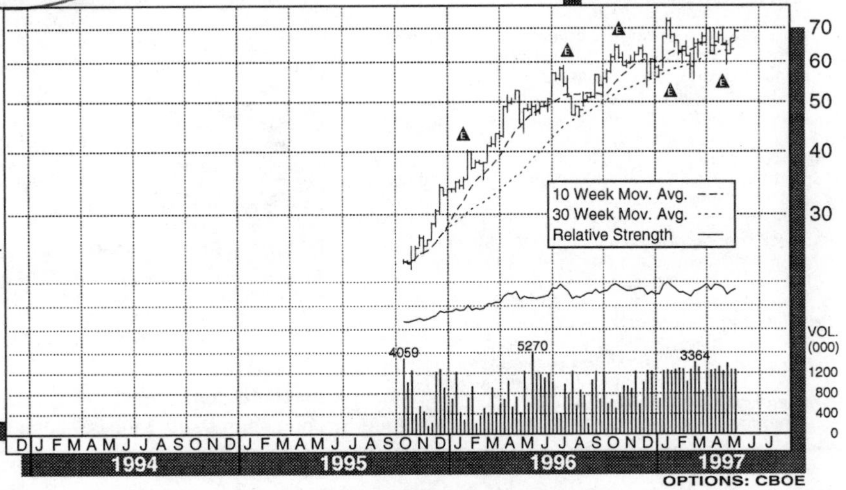
70
60
50
40
30
10 Week Mov. Avg.
30 Week Mov. Avg.
Relative Strength
VOL. (000)
1200
800
400
0
4059
5270
3364
D J F M A M J J A S O N D J F M A M J J A S O N D J F M A M J J A S O N D J F M A M J J
1994
1995
1996
1997

OPTIONS: CBOE

## Overview - 16-APR-97

With a fleet of 30 semisubmersible drilling rigs, 18 of which are located in the Gulf of Mexico, the company owns 23% of the world's semisubmersible rig fleet and 55% of all semisubmersibles currently in the Gulf of Mexico. Utilization rates for semisubmersible rigs are approaching 100% in some regions, and DO continues to benefit from surging dayrates for these rigs. Recent technological advances have made drilling for oil and gas in deepwater areas more economical, and the resulting increase in deepwater drilling activity has placed a premium on rigs capable of drilling in water depths in excess of 2,500 ft. After completion of some upgrade work in 1997, the company will have 12 rigs capable of working in these depths. A recently announced $300 million convertible note offering will allow DO to pursue further rig upgrades or other strategic initiatives.

## Valuation - 16-APR-97

The shares, along with those of other offshore drilling contractors, have pulled back recently on profit taking and an easing of natural gas prices. However, the correction appears overdone, and we expect shares of contract drillers to rebound and substantially outperform the market over the remainder of 1997. With the world's largest semisubmersible rig fleet, DO is leveraged to deepwater drilling activity, making it less vulnerable to volatile natural gas prices. EPS are seen at $3.85 for 1997, but considering recent contract commitments, significant upside earnings potential exists. We recommend the shares for purchase by aggressive investors capable of withstanding the volatility normally associated with the shares of oil and gas drillers.

## Key Stock Statistics

| | | | |
|---|---|---|---|
| S&P EPS Est. 1997 | 3.85 | Tang. Bk. Value/Share | 15.58 |
| P/E on S&P Est. 1997 | 17.9 | Beta | NA |
| S&P EPS Est. 1998 | 5.35 | Shareholders | 100 |
| Dividend Rate/Share | Nil | Market cap. (B) | $ 4.7 |
| Shs. outstg. (M) | 68.4 | Inst. holdings | 42% |
| Avg. daily vol. (M) | 0.408 | | |

Value of $10,000 invested 5 years ago: NA

## Fiscal Year Ending Dec. 31

| | 1998 | 1997 | 1996 | 1995 | 1994 | 1993 |
|---|---|---|---|---|---|---|
| **Revenues (Million $)** | | | | | | |
| 1Q | — | 204.7 | 106.9 | 70.76 | -- | — |
| 2Q | — | — | 147.0 | 76.11 | 148.8 | — |
| 3Q | — | — | 170.6 | 91.70 | 78.90 | — |
| 4Q | — | — | 187.0 | 98.00 | 80.20 | — |
| Yr. | — | — | 611.4 | 336.6 | 307.9 | — |
| **Earnings Per Share ($)** | | | | | | |
| 1Q | — | 0.79 | 0.37 | -- | -- | — |
| 2Q | — | — | 0.53 | -0.07 | -0.16 | — |
| 3Q | — | — | 0.56 | 0.14 | -0.06 | — |
| 4Q | — | — | 0.82 | 0.13 | -0.09 | — |
| Yr. | E5.35 | E3.85 | 2.35 | 0.20 | -0.31 | — |

**Next earnings report expected: mid July**

## Dividend Data

No cash dividends have been paid. The company intends to retain earnings for the development of its business and does not expect to pay cash dividends in the foreseeable future.

This report is for information purposes and should not be considered a solicitation to buy or sell any security. Neither S&P nor any other party guarantee its accuracy or make warranties regarding results from its usage. Redistribution is prohibited without written permission. Copyright © 1997

*A Division of The McGraw-Hill Companies*

STANDARD
&POOR'S
STOCK REPORTS

# Diamond Offshore Drilling, Inc.

**751G**

**17-MAY-97**

## Business Summary - 16-APR-97

Diamond Offshore Drilling is engaged principally in the contract drilling of offshore oil and gas wells. Following the April 1996 acquisition of Arethusa (Off-Shore) Ltd., its fleet of mobile offshore drilling rigs (one of the largest in the world) consisted of 30 semisubmersible rigs, 15 jack-up rigs and one drillship, deployed in the Gulf of Mexico, the North Sea, the Black Sea, South America, Australia and Southeast Asia.

A mobile offshore drilling rig consists of a drilling package mounted on a hull, which is maintained at a specific location during drilling operations. The drilling package typically consists of a power plant, hoisting equipment, a rotary system, tubulars and systems for mud treating and pumping, well control and the handling of bulk materials. The drilling rig also includes living quarters, heliport, cranes and tensioning and compensation systems.

Semisubmersible rigs consist of an upper working and living deck resting on vertical columns connected to lower hull members. Such rigs operate in a semisubmerged position, remaining afloat, off bottom, in a position in which the lower hull is 55 ft. to 90 ft. below the water line, and the upper deck protrudes well above the surface. The rig is typically anchored in position, and remains stable for drilling in the semisubmerged floating position, in part as a result of its wave transparency characteristics at the water line. Three of the company's rigs are fourth-generation semisubmersibles, which are larger and capable of working in harsh environments and operating in water depths of up to 5,000 ft.

Jack-up rigs are mobile, self-elevating drilling platforms equipped with legs that are lowered to the ocean floor until a foundation is established to support the drilling platform. The rig hull includes the drilling rig, jacking system, crew quarters, loading and unloading facilities, storage areas for bulk and liquid materials, heliport and other related equipment. Jack-ups are used extensively for drilling in water depths from 20 ft. to 350 ft.

Drillships (typically self-propelled) are positioned over a drillsite through the use of either an anchoring system or a computer-controlled thruster system similar to those used on semisubmersible rigs. Drillships normally require water depth of at least 200 ft. in order to operate.

In the fourth quarter of 1996, DO sold its land rigs and associated equipment to a subsidiary of DI Industries (ASE; DRL) for approximately $26 million, recording an after-tax gain of about $14 million ($0.20 a share).

## Important Developments

**Apr. '97**—DO agreed to purchase a semisubmersible accommodation vessel for $81 million. The company plans to convert the rig into a drilling unit, at a cost of $160 million to $175 million, beginning no later than March 1998.

## Capitalization

**Long Term Debt:** $400,000,000 (3/97).

### Per Share Data ($)

| (Year Ended Dec. 31) | 1996 | 1995 | 1994 | 1993 | 1992 | 1991 | 1990 | 1989 | 1988 | 1987 |
|---|---|---|---|---|---|---|---|---|---|---|
| Tangible Bk. Val. | 15.58 | 9.86 | 9.61 | NA | NA | NA | NA | NA | NA | NA |
| Cash Flow | 3.57 | 0.92 | NA | NA | NA | NA | NA | NA | NA | NA |
| Earnings | 2.35 | 0.20 | -0.31 | NA | NA | NA | NA | NA | NA | NA |
| Dividends | Nil | Nil | NA | NA | NA | NA | NA | NA | NA | NA |
| Payout Ratio | Nil | Nil | NA | NA | NA | NA | NA | NA | NA | NA |
| Prices - High | 65 | 34½ | NA | NA | NA | NA | NA | NA | NA | NA |
| - Low | 33¼ | 23⅜ | NA | NA | NA | NA | NA | NA | NA | NA |
| P/E Ratio - High | 28 | NM | NA | NA | NA | NA | NA | NA | NA | NA |
| - Low | 14 | NM | NA | NA | NA | NA | NA | NA | NA | NA |

### Income Statement Analysis (Million $)

| | 1996 | 1995 | 1994 | 1993 | 1992 | 1991 | 1990 | 1989 | 1988 | 1987 |
|---|---|---|---|---|---|---|---|---|---|---|
| Revs. | 611 | 337 | 308 | 288 | 215 | 64.0 | 41.0 | NA | NA | NA |
| Oper. Inc. | 254 | 63.2 | 39.0 | 48.1 | 0.3 | -1.3 | -8.4 | NA | NA | NA |
| Depr. | 75.8 | 52.9 | 55.4 | 46.8 | 49.7 | 14.5 | 10.1 | NA | NA | NA |
| Int. Exp. | 2.3 | 27.1 | 31.3 | 25.9 | 28.6 | 7.3 | 0.9 | NA | NA | NA |
| Pretax Inc. | 213 | -13.8 | -46.4 | -21.7 | -78.0 | -22.6 | -19.1 | NA | NA | NA |
| Eff. Tax Rate | 31% | NM | NM | NM | NM | NM | NM | NA | NA | NA |
| Net Inc. | 146 | -7.0 | -34.8 | -16.6 | -53.4 | -26.6 | -21.6 | NA | NA | NA |

### Balance Sheet & Other Fin. Data (Million $)

| | 1996 | 1995 | 1994 | 1993 | 1992 | 1991 | 1990 | 1989 | 1988 | 1987 |
|---|---|---|---|---|---|---|---|---|---|---|
| Cash | 28.2 | 15.3 | NA | NA | NA | NA | NA | NA | NA | NA |
| Curr. Assets | 243 | 116 | 105 | NA | NA | NA | NA | NA | NA | NA |
| Total Assets | 1,575 | 618 | 588 | NA | NA | NA | NA | NA | NA | NA |
| Curr. Liab. | 12.8 | 52.3 | 42.3 | NA | NA | NA | NA | NA | NA | NA |
| LT Debt | 63.0 | Nil | Nil | NA | NA | NA | NA | NA | NA | NA |
| Common Eqty. | 1,195 | 493 | 481 | NA | NA | NA | NA | NA | NA | NA |
| Total Cap. | 1,434 | 566 | 481 | NA | NA | NA | NA | NA | NA | NA |
| Cap. Exp. | 267 | 66.6 | 21.1 | 14.3 | 16.2 | NA | NA | NA | NA | NA |
| Cash Flow | 222 | 45.8 | 20.6 | 30.2 | -3.7 | -12.1 | -11.5 | NA | NA | NA |
| Curr. Ratio | 1.9 | 2.2 | 2.5 | NA | NA | NA | NA | NA | NA | NA |
| % LT Debt of Cap. | 4.4 | Nil | Nil | NA | NA | NA | NA | NA | NA | NA |
| % Net Inc.of Revs. | 23.9 | NM | NM | NM | NM | NM | NM | NA | NA | NA |
| % Ret. on Assets | 13.4 | NM | NA | NA | NA | NA | NA | NA | NA | NA |
| % Ret. on Equity | 17.4 | NM | NA | NA | NA | NA | NA | NA | NA | NA |

Data as orig. reptd.; bef. results of disc. opers. and/or spec. items. Per share data adj. for stk. divs. as of ex-div. date. E-Estimated. NA-Not Available. NM-Not Meaningful. NR-Not Ranked.

**Office**—15415 Katy Freeway, Houston, TX 77094. **Tel**—(281) 492-5300. **Pres & CEO**—R. E. Rose. **SVP & CFO**—L. R. Dickerson. **VP & Secy**—R. L. Lionberger. **Dirs**—H. C. Hofmann, A. Rebell, R. E. Rose, J. S. Tisch, R. S. Troubh. **Incorporated**—in Delaware in 1989. **Empl**— 3,770. **S&P Analyst:** Norman Rosenberg

# Dollar General

# 763M

NYSE Symbol **DG**

In S&P MidCap 400

**19-MAY-97**

**Industry:** Retail (Discounters)

**Summary:** This discount retailer sells inexpensive soft and hard goods to low-, middle- and fixed-income families through more than 2,860 stores in small communities in 24 states.

**S&P Opinion: Accumulate (★★★★)**

| | |
|---|---|
| Recent Price • 30⅜ | Yield • 0.7% |
| 52 Wk Range • 35⅜-19 | 12-Mo. P/E • 28.4 |

**Quantitative Evaluations**

Outlook
(1 Lowest—5 Highest)
• **4**

Fair Value
• **36⅜**

Risk
• **Average**

Earn./Div. Rank
• **A+**

Technical Eval.
• **Bullish** since 3/96

Rel. Strength Rank
(1 Lowest—99 Highest)
• **45**

Insider Activity
• **Neutral**

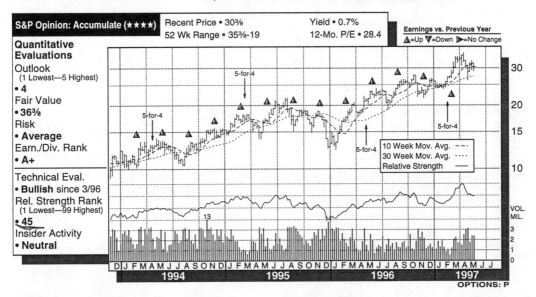

Earnings vs. Previous Year
▲=Up ▼=Down ▶=No Change

10 Week Mov. Avg. - - -
30 Week Mov. Avg. ······
Relative Strength ——

OPTIONS: P

## Overview - 19-MAY-97

Total sales in FY 98 (Jan.) should rise about 24%, reflecting 350 new units, with Texas the largest growth area. Same-store sales should advance 6%. Gross margins should narrow, reflecting a shift in the sales mix toward lower-margin hardlines. However, an improved distribution system should boost the company's in-stock position. SG&A expenses should decline as a percentage of sales, aided by tight control of costs, offset somewhat by increased operating expenses from a larger store base. Interest expense should remain flat. Favorable consumer response to better merchandise selection and to DG's commitment to everyday low pricing, accelerated new store development, aggressive overhead cost controls, and increased use of cost-effective information technology should fuel continued 20%-plus annual sales and earnings growth for the foreseeable future. In spite of an aggressive capital expenditure program, the company has excess cash flow, and has just completed a two million share repurchase program.

## Valuation - 19-MAY-97

The shares have run up in price thus far in 1997, buoyed by strong same-store sales gains. We anticipate that the low-priced, bargain sector of retailing will continue to outpace the moderate-priced group, with less retail square footage devoted to this segment of retailing. We are projecting a 25% increase in EPS for FY 98, slowing to 20% in FY 99. The more moderate gain projected for EPS reflects the larger store base and more conservative assumptions of 5% gains in same-store sales. The company's strong balance sheet is a plus. The shares have appeal for superior long-term appreciation.

## Key Stock Statistics

| | | | |
|---|---|---|---|
| S&P EPS Est. 1998 | 1.30 | Tang. Bk. Value/Share | 5.42 |
| P/E on S&P Est. 1998 | 23.4 | Beta | 0.40 |
| S&P EPS Est. 1999 | 1.55 | Shareholders | 3,500 |
| Dividend Rate/Share | 0.20 | Market cap. (B) | $ 3.3 |
| Shs. outstg. (M) | 108.6 | Inst. holdings | 51% |
| Avg. daily vol. (M) | 0.520 | | |

Value of $10,000 invested 5 years ago: $ 62,299

## Fiscal Year Ending Jan. 31

| | 1998 | 1997 | 1996 | 1995 | 1994 | 1993 |
|---|---|---|---|---|---|---|
| **Revenues (Million $)** | | | | | | |
| 1Q | 520.0 | 455.9 | 343.4 | 287.0 | 221.8 | 189.0 |
| 2Q | — | 494.4 | 408.2 | 317.3 | 255.6 | 217.0 |
| 3Q | — | 509.0 | 437.2 | 359.4 | 272.6 | 224.0 |
| 4Q | — | 675.2 | 575.4 | 484.8 | 383.1 | 292.0 |
| Yr. | — | 2,134 | 1,764 | 1,449 | 1,133 | 921.0 |
| **Earnings Per Share ($)** | | | | | | |
| 1Q | 0.17 | 0.14 | 0.10 | 0.09 | 0.06 | 0.04 |
| 2Q | E0.25 | 0.20 | 0.16 | 0.13 | 0.09 | 0.07 |
| 3Q | E0.30 | 0.24 | 0.18 | 0.16 | 0.10 | 0.08 |
| 4Q | E0.57 | 0.47 | 0.35 | 0.30 | 0.21 | 0.16 |
| Yr. | E1.30 | 1.04 | 0.80 | 0.69 | 0.46 | 0.34 |

**Next earnings report expected: mid May**

**Dividend Data** (Dividends have been paid since 1975.)

| Amount ($) | Date Decl. | Ex-Div. Date | Stock of Record | Payment Date |
|---|---|---|---|---|
| 0.050 | Nov. 18 | Nov. 27 | Dec. 02 | Dec. 16 '96 |
| 5-for-4 | Jan. 13 | Feb. 13 | Feb. 03 | Feb. 12 '97 |
| 0.050 | Jan. 13 | Feb. 19 | Feb. 21 | Mar. 10 '97 |
| 0.050 | Mar. 24 | May. 16 | May. 20 | Jun. 10 '97 |

This report is for information purposes and should not be considered a solicitation to buy or sell any security. Neither S&P nor any other party guarantee its accuracy or make warranties regarding results from its usage. Redistribution is prohibited without written permission. Copyright © 1997

A Division of The McGraw-Hill Companies

## Business Summary - 19-MAY-97

Dollar General Corporation operates a chain of more than 2,734 small, self-service discount stores. The stores feature, at greatly reduced prices, a focused assortment of both brand name and irregular soft and hard goods.

Contributions to sales in recent fiscal years (Jan.) were:

|  | FY 97 | FY 96 |
|---|---|---|
| Soft goods (mainly apparel) | 25% | 30% |
| Hard goods | 75% | 70% |

The company's strategy is to provide a focused assortment of basic quality merchandise at everyday low prices to low-, middle- and fixed-income families. The majority of the products in Dollar General stores are priced at $1 with the most expensive item generally priced at $35. Nearly 50% of the products are $1 or less. In recent years, the company has shifted its merchandise mix focus to hard goods.

Irregular, overrun and closeout merchandise accounted for 5% of merchandise sales in FY 96 (Jan.). About 20% of softline merchandise consisted of brand name merchandise and 40% of hard line goods.

DG ended FY 97 with a total of 2,734 stores in operation. The stores were located in 24 states, with the greatest concentrations in Texas (356), Tennessee (192 stores), Kentucky (166), Illinois (161), West Virginia (140), Texas (277), Florida (175), Kentucky (166), Missouri (161), Indiana (143), Ohio (141) and Virginia (140). The typical store is relatively small (6,400 sq. ft. average size), and is located in a community of fewer than 25,000 people. About 65% of stores are located in strip shopping centers, with the remainder in freestanding and downtown buildings.

## Important Developments

May. '97—Same-store sales in the FY 97 first quarter rose 3.8%, year to year. DG said sales gains would slow in the first half of FY 98, reflecting reduced advertising and store remerchandising, Expenses should remain well controlled, and sales should rebound in the second half. The sales mix continued to shift toward hardlines, which accounted for 80.0%, versus 72.8% in the FY 96 period. Gross margins widened to 27.28%, from 27.06%. Operating expenses declined to 21.22% of sales, from 21.49%. Net income rose 28%, to $19.3 million. The company opened 360 new stores and closed 42 units in FY 97. Capital expenditures totaled $84.4 million, up 40% from the level in FY 96. DG completed the repurchase of two million common shares by the end of the third quarter.

## Capitalization

**Long Term Obligs.:** $1,807,000 (5/2/97).
**Series A Conv. Jr. Pfd. Stk.:** 1,715,742 shs. (no par). 6.25 votes ea.; held by C. Turner Jr.

### Per Share Data ($)

| (Year Ended Jan. 31) | 1997 | 1996 | 1995 | 1994 | 1993 | 1992 | 1991 | 1990 | 1989 | 1988 |
|---|---|---|---|---|---|---|---|---|---|---|
| Tangible Bk. Val. | 5.42 | 4.65 | 3.66 | 2.33 | 1.90 | 1.55 | 1.37 | 1.26 | 1.17 | 1.13 |
| Cash Flow | 1.62 | 1.26 | 0.84 | 0.57 | 0.42 | 0.28 | 0.22 | 0.19 | 0.17 | 0.14 |
| Earnings | 1.04 | 0.80 | 0.68 | 0.46 | 0.34 | 0.21 | 0.15 | 0.13 | 0.10 | 0.07 |
| Dividends | 0.19 | 0.15 | 0.10 | 0.07 | 0.05 | 0.04 | 0.04 | 0.04 | 0.04 | 0.04 |
| Payout Ratio | 18% | 19% | 14% | 14% | 14% | 19% | 25% | 30% | 36% | 57% |
| Cal. Yrs. | 1996 | 1995 | 1994 | 1993 | 1992 | 1991 | 1990 | 1989 | 1988 | 1987 |
| Prices - High | 27⅞ | 21¾ | 15⅝ | 13⅞ | 8⅛ | 5⅛ | 2³⁄₁₆ | 2⁷⁄₁₆ | 2⅛ | 2¾ |
|     - Low | 12⅜ | 12½ | 10 | 6⅞ | 4½ | 1⁷⁄₁₆ | 1⅜ | 1⅝ | 1¹⁄₁₆ | ⅞ |
| P/E Ratio - High | 27 | 27 | 23 | 31 | 24 | 24 | 14 | 19 | 20 | 41 |
|     - Low | 12 | 16 | 15 | 15 | 13 | 7 | 9 | 13 | 10 | 14 |

### Income Statement Analysis (Million $)

| | 1997 | 1996 | 1995 | 1994 | 1993 | 1992 | 1991 | 1990 | 1989 | 1988 |
|---|---|---|---|---|---|---|---|---|---|---|
| Revs. | 2,134 | 1,765 | 1,449 | 1,133 | 921 | 754 | 653 | 615 | 613 | 588 |
| Oper. Inc. | 221 | 174 | 138 | 91.9 | 69.1 | 44.5 | 34.7 | 32.3 | 28.4 | 25.2 |
| Depr. | 31.0 | 25.2 | 17.3 | 11.7 | 8.2 | 6.7 | 6.7 | 6.0 | 6.0 | 6.9 |
| Int. Exp. | 4.7 | 7.4 | 2.8 | 2.2 | 2.7 | 3.1 | 4.9 | 5.8 | 6.3 | 6.8 |
| Pretax Inc. | 185 | 142 | 118 | 75.0 | 58.2 | 34.7 | 23.1 | 20.3 | 16.2 | 11.6 |
| Eff. Tax Rate | 38% | 38% | 38% | 38% | 39% | 38% | 37% | 39% | 38% | 44% |
| Net Inc. | 115 | 87.8 | 73.6 | 48.6 | 35.6 | 21.5 | 14.6 | 12.4 | 10.0 | 6.5 |

### Balance Sheet & Other Fin. Data (Million $)

| | 1997 | 1996 | 1995 | 1994 | 1993 | 1992 | 1991 | 1990 | 1989 | 1988 |
|---|---|---|---|---|---|---|---|---|---|---|
| Cash | 6.6 | 4.3 | 33.0 | 35.4 | 25.0 | 7.9 | 3.9 | 6.5 | 5.7 | 7.3 |
| Curr. Assets | 505 | 516 | 410 | 315 | 256 | 192 | 168 | 155 | 183 | 190 |
| Total Assets | 718 | 680 | 541 | 397 | 316 | 237 | 208 | 194 | 210 | 225 |
| Curr. Liab. | 224 | 254 | 209 | 148 | 117 | 62.4 | 55.1 | 45.1 | 52.4 | 61.4 |
| LT Debt | 2.6 | 3.3 | 4.8 | 5.7 | 7.0 | 21.2 | 19.1 | 26.8 | 45.6 | 48.9 |
| Common Eqty. | 485 | 419 | 323 | 241 | 190 | 151 | 132 | 121 | 112 | 109 |
| Total Cap. | 494 | 426 | 332 | 249 | 199 | 175 | 153 | 149 | 158 | 163 |
| Cap. Exp. | 84.4 | 60.5 | 65.8 | 35.0 | 24.7 | 12.8 | 8.9 | 17.0 | 4.5 | 4.8 |
| Cash Flow | 144 | 111 | 90.1 | 60.3 | 43.8 | 28.2 | 21.3 | 18.4 | 16.0 | 13.4 |
| Curr. Ratio | 2.2 | 2.0 | 2.0 | 2.1 | 2.2 | 3.1 | 3.1 | 3.4 | 3.5 | 3.1 |
| % LT Debt of Cap. | 0.5 | 0.8 | 1.4 | 2.3 | 3.5 | 12.1 | 12.5 | 18.0 | 28.9 | 29.9 |
| % Net Inc.of Revs. | 5.4 | 5.0 | 5.1 | 4.3 | 3.9 | 2.9 | 2.2 | 2.0 | 1.6 | 1.1 |
| % Ret. on Assets | 16.5 | 14.4 | 16.7 | 13.4 | 12.7 | 9.6 | 7.3 | 6.1 | 4.6 | 2.9 |
| % Ret. on Equity | 24.9 | 23.1 | 27.5 | 22.3 | 20.6 | 15.1 | 11.6 | 10.6 | 9.1 | 6.0 |

Data as orig. reptd.; bef. results of disc. opers. and/or spec. items. Per share data adj. for stk. divs. as of ex-div. date. Bk. val. figs. in Per Share Data tbl. incl. intangibles. E-Estimated. NA-Not Available. NM-Not Meaningful. NR-Not Ranked.

**Office**—104 Woodmont Blvd., Suite 500, Nashville, TN 37205. **Tel**—(615) 783-2000. **Chrmn & CEO**—C. Turner, Jr. **Pres**—B. W. Krysiak. **Investor Contact**—Kiley Fleming. **Dirs**—J. L. Clayton, R. D. Dickson, J. B. Holland, B. M. Knuckes, W. N. Rasmussen, C. Turner, C. Turner Jr., D. M. Wilds, W. S. Wire II. **Transfer Agent**—Registrar & Transfer Co. Cranford, NJ. **Incorporated**—in Kentucky in 1955. **Empl**— 25,400. **S&P Analyst:** Karen J. Sack, CFA

# STANDARD &POOR'S
### STOCK REPORTS

# EMC Corp.

# 789D
NYSE Symbol **EMC**

**In S&P 500**

**17-MAY-97**

**Industry:**
Computers (Peripher-als)

**Summary:** This company makes high performance, high reliability storage systems for the mainframe, open systems and networking computer markets as well as for the midrange storage market.

| | |
|---|---|
| **S&P Opinion: Buy (★★★★)** | |

| Recent Price • 39⅜ | Yield • Nil |
|---|---|
| 52 Wk Range • 41¾-16½ | 12-Mo. P/E • 23.7 |

**Quantitative Evaluations**

**Outlook**
(1 Lowest—5 Highest)
• **5**

**Fair Value**
• **56¼**

**Risk**
• **Average**

**Earn./Div. Rank**
• **B**

**Technical Eval.**
• **Bearish** since 1/94

**Rel. Strength Rank**
(1 Lowest—99 Highest)
• **80**

**Insider Activity**
• **Neutral**

**Earnings vs. Previous Year**
▲=Up ▼=Down ▷=No Change

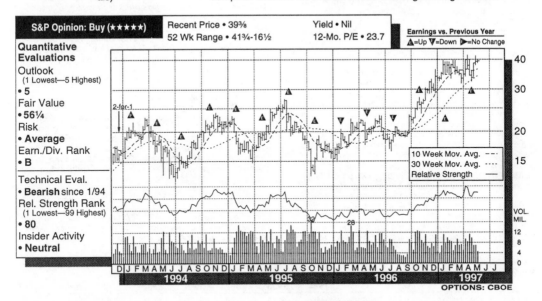

10 Week Mov. Avg. ---
30 Week Mov. Avg. ····
Relative Strength —

OPTIONS: CBOE

---

## Overview - 23-APR-97

Revenues are expected to advance over 20% in the final three quarters of 1997 and into 1998, reflecting particularly strong demand for the company's client/server-based storage subsystems for the open systems and networked computer markets, as well as ongoing demand for Symmetrix storage systems for the mainframe environment, where the company continues to gain market share. Revenues derived from the open systems market should overtake those derived from the mainframe market in the second quarter of 1997. Revenues from software products should add to growth. Contributions from alliances and relationships with major computer industry players should also aid results. Margins are expected to widen slightly on volume related efficiencies, more modest price erosion, a more favorable revenue mix and ongoing cost controls. Earnings should benefit from the higher revenues and wider margins.

## Valuation - 23-APR-97

The shares of this leading supplier of storage solutions have moved steadily higher over the past five months, aided by new products and signs of a better pricing environment. EMC's storage subsystems offer very attractive price/performance features. The company continues to gain share in the core mainframe storage market and has extended its product line to serve the open systems and networked computing markets, as well as the storage software segment. We view favorably the more modest pricing environment in EMC's markets, as well as the company's refreshed product line. We expect the shares to outperform the market over the next six to 12 months.

## Key Stock Statistics

| | | | |
|---|---|---|---|
| S&P EPS Est. 1997 | 1.95 | Tang. Bk. Value/Share | 6.73 |
| P/E on S&P Est. 1997 | 20.2 | Beta | 1.31 |
| S&P EPS Est. 1998 | 2.40 | Shareholders | 4,500 |
| Dividend Rate/Share | Nil | Market cap. (B) | $ 9.7 |
| Shs. outstg. (M) | 245.8 | Inst. holdings | 70% |
| Avg. daily vol. (M) | 1.376 | | |

Value of $10,000 invested 5 years ago: $ 188,399

### Fiscal Year Ending Dec. 31

| | 1998 | 1997 | 1996 | 1995 | 1994 | 1993 |
|---|---|---|---|---|---|---|
| **Revenues (Million $)** | | | | | | |
| 1Q | — | 618.4 | 521.5 | 448.1 | 267.1 | 138.8 |
| 2Q | — | — | 545.0 | 478.5 | 308.1 | 179.5 |
| 3Q | — | — | 550.8 | 475.5 | 371.6 | 215.8 |
| 4Q | — | — | 656.4 | 519.2 | 430.7 | 248.6 |
| Yr. | — | — | 2,274 | 1,921 | 1,377 | 782.6 |
| **Earnings Per Share ($)** | | | | | | |
| 1Q | — | 0.44 | 0.34 | 0.35 | 0.23 | 0.08 |
| 2Q | — | E0.47 | 0.36 | 0.38 | 0.26 | 0.14 |
| 3Q | — | E0.51 | 0.37 | 0.35 | 0.32 | 0.19 |
| 4Q | — | E0.53 | 0.50 | 0.26 | 0.36 | 0.23 |
| Yr. | E2.40 | E1.95 | 1.57 | 1.36 | 1.18 | 0.65 |

**Next earnings report expected: mid July**

### Dividend Data

No cash dividends have been paid.

---

This report is for information purposes and should not be considered a solicitation to buy or sell any security. Neither S&P nor any other party guarantee its accuracy or make warranties regarding results from its usage. Redistribution is prohibited without written permission. Copyright © 1997

*A Division of The McGraw-Hill Companies*

STANDARD
&POOR'S
STOCK REPORTS

# EMC Corporation

# 789D
## 17-MAY-97

## Business Summary - 23-APR-97

EMC Corp. designs, manufactures, markets and supports high performance storage products and provides related services for the mainframe, open systems and network computer markets. The company's principal products are based on Integrated Cached Disk Array (ICDA) technology, which combines high speed semiconductor cache memory with an array of industry standard disk drives. The company also offers software products that improve the management of specific EMC systems.

Products include the Symmetrix series of high-speed ICDA-based storage system for the mainframe computer markets. The Symmetrix 5000 product family features storage capacities of up to 3 terabytes, hardware and channel redundancy, full system battery backup, nondisruptive component upgrade and replacement, and remote diagnostic features. Product sales to the mainframe storage market represented 55%, 74% and 85% of 1996, 1995 and 1994 product revenues, respectively.

EMC's Symmetrix 3000 family of ICDA products serves the open systems storage market. Revenues from the open systems market represented about 33% and 11%, respectively, of total product revenues in 1996 and 1995.

Products for the networking market include the ES-CON Director, a high-speed fiber-optic-based network switch designed to connect computers and peripherals within data center environments. In both 1996 and 1995, product sales to the network market represented 8% of EMC's product revenue.

Other products include ICDA-based storage systems for IBM's AS/400 midrange computer market, a line of 8mm tape backup subsystems, and main memory upgrades for selected AS/400 CPU models. EMC also offers services and rental options. Other revenues accounted for 4%, 7% and 13% of product revenues in 1996, 1995 and 1994, respectively.

## Important Developments

**Apr. '97**—EMC said it expected revenue generated from its open systems products to overtake revenue generated by its products for the mainframe market, in the second quarter of 1997. The company recorded $758 million in open systems revenue for 1996, nearly quadruple its 1995 revenue from this market. The company also said its software business was on track to generate revenues of approximately $200 million in 1997.

## Capitalization

**Long Term Debt:** $191,234,000 (12/96), incl. $142,720,000 of conv. sub. notes and $48,514,000 of notes payable and capital lease obligs.

## Per Share Data ($)

| (Year Ended Dec. 31) | 1996 | 1995 | 1994 | 1993 | 1992 | 1991 | 1990 | 1989 | 1988 | 1987 |
|---|---|---|---|---|---|---|---|---|---|---|
| Tangible Bk. Val. | 6.65 | 4.96 | 3.57 | 2.24 | 0.99 | 0.79 | 0.74 | 0.69 | 0.81 | 0.88 |
| Cash Flow | 1.90 | 1.55 | 1.30 | 0.76 | 0.29 | 0.14 | 0.11 | -0.09 | -0.03 | 0.21 |
| Earnings | 1.57 | 1.36 | 1.18 | 0.65 | 0.18 | 0.08 | 0.06 | -0.13 | -0.06 | 0.20 |
| Dividends | Nil | Nil | Nil | Nil | Nil | Nil | Nil | Nil | Nil | Nil |
| Payout Ratio | Nil | Nil | Nil | Nil | Nil | Nil | Nil | Nil | Nil | Nil |
| Prices - High | 36³/₈ | 27³/₈ | 24 | 19¹/₂ | 6¹/₈ | 2³/₁₆ | 1⁵/₈ | 1 | 3¹/₈ | 4⁷/₈ |
| - Low | 15¹/₈ | 13 | 12¹/₂ | 5¹/₈ | 1¹³/₁₆ | ¹³/₁₆ | ⁹/₁₆ | ⁷/₁₆ | ⁵/₈ | 1¹¹/₁₆ |
| P/E Ratio - High | 23 | 20 | 20 | 30 | 34 | 26 | 27 | NM | NM | 24 |
| - Low | 10 | 10 | 11 | 8 | 11 | 10 | 9 | NM | NM | 8 |

## Income Statement Analysis (Million $)

| | 1996 | 1995 | 1994 | 1993 | 1992 | 1991 | 1990 | 1989 | 1988 | 1987 |
|---|---|---|---|---|---|---|---|---|---|---|
| Revs. | 2,274 | 1,878 | 1,377 | 783 | 349 | 232 | 171 | 132 | 123 | 127 |
| Oper. Inc. | 583 | 489 | 383 | 202 | 63.9 | 30.1 | 16.7 | -15.9 | -7.2 | 38.9 |
| Depr. | 86.9 | 53.6 | 32.7 | 21.7 | 17.4 | 9.3 | 7.5 | 5.1 | 3.1 | 1.9 |
| Int. Exp. | 12.0 | 12.9 | 15.3 | 6.0 | 4.8 | 1.9 | 1.9 | 2.8 | 0.9 | 0.9 |
| Pretax Inc. | 519 | 451 | 355 | 180 | 42.3 | 20.1 | 12.5 | -26.1 | -7.6 | 41.8 |
| Eff. Tax Rate | 26% | 28% | 30% | 29% | 32% | 35% | 29% | NM | NM | 32% |
| Net Inc. | 386 | 327 | 251 | 127 | 28.7 | 13.0 | 8.9 | -18.6 | -7.8 | 28.2 |

## Balance Sheet & Other Fin. Data (Million $)

| | 1996 | 1995 | 1994 | 1993 | 1992 | 1991 | 1990 | 1989 | 1988 | 1987 |
|---|---|---|---|---|---|---|---|---|---|---|
| Cash | 727 | 380 | 241 | 345 | 55.1 | 16.8 | 35.5 | 17.8 | 10.1 | 52.5 |
| Curr. Assets | 1,754 | 1,319 | 902 | 650 | 217 | 112 | 104 | 88.0 | 111 | 132 |
| Total Assets | 2,294 | 1,746 | 1,318 | 830 | 321 | 190 | 157 | 137 | 153 | 158 |
| Curr. Liab. | 418 | 359 | 301 | 133 | 76.3 | 44.1 | 28.2 | 14.0 | 25.9 | 22.1 |
| LT Debt | 191 | 246 | 286 | 274 | 75.7 | 15.7 | 15.8 | 15.4 | 6.3 | 6.5 |
| Common Eqty. | 1,637 | 1,140 | 728 | 419 | 158 | 126 | 108 | 98.0 | 115 | 123 |
| Total Cap. | 1,874 | 1,386 | 1,014 | 693 | 239 | 146 | 128 | 117 | 127 | 135 |
| Cap. Exp. | 126 | 92.0 | 109 | 51.3 | 28.5 | 19.6 | 16.2 | 9.0 | 15.3 | 6.2 |
| Cash Flow | 473 | 380 | 283 | 149 | 46.1 | 22.3 | 16.3 | -13.5 | -4.7 | 30.1 |
| Curr. Ratio | 4.2 | 3.7 | 3.0 | 4.9 | 2.8 | 2.5 | 3.7 | 6.3 | 4.3 | 6.0 |
| % LT Debt of Cap. | 10.2 | 17.7 | 28.2 | 39.5 | 31.7 | 10.8 | 12.3 | 13.2 | 5.0 | 4.8 |
| % Net Inc.of Revs. | 17.0 | 17.4 | 18.2 | 16.2 | 8.2 | 5.6 | 5.2 | NM | NM | 22.2 |
| % Ret. on Assets | 19.1 | 21.3 | 22.8 | 20.9 | 11.2 | 7.4 | 6.0 | NM | NM | 22.8 |
| % Ret. on Equity | 27.8 | 35.0 | 42.7 | 41.6 | 20.0 | 11.0 | 8.5 | NM | NM | 28.8 |

Data as orig. reptd.; bef. results of disc. opers. and/or spec. items. Per share data adj. for stk. divs. as of ex-div. date. E-Estimated. NA-Not Available. NM-Not Meaningful. NR-Not Ranked.

**Office**—171 South St., Hopkinton, MA 01748-9103. **Tel**—(508) 435-1000.**Website**—http://www.emc.com **Chrmn**—R. J. Egan. **Pres & CEO**—M. C. Ruettgers. **VP & CFO**—C. G. Patteson. **Dirs**—M. J. Cronin, J. F. Cunningham, J. R. Egan, M. E. Egan, R. J. Egan, W. P. Fitzgerald, J. Oliveri, M. C. Ruettgers. **Transfer Agent & Registrar**—State Street Bank & Trust Co., Boston. **Incorporated**—in Massachusetts in 1979. **Empl**— 4,800. **S&P Analyst:** Peter C. Wood, CFA

# Electronics for Imaging 3791K

Nasdaq Symbol **EFII**

**17-MAY-97**

**Industry:** Computer (Software & Services)

**Summary:** This company designs and markets products that enable high-quality color printing in short production runs.

| S&P Opinion: Avoid (★★) | Recent Price • 43¼ | Yield • Nil |
| --- | --- | --- |
| | 52 Wk Range • 49⅜-22⅝ | 12-Mo. P/E • 34.1 |

**Quantitative Evaluations**

Outlook
(1 Lowest—5 Highest)
• **5**

Fair Value
• **64¼**

Risk
• **Average**

Earn./Div. Rank
• **NR**

Technical Eval.
• **Bullish** since 6/94

Rel. Strength Rank
(1 Lowest—99 Highest)
• **69**

Insider Activity
• **Neutral**

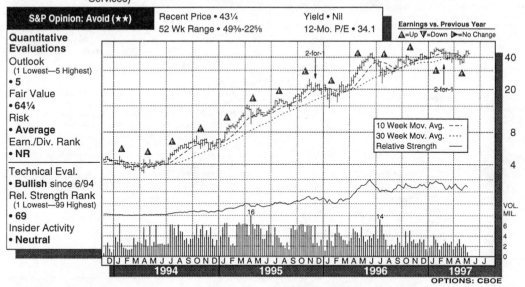

Earnings vs. Previous Year
▲=Up ▼=Down ▶=No Change

10 Week Mov. Avg. - - -
30 Week Mov. Avg. ·····
Relative Strength —

OPTIONS: CBOE

## Overview - 16-APR-97

EFII's Fiery Color Servers family integrates hardware and software technologies required to turn digital color copiers and desktop printers into high-quality color printers. First shipped in 1991, more than 50,000 Fiery Color Servers and Fiery Color Controllers have been sold and installed in leading corporations, advertising agencies, graphic design studios and print-for-pay businesses. The Fiery product lines have accounted for virtually all product revenues, which raises the concern that the company offers a limited product line. EFII has significant relationships with Canon, Digital Equipment, IBM, Eastman Kodak, Minolta, Oce, Ricoh and Xerox. Sales to Canon, Xerox, Ricoh and Minolta accounted for approximately 92% of 1996 revenues and about 84% of accounts receivable. On a positive note, the company has a pristine balance sheet, with no long term debt, healthy liquidity ratios, and high inventory turnover.

## Valuation - 16-APR-97

Revenue growth has exceeded 50% in recent periods, but fell to 43% in 1997's first quarter and we forecast revenues to grow 42% in 1997. The high revenue growth is being driven by the expanded use of color technology in short production runs and the lower percentage number is due to the increasing revenue base. Gross margins rose to 55% in the first quarter due to a more favorable mix and from lower component costs and should remain stable in the mid 50% level for the rest of the year. However, earnings will be somewhat restricted by marketing and R&D costs needed to keep EFII's technology on the cutting edge. Although earnings should grow 46% in 1997, with the shares trading at a lofty 23X our recently upwardly revised 1997 EPS estimate of $1.65, we view the stock as highly valued and therefore potentially vulnerable.

## Key Stock Statistics

| | | | |
| --- | --- | --- | --- |
| S&P EPS Est. 1997 | 1.65 | Tang. Bk. Value/Share | 4.84 |
| P/E on S&P Est. 1997 | 26.2 | Beta | NA |
| S&P EPS Est. 1998 | 1.95 | Shareholders | 300 |
| Dividend Rate/Share | Nil | Market cap. (B) | $ 2.2 |
| Shs. outstg. (M) | 51.8 | Inst. holdings | 86% |
| Avg. daily vol. (M) | 0.345 | | |

Value of $10,000 invested 5 years ago: NA

### Fiscal Year Ending Dec. 31

| | 1998 | 1997 | 1996 | 1995 | 1994 | 1993 |
| --- | --- | --- | --- | --- | --- | --- |
| **Revenues (Million $)** | | | | | | |
| 1Q | — | 91.01 | 63.65 | 40.36 | 27.31 | 19.40 |
| 2Q | — | — | 69.05 | 44.80 | 30.21 | 20.93 |
| 3Q | — | — | 75.12 | 48.50 | 32.58 | 23.10 |
| 4Q | — | — | 90.20 | 56.79 | 40.29 | 26.10 |
| Yr. | — | — | 298.0 | 190.4 | 130.4 | 89.53 |
| **Earnings Per Share ($)** | | | | | | |
| 1Q | — | 0.37 | 0.24 | 0.13 | 0.08 | 0.06 |
| 2Q | — | E0.39 | 0.25 | 0.15 | 0.09 | 0.06 |
| 3Q | — | E0.42 | 0.29 | 0.19 | 0.10 | 0.07 |
| 4Q | — | E0.47 | 0.36 | 0.23 | 0.15 | 0.08 |
| Yr. | E1.95 | E1.65 | 1.13 | 0.70 | 0.43 | 0.26 |

Next earnings report expected: **mid July**

## Dividend Data

| Amount ($) | Date Decl. | Ex-Div. Date | Stock of Record | Payment Date |
| --- | --- | --- | --- | --- |
| 2-for-1 | Jan. 23 | Feb. 21 | Feb. 10 | Feb. 20 '97 |

This report is for information purposes and should not be considered a solicitation to buy or sell any security. Neither S&P nor any other party guarantee its accuracy or make warranties regarding results from its usage. Redistribution is prohibited without written permission. Copyright © 1997

*A Division of The* **McGraw·Hill** *Companies*

STANDARD
&POOR'S
STOCK REPORTS

**Electronics for Imaging, Inc.**

**3791K**

**17-MAY-97**

## Business Summary - 16-APR-97

Electronics for Imaging (EFII) was founded to develop innovative solutions to enable color desktop publishing. Its systems and software permit users to produce color documents easily, quickly and cost-effectively in the office on a range of peripheral devices

To provide desktop users with cost-effective, short-run color printing on a system that has sufficient memory and processing power to handle color images on a network, the company developed the Fiery Color Server, which enables a plain paper color copier to also function as a high performance color PostScript printer. Additionally, the company has developed and manufactures variations of the Fiery Color Servers for wide-format inkjet printers and Fiery Color Controllers, which are an embedded solution to enable color printing on desktop color laser printers. With over 50,000 units installed worldwide, Fiery Color Servers and Fiery Color Controllers are used by leading corporations, advertising agencies, graphic design studios, and print-for-pay businesses.

EFII has established distribution partnerships with leading color copier makers, including Canon, Kodak, Xerox, Minolta and Ricoh, and through certain Canon subsidiaries and dealers. EFII's strategy is to expand its product line by developing new and better equipment, seek additional relationships with key industry players and to further develop its existing relationships, and to leverage its expertise in color technology.

The company launched its first generation Fiery Color

Server in August 1991 and by March 1995, introduced its third generation of the Fiery Color Server, the Fiery XJ. This new product line was designed to provide the fastest document processing time available in the short-run color printing industry. In 1996, EFII enhanced the XJ product line and launched the Fiery XJ+, which provides faster document processing times. Also in 1996, the company began shipping Fiery XJ printer Controllers (marketed under the name Fiery XJe) to IBM, Canon and Digital. In October 1996, EFII announced the Fiery XJ-W, a controller for wide-format color printers. In December 1996, the company released the first Fiery SI, a stand-alone color server that combines Fiery qualities to print business documents.

In March 1997, EFII and Kinko's, a leading print-for-pay chain store business, signed a letter of intent to enter into a worldwide strategic technology alliance. Kinko's will purchase Fiery Controllers and EFII will provide Kinko's with solutions designed specifically for its stores and help with sales and marketing efforts in providing digital output services.

International sales, primarily in Europe and Japan, accounted for about 51% of product revenue in 1996. R&D spending amounted to $22.4 million in 1996 (7.5% of sales), up from $12.9 million in 1995 (6.8%).

### Capitalization

**Long Term Debt:** None (3/97).

**Options:** To buy 6,085,438 shs. at $4.89 to $25.80 a sh. (12/96).

### Per Share Data ($)

| (Year Ended Dec. 31) | 1996 | 1995 | 1994 | 1993 | 1992 | 1991 | 1990 | 1989 | 1988 | 1987 |
|---|---|---|---|---|---|---|---|---|---|---|
| Tangible Bk. Val. | 4.84 | 3.28 | 2.37 | 1.90 | 1.24 | -0.13 | NA | NA | NA | NA |
| Cash Flow | 1.23 | 0.79 | 0.49 | 0.30 | 0.23 | 0.04 | NA | NA | NA | NA |
| Earnings | 1.13 | 0.71 | 0.43 | 0.26 | 0.19 | 0.03 | NA | NA | NA | NA |
| Dividends | Nil | Nil | Nil | Nil | Nil | Nil | NA | NA | NA | NA |
| Payout Ratio | Nil | Nil | Nil | Nil | Nil | Nil | NA | NA | NA | NA |
| Prices - High | 44⅛ | 25⅛ | 7⅜ | 5⅝ | 6 | NA | NA | NA | NA | NA |
| - Low | 13⅜ | 6 | 3⅜ | 3½ | 3¼ | NA | NA | NA | NA | NA |
| P/E Ratio - High | 39 | 36 | 17 | 22 | 32 | NA | NA | NA | NA | NA |
| - Low | 12 | 9 | 8 | 13 | 17 | NA | NA | NA | NA | NA |

### Income Statement Analysis (Million $)

| | 1996 | 1995 | 1994 | 1993 | 1992 | 1991 | 1990 | 1989 | 1988 | 1987 |
|---|---|---|---|---|---|---|---|---|---|---|
| Revs. | 298 | 191 | 130 | 89.5 | 53.7 | 16.4 | NA | NA | NA | NA |
| Oper. Inc. | 95.3 | 56.5 | 33.5 | 20.6 | 9.2 | 0.7 | NA | NA | NA | NA |
| Depr. | 5.5 | 3.4 | 3.1 | 1.9 | 1.5 | 0.6 | NA | NA | NA | NA |
| Int. Exp. | Nil | NM | NA | NA | NA | NA | NA | NA | NA | NA |
| Pretax Inc. | 97.2 | 58.6 | 33.3 | 20.6 | 8.8 | 0.8 | NA | NA | NA | NA |
| Eff. Tax Rate | 36% | 36% | 36% | 38% | 25% | 19% | NA | NA | NA | NA |
| Net Inc. | 62.2 | 37.5 | 21.3 | 12.8 | 6.6 | 0.6 | NA | NA | NA | NA |

### Balance Sheet & Other Fin. Data (Million $)

| | 1996 | 1995 | 1994 | 1993 | 1992 | 1991 | 1990 | 1989 | 1988 | 1987 |
|---|---|---|---|---|---|---|---|---|---|---|
| Cash | 72.0 | 46.0 | 107 | 79.5 | 45.2 | 3.0 | NA | NA | NA | NA |
| Curr. Assets | 287 | 188 | 130 | 99 | 54.8 | 4.6 | NA | NA | NA | NA |
| Total Assets | 299 | 195 | 135 | 104 | 58.5 | 6.5 | NA | NA | NA | NA |
| Curr. Liab. | 50.0 | 30.5 | 21.9 | 15.7 | 11.1 | 6.6 | NA | NA | NA | NA |
| LT Debt | Nil | NM | Nil | Nil | Nil | 1.6 | NA | NA | NA | NA |
| Common Eqty. | 249 | 164 | 114 | 88.3 | 47.4 | -1.7 | NA | NA | NA | NA |
| Total Cap. | 249 | 164 | 114 | 88.3 | 47.4 | -0.1 | NA | NA | NA | NA |
| Cap. Exp. | 10.7 | 4.5 | 2.8 | 3.2 | 3.2 | 1.6 | NA | NA | NA | NA |
| Cash Flow | 67.7 | 40.9 | 24.4 | 14.6 | 8.1 | 1.2 | NA | NA | NA | NA |
| Curr. Ratio | 5.7 | 6.2 | 5.9 | 6.3 | 4.9 | 0.7 | NA | NA | NA | NA |
| % LT Debt of Cap. | Nil | NM | Nil | Nil | Nil | NM | NA | NA | NA | NA |
| % Net Inc.of Revs. | 20.9 | 19.7 | 16.3 | 14.2 | 12.3 | 3.8 | NA | NA | NA | NA |
| % Ret. on Assets | 25.2 | 22.7 | 17.5 | 14.6 | 17.1 | NA | NA | NA | NA | NA |
| % Ret. on Equity | 30.1 | 27.0 | 20.8 | 17.5 | NM | NA | NA | NA | NA | NA |

Data as orig. reptd.; bef. results of disc. opers. and/or spec. items. Per share data adj. for stk. divs. as of ex-div. date. E-Estimated. NA-Not Available. NM-Not Meaningful. NR-Not Ranked.

**Office**—2855 Campus Drive, San Mateo, CA 94403. **Tel**—(415) 286-8600. **Fax**—(415) 286-8544. **Website**—http://www.efi.com **Chrmn**—E. Arazi. **Pres & CEO**—D. Avida. **Dirs**—E. Arazi, D. Avida, G. Cogan, I. Federman, J.L. Gassee, T. I. Unterberg. **Transfer Agent & Registrar**—First National Bank of Boston. **Incorporated**—in Delaware in 1988. **Empl**— 370. **S&P Analyst:** Ted Groesbeck

**17-MAY-97**

**Industry:** Oil & Gas (Drilling & Equipment)

**Summary:** This international contract drilling company also provides marine transportation services to the oil and gas industry.

| S&P Opinion: Buy (★★★★) | Recent Price • 47<br>52 Wk Range • 58-26¾ | Yield • Nil<br>12-Mo. P/E • 27.5 |
|---|---|---|

**Quantitative Evaluations**

Outlook
(1 Lowest—5 Highest)
• **5**

Fair Value
• **66¾**

Risk
• **Average**

Earn./Div. Rank
• **B-**

Technical Eval.
• **Bullish** since 3/95

Rel. Strength Rank
(1 Lowest—99 Highest)
• **36**

Insider Activity
• **Neutral**

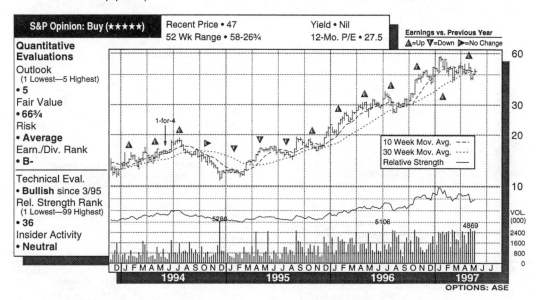

**Earnings vs. Previous Year**
▲=Up ▼=Down ▷=No Change

10 Week Mov. Avg. ---
30 Week Mov. Avg. ·····
Relative Strength —

OPTIONS: ASE

## Overview - 17-APR-97

ENSCO's 1997 and 1998 earnings will benefit from increased spending on the upstream and the recent acquisition of Dual Drilling Co. The company's contract drilling and marine transportation divisions are seeing utilization levels rise as a result of strong demand for offshore jackup and platform rigs as well as marine support vessels, particularly in the Gulf of Mexico, where the company has a large concentration of its rigs and vessels. In 1996, operating profit in the contract drilling segment more than doubled, and we believe margins will continue to improve through year-end 1997. The recent strength in the price of, and demand for, natural gas domestically bodes well for increased profits for contract drillers. By targeting the high end of the rig and boat markets, ESV has consistently achieved superior operating earnings results and we expect this trend to continue.

## Valuation - 17-APR-97

The DUAL acquisition gives ENSCO exposure to the fast growing S.E. Asia market, making this the most attractive pick among the contract drilling group. Importantly, all of DUAL's rigs were built after 1980. We expect the stock to rise by at least 20% over the next year as a result of firming day-rates for the company's rig and boat fleet. The highly-leveraged nature of the business will allow nearly 85% of incremental dayrates to reach the bottom line. ENSCO clearly has a premium fleet of jackup and platform rigs. Following recent upgrades, all 34 jackup rigs have top drives and independent leg designs. And 18 of the rigs are zero discharge rigs, suited for environmentally sensitive areas. We believe the shares should outperform the market handily in 1997.

## Key Stock Statistics

| | | | |
|---|---|---|---|
| S&P EPS Est. 1997 | 2.45 | Tang. Bk. Value/Share | 11.93 |
| P/E on S&P Est. 1997 | 19.2 | Beta | 0.19 |
| S&P EPS Est. 1998 | 3.40 | Shareholders | 2,800 |
| Dividend Rate/Share | Nil | Market cap. (B) | $ 3.3 |
| Shs. outstg. (M) | 70.9 | Inst. holdings | 78% |
| Avg. daily vol. (M) | 0.742 | | |

Value of $10,000 invested 5 years ago: $ 82,727

### Fiscal Year Ending Dec. 31

| | 1998 | 1997 | 1996 | 1995 | 1994 | 1993 |
|---|---|---|---|---|---|---|
| **Revenues (Million $)** | | | | | | |
| 1Q | — | 161.6 | 84.55 | 61.13 | 65.40 | 51.80 |
| 2Q | — | — | 97.25 | 62.43 | 67.10 | 58.30 |
| 3Q | — | — | 134.6 | 71.80 | 63.20 | 65.70 |
| 4Q | — | — | 152.4 | 83.77 | 66.40 | 70.50 |
| Yr. | — | — | 468.8 | 279.1 | 262.0 | 246.2 |
| **Earnings Per Share ($)** | | | | | | |
| 1Q | — | 0.51 | 0.24 | 0.12 | 0.18 | -0.12 |
| 2Q | — | E0.59 | 0.34 | 0.11 | 0.17 | 0.04 |
| 3Q | — | E0.65 | 0.38 | 0.18 | 0.12 | 0.12 |
| 4Q | — | E0.70 | 0.45 | 0.28 | 0.14 | 0.16 |
| Yr. | E3.40 | E2.45 | 1.44 | 0.69 | 0.61 | 0.32 |

Next earnings report expected: mid July

### Dividend Data

No common dividends have been paid. A one-for-four reverse stock split was effected June 1, 1994. In February 1995, a shareholder rights plan was adopted.

This report is for information purposes and should not be considered a solicitation to buy or sell any security. Neither S&P nor any other party guarantee its accuracy or make warranties regarding results from its usage. Redistribution is prohibited without written permission. Copyright © 1997    *A Division of The McGraw·Hill Companies*

## Business Summary - 17-APR-97

ENSCO International Inc. (formerly Energy Service Co., Inc. and before that, Blocker Energy Corp.) is engaged in domestic and international contract drilling of oil and gas wells, both onshore and offshore, and marine transportation services for offshore oil and gas exploration and production companies. It also owns Penrod Holding Corp., an international offshore contract drilling company.

ENSCO acquired Dual Drilling Co. for about 10.1 million common shares in June 1996. The company also acquired a single jackup drilling rig located in Southeast Asia in November 1996. After the acquisitions, ESV had 23 jackup rigs in the Gulf of Mexico, 10 barge rigs in Venezuela, eight platform rigs, six jackup rigs in the North Sea and five jackup rigs in Asia.

In 1988, ESV entered the marine transportation business through wholly owned ENSCO Marine Co., which bought 14 supply boats for use in the Gulf of Mexico. The company currently has a fleet of 37 vessels, consisting of six anchor handling tug supply vessels, 23 supply vessels and eight mini-supply vessels. All of the company's marine transportation vessels are currently in the Gulf of Mexico. The tug supply vessels support semi-submersible rigs and large offshore construction projects, or provide towing services, while the supply vessels support general drilling and production activity by ferrying supplies from land, and between offshore rigs.

Effective September 30, 1995, ESV exited the technical services business through the sale of its wholly owned subsidiary, ENSCO Technology Co., which provides horizontal drilling services to the petroleum industry in the U.S. and Canada. Horizontal drilling enhances oil and gas recovery from certain types of producing reservoirs. The purchase price consisted of $11.8 million in cash, a promissory note for $3.6 million, a convertible promissory note for $2.5 million and the assumption of $1.9 million of liabilities.

In 1990, the company discontinued its oil and gas operations, resulting in a $5.6 million loss. It disposed of supply operations in 1993, and sold its domestic land rig business in 1994. ESV now focuses on expansion of its offshore contract drilling and marine transportation businesses.

### Important Developments

**Apr. '97**—ENSCO reported EPS of $0.51, on 17% more shares outstanding, in the first quarter of 1997, up from $0.24 in 1996's first quarter. Results were aided by higher average dayrates for the company's drilling rigs and marine transportation vessels, as well as the inclusion of revenues from the acquisition of Dual Drilling Co., completed in June 1996. Offshore rig dayrates averaged $34,653 in 1997's first quarter, versus $26,266 in the first quarter of 1996. Marine vessel dayrates averaged $6,791, versus $4,120 in 1996's first quarter.

### Capitalization

**Long Term Debt:** $235,590,000 (3/97).

| Per Share Data ($)<br>(Year Ended Dec. 31) | 1996 | 1995 | 1994 | 1993 | 1992 | 1991 | 1990 | 1989 | 1988 | 1987 |
|---|---|---|---|---|---|---|---|---|---|---|
| Tangible Bk. Val. | 10.43 | 8.65 | 7.66 | 6.36 | 4.68 | 5.68 | 6.20 | 5.92 | 5.40 | 5.48 |
| Cash Flow | 2.67 | 1.65 | 1.54 | 1.04 | -0.60 | 0.08 | 0.28 | 0.28 | 0.24 | -0.24 |
| Earnings | 1.44 | 0.69 | 0.61 | 0.32 | -1.12 | -0.56 | -0.32 | -0.44 | -0.08 | -0.60 |
| Dividends | Nil | Nil | Nil | Nil | Nil | Nil | Nil | Nil | Nil | Nil |
| Payout Ratio | Nil | Nil | Nil | Nil | Nil | Nil | Nil | Nil | Nil | Nil |
| Prices - High | 50⅛ | 23 | 19¼ | 16¼ | 8 | 13 | 21 | 18 | 14½ | 31 |
|    - Low | 20 | 11¼ | 10¾ | 3½ | 4 | 5 | 8 | 7½ | 6½ | 3½ |
| P/E Ratio - High | 35 | 33 | 32 | 51 | NM | NM | NM | NM | NM | NM |
|    - Low | 14 | 16 | 18 | 11 | NM | NM | NM | NM | NM | NM |

### Income Statement Analysis (Million $)

| | 1996 | 1995 | 1994 | 1993 | 1992 | 1991 | 1990 | 1989 | 1988 | 1987 |
|---|---|---|---|---|---|---|---|---|---|---|
| Revs. | 469 | 279 | 262 | 246 | 162 | 207 | 175 | 159 | 127 | 48.0 |
| Oper. Inc. | 231 | 114 | 106 | 66.3 | Nil | 10.3 | 7.2 | 11.9 | -2.8 | -3.9 |
| Depr. | 81.9 | 58.4 | 54.2 | 30.1 | 15.7 | 15.3 | 12.1 | 12.3 | 6.2 | 4.6 |
| Int. Exp. | 20.9 | 16.6 | 14.1 | 10.5 | 4.5 | 4.2 | 5.0 | 6.0 | 6.4 | 1.1 |
| Pretax Inc. | 143 | 47.3 | 43.9 | 29.6 | -26.8 | -8.0 | -1.5 | -2.4 | 3.5 | -8.0 |
| Eff. Tax Rate | 31% | 7.20% | 8.60% | 20% | NM | NM | NM | NM | 61% | NM |
| Net Inc. | 95.4 | 41.8 | 37.2 | 16.7 | -29.6 | -8.7 | -1.9 | -2.6 | 1.4 | -8.0 |

### Balance Sheet & Other Fin. Data (Million $)

| | 1996 | 1995 | 1994 | 1993 | 1992 | 1991 | 1990 | 1989 | 1988 | 1987 |
|---|---|---|---|---|---|---|---|---|---|---|
| Cash | 80.7 | 82.0 | 154 | 128 | 25.5 | 29.5 | 46.9 | 30.2 | 33.1 | 23.7 |
| Curr. Assets | 211 | 166 | 212 | 193 | 79.0 | 85.0 | 112 | 87.0 | 93.0 | 57.0 |
| Total Assets | 1,315 | 822 | 775 | 691 | 283 | 315 | 293 | 275 | 253 | 134 |
| Curr. Liab. | 104 | 86.8 | 88.2 | 65.9 | 40.1 | 44.9 | 37.7 | 30.2 | 41.4 | 28.9 |
| LT Debt | 259 | 159 | 162 | 126 | 23.6 | 31.0 | 31.0 | 49.0 | 44.0 | 15.0 |
| Common Eqty. | 846 | 531 | 488 | 384 | 143 | 165 | 149 | 115 | 87.0 | 86.0 |
| Total Cap. | 1,178 | 717 | 678 | 609 | 238 | 268 | 255 | 245 | 211 | 105 |
| Cap. Exp. | 176 | 143 | 153 | 384 | 4.0 | 44.6 | 15.4 | 19.0 | 98.3 | 45.8 |
| Cash Flow | 177 | 100 | 89.2 | 42.6 | -18.2 | 2.0 | 5.4 | 4.7 | 4.0 | -3.3 |
| Curr. Ratio | 2.0 | 1.9 | 2.4 | 2.9 | 2.0 | 1.9 | 3.0 | 2.9 | 2.2 | 2.0 |
| % LT Debt of Cap. | 22.0 | 22.2 | 24.0 | 20.7 | 9.9 | 11.7 | 12.0 | 20.2 | 20.7 | 14.4 |
| % Net Inc.of Revs. | 20.3 | 15.0 | 14.2 | 6.8 | NM | NM | NM | NM | 1.1 | NM |
| % Ret. on Assets | 8.9 | 6.0 | 4.9 | 2.8 | NM | NM | NM | NM | 0.7 | NM |
| % Ret. on Equity | 13.9 | 9.4 | 7.7 | 3.8 | NM | NM | NM | NM | NM | NM |

Data as orig. reptd.; bef. results of disc. opers. and/or spec. items. Per share data adj. for stk. divs. as of ex-div. date. E-Estimated. NA-Not Available. NM-Not Meaningful. NR-Not Ranked.

**Office**—2700 Fountain Place, 1445 Ross Ave., Dallas, TX 75202-2792. **Tel**—(214) 922-1500. **Chrmn, Pres & CEO**—C. F. Thorne. **SVP & COO**—R. A. Wilson. **VP & CFO**—C. C. Gaut. **Investor Contact**—Richard A. LeBlanc. **Secy**—W. S. Chadwick, Jr. **Dirs**—C. I. Fields, O. D. Gaither, G. W. Haddock, D. S. Hammett, T. L. Kelly II, M. H. Meyerson, C. F. Thorne, R. A. Wilson. **Transfer Agent & Registrar**—American Stock Transfer & Trust Co., NYC. **Incorporated**—in Texas in 1975; reincorporated in Delaware in 1987. **Empl**— 2,300. **S&P Analyst:** Norman Rosenberg

# STANDARD &POOR'S
## STOCK REPORTS

# Express Scripts

## 3819L
### Nasdaq Symbol ESRX
### In S&P SmallCap 600

**20-MAY-97**

**Industry:** Health Care (Managed Care)

**Summary:** This company offers prescription benefits management, eyecare, infusion therapy and disease state management support services.

**S&P Opinion: Accumulate (★★★★)**

Recent Price • 41½
52 Wk Range • 51½-26½

Yield • Nil
12-Mo. P/E • 24.4

**Earnings vs. Previous Year**
▲=Up ▼=Down ▶=No Change

### Quantitative Evaluations

**Outlook**
(1 Lowest—5 Highest)
• 5

**Fair Value**
• 94⅜

**Risk**
• Average

**Earn./Div. Rank**
• NR

**Technical Eval.**
• Bullish since 5/97

**Rel. Strength Rank**
(1 Lowest—99 Highest)
• 90

**Insider Activity**
• NA

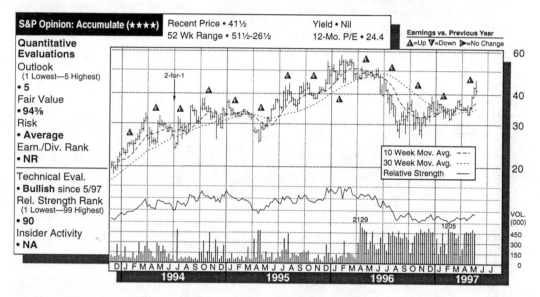

10 Week Mov. Avg. — ·—
30 Week Mov. Avg. ·······
Relative Strength ——

VOL. (000)

## Overview - 19-MAY-97

Revenue growth for the balance of 1997 should remain above 40%, reflecting sharp enrollment growth in the pharmacy benefits management (PBM) business, along with strong contributions from the vision and infusion therapy segments. Most significant should be the commencement (effective March 1997) of a three-year contract to provide PBM services to about 500,000 members of RightCHOICE Managed Care Inc., a subsidiary of Blue Cross & Blue Shield of Missouri. Gross profit margins may remain under pressure as competition within the PBM business continues to intensify, but we anticipate that gross margins will stabilize at about 10% in 1997 and 1998. Increased penetration in the vision care and infusion therapy areas should provide some margin support, however, and EPS growth should settle in the 25% range through 1998.

## Valuation - 19-MAY-97

We recently initiated coverage of ESRX with an Accumulate opinion, in the belief that the shares should modestly outperform the S&P 500 during 1997. Based on a recent P/E of about 20 times our 1997 EPS estimate, and 16 times our 1998 forecast, the stock looks underpriced relative to expected profit growth. We do have some concerns regarding future margin levels as ongoing consolidation within the managed care industry may result in the loss of some contracts and heightened competition for contracts with the remaining large HMOs. These pressures will likely slow the rate of EPS expansion, but we continue to look for growth in excess of 25% as the company seeks out smaller HMO contracts and broadens its service offerings to areas outside of its core PBM business. Common share buybacks should provide additional EPS support.

## Key Stock Statistics

| | | | |
|---|---|---|---|
| S&P EPS Est. 1997 | 2.05 | Tang. Bk. Value/Share | 10.07 |
| P/E on S&P Est. 1997 | 20.2 | Beta | NA |
| S&P EPS Est. 1998 | 2.55 | Shareholders | 200 |
| Dividend Rate/Share | Nil | Market cap. (B) | $0.668 |
| Shs. outstg. (M) | 16.5 | Inst. holdings | 39% |
| Avg. daily vol. (M) | 0.129 | | |

Value of $10,000 invested 5 years ago: NA

### Fiscal Year Ending Dec. 31

| | 1997 | 1996 | 1995 | 1994 | 1993 | 1992 |
|---|---|---|---|---|---|---|
| **Revenues (Million $)** | | | | | | |
| 1Q | 262.0 | 168.4 | 118.0 | 83.08 | 26.70 | 14.90 |
| 2Q | — | 184.7 | 135.1 | 89.97 | 29.50 | 16.90 |
| 3Q | — | 194.3 | 138.5 | 100.7 | 30.70 | 18.70 |
| 4Q | — | 226.2 | 152.8 | 110.8 | 33.40 | 20.40 |
| Yr. | — | 773.6 | 544.5 | 384.5 | 120.3 | 70.90 |
| **Earnings Per Share ($)** | | | | | | |
| 1Q | 0.46 | 0.36 | 0.28 | 0.18 | 0.11 | 0.08 |
| 2Q | E0.50 | 0.39 | 0.30 | 0.20 | 0.13 | 0.10 |
| 3Q | E0.53 | 0.42 | 0.31 | 0.22 | 0.15 | 0.09 |
| 4Q | E0.56 | 0.43 | 0.31 | 0.24 | 0.16 | 0.10 |
| Yr. | E2.05 | 1.60 | 1.20 | 0.84 | 0.55 | 0.36 |

Next earnings report expected: late July

## Dividend Data

No cash dividends have been paid. A two-for-one stock split was effected in June 1994.

This report is for information purposes and should not be considered a solicitation to buy or sell any security. Neither S&P nor any other party guarantee its accuracy or make warranties regarding results from its usage. Redistribution is prohibited without written permission. Copyright © 1997

A Division of The McGraw-Hill Companies

STANDARD
&POOR'S
STOCK REPORTS

# Express Scripts, Inc.

# 3819L
## 20-MAY-97

## Business Summary - 19-MAY-97

Express Scripts, a leading pharmacy benefits manager (PBM), ranks among the fastest-growing companies in America, reflecting surging demand among managed care organizations, third-party administrators, employer groups and union-sponsored benefit plans for services intended to control surging pharmaceutical costs. As of March 31, 1997, the company provided PBM programs to nearly 11,000,000 individuals.

The company's PBM unit manages outpatient prescription drug usage through the application of managed care principles and advanced information technologies. Core services include retail pharmacy network administration; formulary administration; electronic point-of-sale claims processing; drug utilization review; mail pharmacy service; and benefit plan design consultation. About 82% of the members served have access to prescription drugs through one of the company's retail pharmacy networks and mail pharmacy facilities.

Express Scripts also offers advanced PBM services, including the development of formulary compliance and therapeutic substitution programs; therapy management services such as prior authorization, therapy guidelines, step therapy protocols and disease management interventions; and sophisticated management information reporting and analytic capabilities.

About 67% of net revenues in 1996 came from pharmacy network and claims administration services, while 29% were from mail pharmacy services. The number of claims processed by ESRX through its pharmacy networks reached 57.8 million in 1996, up from 42.9 million in 1995, while the number of mail prescriptions processed rose to 2.8 million from 2.1 million.

The company is a major provider of PBM services to the managed care industry, including several large HMOs. some of its largest customers include FHP Inc., NYLCare Health Plans Inc., and Coventry Corp. As of January 1, 1997, about 51% of the members receiving PBM services are enrolled in HMOs.

ESRX also offers a managed vision care program through a network of approximately 5,500 providers, primarily optometrists and a smaller number of ophthalmologists. Several providers offer service at multiple locations, thereby allowing members to access the vision care product at about 7,500 locations in 49 states. The providers have agreed to provide, at specific rates, a routine vision exam and eyeware to members of ESRX's managed vision care plan.

Outpatient infusion services include administration of prescription drugs and other products by catheter, feeding tube or intravenously at the home, a doctor's office or freestanding center. These services benefit managed care clients by reducing the length of hospital stays.

## Capitalization

**Long Term Debt:** None (3/97).
**Class A Common Stock:** 8,974,000 shs. (12/96).
**Class B Common Stock:** 7,510,000 shs. (12/96).

## Per Share Data ($)

| (Year Ended Dec. 31) | 1996 | 1995 | 1994 | 1993 | 1992 | 1991 | 1990 | 1989 | 1988 | 1987 |
|---|---|---|---|---|---|---|---|---|---|---|
| Tangible Bk. Val. | 10.07 | 5.15 | 3.56 | 2.60 | 2.05 | 0.33 | NA | NA | NA | NA |
| Cash Flow | 2.01 | 1.48 | 1.06 | 0.68 | 0.44 | 0.34 | NA | NA | NA | NA |
| Earnings | 1.60 | 1.20 | 0.84 | 0.55 | 0.36 | 0.28 | NA | NA | NA | NA |
| Dividends | Nil | Nil | Nil | Nil | Nil | Nil | NA | NA | NA | NA |
| Payout Ratio | Nil | Nil | Nil | Nil | Nil | Nil | NA | NA | NA | NA |
| Prices - High | 58 | 55 | 38¼ | 23½ | 16½ | NA | NA | NA | NA | NA |
| - Low | 26½ | 25 | 22 | 9⅜ | 6¼ | NA | NA | NA | NA | NA |
| P/E Ratio - High | 36 | 46 | 46 | 43 | 46 | NA | NA | NA | NA | NA |
| - Low | 17 | 21 | 26 | 17 | 17 | NA | NA | NA | NA | NA |

## Income Statement Analysis (Million $)

| | 1996 | 1995 | 1994 | 1993 | 1992 | 1991 | 1990 | 1989 | 1988 | 1987 |
|---|---|---|---|---|---|---|---|---|---|---|
| Revs. | 774 | 544 | 385 | 120 | 71.0 | 47.0 | NA | NA | NA | NA |
| Oper. Inc. | 46.3 | 33.3 | 23.8 | 14.8 | 8.3 | 5.3 | NA | NA | NA | NA |
| Depr. | 6.7 | 4.4 | 3.3 | 2.0 | 1.0 | 0.7 | NA | NA | NA | NA |
| Int. Exp. | 0.1 | 0.1 | 0.1 | 0.1 | 0.1 | 0.2 | NA | NA | NA | NA |
| Pretax Inc. | 43.1 | 29.6 | 20.8 | 13.0 | 7.4 | 4.7 | NA | NA | NA | NA |
| Eff. Tax Rate | 39% | 38% | 39% | 38% | 37% | 38% | NA | NA | NA | NA |
| Net Inc. | 26.1 | 18.3 | 12.7 | 8.1 | 4.6 | 2.9 | NA | NA | NA | NA |

## Balance Sheet & Other Fin. Data (Million $)

| | 1996 | 1995 | 1994 | 1993 | 1992 | 1991 | 1990 | 1989 | 1988 | 1987 |
|---|---|---|---|---|---|---|---|---|---|---|
| Cash | 79.6 | 11.5 | 5.7 | 2.0 | 11.8 | 3.5 | NA | NA | NA | NA |
| Curr. Assets | 263 | 144 | 92.8 | 63.3 | 40.1 | 16.6 | NA | NA | NA | NA |
| Total Assets | 300 | 164 | 108 | 75.4 | 45.4 | 20.2 | NA | NA | NA | NA |
| Curr. Liab. | 135 | 86.0 | 55.9 | 37.1 | 15.7 | 16.8 | NA | NA | NA | NA |
| LT Debt | Nil | Nil | Nil | Nil | Nil | Nil | NA | NA | NA | NA |
| Common Eqty. | 164 | 77.4 | 52.5 | 38.3 | 29.7 | 3.4 | NA | NA | NA | NA |
| Total Cap. | 166 | 78.3 | 52.5 | 38.3 | 29.7 | 3.4 | NA | NA | NA | NA |
| Cap. Exp. | 9.5 | 8.1 | 6.3 | 7.1 | 2.5 | 1.8 | NA | NA | NA | NA |
| Cash Flow | 32.9 | 22.7 | 16.0 | 10.0 | 5.6 | 3.6 | NA | NA | NA | NA |
| Curr. Ratio | 2.0 | 1.7 | 1.7 | 1.7 | 2.6 | 1.0 | NA | NA | NA | NA |
| % LT Debt of Cap. | Nil | Nil | Nil | Nil | Nil | Nil | NA | NA | NA | NA |
| % Net Inc.of Revs. | 3.4 | 3.4 | 3.3 | 6.7 | 6.5 | 6.1 | NA | NA | NA | NA |
| % Ret. on Assets | 11.3 | 13.4 | 13.8 | 13.3 | 12.6 | NA | NA | NA | NA | NA |
| % Ret. on Equity | 21.7 | 28.2 | 28.0 | 23.7 | 26.9 | NA | NA | NA | NA | NA |

Data as orig. reptd.; bef. results of disc. opers. and/or spec. items. Per share data adj. for stk. divs. as of ex-div. date. E-Estimated. NA-Not Available. NM-Not Meaningful. NR-Not Ranked.

**Office**—14000 Riverport Dr., Maryland Heights, MO 63043. **Tel**—(314) 770-1666. **Website**—http://www.express-scripts.com **Chrmn**—H. L. Waltman. **Pres & CEO**—B. A. Toan. **EVP-CFO & Treas**—S. L. Bascomb. **SVP-Secy**—T. M. Boudreau. **Dirs**—H. Atkins, B.N. Del Bello, R.M. Kernan Jr., R.A. Norling, F.J. Sievert, N. Steinig, S. Sternberg, B.A. Toan, H.L. Waltman, N. Zachary. **Transfer Agent & Registrar**—American Stock Transfer & Trust Co., NYC. **Incorporated**—in Missouri in 1986; reincorporated in Delaware in 1992. **Empl**— 1,477. **S&P Analyst:**  Robert M. Gold

# Fair, Isaac & Co.

## 852V

NYSE Symbol **FIC**

In S&P SmallCap 600

**17-MAY-97**

**Industry:**
Services (Data Processing)

**Summary:** FIC is a leading developer of predictive models, software systems, and marketing database management and decision services used in the credit, insurance and marketing industries.

## Quantitative Evaluations

**Outlook**
(1 Lowest—5 Highest)
• **5**

**Fair Value**
• **46**

**Risk**
• **Average**

**Earn./Div. Rank**
• **B+**

**Technical Eval.**
• **NA**

**Rel. Strength Rank**
(1 Lowest—99 Highest)
• **59**

**Insider Activity**
• **Unfavorable**

Recent Price • 36⅝    Yield • 0.2%
52 Wk Range • 50-29⅜    12-Mo. P/E • 26.3

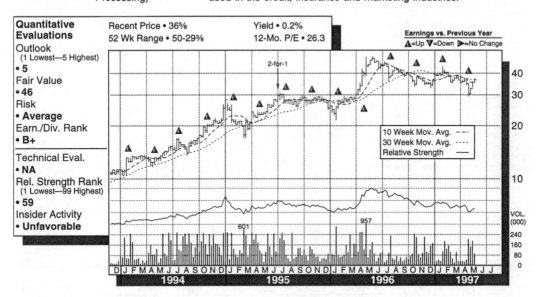

Earnings vs. Previous Year
▲=Up ▼=Down ▶=No Change

10 Week Mov. Avg. ----
30 Week Mov. Avg. ·····
Relative Strength ——

## Business Profile - 29-APR-97

By winning accounts with large banks and other credit issuers, FIC has achieved above average annual compound revenue growth of 34% over the past five fiscal years, when the U.S. bankcard industry was slowing and banks were consolidating. Now, it believes it ranks first or second in all of its product categories. FIC has grown by expanding product functionality and entering new markets such as insurance, small business and mortgage lending, but caveats include potential government regulation and dependence on a few large credit bureaus.

## Operational Review - 29-APR-97

Total revenues in the first half of FY 97 (Sep.) rose 30%, year to year, reflecting strong growth in all of the company's strategic business units, including over 25% growth in credit, over 50% growth at DynaMark, and close to 100% growth in insurance products. Gross margins widened, but following a 35% increase in general and administrative expense and a more-than-doubling of R&D expense, the gain in operating income was held to 19%. Net income gained 21%, to $9,577,000 ($0.74 a share), from $7,897,000 ($0.62).

## Stock Performance - 16-MAY-97

In the past 30 trading days, FIC's shares have increased 2%, compared to a 9% rise in the S&P 500. Average trading volume for the past five days was 17,620 shares, compared with the 40-day moving average of 18,979 shares.

## Key Stock Statistics

| | | | |
|---|---|---|---|
| Dividend Rate/Share | 0.08 | Shareholders | 200 |
| Shs. outstg. (M) | 12.7 | Market cap. (B) | $0.464 |
| Avg. daily vol. (M) | 0.031 | Inst. holdings | 27% |
| Tang. Bk. Value/Share | 5.48 | | |
| Beta | 0.40 | | |

Value of $10,000 invested 5 years ago: $ 71,550

### Fiscal Year Ending Sep. 30

| | 1997 | 1996 | 1995 | 1994 | 1993 | 1992 |
|---|---|---|---|---|---|---|
| **Revenues (Million $)** | | | | | | |
| 1Q | 41.53 | 32.63 | 25.63 | 21.02 | 13.35 | 8.73 |
| 2Q | 46.46 | 35.28 | 26.38 | 21.00 | 15.08 | 9.97 |
| 3Q | — | 37.12 | 28.67 | 22.64 | 17.90 | 10.78 |
| 4Q | — | 43.73 | 33.19 | 25.51 | 20.34 | 13.13 |
| Yr. | — | 148.8 | 113.9 | 90.28 | 66.67 | 42.61 |
| **Earnings Per Share ($)** | | | | | | |
| 1Q | 0.35 | 0.28 | 0.22 | 0.19 | 0.10 | 0.06 |
| 2Q | 0.39 | 0.34 | 0.23 | 0.17 | 0.09 | 0.08 |
| 3Q | — | 0.34 | 0.25 | 0.21 | 0.11 | 0.08 |
| 4Q | — | 0.31 | 0.30 | 0.24 | 0.13 | 0.11 |
| Yr. | — | 1.27 | 1.00 | 0.80 | 0.43 | 0.33 |

**Next earnings report expected: mid July**

**Dividend Data** (Dividends have been paid since 1989.)

| Amount ($) | Date Decl. | Ex-Div. Date | Stock of Record | Payment Date |
|---|---|---|---|---|
| 0.020 | May. 29 | Jun. 06 | Jun. 10 | Jun. 24 '96 |
| 0.020 | Aug. 13 | Aug. 22 | Aug. 26 | Sep. 10 '96 |
| 0.020 | Nov. 18 | Nov. 27 | Dec. 02 | Dec. 18 '96 |
| 0.020 | Feb. 04 | Feb. 18 | Feb. 20 | Mar. 06 '97 |

This report is for information purposes and should not be considered a solicitation to buy or sell any security. Neither S&P nor any other party guarantee its accuracy or make warranties regarding results from its usage. Redistribution is prohibited without written permission. Copyright © 1997    A Division of The McGraw-Hill Companies

STANDARD
&POOR'S
STOCK REPORTS

**Fair, Isaac and Company, Incorporated**

**852V**

17-MAY-97

## Business Summary - 29-APR-97

Fair, Isaac and Company has been a pioneer in the development of statistical tools, called scoring algorithms, used mainly by grantors of credit to evaluate prospective credit customers, applicants for credit and existing credit customers. The company also produces software and stand-alone computers for the implementation of its scoring algorithms.

The company's best-known product, the Credit Application Scoring Algorithm, is used to calculate the risk of lending to individual credit applicants. The company's user base of about 500 companies includes more than 75 of the 100 largest banks in the U.S., each of the major travel and entertainment card companies, 20 banks in the U.K., several of the largest banks in Canada, 12 oil companies, more than 40 finance companies and more than 40 retailers. Products and services sold to the consumer credit industry have traditionally accounted for most of Fair, Isaac's revenues, but the company is actively promoting its products and services to other segments of the credit industry, including mortgage and small business lending; and to non-credit industries--particularly personal lines insurance and direct marketing. Consumer credit and direct marketing accounted for 83% and 14%, respectively, of Fair, Isaac's revenues in FY 96 (Sep.).

Other key product offerings include: Behavior Scoring Algorithms, which permit managements to define rules for treatment of existing credit customers on an ongoing basis; PreScore Algorithms, used for screening mailings that solicit credit applications; and Automated Strategic Application Processing (ASAP) systems, which are stand-alone assemblies of hardware and software that automate the processing of credit applications.

The company's most advanced product is the Adaptive Control System, now generally marketed under the name TRIAD. An Adaptive Control System is a complex of behavior scoring algorithms, computer software and account management strategy addressed to one or more aspects of the management of a consumer credit or similar portfolio.

DynaMark Inc., acquired in 1992, is engaged in developing and managing marketing databases.

The percentage of revenues derived from customers outside the United States was approximately 15% in FY 96, 13% in FY 95, and 14% in FY 94.

In September 1996, FIC expanded its credit management consulting services with the acquisition of Credit & Risk Management Associates, Inc. (CRMA), a provider of consulting services, MIS and organizational support for credit issuers, lenders, utilities and telecommunications firms.

### Capitalization

**Long Term Debt:** $1,552,000 of cap. lease obligs. (12/96).

### Per Share Data ($)

| (Year Ended Sep. 30) | 1996 | 1995 | 1994 | 1993 | 1992 | 1991 | 1990 | 1989 | 1988 | 1987 |
|---|---|---|---|---|---|---|---|---|---|---|
| Tangible Bk. Val. | 5.48 | 4.20 | 3.30 | 2.49 | 2.37 | 2.03 | 1.80 | 1.68 | 1.54 | 1.33 |
| Cash Flow | 1.88 | 1.50 | 1.14 | 0.69 | 0.41 | 0.32 | 0.21 | 0.22 | 0.24 | 0.25 |
| Earnings | 1.27 | 1.00 | 0.80 | 0.43 | 0.33 | 0.24 | 0.14 | 0.17 | 0.21 | 0.21 |
| Dividends | 0.08 | 0.08 | 0.07 | 0.07 | 0.07 | 0.05 | 0.05 | 0.05 | Nil | Nil |
| Payout Ratio | 6% | 8% | 9% | 16% | 20% | 21% | 35% | 28% | Nil | Nil |
| Prices - High | 50 | 30³/₄ | 28⁵/₈ | 11¹/₄ | 8 | 6 | 3³/₈ | 4¹/₂ | 4¹/₈ | 5¹/₄ |
|     - Low | 21¹/₂ | 17 | 10¹/₂ | 5⁷/₈ | 4³/₄ | 2³/₈ | 2¹/₄ | 2¹/₂ | 2¹/₄ | 1⁷/₈ |
| P/E Ratio - High | 39 | 31 | 36 | 26 | 24 | 26 | 24 | 26 | 20 | 25 |
|     - Low | 17 | 17 | 13 | 14 | 14 | 10 | 16 | 15 | 11 | 9 |

### Income Statement Analysis (Million $)

| | 1996 | 1995 | 1994 | 1993 | 1992 | 1991 | 1990 | 1989 | 1988 | 1987 |
|---|---|---|---|---|---|---|---|---|---|---|
| Revs. | 149 | 114 | 90.3 | 66.7 | 42.6 | 31.8 | 25.5 | 23.2 | 21.0 | 18.1 |
| Oper. Inc. | 35.8 | 26.0 | 20.1 | 12.2 | 6.6 | 4.0 | 1.7 | 2.4 | 3.1 | 3.9 |
| Depr. | 7.9 | 6.2 | 4.3 | 3.1 | 1.0 | 0.9 | 0.8 | 0.6 | 0.4 | 0.4 |
| Int. Exp. | 0.1 | 0.2 | 0.2 | 0.3 | NM | Nil | Nil | Nil | 0.0 | Nil |
| Pretax Inc. | 27.2 | 21.4 | 16.6 | 8.6 | 6.7 | 4.4 | 2.3 | 3.2 | 3.7 | 4.0 |
| Eff. Tax Rate | 41% | 41% | 39% | 39% | 41% | 37% | 33% | 38% | 36% | 48% |
| Net Inc. | 16.2 | 12.7 | 10.0 | 5.3 | 3.9 | 2.8 | 1.6 | 2.0 | 2.4 | 2.1 |

### Balance Sheet & Other Fin. Data (Million $)

| | 1996 | 1995 | 1994 | 1993 | 1992 | 1991 | 1990 | 1989 | 1988 | 1987 |
|---|---|---|---|---|---|---|---|---|---|---|
| Cash | 15.7 | 8.3 | 14.9 | 10.7 | 12.1 | 16.3 | 17.2 | 13.5 | 14.3 | 10.2 |
| Curr. Assets | 61.5 | 47.8 | 38.3 | 32.0 | 24.7 | 24.6 | 24.4 | 20.8 | 21.9 | 19.4 |
| Total Assets | 113 | 88.3 | 70.9 | 54.2 | 41.9 | 31.4 | 27.6 | 25.9 | 24.5 | 21.3 |
| Curr. Liab. | 28.2 | 23.4 | 21.8 | 17.3 | 11.4 | 8.1 | 7.3 | 5.7 | 5.2 | 3.2 |
| LT Debt | 1.6 | 1.9 | 2.3 | 2.7 | 2.7 | Nil | Nil | Nil | Nil | Nil |
| Common Eqty. | 78.3 | 56.1 | 42.9 | 31.5 | 26.6 | 22.3 | 19.7 | 18.4 | 16.8 | 14.8 |
| Total Cap. | 80.9 | 64.9 | 45.3 | 34.2 | 29.3 | 22.3 | 20.1 | 19.8 | 18.9 | 17.9 |
| Cap. Exp. | 1.7 | 10.7 | 5.3 | 5.7 | 6.2 | 1.0 | 1.0 | 1.3 | 0.6 | 0.6 |
| Cash Flow | 24.0 | 18.9 | 14.3 | 8.4 | 4.9 | 3.7 | 2.4 | 2.6 | 2.8 | 2.5 |
| Curr. Ratio | 2.2 | 2.0 | 1.8 | 1.8 | 2.2 | 3.0 | 3.3 | 3.6 | 4.2 | 6.1 |
| % LT Debt of Cap. | 2.0 | 2.9 | 5.2 | 8.0 | 9.1 | Nil | Nil | Nil | Nil | Nil |
| % Net Inc.of Revs. | 10.9 | 11.2 | 11.1 | 7.9 | 9.2 | 8.7 | 6.1 | 8.5 | 11.3 | 11.4 |
| % Ret. on Assets | 16.1 | 16.0 | 15.8 | 10.8 | 10.6 | 9.3 | 5.8 | 7.8 | 10.5 | 12.1 |
| % Ret. on Equity | 24.1 | 25.7 | 26.6 | 17.9 | 15.9 | 13.1 | 8.2 | 11.2 | 15.1 | 20.2 |

Data as orig. reptd.; bef. results of disc. opers. and/or spec. items. Per share data adj. for stk. divs. as of ex-div. date. E-Estimated. NA-Not Available. NM-Not Meaningful. NR-Not Ranked.

**Office**—120 N. Redwood Dr., San Rafael, CA 94903-1996. **Tel**—(415) 472-2211. **Chrmn**—R. M. Oliver. **Pres & CEO**—L. E. Rosenberger. **EVP & COO**—J. D. Woldrich. **SVP & CFO**—P. Cole **VP & Secy**—P. L. McCorkell. **Dirs**—A. G. Battle, B. J. Brooks, H. R. Heller, G. R. Henshaw, D. S. P. Hopkins, R. M. Oliver, L. E. Rosenberger, R. D. Sanderson, J. D. Woldrich. **Transfer Agent & Registrar**—Chemical Trust Co. of California, SF. **Incorporated**—in Delaware in 1987. **Empl**— 1,037. **S&P Analyst:** Adam Penn

# Federal Home Loan Mortgage    865T

NYSE Symbol **FRE**

In S&P 500

**17-MAY-97**

**Industry:**
Financial (Diversified)

**Summary:** Federal Home Loan Mortgage ("Freddie Mac"), a corporate instrumentality of the U.S. government, buys mortgages from lenders in order to increase the supply of funds for housing.

| | | |
|---|---|---|
| **S&P Opinion: Accumulate (★★★★)** | Recent Price • 32½ | Yield • 1.2% |
| | 52 Wk Range • 33⅞-20⅛ | 12-Mo. P/E • 19.0 |

**Quantitative Evaluations**

**Outlook**
(1 Lowest—5 Highest)
• **2+**

**Fair Value**
• **30**

**Risk**
• **Low**

**Earn./Div. Rank**
• **NR**

**Technical Eval.**
• **Bullish** since 2/95

**Rel. Strength Rank**
(1 Lowest—99 Highest)
• **80**

**Insider Activity**
• **NA**

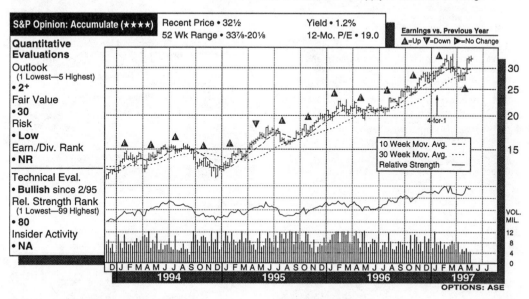

Earnings vs. Previous Year
▲=Up ▼=Down ▶=No Change

10 Week Mov. Avg. ---
30 Week Mov. Avg. ·····
Relative Strength —

4-for-1

VOL.
MIL.

OPTIONS: ASE

## Overview - 16-APR-97

Share earnings are projected to grow steadily at percentages in the low teens range over the next three to five years. The main factor expected to benefit earnings is expansion of the retained mortgage portfolio Freddie Mac holds for its own account. At March 31, 1997, this portfolio totaled $144.4 billion, up from $117.3 billion a year earlier. FRE should continue to expand this portfolio through new mortgage purchases due to growth in the level of mortgage debt outstanding, its access to low-cost financing by virtue of its quasi-agency status, and the fact that it only owns a small share of total mortgage debt. Only modest gains are seen in the company's securitization operations, reflecting the large balance of mortgages already securitized and a reduced need by well-capitalized thrifts to hold MBS in their portfolios.

## Valuation - 16-APR-97

Freddie Mac shares are a solid, long-term core holding. Although the stock was recently trading at a P/E of about 14X projected 1997 EPS, below the market average, we expect the company to boost earnings at low double digit rates on average for the foreseeable future, above the growth rate of the overall market. We attach a high degree of confidence to our growth outlook, as FRE enjoys competitive endowments such as access to financing only modestly above treasury rates (because of its quasi-agency status) and a low cost structure, resulting from economies of scale inherent in its businesses. In addition, total mortgage debt outstanding is increasing. The company typically generates an impressive return on equity of 20%, much better than that of other financial concerns. Lastly, credit quality trends are positive.

## Key Stock Statistics

| | | | |
|---|---|---|---|
| S&P EPS Est. 1997 | 1.90 | Tang. Bk. Value/Share | 7.68 |
| P/E on S&P Est. 1997 | 17.1 | Beta | 1.72 |
| Dividend Rate/Share | 0.40 | Shareholders | 1,900 |
| Shs. outstg. (M) | 695.0 | Market cap. (B) | $ 22.6 |
| Avg. daily vol. (M) | 0.935 | Inst. holdings | 78% |

Value of $10,000 invested 5 years ago: $ 30,830

### Fiscal Year Ending Dec. 31

| | 1997 | 1996 | 1995 | 1994 | 1993 | 1992 |
|---|---|---|---|---|---|---|
| **Revenues (Million $)** | | | | | | |
| 1Q | 3,844 | 2,749 | 2,143 | 1,574 | 1,165 | 1,071 |
| 2Q | — | 2,995 | 2,305 | 1,626 | 1,318 | 1,099 |
| 3Q | — | 3,137 | 2,489 | 1,779 | 1,382 | 1,104 |
| 4Q | — | 3,235 | 2,582 | 1,944 | 1,591 | 1,187 |
| Yr. | — | 12,116 | 9,519 | 6,923 | 5,456 | 4,461 |
| **Earnings Per Share ($)** | | | | | | |
| 1Q | 0.44 | 0.40 | 0.33 | 0.36 | 0.26 | 0.19 |
| 2Q | E0.46 | 0.43 | 0.34 | 0.32 | 0.24 | 0.22 |
| 3Q | E0.49 | 0.41 | 0.36 | 0.32 | 0.26 | 0.21 |
| 4Q | E0.51 | 0.43 | 0.38 | 0.32 | 0.26 | 0.20 |
| Yr. | E1.90 | 1.67 | 1.42 | 1.33 | 1.02 | 0.82 |

### Next earnings report expected: mid July

**Dividend Data** (Dividends have been paid since 1989.)

| Amount ($) | Date Decl. | Ex-Div. Date | Stock of Record | Payment Date |
|---|---|---|---|---|
| 0.350 | Sep. 06 | Sep. 12 | Sep. 16 | Sep. 30 '96 |
| 0.350 | Dec. 06 | Dec. 12 | Dec. 16 | Dec. 31 '96 |
| 4-for-1 | Dec. 06 | Jan. 13 | Dec. 31 | Jan. 10 '97 |
| 0.100 | Mar. 07 | Mar. 13 | Mar. 17 | Mar. 31 '97 |

This report is for information purposes and should not be considered a solicitation to buy or sell any security. Neither S&P nor any other party guarantee its accuracy or make warranties regarding results from its usage. Redistribution is prohibited without written permission. Copyright © 1997

*A Division of The McGraw-Hill Companies*

## Business Summary - 16-APR-97

The Federal Home Loan Mortgage Corp., better known as Freddie Mac, is one of two public government-sponsored enterprises (the other being rival Fannie Mae) formed to promote home ownership by increasing the availability of mortgage financing. The company was originally part of the Federal Home Loan Bank Board, which was dismantled under the S & L bailout law of 1989. Of its 18 directors, 13 are elected by stockholders and five are picked by the President. Freddie Mac has two principal business segments.

In its portfolio business, Freddie Mac functions quite similarly to a savings and loan which originates home mortgage loans to hold for its own account. The major differences are that (1) Freddie Mac uses capital markets borrowings to finance its mortgage purchases whereas the thrift uses retail savings and (2) Freddie Mac purchases mortgages from various lenders while the thrift actually issues the homebuyer a mortgage.

The term "retained mortgage portfolio" is intended to indicate that these mortgages are "warehoused" (i.e. held) as a long-term investment for their valuable interest income. This business is quite profitable for Freddie because its cost of funds is in one sense subsidized by its quasi-agency status. The retained portfolio business generates some two-thirds of the company's profits. At December 31, 1996 Freddie Mac's retained mortgage portfolio totaled some $137.5 billion, about one-fifth as large as Fannie Mae's retained mortgage portfolio.

The company's mortgage backed security (MBS) operation is best illustrated by an example. Typically, a bank or thrift will decide it prefers to hold MBS as opposed to originated loans. The institution then gives the loan, or more often a pool of loans, to Freddie Mac, who gives the lender MBS in return. Both parties win. Freddie Mac receives a fee of about one-fifth of 1% to guarantee the principal and interest on the MBS. And the lender has a nearly risk free instrument on which it receives principal and interest payments. Freddie Mac makes money in this business because its loss rate is very low-- people will default on all sorts of bills but the basic need for shelter provides a powerful incentive to keep the mortgage more or less current.

Nonperforming single family loans amounted to 0.58% of the total portfolio at December 31, 1996, down from 0.60% a year earlier. Apartment delinquencies and foreclosures were 1.96% of the total portfolio, based on principal balances, versus 2.88% a year earlier.

According to a study by the Office of Management and Budget, mortgage rates are about 0.25-0.50% lower because Freddie Mac and its rival Fannie Mae exist in the form and size they do.

## Capitalization

**Short Term Debt:** $68,262,000,000 (3/97).
**Long Term Debt:** $85,359,000,000 (3/97).
**Noncum. Preferred Stock:** $837,300,000.

### Per Share Data ($)

| (Year Ended Dec. 31) | 1996 | 1995 | 1994 | 1993 | 1992 | 1991 | 1990 | 1989 | 1988 | 1987 |
|---|---|---|---|---|---|---|---|---|---|---|
| Tangible Bk. Val. | 9.63 | 7.38 | 6.45 | 4.95 | 4.17 | 3.56 | 2.97 | 2.66 | NA | NA |
| Earnings | 1.67 | 1.42 | 1.33 | 1.02 | 0.82 | 0.77 | 0.57 | 0.55 | 0.48 | 0.38 |
| Dividends | 0.35 | 0.30 | 0.26 | 0.22 | 0.19 | 0.17 | 0.13 | 0.13 | NA | NA |
| Payout Ratio | 21% | 21% | 20% | 22% | 23% | 22% | 23% | 24% | NA | NA |
| Prices - High | 29¼ | 20⅞ | 15¾ | 14¼ | 12⅜ | 11⅝ | 6⅞ | 8¾ | 4⅜ | NA |
| - Low | 19⅛ | 12½ | 11¾ | 11⅜ | 8½ | 3¾ | 2½ | 4⅛ | 3¾ | NA |
| P/E Ratio - High | 18 | 15 | 12 | 14 | 15 | 15 | 12 | 16 | 9 | NA |
| - Low | 11 | 9 | 9 | 11 | 10 | 5 | 4 | 7 | 8 | NA |

### Income Statement Analysis (Million $)

| | 1996 | 1995 | 1994 | 1993 | 1992 | 1991 | 1990 | 1989 | 1988 | 1987 |
|---|---|---|---|---|---|---|---|---|---|---|
| Interest On: Mtges. | 9,038 | 6,505 | 4,528 | 3,296 | 2,608 | 2,332 | 2,053 | 2,016 | 1,569 | 1,194 |
| Interest On: Invest. | 1,745 | 1,888 | 1,287 | 1,127 | 917 | 1,095 | 1,258 | 1,169 | 833 | 627 |
| Int. Exp. | 8,241 | 6,997 | 4,703 | 3,571 | 2,830 | 2,744 | 2,692 | 2,668 | 1,910 | 1,422 |
| Guaranty Fees | 1,249 | 1,087 | 1,108 | 1,033 | 936 | 792 | 654 | 572 | 465 | NA |
| Loan Loss Prov. | 320 | 255 | 200 | 300 | 473 | 431 | 474 | 260 | 204 | NA |
| Admin. Exp. | 440 | 395 | 379 | 361 | 329 | 287 | 243 | 217 | 194 | NA |
| Pretax Inc. | 1,797 | 1,586 | 1,482 | 1,128 | 901 | 800 | 587 | 628 | 554 | 480 |
| Eff. Tax Rate | 30% | 31% | 31% | 30% | 31% | 31% | 30% | 30% | 31% | 37% |
| Net Inc. | 1,243 | 1,091 | 1,027 | 786 | 622 | 555 | 414 | 437 | 381 | 301 |

### Balance Sheet & Other Fin. Data (Million $)

| | 1996 | 1995 | 1994 | 1993 | 1992 | 1991 | 1990 | 1989 | 1988 | 1987 |
|---|---|---|---|---|---|---|---|---|---|---|
| Mtges. | 137,520 | 107,411 | 72,295 | 55,732 | 33,523 | 26,537 | 21,395 | 21,329 | 16,815 | NA |
| Invest. | 16,331 | 13,962 | 17,808 | 18,223 | 12,542 | 9,956 | 11,012 | 5,765 | 9,107 | NA |
| Cash & Equiv. | 9,141 | 7,483 | 11,442 | 3,216 | 6,453 | 7,987 | 4,859 | 5,397 | 5,525 | 4,670 |
| Total Assets | 173,866 | 137,181 | 106,199 | 83,880 | 59,502 | 46,860 | 40,579 | 35,462 | 34,352 | 25,674 |
| ST Debt | 80,105 | 62,141 | 47,303 | 17,999 | 12,854 | 17,239 | 19,959 | 16,673 | 18,847 | 12,801 |
| LT Debt | 76,386 | 57,820 | 48,984 | 31,994 | 16,777 | 13,023 | 10,982 | 9,474 | 8,035 | 6,746 |
| Equity | 6,685 | 5,000 | 4,300 | 3,574 | 3,008 | 2,566 | 2,136 | 1,916 | 1,584 | 1,182 |
| % Ret. on Assets | 0.8 | 0.9 | 1.1 | 1.1 | 1.2 | 1.2 | 1.1 | 1.3 | 1.3 | 1.2 |
| % Ret. on Equity | 18.5 | 22.1 | 24.4 | 21.4 | 21.2 | 23.6 | 20.4 | 25.0 | 27.5 | 28.2 |
| Equity/Assets Ratio | 4.0 | 3.8 | 4.2 | 4.6 | 5.2 | 5.4 | 5.3 | 5.0 | 4.6 | NA |
| Price Times Book Value: | | | | | | | | | | |
| Hi | 3.0 | 2.8 | 2.4 | 2.9 | 2.5 | 3.3 | 2.3 | 3.3 | NA | NA |
| Low | 1.2 | 1.7 | 1.8 | 2.3 | 1.7 | 1.0 | 0.9 | 1.5 | NA | NA |

Data as orig. reptd.; bef. results of disc opers. and/or spec. items. Per share data adj. for stk. divs. as of ex-div. date. E-Estimated. NA-Not Available. NM-Not Meaningful. NR-Not Ranked.

**Office**—8200 Jones Branch Drive, McLean, VA 22102. **Tel**—(703) 903-2000. **Website**—http://www.freddiemac.com **Chrmn & CEO**—L. C. Brendsel. **Pres**—D. W. Glenn. **VP & Secy**—M. E. Mater. **Investor Contact**—Paul Scarpetta (703-903-2798). **Dirs**—L. C. Brendsel, D. DeConcini, D. W. Glenn, G. D Gould, J. M. Hultin, H. Kaufman, J. B. McCoy, J. F. Montgomery, J. B. Nutter, R. E. Palmer, R. F. Poe, D. J. Schuenke, C. Selx, W. J. Turner, H. F. Woods. **Transfer Agent & Registrar**—ChaseMellon Shareholder Services, NYC. **Incorporated**—under the laws of the United States in 1970. **Empl**—3,000. **S&P Analyst:** Paul L. Huberman, CFA

**17-MAY-97**

**Industry:**
Financial (Diversified)

**Summary:** "Fannie Mae," a U.S. government-sponsored company, uses mostly borrowed funds to buy a variety of mortgages, thereby creating a secondary market for mortgage lenders.

**S&P Opinion: Accumulate (★★★★)**

| | |
|---|---|
| Recent Price • 42 | Yield • 2.0% |
| 52 Wk Range • 44-29⅛ | 12-Mo. P/E • 16.4 |

**Quantitative Evaluations**

**Outlook**
(1 Lowest—5 Highest)
• **2+**

**Fair Value**
• **40½**

**Risk**
• **Average**

**Earn./Div. Rank**
• **A**

**Technical Eval.**
• **Bullish** since 4/95

**Rel. Strength Rank**
(1 Lowest—99 Highest)
• **68**

**Insider Activity**
• **NA**

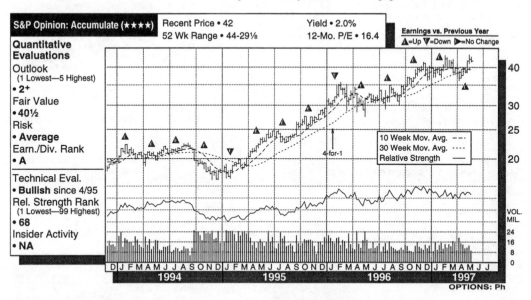

Earnings vs. Previous Year
▲=Up ▼=Down ►=No Change

10 Week Mov. Avg. – – –
30 Week Mov. Avg. ·······
Relative Strength ——

4-for-1

1994   1995   1996   1997

VOL. MIL.

OPTIONS: Ph

## Overview - 11-APR-97

Fannie Mae should increase its earnings per share 10% to 15% a year for the foreseeable future (excluding nonrecurring expenses such as a charitable contribution in 1995). This outlook reflects projected growth in the mortgage portfolio Fannie Mae holds for its own account (about two-thirds of profits). FNM should expand this portfolio about 10%-13% in 1997, based on projected growth of 7% to 9% in mortgage debt, home price inflation and FNM's plans to increase its purchases of mortgage-backed securities. The mortgage-backed securities segment (about one-third of net income) is growing more slowly, partly reflecting the fact that a high percentage of mortgages has already been securitized and reduced demand for MBS on the part of certain financial institutions. No major increase in credit provisioning is likely, given the company's strong reserve position. Long-term prospects are further enhanced by share repurchases.

## Valuation - 11-APR-97

Fannie Mae, which we regard as a solid core holding, carries an accumulate recommendation. The company enjoys favorable long-term growth prospects, a result of projected increases in mortgage debt outstanding, new housing initiatives and its access to low-cost financing by virtue of its quasi-agency status. Another positive is the fact that Fannie Mae faces only one competitor in its major markets. The company typically generates a high return on shareholders' equity. The stock is selling at a P/E ratio of about 13 on projected 1997 earnings per share of $2.80, below the market's P/E. Given the company's strengths, we believe the shares deserve a richer P/E multiple.

## Key Stock Statistics

| | | | |
|---|---|---|---|
| S&P EPS Est. 1997 | 2.80 | Tang. Bk. Value/Share | 11.10 |
| P/E on S&P Est. 1997 | 15.0 | Beta | 1.56 |
| Dividend Rate/Share | 0.84 | Shareholders | 19,000 |
| Shs. outstg. (M) | 1061.0 | Market cap. (B) | $ 44.6 |
| Avg. daily vol. (M) | 2.183 | Inst. holdings | 79% |

Value of $10,000 invested 5 years ago: $ 27,593

## Fiscal Year Ending Dec. 31

| | 1997 | 1996 | 1995 | 1994 | 1993 | 1992 |
|---|---|---|---|---|---|---|
| **Revenues (Million $)** | | | | | | |
| 1Q | — | 6,065 | 5,290 | 4,304 | 2,863 | 3,470 |
| 2Q | — | 6,146 | 5,452 | 4,496 | 3,897 | 3,642 |
| 3Q | — | 6,317 | 5,631 | 4,735 | 4,071 | 3,670 |
| 4Q | — | 6,526 | 5,866 | 5,038 | 4,222 | 3,777 |
| Yr. | — | 25,054 | 22,250 | 18,573 | 16,053 | 14,559 |
| **Earnings Per Share ($)** | | | | | | |
| 1Q | 0.67 | 0.61 | 0.51 | 0.50 | 0.44 | 0.35 |
| 2Q | E0.69 | 0.61 | 0.52 | 0.50 | 0.45 | 0.38 |
| 3Q | E0.71 | 0.63 | 0.55 | 0.49 | 0.48 | 0.39 |
| 4Q | E0.73 | 0.65 | 0.37 | 0.47 | 0.49 | 0.39 |
| Yr. | E2.80 | 2.50 | 1.96 | 1.95 | 1.86 | 1.50 |

**Next earnings report expected: mid July**

**Dividend Data** (Dividends have been paid since 1956.)

| Amount ($) | Date Decl. | Ex-Div. Date | Stock of Record | Payment Date |
|---|---|---|---|---|
| 0.190 | Jul. 16 | Jul. 29 | Jul. 31 | Aug. 25 '96 |
| 0.190 | Oct. 15 | Oct. 29 | Oct. 31 | Nov. 25 '96 |
| 0.210 | Jan. 21 | Jan. 29 | Jan. 31 | Feb. 25 '97 |
| 0.210 | Apr. 15 | Apr. 28 | Apr. 30 | May. 25 '97 |

This report is for information purposes and should not be considered a solicitation to buy or sell any security. Neither S&P nor any other party guarantee its accuracy or make warranties regarding results from its usage. Redistribution is prohibited without written permission. Copyright © 1997 | A Division of The McGraw·Hill Companies

## Business Summary - 11-APR-97

The Federal National Mortgage Association, more commonly known as "Fannie Mae," is a government-sponsored enterprise, chartered by Congress to increase the availability of mortgage credit for homebuyers. Its mission, in essence, is to increase the rate of home ownership--which in turn makes American society more stable. The company's predecessor was formed during the Great Depression to make home ownership possible during a time when it was nearly impossible for people in certain parts of the country to obtain a mortgage. The company basically operates in two business segments.

In its retained portfolio business, which accounts for about two-thirds of profits, the company buys a variety of mortgages from banks, thrifts, mortgage bankers and others for its own account. The term "retained" is intended to indicate that Fannie Mae holds these mortgages for investment just as an S & L, which originates mortgages, holds mortgages in its own portfolio. The company finances its mortgage purchases by debt offerings of various maturities. This business activity is especially profitable because FNM enjoys access to low-cost funds by virtue of its quasi-agency status, that is, investors believe there is a very low risk of default on the company's bonds because, in the event of trouble, the government would probably step in and make good on the obligation. Fannie Mae is an ex-

tremely large company. As an indication of the company's size, at the end of 1995, Fannie Mae owned $253.5 billion of mortgages, equal to some 6.5% of the total mortgages outstanding nationwide.

In its securitization operations, which account for much of the remaining profits, the company swaps mortgage-backed securities for mortgages with various lending institutions and in the process earns a fee of about one-fifth of 1% or 0.20%. One reason lenders would swap loans for MBS is that the latter add to its liquidity. Fannie Mae essentially functions as a "mortgage insurer" to the extent that it accepts the risk of default on the mortgage in exchange for a fee or a premium.

Finally, the company earns a small amount for guaranteeing complex mortgage-backed securities that are put together by Wall Street firms.

Although FNM is highly profitable in a variety of interest rate environments, Congress is constantly concerned about its risk exposure on the $800 billion of mortgages and mortgage-backed securities outstanding--since the U. S. government ultimately would have to make good on large scale defaults. Therefore, Congress has established capital standards, which the company meets.

### Capitalization

**Short Term Debt:** $159,071,000,000 (3/97).
**Long Term Debt:** $177,103,000,000 (3/97).
**Preferred Stock:** $1,000,000,000.

### Per Share Data ($)

| (Year Ended Dec. 31) | 1996 | 1995 | 1994 | 1993 | 1992 | 1991 | 1990 | 1989 | 1988 | 1987 |
|---|---|---|---|---|---|---|---|---|---|---|
| Tangible Bk. Val. | 11.10 | 10.04 | 8.74 | 7.39 | 6.20 | 5.08 | 4.14 | 3.13 | 2.39 | 1.92 |
| Earnings | 2.50 | 1.94 | 1.95 | 1.86 | 1.50 | 1.33 | 1.13 | 0.79 | 0.54 | 0.39 |
| Dividends | 0.76 | 0.68 | 0.60 | 0.46 | 0.35 | 0.26 | 0.18 | 0.11 | 0.06 | 0.03 |
| Payout Ratio | 30% | 35% | 31% | 25% | 23% | 20% | 16% | 14% | 11% | 8% |
| Prices - High | 41⅝ | 31½ | 22⅝ | 21½ | 19⅜ | 17⅜ | 11⅛ | 11⅝ | 4⅜ | 4 |
| - Low | 27½ | 17¼ | 17 | 18¼ | 13¾ | 8⅛ | 6¼ | 4¼ | 2⁷/₁₆ | 2⅛ |
| P/E Ratio - High | 17 | 16 | 12 | 12 | 13 | 13 | 10 | 15 | 8 | 10 |
| - Low | 11 | 9 | 9 | 10 | 9 | 6 | 6 | 5 | 5 | 5 |

### Income Statement Analysis (Million $)

| | 1996 | 1995 | 1994 | 1993 | 1992 | 1991 | 1990 | 1989 | 1988 | 1987 |
|---|---|---|---|---|---|---|---|---|---|---|
| Interest On: Mtges. | 20,560 | 18,154 | 15,851 | 13,957 | 12,651 | 11,603 | 10,958 | 10,103 | 9,629 | 9,586 |
| Interest On: Invest. | 3,212 | 2,917 | 1,496 | 876 | 884 | 990 | 1,111 | 977 | 597 | 257 |
| Int. Exp. | 20,180 | 18,024 | 14,524 | 12,300 | 11,476 | 10,815 | 10,476 | 9,889 | 9,389 | 8,953 |
| Guaranty Fees | 1,196 | 0.0 | 1,083 | 961 | 834 | 675 | 536 | 408 | 328 | 263 |
| Loan Loss Prov. | 195 | 140 | 155 | 175 | 320 | 370 | 310 | 310 | 365 | 360 |
| Admin. Exp. | 560 | 546 | 525 | 443 | 381 | 319 | 286 | 254 | 218 | 197 |
| Pretax Inc. | 3,905 | 2,995 | 3,146 | 3,005 | 2,382 | 2,081 | 1,647 | 1,104 | 663 | 568 |
| Eff. Tax Rate | 30% | 28% | 32% | 32% | 31% | 30% | 29% | 27% | 24% | 34% |
| Net Inc. | 2,754 | 2,155 | 2,141 | 2,042 | 1,649 | 1,455 | 1,173 | 807 | 507 | 376 |

### Balance Sheet & Other Fin. Data (Million $)

| | 1996 | 1995 | 1994 | 1993 | 1992 | 1991 | 1990 | 1989 | 1988 | 1987 |
|---|---|---|---|---|---|---|---|---|---|---|
| Mtges. | 286,259 | 252,588 | 220,525 | 189,892 | 156,021 | 126,486 | 113,875 | 107,756 | 99,867 | 93,470 |
| Invest. | 56,606 | 57,273 | 46,335 | 21,396 | 14,786 | 10,999 | 9,868 | 6,656 | 5,289 | 3,468 |
| Cash & Equiv. | 850 | 318 | 231 | 977 | 3,194 | 4,178 | 5,214 | 2,859 | 2,457 |  |
| Total Assets | 351,041 | 316,550 | 272,508 | 216,979 | 180,978 | 147,072 | 133,113 | 124,315 | 112,258 | 103,459 |
| ST Debt | 159,900 | 146,153 | 112,602 | 71,950 | 56,404 | 34,608 | 38,453 | 36,346 | 36,599 | 29,718 |
| LT Debt | 171,370 | 153,021 | 144,628 | 129,162 | 109,896 | 99,329 | 84,950 | 79,718 | 68,860 | 67,339 |
| Equity | 12,773 | 10,959 | 9,541 | 8,052 | 6,774 | 5,547 | 3,941 | 2,991 | 2,260 | 1,811 |
| % Ret. on Assets | 0.8 | 0.7 | 0.9 | 1.0 | 1.0 | 1.0 | 0.9 | 0.7 | 0.5 | 0.4 |
| % Ret. on Equity | 23.9 | 21.0 | 24.3 | 27.5 | 26.8 | 30.7 | 33.8 | 30.7 | 24.9 | 25.1 |
| Equity/Assets Ratio | 3.4 | 3.5 | 3.6 | 3.7 | 3.8 | 3.4 | 2.7 | 2.2 | 1.9 | NA |
| Price Times Book Value: | | | | | | | | | | |
| Hi | 3.8 | 3.1 | 2.6 | 2.9 | 3.1 | 3.4 | 2.7 | 3.7 | 1.8 | 2.1 |
| Low | 2.5 | 1.7 | 1.9 | 2.5 | 2.2 | 1.6 | 1.5 | 1.3 | 1.0 | 1.1 |

Data as orig. reptd.; bef. results of disc. opers. and/or spec. items. Per share data adj. for stk. divs. as of ex-div. date. E-Estimated. NA-Not Available. NM-Not Meaningful. NR-Not Ranked.

**Office**—3900 Wisconsin Ave. N.W., Washington, DC 20016. **Tel**—(202) 752-7000. **Website**—http://www.fanniemae.com **Chrmn & CEO**—J. A. Johnson. **Pres**—L. M. Small. **EVP-CFO**—J. T. Howard. **EVP-Secy**—C. S. Bernstein. **Investor Contact**—Jayne Shontell (202-752-7115). **Dirs**—F. M. Beck, R. E. Birk, E. Broad, W. M. Daley, T. P. Gerrity, J. A. Johnson, T. A. Leonard, V. A. Mai, A. McLaughlin, R. D. Parsons, F. D. Raines, J. R. Sasso, A. Shusta, L. M. Small, C. J. Sumner, J. H. Villarreal, K. H. Williams. **Incorporated**—under the laws of the United States in 1938. **Empl**—3,400. **S&P Analyst:** Paul L. Huberman, CFA

# STANDARD &POOR'S
STOCK REPORTS

# Franklin Resources

**922Q**

NYSE Symbol **BEN**

In S&P MidCap 400

**17-MAY-97**

**Industry:** Investment Management

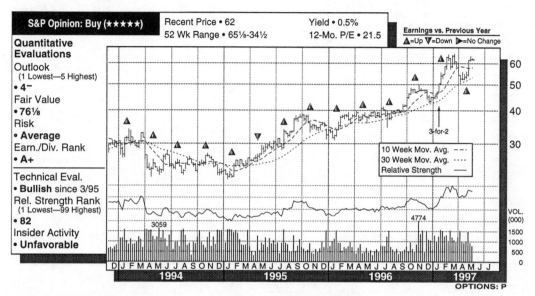

**Summary:** Franklin Resources is one of the world's largest publicly traded independent asset managers.

| S&P Opinion: Buy (★★★★) | Recent Price • 62 | Yield • 0.5% |
| --- | --- | --- |
| | 52 Wk Range • 65⅛-34½ | 12-Mo. P/E • 21.5 |

**Quantitative Evaluations**

**Outlook** (1 Lowest—5 Highest)
• **4⁻**

**Fair Value**
• **76⅛**

**Risk**
• **Average**

**Earn./Div. Rank**
• **A+**

**Technical Eval.**
• **Bullish** since 3/95

**Rel. Strength Rank** (1 Lowest—99 Highest)
• **82**

**Insider Activity**
• **Unfavorable**

**Earnings vs. Previous Year**
▲=Up ▼=Down ▶=No Change

10 Week Mov. Avg. - - -
30 Week Mov. Avg. · · · ·
Relative Strength ——

3-for-2

OPTIONS: P

## Overview - 24-APR-97

Solid earnings-per-share growth in the low double-digit range is expected for FY 98 (Sep.). Contributors to the anticipated profit growth include the acquisition of Heine Securities, the ongoing reinvestment of dividends and interest by existing fundholders, greater retirement savings by the baby boom generation, and improved sales of international funds. Stock funds have been the company's best selling product in recent periods. Margins, which are extremely wide, could expand further, based on anticipated growth in assets under management. Because of goodwill resulting from the Heine deal, cash flow will be considerably greater than net income. The major risk is the direction of financial markets. If, for example, the stock market declined, assets under management and thus advisory fees would also fall.

## Valuation - 24-APR-97

The shares carry a buy recommendation. Franklin enjoys a favorable long-term growth outlook, aided by the purchase of Heine Securities, which broadens its range of product offerings, adds funds with excellent track records, and opens up a new channel of distribution. Other contributors to the projected growth include increased retirement savings by the baby boom generation, and the highly attractive economics of the investment management business. Valuation levels are attractive. The stock trades at a P/E ratio of about 15 on projected FY 97 earnings per share. In addition, the company enjoyed pretax margins of 28% in the latest quarter and a return on equity of over 20%, both of which compare very favorably to industrial concerns. One risk is the level of the stock market, as fees are computed as a percentage of assets under management.

## Key Stock Statistics

| | | | |
| --- | --- | --- | --- |
| S&P EPS Est. 1997 | 3.20 | Tang. Bk. Value/Share | 6.30 |
| P/E on S&P Est. 1997 | 19.4 | Beta | 1.84 |
| S&P EPS Est. 1998 | 3.65 | Shareholders | 2,000 |
| Dividend Rate/Share | 0.32 | Market cap. (B) | $ 7.8 |
| Shs. outstg. (M) | 126.1 | Inst. holdings | 34% |
| Avg. daily vol. (M) | 0.206 | | |

Value of $10,000 invested 5 years ago: $ 34,240

## Fiscal Year Ending Sep. 30

| | 1998 | 1997 | 1996 | 1995 | 1994 | 1993 |
| --- | --- | --- | --- | --- | --- | --- |
| **Revenues (Million $)** | | | | | | |
| 1Q | — | 440.0 | 342.6 | 208.2 | 198.5 | 126.9 |
| 2Q | — | 521.9 | 393.8 | 199.8 | 213.6 | 153.6 |
| 3Q | — | — | 395.4 | 212.7 | 204.9 | 162.7 |
| 4Q | — | — | 390.8 | 225.1 | 209.9 | 197.5 |
| Yr. | — | — | 1,523 | 845.3 | 826.9 | 640.7 |
| **Earnings Per Share ($)** | | | | | | |
| 1Q | — | 0.76 | 0.59 | 0.51 | 0.47 | 0.29 |
| 2Q | — | 0.80 | 0.61 | 0.51 | 0.55 | 0.34 |
| 3Q | — | E0.81 | 0.65 | 0.56 | 0.48 | 0.36 |
| 4Q | — | E0.83 | 0.67 | 0.59 | 0.51 | 0.43 |
| Yr. | E3.65 | E3.20 | 2.52 | 2.16 | 2.00 | 1.41 |

**Next earnings report expected: late July**

**Dividend Data** (Dividends have been paid since 1981.)

| Amount ($) | Date Decl. | Ex-Div. Date | Stock of Record | Payment Date |
| --- | --- | --- | --- | --- |
| 0.110 | Sep. 10 | Sep. 25 | Sep. 27 | Oct. 14 '96 |
| 0.080 | Dec. 16 | Dec. 27 | Dec. 31 | Jan. 15 '97 |
| 3-for-2 | Dec. 16 | Jan. 15 | Dec. 31 | Jan. 14 '97 |
| 0.080 | Mar. 18 | Mar. 26 | Mar. 31 | Apr. 15 '97 |

This report is for information purposes and should not be considered a solicitation to buy or sell any security. Neither S&P nor any other party guarantee its accuracy or make warranties regarding results from its usage. Redistribution is prohibited without written permission. Copyright © 1997

*A Division of The McGraw-Hill Companies*

STANDARD
&POOR'S
STOCK REPORTS

# Franklin Resources, Inc.

**922Q**

**17-MAY-97**

## Business Summary - 24-APR-97

Franklin Resources is one of the largest mutual fund management companies in the U. S. with over $180 billion in assets under management at December 31, 1996. In essence, the company manages assets for individuals who have sent in their money. Franklin is an extremely profitable company, owing mainly to the attractive economics of the investment management business. The company receives a fee of some 0.63% on a huge balance of funds, or $884 million in FY 96 (Sep.), but its costs amount to little more than renting office space and paying its employees. Assets under mangement broke down as follows at the end of the last two fiscal years:

| | 9/96 | 9/95 |
|---|---|---|
| Fixed Income: | | |
| Tax-free income | 28% | 31% |
| U.S. government fixed income | 10% | 11% |
| Money fund | 2% | 2% |
| Global/int'l fixed income | 2% | 2% |
| Equity and Income: | | |
| Global/int'l equity | 31% | 28% |
| U.S. equity/income | 13% | 13% |
| Institutional | 14% | 13% |

The company has a leading share of fixed income mutual funds, particularly California municipal bonds. Franklin was one of the first mutual fund organizations to offer investors a California muni fund. Investors in municipal bond funds are often wealthy people in high tax brackets.

The company's international equity funds were acquired in 1992 with the purchase of Templeton Galbraith Hansberger, a firm run by legendary investor Sir John Templeton, who pioneered international investing. These funds boast excellent long-term performance records, although John Templeton has retired from active duty. In November 1996, the company acquired Heine Securities, which owns the Short Hills, N. J.-based Mutual Series of mutual funds run by famed value investor Michael Price. This deal rounded out the company's fund offering to include a domestic equity line-up. The company paid $618 million for the complex, which had $17 billion of assets under management.

Two important facts about Franklin are that Charles and Rupert Johnson, the Chairman and Executive Vice President, respectively, own some 34.5% of the stock outstanding, and that the funds, prior to the Heine deal, had been sold with a load charge primarily through the broker-dealer community.

## Capitalization

**Long Term Debt:** $468,320,000 (12/96).

## Per Share Data ($)

| (Year Ended Sep. 30) | 1996 | 1995 | 1994 | 1993 | 1992 | 1991 | 1990 | 1989 | 1988 | 1987 |
|---|---|---|---|---|---|---|---|---|---|---|
| Tangible Bk. Val. | 6.30 | 4.13 | 2.06 | 0.19 | 3.99 | 3.11 | 2.46 | 1.85 | 1.28 | 0.87 |
| Cash Flow | 2.84 | 2.55 | NA | NA | NA | NA | NA | NA | NA | NA |
| Earnings | 2.52 | 2.16 | 2.00 | 1.41 | 1.06 | 0.84 | 0.76 | 0.67 | 0.56 | 0.49 |
| Dividends | 0.29 | 0.27 | 0.27 | 0.19 | 0.17 | 0.15 | 0.13 | 0.10 | 0.09 | 0.05 |
| Payout Ratio | 12% | 12% | 11% | 13% | 16% | 18% | 18% | 15% | 17% | 10% |
| Prices - High | 49¾ | 38⅝ | 34 | 34⅝ | 26 | 18⅞ | 12 | 10 | 5¼ | 9½ |
|     - Low | 30⅞ | 22 | 22⅜ | 21⅜ | 15⅛ | 9¾ | 7½ | 5 | 3¾ | 2⅝ |
| P/E Ratio - High | 20 | 18 | 17 | 24 | 25 | 23 | 16 | 15 | 10 | 19 |
|     - Low | 12 | 10 | 11 | 15 | 14 | 12 | 10 | 8 | 7 | 5 |

## Income Statement Analysis (Million $)

| | | | | | | | | | | |
|---|---|---|---|---|---|---|---|---|---|---|
| Commissions | NA | 37.1 | 96.6 | 87.1 | 30.3 | 24.4 | 23.0 | 20.4 | 18.8 | 29.1 |
| Int. Inc. | NA | NA | NA | NA | NA | NA | NA | NA | NA | NA |
| Total Revs. | 1,523 | 874 | 827 | 641 | 385 | 318 | 288 | 253 | 203 | 207 |
| Int. Exp. | 36.9 | 39.8 | 9.4 | 9.4 | 12.7 | 11.6 | NA | NA | NA | NA |
| Pretax Inc. | 456 | 387 | 363 | 274 | 205 | 163 | 144 | 130 | 109 | 113 |
| Eff. Tax Rate | 31% | 31% | 31% | 36% | 39% | 40% | 38% | 39% | 39% | 48% |
| Net Inc. | 315 | 269 | 251 | 175 | 124 | 98.2 | 89.4 | 78.6 | 66.3 | 58.9 |

## Balance Sheet & Other Fin. Data (Million $)

| | | | | | | | | | | |
|---|---|---|---|---|---|---|---|---|---|---|
| Total Assets | 2,374 | 2,245 | 1,738 | 1,582 | 834 | 579 | 479 | 394 | 177 | 138 |
| Cash Items | 502 | 246 | 210 | 303 | 2.8 | 3.9 | 1.7 | 1.1 | 1.0 | 0.4 |
| Receivables | 188 | 149 | 51.7 | 248 | 171 | 119 | 83.0 | 85.0 | 23.0 | 19.0 |
| Secs. Owned | 199 | 233 | 189 | 217 | 598 | 408 | 351 | 277 | 120 | 92.0 |
| Sec. Borrowed | Nil | Nil | Nil | Nil | Nil | Nil | Nil | Nil | Nil | Nil |
| Due Brokers & Cust. | Nil | 118 | 127 | 91.7 | 34.6 | 35.9 | 32.0 | 28.4 | 6.6 | 9.0 |
| Other Liabs. | 574 | 584 | 297 | 355 | 177 | 174 | 154 | 143 | 18.0 | 21.0 |
| Capitalization: | | | | | | | | | | |
| Debt | 400 | 382 | 384 | 455 | 156 | 5.6 | 4.2 | 6.1 | 2.6 | 3.6 |
| Equity | 1,401 | 1,161 | 931 | 720 | 467 | 363 | 289 | 217 | 150 | 105 |
| Total | 1,800 | 1,543 | 1,314 | 1,175 | 623 | 369 | 293 | 223 | 153 | 108 |
| % Return On Revs. | 20.3 | 30.8 | 30.4 | 27.4 | 32.2 | 30.9 | 31.1 | 31.0 | 32.7 | 28.5 |
| % Ret. on Assets | 13.6 | 12.8 | 15.1 | 14.5 | 17.6 | 18.6 | 20.5 | 21.9 | 42.1 | 52.1 |
| % Ret. on Equity | 24.6 | 25.8 | 30.4 | 29.6 | 29.9 | 30.1 | 35.4 | 42.9 | 52.0 | 74.9 |

Data as orig. reptd.; bef. results of disc. opers. and/or spec. items. Per share data adj. for stk. divs. as of ex-div. date. E-Estimated. NA-Not Available. NM-Not Meaningful. NR-Not Ranked.

**Office**—777 Mariners Island Blvd., San Mateo, CA 94404. **Tel**—(415) 312-2000. **Pres & CEO**—C. B. Johnson. **EVP & Secy**—H. E. Burns. **SVP, Treas & CFO**—M. L. Flanagan. **Investor Contact**—Alex W. Peters (415-312-6521). **Dirs**—H. E. Burns, J. R. Grosvenor, F. W. Hellman, C. B. Johnson, C. E. Johnson, R. H. Johnson Jr., H. O. Kline, P. M. Sacerdote, L. E. Woodworth. **Transfer Agent & Registrar**—Bank of New York, NYC. **Incorporated**—in Delaware in 1969. **Empl**— 4,900. **S&P Analyst:** Paul L. Huberman, CFA

# Frontier Insurance Group 926M

NYSE Symbol **FTR**

In S&P SmallCap 600

**17-MAY-97**

**Industry:**
Insurance (Property-Casualty)

**Summary:** Through subsidiaries, this holding company conducts business as a specialty property and casualty insurer and reinsurer. Principal lines include medical and dental malpractice.

## Quantitative Evaluations

| | |
|---|---|
| Recent Price • 53⅝ | Yield • 1.0% |
| 52 Wk Range • 54⅞-30½ | 12-Mo. P/E • 18.2 |

**Outlook**
(1 Lowest—5 Highest)
• **3⁻**

**Fair Value**
• **54¾**

**Risk**
• **Low**

**Earn./Div. Rank**
• **B+**

**Technical Eval.**
• **Bullish** since 4/95

**Rel. Strength Rank**
(1 Lowest—99 Highest)
• **89**

**Insider Activity**
• **Unfavorable**

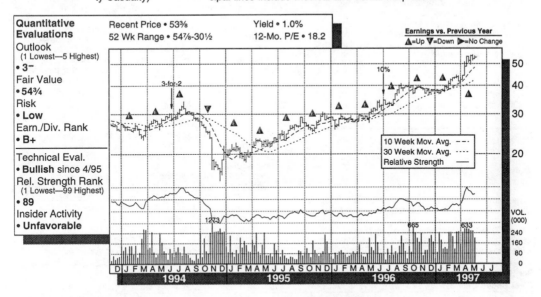

## Business Profile - 16-MAY-97

This well diversified specialty insurer's performance has been bolstered in recent periods by enhanced underwriting efficiency, higher premiums, and its ability to provide products to underserved markets. The company's growth strategy calls for the development of new insurance programs, the expansion of existing lines of business, and the acquisition of other specialty insurers. Frontier recently agreed to acquire Lyndon Property Insurance Co., which provides niche insurance products for financial institutions and other specialty markets, in a transaction that is expected to close during the second quarter of 1997. Frontier's minimum profitability objective is a 15% return on equity, which it has, historically, surpassed.

## Operational Review - 16-MAY-97

For the three months ended March 31, 1997, total revenues climbed 34%, year to year, fueled by a 33% increase in net premiums earned and a 53% rise in net investment income. Total expenses grew 36%, reflecting higher losses and loss adjustment costs, and increased policy acquisition, underwriting and other expenses. After taxes at 29.3%, versus 27.3%, net income advanced 28%, to $11,904,000 ($0.81 a share, on 2.4% more shares; $0.76 fully diluted), from $9,264,000 ($0.65; no dilution).

## Stock Performance - 16-MAY-97

In the past 30 trading days, FTR's shares have increased 20%, compared to a 9% rise in the S&P 500. Average trading volume for the past five days was 39,600 shares, compared with the 40-day moving average of 83,238 shares.

## Key Stock Statistics

| | | | |
|---|---|---|---|
| Dividend Rate/Share | 0.52 | Shareholders | 900 |
| Shs. outstg. (M) | 14.7 | Market cap. (B) | $0.785 |
| Avg. daily vol. (M) | 0.078 | Inst. holdings | 49% |
| Tang. Bk. Value/Share | 17.54 | | |
| Beta | 1.06 | | |

Value of $10,000 invested 5 years ago: $ 40,586

### Fiscal Year Ending Dec. 31

| | 1997 | 1996 | 1995 | 1994 | 1993 | 1992 |
|---|---|---|---|---|---|---|
| **Revenues (Million $)** | | | | | | |
| 1Q | — | 66.80 | 51.77 | 41.16 | 36.78 | 27.58 |
| 2Q | — | 75.30 | 53.91 | 37.95 | 34.80 | 30.00 |
| 3Q | — | 79.77 | 58.07 | 46.44 | 36.14 | 32.65 |
| 4Q | — | 83.05 | 62.65 | 54.43 | 31.44 | 36.50 |
| Yr. | — | 305.0 | 226.4 | 180.0 | 139.2 | 126.7 |
| **Earnings Per Share ($)** | | | | | | |
| 1Q | 0.81 | 0.65 | 0.48 | 0.47 | 0.47 | 0.40 |
| 2Q | — | 0.68 | 0.55 | 0.52 | 0.51 | 0.42 |
| 3Q | — | 0.66 | 0.57 | -0.35 | 0.42 | 0.35 |
| 4Q | — | 0.79 | 0.58 | 0.55 | 0.45 | 0.44 |
| Yr. | — | 2.77 | 2.18 | 1.19 | 1.85 | 1.61 |

**Next earnings report expected: mid August**

**Dividend Data** (Dividends have been paid since 1992.)

| Amount ($) | Date Decl. | Ex-Div. Date | Stock of Record | Payment Date |
|---|---|---|---|---|
| 0.130 | May. 23 | Jun. 26 | Jun. 28 | Jul. 19 '96 |
| 0.130 | Aug. 16 | Sep. 26 | Sep. 30 | Oct. 18 '96 |
| 0.130 | Nov. 29 | Dec. 24 | Dec. 27 | Jan. 16 '97 |
| 0.130 | Mar. 03 | Mar. 20 | Mar. 24 | Apr. 21 '97 |

This report is for information purposes and should not be considered a solicitation to buy or sell any security. Neither S&P nor any other party guarantee its accuracy or make warranties regarding results from its usage. Redistribution is prohibited without written permission. Copyright © 1997

*A Division of The McGraw·Hill Companies*

## Business Summary - 16-MAY-97

Frontier Insurance Group, an insurance holding company, operates through thirteen direct or indirect wholly-owned subsidiaries, including its five principal subsidiaries: Frontier Insurance Co., Frontier Pacific Insurance Co., Medical Professional Liability Agency, Inc., Pioneer Claim Management Inc. and Spencer Douglass Insurance Associates. The company, a specialty property and casualty insurer and reinsurer, performs claims adjusting and management services, and acts as an insurance agent and broker. At December 31, 1996, it was licensed in 49 states, the District of Columbia, Puerto Rico and the Virgin Islands.

Net premiums written in 1996 totaled $311.9 million ($220.8 million in 1995), and were divided:

|                                         | 1996  | 1995  |
| --------------------------------------- | ----- | ----- |
| Medical malpractice (including dental)  | 38.4% | 45.0% |
| General liability                       | 30.1% | 25.8% |
| Surety                                  | 18.2% | 19.7% |
| Workers' compensation                   | 2.0%  | 4.5%  |
| Other                                   | 11.3% | 5.0%  |

The company's underwriting strategy is to identify niche markets that are unattractive to other insurers and that Frontier believes afford favorable opportunities for profitability due to limited potential competition and its innovative underwriting services. FTR directly underwrites specialty niche-market programs including pre-ferred-risk malpractice for physicians, chiropractors and dentists. At 1996 year-end, about 17,500 physicians and 4,900 dentists were insured under the company's medical and dental malpractice insurance programs. FTR also directly underwrites workers' compensation, general liability, surety bonds for small contractors, product liability and custom bonds.

The company directly underwrites general liability coverage for day care centers, small commercial businesses and contractors, and for a variety of farm and agricultural risks. FTR also underwrites pest control operators, fire protection equipment dealers and installers, and security guards. The company underwrites umbrella coverage up to $5 million over underlying $1 million general liability coverage.

## Important Developments

**Mar. '97**—FTR agreed to acquire, in an all-cash transaction, Lyndon Property Insurance Co. and its six subsidiaries from Mercury Finance Co., for $92 million. The transaction, which is subject to regulatory approvals, is expected to close during the second quarter of 1997. Lyndon provides niche products for financial institutionsand other specialty markets, including credit-related insurance, residual value, extended service contracts, and collateral protection coverages.

## Capitalization

**Long Term Debt:** $167,000,000 (12/96).

### Per Share Data ($)

| (Year Ended Dec. 31) | 1996 | 1995 | 1994 | 1993 | 1992 | 1991 | 1990 | 1989 | 1988 | 1987 |
| -------------------- | ---- | ---- | ---- | ---- | ---- | ---- | ---- | ---- | ---- | ---- |
| Tangible Bk. Val.    | 17.54 | 16.04 | 13.32 | 13.04 | 8.99 | 7.75 | 5.33 | 4.18 | 3.16 | 2.36 |
| Oper. Earnings       | 2.70 | 2.18 | 1.25 | 1.84 | 1.59 | 1.33 | 1.15 | 0.96 | 0.79 | 0.60 |
| Earnings             | 2.77 | 2.18 | 1.19 | 1.85 | 1.60 | 1.38 | 1.16 | 1.01 | 0.78 | 0.59 |
| Dividends            | 0.50 | 0.44 | 0.42 | 0.35 | 0.32 | Nil | Nil | Nil | Nil | Nil |
| Payout Ratio         | 18% | 20% | 35% | 19% | 20% | Nil | Nil | Nil | Nil | Nil |
| Prices - High        | 41⅛ | 30⅝ | 34⅛ | 30¼ | 24⅛ | 14⅝ | 15¾ | 9⅜ | 5¼ | 4⅜ |
|    - Low | 25⅝ | 18⅜ | 15¼ | 22¼ | 13½ | 8⅜ | 6¾ | 4⅞ | 2½ | 2⅜ |
| P/E Ratio - High     | 15 | 14 | 29 | 16 | 15 | 11 | 14 | 9 | 7 | 7 |
|    - Low | 9 | 8 | 13 | 12 | 8 | 6 | 6 | 5 | 3 | 4 |

### Income Statement Analysis (Million $)

|                 | 1996 | 1995 | 1994 | 1993 | 1992 | 1991 | 1990 | 1989 | 1988 | 1987 |
| --------------- | ---- | ---- | ---- | ---- | ---- | ---- | ---- | ---- | ---- | ---- |
| Premium Inc.    | 266 | 196 | 157 | 116 | 105 | 78.0 | 72.3 | 55.0 | 39.3 | 32.0 |
| Net Invest. Inc.| 37.2 | 30.0 | 24.5 | 22.5 | 19.9 | 15.9 | 12.1 | 8.6 | 6.0 | 4.1 |
| Oth. Revs.      | 0.1 | 0.2 | -1.2 | 0.3 | 1.7 | 2.3 | 1.6 | Nil | Nil | Nil |
| Total Revs.     | 305 | 226 | 180 | 139 | 127 | 96.3 | 86.0 | 63.6 | 45.3 | 36.1 |
| Pretax Inc.     | 56.5 | 43.3 | 21.3 | 30.3 | 25.2 | 20.1 | 14.7 | 12.8 | 10.0 | 6.9 |
| Net Oper. Inc.  | NA | 31.2 | 17.9 | 23.0 | NA | NA | 10.4 | 9.2 | 7.4 | 5.5 |
| Net Inc.        | 40.0 | 31.2 | 17.0 | 23.2 | 19.0 | 15.0 | 10.8 | 9.4 | 7.2 | 5.5 |

### Balance Sheet & Other Fin. Data (Million $)

|                       | 1996 | 1995 | 1994 | 1993 | 1992 | 1991 | 1990 | 1989 | 1988 | 1987 |
| --------------------- | ---- | ---- | ---- | ---- | ---- | ---- | ---- | ---- | ---- | ---- |
| Cash & Equiv.         | 8.3 | 12.6 | 11.4 | 17.8 | 5.0 | 14.4 | 4.1 | 3.8 | 2.8 | 4.0 |
| Premiums Due          | 76.6 | 50.0 | 41.1 | 28.4 | 28.2 | 24.7 | 26.6 | 18.0 | 18.4 | 14.1 |
| Invest. Assets: Bonds | 685 | 521 | 346 | 276 | 242 | 208 | 153 | 114 | 72.0 | 49.0 |
| Invest. Assets: Stocks| 16.2 | 21.0 | 48.7 | 7.5 | 9.9 | 1.1 | 3.8 | 4.9 | 6.2 | 5.2 |
| Invest. Assets: Loans | Nil | Nil | Nil | Nil | Nil | Nil | Nil | Nil | Nil | Nil |
| Invest. Assets: Total | 702 | 553 | 408 | 344 | 262 | 235 | 165 | 131 | 90.0 | 60.0 |
| Deferred Policy Costs | 32.8 | 18.8 | 13.2 | 6.8 | 5.9 | 3.2 | 2.2 | Nil | Nil | 0.1 |
| Total Assets          | 1,246 | 773 | 599 | 522 | 341 | 300 | 215 | 170 | 122 | 90.0 |
| Debt                  | NM | 25.0 | Nil | Nil | Nil | Nil | Nil | Nil | Nil | Nil |
| Common Eqty.          | 269 | 230 | 190 | 186 | 107 | 91.2 | 49.7 | 39.0 | 29.4 | 22.0 |
| Prop. & Cas. Loss Ratio | NA | NA | 70.8 | 66.7 | 71.2 | 69.7 | 73.7 | 75.1 | 75.6 | 71.2 |
| Prop. & Cas. Expense Ratio | NA | NA | 27.0 | 26.5 | 25.6 | 26.3 | 24.0 | 23.7 | 17.8 | 16.8 |
| Prop. & Cas. Combined Ratio | 90.9 | 91.5 | 97.8 | 93.3 | 96.8 | 96.0 | 97.7 | 98.8 | 93.4 | 88.0 |
| % Return On Revs.     | 13.1 | 13.8 | 9.4 | 16.7 | 15.0 | 15.6 | 12.5 | 14.8 | 16.3 | 15.2 |
| % Ret. on Equity      | 16.1 | 14.9 | 9.1 | 15.8 | 19.2 | 21.3 | 24.3 | 27.5 | 28.8 | 28.5 |

Data as orig. reptd.; bef. results of disc. opers. and/or spec. items. Per share data adj. for stk. divs. as of ex-div. date. E-Estimated. NA-Not Available. NM-Not Meaningful. NR-Not Ranked.

**Office**—195 Lake Louise Marie Rd., Rock Hill, NY 12775-8000. **Tel**—(914) 796-2100. **Chrmn & CEO**—W. A. Rhulen. **Secy**—J. P. Loughlin. **Investor Contact**—Linda Markovits. **Dirs**—A. Gerry, D. C. Moat, L. E. O'Brien, P. L. Rhulen, W. A. Rhulen. **Transfer Agent & Registrar**—American Stock Transfer & Trust Co., NYC. **Incorporated**—in Delaware in 1986. **Empl**— 749. **S&P Analyst:** Thomas C. Ferguson

**17-MAY-97**    **Industry:** Specialty Printing

**Summary:** This company is an independent provider of research and analysis of the computer hardware, software, communications and related technologies industries.

| Quantitative Evaluations | | |
|---|---|---|
| **Outlook** (1 Lowest—5 Highest) • **NA** | Recent Price • 28⅝ | Yield • Nil |
| **Fair Value** • **NA** | 52 Wk Range • 42¼-19¾ | 12-Mo. P/E • 95.4 |
| **Risk** • **High** | | |
| **Earn./Div. Rank** • **NR** | | |
| **Technical Eval.** • **Bearish** since 2/97 | | |
| **Rel. Strength Rank** (1 Lowest—99 Highest) • **73** | | |
| **Insider Activity** • **NA** | | |

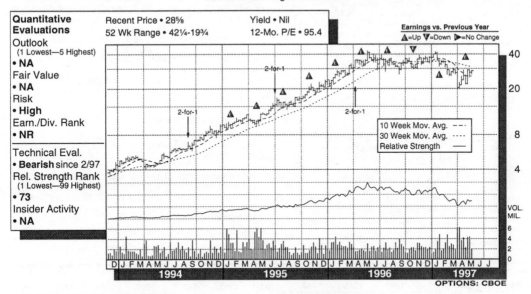

Earnings vs. Previous Year
▲=Up ▼=Down ▶=No Change

10 Week Mov. Avg. ---
30 Week Mov. Avg. ·····
Relative Strength —

VOL. MIL.

1994   1995   1996   1997

OPTIONS: CBOE

## Business Profile - 22-APR-97

The company's core business is researching and analyzing information technology industry developments, packaging its analysis into subscription-based products, and distributing these products through print and electronic media. Its strategy has been to focus on its core businesses, target users of information technology, increase market penetration, and develop new products through internal development and acquisitions. As a result of recent global expansion initiatives, international revenues now account for approximately 35% of the company total. GART is seeking growth opportunities through further expansion of its international client base, continued penetration of its current client base, and the attraction of new business.

## Operational Review - 22-APR-97

Revenues in the first half of FY 97 advanced 31%, year to year, reflecting a 28% gain in research, advisory and benchmarking services and a 40% gain in other revenues, primarily from the company's technology-based training business. Lower SG&A expense as a percentage of sales outweighed lower gross margins; operating income was up 49%. Aided by the absence of a $1.7 million acquisition-related charge recorded in the FY 96 period and higher net interest income, net income was up 60%, to $37,242,000 ($0.37 a share), from $23,205,000 ($0.24).

## Stock Performance - 16-MAY-97

In the past 30 trading days, GART's shares have increased 33%, compared to a 9% rise in the S&P 500. Average trading volume for the past five days was 383,840 shares, compared with the 40-day moving average of 909,290 shares.

## Key Stock Statistics

| | | | |
|---|---|---|---|
| Dividend Rate/Share | Nil | Shareholders | 300 |
| Shs. outstg. (M) | 93.8 | Market cap. (B) | $ 2.7 |
| Avg. daily vol. (M) | 0.633 | Inst. holdings | 40% |
| Tang. Bk. Value/Share | 0.61 | | |
| Beta | NA | | |

Value of $10,000 invested 5 years ago: NA

### Fiscal Year Ending Sep. 30

| | 1998 | 1997 | 1996 | 1995 | 1994 | 1993 |
|---|---|---|---|---|---|---|
| **Revenues (Million $)** | | | | | | |
| 1Q | — | 125.4 | 96.47 | 55.65 | 40.08 | — |
| 2Q | — | 119.1 | 90.83 | 50.74 | 38.45 | — |
| 3Q | — | — | 97.41 | 58.78 | 46.00 | — |
| 4Q | — | — | 110.0 | 63.98 | 46.00 | — |
| Yr. | — | — | 394.7 | 229.1 | 169.0 | 122.5 |
| **Earnings Per Share ($)** | | | | | | |
| 1Q | — | 0.19 | 0.12 | 0.08 | 0.05 | — |
| 2Q | — | 0.18 | 0.12 | 0.07 | 0.04 | — |
| 3Q | — | — | 0.13 | 0.07 | 0.04 | — |
| 4Q | — | — | -0.18 | 0.07 | 0.04 | — |
| Yr. | — | — | 0.17 | 0.28 | 0.16 | 0.07 |

**Next earnings report expected: mid July**

## Dividend Data

No cash dividends have been paid. A 2-for-1 stock split was effected on March 29, 1996.

This report is for information purposes and should not be considered a solicitation to buy or sell any security. Neither S&P nor any other party guarantee its accuracy or make warranties regarding results from its usage. Redistribution is prohibited without written permission. Copyright © 1997    A Division of The **McGraw-Hill** Companies

STANDARD
&POOR'S
STOCK REPORTS

# Gartner Group

**3945N**

**17-MAY-97**

## Business Summary - 22-APR-97

Gartner Group, Inc. is a leading independent provider of research and analysis of the computer hardware, software, communications and related technology industries (collectively, the information technology or IT industry). The company's core business is researching and analyzing significant IT industry developments, packaging such analysis into annually renewable subscription-based products, and distributing these products through print and electronic media. Revenues in recent fiscal years (Sep.) were derived as follows:

|  | FY 96 | FY 95 |
|---|---|---|
| Continuous Services | 78% | 85% |
| Other, principally consulting and conferences | 22% | 15% |

As of March 31, 1997, there were about 7,775 client organizations subscribing to GART's continuous service products (annually renewable subscription services). Products are generally grouped into three categories of technology: application, direction and management. Training on technology is a fourth product group. Continuous service products highlight industry developments, review new products and technologies and analyze industry trends within a particular technology or market sector. The company currently offers about 80 continuous service products.

Each subscriber to a continuous service receives research notes on several topics, periodic strategic analysis reports, GartnerFLASH (late-breaking analysis of recent important events and new research) on a weekly basis, a monthly research review of industry trends and developments, audio conference calls on specific topics of interest, telephone consultations, and a direct hot line for client access to GART research and resources.

The company also provides a number of other products and services, including individual reports on industry topics, private speaking engagements, and consulting services and events. Consulting services provide customized project consulting on IT deployment issues. Events include industry conferences, seminars and briefings.

## Important Developments

**Apr. '97**—In reporting FY 97 (Sep.) second quarter results, Gartner said it acquired two Australia-based companies during the quarter, adding to its local product line in the Asia/Pacific region. As a result of these acquisitions and other global expansion initiatives, the company reported that international business currently accounts for approximately 35% of its total revenues.

## Capitalization

**Long Term Liabilities:** $2,115,000 (3/97).

### Per Share Data ($)

| (Year Ended Sep. 30) | 1996 | 1995 | 1994 | 1993 | 1992 | 1991 | 1990 | 1989 | 1988 | 1987 |
|---|---|---|---|---|---|---|---|---|---|---|
| Tangible Bk. Val. | 0.61 | 0.32 | NM | NA | NA | NA | NA | NA | NA | NA |
| Cash Flow | 0.30 | 0.37 | 0.24 | 0.16 | NA | NA | NA | NA | NA | NA |
| Earnings | 0.17 | 0.28 | 0.17 | 0.06 | NA | NA | NA | NA | NA | NA |
| Dividends | Nil | Nil | Nil | Nil | NA | NA | NA | NA | NA | NA |
| Payout Ratio | Nil | Nil | Nil | Nil | NA | NA | NA | NA | NA | NA |
| Prices - High | 43⅛ | 24⅛ | 9⅞ | 4⅝ | NA | NA | NA | NA | NA | NA |
|    - Low | 19¾ | 8⅞ | 4 | 2¾ | NA | NA | NA | NA | NA | NA |
| P/E Ratio - High | NM | 86 | 58 | 77 | NA | NA | NA | NA | NA | NA |
|    - Low | NM | 32 | 24 | 46 | NA | NA | NA | NA | NA | NA |

### Income Statement Analysis (Million $)

| | 1996 | 1995 | 1994 | 1993 | 1992 | 1991 | 1990 | 1989 | 1988 | 1987 |
|---|---|---|---|---|---|---|---|---|---|---|
| Revs. | 395 | 229 | 169 | 123 | NA | NA | NA | NA | NA | NA |
| Oper. Inc. | 97.2 | 51.3 | 34.7 | 21.0 | NA | NA | NA | NA | NA | NA |
| Depr. | 12.9 | 8.1 | 7.3 | 6.4 | NA | NA | NA | NA | NA | NA |
| Int. Exp. | Nil | 0.2 | 0.2 | 2.4 | NA | NA | NA | NA | NA | NA |
| Pretax Inc. | 53.1 | 45.6 | 27.3 | 10.2 | NA | NA | NA | NA | NA | NA |
| Eff. Tax Rate | 69% | 44% | 45% | 53% | NA | NA | NA | NA | NA | NA |
| Net Inc. | 16.4 | 25.5 | 15.0 | 4.8 | NA | NA | NA | NA | NA | NA |

### Balance Sheet & Other Fin. Data (Million $)

| | 1996 | 1995 | 1994 | 1993 | 1992 | 1991 | 1990 | 1989 | 1988 | 1987 |
|---|---|---|---|---|---|---|---|---|---|---|
| Cash | 127 | 91.1 | 50.7 | NA | NA | NA | NA | NA | NA | NA |
| Curr. Assets | 310 | 218 | 165 | NA | NA | NA | NA | NA | NA | NA |
| Total Assets | 444 | 301 | 233 | NA | NA | NA | NA | NA | NA | NA |
| Curr. Liab. | 291 | 212 | 171 | NA | NA | NA | NA | NA | NA | NA |
| LT Debt | Nil | Nil | 6.4 | NA | NA | NA | NA | NA | NA | NA |
| Common Eqty. | 150 | 85.5 | 49.0 | NA | NA | NA | NA | NA | NA | NA |
| Total Cap. | 150 | 85.5 | 55.4 | NA | NA | NA | NA | NA | NA | NA |
| Cap. Exp. | 15.6 | 14.5 | 4.1 | 2.9 | NA | NA | NA | NA | NA | NA |
| Cash Flow | 29.3 | 33.6 | 22.3 | 11.2 | NA | NA | NA | NA | NA | NA |
| Curr. Ratio | 1.1 | 1.0 | 1.0 | NA | NA | NA | NA | NA | NA | NA |
| % LT Debt of Cap. | Nil | Nil | 11.6 | NA | NA | NA | NA | NA | NA | NA |
| % Net Inc.of Revs. | 4.2 | 11.1 | 8.9 | 3.9 | NA | NA | NA | NA | NA | NA |
| % Ret. on Assets | 4.2 | 9.6 | NA | NA | NA | NA | NA | NA | NA | NA |
| % Ret. on Equity | 14.6 | 38.0 | NA | NA | NA | NA | NA | NA | NA | NA |

Data as orig. reptd.; bef. results of disc. opers. and/or spec. items. Per share data adj. for stk. divs. as of ex-div. date. E-Estimated. NA-Not Available. NM-Not Meaningful. NR-Not Ranked.

**Office**—P.O. Box 10212, 56 Top Gallant Rd., Stamford, CT 06904-0096.**Tel**—(203) 964-0096. **Website**—http://www.gartnet.com **Chrmn, Pres & CEO**—M. A. Fernandez. **EVP & COO**—W. T. Clifford. **EVP, CFO, Treas & Secy**—J. F. Halligan. **Dirs**—M. A. Fernandez, W. O. Grabe, M. D. Hopper, J. P. Imlay, Jr., S. G. Pagliuca, D. G. Sisco.**Transfer Agent**—Boston EquiServe.**Incorporated**—in Delaware. **Empl**— 0. **S&P Analyst:** Adam Penn

# Gateway 2000, Inc.  3947P
### Nasdaq Symbol GATE

**19-MAY-97**

**Industry:** Computers (Hardware)

**Summary:** Gateway 2000 is a leading direct marketer of personal computers in the U.S.

| S&P Opinion: Accumulate (★★★★) | Recent Price • 69¾ | Yield • Nil |
|---|---|---|
| | 52 Wk Range • 70⅜-27¾ | 12-Mo. P/E • 20.4 |

**Quantitative Evaluations**

Outlook (1 Lowest—5 Highest)
• 5

Fair Value
• 90⅞

Risk
• High

Earn./Div. Rank
• NR

Technical Eval.
• **Bearish** since 5/96

Rel. Strength Rank (1 Lowest—99 Highest)
• 96

Insider Activity
• Neutral

**Earnings vs. Previous Year**
▲=Up ▼=Down ▶=No Change

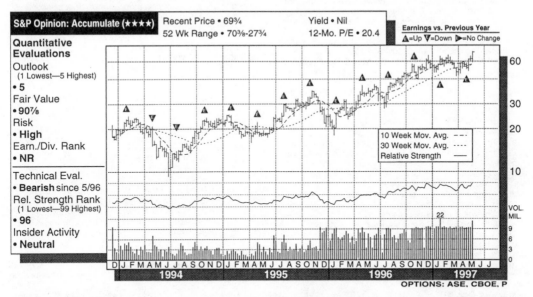

10 Week Mov. Avg. ----
30 Week Mov. Avg. ·······
Relative Strength ——

OPTIONS: ASE, CBOE, P

## Overview - 19-MAY-97

Revenues should grow more than 20% in 1997, benefiting from strong underlying PC demand and new products and feature sets. Demand for PC's is being driven by falling prices, more powerful Pentium Pro processors from Intel and a new release of Windows NT software from Microsoft. Growth is also expected to be fueled by Intel's new MMX-enabled processors, which are expected to improve greatly the graphics and video capabilities of PCs. Gross margins should remain flat during 1997, as higher margin desktop and portable products offset slightly higher component costs. Although the company is expected to aggressively support staff, marketing and international expansion programs, growth in selling, general and administrative expense is expected to trail the revenue rise. Earnings in 1997 should reach $4.00 a share, up 25% from 1996's $3.21.

## Valuation - 19-MAY-97

We recently raised our opinion to accumulate from hold. Based on our EPS estimate of $5.00 for 1998, the shares trade at roughly 14X earnings, which we view as attractive, given the 25% EPS growth we see for 1997 and 1998. Gateway 2000 has a strong niche position, and enjoys the inherent advantages of the direct business model. The company is also making strides in gaining greater penetration in major accounts and in international markets (which are expected to grow at a faster rate versus the U.S. over the next several years, given their relative immaturity). We believe these opportunities could result in future earnings surprises.

## Key Stock Statistics

| | | | |
|---|---|---|---|
| S&P EPS Est. 1997 | 4.00 | Tang. Bk. Value/Share | 10.63 |
| P/E on S&P Est. 1997 | 17.4 | Beta | NA |
| S&P EPS Est. 1998 | 5.00 | Shareholders | 2,200 |
| Dividend Rate/Share | Nil | Market cap. (B) | $ 5.4 |
| Shs. outstg. (M) | 76.8 | Inst. holdings | 35% |
| Avg. daily vol. (M) | 2.961 | | |

Value of $10,000 invested 5 years ago: NA

### Fiscal Year Ending Dec. 31

| | 1997 | 1996 | 1995 | 1994 | 1993 | 1992 |
|---|---|---|---|---|---|---|
| **Revenues (Million $)** | | | | | | |
| 1Q | 1,418 | 1,142 | 776.0 | 615.9 | 421.0 | 236.9 |
| 2Q | — | 1,137 | 766.4 | 616.5 | 364.7 | 248.6 |
| 3Q | — | 1,203 | 888.7 | 644.4 | 400.0 | 267.8 |
| 4Q | — | 1,553 | 1,245 | 824.3 | 545.9 | 353.7 |
| Yr. | — | 5,035 | 3,676 | 2,701 | 1,732 | 1,107 |
| **Earnings Per Share ($)** | | | | | | |
| 1Q | E0.86 | 0.65 | 0.49 | 0.32 | 0.37 | 0.24 |
| 2Q | E0.90 | 0.66 | 0.44 | 0.05 | 0.27 | 0.23 |
| 3Q | E1.03 | 0.78 | 0.52 | 0.35 | 0.33 | 0.25 |
| 4Q | E1.21 | 1.12 | 0.74 | 0.50 | 0.43 | 0.31 |
| Yr. | E4.00 | 3.21 | 2.19 | 1.22 | 1.41 | 1.03 |

**Next earnings report expected: late July**

### Dividend Data

No cash dividends have been paid.

This report is for information purposes and should not be considered a solicitation to buy or sell any security. Neither S&P nor any other party guarantee its accuracy or make warranties regarding results from its usage. Redistribution is prohibited without written permission. Copyright © 1997 | A Division of The McGraw-Hill Companies

## Business Summary - 19-MAY-97

Gateway 2000 is the fifth largest PC (personal computer) supplier in the U.S. Like Dell, Gateway 2000 sells directly to users, primarily targeting experienced PC users who are willing to buy a computer unseen, provided the price is right. However, the company is making progress in recent efforts to boost major account sales as well, which has helped it grow market share over the past year. Gateway 2000's share of the U.S. market for PCs in the first quarter of 1997 grew to 6.5% (according to International Data Corp.), compared with 5.8% in the first quarter of 1996. GATE has a less significant share of the world wide market, although part of the company's growth strategy is to expand its international operations. The U.S. accounted for some 84% of Gateway 2000's total 1996 revenues.

Gateway 2000 has a niche position with "PC enthusiasts." The company primarily advertises through computer trade publications, and maintains a close relationship with its customers to achieve greater responsiveness and better service. Customers can have their PCs custom-configured by GATE, with a choice of microprocessors of varying clock speeds, memory and storage capacities, as well as other options. The company estimates that approximately 50% of its business comes from repeat buyers of its PC, or based on word-of-mouth from previous buyers. Gateway 2000 has also built strong brand recognition, represented with its trademark black-and-white spot cow design on its product packaging.

The company believes the direct selling business model, versus indirect (or using the retail channel) helps promote such customer loyalty and brand awareness. Other advantages of the direct model include: the ability to offer product at a more competitive price, since the vendor is able to avoid the traditional markups and the inventory and occupancy costs associated with traditional retail channels; in addition, the risk of inventory obsolescence is reduced. Furthermore, to combat hesitancy among consumers to purchase a computer unseen, Gateway 2000 has opened several Country Stores across the U.S. where potential buyers can "test drive" the product.

Gateway 2000 also stands out as, generally, one of the first PC makers to incorporate Intel Corp.'s latest and greatest microprocessor into its product line. In fact, Gateway 2000's most recently announced new additions to its product line based on Intel's latest processor, the Pentium II, the same day Intel launched the new processor. GATE's Pentium-based desktops accounted for nearly 85% of its sales in 1996, increasing form 76% in 1996. As such, Gateway revenues are also vulnerable to any potential microprocessor shipment delays from Intel. Portable computer sales account for much less of Gateway 2000's revenues, representing only about 9% of total 1996 revenues, and were just 5% in 1995.

## Capitalization

**Long Term Debt:** $6,599,000 (3/97).

### Per Share Data ($)

| (Year Ended Dec. 31) | 1996 | 1995 | 1994 | 1993 | 1992 | 1991 | 1990 | 1989 | 1988 | 1987 |
|---|---|---|---|---|---|---|---|---|---|---|
| Tangible Bk. Val. | 10.63 | 7.45 | 5.20 | 3.87 | 2.30 | NA | NA | NA | NA | NA |
| Cash Flow | 4.00 | 2.67 | 1.45 | 1.52 | 1.10 | NA | NA | NA | NA | NA |
| Earnings | 3.21 | 2.19 | 1.22 | 1.41 | 1.03 | NA | NA | NA | NA | NA |
| Dividends | Nil | Nil | Nil | Nil | Nil | NA | NA | NA | NA | NA |
| Payout Ratio | Nil | Nil | Nil | Nil | Nil | NA | NA | NA | NA | NA |
| Prices - High | 66¼ | 37½ | 24¾ | 21½ | NA | NA | NA | NA | NA | NA |
|    - Low | 18 | 16 | 9¼ | 15 | NA | NA | NA | NA | NA | NA |
| P/E Ratio - High | 21 | 17 | 20 | 15 | NA | NA | NA | NA | NA | NA |
|    - Low | 6 | 7 | 8 | 11 | NA | NA | NA | NA | NA | NA |

### Income Statement Analysis (Million $)

| | 1996 | 1995 | 1994 | 1993 | 1992 | 1991 | 1990 | 1989 | 1988 | 1987 |
|---|---|---|---|---|---|---|---|---|---|---|
| Revs. | 5,035 | 3,676 | 2,701 | 1,732 | 1,107 | NA | NA | NA | NA | NA |
| Oper. Inc. | 418 | 287 | 159 | 157 | 108 | NA | NA | NA | NA | NA |
| Depr. | 61.8 | 38.1 | 18.0 | 8.0 | 4.9 | NA | NA | NA | NA | NA |
| Int. Exp. | Nil | Nil | NA | NA | NA | NA | NA | NA | NA | NA |
| Pretax Inc. | 383 | 262 | 146 | 154 | 106 | NA | NA | NA | NA | NA |
| Eff. Tax Rate | 35% | 34% | 34% | 35% | 34% | NA | NA | NA | NA | NA |
| Net Inc. | 251 | 173 | 96.0 | 100 | 70.0 | NA | NA | NA | NA | NA |

### Balance Sheet & Other Fin. Data (Million $)

| | 1996 | 1995 | 1994 | 1993 | 1992 | 1991 | 1990 | 1989 | 1988 | 1987 |
|---|---|---|---|---|---|---|---|---|---|---|
| Cash | 516 | 169 | 244 | 132 | NA | NA | NA | NA | NA | NA |
| Curr. Assets | 1,318 | 866 | 659 | 501 | 247 | NA | NA | NA | NA | NA |
| Total Assets | 1,673 | 1,124 | 771 | 564 | 269 | NA | NA | NA | NA | NA |
| Curr. Liab. | 800 | 525 | 349 | 255 | 137 | NA | NA | NA | NA | NA |
| LT Debt | 7.2 | 10.8 | 27.1 | 29.1 | 11.8 | NA | NA | NA | NA | NA |
| Common Eqty. | 816 | 555 | 376 | 280 | 129 | NA | NA | NA | NA | NA |
| Total Cap. | 823 | 573 | 410 | 309 | 143 | NA | NA | NA | NA | NA |
| Cap. Exp. | 86.0 | 77.5 | 29.0 | 35.9 | 14.3 | NA | NA | NA | NA | NA |
| Cash Flow | 312 | 211 | 114 | 108 | 75.0 | NA | NA | NA | NA | NA |
| Curr. Ratio | 1.6 | 1.6 | 1.9 | 2.0 | 1.8 | NA | NA | NA | NA | NA |
| % LT Debt of Cap. | 0.9 | 1.9 | 6.7 | 9.4 | 9.6 | NA | NA | NA | NA | NA |
| % Net Inc.of Revs. | 5.0 | 4.7 | 3.6 | 5.8 | 6.3 | NA | NA | NA | NA | NA |
| % Ret. on Assets | 17.9 | 18.3 | 14.4 | 24.0 | 35.4 | NA | NA | NA | NA | NA |
| % Ret. on Equity | 36.6 | 37.2 | 29.3 | 48.8 | 72.5 | NA | NA | NA | NA | NA |

Data as orig. reptd.; bef. results of disc. opers. and/or spec. items. Per share data adj. for stk. divs. as of ex-div. date. E-Estimated. NA-Not Available. NM-Not Meaningful. NR-Not Ranked.

**Office**—610 Gateway Drive, N. Sioux City, S.D. 57049-2000. **Tel**— (605) 232-2000.**Website**— http://www.gw2k.com**Chrmn & CEO**—T. W. Waitt. **Pres & COO**—R. D. Snyder.**SVP, CFO & Treas**—D. J. McKittrick. **Dirs**—C. G. Carey, J. W. Cravens, G. H. Krauss, D. L. Lacey, J. F. McCann, R. D. Snyder, T. W. Waitt. **Transfer Agent & Registrar**—Norwest Bank Minnesota, N.A. **Incorporated**—in Iowa in 1986, reincorporated in South Dakota in 1989 and Delaware in 1991. **Empl**— 9,700. **S&P Analyst:** Megan Graham Hackett

# General Electric     966

NYSE Symbol **GE**

In S&P 500

**19-MAY-97**

**Industry:** Electrical Equipment

**Summary:** GE's major businesses include aircraft engines, medical systems, power systems, broadcasting, appliances, lighting and financial services.

| S&P Opinion: Buy (★★★★★) | Recent Price • 60½ | Yield • 1.7% |
|---|---|---|
| | 52 Wk Range • 62⅜-39 | 12-Mo. P/E • 26.8 |

**Earnings vs. Previous Year**
▲=Up ▼=Down ▶=No Change

## Quantitative Evaluations

**Outlook**
(1 Lowest—5 Highest)
• **1+**

**Fair Value**
• **79¼**

**Risk**
• **Low**

**Earn./Div. Rank**
• **A+**

**Technical Eval.**
• **Bullish** since 12/94

**Rel. Strength Rank**
(1 Lowest—99 Highest)
• **89**

**Insider Activity**
• **NA**

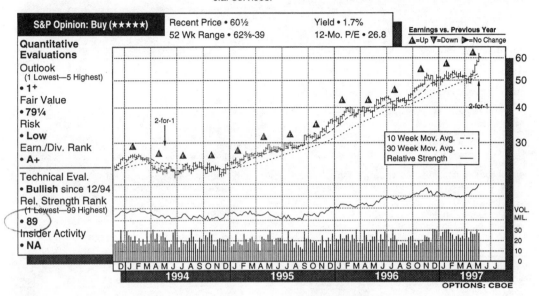

10 Week Mov. Avg. ----
30 Week Mov. Avg. ·····
Relative Strength ——

OPTIONS: CBOE

## Overview - 19-MAY-97

Revenues are expected to rise about 10% in 1997 from those of 1996, reflecting favorable trends in key businesses, emphasis on international expansion, acquisitions, and a concerted effort to boost aftermarket repair and services revenues from GE's traditional manufacturing businesses. The focus on service will be most visible in the aircraft engine, medical equipment and power generation businesses. At the original equipment end of the business, aircraft engines should benefit from a sharp increase in market share. NBC will continue to be aided by strong ratings and special event broadcasts. Financial services should continue to expand at a 20% annual rate, aided by aggressive marketing and acquisitions. GE's consolidated earnings should benefit from improved margins on greater volume, improved manufacturing efficiencies and strong cost control programs.

## Valuation - 19-MAY-97

We continue to recommend purchase of the shares of this diversified powerhouse. GE has long established itself as a well managed company that delivers consistent earnings growth. As a result, the shares have been awarded an above-average P/E multiple. Despite this premium valuation, we think that the shares remain attractive. GE actively manages its portfolio of businesses, retaining leaders and divesting those lacking promise. This has enabled GE to achieve consistently robust growth, which should continue. The primary risk facing GE is a broad deterioration in economic conditions; however, given its focus on rapid international expansion, we see the downside risk as minimal. Substantial share repurchases and a rising dividend enhance the shares' appeal. The stock was recently split 2-for-1.

## Key Stock Statistics

| | | | |
|---|---|---|---|
| S&P EPS Est. 1997 | 2.42 | Tang. Bk. Value/Share | 4.09 |
| P/E on S&P Est. 1997 | 24.9 | Beta | 1.14 |
| S&P EPS Est. 1998 | 2.70 | Shareholders | 493,000 |
| Dividend Rate/Share | 1.04 | Market cap. (B) | $198.5 |
| Shs. outstg. (M) | 3280.4 | Inst. holdings | 49% |
| Avg. daily vol. (M) | 5.628 | | |

Value of $10,000 invested 5 years ago: $ 35,916

### Fiscal Year Ending Dec. 31

| | 1997 | 1996 | 1995 | 1994 | 1993 | 1992 |
|---|---|---|---|---|---|---|
| **Revenues (Million $)** | | | | | | |
| 1Q | 20,157 | 17,098 | 15,126 | 12,657 | 12,900 | 12,430 |
| 2Q | — | 19,066 | 17,809 | 14,768 | 14,761 | 14,200 |
| 3Q | — | 20,021 | 17,341 | 14,481 | 14,858 | 14,210 |
| 4Q | — | 22,994 | 19,752 | 17,791 | 18,087 | 16,230 |
| Yr. | — | 79,179 | 70,028 | 60,108 | 60,562 | 57,073 |
| **Earnings Per Share ($)** | | | | | | |
| 1Q | 0.51 | 0.46 | 0.40 | 0.36 | 0.32 | 0.28 |
| 2Q | E0.63 | 0.57 | 0.51 | 0.46 | 0.19 | 0.33 |
| 3Q | E0.60 | 0.54 | 0.48 | 0.43 | 0.35 | 0.29 |
| 4Q | E0.69 | 0.63 | 0.56 | 0.50 | 0.43 | 0.36 |
| Yr. | E2.42 | 2.20 | 1.95 | 1.73 | 1.30 | 1.26 |

### Next earnings report expected: mid July

**Dividend Data** (Dividends have been paid since 1899.)

| Amount ($) | Date Decl. | Ex-Div. Date | Stock of Record | Payment Date |
|---|---|---|---|---|
| 0.460 | Sep. 13 | Sep. 26 | Sep. 30 | Oct. 25 '96 |
| 0.520 | Dec. 19 | Dec. 27 | Dec. 31 | Jan. 27 '97 |
| 0.520 | Feb. 07 | Mar. 04 | Mar. 06 | Apr. 25 '97 |
| 2-for-1 | Mar. 17 | May. 12 | Apr. 28 | May. 09 '97 |

This report is for information purposes and should not be considered a solicitation to buy or sell any security. Neither S&P nor any other party guarantee its accuracy or make warranties regarding results from its usage. Redistribution is prohibited without written permission. Copyright © 1997

*A Division of The McGraw·Hill Companies*

STANDARD
&POOR'S
STOCK REPORTS

**General Electric Company**

**966**

**19-MAY-97**

## Business Summary - 19-MAY-97

This diverse company has the highest market capitalization of any public company. GE's interests include a broad range of services, technology and manufacturing industries. GE's senior management has proven adept at defining broad themes which lower level managers implement. Key to GE's business plan is the requirement that businesses be first or second in market share in their industries. Businesses that aren't leaders are divested.

Presently, six themes are being pursued: quality, globalization, service, information technology and consumer wealth accumulation and protection. Quality involves a company-wide initiative to boost quality and lower costs.The company believes that this should boost margins in 1997 and 1998 as hundreds of projects underway mature. Globalization is the pursuit of rapid growth in overseas markets. Already more than 40% of GE's revenues (including exports), and 32% of profits are derived overseas.

Service aims to capture a larger part of the recurring revenue stream tied to aftermarket service of manufactured products. This strategy is having the largest impact on aircraft engines, medical equipment, power generation and locomotives. Information technology is developing information services units such as GE's media and satellite leasing businesses, as well as applying information technology in all units to improve their competitiveness. Consumer wealth accumulation addresses the growing demand for financial, insurance, health care and other needs of aging baby-boomers.

Segment contributions in 1996 (profits in million $):

|  | Revs. | Profits |
|---|---|---|
| Aircraft engines | 7.6% | $1,225 |
| Appliances | 7.7% | 750 |
| Broadcasting | 6.3% | 953 |
| Industrial products & systems | 12.6% | 1,617 |
| Materials | 7.9% | 1,466 |
| Power generation | 8.8% | 1,068 |
| Technical products/services | 5.7% | 849 |
| Financial services | 39.6% | 4,048 |
| Other | 3.8% | 3,088 |

GE operates in two groups: product, service and media businesses and GE Capital Services (GECS). Product, service and media includes 11 businesses: aircraft engines, appliances, lighting, medical systems, NBC, plastics, power systems, electrical distribution and control, information services, motors and industrial systems, and transportation systems. GECS operates 27 financial businesses clustered in equipment management, specialty insurance, consumer services, specialized financing and mid-market financing.

## Capitalization

**Long Term Debt:** $49,246,000,000 (12/96).
**Minority Interest:** $3,007,000,000.

### Per Share Data ($)

| (Year Ended Dec. 31) | 1996 | 1995 | 1994 | 1993 | 1992 | 1991 | 1990 | 1989 | 1988 | 1987 |
|---|---|---|---|---|---|---|---|---|---|---|
| Tangible Bk. Val. | 4.09 | 4.88 | 4.40 | 4.53 | 4.08 | 3.43 | 3.53 | 3.34 | 2.75 | 3.34 |
| Cash Flow | 3.34 | 3.02 | 2.67 | 2.25 | 2.08 | 2.09 | 1.92 | 1.71 | 1.57 | 1.01 |
| Earnings | 2.20 | 1.95 | 1.73 | 1.30 | 1.26 | 1.27 | 1.21 | 1.09 | 0.94 | 0.58 |
| Dividends | 0.95 | 0.85 | 0.74 | 0.63 | 0.58 | 0.52 | 0.48 | 0.43 | 0.36 | 0.33 |
| Payout Ratio | 43% | 43% | 43% | 38% | 46% | 41% | 39% | 39% | 39% | 56% |
| Prices - High | 53⅛ | 36⅝ | 27½ | 26¾ | 21⅞ | 19½ | 18⅞ | 16¼ | 12 | 16⅝ |
| - Low | 34¾ | 25 | 22½ | 20¼ | 18¼ | 13¼ | 12½ | 10⅞ | 9⅝ | 9¾ |
| P/E Ratio - High | 24 | 19 | 16 | 21 | 17 | 15 | 16 | 15 | 13 | 28 |
| - Low | 16 | 13 | 13 | 16 | 14 | 10 | 10 | 10 | 10 | 17 |

### Income Statement Analysis (Million $)

| | 1996 | 1995 | 1994 | 1993 | 1992 | 1991 | 1990 | 1989 | 1988 | 1987 |
|---|---|---|---|---|---|---|---|---|---|---|
| Revs. | 79,179 | 70,028 | 59,316 | 59,827 | 56,274 | 59,379 | 57,662 | 53,884 | 49,414 | 39,315 |
| Oper. Inc. | 22,764 | 20,821 | 16,194 | 16,241 | 15,205 | 15,887 | 15,377 | 13,944 | 11,190 | 5,223 |
| Depr. | 3,785 | 3,594 | 3,207 | 3,261 | 2,818 | 2,832 | 2,508 | 2,256 | 2,266 | 1,544 |
| Int. Exp. | 7,904 | 7,327 | 5,024 | 7,057 | 6,943 | 7,504 | 7,544 | 6,812 | 5,129 | 668 |
| Pretax Inc. | 10,806 | 9,737 | 8,831 | 6,726 | 6,326 | 6,508 | 6,229 | 5,787 | 4,782 | 3,207 |
| Eff. Tax Rate | 33% | 33% | 31% | 32% | 31% | 31% | 30% | 31% | 28% | 34% |
| Net Inc. | 7,280 | 6,573 | 5,915 | 4,424 | 4,305 | 4,435 | 4,303 | 3,939 | 3,386 | 2,119 |

### Balance Sheet & Other Fin. Data (Million $)

| | 1996 | 1995 | 1994 | 1993 | 1992 | 1991 | 1990 | 1989 | 1988 | 1987 |
|---|---|---|---|---|---|---|---|---|---|---|
| Cash | 64,080 | 43,890 | 33,556 | 3,218 | 3,129 | 1,971 | 1,975 | 2,258 | 2,187 | 2,692 |
| Curr. Assets | NA | NA | NA | NA | NA | NA | NA | NA | NA | 15,739 |
| Total Assets | 272,402 | 228,035 | 194,484 | 251,506 | 192,876 | 168,259 | 153,884 | 128,344 | 110,865 | 38,920 |
| Curr. Liab. | NA | 82,001 | 72,854 | 155,729 | 120,475 | 102,611 | 93,022 | 73,902 | 61,800 | 12,671 |
| LT Debt | 49,246 | 51,027 | 36,979 | 28,270 | 25,376 | 22,682 | 21,043 | 16,110 | 15,082 | 4,491 |
| Common Eqty. | 31,125 | 29,609 | 26,387 | 25,824 | 23,459 | 21,683 | 21,680 | 20,890 | 18,466 | 16,480 |
| Total Cap. | 91,651 | 90,972 | 70,418 | 60,859 | 54,719 | 49,392 | 47,746 | 41,544 | 37,902 | 21,352 |
| Cap. Exp. | 7,760 | 6,447 | 7,492 | 4,739 | 4,824 | 5,000 | 4,523 | 5,474 | 3,681 | 1,778 |
| Cash Flow | 11,065 | 10,162 | 9,122 | 7,685 | 7,123 | 7,267 | 6,811 | 6,195 | 5,652 | 3,663 |
| Curr. Ratio | NA | NA | NA | NA | NA | NA | NA | NA | NA | 1.2 |
| % LT Debt of Cap. | 53.7 | 56.1 | 52.5 | 46.5 | 46.4 | 45.9 | 44.1 | 38.8 | 39.8 | 21.0 |
| % Net Inc.of Revs. | 9.2 | 9.4 | 10.0 | 7.4 | 7.7 | 7.5 | 7.5 | 7.3 | 6.9 | 5.4 |
| % Ret. on Assets | 2.9 | 3.2 | 2.7 | 2.0 | 2.4 | 2.8 | 3.1 | 3.3 | 4.5 | 5.8 |
| % Ret. on Equity | 24.0 | 23.5 | 22.7 | 18.0 | 19.2 | 20.6 | 20.6 | 20.0 | 19.4 | 13.5 |

Data as orig. reptd.; bef. results of disc. opers. and/or spec. items. Per share data adj. for stk. divs. as of ex-div. date. E-Estimated. NA-Not Available. NM-Not Meaningful. NR-Not Ranked.

**Office**—3135 Easton Turnpike, Fairfield, CT 06431. **Tel**—(203) 373-2211. **Website**—http://www.ge.com **Chrmn & CEO**—J. F. Welch Jr. **VP & Secy**—B. W. Heineman Jr. **SVP-Fin & CFO**—D. D. Dammerman. **Investor Contact**—Mark Begor (203-373-2816). **Dirs**—D. W. Calloway, S. S. Cathcart, D. D. Dammerman, P. Fresco, C. X. Gonzalez, R. E. Mercer, G. G. Michelson, S. Nunn, J. D. Opie, R. S. Penske, B. S. Preiskel, F. H. T. Rhodes, A. C. Sigler, D. A. Warner III, J. F. Welch Jr. **Transfer Agent & Registrar**—Bank of New York, NYC. **Incorporated**—In New York in 1892. **Empl**— 239,000. **S&P Analyst:** Joshua M. Harari, CFA.

# Green Tree Financial        1063

NYSE Symbol **GNT**

In S&P 500

**19-MAY-97**

**Industry:** Consumer Finance

**Summary:** This company primarily originates, pools, sells and services conditional sales contracts for manufactured homes, home improvements, consumer products and commercial products.

**S&P Opinion: Accumulate (★★★★)**

| | |
|---|---|
| Recent Price • 33¼ | Yield • 0.9% |
| 52 Wk Range • 42½-26¾ | 12-Mo. P/E • 14.0 |

**Earnings vs. Previous Year**
▲=Up ▼=Down ▶=No Change

**Quantitative Evaluations**

Outlook
(1 Lowest—5 Highest)
• **5**

Fair Value
• **40¼**

Risk
• **Average**

Earn./Div. Rank
• **A**

Technical Eval.
• **Bearish** since 4/97

Rel. Strength Rank
(1 Lowest—99 Highest)
• **44**

Insider Activity
• **Neutral**

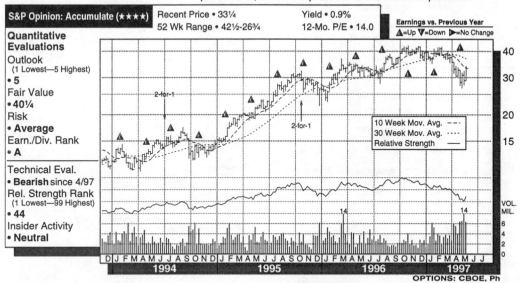

10 Week Mov. Avg. - - -
30 Week Mov. Avg. · · · ·
Relative Strength —

OPTIONS: CBOE, Ph

## Overview - 19-MAY-97

Manufactured housing loan origination growth is expected to be somewhat lower than the 13% rise in 1997, but still remain above projections for manufactured housing unit volume due to steady market share and growth in the average contract size due to a shift to more land-plus-home contracts and price increases by manufacturers. An expanding network of financing relationships with contractors, remodelers and dealers should lead to an increased contribution from the home improvement segment. In addition, the rapid expansion of faster growing consumer and commercial product segments will add to origination volume. Servicing income should advance along with a greater volume of loans sold. A commensurate increase in general and administrative expenses to support expanded operations is anticipated. GNT's high margins and return on equity reflect its focus on a geographically diverse niche business, favorable pricing and efficient operations.

## Valuation - 19-MAY-97

Higher interest rates took their usual toll on the shares of financial companies during the first quarter of 1997, with GNT's declining 13%. While the growth rate for manufactured housing originations has slowed, it is expected to remain in the high single or low double-digits in 1997. The company's roughly two-thirds share of the origination volume in that market, however, has made further market share gains difficult to attain. A continuing expansion of product-type financings outside the traditional manufactured housing market will help boost the level of originations, as these items begin to account for a larger portion of total origination volume. Based on a sustainable above-average growth rate, the shares, trading at about 11 times estimated 1997 earnings, are worthwhile to accumulate for long-term accounts.

## Key Stock Statistics

| | | | |
|---|---|---|---|
| S&P EPS Est. 1997 | 2.95 | Tang. Bk. Value/Share | 8.61 |
| P/E on S&P Est. 1997 | 11.3 | Beta | 1.38 |
| S&P EPS Est. 1998 | 3.55 | Shareholders | 1,100 |
| Dividend Rate/Share | 0.30 | Market cap. (B) | $ 4.6 |
| Shs. outstg. (M) | 139.1 | Inst. holdings | 77% |
| Avg. daily vol. (M) | 2.159 | | |

Value of $10,000 invested 5 years ago: $ 71,435

## Fiscal Year Ending Dec. 31

| | 1997 | 1996 | 1995 | 1994 | 1993 | 1992 |
|---|---|---|---|---|---|---|
| **Revenues (Million $)** | | | | | | |
| 1Q | 267.2 | 168.1 | 128.2 | 104.8 | 66.65 | — |
| 2Q | — | 196.1 | 153.3 | 112.3 | 70.12 | — |
| 3Q | — | 219.7 | 174.4 | 126.1 | 98.93 | — |
| 4Q | — | 340.2 | 255.5 | 154.3 | 118.5 | 67.71 |
| Yr. | — | 924.1 | 711.3 | 497.4 | 366.7 | 246.6 |
| **Earnings Per Share ($)** | | | | | | |
| 1Q | 0.65 | 0.48 | 0.36 | 0.28 | 0.18 | 0.11 |
| 2Q | — | 0.54 | 0.44 | 0.32 | 0.23 | 0.16 |
| 3Q | — | 0.61 | 0.51 | 0.38 | 0.25 | 0.19 |
| 4Q | — | 0.58 | 0.50 | 0.33 | 0.24 | 0.14 |
| Yr. | E2.95 | 2.20 | 1.81 | 1.30 | 0.90 | 0.60 |

**Next earnings report expected: mid July**

**Dividend Data** (Dividends have been paid since 1986.)

| Amount ($) | Date Decl. | Ex-Div. Date | Stock of Record | Payment Date |
|---|---|---|---|---|
| 0.063 | Sep. 03 | Sep. 11 | Sep. 15 | Sep. 30 '96 |
| 0.075 | Oct. 22 | Dec. 11 | Dec. 15 | Dec. 31 '96 |
| 0.075 | Feb. 11 | Mar. 12 | Mar. 14 | Mar. 31 '97 |
| 0.075 | May. 13 | Jun. 11 | Jun. 13 | Jun. 30 '97 |

This report is for information purposes and should not be considered a solicitation to buy or sell any security. Neither S&P nor any other party guarantee its accuracy or make warranties regarding results from its usage. Redistribution is prohibited without written permission. Copyright © 1997   *A Division of The* **McGraw·Hill** *Companies*

## Business Summary - 19-MAY-97

Green Tree Financial is a diversified financial services company that provides financing for manufactured homes, home equity, home improvements, consumer products and equipment and provides consumer and commercial revolving credit. It also markets physical damage and term mortgage life insurance relating to the contracts it services. GNT operates through regional service centers located throughout the U.S.

The majority of the sales contracts for manufactured home purchases are financed on a conventional basis, with a small number of units insured by the FHA or partially guaranteed by the VA. Consumer products are financed using instalment sales contracts. In recent years, GNT has expanded the product types it finances to include motorcycles, marine products, certain musical instruments, horse and utility trailers, sport vehicles and recreational vehicles. The company also provides inventory financing to dealers, manufacturers and distributors of various consumer and commercial products, and in 1996 began providing home equity and revolving credit financing.

During 1996, the company originated a total of 286,731 contracts (221,361 the year before) with a value of $7.6 billion ($5.3 billion). Manufactured housing contracts accounted for 64% of the total value, home improvement/home equity for 20%, and consumer and other for 16%.

The company securitizes substantially all of the contracts it originates, retaining the servicing on the contracts. Conventional manufactured housing contracts are pooled and structured into asset-backed securities that are then sold in the public securities market. GNT's FHA-insured and VA-guaranteed manufactured home contracts are converted into GNMA certificates and sold in the secondary market. At year-end 1996, GNT's servicing portfolio totaled $19.0 billion (up from $13.3 billion at year-end 1995).

The company records income at the time of the sale of its loan contracts, taking the present value of future cash flows into income.

## Important Developments

**Apr. '97**—The company reported that finance volume in the first quarter of 1997 rose 58%, year to year, to $2.9 billion, aided by increases of 13% for manufactured housing, 290% for home improvement/home equity, 131% for consumer finance and 37% for commercial finance. Green Tree noted that it completed four public sales of asset-backed securities during the first quarter of 1997 totaling $1.8 billion.

**Dec. '96**—GNT said it completed the acquisition of the Manufacturer and Dealer Services division from FINOVA Group, Inc. for about $620 million. The division is a leading provider of vendor-oriented sales finance programs involving leasing and financing products for small business equipment purchasers.

## Capitalization

**Long Term Debt:** $762,529,000 (12/96).

| Per Share Data ($) (Year Ended Dec. 31) | 1996 | 1995 | 1994 | 1993 | 1992 | 1991 | 1990 | 1989 | 1988 | 1987 |
|---|---|---|---|---|---|---|---|---|---|---|
| Tangible Bk. Val. | 8.59 | 6.78 | 5.34 | 4.08 | 2.46 | 0.97 | 0.50 | 0.26 | 0.10 | 0.48 |
| Earnings | 2.20 | 1.81 | 1.30 | 0.90 | 0.60 | 0.50 | 0.29 | 0.22 | 0.18 | 0.21 |
| Dividends | 0.26 | 0.20 | 0.12 | 0.08 | 0.08 | 0.08 | 0.08 | 0.08 | 0.08 | 0.06 |
| Payout Ratio | 12% | 11% | 9% | 9% | 13% | 15% | 26% | 34% | 41% | 29% |
| Prices - High | 42 1/2 | 32 3/8 | 17 1/2 | 15 5/8 | 6 1/2 | 5 7/8 | 2 5/16 | 2 5/16 | 2 3/16 | 4 3/4 |
| - Low | 23 | 14 3/4 | 10 3/4 | 5 3/4 | 3 3/4 | 1 1/8 | 1 1/16 | 11/16 | 1 3/16 | 1 1/2 |
| P/E Ratio - High | 19 | 18 | 13 | 17 | 11 | 12 | 8 | 9 | 12 | 22 |
| - Low | 10 | 8 | 8 | 6 | 6 | 2 | 4 | 3 | 6 | 7 |
| **Income Statement Analysis (Million $)** | | | | | | | | | | |
| Total Revs. | 924 | 711 | 497 | 367 | 247 | 215 | 176 | 144 | 134 | 143 |
| Int. Exp. | 70.1 | 57.3 | 41.6 | 51.2 | 44.9 | 49.0 | 51.2 | 44.1 | 37.8 | 34.5 |
| Exp./Op. Revs. | 46% | 42% | 39% | 45% | 52% | 57% | 66% | 67% | 68% | 63% |
| Pretax Inc. | 498 | 410 | 302 | 201 | 119 | 92.2 | 59.4 | 47.7 | 43.3 | 52.6 |
| Eff. Tax Rate | 38% | 38% | 40% | 42% | 39% | 39% | 39% | 39% | 37% | 39% |
| Net Inc. | 309 | 254 | 181 | 116 | 72.5 | 56.7 | 36.5 | 29.4 | 27.4 | 32.4 |
| **Balance Sheet & Other Fin. Data (Million $)** | | | | | | | | | | |
| Cash & Secs. | 625 | 475 | 623 | 315 | 239 | 181 | 113 | 39.0 | 72.0 | 141 |
| Loans | 2,475 | 906 | 700 | 843 | 532 | 438 | 420 | 349 | 298 | 338 |
| Total Assets | 3,792 | 2,384 | 1,772 | 1,740 | 1,034 | 876 | 789 | 711 | 645 | 691 |
| ST Debt | NA | NA | NA | NA | NA | NA | NA | NA | NA | NA |
| Capitalization: | | | | | | | | | | |
| Debt | 763 | 384 | 309 | 515 | 376 | 361 | 279 | 283 | 277 | 254 |
| Equity | 1,245 | 925 | 726 | 549 | 299 | 94.0 | 49.0 | 28.0 | 14.0 | 54.0 |
| Total | 2,008 | 1,309 | 1,035 | 1,064 | 675 | 599 | 471 | 454 | 435 | 452 |
| Price Times Bk. Val.: High | 4.9 | 4.8 | 3.3 | 3.8 | 2.6 | 6.1 | 4.6 | 8.9 | 21.3 | 9.8 |
| Price Times Bk. Val.: Low | 2.7 | 2.2 | 2.0 | 1.4 | 1.5 | 1.2 | 2.1 | 2.7 | 11.6 | 3.1 |
| % Return On Revs. | 33.5 | 35.7 | 36.4 | 31.8 | 29.4 | 26.4 | 20.8 | 20.4 | 20.5 | 22.7 |
| % Ret. on Assets | 10.0 | 12.2 | 1.0 | 8.0 | 7.0 | 7.0 | 4.9 | 4.3 | 4.3 | 4.9 |
| % Ret. on Equity | 28.5 | 30.8 | 28.4 | 27.3 | 33.6 | 66.2 | 70.9 | 95.1 | 52.7 | 32.0 |
| Loans/Equity | 1.6 | 1.8 | 1.2 | 1.8 | 1.8 | 1.9 | 2.1 | 1.9 | 1.7 | 1.5 |

Data as orig. reptd.; bef. results of disc opers. and/or spec. items. Per share data adj. for stk. divs. as of ex-div. date. E-Estimated. NA-Not Available. NM-Not Meaningful. NR-Not Ranked.

**Office**—1100 Landmark Towers, 345 Saint Peter St., Saint Paul, MN 55102-1639. **Tel**—(612) 293-3400. **Fax**—(612) 293-5746. **Chrmn & CEO**—L. M. Coss.**Pres & COO**—R. D. Potts. **EVP & CFO**—E. L. Finn. **SVP & Secy**—J. H. Gottesman.**VP & Investor Contact**—John A. Dolphin. **Dirs**—L. M. Coss, R. G. Evans, W. M. McGee, R. S. Nickoloff, R. D. Potts. **Transfer Agent & Registrar**—Firstar Trust Co., Milwaukee.**Incorporated**—in Minnesota in 1975. **Empl**—4,082. **S&P Analyst:** Stephen R. Biggar

# HBO & Company   4071
### Nasdaq Symbol HBOC

**17-MAY-97**

**Industry:** Computer (Software & Services)

**Summary:** This company is a leading provider of information systems for the healthcare industry.

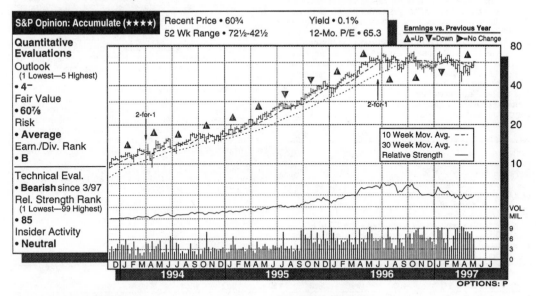

**S&P Opinion: Accumulate (★★★★)**

| Recent Price • 60¾ | Yield • 0.1% |
| 52 Wk Range • 72½-42½ | 12-Mo. P/E • 65.3 |

**Earnings vs. Previous Year**
▲=Up ▼=Down ▶=No Change

**Quantitative Evaluations**

Outlook (1 Lowest—5 Highest)
• 4-

Fair Value
• 60⅞

Risk
• **Average**

Earn./Div. Rank
• **B**

Technical Eval.
• **Bearish** since 3/97

Rel. Strength Rank (1 Lowest—99 Highest)
• 85

Insider Activity
• **Neutral**

10 Week Mov. Avg. ----
30 Week Mov. Avg. ·····
Relative Strength ——

2-for-1

2-for-1

VOL. MIL.

OPTIONS: P

## Overview - 09-APR-97

Revenues are expected to rise over 20% in 1997, aided by continued demand for the company's software products and remote processing, maintenance and other services, aided by a growing installed base. The cost-effective and productivity enhancing nature of the company's products make them particularly attractive to the cost-conscious health care industry. Margins are expected to widen on volume efficiencies, a more favorable revenue mix and well controlled costs. A large and growing backlog adds to the predictability of sales and earnings growth. Earnings comparisons should benefit from the strong sales, wider margins and absence of the following per share acquisition related charges: $0.22 in the fourth quarter of 1996; $0.17 in the third quarter of 1996; $0.07 (adjusted) in the third quarter of 1995, and $1.15 (adjusted) in the second quarter of 1995.

## Valuation - 09-APR-97

The stock of this major provider of computer-based information systems to healthcare organizations advanced over 50% in 1996, far outpacing the broader stock market, aided by continued strong earnings gains and increased predictability associated with those earnings. The company continues to strengthen its competitive position, releasing new products, enhancing existing products, making strategic acquisitions and adding to its salesforce. Earnings are expected to grow much faster than the market, and the balance sheet is very strong. Trading at about 34 times our 1997 earnings estimate, the shares rightly command their premium valuation. In light of the earnings growth we project, the shares are expected to outperform the market in the coming months.

## Key Stock Statistics

| | | | |
|---|---|---|---|
| S&P EPS Est. 1997 | 1.60 | Tang. Bk. Value/Share | 3.83 |
| P/E on S&P Est. 1997 | 38.0 | Beta | 1.49 |
| S&P EPS Est. 1998 | 2.10 | Shareholders | 2,500 |
| Dividend Rate/Share | 0.08 | Market cap. (B) | $ 5.5 |
| Shs. outstg. (M) | 90.9 | Inst. holdings | 87% |
| Avg. daily vol. (M) | 1.471 | | |

Value of $10,000 invested 5 years ago: $ 214,769

## Fiscal Year Ending Dec. 31

| | 1998 | 1997 | 1996 | 1995 | 1994 | 1993 |
|---|---|---|---|---|---|---|
| **Revenues (Million $)** | | | | | | |
| 1Q | — | 219.9 | 172.5 | 99.2 | 67.51 | 52.31 |
| 2Q | — | — | 193.3 | 109.9 | 78.34 | 57.47 |
| 3Q | — | — | 206.4 | 137.9 | 85.94 | 62.20 |
| 4Q | — | — | 224.3 | 148.6 | 95.41 | 65.16 |
| Yr. | — | — | 796.6 | 495.6 | 327.2 | 237.1 |
| **Earnings Per Share ($)** | | | | | | |
| 1Q | — | 0.38 | 0.24 | 0.15 | 0.08 | 0.05 |
| 2Q | — | E0.40 | 0.28 | -0.86 | 0.09 | 0.07 |
| 3Q | — | E0.40 | 0.15 | 0.11 | 0.11 | 0.08 |
| 4Q | — | E0.42 | 0.13 | 0.21 | 0.13 | 0.10 |
| Yr. | E2.10 | E1.60 | 0.79 | -0.33 | 0.43 | 0.29 |

**Next earnings report expected: mid July**

**Dividend Data** (Dividends have been paid since 1982.)

| Amount ($) | Date Decl. | Ex-Div. Date | Stock of Record | Payment Date |
|---|---|---|---|---|
| 0.020 | Aug. 13 | Sep. 26 | Sep. 30 | Oct. 22 '96 |
| 0.020 | Nov. 12 | Dec. 27 | Dec. 31 | Jan. 20 '97 |
| 0.020 | Feb. 11 | Mar. 26 | Mar. 31 | Apr. 22 '97 |
| 0.020 | May. 12 | Jun. 26 | Jun. 30 | Jul. 21 '97 |

This report is for information purposes and should not be considered a solicitation to buy or sell any security. Neither S&P nor any other party guarantee its accuracy or make warranties regarding results from its usage. Redistribution is prohibited without written permission. Copyright © 1997

*A Division of The McGraw-Hill Companies*

## Business Summary - 09-APR-97

Healthcare service providers and insurers have tuned into HBO in increasing numbers. No, we're not referring to the famed pay-TV service. HBO & Co. (Nasdaq: HBOC), no relation to the cable network, has developed computer-based information systems tailored to manage the complex requirements of today's healthcare service providers and payers. HBOC's offerings help keep track of patient records through the disparate locations in which healthcare services are provided. In addition, its products and services address the increasing information needs of employers, insurance firms and government agencies as they seek data regarding the delivery and cost of healthcare services.

HBOC provides products and services in three distinct segments: software, hardware and services. Revenues in recent years:

|  | 1996 | 1995 |
|---|---|---|
| Software | 30% | 28% |
| Hardware | 16% | 14% |
| Services | 54% | 58% |

Software products consist of applications for six areas of information access and delivery: acute-care (hospital), infrastructure, and clinical, practice, access and enterprise management.

Acute-care hospital products such as the STAR, HealthQuest and Surgi-Server transaction and decision support systems, include applications for patient care, laboratory, pharmacy, radiology, financials and manage-ment decision-making. Infrastructure products include both Pathways Interface Manager, which coordinates the flow of information, often from different places, throughout the entire health care information system and Pathways Health Network Server, which stores all patient information for access throughout the enterprise. Clinical, practice and access management solutions include Pathways products, which allow users to document and access patient information and schedule and manage the delivery of healthcare services. Enterprise Management products include Pathways Managed Care, which manages contractual arrangements between providers, payers and patients; Pathways Contract Management, which monitors and manages contracts for providers with significant managed care volumes; and TRENDSTAR accounting programs.

HBOC offers installation and implemetation services for these software products. It also offers software maintenance and enhancement services, as well as custom programming and system modifications to meet special customer requirements.

The company continues to make strategic acquisitons to bolster its presence in niche areas. In February 1997, HBOC signed a definitive agreement to acquire AMISYS Managed Care Systems (annual revenues of about $46 million), a provider of information systems for managed care entities, for about $165 million in stock.

### Capitalization

**Long Term Debt:** $192,000 (12/96).

### Per Share Data ($)

| (Year Ended Dec. 31) | 1996 | 1995 | 1994 | 1993 | 1992 | 1991 | 1990 | 1989 | 1988 | 1987 |
|---|---|---|---|---|---|---|---|---|---|---|
| Tangible Bk. Val. | 3.84 | 1.68 | 0.54 | 0.85 | 0.68 | 0.40 | 0.49 | 0.56 | 0.47 | 0.33 |
| Cash Flow | 1.32 | 0.07 | 0.60 | 0.39 | 0.31 | 0.13 | 0.33 | 0.45 | 0.44 | 0.39 |
| Earnings | 1.19 | 0.72 | 0.43 | 0.29 | 0.22 | -0.05 | 0.13 | 0.25 | 0.20 | 0.15 |
| Dividends | 0.08 | 0.08 | 0.08 | 0.08 | 0.08 | 0.08 | 0.08 | 0.08 | 0.08 | 0.05 |
| Payout Ratio | 7% | 11% | 19% | 25% | 34% | NM | 60% | 30% | 36% | 32% |
| Prices - High | 72½ | 43¼ | 18⅜ | 11⅝ | 6½ | 3 | 3¾ | 4⅛ | 2⅞ | 3⅜ |
| - Low | 32¾ | 16½ | 9⅜ | 4¼ | 2⅜ | 1¼ | 1 | 2⅜ | 1½ | 1³/₁₆ |
| P/E Ratio - High | 61 | 60 | 43 | 39 | 30 | NM | 30 | 17 | 14 | 22 |
| - Low | 28 | 23 | 22 | 14 | 11 | NM | 8 | 9 | 7 | 8 |

### Income Statement Analysis (Million $)

| | 1996 | 1995 | 1994 | 1993 | 1992 | 1991 | 1990 | 1989 | 1988 | 1987 |
|---|---|---|---|---|---|---|---|---|---|---|
| Revs. | 797 | 496 | 327 | 237 | 202 | 171 | 201 | 204 | 187 | 175 |
| Oper. Inc. | 229 | 126 | 59.9 | 37.3 | 26.1 | 17.9 | 27.4 | 37.6 | 35.6 | 36.9 |
| Depr. | 49.2 | 30.2 | 11.9 | 6.1 | 5.7 | 10.2 | 12.0 | 12.5 | 14.5 | 20.4 |
| Int. Exp. | Nil | NA | NA | 1.5 | 1.2 | 2.3 | 3.4 | 2.4 | 2.9 | 1.3 |
| Pretax Inc. | 122 | -42.0 | 47.0 | 30.5 | 19.9 | -4.3 | 10.7 | 23.5 | 19.0 | 21.0 |
| Eff. Tax Rate | 40% | NM | 40% | 40% | 34% | NM | 33% | 34% | 34% | 37% |
| Net Inc. | 74.0 | -25.2 | 28.2 | 18.3 | 13.1 | -2.9 | 7.1 | 15.5 | 12.5 | 13.3 |

### Balance Sheet & Other Fin. Data (Million $)

| | 1996 | 1995 | 1994 | 1993 | 1992 | 1991 | 1990 | 1989 | 1988 | 1987 |
|---|---|---|---|---|---|---|---|---|---|---|
| Cash | 160 | 65.3 | 5.8 | 23.2 | 7.6 | 2.7 | 2.3 | 4.7 | 4.5 | 5.7 |
| Curr. Assets | 520 | 252 | 123 | 73.2 | 69.2 | 70.7 | 70.2 | 58.1 | 44.3 | 43.9 |
| Total Assets | 849 | 535 | 234 | 119 | 103 | 103 | 123 | 114 | 101 | 102 |
| Curr. Liab. | 316 | 205 | 131 | 59.6 | 54.6 | 53.2 | 51.0 | 63.0 | 49.8 | 47.0 |
| LT Debt | 0.2 | 0.6 | Nil | NA | Nil | 20.0 | 37.5 | 6.8 | 10.0 | 19.2 |
| Common Eqty. | 525 | 319 | 91.5 | 50.0 | 40.8 | 22.6 | 26.7 | 32.5 | 28.5 | 19.5 |
| Total Cap. | 525 | 320 | 101 | 59.0 | 48.0 | 50.0 | 72.0 | 51.0 | 51.0 | 55.0 |
| Cap. Exp. | 20.8 | 11.2 | 5.7 | 8.6 | 4.4 | 6.4 | 10.6 | 7.6 | 13.4 | 15.3 |
| Cash Flow | 123 | 5.0 | 40.1 | 24.4 | 18.8 | 7.3 | 19.1 | 28.0 | 27.0 | 33.7 |
| Curr. Ratio | 1.6 | 1.2 | 0.9 | 1.2 | 1.3 | 1.3 | 1.4 | 0.9 | 0.9 | 0.9 |
| % LT Debt of Cap. | Nil | 0.2 | Nil | NA | Nil | 40.0 | 52.0 | 13.3 | 19.7 | 35.0 |
| % Net Inc.of Revs. | 9.3 | NM | 8.6 | 7.7 | 6.5 | NM | 3.5 | 7.6 | 6.7 | 7.6 |
| % Ret. on Assets | 9.9 | NM | 15.6 | 16.7 | 12.3 | NM | 6.2 | 14.6 | 12.3 | 14.4 |
| % Ret. on Equity | 15.8 | NM | 38.8 | 40.8 | 40.4 | NM | 24.9 | 51.6 | 52.0 | 38.0 |

Data as orig. reptd.; bef. results of disc. opers. and/or spec. items. Per share data adj. for stk. divs. as of ex-div. date. E-Estimated. NA-Not Available. NM-Not Meaningful. NR-Not Ranked.

**Office**—301 Perimeter Center North, Atlanta, GA 30346. **Tel**—(404) 393-6000. **Website**—http://www.hboc.com **Chrmn**—H. T. Green, Jr. **Pres & CEO**—C. W. McCall. **SVP-Fin & CFO**—J. P. Gilbertson. **VP & Secy**—J. M. Lapine. **Investor Contact**—Anne Davenport. **Dirs**— A. C. Eckert III, H. T. Green, Jr., P. A. Incarnati, A. F. Irby III, G. E. Mayo, C. W. McCall, J. V. Napier, C. E. Thoele, D. Wegmiller. **Transfer Agent & Registrar**—Trust Co. Bank, Atlanta. **Incorporated**—in Delaware in 1974. **Empl**— 4,400. **S&P Analyst:** Peter C. Wood, CFA

**22-MAY-97**

**Industry:** Insurance (Property-ty-Casualty)

**Summary:** HCC specializes in aviation, marine, energy, property and health and accident insurance through its subsidiaries in the U.S. and Jordan.

## Quantitative Evaluations

**Outlook** (1 Lowest—5 Highest)
- **NA**

**Fair Value**
- **NA**

**Risk**
- **Average**

**Earn./Div. Rank**
- **NR**

**Technical Eval.**
- **Bearish** since 3/97

**Rel. Strength Rank** (1 Lowest—99 Highest)
- **33**

**Insider Activity**
- **NA**

Recent Price • 24¾

52 Wk Range • 32¾-19⅛

Yield • 0.5%

12-Mo. P/E • 29.1

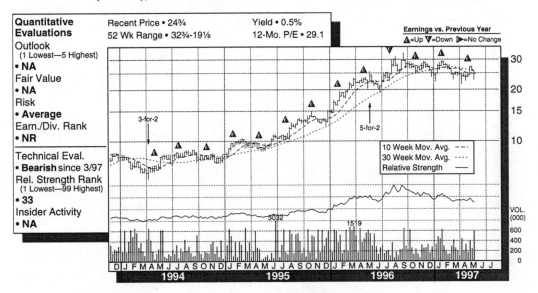

**Earnings vs. Previous Year**
▲=Up ▼=Down ▶=No Change

- 10 Week Mov. Avg. — - —
- 30 Week Mov. Avg. - - - -
- Relative Strength ——

## Business Profile - 20-MAY-97

In recent years, HCC has substantially increased its capital and surplus through the issuance of equity securities, incurrence of debt, and earnings, thereby enabling it to increase its underwriting capacity. The company has utilized this additional capital by increasing underwriting activity across many of its core lines of business, emphasizing lines of business and individual opportunities with the most favorable underwriting characteristics at a particular point in time. In each line of business, HCC also cedes premiums through the purchase of reinsurance in types and amounts appropriate to the line of business, market conditions and its desired net risk retention profile.

## Operational Review - 20-MAY-97

Based on a brief report, total revenues in the three months ended March 31, 1997, advanced 6.2%, year to year. Gross written premiums increased 29%, reflecting a few large policies written in the quarter, while net written premiums decreased 34%, on a reduction in marine gross written premiums. Fee and commission income rose 31%, as a result of the higher proportion of ceded premiums plus several large individual transactions in the quarter. Net investment income was up 13%. Net income advanced 20%, to $11,403,000 ($0.31 a share, on 4.7% more shares), from $9,464,000 ($0.27).

## Stock Performance - 16-MAY-97

In the past 30 trading days, HCC's shares have increased 3%, compared to a 9% rise in the S&P 500. Average trading volume for the past five days was 117,460 shares, compared with the 40-day moving average of 61,872 shares.

## Key Stock Statistics

| | | | |
|---|---|---|---|
| Dividend Rate/Share | 0.12 | Shareholders | 100 |
| Shs. outstg. (M) | 36.2 | Market cap. (B) | $0.895 |
| Avg. daily vol. (M) | 0.067 | Inst. holdings | 52% |
| Tang. Bk. Value/Share | 6.71 | | |
| Beta | NA | | |

Value of $10,000 invested 5 years ago: NA

### Fiscal Year Ending Dec. 31

| | 1997 | 1996 | 1995 | 1994 | 1993 | 1992 |
|---|---|---|---|---|---|---|
| **Revenues (Million $)** | | | | | | |
| 1Q | 39.80 | 37.48 | 21.89 | 13.49 | 9.21 | — |
| 2Q | — | 37.68 | 24.77 | 14.17 | 9.53 | — |
| 3Q | — | 35.57 | 24.86 | 14.71 | 10.55 | — |
| 4Q | — | 41.42 | 27.67 | 17.50 | 11.86 | — |
| Yr. | — | 152.3 | 99.2 | 59.87 | 41.15 | 29.10 |
| **Earnings Per Share ($)** | | | | | | |
| 1Q | 0.31 | 0.27 | 0.18 | 0.12 | 0.08 | — |
| 2Q | — | -0.11 | 0.20 | 0.15 | 0.12 | — |
| 3Q | — | 0.31 | 0.20 | 0.17 | 0.12 | — |
| 4Q | — | 0.35 | 0.26 | 0.18 | 0.13 | — |
| Yr. | — | 0.81 | 0.84 | 0.62 | 0.45 | 0.21 |

**Next earnings report expected: mid July**

**Dividend Data** (Dividends have been paid since 1996.)

| Amount ($) | Date Decl. | Ex-Div. Date | Stock of Record | Payment Date |
|---|---|---|---|---|
| 0.020 | Jun. 18 | Jun. 27 | Jul. 01 | Jul. 15 '96 |
| 0.020 | Sep. 16 | Sep. 27 | Oct. 01 | Oct. 15 '96 |
| 0.020 | Dec. 23 | Dec. 30 | Jan. 02 | Jan. 10 '97 |
| 0.030 | Mar. 24 | Mar. 27 | Apr. 01 | Apr. 11 '97 |

This report is for information purposes and should not be considered a solicitation to buy or sell any security. Neither S&P nor any other party guarantee its accuracy or make warranties regarding results from its usage. Redistribution is prohibited without written permission. Copyright © 1997

*A Division of The McGraw-Hill Companies*

## Business Summary - 20-MAY-97

HCC Insurance Holdings, Inc., through its subsidiaries, provides specialized property and casualty insurance to commercial customers, underwritten on both a direct and reinsurance basis, and, to a lesser extent, insurance agency services. The company's underwriting activities are focused on providing aviation, marine, property, offshore energy and accident and health insurance on a worldwide basis and international reinsurance on these same lines of business.

HCC's revenues in recent years were derived as follows:

|  | 1996 | 1995 |
|---|---|---|
| Net earned premium | 61% | 63% |
| Net investment income | 10% | 10% |
| Net realized investment gain | 4% | 1% |
| Fee and commission income | 25% | 26% |

Houston Casualty Co., the company's principal insurance company subsidiary, operates worldwide, specializing in marketing and servicing complicated, high value, structured insurance and reinsurance programs placed on behalf of domestic and foreign clients which cover large, ocean marine fleet; complex, multinational, energy businesses; international aviation operations; and large international property accounts.

Gross written premium totaled $230,755,000 in 1996, compared with $238,958,000 in 1995; the decline reflected dropoffs in marine, offshore energy, and property lines. Gross written premium by line of business was divided as follows in 1996: aviation 31%, marine 12%, offshore energy 4%, property 51%, accident and health 1% and reinsurance 1%.

HCC's operating philosophy is to maximize underwriting profit while preserving the integrity of shareholders' equity. The company concentrates its writings in selected, narrowly defined lines of business in which it believes there is a substantial opportunity to achieve underwriting profits. HCC primarily underwrites first party, physical damage coverages and lines of business which have relatively short lead times between the occurrence of an insured event and the reporting of claims.

### Important Developments

**Jan. '97**—HCC acquired the occupational accident business of TRM International, Inc. for 266,667 common shares and $6.55 million in cash.
**Nov. '96**—The company acquired North American Special Risk Associates, Inc. group of companies (NASRA) for 1,136,400 common shares and $1.7 million in cash. NASRA provides underwriting and claims management services to insurance and reinsurance companies primarily in occupational accident insurance for self-employed truckers.

### Capitalization

**Notes Payable:** $16,500,000 (12/96).

## Per Share Data ($)

| (Year Ended Dec. 31) | 1996 | 1995 | 1994 | 1993 | 1992 | 1991 | 1990 | 1989 | 1988 | 1987 |
|---|---|---|---|---|---|---|---|---|---|---|
| Tangible Bk. Val. | 6.71 | 6.65 | 4.65 | 4.26 | NA | NA | NA | NA | NA | NA |
| Oper. Earnings | NA | NA | 0.58 | 0.40 | NA | NA | NA | NA | NA | NA |
| Earnings | 0.81 | 0.84 | 0.62 | 0.45 | 0.21 | 0.08 | Nil | NA | NA | NA |
| Dividends | 0.06 | Nil | Nil | Nil | Nil | Nil | Nil | NA | NA | NA |
| Payout Ratio | 7% | Nil | Nil | Nil | Nil | Nil | Nil | NA | NA | NA |
| Prices - High | 32¾ | 15¼ | 8⅞ | 9½ | 5⅜ | NA | NA | NA | NA | NA |
| - Low | 14½ | 7⅞ | 6 | 4⅜ | 3¼ | NA | NA | NA | NA | NA |
| P/E Ratio - High | 40 | 18 | 14 | 21 | 25 | NA | NA | NA | NA | NA |
| - Low | 18 | 9 | 10 | 10 | 15 | NA | NA | NA | NA | NA |

## Income Statement Analysis (Million $)

| | 1996 | 1995 | 1994 | 1993 | 1992 | 1991 | 1990 | 1989 | 1988 | 1987 |
|---|---|---|---|---|---|---|---|---|---|---|
| Premium Inc. | 93.3 | 80.0 | 46.8 | 32.7 | 24.5 | 21.2 | 15.2 | NA | NA | NA |
| Net Invest. Inc. | 15.4 | 12.2 | 8.6 | 4.9 | 2.4 | 1.9 | 2.0 | NA | NA | NA |
| Oth. Revs. | 43.5 | 7.0 | 4.4 | 3.5 | 2.3 | 0.6 | 0.6 | NA | NA | NA |
| Total Revs. | 152 | 99 | 59.9 | 41.1 | 29.1 | 23.8 | 17.8 | NA | NA | NA |
| Pretax Inc. | 36.6 | 31.0 | 17.8 | 10.5 | 3.8 | 1.5 | 1.8 | NA | NA | NA |
| Net Oper. Inc. | NA | NA | NA | NA | NA | NA | NA | NA | NA | NA |
| Net Inc. | 29.3 | 22.3 | 13.4 | 8.0 | 2.9 | 1.5 | 1.5 | NA | NA | NA |

## Balance Sheet & Other Fin. Data (Million $)

| | 1996 | 1995 | 1994 | 1993 | 1992 | 1991 | 1990 | 1989 | 1988 | 1987 |
|---|---|---|---|---|---|---|---|---|---|---|
| Cash & Equiv. | 47.6 | 3.1 | 2.5 | 2.0 | NA | NA | NA | NA | NA | NA |
| Premiums Due | 139 | 75.3 | 68.9 | 29.9 | 11.2 | 16.8 | 9.0 | NA | NA | NA |
| Invest. Assets: Bonds | 265 | 235 | 152 | 121 | NA | NA | NA | NA | NA | NA |
| Invest. Assets: Stocks | 2.4 | 13.8 | 13.6 | 11.4 | NA | NA | NA | NA | NA | NA |
| Invest. Assets: Loans | Nil | 0.1 | 0.4 | 0.4 | NA | NA | NA | NA | NA | NA |
| Invest. Assets: Total | 320 | 290 | 192 | 155 | 71.0 | 34.0 | 31.0 | NA | NA | NA |
| Deferred Policy Costs | 16.8 | 16.4 | 13.1 | 5.5 | NA | NA | NA | NA | NA | NA |
| Total Assets | 746 | 580 | 458 | 295 | 162 | 142 | 111 | NA | NA | NA |
| Debt | 16.5 | 16.3 | 44.3 | 28.3 | 3.5 | 7.5 | 9.0 | NA | NA | NA |
| Common Eqty. | 24.0 | 189 | 108 | 87.0 | 40.0 | 9.0 | 8.0 | NA | NA | NA |
| Prop. & Cas. Loss Ratio | 56.4 | 63.4 | 64.6 | 66.7 | 66.2 | 56.3 | 48.4 | NA | NA | NA |
| Prop. & Cas. Expense Ratio | 15.6 | 11.5 | 10.2 | 14.4 | 21.7 | 40.9 | 40.2 | NA | NA | NA |
| Prop. & Cas. Combined Ratio | 72.0 | 74.9 | 74.8 | 81.1 | 87.4 | 97.2 | 109.5 | NA | NA | NA |
| % Return On Revs. | 19.2 | 22.5 | 22.4 | 19.5 | 10.0 | 6.3 | 8.4 | NA | NA | NA |
| % Ret. on Equity | 13.4 | 15.0 | 13.7 | 12.6 | 7.3 | 7.9 | NA | NA | NA | NA |

Data as orig. reptd.; bef. results of disc. opers. and/or spec. items. Per share data adj. for stk. divs. as of ex-div. date. E-Estimated. NA-Not Available. NM-Not Meaningful. NR-Not Ranked.

**Office**—13403 Northwest Freeway, Houston, TX 77040-6094. **Tel**—(713) 690-7300. **Chrmn & CEO**—S. L. Way. **Pres**—S. J. Lockwood.**EVP, CFO & Secy**—F. J. Bramanti. **Dirs**—J. M. Berry, F. J. Bramanti, M. A. Buechler, P. B. Collins, J. R. Dickerson, E. H. Frank III, A. W. Fulkerson, W. S. Jabsheh, W. J. Lack, S. J. Lockwood, P. B. Smith, W. L. Suydam, L. E. Tuffly, S. L. Way, H. T. Wilson. **Transfer Agent & Registrar**—First Interstate Bank of Texas, Houston. **Incorporated**—in Delaware in 1991.**Empl**— 331. **S&P Analyst:** M.I.

**17-MAY-97**

**Industry:**
Health Care (Hospital Management)

**Summary:** This company operates a rapidly growing network of general acute-care hospitals located primarily in nonurban areas in the Southeast and Southwest.

| | |
|---|---|
| **S&P Opinion: Buy (★★★★)** | Recent Price • 28½    Yield • Nil |
| | 52 Wk Range • 30-16¾    12-Mo. P/E • 32.8 |

**Quantitative Evaluations**

**Outlook**
(1 Lowest—5 Highest)
• **5**

**Fair Value**
• **35¾**

**Risk**
• **Average**

**Earn./Div. Rank**
• **B+**

**Technical Eval.**
• **Bullish** since 5/93

**Rel. Strength Rank**
(1 Lowest—99 Highest)
• **79**

**Insider Activity**
• **NA**

**Earnings vs. Previous Year**
▲=Up ▼=Down ▷=No Change

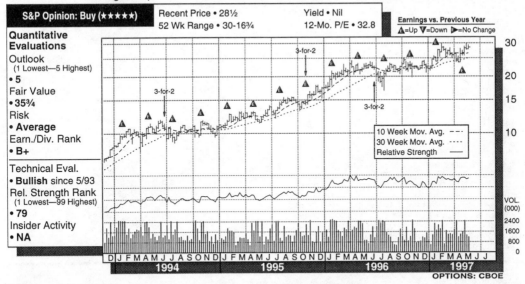

10 Week Mov. Avg. — — —
30 Week Mov. Avg. ·······
Relative Strength ——

OPTIONS: CBOE

## Overview - 23-APR-97

HMA has a long history of successfully acquiring underperforming hospitals in non-urban or rural markets, and implementing its own operating strategies in order to restore profitability. These facilities were often underutilized by local physicians and patients, had severe capital constraints and were heavily leveraged prior to acquisition. However, the company only seeks out those facilities which have the potential to become the sole or dominant provider in its market, and those markets must have a solid physician base from which the company can recruit. Through cost-cutting and revenue building initiatives, management is typically able to restore positive cash flow to these facilities within six months, and operating margins are expected to be at HMA's corporate average within three years.

## Valuation - 23-APR-97

Despite ongoing concerns regarding potential Medicare cutbacks, along with negative sentiment resulting from the recently-disclosed federal investigation of industry leader Columbia/HCA, we maintain a bullish view on the for-profit hospital sector and feel that HMA represents one of the premier investments in the group. The company generated outstanding results in the second quarter of FY 97 (Sep.), aided by a nearly 30% top-line gain. Operating (EBITDA) margins reached 26.5% in the quarter, far above the industry average of about 17%. Following the earnings release, we raised our FY 97 earnings forecast by $0.05 to $1.00, and now see FY 98 EPS of $1.20. Although many state regulators are aggressively challenging mergers between the investor-owned and tax-exempt hospitals, we expect HMA to pursue additional mergers in coming months, while performance at existing sites should remain strong. The stock remains attractive at 22 times our FY 98 forecast.

## Key Stock Statistics

| | | | |
|---|---|---|---|
| S&P EPS Est. 1997 | 1.00 | Tang. Bk. Value/Share | 3.95 |
| P/E on S&P Est. 1997 | 28.5 | Beta | 1.59 |
| S&P EPS Est. 1998 | 1.20 | Shareholders | 1,400 |
| Dividend Rate/Share | Nil | Market cap. (B) | $ 3.1 |
| Shs. outstg. (M) | 107.1 | Inst. holdings | 83% |
| Avg. daily vol. (M) | 0.339 | | |

Value of $10,000 invested 5 years ago: $ 56,766

### Fiscal Year Ending Sep. 30

| | 1998 | 1997 | 1996 | 1995 | 1994 | 1993 |
|---|---|---|---|---|---|---|
| **Revenues (Million $)** | | | | | | |
| 1Q | — | 199.2 | 151.9 | 115.4 | 101.5 | 79.83 |
| 2Q | — | 237.8 | 184.8 | 144.8 | 115.8 | 87.62 |
| 3Q | — | — | 184.4 | 137.0 | 112.5 | 89.88 |
| 4Q | — | — | 193.2 | 133.9 | 108.6 | 89.44 |
| Yr. | — | — | 714.3 | 531.1 | 438.4 | 346.8 |
| **Earnings Per Share ($)** | | | | | | |
| 1Q | — | 0.18 | 0.14 | 0.11 | 0.08 | 0.05 |
| 2Q | — | 0.29 | 0.23 | 0.17 | 0.14 | 0.09 |
| 3Q | — | E0.28 | 0.22 | 0.17 | 0.14 | 0.10 |
| 4Q | — | E0.25 | 0.19 | 0.13 | 0.11 | 0.07 |
| Yr. | E1.20 | E1.00 | 0.76 | 0.59 | 0.46 | 0.33 |

**Next earnings report expected: mid July**

### Dividend Data

| Amount ($) | Date Decl. | Ex-Div. Date | Stock of Record | Payment Date |
|---|---|---|---|---|
| 3-for-2 | Jun. 03 | Jun. 17 | May. 31 | Jun. 14 '96 |

This report is for information purposes and should not be considered a solicitation to buy or sell any security. Neither S&P nor any other party guarantee its accuracy or make warranties regarding results from its usage. Redistribution is prohibited without written permission. Copyright © 1997    A Division of The McGraw-Hill Companies

## Business Summary - 23-APR-97

Health Management Associates has emerged as the leading operator of acute care hospitals in non-urban and rural areas of the U.S., with a primary focus on markets in the southeast and southwest regions.

Founded in 1977 to own, lease and manage hospitals throughout the country, HMA shifted its operating strategy in 1983 to focus on acquiring, improving and operating underperforming hospitals in high-growth, non-urban areas exhibiting favorable demographics and strong physician bases. These hospitals must have the potential to become the sole or dominant medical provider in its market. As of mid-April 1997, HMA was operating 26 hospitals 11 states with a total of 3,078 licensed beds.

The company's acute-care hospitals offer a broad range of medical and surgical services, including inpatient care, intensive and cardiac care, diagnostic services and emergency services that are physician-staffed 24 hours a day, seven days a week. HMA also provides outpatient services such as one-day surgery, laboratory, X-ray, respiratory therapy, cardiology and physical therapy. Some of the hospitals provide specialty services such as oncology, radiation therapy, CT scanning, MRI imaging, lithotripsy and full-service obstetrics. The company seeks to provide at least 90% of the acute care needs of each community in its service areas, thereby reducing out-migration of potential patients to hospitals in larger urban areas.

Psychiatric care is provided in four hospitals: one 80-bed hospital, one 66-bed hospital, one 100-bed hospital (with 60 adolescent beds and 40 geriatric beds), and one 60-bed child/adolescent hospital.

HMA pursues a strategy of efficiently and profitably operating its existing base of facilities and selectively acquiring 100- to 300-bed acute-care hospitals in nonurban communities in market areas of 40,000 to 300,000 people in the southeastern and southwestern U.S.

Many of these facilities are unprofitable at the time of acquisition, and the company immediately employs an executive director and controller, implements its proprietary management information system, recruits physicians, induces strict cost control measures with respect to hospital staffing and volume purchasing, and spending the required capital to upgrade the facility and equipment. HMA operates each acquired hospital to maximize operating margins and return on capital within the first 36 months of operation, a time period which the company believes is sufficient to fully implement the plan of improvement.

In FY 96, Medicare provided 52% of patient service revenues, Medicaid 13% and private and other sources 35%.

### Capitalization

**Long Term Debt:** $68,700,000 (12/96).

### Per Share Data ($)

| (Year Ended Sep. 30) | 1996 | 1995 | 1994 | 1993 | 1992 | 1991 | 1990 | 1989 | 1988 | 1987 |
|---|---|---|---|---|---|---|---|---|---|---|
| Tangible Bk. Val. | 3.95 | 3.07 | 2.45 | 1.91 | 1.42 | 0.89 | 0.34 | 0.26 | NA | NA |
| Cash Flow | 1.01 | 0.77 | 0.61 | 0.45 | 0.36 | 0.30 | 0.23 | 0.16 | NA | NA |
| Earnings | 0.76 | 0.59 | 0.46 | 0.32 | 0.23 | 0.16 | 0.07 | 0.03 | NA | NA |
| Dividends | Nil | Nil | Nil | Nil | Nil | Nil | Nil | Nil | NA | NA |
| Payout Ratio | Nil | Nil | Nil | Nil | Nil | Nil | Nil | Nil | NA | NA |
| Prices - High | 25 | 15⅝ | 11⅞ | 8⅝ | 5⅝ | 5¼ | NA | NA | NA | NA |
|    - Low | 16¾ | 10½ | 8 | 3⅛ | 3¾ | 2⅛ | NA | NA | NA | NA |
| P/E Ratio - High | 33 | 27 | 26 | 27 | 25 | 34 | NA | NA | NA | NA |
|    - Low | 22 | 18 | 17 | 10 | 16 | 14 | NA | NA | NA | NA |

### Income Statement Analysis (Million $)

| | | | | | | | | | | |
|---|---|---|---|---|---|---|---|---|---|---|
| Revs. | 714 | 531 | 438 | 347 | 278 | 226 | 192 | 142 | NA | NA |
| Oper. Inc. | 169 | 128 | 102 | 74.1 | 58.2 | 46.8 | 36.5 | 27.5 | NA | NA |
| Depr. | 27.2 | 20.6 | 16.2 | 12.8 | 12.6 | 10.9 | 9.7 | 7.9 | NA | NA |
| Int. Exp. | 3.5 | 3.6 | 4.3 | 4.8 | 7.2 | 14.1 | 17.8 | 16.5 | NA | NA |
| Pretax Inc. | 138 | 104 | 81.7 | 56.4 | 38.4 | 21.8 | 9.2 | 4.1 | NA | NA |
| Eff. Tax Rate | 39% | 39% | 40% | 43% | 43% | 45% | 49% | 52% | NA | NA |
| Net Inc. | 84.1 | 63.3 | 49.1 | 32.2 | 21.9 | 12.0 | 4.6 | 2.0 | NA | NA |

### Balance Sheet & Other Fin. Data (Million $)

| | | | | | | | | | | |
|---|---|---|---|---|---|---|---|---|---|---|
| Cash | 31.2 | 75.3 | 109 | 74.4 | 25.2 | 0.2 | 3.0 | 0.2 | NA | NA |
| Curr. Assets | 178 | 173 | 178 | 119 | 57.9 | 41.3 | 40.7 | 34.8 | NA | NA |
| Total Assets | 592 | 467 | 399 | 326 | 243 | 229 | 216 | 189 | NA | NA |
| Curr. Liab. | 70.9 | 50.6 | 39.6 | 43.2 | 35.3 | 32.7 | 31.0 | 25.4 | NA | NA |
| LT Debt | 68.7 | 67.7 | 76.0 | 78.0 | 63.0 | 112 | 160 | 144 | NA | NA |
| Common Eqty. | 418 | 318 | 253 | 193 | 135 | 76.0 | 21.0 | 16.0 | NA | NA |
| Total Cap. | 505 | 404 | 348 | 273 | 201 | 191 | 183 | 161 | NA | NA |
| Cap. Exp. | 41.2 | 22.9 | 40.6 | 34.3 | 14.5 | 23.0 | 31.3 | 14.9 | NA | NA |
| Cash Flow | 111 | 83.9 | 65.3 | 45.1 | 34.5 | 22.9 | 14.3 | 9.9 | NA | NA |
| Curr. Ratio | 2.5 | 3.4 | 4.5 | 2.7 | 1.6 | 1.3 | 1.3 | 1.4 | NA | NA |
| % LT Debt of Cap. | 13.6 | 16.8 | 21.8 | 28.5 | 31.4 | 58.9 | 87.0 | 89.2 | NA | NA |
| % Net Inc.of Revs. | 11.8 | 11.9 | 11.2 | 9.3 | 7.9 | 5.3 | 2.4 | 1.4 | NA | NA |
| % Ret. on Assets | 15.9 | 14.6 | 13.4 | 11.1 | 8.7 | 4.6 | 2.3 | NA | NA | NA |
| % Ret. on Equity | 22.9 | 22.2 | 21.8 | 19.2 | 19.8 | 23.0 | 24.7 | NA | NA | NA |

Data as orig. reptd.; bef. results of disc. opers. and/or spec. items. Per share data adj. for stk. divs. as of ex-div. date. E-Estimated. NA-Not Available. NM-Not Meaningful. NR-Not Ranked.

**Office**—5811 Pelican Bay Blvd., Suite 500, Naples, FL 33963-2710. **Tel**—(941) 598-3131. **Chrmn & CEO**—W. J. Schoen. **Vice Chrmn**—E. P. Holland. **Pres & COO**—J. V. Vumbacco.**SVP-Fin**—S. M. Ray. **Dirs**—K. P. Dauten, E. P. Holland, R. A. Knox, C. R. Lees, K. D. Lewis, W. E. Mayberry, W. J. Schoen. **Transfer Agent & Registrar**—First Union National Bank of North Carolina, Charlotte. **Incorporated**—in Delaware in 1979. **Empl**— 9,000. **S&P Analyst:** Robert M. Gold

# STANDARD &POOR'S
### STOCK REPORTS
# Hewlett-Packard
# 1137
NYSE Symbol **HWP**

**In S&P 500**

**20-MAY-97** Industry: Computers (Hardware)

**Summary:** Hewlett-Packard is a leading manufacturer of computer products, including printers, servers, workstations and PCs. The company also offers a vast service and support network.

| S&P Opinion: Hold (★★★) | Recent Price • 52¾ | Yield • 1.1% |
| | 52 Wk Range • 60-37¾ | 12-Mo. P/E • 20.0 |

**Quantitative Evaluations**

**Outlook** (1 Lowest—5 Highest)
• **4**

**Fair Value**
• **66¼**

**Risk**
• **Average**

**Earn./Div. Rank**
• **A**

**Technical Eval.**
• **Bullish** since 5/97

**Rel. Strength Rank** (1 Lowest—99 Highest)
• **37**

**Insider Activity**
• **Unfavorable**

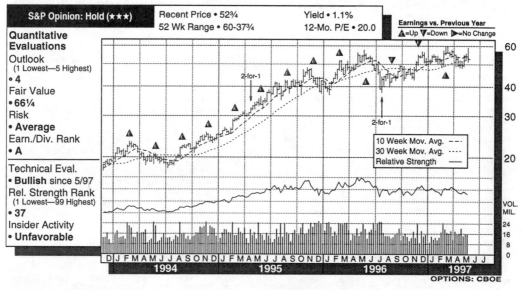

Earnings vs. Previous Year ▲=Up ▼=Down ▶=No Change

10 Week Mov. Avg. – – –
30 Week Mov. Avg. - - - -
Relative Strength —

OPTIONS: CBOE

## Overview - 19-MAY-97

Revenues are estimated to grow 11% during FY 97 (Oct.), primarily on strength expected in the second half of the year, as HWP benefits from easier year over year comparisons (versus difficult comparisons in the first half), and new product introductions. The company's recently introduced Windows NT workstations, and entry level and mid-range servers have been well received and we see further growth ahead. Gross margins are expected to remain under pressure, reflecting a greater proportion of less profitable PC and printer sales, and ongoing price competition in all of HWP's businesses. Nevertheless, HWP's efforts to control costs through improved supply-chain management have been encouraging. We expect HWP to devote considerable energy to controlling operating expenses, particularly as revenue and order growth slow from the heightened levels of the past few years.

## Valuation - 19-MAY-97

We recently downgraded HWP to neutral from accumulate. The company's Q1 revenue and order growth rates at 5% and 3%, respectively, were well below expectations. The slower order rate resulted in our reduced expectations for revenue growth in the second half of the year, although these revenues will have easier year over year comparisons than those of the first half. Meanwhile, HWP has managed to improve gross margins and control expenses despite the slowdown. With favorable reviews of HWP's new products and several others likely to begin boosting revenues in FY 98, we continue to like the shares longer term. However, at 15X our FY 98 EPS of $3.55, we believe the shares will perform in line with the overall market.

## Key Stock Statistics

| | | | |
|---|---|---|---|
| S&P EPS Est. 1997 | 3.15 | Tang. Bk. Value/Share | 13.25 |
| P/E on S&P Est. 1997 | 16.7 | Beta | 1.67 |
| S&P EPS Est. 1998 | 3.55 | Shareholders | 92,100 |
| Dividend Rate/Share | 0.56 | Market cap. (B) | $ 53.7 |
| Shs. outstg. (M) | 1016.2 | Inst. holdings | 48% |
| Avg. daily vol. (M) | 4.245 | | |

Value of $10,000 invested 5 years ago: $ 39,212

### Fiscal Year Ending Oct. 31

| | 1997 | 1996 | 1995 | 1994 | 1993 | 1992 |
|---|---|---|---|---|---|---|
| **Revenues (Million $)** | | | | | | |
| 1Q | 10,295 | 9,288 | 7,304 | 5,682 | 4,573 | 3,863 |
| 2Q | 10,340 | 9,880 | 7,428 | 6,254 | 5,096 | 4,183 |
| 3Q | — | 9,105 | 7,739 | 6,053 | 4,961 | 4,040 |
| 4Q | — | 10,147 | 9,048 | 7,002 | 5,687 | 4,324 |
| Yr. | — | 38,420 | 31,519 | 24,991 | 20,317 | 16,410 |
| **Earnings Per Share ($)** | | | | | | |
| 1Q | 0.87 | 0.75 | 0.57 | 0.36 | 0.26 | 0.30 |
| 2Q | 0.75 | 0.69 | 0.55 | 0.39 | 0.35 | 0.32 |
| 3Q | E0.70 | 0.40 | 0.54 | 0.33 | 0.26 | 0.19 |
| 4Q | E0.82 | 0.62 | 0.65 | 0.46 | 0.29 | 0.07 |
| Yr. | E3.15 | 2.46 | 2.31 | 1.54 | 1.16 | 0.87 |

**Next earnings report expected: mid May**

**Dividend Data** (Dividends have been paid since 1965.)

| Amount ($) | Date Decl. | Ex-Div. Date | Stock of Record | Payment Date |
|---|---|---|---|---|
| 0.120 | Jul. 19 | Sep. 23 | Sep. 25 | Oct. 16 '96 |
| 0.120 | Nov. 22 | Dec. 20 | Dec. 24 | Jan. 15 '97 |
| 0.120 | Jan. 31 | Mar. 24 | Mar. 26 | Apr. 16 '97 |
| 0.140 | May. 16 | Jun. 16 | Jun. 18 | Jul. 09 '97 |

This report is for information purposes and should not be considered a solicitation to buy or sell any security. Neither S&P nor any other party guarantee its accuracy or make warranties regarding results from its usage. Redistribution is prohibited without written permission. Copyright © 1997

*A Division of The* **McGraw·Hill** *Companies*

## Business Summary - 19-MAY-97

Hewlett-Packard produces a broad range of computer systems and peripherals and electronic instruments and measurement products. The company derived 14% of its revenues in FY 96 (Oct.) from servicing its equipment, systems and peripherals. Orders originating outside of the U.S. accounted for 56% of total orders in FY 96, up from 55% in FY 95.

Computer products, service and support (82% of FY 96 revenues) include the HP 9000 series, a line of UNIX-based workstations and multiuser systems for both technical and commercial users; the HP Vectra series of IBM-compatible personal computers for businesses; and the HP Pavilion family of computers for the home. The 9000 family is based on the company's Precision Architecture reduced instruction set computing (PA-RISC) microprocessor design. Peripheral products include printers, such as the HP LaserJet and DeskJet families; plotters and page scanners; and video display terminals. The company offers software programming services, network services, distributed systems services and data management services.

Electronic test and measurement instrumentation, systems and services (10%) include voltmeters and multimeters, counters, oscilloscopes and logic analyzers, signal generators and specialized communications test equipment.

Medical electronic equipment and services (4%) include continuous monitoring systems for critical care patients, medical data management systems and fetal monitors.

Chemical analysis and service (2%) includes gas and liquid chromatographs, mass spectrometers and spectrophotometers.

Electronic components (2%) include microwave semiconductor and optoelectronic devices sold primarily to original equipment manufacturers.

## Important Developments

**Feb. '97**—The company introduced new entry-level models of its HP Vectra 500 Series PC, with prices starting as low as $1,094. The entry level model includes 16MB RAM, a 133 Mhz Intel Pentium processor, 256KB cache and a 1.2GB hard drive.
**Oct. '96**—HWP introduced the new PA-8200 family of 64-bit microprocessors, which is expected to boost application performance by an average of 50%.
**Sep. '96**—HWP introduced its HP 9000 enterprise server family, which runs on its PA-8000 microprocessor. Separately, the company introduced a new series of PC servers targeted at small and medium-sized businesses. In August, the company unveiled the HP Vectra XW personal workstation, designed for the emerging Windows NT/Pentium Pro workstation market.

## Capitalization

**Long Term Debt:** $2,495,000,000 (3/97).

| Per Share Data ($) (Year Ended Oct. 31) | 1996 | 1995 | 1994 | 1993 | 1992 | 1991 | 1990 | 1989 | 1988 | 1987 |
|---|---|---|---|---|---|---|---|---|---|---|
| Tangible Bk. Val. | 13.25 | 11.61 | 9.22 | 7.80 | 6.86 | 7.22 | 6.52 | 5.31 | 4.84 | 4.88 |
| Cash Flow | 3.69 | 3.40 | 2.50 | 1.89 | 1.54 | 1.31 | 1.27 | 1.34 | 1.20 | 0.96 |
| Earnings | 2.46 | 2.32 | 1.54 | 1.16 | 0.87 | 0.76 | 0.76 | 0.88 | 0.84 | 0.63 |
| Dividends | 0.46 | 0.38 | 0.28 | 0.22 | 0.18 | 0.12 | 0.10 | 0.09 | 0.07 | 0.06 |
| Payout Ratio | 19% | 16% | 18% | 19% | 21% | 16% | 14% | 10% | 8% | 9% |
| Prices - High | 57¾ | 48⅜ | 25⅝ | 22⅜ | 21¼ | 14⅜ | 12⅝ | 15⅜ | 16⅜ | 18⅜ |
| - Low | 36⅞ | 24½ | 18 | 16⅛ | 12⅝ | 7½ | 6¼ | 10⅛ | 11 | 9 |
| P/E Ratio - High | 23 | 21 | 17 | 19 | 24 | 19 | 16 | 17 | 19 | 29 |
| - Low | 15 | 11 | 12 | 14 | 14 | 10 | 8 | 11 | 13 | 14 |
| **Income Statement Analysis (Million $)** | | | | | | | | | | |
| Revs. | 38,420 | 31,519 | 24,991 | 20,317 | 16,410 | 14,494 | 13,233 | 11,899 | 9,831 | 8,090 |
| Oper. Inc. | 5,023 | 4,707 | 3,555 | 2,622 | 2,183 | 1,890 | 1,650 | 1,630 | 1,572 | 1,354 |
| Depr. | 1,297 | 1,139 | 1,006 | 743 | 673 | 555 | 488 | 435 | 353 | 342 |
| Int. Exp. | 327 | 206 | 155 | 121 | 96.0 | 130 | 172 | 126 | 77.0 | 50.0 |
| Pretax Inc. | 3,694 | 3,632 | 2,423 | 1,783 | 1,325 | 1,127 | 1,056 | 1,151 | 1,142 | 962 |
| Eff. Tax Rate | 30% | 33% | 34% | 34% | 34% | 33% | 30% | 28% | 29% | 33% |
| Net Inc. | 2,586 | 2,433 | 1,599 | 1,177 | 881 | 755 | 739 | 829 | 816 | 644 |
| **Balance Sheet & Other Fin. Data (Million $)** | | | | | | | | | | |
| Cash | 3,327 | 2,616 | 2,478 | 1,644 | 1,035 | 1,120 | 1,106 | 926 | 918 | 2,645 |
| Curr. Assets | 17,991 | 16,239 | 12,509 | 10,236 | 7,679 | 6,716 | 6,510 | 5,731 | 4,420 | 5,490 |
| Total Assets | 27,699 | 24,427 | 19,567 | 16,736 | 13,700 | 11,973 | 11,395 | 10,075 | 7,497 | 8,133 |
| Curr. Liab. | 10,623 | 10,944 | 8,230 | 6,868 | 5,094 | 4,063 | 4,443 | 3,743 | 2,570 | 2,735 |
| LT Debt | 2,579 | 663 | 547 | 667 | 425 | 188 | 139 | 474 | 61.0 | 88.0 |
| Common Eqty. | 13,438 | 11,839 | 9,926 | 8,511 | 7,499 | 7,269 | 6,363 | 5,446 | 4,533 | 5,022 |
| Total Cap. | 16,017 | 12,502 | 10,473 | 9,209 | 7,973 | 7,700 | 6,763 | 6,168 | 4,770 | 5,264 |
| Cap. Exp. | 2,201 | 1,601 | 1,257 | 1,489 | 1,032 | 862 | 955 | 915 | 648 | 507 |
| Cash Flow | 3,883 | 3,572 | 2,605 | 1,920 | 1,554 | 1,310 | 1,305 | 1,264 | 1,169 | 986 |
| Curr. Ratio | 1.7 | 1.5 | 1.5 | 1.5 | 1.5 | 1.7 | 1.5 | 1.5 | 1.7 | 2.0 |
| % LT Debt of Cap. | 16.1 | 5.3 | 5.2 | 7.2 | 5.3 | 2.4 | 2.1 | 7.7 | 1.3 | 1.7 |
| % Net Inc.of Revs. | 6.7 | 7.7 | 6.4 | 5.8 | 5.4 | 5.2 | 5.6 | 7.0 | 8.3 | 8.0 |
| % Ret. on Assets | 9.9 | 11.1 | 8.8 | 7.7 | 6.9 | 6.4 | 6.8 | 9.4 | 11.0 | 8.9 |
| % Ret. on Equity | 20.5 | 22.4 | 17.3 | 14.7 | 11.9 | 10.9 | 12.4 | 16.5 | 17.9 | 13.7 |

Data as orig. reptd.; bef. results of disc. opers. and/or spec. items. Per share data adj. for stk. divs. as of ex-div. date. E-Estimated. NA-Not Available. NM-Not Meaningful. NR-Not Ranked.

**Office**—3000 Hanover St., Palo Alto, CA 94304. **Tel**—(415) 857-1501. **Website**—http://www.hp.com **Chrmn, Pres & CEO**—L. E. Platt. **EVP-Fin & CFO**—R. P. Wayman. **Secy**—D. C. Nordlund. **Investor Contact**—Steve Beitler. **Dirs**—T. E. Everhart, J. B. Fery, S. Ginn, J.-P. G. Gimon, R. A. Hackborn, W. B. Hewlett, G. A. Keyworth II, D. M. Lawrence, P. F. Miller Jr., S. P. Orr, D. E. Petersen, L. E. Platt, R. P. Wayman. **Transfer Agent & Registrar**—Harris Trust & Savings Bank, Chicago. **Incorporated**—in California in 1947. **Empl**— 114,600. **S&P Analyst:** Megan Graham Hackett

# STANDARD &POOR'S
## STOCK REPORTS

# HFS Inc.

## 1081E
### NYSE Symbol HFS
### In S&P 500

**19-MAY-97**

**Industry:** Services (Commercial & Consumer)

**Summary:** HFS is the world's largest franchisor of hotels and residential real estate brokerage offices, and also owns other service industry businesses.

---

**S&P Opinion: Hold (★★★)**

| | |
|---|---|
| Recent Price • 56½ | Yield • Nil |
| 52 Wk Range • 79⅞-49⅛ | 12-Mo. P/E • 37.7 |

**Quantitative Evaluations**

**Outlook** (1 Lowest—5 Highest)
• 5

**Fair Value**
• 112

**Risk**
• Average

**Earn./Div. Rank**
• NR

**Technical Eval.**
• **Bearish** since 3/97

**Rel. Strength Rank** (1 Lowest—99 Highest)
• 21

**Insider Activity**
• Neutral

Earnings vs. Previous Year
▲=Up ▼=Down ►=No Change

10 Week Mov. Avg. – – –
30 Week Mov. Avg. ‥‥‥
Relative Strength —

OPTIONS: ASE, CBOE

---

## Overview - 19-MAY-97

This leading franchisor of hotels and real estate brokerage offices has aggressively expanded into other service businesses. In April 1997, HFS acquired PHH Corp.--whose businesses include corporate real estate services (largely relocation), vehicle management services, and mortgage banking services--through a stock-swap transaction valued at about $1.8 billion. Our 1997 earnings estimate excludes a one-time second quarter charge of about $0.86/share in connection with the merger; related cost savings are expected in the future. Also, in late 1996, HFS acquired car rental company Avis Inc. and Resorts Condominiums International, which is the world's largest provider of exchange programs for timeshare owners and resorts. Overall, with its emphasis on providing services to franchisees and customers in the travel and real estate industries, we expect that HFS will have various cross-promotional opportunities among its various businesses. In addition, this fast growing company is likely to benefit from economies of scale, as rising revenues are spread over a cost base that increases less rapidly.

## Valuation - 19-MAY-97

We recently lowered our opinion on the stock of this rapidly growing services company to "hold," from "accumulate." This reflected concern about HFS's future ability to make acquisitions which will have sizable additive impact on earnings per share, and the lack of a positive surprise in 1997's first quarter EPS. However, HFS's strategy of making acquisitions, building brands and revenues, and generating economies of scale, has generally been successful in recent years, and the shares have some appeal. Due to a large amount of non-cash depreciation or amortization expense, we expect that reported earnings will significantly understate the company's ability to generate cash.

## Key Stock Statistics

| | | | |
|---|---|---|---|
| S&P EPS Est. 1997 | 2.60 | Tang. Bk. Value/Share | NM |
| P/E on S&P Est. 1997 | 21.7 | Beta | NA |
| S&P EPS Est. 1998 | 3.35 | Shareholders | 500 |
| Dividend Rate/Share | Nil | Market cap. (B) | $ 9.0 |
| Shs. outstg. (M) | 158.5 | Inst. holdings | 78% |
| Avg. daily vol. (M) | 1.180 | | |

Value of $10,000 invested 5 years ago: NA

### Fiscal Year Ending Dec. 31

| | 1997 | 1996 | 1995 | 1994 | 1993 | 1992 |
|---|---|---|---|---|---|---|
| **Revenues (Million $)** | | | | | | |
| 1Q | 348.0 | 124.6 | 74.15 | 64.29 | 47.94 | 38.60 |
| 2Q | — | 179.7 | 96.33 | 81.04 | 65.87 | 56.40 |
| 3Q | — | 245.8 | 129.3 | 95.02 | 82.07 | 61.70 |
| 4Q | — | 249.0 | 113.3 | 72.21 | 61.19 | 46.30 |
| Yr. | — | 799.0 | 413.0 | 312.5 | 257.1 | 204.4 |
| **Earnings Per Share ($)** | | | | | | |
| 1Q | 0.41 | 0.20 | 0.12 | 0.10 | 0.05 | 0.02 |
| 2Q | — | 0.31 | 0.19 | 0.14 | 0.10 | 0.08 |
| 3Q | — | 0.44 | 0.25 | 0.19 | 0.13 | 0.10 |
| 4Q | — | 0.34 | 0.18 | 0.11 | 0.07 | 0.03 |
| Yr. | E2.60 | 1.29 | 0.74 | 0.53 | 0.35 | 0.23 |

**Next earnings report expected: late July**

### Dividend Data

HFS is expected to retain any earnings for development and expansion of its business and repayment of debt, and is not expected to pay cash dividends on the common stock in the foreseeable future. A two-for-one stock split was effected in April 1994. Shareholders of record November 14, 1994, received one common share of National Gaming Corp., a corporation formed to hold the company's casino development business, for every 10 HFS shares held.

---

This report is for information purposes and should not be considered a solicitation to buy or sell any security. Neither S&P nor any other party guarantee its accuracy or make warranties regarding results from its usage. Redistribution is prohibited without written permission. Copyright © 1997

*A Division of The McGraw-Hill Companies*

STANDARD
&POOR'S
STOCK REPORTS

HFS Inc.

# 1081E
## 19-MAY-97

## Business Summary - 19-MAY-97

Affiliates of this fast-growing service company are looking to provide consumers with shelter and transportation. HFS Inc. (formerly known as Hospitality Franchise Systems), is the world's largest franchisor of hotels and residential real estate brokerage offices, and also owns rental car company Avis Inc. and timeshare business Resorts Condominiums International, and service provider PHH Corp.

HFS, which was formed in 1990 and became a publicly owned company in 1992, has grown largely through acquisitions. In 1996, HFS completed acquisitions--paid for with cash, stock and debt--which had a total value of more than $2 billion. A portion of the financing was provided by $1.2 billion of net proceeds from a May 1996 stock offering. Also, in April 1997, HFS completed a stock-swap acquisition of PHH Corp.

HFS operates eight franchise lodging systems: Days Inn, Ramada (in the U.S.), Howard Johnson Super 8, Villager Lodge, Knights Inn, Travelodge (in North America; acquired in January 1996), and Wingate Inn. It licenses hotel operators to use its brand names, but does not itself own or operate hotels. As of year-end 1996, HFS's lodging franchise systems included about 5,400 properties with more than 495,000 rooms. The two largest lodging franchise systems, Days Inn and Ramada, both have more than 100,000 rooms.

HFS's position as a franchisor of real estate brokerage offices was largely built through a series of acquisitions made in 1995-96. As of year-end 1996, HFS's real estate franchise system business, which includes the Century 21, ERA, and Coldwell Banker brands, had about 11,350 franchised offices in various parts of the world.

In October 1996, HFS acquired rental car company Avis Inc. in a transaction valued at about $800 million. An initial public stock offering related to a portion of the Avis business is expected to occur later in 1997. Also, in November 1996, HFS acquired timeshare company Resort Condominiums International, Inc. (RCI), through a cash-and-stock transaction valued at about $625 million, plus future contingency payments of up to $200 million over the next five years. RCI is the world's largest provider of exchange programs for timeshare owners and resorts around the world. More recently, in April 1997, HFS acquired PHH Corp. in a stock-swap exchange valued at about $1.8 billion. PHH's operations include corporate real estate services (principally relocation); vehicle management services; and mortgage banking services.

HFS also has a preferred vendor program under which various businesses provide significant discounts, commissions, and co-marketing revenue to franchisees, plus fees to HFS, in exchange for being designated as preferred providers of goods or services to hotel owners, franchisees and/or customers of franchisees.

### Capitalization

**Long Term Debt:** $748,421,000 (12/96).

### Per Share Data ($)

| (Year Ended Dec. 31) | 1996 | 1995 | 1994 | 1993 | 1992 | 1991 | 1990 | 1989 | 1988 | 1987 |
|---|---|---|---|---|---|---|---|---|---|---|
| Tangible Bk. Val. | NM | NM | NM | -3.78 | -2.30 | -2.98 | NA | NA | NA | NA |
| Cash Flow | 1.78 | 0.97 | 0.76 | 0.54 | 0.39 | 0.07 | NA | NA | NA | NA |
| Earnings | 1.34 | 0.73 | 0.53 | 0.34 | 0.22 | -0.10 | NA | NA | NA | NA |
| Dividends | Nil | Nil | Nil | Nil | Nil | NA | NA | NA | NA | NA |
| Payout Ratio | Nil | Nil | Nil | Nil | Nil | NA | NA | NA | NA | NA |
| Prices - High | 79⅞ | 41⅛ | 16¾ | 13½ | 5⅛ | NA | NA | NA | NA | NA |
| - Low | 36½ | 12½ | 10⅜ | 4¾ | 4 | NA | NA | NA | NA | NA |
| P/E Ratio - High | 60 | 56 | 32 | 39 | 23 | NA | NA | NA | NA | NA |
| - Low | 27 | 17 | 20 | 14 | 18 | NA | NA | NA | NA | NA |

### Income Statement Analysis (Million $)

| | 1996 | 1995 | 1994 | 1993 | 1992 | 1991 | 1990 | 1989 | 1988 | 1987 |
|---|---|---|---|---|---|---|---|---|---|---|
| Revs. | 799 | 413 | 292 | 257 | 203 | 197 | NA | NA | NA | NA |
| Oper. Inc. | 388 | 196 | 112 | 88.6 | 64.1 | 36.0 | NA | NA | NA | NA |
| Depr. | 71.4 | 32.1 | 23.7 | 19.2 | 14.9 | 14.8 | NA | NA | NA | NA |
| Int. Exp. | 32.8 | 20.1 | 18.7 | 20.2 | 25.1 | 33.5 | NA | NA | NA | NA |
| Pretax Inc. | 284 | 137 | 90.6 | 60.7 | 28.7 | -8.0 | NA | NA | NA | NA |
| Eff. Tax Rate | 40% | 40% | 41% | 43% | 31% | NM | NA | NA | NA | NA |
| Net Inc. | 170 | 79.7 | 53.5 | 34.3 | 19.9 | -8.5 | NA | NA | NA | NA |

### Balance Sheet & Other Fin. Data (Million $)

| | 1996 | 1995 | 1994 | 1993 | 1992 | 1991 | 1990 | 1989 | 1988 | 1987 |
|---|---|---|---|---|---|---|---|---|---|---|
| Cash | 55.8 | 16.1 | 6.0 | 16.9 | 25.1 | NA | NA | NA | NA | NA |
| Curr. Assets | 469 | 168 | 76.4 | 79.5 | 80.2 | NA | NA | NA | NA | NA |
| Total Assets | 4,289 | 1,166 | 774 | 736 | 545 | 530 | NA | NA | NA | NA |
| Curr. Liab. | 715 | 125 | 70.0 | 49.9 | 69.6 | NA | NA | NA | NA | NA |
| LT Debt | 748 | 301 | 347 | 348 | 236 | 245 | NA | NA | NA | NA |
| Common Eqty. | 2,477 | 560 | 281 | 267 | 227 | 211 | NA | NA | NA | NA |
| Total Cap. | 3,307 | 944 | 700 | 680 | 470 | NA | NA | NA | NA | NA |
| Cap. Exp. | 41.2 | 24.5 | 11.4 | 8.3 | 6.4 | NA | NA | NA | NA | NA |
| Cash Flow | 241 | 112 | 77.2 | 53.5 | 32.5 | 6.3 | NA | NA | NA | NA |
| Curr. Ratio | 0.7 | 1.3 | 1.1 | 1.6 | 1.2 | NA | NA | NA | NA | NA |
| % LT Debt of Cap. | 22.6 | 31.2 | 49.6 | 51.1 | 50.3 | NA | NA | NA | NA | NA |
| % Net Inc.of Revs. | 21.3 | 19.3 | 18.3 | 14.0 | 10.0 | NM | NA | NA | NA | NA |
| % Ret. on Assets | 6.2 | 8.2 | 6.9 | 5.3 | 4.2 | NA | NA | NA | NA | NA |
| % Ret. on Equity | 11.2 | 19.0 | 19.1 | 13.7 | 8.7 | NA | NA | NA | NA | NA |

Data as orig. reptd.; bef. results of disc. opers. and/or spec. items. Per share data adj. for stk. divs. as of ex-div. date. E-Estimated. NA-Not Available. NM-Not Meaningful. NR-Not Ranked.

**Office**—339 Jefferson Rd., Parsippany, NJ 07054. **Tel**—(201) 428-9700. **Chrmn & CEO**—H. R. Silverman. **Vice Chrmn & CFO**—M. P. Monaco. **SVP & Treas**—T. Kridler. **Secy**—J. M. Murphy. **SVP & Investor Contact**—Michael Wargotz (201-952-8444). **Dirs**— J. E. Buckman, C. DeHaan, M. L. Edelman, S. P. Holmes, R. D. Kunisch, M. P. Monaco, R. E. Nederlander, R. W. Pittman, E. J. Rosenwald, Jr., L. Schutzman, H. R. Silverman, R. F. Smith, J. D. Snodgrass. **Transfer Agent & Registrar**—Mellon Securities Trust Co., Ridgefield Park, NJ. **Incorporated**—in Delaware in 1990. **Empl**— 2,100. **S&P Analyst:** Tom Graves, CFA

**17-MAY-97**

**Industry:** Retail (Building Supplies)

**Summary:** HD operates a chain of more than 512 retail warehouse-type stores, selling a wide variety of home improvement products for the do-it-yourself and home remodeling markets.

| S&P Opinion: Buy (★★★★) | Recent Price • 59⅝ | Yield • 0.4% |
|---|---|---|
| | 52 Wk Range • 60⅝-47¾ | 12-Mo. P/E • 30.7 |

**Quantitative Evaluations**

**Outlook** (1 Lowest—5 Highest)
• **4**

**Fair Value**
• **67**

**Risk**
• **Average**

**Earn./Div. Rank**
• **A+**

**Technical Eval.**
• **Bullish** since 3/97

**Rel. Strength Rank** (1 Lowest—99 Highest)
• **75**

**Insider Activity**
• **Unfavorable**

**Earnings vs. Previous Year**
▲=Up ▼=Down ▷=No Change

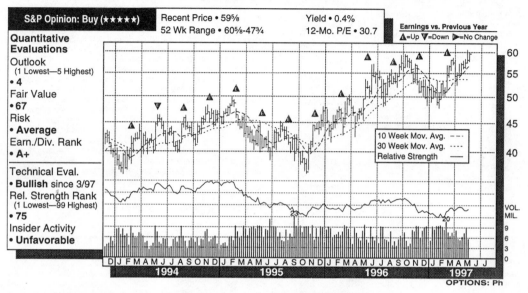

10 Week Mov. Avg. — — —
30 Week Mov. Avg. ········
Relative Strength ———

OPTIONS: Ph

## Overview - 16-MAY-97

Revenue growth of this leading home improvement retailer should be about 25% in FY 98 (Jan.), mainly fueled by the company's ongoing aggressive expansion program. About 111 new units are planned for FY 98. Same-unit sales should rise about 6%. Operating income should increase about 24%. HD has addditional room for growth in the highly fragmented, $134 billion do-it-yourself home improvement industry, with only a 14% share of the market. The industry is projected to grow at an annual 5% rate through the end of the decade. The bulk of the growth should come from the estimated 75 million older homes that will need to be repaired. HD plans to operate 900 stores by the end of 1999. The $1 billion proceeds from the October 1996 sale of 3.25% convertible subordinated notes were used in part to repay outstanding commercial paper obligations, and will also finance a portion of the company's capital expenditure program, including store expansions and renovations.

## Valuation - 16-MAY-97

The shares have rebounded from a year-end selloff, with continued solid gains in same-store sales and an EPS gain slightly better than expected in FY 97. With plans to expand the company's store base by 25% annually over the next few years, Home Depot is building substantially on its already dominant position in the do-it-yourself market. As a result, EPS should continue to grow in the 23% to 25% range over the next few years. The shares warrant a premium P/E multiple to the market, in line with the company's outstanding earnings record and well defined growth prospects.

## Key Stock Statistics

| | | | |
|---|---|---|---|
| S&P EPS Est. 1998 | 2.40 | Tang. Bk. Value/Share | 12.21 |
| P/E on S&P Est. 1998 | 24.8 | Beta | 0.70 |
| Dividend Rate/Share | 0.24 | Shareholders | 77,700 |
| Shs. outstg. (M) | 485.7 | Market cap. (B) | $ 29.0 |
| Avg. daily vol. (M) | 1.399 | Inst. holdings | 56% |

Value of $10,000 invested 5 years ago: $ 18,007

## Fiscal Year Ending Jan. 31

| | 1998 | 1997 | 1996 | 1995 | 1994 | 1993 |
|---|---|---|---|---|---|---|
| **Revenues (Million $)** | | | | | | |
| 1Q | — | 4,362 | 3,569 | 2,872 | 2,180 | 1,640 |
| 2Q | — | 5,293 | 4,152 | 3,287 | 2,454 | 1,856 |
| 3Q | — | 4,922 | 3,998 | 3,240 | 2,317 | 1,834 |
| 4Q | — | 4,959 | 3,752 | 3,077 | 2,287 | 1,818 |
| Yr. | — | 19,536 | 15,470 | 12,477 | 9,239 | 7,148 |
| **Earnings Per Share ($)** | | | | | | |
| 1Q | — | 0.41 | 0.34 | 0.31 | 0.34 | 0.18 |
| 2Q | — | 0.56 | 0.45 | 0.39 | 0.30 | 0.23 |
| 3Q | — | 0.46 | 0.37 | 0.31 | 0.23 | 0.19 |
| 4Q | — | 0.52 | 0.39 | 0.32 | 0.25 | 0.21 |
| Yr. | E2.40 | 1.94 | 1.54 | 1.32 | 1.01 | 0.81 |

**Next earnings report expected: mid May**

**Dividend Data** (Dividends have been paid since 1987.)

| Amount ($) | Date Decl. | Ex-Div. Date | Stock of Record | Payment Date |
|---|---|---|---|---|
| 0.060 | May. 29 | Jun. 07 | Jun. 11 | Jun. 25 '96 |
| 0.060 | Aug. 27 | Sep. 10 | Sep. 12 | Sep. 26 '96 |
| 0.060 | Nov. 13 | Dec. 03 | Dec. 05 | Dec. 19 '96 |
| 0.060 | Feb. 27 | Mar. 11 | Mar. 13 | Mar. 27 '97 |

This report is for information purposes and should not be considered a solicitation to buy or sell any security. Neither S&P nor any other party guarantee its accuracy or make warranties regarding results from its usage. Redistribution is prohibited without written permission. Copyright © 1997

*A Division of The McGraw-Hill Companies*

## Business Summary - 16-MAY-97

Home Depot is a do-it-yourselfer's paradise. Founded in 1978, The Home Depot is the world's largest home improvement retailer and currently has garnered about 14% of the U.S. $135 billion home improvement industry. The company operates retail warehouse-type stores selling a wide assortment of building materials and home improvement products, primarily to the do-it-yourself and home remodeling markets. At February 2, 1997, it was operating 483 stores in 28 states, mostly in California, Florida and Texas, and 24 stores in Canada.

Stores average 105,000 sq. ft., plus 20,000 to 28,000 sq. ft. of garden center and storage space. They stock 40,000 to 50,000 product items. HD's strategy is to provide a broad range of merchandise, consisting of many different kinds of building and home improvement materials, at competitive prices. The company trains its employees to be knowledgeable about the products in the stores; they may also have trade skills or direct experience in using the products.

Growth opportunities remain in existing and as yet untapped markets in the U.S. HD plans to expand its square footage base by 21% to 22% a year for the foreseeable future. In FY 97 (Jan.), store openings of 111 units and 7 relocations are planned.

The EXPO Design Centers, with about 144,000 sq. ft. of selling space, are a test concept, marketing upscale interior design products. The company currently operates five units and continues to finetune the concept.

In 1994, HD acquired a 75% interest in Canada's Aikenhead's Home Improvement Warehouse chain from Molson Cos. Ltd., for $160 million. Beginning in the year 2000, it has the right to acquire the remaining 25%. The chain, known as Home Depot Canada, currently operates 24 warehouse-style stores in Canada. In an attempt to strengthen its position in the $10 billion direct mail marketing of maintenance, repair and operations products to the U.S. building and facilities management markets, the company acquired the $130 million (in revenues) Maintenance Warehouse/America Corp. in March 1997. The company believes that the Home Depot concept is ripe for global expansion. In early 1998, a Home Depot store is planned in Santiago, Chile, as a prelude to expansion in Latin America. The company has formed a joint venture with S.A.C.I. Falabella, the largest departmnent store chain in Chile.

## Capitalization

**Long Term Debt:** $1,246,593,000 (2/2/97).

### Per Share Data ($)

| (Year Ended Jan. 31) | 1997 | 1996 | 1995 | 1994 | 1993 | 1992 | 1991 | 1990 | 1989 | 1988 |
|---|---|---|---|---|---|---|---|---|---|---|
| Tangible Bk. Val. | 12.21 | 10.27 | 7.40 | 6.22 | 5.15 | 3.95 | 1.87 | 1.42 | 1.07 | 0.89 |
| Cash Flow | 2.40 | 1.91 | 1.54 | 1.20 | 0.96 | 0.73 | 0.54 | 0.38 | 0.26 | 0.20 |
| Earnings | 1.94 | 1.54 | 1.32 | 1.01 | 0.82 | 0.60 | 0.45 | 0.32 | 0.22 | 0.17 |
| Dividends | 0.23 | 0.19 | 0.15 | 0.12 | 0.08 | 0.05 | 0.04 | 0.02 | 0.02 | 0.01 |
| Payout Ratio | 12% | 12% | 11% | 12% | 10% | 9% | 8% | 8% | 7% | 5% |
| Cal. Yrs. | 1996 | 1995 | 1994 | 1993 | 1992 | 1991 | 1990 | 1989 | 1988 | 1987 |
| Prices - High | 59½ | 50 | 48¼ | 50⅞ | 51½ | 35⅛ | 14½ | 8½ | 4¾ | 4⅛ |
| - Low | 41½ | 36⅝ | 36½ | 35 | 29¾ | 11⅝ | 7⅝ | 4¼ | 2⅝ | 1¾ |
| P/E Ratio - High | 31 | 32 | 48 | 50 | 63 | 58 | 32 | 27 | 21 | 25 |
| - Low | 21 | 24 | 36 | 35 | 36 | 19 | 17 | 13 | 12 | 11 |

### Income Statement Analysis (Million $)

| | 1997 | 1996 | 1995 | 1994 | 1993 | 1992 | 1991 | 1990 | 1989 | 1988 |
|---|---|---|---|---|---|---|---|---|---|---|
| Revs. | 19,536 | 15,470 | 12,477 | 9,239 | 7,148 | 5,137 | 3,815 | 2,759 | 2,000 | 1,454 |
| Oper. Inc. | 1,766 | 1,361 | 1,117 | 793 | 615 | 434 | 300 | 205 | 141 | 109 |
| Depr. | 232 | 181 | 130 | 85.9 | 65.6 | 52.3 | 34.4 | 20.5 | 14.4 | 10.6 |
| Int. Exp. | 39.0 | 25.0 | 53.5 | 44.6 | 48.6 | 24.0 | 31.1 | 18.3 | 4.5 | 6.0 |
| Pretax Inc. | 1,543 | 1,195 | 980 | 737 | 576 | 396 | 260 | 182 | 126 | 96.0 |
| Eff. Tax Rate | 39% | 39% | 38% | 38% | 37% | 37% | 37% | 39% | 39% | 43% |
| Net Inc. | 938 | 732 | 605 | 457 | 363 | 249 | 163 | 112 | 77.0 | 54.0 |

### Balance Sheet & Other Fin. Data (Million $)

| | 1997 | 1996 | 1995 | 1994 | 1993 | 1992 | 1991 | 1990 | 1989 | 1988 |
|---|---|---|---|---|---|---|---|---|---|---|
| Cash | 558 | 108 | 58.0 | 431 | 414 | 395 | 137 | 135 | 16.0 | 26.0 |
| Curr. Assets | 3,709 | 2,672 | 2,133 | 1,967 | 1,562 | 1,158 | 714 | 566 | 337 | 257 |
| Total Assets | 9,342 | 7,354 | 5,778 | 4,701 | 3,932 | 2,510 | 1,640 | 1,118 | 699 | 528 |
| Curr. Liab. | 1,842 | 1,416 | 1,214 | 973 | 755 | 534 | 413 | 292 | 194 | 147 |
| LT Debt | 1,247 | 720 | 983 | 882 | 844 | 271 | 531 | 303 | 108 | 52.0 |
| Common Eqty. | 5,955 | 4,988 | 3,442 | 2,814 | 2,304 | 1,691 | 683 | 512 | 383 | 321 |
| Total Cap. | 7,366 | 5,822 | 4,496 | 3,724 | 3,164 | 1,969 | 1,222 | 825 | 504 | 381 |
| Cap. Exp. | 1,194 | 1,278 | 1,101 | 900 | 437 | 432 | 398 | 205 | 105 | 90.0 |
| Cash Flow | 1,170 | 913 | 734 | 543 | 428 | 301 | 196 | 132 | 91.0 | 65.0 |
| Curr. Ratio | 2.0 | 1.9 | 1.8 | 2.0 | 2.1 | 2.2 | 1.7 | 1.9 | 1.7 | 1.8 |
| % LT Debt of Cap. | 16.9 | 16.9 | 21.9 | 23.7 | 26.7 | 13.7 | 43.4 | 36.7 | 21.3 | 13.7 |
| % Net Inc.of Revs. | 4.8 | 4.7 | 4.8 | 5.0 | 5.1 | 4.9 | 4.3 | 4.1 | 3.8 | 3.7 |
| % Ret. on Assets | 11.2 | 11.1 | 11.5 | 10.5 | 11.0 | 11.2 | 11.7 | 12.2 | 12.4 | 11.0 |
| % Ret. on Equity | 17.1 | 17.4 | 19.2 | 17.8 | 17.8 | 19.9 | 27.0 | 24.8 | 21.7 | 21.2 |

Data as orig. reptd.; bef. results of disc. opers. and/or spec. items. Per share data adj. for stk. divs. as of ex-div. date. E-Estimated. NA-Not Available. NM-Not Meaningful. NR-Not Ranked.

**Office**—2727 Paces Ferry Rd., Atlanta, GA 30339. **Tel**—(770) 433-8211. **Chrmn, CEO & Secy**—B. Marcus. **Pres**—A. M. Blank. **EVP & CAO**—R. M. Brill.**CFO**—M. L. Day. **Investor Contact**—Kim Schreckengost. **Dirs**—A. M. Blank, F. Borman, R. M. Brill, J. L. Clendenin, B. R. Cox, M. A. Hart III, J. W. Inglis, D. R. Keough, K. G. Langone, B. Marcus, M. F. Wilson. **Transfer Agent & Registrar**—First National Bank of Boston. **Incorporated**—in Delaware in 1978. **Empl**—98,000. **S&P Analyst:** Karen J. Sack, CFA

**17-MAY-97**

Industry:
Consumer Finance

**Summary:** This company is a major provider of consumer financial services in the U.S., Canada and the U.K.

| S&P Opinion: Accumulate (★★★★) | Recent Price • 89⅝ | Yield • 1.7% |
|---|---|---|
| | 52 Wk Range • 108¼-67⅞ | 12-Mo. P/E • 16.2 |

**Quantitative Evaluations**

Outlook
(1 Lowest—5 Highest)
• **3+**

Fair Value
• **90½**

Risk
• **Low**

Earn./Div. Rank
• **B+**

Technical Eval.
• **Bullish** since 7/94

Rel. Strength Rank
(1 Lowest—99 Highest)
• **47**

Insider Activity
• **Favorable**

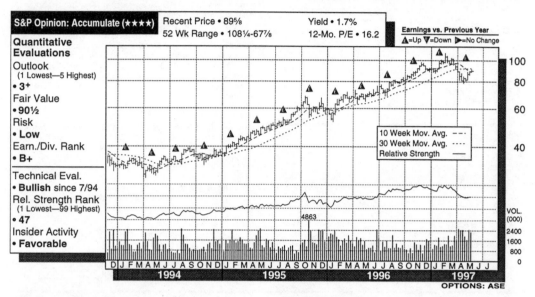

Earnings vs. Previous Year
▲=Up ▼=Down ▶=No Change

10 Week Mov. Avg. ---
30 Week Mov. Avg. ·····
Relative Strength —

4863

VOL. (000)

OPTIONS: ASE

## Overview - 13-MAY-97

Earnings growth in 1997 should be driven by further gains in managed loans, a focus on more profitable businesses, and continued efficiency improvements. Receivables growth received a substantial boost from the June 1996 acquisition of the Union Privilege affinity credit card portfolio from Bank of New York; the acquisition was part of an effort to focus on higher return businesses. Double-digit growth in credit card receivables should return as the company resumes mailings, which were suspended to concentrate on the integration of Union Privilege. Margins are expected to widen modestly, on a more favorable portfolio mix. The sale of certain businesses and a restructuring of consumer banking operations will allow the company to concentrate on its most profitable ventures. Credit quality remains strong, although chargeoffs will increase with further seasoning of the portfolio and a higher proportion of unsecured loans. Overall, earnings growth is projected at about 20% for 1997. Internal financial targets for 1997 include a return on equity of 20% and an efficiency ratio of better than 40%.

## Valuation - 13-MAY-97

Given the expectation of continuing earnings gains following significant strides in improving efficiency and targeting more profitable businesses, the shares are rated accumulate. The company's credit card business received a substantial boost from the acquisition of the AFL-CIO Union Privilege portfolio. Aided by strong receivables growth, healthier margins and efficiency improvement, earnings are expected to rise about 20% in 1997. Trading at 14X our 1997 EPS estimate of $6.40, the shares are recommended for above-average appreciation in the year ahead.

## Key Stock Statistics

| | | | |
|---|---|---|---|
| S&P EPS Est. 1997 | 6.40 | Tang. Bk. Value/Share | 20.21 |
| P/E on S&P Est. 1997 | 14.0 | Beta | 1.02 |
| S&P EPS Est. 1998 | 7.65 | Shareholders | 10,900 |
| Dividend Rate/Share | 1.56 | Market cap. (B) | $ 8.7 |
| Shs. outstg. (M) | 97.3 | Inst. holdings | 68% |
| Avg. daily vol. (M) | 0.438 | | |

Value of $10,000 invested 5 years ago: $ 40,824

### Fiscal Year Ending Dec. 31

| | 1998 | 1997 | 1996 | 1995 | 1994 | 1993 |
|---|---|---|---|---|---|---|
| **Revenues (Million $)** | | | | | | |
| 1Q | — | 1,173 | 1,175 | 1,246 | 1,129 | 1,076 |
| 2Q | — | — | 1,307 | 1,341 | 1,132 | 1,080 |
| 3Q | — | — | 1,242 | 1,313 | 1,143 | 1,156 |
| 4Q | — | — | 1,335 | 1,245 | 1,200 | 1,143 |
| Yr. | — | — | 5,059 | 5,144 | 4,603 | 4,455 |
| **Earnings Per Share ($)** | | | | | | |
| 1Q | — | 1.30 | 1.08 | 0.91 | 0.74 | 0.62 |
| 2Q | — | — | 1.22 | 1.00 | 0.81 | 0.67 |
| 3Q | — | — | 1.38 | 1.11 | 0.90 | 0.72 |
| 4Q | — | — | 1.63 | 1.29 | 1.07 | 0.90 |
| Yr. | E7.65 | E6.40 | 5.31 | 4.31 | 3.52 | 2.91 |

Next earnings report expected: late July

**Dividend Data** (Dividends have been paid since 1926.)

| Amount ($) | Date Decl. | Ex-Div. Date | Stock of Record | Payment Date |
|---|---|---|---|---|
| 0.390 | Jul. 09 | Sep. 26 | Sep. 30 | Oct. 15 '96 |
| 0.390 | Nov. 12 | Dec. 27 | Dec. 31 | Jan. 15 '97 |
| 0.390 | Mar. 11 | Mar. 26 | Mar. 31 | Apr. 15 '97 |
| 0.390 | May. 14 | Jun. 26 | Jun. 30 | Jul. 15 '97 |

This report is for information purposes and should not be considered a solicitation to buy or sell any security. Neither S&P nor any other party guarantee its accuracy or make warranties regarding results from its usage. Redistribution is prohibited without written permission. Copyright © 1997

*A Division of The McGraw·Hill Companies*

STANDARD
&POOR'S
STOCK REPORTS

# Household International, Inc.

**1160**

17-MAY-97

## Business Summary - 13-MAY-97

Household International Inc. is a major provider of consumer financial services in the U.S., Canada and the U.K. During 1995, it sold its non-Illinois consumer bank branches, its traditional first mortgage business and its individual life and annuity product lines. The company's business strategy is to concentrate on high return businesses that provide profitable growth, such as consumer finance and credit cards, work to improve efficiency by controlling costs and increasing revenues, aggressively manage credit risk and conservatively manage its balance sheet.

Total receivables owned of $24.1 billion at 1996 year end, up from $21.7 billion a year earlier, were divided:

|  | 1996 | 1995 |
|---|---|---|
| First mortgage | 3% | 10% |
| Home equity | 15% | 19% |
| Visa/Mastercard | 36% | 25% |
| Merchant participation | 21% | 17% |
| Other unsecured | 21% | 23% |
| Commercial | 4% | 6% |

Household Finance Corp., the oldest and largest independent consumer finance company in the U.S., offers a variety of secured and unsecured lending products to middle-income customers through a network of 526 branch lending offices throughout the U.S. Operations are focused primarily on home equity loans and unsecured credit products.

Household Retail Services (HRS) is a revolving credit merchant participation business that purchases and services merchants' revolving charge accounts resulting from consumer purchases of electronics, furniture, appliances, home improvement products and other durable merchandise. HRS believes that it is the second largest provider of private-label credit cards in the U.S.

Household Credit Services (HCS) markets Visa/Mastercard credit cards issued by one of the company's subsidiary national credit card banks, Household Bank, f.s.b., or other financial institutions affiliated with Household International. HCS had $18.1 billion of Visa/Mastercard receivables owned and serviced at 1996 year end. In June 1996, HI acquired the AFL-CIO's $3.4 billion Union Privilege affinity credit card portfolio, which made it the sixth largest issuer of VISA/Mastercards in the U.S.

Household Bank, a federally chartered savings bank, sold its banking operations in California, Maryland, Virginia, Ohio and Indiana in 1995, and in 1996 sold its Illinois-based bank branches. Household Bank will continue to offer credit cards, consumer and student loans through other distribution channels.

In connection with its consumer lending operations, the company also makes available credit life, credit accident and health, term and specialty insurance products to its customers.

### Capitalization

**Long Term Debt:** $14,802,000,000 (12/96).
**Preferred Stock:** $205,000,000.
**Redeem. Pfd. Securities:** $175,000,000.

### Per Share Data ($)

| (Year Ended Dec. 31) | 1996 | 1995 | 1994 | 1993 | 1992 | 1991 | 1990 | 1989 | 1988 | 1987 |
|---|---|---|---|---|---|---|---|---|---|---|
| Tangible Bk. Val. | 20.21 | 21.70 | 15.35 | 16.78 | 13.52 | 12.72 | 12.55 | 16.91 | 16.79 | 13.71 |
| Earnings | 5.30 | 4.31 | 3.52 | 2.91 | 1.96 | 1.58 | 3.03 | 2.93 | 2.49 | 2.78 |
| Dividends | 1.46 | 1.31 | 1.23 | 1.17 | 1.14 | 1.11 | 1.08 | 1.07 | 1.04 | 0.96 |
| Payout Ratio | 28% | 30% | 35% | 40% | 58% | 71% | 36% | 36% | 42% | 35% |
| Prices - High | 98⅛ | 68⅜ | 39¾ | 40½ | 30¼ | 31½ | 26⅝ | 32¾ | 30½ | 31¼ |
|    - Low | 52 | 35⅞ | 28½ | 27 | 20¾ | 13¾ | 9¾ | 23¼ | 19¾ | 16¼ |
| P/E Ratio - High | 19 | 16 | 11 | 14 | 15 | 20 | 9 | 11 | 12 | 11 |
|    - Low | 10 | 8 | 8 | 9 | 11 | 9 | 3 | 8 | 8 | 6 |

### Income Statement Analysis (Million $)

| | 1996 | 1995 | 1994 | 1993 | 1992 | 1991 | 1990 | 1989 | 1988 | 1987 |
|---|---|---|---|---|---|---|---|---|---|---|
| Total Revs. | 5,058 | 5,144 | 4,603 | 4,455 | 4,181 | 4,594 | 4,320 | 3,490 | 2,637 | 3,441 |
| Int. Exp. | 1,521 | 1,557 | 1,243 | 1,150 | 1,420 | 1,887 | 2,026 | 1,708 | 1,219 | 893 |
| Exp./Op. Revs. | 58% | 85% | 89% | 90% | 93% | 96% | 92% | 91% | 89% | NA |
| Pretax Inc. | 822 | 754 | 528 | 451 | 278 | 200 | 349 | 333 | 292 | 341 |
| Eff. Tax Rate | 35% | 40% | 30% | 34% | 31% | 25% | 33% | 34% | 37% | 35% |
| Net Inc. | 539 | 453 | 368 | 299 | 191 | 150 | 235 | 218 | 184 | 222 |

### Balance Sheet & Other Fin. Data (Million $)

| | 1996 | 1995 | 1994 | 1993 | 1992 | 1991 | 1990 | 1989 | 1988 | 1987 |
|---|---|---|---|---|---|---|---|---|---|---|
| Cash & Secs. | 2,521 | 4,909 | 9,546 | 9,113 | 7,646 | 6,710 | 5,332 | 4,367 | 3,359 | 2,243 |
| Loans | 24,067 | 21,732 | 20,556 | 19,563 | 18,961 | 18,987 | 22,194 | 20,017 | 16,123 | 13,096 |
| Total Assets | 29,595 | 29,219 | 34,338 | 32,961 | 31,128 | 29,982 | 29,455 | 26,163 | 21,032 | 16,986 |
| ST Debt | 6,428 | 6,659 | 4,372 | 5,642 | 5,253 | 4,142 | 5,681 | 6,865 | 5,702 | NA |
| Capitalization: | | | | | | | | | | |
| Debt | 14,802 | 11,228 | 10,274 | 9,114 | 9,015 | 9,595 | 9,561 | 7,916 | 6,560 | 6,265 |
| Equity | 2,941 | 2,691 | 2,200 | 2,078 | 1,608 | 1,525 | 1,344 | 1,194 | 1,174 | 1,008 |
| Total | 17,538 | 14,124 | 13,117 | 11,531 | 10,959 | 11,624 | 11,374 | 9,490 | 7,734 | 7,356 |
| Price Times Bk. Val.: High | 4.9 | 3.2 | 2.6 | 2.4 | 2.2 | 2.5 | 2.1 | 1.9 | 1.8 | 2.3 |
| Price Times Bk. Val.: Low | 2.6 | 1.7 | 1.9 | 1.6 | 1.5 | 1.1 | 0.8 | 1.4 | 1.2 | 1.4 |
| % Return On Revs. | 10.6 | 8.8 | 8.0 | 6.7 | 4.6 | 3.3 | 5.4 | 6.3 | 7.0 | 6.4 |
| % Ret. on Assets | 1.8 | 1.4 | 1.1 | 0.9 | 0.6 | 0.5 | 0.8 | 0.9 | 1.0 | 1.5 |
| % Ret. on Equity | 19.1 | 17.5 | 16.0 | 14.2 | 10.6 | 9.0 | 17.7 | 18.4 | 15.9 | 19.4 |
| Loans/Equity | 12.2 | 11.6 | 9.4 | 10.5 | 11.8 | 14.2 | 16.6 | 15.3 | 13.5 | 10.4 |

Data as orig. reptd.; bef. results of disc. opers. and/or spec. items. Per share data adj. for stk. divs. as of ex-div. date. E-Estimated. NA-Not Available. NM-Not Meaningful. NR-Not Ranked.

**Office**—2700 Sanders Rd., Prospect Heights, IL 60070-2799. **Tel**—(847) 564-5000. **Chrmn & CEO**—W. F. Aldinger. **EVP & CFO**—D. A. Schoenholz. **Investor Contact**—Craig A. Streem (847-564-6053). **Dirs**—W. F. Aldinger, R. J. Darnall, G. G. Dillon, J. A. Edwardson, M. J. Evans, D. Fishburn, C. F. Freidheim Jr., L. E. Levy, G. A. Lorch, J. D. Nichols, J. B. Pitblado, S. J. Stewart, L. W. Sullivan, R. C. Tower. **Transfer Agent & Registrar**—Harris Trust and Savings Bank, Chicago. **Incorporated**—in Delaware in 1925. **Empl**—14,700. **S&P Analyst:** Stephen R. Biggar

**22-MAY-97**

**Industry:** Computers (Peripherals)

**Summary:** This company manufactures lead wire assemblies for the disk drive industry.

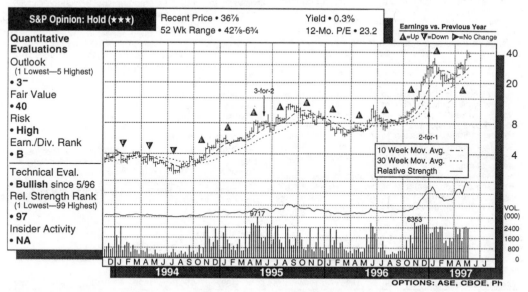

| S&P Opinion: Hold (★★★) | | |
|---|---|---|
| Recent Price • 36⅞ | Yield • 0.3% | |
| 52 Wk Range • 42⅞-6¾ | 12-Mo. P/E • 23.2 | |

**Quantitative Evaluations**

Outlook
(1 Lowest—5 Highest)
• **3⁻**

Fair Value
• **40**

Risk
• **High**

Earn./Div. Rank
• **B**

Technical Eval.
• **Bullish** since 5/96

Rel. Strength Rank
(1 Lowest—99 Highest)
• **97**

Insider Activity
• **NA**

Earnings vs. Previous Year
▲=Up ▼=Down ▶=No Change

10 Week Mov. Avg. — - —
30 Week Mov. Avg. ·········
Relative Strength ———

3-for-2
2-for-1
9717
6353

VOL. (000)

OPTIONS: ASE, CBOE, Ph

## Overview - 21-MAY-97

Revenues in the first half of FY 97 (Sep.) surged 144%, year to year, led by increased shipments of lead wire assemblies for magneto resistive (MR) disk drives, including its Wire Alignment Tab (WAT) product, and the inclusion of Litchfield Precision Components. Operating margins widened in the period, reflecting a more favorable product mix and a strong showing at Litchfield Precision. Results also benefited from a profit at InnoMedica, INVX's medical products unit, during the second quarter, though InnoMedica is not expected to post an overall profit in FY 97. The disk drive industry continues to project strong demand through the rest of the decade, where growth in inductive heads is expected to be moderate and shipments of MR heads is projected to substantially exceed the disk drive industry's 20% long term growth rate. INVX should benefit from the trend toward MR technology and the fact that MR heads require twice as many conductors as do inductive heads.

## Valuation - 21-MAY-97

We recently downgraded the shares from buy to hold on a price basis, as the shares have risen dramatically since our last upgrade. Net income in the first half surged to $16.3 million from $5.7 million a year earlier. We continue to view the company favorably, as industry fundamentals are strong, and we expect to see continued healthy revenue and earnings gains for this maker of lead wire assemblies. Demand for INVX's products is currently outpacing supply, and the company is rapidly expanding production. By December 1997, Innovex plans to be delivering 18 million wire sets per week, up from 11 million currently. With the shares trading at 15X our FY 97 estimate of $2.45 a share, we view the stock as adequately valued.

## Key Stock Statistics

| | | | |
|---|---|---|---|
| S&P EPS Est. 1997 | 2.45 | Tang. Bk. Value/Share | 3.24 |
| P/E on S&P Est. 1997 | 15.1 | Beta | 1.98 |
| S&P EPS Est. 1998 | 3.00 | Shareholders | 500 |
| Dividend Rate/Share | 0.12 | Market cap. (B) | $0.449 |
| Shs. outstg. (M) | 14.4 | Inst. holdings | 59% |
| Avg. daily vol. (M) | 0.600 | | |

Value of $10,000 invested 5 years ago: $ 411,333

### Fiscal Year Ending Sep. 30

| | 1997 | 1996 | 1995 | 1994 | 1993 | 1992 |
|---|---|---|---|---|---|---|
| **Revenues (Million $)** | | | | | | |
| 1Q | 29.31 | 13.11 | 9.98 | 5.66 | 5.87 | 5.91 |
| 2Q | 38.39 | 14.67 | 11.69 | 6.45 | 7.10 | 8.94 |
| 3Q | — | 19.25 | 14.03 | 8.44 | 7.15 | 9.80 |
| 4Q | — | 22.53 | 14.50 | 10.01 | 6.48 | 10.57 |
| Yr. | — | 69.57 | 50.19 | 30.56 | 26.60 | 35.21 |
| **Earnings Per Share ($)** | | | | | | |
| 1Q | 0.42 | 0.19 | 0.11 | 0.04 | 0.06 | -0.04 |
| 2Q | 0.66 | 0.21 | 0.15 | 0.04 | 0.08 | 0.01 |
| 3Q | E0.67 | 0.24 | 0.21 | 0.07 | 0.08 | 0.05 |
| 4Q | E0.70 | 0.26 | 0.23 | 0.11 | 0.05 | 0.03 |
| Yr. | E2.45 | 0.90 | 0.70 | 0.26 | 0.27 | 0.06 |

**Next earnings report expected: mid July**

**Dividend Data** (Dividends have been paid since 1993.)

| Amount ($) | Date Decl. | Ex-Div. Date | Stock of Record | Payment Date |
|---|---|---|---|---|
| 0.045 | Oct. 24 | Nov. 13 | Nov. 17 | Nov. 27 '96 |
| 2-for-1 | Nov. 27 | Dec. 24 | Dec. 16 | Dec. 23 '96 |
| 0.030 | Jan. 22 | Feb. 10 | Feb. 12 | Feb. 26 '97 |
| 0.030 | Apr. 25 | May. 12 | May. 14 | May. 28 '97 |

This report is for information purposes and should not be considered a solicitation to buy or sell any security. Neither S&P nor any other party guarantee its accuracy or make warranties regarding results from its usage. Redistribution is prohibited without written permission. Copyright © 1997 | A Division of The **McGraw·Hill** Companies

## Business Summary - 21-MAY-97

Innovex, Inc., through its largest division, the Precision Products division, designs, develops and manufactures specialty components, primarily lead wire assemblies, for the disk drive industry. In May 1996, INVX acquired privately held Litchfield Precision Components, Inc., a designer and manufacturer of intricate flexible circuitry, chemically machined parts, and film and optical components. Litchfield is now a division of the company, and accounted for 8.4% of FY 96 (Sep.) revenues. The company also makes pacemaker lead wires and other medical devices, and software for document storage retrieval and management.

The Precision Products division produces a variety of small, thin-wire computer subassemblies that often involve specialized tasks and cannot be economically produced by its customers. Products are manufactured according to individual customer orders and specifications. Lead assembly sales constituted 80% of consolidated revenues from continuing operations in the past three fiscal years.

The InnoMedica medical products division was formed in FY 93 to provide greater strategic direction and business discipline to the company's emerging medical business. The division provides pacing/defibrillation leads and adapters for implantable bradycardia and tachycardia devices. The division also makes other customized medical products and performs customized development for OEMs. In September 1993, the assets of Daig Corp.'s permanent pacemaker lead wire and adapter business were purchased for an undisclosed amount of cash; Possis Medical, Inc.'s pacemaker lead wire business was purchased in March 1994.

In November 1993, Innovex bought from Syntactic Analyzer, Inc. and ZH Computer, Inc. a technologically advanced software product line for preparing indexes and abstracts of documents stored in computer hard drives and CD-ROM systems, for $835,000. A new wholly owned subsidiary, Iconovex, currently handles the software business. In April 1995, AnchorPage, an automatic hypertext software program for use with the Internet, was unveiled.

Exports, principally to Pacific Rim customers, accounted for 74% of net sales in FY 96, down from 78% in FY 95. Five customers accounted for 82% of total revenues in the past three fiscal years.

### Important Developments

**Apr. '97**—Innovex reported a 162% year to year increase in FY 97 second quarter revenues, reflecting an acquisition, high demand in the computer disk drive market and continued strength in the Wire Alignment Tab (WAT) product. Net income more than tripled, to $10,056,369 ($0.66 a share), from $2,956,264 ($0.21, as adjusted).

### Capitalization

**Long Term Debt:** $1,010,945 (3/97).

## Per Share Data ($)

| (Year Ended Sep. 30) | 1996 | 1995 | 1994 | 1993 | 1992 | 1991 | 1990 | 1989 | 1988 | 1987 |
|---|---|---|---|---|---|---|---|---|---|---|
| Tangible Bk. Val. | 6.48 | 2.55 | 1.82 | 1.65 | 1.42 | 1.41 | 1.36 | 1.23 | 1.15 | 0.86 |
| Cash Flow | 1.94 | 0.91 | 0.40 | 0.37 | 0.96 | 0.14 | 0.20 | 0.14 | 0.19 | 0.16 |
| Earnings | 0.90 | 0.70 | 0.26 | 0.27 | 0.06 | 0.05 | 0.13 | 0.08 | 0.13 | 0.10 |
| Dividends | 0.09 | 0.08 | 0.07 | 0.07 | Nil | Nil | Nil | Nil | Nil | Nil |
| Payout Ratio | 10% | 11% | 28% | 24% | Nil | Nil | Nil | Nil | Nil | Nil |
| Prices - High | 30¼ | 12⅜ | 5⅝ | 4½ | 1¾ | 1¹³⁄₁₆ | 1⁹⁄₁₆ | 1⅝ | 1¹⁵⁄₁₆ | 4⅞ |
| - Low | 5⅞ | 4¾ | 2½ | 1¹¹⁄₁₆ | ¹⁵⁄₁₆ | ¹³⁄₁₆ | 1 | 1 | 1⅛ | 1 |
| P/E Ratio - High | 34 | 18 | 21 | 16 | 31 | 37 | 12 | 19 | 14 | 47 |
| - Low | 6 | 7 | 10 | 6 | 16 | 17 | 8 | 12 | 9 | 10 |

## Income Statement Analysis (Million $)

| | 1996 | 1995 | 1994 | 1993 | 1992 | 1991 | 1990 | 1989 | 1988 | 1987 |
|---|---|---|---|---|---|---|---|---|---|---|
| Revs. | 69.6 | 50.1 | 30.6 | 26.6 | 35.2 | 35.0 | 34.4 | 28.2 | 26.0 | 20.5 |
| Oper. Inc. | 22.0 | 17.4 | 6.9 | 6.7 | 3.4 | 2.0 | 3.7 | 2.2 | 3.2 | 2.6 |
| Depr. | 3.6 | 3.1 | 2.0 | 1.3 | 1.4 | 1.1 | 1.0 | 0.8 | 0.7 | 0.6 |
| Int. Exp. | 0.1 | 0.1 | 0.1 | 0.1 | 0.1 | 0.1 | 0.1 | 0.1 | 0.1 | 0.1 |
| Pretax Inc. | 18.7 | 14.8 | 5.2 | 5.6 | 1.1 | 0.8 | 2.5 | 1.7 | 2.7 | 2.3 |
| Eff. Tax Rate | 30% | 32% | 32% | 34% | 33% | 18% | 34% | 35% | 32% | 38% |
| Net Inc. | 13.1 | 10.0 | 3.5 | 3.7 | 0.8 | 0.7 | 1.7 | 1.1 | 1.8 | 1.3 |

## Balance Sheet & Other Fin. Data (Million $)

| | 1996 | 1995 | 1994 | 1993 | 1992 | 1991 | 1990 | 1989 | 1988 | 1987 |
|---|---|---|---|---|---|---|---|---|---|---|
| Cash | 21.8 | 22.4 | 13.1 | 9.5 | 4.2 | 2.9 | 2.6 | 1.8 | 2.4 | 5.2 |
| Curr. Assets | 42.0 | 32.2 | 21.0 | 19.2 | 18.1 | 15.8 | 16.4 | 14.9 | 13.5 | 14.7 |
| Total Assets | 58.2 | 41.2 | 29.9 | 26.6 | 25.2 | 22.9 | 22.5 | 20.4 | 18.7 | 19.1 |
| Curr. Liab. | 8.5 | 3.9 | 3.4 | 2.2 | 5.2 | 3.0 | 3.2 | 3.4 | 2.6 | 3.2 |
| LT Debt | 1.1 | 1.2 | 1.5 | 1.9 | 0.9 | 1.0 | 1.1 | 0.6 | 0.6 | 0.2 |
| Common Eqty. | 48.4 | 36.0 | 24.7 | 22.2 | 18.7 | 18.6 | 17.9 | 16.2 | 15.2 | 13.1 |
| Total Cap. | 49.5 | 37.2 | 26.6 | 24.4 | 20.0 | 19.9 | 19.3 | 17.0 | 16.0 | 15.9 |
| Cap. Exp. | 4.2 | 3.0 | 1.8 | 4.0 | 1.9 | 2.3 | 2.0 | 0.9 | 1.4 | 1.1 |
| Cash Flow | 14.0 | 13.1 | 5.5 | 4.9 | 2.2 | 1.8 | 2.7 | 1.9 | 2.5 | 2.0 |
| Curr. Ratio | 4.9 | 8.3 | 6.2 | 8.7 | 3.5 | 5.2 | 5.1 | 4.4 | 5.1 | 4.6 |
| % LT Debt of Cap. | 2.2 | 3.1 | 5.8 | 7.7 | 4.5 | 5.2 | 6.0 | 3.6 | 4.1 | 1.0 |
| % Net Inc.of Revs. | 18.9 | 20.0 | 11.5 | 13.7 | 2.1 | 1.9 | 4.8 | 3.9 | 7.0 | 6.4 |
| % Ret. on Assets | 26.4 | 28.1 | 12.4 | 14.0 | 3.1 | 2.9 | 7.8 | 5.6 | 9.5 | 7.1 |
| % Ret. on Equity | 31.1 | 32.9 | 14.9 | 17.7 | 4.0 | 3.6 | 9.8 | 6.9 | 12.7 | 10.3 |

Data as orig. reptd.; bef. results of disc. opers. and/or spec. items. Per share data adj. for stk. divs. as of ex-div. date. E-Estimated. NA-Not Available. NM-Not Meaningful. NR-Not Ranked.

**Office**—1313 S. Fifth St., Hopkins, MN 55343-9904. **Tel**—(612) 938-4155. **Website**—http://www.innovexinc.com **Chrmn & CEO**—T. W. Haley. **VP Fin**—D. W. Keller. **Secy**—M. E. Curtin. **Dirs**—G. M. Bestler, M. E. Curtin, W. K. Drake, T. W. Haley, W. J. Miller, M. C. Slagle. **Transfer Agent & Registrar**—Norwest Bank Minnesota, South St. Paul. **Incorporated**—in Minnesota in 1972. **Empl**— 834. **S&P Analyst:** M. Basham, T. Groesbeck

# STANDARD &POOR'S
STOCK REPORTS

## Intel Corp.

### 4249H
Nasdaq Symbol **INTC**

**In S&P 500**

**19-MAY-97**

**Industry:** Electronics (Semiconductors)

**Summary:** Intel is the world's largest manufacturer of microprocessors, the central processing unit of a PC. Various other products that enhance a PC's capabilities are also produced.

| S&P Opinion: Buy (★★★★) | Recent Price • 155⅛ | Yield • 0.1% |
| --- | --- | --- |
| | 52 Wk Range • 165-64⅛ | 12-Mo. P/E • 22.2 |

**Earnings vs. Previous Year**
▲=Up ▼=Down ▶=No Change

**Quantitative Evaluations**

Outlook (1 Lowest—5 Highest)
• **4**

Fair Value
• **199**

Risk
• **Average**

Earn./Div. Rank
• **B+**

Technical Eval.
• **Bullish** since 5/97

Rel. Strength Rank (1 Lowest—99 Highest)
• **76**

Insider Activity
• **Neutral**

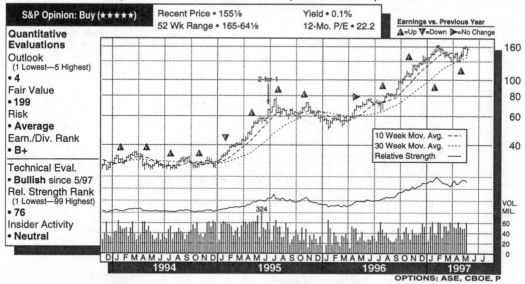

10 Week Mov. Avg. – – –
30 Week Mov. Avg. ·····
Relative Strength ——

OPTIONS: ASE, CBOE, P

## Overview - 19-MAY-97

We see revenues growing 30% in 1997, on strong worldwide demand for personal computers (PCs), and continued industrywide embrace of INTC's Pentium and Pentium Pro microprocessor families, which have minimal competition (see below), and Intel's MMX multimedia technology. We expect demand for the high-end Pentium Pro to grow, fueled by price reductions on the chip as Intel rolls out its new Pentium II targeted at high-end desktops in May. We also see further growth for the Pentium with MMX technology, as it continues to find strong acceptance from consumers looking for improved graphics performance. Margins should be in the 60% range, as a better mix of processors is offset somewhat by less profitable board level products, reflecting Intel's ramp of its new Pentium processors. R&D and marketing costs will grow sharply, as Intel seeks to maintain its dominant position in the industry.

## Valuation - 19-MAY-97

The shares have retreated into a trading range after soaring in late 1996 on Intel's surging revenue and EPS performance in 1996's second half, and on prospects for a strong upgrade cycle in 1997. The shares have stalled since January, however, primarily due to exaggerated concerns over competition from Advanced Micro Devices and Cyrix. Most industry experts agree that Intel's dominance in the industry will continue. We see Intel as the principal benefactor of the current upgrade cycle, which should gain momentum given: aggressive pricing by OEM manufacturers; Intel's own strong pricing strategy as it transitions to its Pentium II desktop microprocessors; and the popularity of Windows NT. We recently raised our 1997 estimate to $9.00 from $7.45, on the strength of Intel's first quarter earnings report. We believe Intel's current valuation offers investors above average appreciation potential.

## Key Stock Statistics

| | | | |
| --- | --- | --- | --- |
| S&P EPS Est. 1997 | 9.00 | Tang. Bk. Value/Share | 20.55 |
| P/E on S&P Est. 1997 | 17.2 | Beta | 1.47 |
| S&P EPS Est. 1998 | 10.75 | Shareholders | 124,000 |
| Dividend Rate/Share | 0.20 | Market cap. (B) | $126.8 |
| Shs. outstg. (M) | 817.5 | Inst. holdings | 57% |
| Avg. daily vol. (M) | 12.124 | | |

Value of $10,000 invested 5 years ago: $ 128,208

### Fiscal Year Ending Dec. 31

| | 1997 | 1996 | 1995 | 1994 | 1993 | 1992 |
| --- | --- | --- | --- | --- | --- | --- |
| **Revenues (Million $)** | | | | | | |
| 1Q | 6,448 | 4,644 | 3,557 | 2,660 | 2,024 | 1,241 |
| 2Q | — | 4,621 | 3,894 | 2,770 | 2,130 | 1,320 |
| 3Q | — | 5,142 | 4,171 | 2,863 | 2,240 | 1,426 |
| 4Q | — | 6,440 | 4,580 | 3,228 | 2,389 | 1,856 |
| Yr. | — | 20,847 | 16,202 | 11,521 | 8,782 | 5,844 |
| **Earnings Per Share ($)** | | | | | | |
| 1Q | 2.20 | 1.02 | 1.02 | 0.70 | 0.62 | 0.22 |
| 2Q | E2.16 | 1.17 | 0.99 | 0.73 | 0.65 | 0.25 |
| 3Q | E2.21 | 1.48 | 1.05 | 0.76 | 0.66 | 0.28 |
| 4Q | E2.43 | 2.13 | 0.98 | 0.43 | 0.68 | 0.50 |
| Yr. | E9.00 | 5.81 | 4.03 | 2.62 | 2.60 | 1.24 |

**Next earnings report expected: mid July**

### Dividend Data (Dividends have been paid since 1992.)

| Amount ($) | Date Decl. | Ex-Div. Date | Stock of Record | Payment Date |
| --- | --- | --- | --- | --- |
| 0.050 | May. 22 | Jul. 30 | Aug. 01 | Sep. 01 '96 |
| 0.050 | Sep. 18 | Oct. 30 | Nov. 01 | Dec. 01 '96 |
| 0.050 | Nov. 13 | Jan. 29 | Feb. 01 | Mar. 01 '97 |
| 0.050 | Mar. 26 | Apr. 29 | May. 01 | Jun. 01 '97 |

This report is for information purposes and should not be considered a solicitation to buy or sell any security. Neither S&P nor any other party guarantee its accuracy or make warranties regarding results from its usage. Redistribution is prohibited without written permission. Copyright © 1997

*A Division of The McGraw-Hill Companies*

# Intel Corporation



## Business Summary - 19-MAY-97

With an overwhelming market share of some 95% in 1996, as measured by Dataquest Inc., Intel is by far the leader in sales of X86 microprocessors for PCs (personal computers).

INTC's product strategy is twofold: the company offers OEMs (original equipment manufacturers) a wide range of PC building-block products to meet their needs, and offers PC users products that expand the capability of their systems and networks.

Intel introduced the first microprocessor in 1971. A microprocessor is essentially the "brains" (the central processing unit) of a PC, processing system data and controlling the other devices in the system. INTC's fifth generation Pentium line was the most popular processor in 1995, eclipsing the 486 family in unit volume in the third quarter. Intel introduced its sixth-generation microprocessor in November 1995, the Pentium Pro. This high-end chip is mostly targeted for use in workstations, high-end desktop systems and servers.

In May 1997, Intel will launch its latest technology, the Pentium II processor. Pentium II will use a Dual Independent Bus (DIB) architecture targeted at addressing bandwidth constraints limiting the output and performance of processors. Initially, Pentium II should offer clock speeds of 400 MHz, or double the processing speed of the fastest Pentiums currently in use. By the year 2000, the combination of the DIB architecture, the Pentium II processor systems, and a new feature called an Accelerator Graphics Port, is expected to enable the bandwidth to scale with the processor to reach clock speeds of 500 MHz. Pentium II will incorporate Intel's MMX media enhancement technology, as will all of Intel's chips by early 1998.

Intel also produces chipsets, which support and extend the graphic and other capabilities of microprocessors; embedded chips, which provide devices like wireless communications devices, printers, copiers, fax machines with computing power; and flash memory chips used to store computer data.

INTC is offering an increasing number of networking products. These include its EtherExpress family of adapters and LANDesk line of network management products. ProShare personal conferencing products let two users view and manipulate the same documents simultaneously and, in some cases, see real-time video images of each other.

Manufacturing and test facilities are located in Chandler, AZ; Aloha and Hillsboro, OR; Santa Clara and Folsom, CA; Rio Rancho, NM; Las Piedras, Puerto Rico; Jerusalem, Israel; Leixlip, Ireland; Penang, Malaysia; and Manila, Philippines. In 1996, foreign business contributed 58% of sales and 36% of operating income.

## Capitalization

**Long Term Debt:** $481,000,000 (3/97).

| Per Share Data ($) (Year Ended Dec. 31) | 1996 | 1995 | 1994 | 1993 | 1992 | 1991 | 1990 | 1989 | 1988 | 1987 |
|---|---|---|---|---|---|---|---|---|---|---|
| Tangible Bk. Val. | 20.55 | 14.79 | 11.22 | 8.97 | 6.51 | 5.42 | 4.50 | 3.46 | 2.88 | 1.94 |
| Cash Flow | 7.93 | 5.58 | 3.79 | 3.41 | 1.85 | 1.48 | 1.17 | 0.84 | 0.92 | 0.48 |
| Earnings | 5.81 | 4.03 | 2.62 | 2.60 | 1.24 | 0.98 | 0.80 | 0.52 | 0.63 | 0.24 |
| Dividends | 0.18 | 0.14 | 0.11 | 0.17 | 0.03 | Nil | Nil | Nil | Nil | Nil |
| Payout Ratio | 3% | 3% | 4% | 7% | 2% | Nil | Nil | Nil | Nil | Nil |
| Prices - High | 141½ | 78⅜ | 36¾ | 37⅛ | 22⅞ | 14⅞ | 13 | 9 | 9⅜ | 10½ |
| - Low | 49¾ | 31½ | 28 | 21⅜ | 11⅝ | 9½ | 7 | 5¾ | 4⅞ | 3½ |
| P/E Ratio - High | 24 | 19 | 14 | 14 | 18 | 15 | 16 | 17 | 15 | 43 |
| - Low | 9 | 8 | 11 | 8 | 9 | 10 | 9 | 11 | 8 | 14 |
| **Income Statement Analysis (Million $)** | | | | | | | | | | |
| Revs. | 20,847 | 16,202 | 11,521 | 8,782 | 5,844 | 4,779 | 3,921 | 3,127 | 2,875 | 1,907 |
| Oper. Inc. | 9,441 | 6,623 | 4,863 | 4,109 | 2,043 | 1,498 | 1,151 | 794 | 805 | 417 |
| Depr. | 1,888 | 1,371 | 1,028 | 717 | 518 | 418 | 292 | 237 | 211 | 171 |
| Int. Exp. | 58.0 | 75.0 | 84.0 | 58.0 | 66.0 | 88.0 | 102 | 102 | 78.0 | 63.0 |
| Pretax Inc. | 7,934 | 5,638 | 3,603 | 3,530 | 1,569 | 1,195 | 986 | 583 | 629 | 288 |
| Eff. Tax Rate | 35% | 37% | 37% | 35% | 32% | 32% | 34% | 33% | 28% | 39% |
| Net Inc. | 5,157 | 3,566 | 2,288 | 2,295 | 1,067 | 819 | 650 | 391 | 453 | 176 |
| **Balance Sheet & Other Fin. Data (Million $)** | | | | | | | | | | |
| Cash | 7,907 | 2,458 | 2,410 | 3,136 | 2,835 | 2,277 | 1,785 | 1,090 | 971 | 619 |
| Curr. Assets | 13,684 | 8,097 | 6,167 | 5,802 | 4,691 | 3,604 | 3,119 | 2,163 | 1,970 | 1,431 |
| Total Assets | 23,765 | 17,504 | 13,816 | 11,344 | 8,089 | 6,292 | 5,376 | 3,994 | 3,550 | 2,597 |
| Curr. Liab. | 4,863 | 3,619 | 3,024 | 2,433 | 1,842 | 1,228 | 1,314 | 921 | 934 | 882 |
| LT Debt | 728 | 400 | 392 | 426 | 2.5 | 363 | 345 | 412 | 479 | 298 |
| Common Eqty. | 1,687 | 12,140 | 9,267 | 7,500 | 5,445 | 4,418 | 3,592 | 2,549 | 2,080 | 1,306 |
| Total Cap. | 18,597 | 13,160 | 10,048 | 8,223 | 5,874 | 4,924 | 4,063 | 3,073 | 2,616 | 1,715 |
| Cap. Exp. | 3,024 | 3,550 | 2,441 | 1,933 | 1,228 | 948 | 680 | 422 | 477 | 302 |
| Cash Flow | 7,045 | 4,937 | 3,316 | 3,012 | 1,584 | 1,237 | 943 | 628 | 664 | 347 |
| Curr. Ratio | 2.8 | 2.2 | 2.0 | 2.4 | 2.5 | 2.9 | 2.4 | 2.3 | 2.1 | 1.6 |
| % LT Debt of Cap. | 3.9 | 3.0 | 3.9 | 5.2 | 4.2 | 7.4 | 8.5 | 13.4 | 18.3 | 17.4 |
| % Net Inc.of Revs. | 24.7 | 22.0 | 19.9 | 26.1 | 18.3 | 17.1 | 16.6 | 12.5 | 15.8 | 9.2 |
| % Ret. on Assets | 25.0 | 22.8 | 18.3 | 23.6 | 14.7 | 13.9 | 13.4 | 10.3 | 14.3 | 7.5 |
| % Ret. on Equity | 35.6 | 33.3 | 27.4 | 35.5 | 35.5 | 20.2 | 20.5 | 16.7 | 26.0 | 13.6 |

Data as orig. reptd.; bef. results of disc. opers. and/or spec. items. Per share data adj. for stk. divs. as of ex-div. date. E-Estimated. NA-Not Available. NM-Not Meaningful. NR-Not Ranked.

**Office**—2200 Mission College Blvd., Santa Clara, CA 95052-8119. **Tel**—(408) 765-8080. **Chrmn emeritus**—G. E. Moore. **Chrmn & CEO**—A. S. Grove. **Pres**—C. R. Barrett. **Investor Contact**—Gordon Casey.**VP & CFO**—A. D. Bryant,**VP & Secy**—F. T. Dunlap, Jr. **Dirs**—C. R. Barrett, J.P. Browne, W. H. Chen, A. S. Grove, D. J. Guzy, R. Hodgson, S. Kaplan, G. E. Moore, M. Palevsky, A. Rock, J. E. Shaw, L. L. Vadasz, D. B. Yoffie, C. E. Young. **Transfer Agent & Registrar**—Harris Trust and Savings Bank. **Incorporated**—in California in 1968. **Empl**— 48,500. **S&P Analyst:** Megan Graham Hackett

**17-MAY-97**

**Industry:** Health Care (Diversi-fied)

**Summary:** The world's largest and most comprehensive health care company, J&J offers a broad line of drugs, consumer products and other medical and dental items.

| S&P Opinion: Buy (★★★★) | Recent Price • 60¼ | Yield • 1.5% |
| --- | --- | --- |
| | 52 Wk Range • 62¾-44⅛ | 12-Mo. P/E • 26.7 |

**Earnings vs. Previous Year**
▲=Up ▼=Down ▶=No Change

**Quantitative Evaluations**

**Outlook**
(1 Lowest—5 Highest)
• **1⁻**

**Fair Value**
• **54⅝**

**Risk**
• **Low**

**Earn./Div. Rank**
• **A+**

**Technical Eval.**
• **Bullish** since 5/94

**Rel. Strength Rank**
(1 Lowest—99 Highest)
• **66**

**Insider Activity**
• **Favorable**

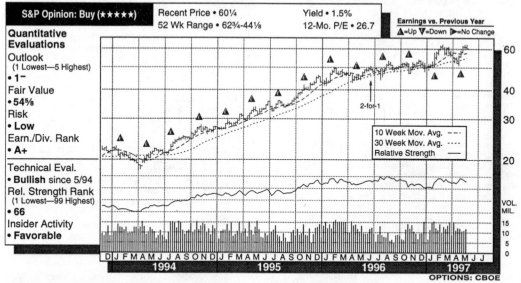

10 Week Mov. Avg. ---
30 Week Mov. Avg. ····
Relative Strength ——

2-for-1

VOL. MIL.

D J F M A M J J A S O N D | J F M A M J J A S O N D | J F M A M J J A S O N D | J F M A M J J

1994   1995   1996   1997

OPTIONS: CBOE

## Overview - 12-MAY-97

Sales in 1997 are expected to advance by about 10%. Pharmaceutical volume should be augmented by gains in newer drugs such as Risperdal anti-psychotic, Propulsid gastrointestinal, Ultram pain reliever, and Sporanox antifungal. Sales of Sporanox should benefit from recent FDA approval for the treatment of thrush, a fungal infection that affects nearly 50% of all HIV-positive persons. In late 1996, FDA clearance was received for Levaquin anti-infective and Topamax anti-epileptic. Sales in the professional group should benefit from continued robust growth in the Palmaz-Schatz coronary stent line, as well as growth in angioplasty, endoscopy and other lines. Consumer sales should benefit from gains in Neutrogena products, Pepcid AC and Tylenol. Despite a projected higher tax rate, margins should widen, on greater volume and pro-ductivity gains.

## Valuation - 12-MAY-97

The shares moved modestly higher in recent months, buoyed by the general market advance and continued robust earnings growth. J&J posted EPS growth of 15% on a sales gain of 7% in the first quarter of 1997. The lower than usual sales gain reflected adverse foreign exchange and sluggish U.S. consumer sales growth. However, profitability benefited from a better product mix and tight cost controls. Gross profit margins in the 1997 quarter rose to 69.0%, from 67.8% the year before. Over the 1995-96 period, higher gross margins and reductions in operating expenses resulted in profit improvement of about $600 million on an annual basis. The company's dominant positions in growing global markets, coupled with renewed focus on new innovative products, should enable J&J to continue to generate su-perior earnings growth in the years ahead. We continue to recommend purchase of the shares.

## Key Stock Statistics

| | | | |
| --- | --- | --- | --- |
| S&P EPS Est. 1997 | 2.45 | Tang. Bk. Value/Share | 5.80 |
| P/E on S&P Est. 1997 | 24.6 | Beta | 1.43 |
| S&P EPS Est. 1998 | 2.80 | Shareholders | 138,500 |
| Dividend Rate/Share | 0.88 | Market cap. (B) | $ 80.3 |
| Shs. outstg. (M) | 1333.6 | Inst. holdings | 56% |
| Avg. daily vol. (M) | 2.223 | | |

Value of $10,000 invested 5 years ago: $ 23,179

### Fiscal Year Ending Dec. 31

| | 1998 | 1997 | 1996 | 1995 | 1994 | 1993 |
| --- | --- | --- | --- | --- | --- | --- |
| **Revenues (Million $)** | | | | | | |
| 1Q | — | 5,715 | 5,334 | 4,496 | 3,690 | 3,560 |
| 2Q | — | — | 5,382 | 4,762 | 3,916 | 3,541 |
| 3Q | — | — | 5,402 | 4,738 | 4,038 | 3,506 |
| 4Q | — | — | 5,502 | 4,846 | 4,090 | 3,531 |
| Yr. | — | — | 21,620 | 18,842 | 15,734 | 14,138 |
| **Earnings Per Share ($)** | | | | | | |
| 1Q | — | 0.68 | 0.60 | 0.51 | 0.43 | 0.39 |
| 2Q | — | E0.67 | 0.60 | 0.51 | 0.43 | 0.38 |
| 3Q | — | E0.62 | 0.56 | 0.48 | 0.41 | 0.35 |
| 4Q | — | E0.48 | 0.42 | 0.36 | 0.29 | 0.26 |
| Yr. | E2.80 | E2.45 | 2.17 | 1.86 | 1.56 | 1.37 |

**Next earnings report expected: mid July**

### Dividend Data (Dividends have been paid since 1905.)

| Amount ($) | Date Decl. | Ex-Div. Date | Stock of Record | Payment Date |
| --- | --- | --- | --- | --- |
| 0.190 | Jul. 15 | Aug. 16 | Aug. 20 | Sep. 10 '96 |
| 0.190 | Oct. 21 | Nov. 15 | Nov. 19 | Dec. 10 '96 |
| 0.190 | Jan. 02 | Feb. 13 | Feb. 18 | Mar. 11 '97 |
| 0.220 | Apr. 24 | May. 16 | May. 20 | Jun. 10 '97 |

This report is for information purposes and should not be considered a solicitation to buy or sell any security. Neither S&P nor any other party guarantee its accuracy or make warranties regarding results from its usage. Redistribution is prohibited without written permission. Copyright © 1997 | _A Division of The McGraw·Hill Companies_

## Business Summary - 12-MAY-97

Well known for household names like Tylenol and Band-Aid adhesive bandages, Johnson & Johnson ranks as the largest and most diversified health care company in the world. J&J traces its roots to James Johnson and Edward Mead Johnson who formed the company over 110 years ago. Today, J&J offers an impressive list of blockbuster prescription drugs, professional products and the broadest line of health-related consumer products. Foreign business accounted for 50% of sales and 43% of profits in 1996. Sales and earnings in 1996 were divided:

|                 | Sales | Profits |
|-----------------|-------|---------|
| Pharmaceuticals | 33%   | 58%     |
| Professional    | 37%   | 33%     |
| Consumer        | 30%   | 9%      |

Despite its immense size, J&J continues to generate robust earnings growth. While helped by an expanding healthcare marketplace, J&J's outstanding success also reflects proficient management who directed the company's growth through well-planned, strategic acquisitions, aggressive R&D spending, and a policy of decentralized management. New product launches and products introduced in new foreign markets over the past five years accounted for 35% of total sales in 1996.

Some of the more noteworthy fast-growing product lines developed in recent years have been Risperdal anti-psychotic and Sporonox antifungal drugs, the LifeScan home glucose monitoring system and the Palmaz-Schatz coronary stent used after angioplasty procedures. These and similar products enabled J&J to chalk up compound EPS growth of about 15% over the 1991-96 period.

Although usually thought of as a medical products and hospital supplies firm, J&J derives close to 60% of its profits from a growing list of drugs. Over 80 different prescription drug, contraceptive and veterinary products are sold, 20 of which each generate revenues in excess of $100 million. Some of the big sellers include Procrit red blood stimulant, Propulsid gastrointestinal, Risperdal anti-psychotic and Ortho-Novum oral contraceptive.

Leading positions are also maintained in growing professional and consumer products lines. Professional items include older items such as sutures, wound closure products and surgical accessories, as well as newer products such as coronary stents, angioplasty catheters and disposable contact lenses. Albeit slower growing, J&J's wide list of consumer products such as Tylenol, bandages, toiletries and other items provide a solid base of stability and cash flow.

### Capitalization

**Long Term Debt:** $1,410,000,000 (12/96).

### Per Share Data ($)

| (Year Ended Dec. 31) | 1996 | 1995 | 1994 | 1993 | 1992 | 1991 | 1990 | 1989 | 1988 | 1987 |
|---|---|---|---|---|---|---|---|---|---|---|
| Tangible Bk. Val. | 5.80 | 4.70 | 3.67 | 3.61 | 3.40 | 3.67 | 3.15 | 2.59 | 2.17 | 2.08 |
| Cash Flow | 2.93 | 2.53 | 2.13 | 1.85 | 1.65 | 1.47 | 1.21 | 1.08 | 0.96 | 0.83 |
| Earnings | 2.17 | 1.86 | 1.56 | 1.37 | 1.23 | 1.10 | 0.86 | 0.82 | 0.71 | 0.60 |
| Dividends | 0.74 | 0.64 | 0.57 | 0.51 | 0.44 | 0.39 | 0.33 | 0.28 | 0.24 | 0.20 |
| Payout Ratio | 34% | 34% | 36% | 37% | 36% | 35% | 38% | 34% | 33% | 33% |
| Prices - High | 54 | 46¼ | 28¼ | 25¼ | 29⅜ | 29⅜ | 18½ | 14⅞ | 11 | 13¼ |
|    - Low | 41⅝ | 26⅞ | 18 | 17⅞ | 21½ | 16⅜ | 12¾ | 10⅜ | 8⅝ | 6⅞ |
| P/E Ratio - High | 25 | 25 | 18 | 18 | 24 | 26 | 22 | 18 | 15 | 22 |
|    - Low | 19 | 14 | 12 | 13 | 17 | 15 | 15 | 13 | 12 | 11 |

### Income Statement Analysis (Million $)

| | 1996 | 1995 | 1994 | 1993 | 1992 | 1991 | 1990 | 1989 | 1988 | 1987 |
|---|---|---|---|---|---|---|---|---|---|---|
| Revs. | 21,620 | 18,842 | 15,734 | 14,138 | 13,753 | 12,447 | 11,232 | 9,757 | 9,000 | 8,012 |
| Oper. Inc. | 5,312 | 6,002 | 3,531 | 3,011 | 2,837 | 2,657 | 2,399 | 2,019 | 1,741 | 1,522 |
| Depr. | 1,009 | 857 | 724 | 617 | 560 | 493 | 474 | 358 | 337 | 313 |
| Int. Exp. | 180 | 213 | 186 | 174 | 177 | 175 | 206 | 182 | 135 | 140 |
| Pretax Inc. | 4,033 | 3,317 | 2,681 | 2,332 | 2,207 | 2,038 | 1,623 | 1,514 | 1,396 | 1,193 |
| Eff. Tax Rate | 28% | 28% | 25% | 23% | 26% | 28% | 30% | 29% | 30% | 30% |
| Net Inc. | 2,887 | 2,403 | 2,006 | 1,787 | 1,625 | 1,461 | 1,143 | 1,082 | 974 | 833 |

### Balance Sheet & Other Fin. Data (Million $)

| | 1996 | 1995 | 1994 | 1993 | 1992 | 1991 | 1990 | 1989 | 1988 | 1987 |
|---|---|---|---|---|---|---|---|---|---|---|
| Cash | 2,136 | 1,364 | 704 | 476 | 878 | 792 | 931 | 583 | 660 | 741 |
| Curr. Assets | 9,370 | 7,938 | 6,680 | 5,217 | 5,423 | 4,933 | 4,664 | 3,776 | 3,503 | 3,272 |
| Total Assets | 20,010 | 17,873 | 15,668 | 12,242 | 11,884 | 10,513 | 9,506 | 7,919 | 7,119 | 6,546 |
| Curr. Liab. | 5,184 | 4,388 | 4,266 | 3,212 | 3,427 | 2,689 | 2,623 | 1,927 | 1,868 | 1,763 |
| LT Debt | 1,410 | 2,107 | 2,199 | 1,493 | 1,365 | 1,301 | 1,316 | 1,170 | 1,166 | 733 |
| Common Eqty. | 10,836 | 9,045 | 7,122 | 5,568 | 5,171 | 5,626 | 4,900 | 4,148 | 3,503 | 3,485 |
| Total Cap. | 12,416 | 11,308 | 9,451 | 7,183 | 6,627 | 6,927 | 6,216 | 5,318 | 4,669 | 4,238 |
| Cap. Exp. | 1,373 | 1,256 | 937 | 975 | 1,103 | 987 | 830 | 750 | 664 | 542 |
| Cash Flow | 3,896 | 3,260 | 2,730 | 2,404 | 2,185 | 1,954 | 1,617 | 1,440 | 1,311 | 1,146 |
| Curr. Ratio | 1.8 | 1.8 | 1.6 | 1.6 | 1.6 | 1.8 | 1.8 | 2.0 | 1.9 | 1.9 |
| % LT Debt of Cap. | 11.4 | 18.6 | 23.3 | 20.8 | 20.6 | 18.8 | 21.2 | 22.0 | 25.0 | 17.3 |
| % Net Inc.of Revs. | 13.3 | 12.8 | 12.7 | 12.6 | 11.8 | 11.7 | 10.2 | 11.1 | 10.8 | 10.4 |
| % Ret. on Assets | 15.2 | 14.3 | 14.4 | 15.0 | 14.6 | 14.6 | 13.1 | 14.4 | 14.5 | 13.4 |
| % Ret. on Equity | 29.0 | 29.7 | 31.6 | 33.6 | 30.4 | 27.8 | 25.3 | 28.3 | 28.3 | 26.5 |

Data as orig. reptd.; bef. results of disc. opers. and/or spec. items. Per share data adj. for stk. divs. as of ex-div. date. E-Estimated. NA-Not Available. NM-Not Meaningful. NR-Not Ranked.

**Office**—One Johnson & Johnson Plaza, New Brunswick, NJ 08933. **Tel**—(908) 524-0400. **Website**—http://www.jnj.com **Chrmn & CEO**—R. S. Larsen. **Vice Chrmn**—R. N. Wilson. **VP-Fin & CFO**—C. H. Johnson. **Secy**—P. S. Galloway. **Treas**—R. J. Darretta. **Investor Contact**—David R. Sheffield (800-950-5089). **Dirs**—Sir James W. Black, G. N. Burrow, J. G. Cooney, J. G. Cullen, P.M. Hawley, C. H. Johnson, A. D. Jordan, A. G. Langbo, R. S. Larsen, J. S. Mayo, T. S. Murphy, P. J. Rizzo, M. F. Singer, R. B. Smith, R. N. Wilson. **Transfer Agent & Registrar**—First Chicago Trust Co. of New York, Jersey City, NJ. **Incorporated**—in New Jersey in 1887. **Empl**— 89,300. **S&P Analyst:** H.B. Saftlas

# Jones Apparel Group     1270

NYSE Symbol **JNY**

In S&P MidCap 400

**19-MAY-97**

**Industry:** Textiles (Apparel)

**Summary:** This leader in the women's sportswear, suit and dress businesses sells under its flagship brands Jones New York, Rena Rowan for Saville, and Evan-Picone.

| | |
|---|---|
| **S&P Opinion: Accumulate (★★★★)** | Recent Price • 44½  —  Yield • Nil |
| | 52 Wk Range • 44¾-22⅝  —  12-Mo. P/E • 26.5 |

**Quantitative Evaluations**

Outlook (1 Lowest—5 Highest)
• 3

Fair Value
• 44⅜

Risk
• Average

Earn./Div. Rank
• B+

Technical Eval.
• **Bullish** since 3/95

Rel. Strength Rank (1 Lowest—99 Highest)
• 89

Insider Activity
• Neutral

Earnings vs. Previous Year
▲=Up ▼=Down ▶=No Change

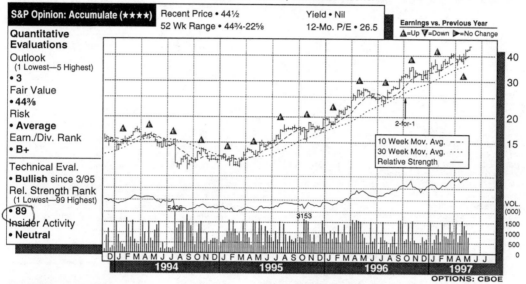

10 Week Mov. Avg. − − −
30 Week Mov. Avg. · · · ·
Relative Strength —

2-for-1

VOL. (000)
1500
1000
500
0

D J F M A M J J A S O N D J F M A M J J A S O N D J F M A M J J A S O N D J F M A M J J
**1994**  **1995**  **1996**  **1997**

OPTIONS: CBOE

## Overview - 19-MAY-97

We expect sales to rise 20% or more in 1997, on strong demand for career and casual sportswear, dresses and suits, and the continued expansion of new and existing shops. All of the company's well-known brand names should report higher volume. The fall 1996 roll-out of the new Lauren Ralph Lauren line is beginning to make a significant contribution to sales growth. Unlike many of its competitors, JNY has consistently responded well to the growing trend by women toward casual and comfortable apparel. Management has focused on identifying and providing the better sportswear market with highly differentiated, quality brands. Margins should increase slightly, on a more profitable mix, mostly as a result of the new Lauren Ralph Lauren line and improved planning and production. We estimate that earnings will rise about 18% to 22% annually for the next several years.

## Valuation - 19-MAY-97

After more than doubling in 1996, the shares climbed another 18% through mid-May 1997, versus a 6.7% gain for index of Apparel (Textiles) companies, and a 12% gain for the S&P 500. Over the past several years, the company has succeeded in boosting its sales and earnings via acquisitions, licensing, and the creation of new lines. We expect JNY's most recently added licensed brand, Lauren Ralph Lauren, to contribute up to $200 million in incremental sales in 1997. Much of the company's success is attributable to management's expertise in providing the right product at the right time, as well as in establishing strong relationships with customers. Given JNY's impressive and steady recent history of earnings improvement, and its well-known brand franchise, we believe that the shares, recently trading at 23X estimated 1997 EPS of $1.90, remain attractive for long-term capital gains.

## Key Stock Statistics

| | | | |
|---|---|---|---|
| S&P EPS Est. 1997 | 1.90 | Tang. Bk. Value/Share | 6.80 |
| P/E on S&P Est. 1997 | 23.4 | Beta | 0.45 |
| Dividend Rate/Share | Nil | Shareholders | 100 |
| Shs. outstg. (M) | 52.2 | Market cap. (B) | $ 2.3 |
| Avg. daily vol. (M) | 0.283 | Inst. holdings | 67% |

Value of $10,000 invested 5 years ago: $ 30,169

### Fiscal Year Ending Dec. 31

| | 1997 | 1996 | 1995 | 1994 | 1993 | 1992 |
|---|---|---|---|---|---|---|
| **Revenues (Million $)** | | | | | | |
| 1Q | 318.0 | 260.4 | 192.0 | 161.7 | 145.1 | 106.0 |
| 2Q | — | 193.3 | 156.3 | 135.7 | 121.6 | 99.0 |
| 3Q | — | 309.0 | 243.5 | 193.7 | 165.7 | 139.0 |
| 4Q | — | 258.4 | 184.6 | 142.1 | 108.7 | 92.38 |
| Yr. | — | 1,021 | 776.4 | 633.3 | 541.2 | 436.6 |
| **Earnings Per Share ($)** | | | | | | |
| 1Q | 0.55 | 0.38 | 0.32 | 0.28 | 0.25 | 0.20 |
| 2Q | E0.29 | 0.25 | 0.21 | 0.18 | 0.16 | 0.14 |
| 3Q | E0.69 | 0.58 | 0.45 | 0.39 | 0.38 | 0.33 |
| 4Q | E0.37 | 0.30 | 0.22 | 0.19 | 0.14 | 0.12 |
| Yr. | E1.90 | 1.51 | 1.20 | 1.04 | 0.93 | 0.79 |

**Next earnings report expected: late July**

### Dividend Data

| Amount ($) | Date Decl. | Ex-Div. Date | Stock of Record | Payment Date |
|---|---|---|---|---|
| 2-for-1 | Aug. 12 | Oct. 03 | Sep. 12 | Oct. 02 '96 |

This report is for information purposes and should not be considered a solicitation to buy or sell any security. Neither S&P nor any other party guarantee its accuracy or make warranties regarding results from its usage. Redistribution is prohibited without written permission. Copyright © 1997   | A Division of The McGraw-Hill Companies

## Business Summary - 19-MAY-97

Jones Apparel Group, Inc. designs, contracts for the manufacture of, and markets a broad range of primarily better priced women's sportswear, suits and dresses. Sales by product category in recent years were:

|  | 1996 | 1995 | 1994 | 1993 |
|---|---|---|---|---|
| Career sportswear | 56% | 57% | 65% | 67% |
| Casual sportswear | 29% | 27% | 17% | 14% |
| Suits, dresses, other | 14% | 16% | 18% | 19% |

In the career sportswear area, the company's flagship label is Jones New York, under which it offers an extensive range of sportswear garments primarily for the career woman's working needs. Jones New York products are sold in petite, misses and women's sizes, and marketed under the Jones New York, Jones New York Petites and Jones New York Woman labels. The Rena Rowan for Saville label was introduced for the spring 1991 season, while shipments of the Jones*Wear career sportswear line began in 1992. The Evan-Picone Career Sportswear line was launched for the spring 1994 season; Jones acquired worldwide rights to the Evan-Picone trademark in November 1993, and the rights to sell career sportswear under the Lauren Ralph Lauren label in October 1995.

Casual sportswear under the Jones New York Sport label, which is offered in misses, petite and women's sizes, includes a collection of weekend and leisure sportswear. Products offered in this line are intended for a less formal working environment as well as for

casual wear. JNY also offers lines of casual apparel under the Jones & Co., Jones Studio, and Jones New York Country labels.

Suits are designed to sell in two price ranges under the brand names Christian Dior (a "bridge" brand that relies on a collaborative design effort between JNY and Christian Dior Paris; the Christian Dior name is used by JNY under a licensing agreement), Jones New York (a better-priced brand) and Saville (upper moderate-priced). Dresses are sold under the Jones New York and Evan-Picone labels.

Products are distributed through 7,700 locations, including department stores (two-thirds of 1996 sales), specialty retailers, and direct mail catalog companies throughout the U.S. and Canada. The company also operates 196 factory outlet stores and four full-price stores.

### Important Developments

**Feb. '97—**JNY said backlog of open orders at March 31, 1997, was up 32% from the level a year earlier. The company noted that it was seeing excellent response to its fall collections, especially Jones New York, Evan-Picone and Rena Rowan for Saville. In addition, based on the continued retail success of the Lauren Ralph Lauren product, JNY anticipated that 1997 sales for the line would exceed $200 million.

### Capitalization

**Long Term Debt:** $12,141,000 (12/96), incl. $12,134,000 of capital lease obligs.

### Per Share Data ($)

| (Year Ended Dec. 31) | 1996 | 1995 | 1994 | 1993 | 1992 | 1991 | 1990 | 1989 | 1988 | 1987 |
|---|---|---|---|---|---|---|---|---|---|---|
| Tangible Bk. Val. | 6.81 | 5.61 | 4.26 | 3.10 | 2.67 | 1.73 | 0.90 | 0.51 | NA | NA |
| Cash Flow | 1.67 | 1.33 | 1.11 | 0.99 | 0.85 | 0.74 | 0.47 | 0.29 | 0.08 | NA |
| Earnings | 1.50 | 1.20 | 1.04 | 0.93 | 0.79 | 0.63 | 0.43 | 0.25 | 0.04 | -0.14 |
| Dividends | Nil | Nil | Nil | Nil | Nil | Nil | Nil | Nil | Nil | Nil |
| Payout Ratio | Nil | Nil | Nil | Nil | Nil | Nil | Nil | Nil | Nil | Nil |
| Prices - High | 37⅜ | 19⅞ | 17⅞ | 20½ | 21 | 15 | NA | NA | NA | NA |
|    - Low | 17⅞ | 11⅜ | 11 | 9⅜ | 11½ | 6⅞ | NA | NA | NA | NA |
| P/E Ratio - High | 25 | 17 | 17 | 22 | 26 | 24 | NA | NA | NA | NA |
|    - Low | 12 | 9 | 11 | 10 | 14 | 11 | NA | NA | NA | NA |

### Income Statement Analysis (Million $)

| | 1996 | 1995 | 1994 | 1993 | 1992 | 1991 | 1990 | 1989 | 1988 | 1987 |
|---|---|---|---|---|---|---|---|---|---|---|
| Revs. | 1,034 | 787 | 642 | 541 | 437 | 334 | 289 | 212 | 170 | 178 |
| Oper. Inc. | 139 | 107 | 92.1 | 82.5 | 70.2 | 54.9 | 36.1 | 25.2 | 11.3 | NA |
| Depr. | 8.9 | 6.7 | 4.2 | 3.6 | 2.7 | 2.1 | 1.7 | 1.9 | 1.9 | NA |
| Int. Exp. | 3.0 | 1.9 | 1.2 | 0.7 | 1.2 | 2.9 | 4.5 | 5.0 | 4.6 | NA |
| Pretax Inc. | 128 | 100 | 87.3 | 79.0 | 66.6 | 50.1 | 31.7 | 18.2 | 3.3 | -12.0 |
| Eff. Tax Rate | 37% | 36% | 37% | 39% | 38% | 32% | 41% | 41% | 45% | NM |
| Net Inc. | 80.8 | 63.5 | 54.9 | 48.4 | 41.3 | 34.1 | 18.7 | 10.7 | 1.8 | -6.0 |

### Balance Sheet & Other Fin. Data (Million $)

| | 1996 | 1995 | 1994 | 1993 | 1992 | 1991 | 1990 | 1989 | 1988 | 1987 |
|---|---|---|---|---|---|---|---|---|---|---|
| Cash | 30.1 | 16.9 | 21.1 | 27.0 | 33.0 | 17.0 | 1.4 | 1.6 | NA | NA |
| Curr. Assets | 390 | 331 | 261 | 212 | 167 | 117 | 80.0 | 60.0 | NA | NA |
| Total Assets | 488 | 401 | 318 | 267 | 185 | 129 | 88.0 | 68.0 | 62.0 | 64.0 |
| Curr. Liab. | 96.0 | 71.0 | 54.4 | 52.8 | 45.1 | 37.7 | 47.9 | 42.2 | NA | NA |
| LT Debt | 12.1 | 10.1 | 8.0 | 9.6 | 4.8 | 5.2 | 4.6 | 5.0 | 5.8 | 17.0 |
| Common Eqty. | 377 | 315 | 249 | 189 | 135 | 85.8 | 35.9 | 20.5 | 11.0 | 8.4 |
| Total Cap. | 389 | 325 | 257 | 199 | 140 | 91.0 | 40.6 | 25.5 | 16.9 | 25.4 |
| Cap. Exp. | 34.1 | 16.0 | 9.5 | 11.6 | 7.1 | 2.5 | 2.0 | 0.6 | 0.3 | NA |
| Cash Flow | 89.8 | 70.2 | 59.1 | 51.9 | 44.0 | 36.2 | 20.4 | 12.7 | 3.7 | NA |
| Curr. Ratio | 4.1 | 4.7 | 4.8 | 4.0 | 3.7 | 3.1 | 1.7 | 1.4 | NA | NA |
| % LT Debt of Cap. | 3.1 | 3.1 | 3.1 | 4.8 | 3.4 | 5.8 | 11.4 | 19.6 | 34.6 | 67.1 |
| % Net Inc.of Revs. | 7.8 | 8.1 | 8.6 | 8.9 | 9.5 | 10.2 | 6.5 | 5.1 | 1.1 | NM |
| % Ret. on Assets | 18.2 | 17.7 | 18.7 | 21.3 | 26.1 | 28.6 | NM | NM | NM | NM |
| % Ret. on Equity | 23.4 | 22.5 | 24.9 | 29.7 | 37.1 | 52.4 | NM | NM | NM | NM |

Data as orig. reptd.; bef. results of disc. opers. and/or spec. items. Per share data adj. for stk. divs. as of ex-div. date. E-Estimated. NA-Not Available. NM-Not Meaningful. NR-Not Ranked.

**Offices—**250 Rittenhouse Circle, Keystone Park, Bristol, PA 19007.**Tel—**(215) 785-4000. **Chrmn—**S. Kimmel. **Vice Chrmn & Secy—**H. J. Goodfriend. **Pres—**J. Nemerov. **CFO & Investor Contact—**Wesley R. Card. **Dirs—**H. Gittis, H. J. Goodfriend, S. Kimmel, I. Samelman, G. Stutz. **Transfer Agent & Registrar—**ChaseMellon Shareholder Services, Ridgefield Park, NJ. **Incorporated—**in Pennsylvania in 1975. **Empl—** 2,945. **S&P Analyst:** Maureen C. Carini

**17-MAY-97**

**Industry:**
Health Care (Drugs - Generic & Other)

**Summary:** This company manufactures and distributes ethical pharmaceuticals, OTC drugs and branded vitamin and nutritional products.

**Quantitative Evaluations**

**Outlook**
(1 Lowest—5 Highest)
• **NA**

**Fair Value**
• **NA**

**Risk**
• **High**

**Earn./Div. Rank**
• **B+**

**Technical Eval.**
• **Bearish** since 12/96

**Rel. Strength Rank**
(1 Lowest—99 Highest)
• **83**

**Insider Activity**
• **Unfavorable**

| Recent Price • 34½ | Yield • 0.2% |
| 52 Wk Range • 50½-21 | 12-Mo. P/E • 44.2 |

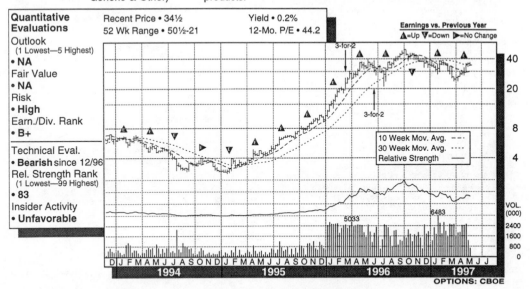

OPTIONS: CBOE

## Business Profile - 14-MAY-97

This emerging specialty pharmaceutical company has experienced an uninterrupted 15-year history of record sales and profits. JMED's strategy has been to build a portfolio of growing products through the acquisition of under-promoted, approved products from other firms. In March 1996, the company purchased the anti-thyroid product Tapazole, from Eli Lilly, and the hypothyroidism product Levoxyl, acquired with the purchase of Daniels Pharmaceuticals in August. These two growing products have allowed the company to add a third sales force focusing on physician-driven prescription marketing. The acquisition of Abana Pharmaceuticals in December 1996 added 55 additional professionals to a sales force that already exceeded 100. The company considers a large sales presence necessary to fuel greater internal growth.

## Operational Review - 14-MAY-97

Based on a brief report, revenue in the three months ended March 31, 1997, advanced 36%, year to year and as restated for acquisitions, reflecting strong overall growth of both hospital pharmaceutical sales and physician driven prescription pharmaceutical sales. Gross margins widened on the greater volume and a more favorable product mix. Net income advanced 117% to $8,118,000 ($0.28 a share, based on 15% more shares), from $3,749,000 ($0.15, as adjusted). Cash and equivalents totaled $52,171,684 at the end of 1996.

## Stock Performance - 16-MAY-97

In the past 30 trading days, JMED's shares have increased 30%, compared to a 9% rise in the S&P 500. Average trading volume for the past five days was 128,900 shares, compared with the 40-day moving average of 403,400 shares.

## Key Stock Statistics

| | | | |
|---|---|---|---|
| Dividend Rate/Share | 0.08 | Shareholders | 500 |
| Shs. outstg. (M) | 28.6 | Market cap. (B) | $0.986 |
| Avg. daily vol. (M) | 0.395 | Inst. holdings | 61% |
| Tang. Bk. Value/Share | 3.24 | | |
| Beta | 2.01 | | |

Value of $10,000 invested 5 years ago: $ 107,585

### Fiscal Year Ending Dec. 31

| | 1997 | 1996 | 1995 | 1994 | 1993 | 1992 |
|---|---|---|---|---|---|---|
| **Revenues (Million $)** | | | | | | |
| 1Q | 29.78 | 21.85 | 11.46 | 12.14 | 6.78 | 5.80 |
| 2Q | — | 25.74 | 13.28 | 11.59 | 12.28 | 5.90 |
| 3Q | — | 26.22 | 15.25 | 12.16 | 12.04 | 5.50 |
| 4Q | — | 26.34 | 16.41 | 11.67 | 12.11 | 6.79 |
| Yr. | — | 100.2 | 56.40 | 47.55 | 43.22 | 24.06 |
| **Earnings Per Share ($)** | | | | | | |
| 1Q | 0.28 | 0.15 | 0.09 | 0.08 | 0.05 | 0.04 |
| 2Q | — | 0.20 | 0.10 | 0.06 | 0.08 | 0.04 |
| 3Q | — | 0.06 | 0.11 | 0.08 | 0.08 | 0.04 |
| 4Q | — | 0.24 | 0.13 | 0.06 | 0.09 | 0.05 |
| Yr. | — | 0.65 | 0.43 | 0.27 | 0.29 | 0.18 |

**Next earnings report expected: late July**

### Dividend Data (Dividends have been paid since 1989.)

| Amount ($) | Date Decl. | Ex-Div. Date | Stock of Record | Payment Date |
|---|---|---|---|---|
| 0.020 | May. 23 | Jun. 13 | Jun. 17 | Jul. 01 '96 |
| 0.020 | Jul. 23 | Sep. 13 | Sep. 17 | Oct. 01 '96 |
| 0.020 | Nov. 06 | Dec. 12 | Dec. 16 | Jan. 02 '97 |
| 0.020 | Feb. 21 | Mar. 20 | Mar. 24 | Apr. 01 '97 |

This report is for information purposes and should not be considered a solicitation to buy or sell any security. Neither S&P nor any other party guarantee its accuracy or make warranties regarding results from its usage. Redistribution is prohibited without written permission. Copyright © 1997

A Division of The McGraw-Hill Companies

STANDARD
&POOR'S
STOCK REPORTS

# Jones Medical Industries, Inc.

**4309**

**17-MAY-97**

## Business Summary - 14-MAY-97

Jones Medical Industries manufactures, markets, distributes and sells critical-care pharmaceuticals and branded vitamin and nutritional supplement products. During 1996, sales of pharmaceuticals and nutritional supplements accounted for approximately 62% and 32% of total sales, respectively. The company distributes about 120 branded drug products and 270 branded vitamin products under its trademarks.

Since it was founded in 1981, JMED has produced 15 uninterrupted years of record sales and profits. This consistent growth has been driven by the acquisition of under-promoted, approved specialty product lines from other firms. This strategy has allowed the company to avoid the risks associated with new drug development and the lengthy and costly FDA approval process. JMED intends to leverage its existing marketing and sales capabilities through additional strategic acquisitions of complementary products and businesses, by expanding and increasing the market share for current products, and by new product introductions.

The company markets its line of critical-care pharmaceutical products to hospitals through a dedicated sales and marketing staff. Products include Thrombin (a topical hemostat used to arrest bleeding), Therevac (a mini-enema product), Brevital Sodium (a short-acting injectable anesthetic for use during surgery), Liqui-Char (an antidote for acute toxin ingestion, used in emer-

gency rooms) and Derma System products (four antibacterial and antimicrobial surgical scrub products and a skin lotion). A significant portion of revenues are also derived from the sale of Tapazole and Levoxyl (both acquired in 1996) for the treatment of thyroid conditions.

Jones sells vitamin and nutritional supplement products under the Bronson and MD Pharmaceutical Vitamins trademarks. The Bronson line of more than 260 vitamin and nutritional supplement products includes multiple vitamins, mineral formulations, single-entity vitamins, antioxidants, personal care products and herbal formulations. Products are offered in tablets, soft-gel capsules, hardshell capsules, chewables and powders. MD Pharmaceutical Vitamins consist of a broad line of branded vitamin products or nutritional supplement items, including multiple vitamins, mineral formulations, single-entity vitamins and antioxidants. These products are marketed to military commissaries.

The company makes pharmaceutical products at facilities in Canton, OH, and St. Louis, MO. Wholly owned GenTrac makes its hemostatic products, including Thrombin, in a Middleton, WI, plant. Vitamin and nutritional supplement products are produced at a facility in Tempe, AZ.

## Capitalization

**Long Term Debt:** None (12/96).

### Per Share Data ($)

| (Year Ended Dec. 31) | 1996 | 1995 | 1994 | 1993 | 1992 | 1991 | 1990 | 1989 | 1988 | 1987 |
|---|---|---|---|---|---|---|---|---|---|---|
| Tangible Bk. Val. | 3.24 | 0.80 | 0.89 | 0.46 | 0.78 | 0.52 | 0.63 | 0.00 | 0.28 | 0.32 |
| Cash Flow | 0.79 | 0.54 | 0.37 | 0.37 | 0.24 | 0.20 | 0.20 | 0.14 | 0.10 | 0.07 |
| Earnings | 0.65 | 0.43 | 0.27 | 0.29 | 0.18 | 0.16 | 0.16 | 0.10 | 0.08 | 0.06 |
| Dividends | 0.08 | 0.05 | 0.04 | 0.04 | 0.03 | 0.03 | 0.02 | 0.02 | 0.00 | Nil |
| Payout Ratio | 12% | 11% | 17% | 14% | 19% | 16% | 13% | 17% | 5% | Nil |
| Prices - High | 50½ | 11 | 6⅞ | 7¾ | 4¼ | 5⅝ | 3⅜ | 2⁷/₁₆ | 1¼ | 1½ |
|    - Low | 10⅜ | 2¾ | 2⅞ | 2¼ | 2⅝ | 2¼ | 2 | 1¹/₁₆ | ¹¹/₁₆ | ⁹/₁₆ |
| P/E Ratio - High | 78 | 26 | 26 | 27 | 24 | 35 | 21 | 24 | 15 | 27 |
|    - Low | 16 | 7 | 11 | 8 | 15 | 14 | 13 | 10 | 8 | 10 |

### Income Statement Analysis (Million $)

| | 1996 | 1995 | 1994 | 1993 | 1992 | 1991 | 1990 | 1989 | 1988 | 1987 |
|---|---|---|---|---|---|---|---|---|---|---|
| Revs. | 100 | 56.4 | 47.5 | 43.2 | 24.1 | 20.5 | 19.7 | 13.3 | 10.2 | 6.8 |
| Oper. Inc. | 38.4 | 17.7 | 11.6 | 11.8 | 6.7 | 5.7 | 5.6 | 3.6 | 2.6 | 1.7 |
| Depr. | 4.0 | 2.4 | 2.2 | 1.8 | 1.3 | 0.9 | 0.8 | 0.6 | 0.4 | 0.2 |
| Int. Exp. | 0.6 | 0.4 | 0.5 | 0.3 | 0.1 | 0.3 | 0.4 | 0.4 | 0.2 | 0.1 |
| Pretax Inc. | 30.4 | 14.9 | 9.0 | 9.9 | 6.0 | 5.2 | 4.8 | 2.7 | 2.0 | 1.5 |
| Eff. Tax Rate | 40% | 38% | 37% | 38% | 38% | 36% | 41% | 41% | 39% | 42% |
| Net Inc. | 18.1 | 9.3 | 5.7 | 6.2 | 3.7 | 3.3 | 2.8 | 1.6 | 1.2 | 0.9 |

### Balance Sheet & Other Fin. Data (Million $)

| | 1996 | 1995 | 1994 | 1993 | 1992 | 1991 | 1990 | 1989 | 1988 | 1987 |
|---|---|---|---|---|---|---|---|---|---|---|
| Cash | 52.2 | 5.4 | 7.2 | 2.3 | 11.8 | 11.1 | 9.5 | 1.3 | 1.0 | 2.5 |
| Curr. Assets | 81.0 | 25.0 | 20.8 | 18.3 | 19.8 | 15.4 | 15.4 | 5.3 | 4.9 | 4.5 |
| Total Assets | 177 | 74.7 | 54.9 | 51.8 | 35.2 | 33.4 | 26.2 | 16.4 | 10.4 | 6.7 |
| Curr. Liab. | 10.0 | 11.6 | 5.8 | 6.3 | 3.8 | 3.3 | 4.6 | 3.3 | 1.3 | 0.3 |
| LT Debt | Nil | 9.1 | 3.8 | 5.4 | 0.5 | 2.7 | 1.5 | 4.4 | 2.0 | 0.5 |
| Common Eqty. | 162 | 49.9 | 39.2 | 31.2 | 24.7 | 20.0 | 19.9 | 8.3 | 7.0 | 5.8 |
| Total Cap. | 167 | 63.1 | 49.1 | 45.5 | 31.4 | 30.1 | 21.5 | 13.1 | 9.1 | 6.4 |
| Cap. Exp. | 7.4 | 4.7 | 3.2 | 4.9 | 0.6 | 0.2 | 0.4 | 0.2 | 0.8 | 0.3 |
| Cash Flow | 22.1 | 11.7 | 7.9 | 7.9 | 5.0 | 4.2 | 3.6 | 2.2 | 1.6 | 1.1 |
| Curr. Ratio | 8.1 | 2.2 | 3.6 | 2.9 | 5.2 | 5.5 | 3.3 | 1.6 | 3.9 | 13.8 |
| % LT Debt of Cap. | Nil | 14.4 | 7.7 | 11.9 | 1.6 | 9.1 | 7.0 | 33.9 | 22.1 | 8.1 |
| % Net Inc.of Revs. | 18.1 | 16.5 | 12.1 | 14.4 | 15.5 | 16.1 | 14.4 | 12.0 | 11.9 | 12.9 |
| % Ret. on Assets | 13.8 | 14.4 | 10.6 | 14.2 | 10.8 | 11.0 | 12.2 | 11.9 | 14.3 | 13.6 |
| % Ret. on Equity | 167.0 | 20.9 | 16.0 | 21.9 | 16.4 | 16.2 | 18.8 | 20.9 | 19.1 | 16.3 |

Data as orig. reptd.; bef. results of disc. opers. and/or spec. items. Per share data adj. for stk. divs. as of ex-div. date. E-Estimated. NA-Not Available. NM-Not Meaningful. NR-Not Ranked.

**Office**—1945 Craig Rd., St. Louis, MO 63146. **Tel**—(314) 576-6100. **Chrmn, Pres & CEO**—D. M. Jones. **EVP, Treas & Secy**—J. A. Jones. **Dirs**—M. T. Bramblett, E. A. Chod, G. A. Franz, D. M. Jones, J. A. Jones, S. L. Lopata, D. A. McLaughlin, T. F. Patton, L. J. Polite Jr. **Transfer Agent**—Mark Twain Bank, St. Louis. **Incorporated**—in Delaware in 1981. **Empl**— 508. **S&P Analyst:** Richard Joy

# STANDARD &POOR'S
## STOCK REPORTS

# Keane, Inc.

**8290**

ASE Symbol **KEA**

In S&P SmallCap 600

**17-MAY-97**

**Industry:** Services (Computer Systems)

**Summary:** Keane designs, develops and manages software for corporations, government agencies and healthcare facilities.

## Quantitative Evaluations

**Outlook** (1 Lowest—5 Highest)
- **3⁻**

**Fair Value**
- **54⅜**

**Risk**
- **Average**

**Earn./Div. Rank**
- **B+**

**Technical Eval.**
- **Bearish** since 9/96

**Rel. Strength Rank** (1 Lowest—99 Highest)
- **99**

**Insider Activity**
- **Neutral**

Recent Price • 53¾
52 Wk Range • 54½-16⅜

Yield • Nil
12-Mo. P/E • 60.4

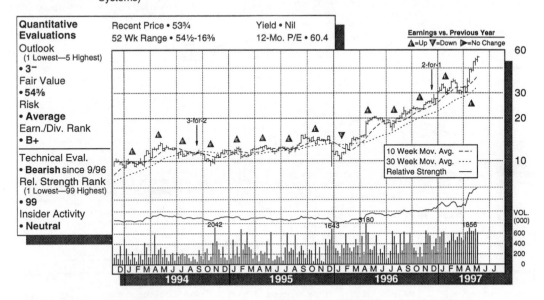

Earnings vs. Previous Year
▲=Up ▼=Down ▶=No Change

10 Week Mov. Avg. — — —
30 Week Mov. Avg. ........
Relative Strength ———

## Business Profile - 15-MAY-97

In March 1997, KEA signed a year 2000 compliance contractto conduct an enterprise assessment of all of LEXIS-NEXIS' mission-critical applications and develop a strategic conversion plan for preparing the company's computing systems, online LEXIS-NEXIS services and all information management software products for the new century. The amount of the contract was not disclosed. The project was expected to be completed by mid-1997. Separately, in February 1997, KEA signed a letter of intent under which Microsoft Corp. will contract its Tucson support facility to KEA. Under the proposed agreement, KEA's Tucson staff would provide technical support by phone to several corporate customers, including Microsoft. KEA has a strong balance sheet, with little long-term debt. Officers and directors own more than 20% of the shares.

## Operational Review - 15-MAY-97

Revenues for the first quarter of 1997 advanced 33%, year to year, reflecting strong demand for strategic services, particularly year 2000 compliance projects and application outsourcing business.Profitability benefited from the higher revenues, and net income moved ahead 83%, to $9.8 million ($0.29 a share, based on 2.2% more shares), from $5.4 million ($0.16, as adjusted for the two-for-one stock split in late 1996).

## Stock Performance - 16-MAY-97

In the past 30 trading days, KEA's shares have increased 77%, compared to a 9% rise in the S&P 500. Average trading volume for the past five days was 139,940 shares, compared with the 40-day moving average of 210,269 shares.

## Key Stock Statistics

| | | | |
|---|---|---|---|
| Dividend Rate/Share | Nil | Shareholders | 800 |
| Shs. outstg. (M) | 32.9 | Market cap. (B) | $ 1.8 |
| Avg. daily vol. (M) | 0.214 | Inst. holdings | 66% |
| Tang. Bk. Value/Share | 4.56 | | |
| Beta | 0.77 | | |

Value of $10,000 invested 5 years ago: $ 143,333

### Fiscal Year Ending Dec. 31

| | 1997 | 1996 | 1995 | 1994 | 1993 | 1992 |
|---|---|---|---|---|---|---|
| **Revenues (Million $)** | | | | | | |
| 1Q | 141.1 | 105.8 | 90.45 | 86.17 | 42.27 | 23.70 |
| 2Q | — | 113.1 | 94.65 | 85.56 | 43.39 | 24.80 |
| 3Q | — | 120.9 | 96.52 | 86.64 | 43.45 | 24.80 |
| 4Q | — | 127.3 | 101.1 | 86.22 | 46.71 | 26.00 |
| Yr. | — | 467.1 | 382.7 | 344.6 | 175.8 | 99.3 |
| **Earnings Per Share ($)** | | | | | | |
| 1Q | 0.29 | 0.17 | 0.16 | 0.14 | 0.09 | 0.07 |
| 2Q | — | 0.19 | 0.17 | 0.15 | 0.09 | 0.08 |
| 3Q | — | 0.19 | 0.15 | 0.15 | 0.10 | 0.07 |
| 4Q | — | 0.21 | 0.11 | 0.14 | 0.10 | 0.07 |
| Yr. | — | 0.76 | 0.59 | 0.57 | 0.38 | 0.28 |

Next earnings report expected: mid July

### Dividend Data

| Amount ($) | Date Decl. | Ex-Div. Date | Stock of Record | Payment Date |
|---|---|---|---|---|
| 2-for-1 | Oct. 24 | Dec. 02 | Nov. 14 | Nov. 29 '96 |

This report is for information purposes and should not be considered a solicitation to buy or sell any security. Neither S&P nor any other party guarantee its accuracy or make warranties regarding results from its usage. Redistribution is prohibited without written permission. Copyright © 1997

*A Division of The McGraw·Hill Companies*

# Keane, Inc.



## Business Summary - 15-MAY-97

Keane is a software services company that designs, develops and manages software for corporations, government agencies and healthcare facilities. The company's services and methodologies are designed to enable clients to leverage their existing information systems (IS) capability and more rapidly and cost-effectively develop and manage mission-critical software applications. Revenue contributions by operating division in recent years:

| | 1996 | 1995 | 1994 |
|---|---|---|---|
| Information services | 94% | 93% | 93% |
| Healthcare services | 6% | 7% | 7% |

During 1996, KEA's five largest clients accounted for 29% of revenues, including 12% from IBM.

The Information services segment provides custom application software design, development and management services for corporations with large and recurring outsourcing needs. Keane delivers (1) application development projects, which include IS planning and assessment, client-server planning and development, and systems migration services; (2) outsourcing services, which include application outsourcing and help desk outsourcing; (3) year 2000 compliance services; and (4) project management training, through which Keane delivers professional training on its project management, estimating and risk management processes.

The Healthcare services (HCS) segment develops, markets and supports patient care and clinical software for large teaching hospitals, hospital chains, community hospitals and long-term healthcare facilities. HCS also provides facilities management services for many of its hospital clients. As of year-end 1996, HCS products were being used by about 385 hospitals and around 625 long-term care facilities.

The company believes that its strengths consist mainly of: (1) long-term client relationships, which create greater opportunities for recurring revenues; (2) a full range of value-added services, which KEA believes differentiates it from many of its competitors; (3) a strong branch office network, which enables it to deliver services proactively and cost-effectively; and (4) disciplined methodologies and best practices, which replicate organizational experience and enable KEA to achieve more reliable and predictable services.

The key elements of KEA's strategy include (1) increasing concentration of project and outsourcing business (including application development and outsourcing, year 2000 compliance and help desk outsourcing); (2) building long-term strategic partnerships with clients (sales people are assigned to a limited number of target accounts to get an in-depth understanding of each client's needs and to build long-term relationships with those clients); and (3) achieving critical mass through a strong branch office network to grow market share.

## Capitalization

**Long Term Debt:** $400,000 of lease obligs. (3/97).

| Per Share Data ($) (Year Ended Dec. 31) | 1996 | 1995 | 1994 | 1993 | 1992 | 1991 | 1990 | 1989 | 1988 | 1987 |
|---|---|---|---|---|---|---|---|---|---|---|
| Tangible Bk. Val. | 4.56 | 3.35 | 4.52 | 3.10 | 1.99 | 1.70 | 1.42 | 0.76 | 0.55 | 0.36 |
| Cash Flow | 1.34 | 1.13 | 0.74 | 0.47 | 0.34 | 0.32 | 0.29 | 0.24 | 0.21 | 0.09 |
| Earnings | 0.76 | 0.59 | 0.57 | 0.38 | 0.28 | 0.27 | 0.25 | 0.20 | 0.17 | 0.05 |
| Dividends | Nil | Nil | Nil | Nil | Nil | Nil | Nil | Nil | Nil | Nil |
| Payout Ratio | Nil | Nil | Nil | Nil | Nil | Nil | Nil | Nil | Nil | Nil |
| Prices - High | $32\frac{7}{8}$ | $15\frac{1}{2}$ | $13\frac{5}{8}$ | $10\frac{1}{2}$ | 6 | $4\frac{3}{4}$ | $4\frac{1}{4}$ | $3\frac{1}{4}$ | $1\frac{3}{16}$ | $\frac{11}{16}$ |
| - Low | $10\frac{1}{8}$ | $9\frac{1}{8}$ | 9 | $5\frac{1}{4}$ | $3\frac{1}{4}$ | 3 | $2\frac{7}{8}$ | 1 | $\frac{1}{2}$ | $\frac{7}{16}$ |
| P/E Ratio - High | 43 | 26 | 24 | 28 | 21 | 18 | 17 | 16 | 7 | 15 |
| - Low | 13 | 15 | 16 | 14 | 12 | 11 | 11 | 5 | 3 | 9 |
| **Income Statement Analysis (Million $)** | | | | | | | | | | |
| Revs. | 467 | 383 | 345 | 176 | 99 | 95.6 | 93.0 | 77.2 | 60.0 | 43.5 |
| Oper. Inc. | 62.4 | 49.0 | 36.0 | 18.7 | 10.9 | 9.8 | 9.3 | 7.1 | 5.8 | 2.8 |
| Depr. | 19.3 | 17.8 | 4.8 | 2.2 | 1.3 | 1.0 | 0.9 | 0.7 | 0.7 | 0.9 |
| Int. Exp. | 0.4 | 0.5 | 2.8 | 0.8 | 0.0 | 0.0 | 0.1 | 0.3 | 0.2 | 0.3 |
| Pretax Inc. | 44.3 | 32.6 | 28.5 | 15.6 | 10.4 | 9.5 | 8.8 | 6.0 | 4.8 | 1.6 |
| Eff. Tax Rate | 43% | 41% | 43% | 42% | 40% | 38% | 41% | 41% | 41% | 46% |
| Net Inc. | 25.4 | 19.3 | 16.2 | 9.1 | 6.3 | 5.9 | 5.2 | 3.6 | 2.9 | 0.9 |
| **Balance Sheet & Other Fin. Data (Million $)** | | | | | | | | | | |
| Cash | 69.1 | 33.2 | 26.3 | 24.1 | 25.7 | 19.7 | 12.6 | 0.1 | 0.3 | 0.1 |
| Curr. Assets | 172 | 120 | 100 | 51.9 | 42.3 | 35.1 | 26.9 | 16.0 | 11.3 | 9.3 |
| Total Assets | 235 | 194 | 179 | 100 | 49.3 | 41.1 | 34.1 | 24.8 | 16.7 | 13.9 |
| Curr. Liab. | 35.4 | 21.6 | 24.4 | 12.3 | 5.7 | 4.8 | 4.3 | 7.2 | 4.0 | 4.4 |
| LT Debt | 3.2 | 5.5 | 7.5 | 4.3 | 0.1 | 0.0 | 0.1 | 4.6 | 2.4 | 1.5 |
| Common Eqty. | 197 | 167 | 144 | 83.1 | 43.4 | 36.2 | 29.6 | 12.9 | 9.0 | 7.8 |
| Total Cap. | 200 | 173 | 155 | 87.4 | 43.6 | 36.3 | 29.8 | 17.6 | 12.7 | 9.5 |
| Cap. Exp. | 4.1 | 5.7 | 3.6 | 1.8 | 1.0 | 1.2 | 1.0 | 1.0 | 0.8 | 0.4 |
| Cash Flow | 44.6 | 37.0 | 21.0 | 11.3 | 7.6 | 6.9 | 6.0 | 4.2 | 3.6 | 1.7 |
| Curr. Ratio | 4.9 | 5.6 | 4.1 | 4.2 | 7.4 | 7.3 | 6.3 | 2.2 | 2.9 | 2.1 |
| % LT Debt of Cap. | 1.6 | 3.2 | 4.8 | 4.9 | 0.3 | Nil | 0.5 | 26.3 | 18.8 | 15.9 |
| % Net Inc.of Revs. | 5.4 | 5.0 | 4.7 | 5.2 | 6.3 | 6.2 | 5.6 | 4.6 | 4.8 | 2.0 |
| % Ret. on Assets | 11.8 | 10.3 | 10.9 | 11.3 | 13.8 | 15.5 | 16.0 | 16.9 | 19.7 | 6.1 |
| % Ret. on Equity | 13.9 | 12.4 | 13.3 | 13.3 | 15.6 | 17.7 | 22.8 | 32.1 | 36.0 | 12.1 |

Data as orig. reptd.; bef. results of disc. opers. and/or spec. items. Per share data adj. for stk. divs. as of ex-div. date. E-Estimated. NA-Not Available. NM-Not Meaningful. NR-Not Ranked.

**Office**—Ten City Square, Boston, MA 02129. **Tel**—(617) 241-9200. **Website**—http://www.keane.com **Pres & CEO**—J. F. Keane. **VP-Fin**—W. A. Cataldo. **Dirs**—P. J. Harkins, W. R. Hindle Jr., J. F. Keane, J. F. Rockart, R. A. Shafto. **Transfer Agent & Registrar**—Boston EquiServe, Boston. **Incorporated**—in Massachusetts in 1967. **Empl**— 6,018. **S&P Analyst:** N. J. DeVita

# STANDARD &POOR'S
## STOCK REPORTS

# Kohl's Corp.

# 1309J
NYSE Symbol **KSS**

In S&P MidCap 400

**19-MAY-97**

**Industry:**
Retail (Department Stores)

**Summary:** This company operates more than 150 specialty department stores, primarily in the Midwest, featuring moderately priced apparel, shoes, accessories and products for the home.

| S&P Opinion: Hold (★★★) | Recent Price • 50½ | Yield • Nil | Earnings vs. Previous Year |
| --- | --- | --- | --- |
| | 52 Wk Range • 51¾-26¾ | 12-Mo. P/E • 36.3 | ▲=Up ▼=Down ▷=No Change |

**Quantitative Evaluations**

**Outlook**
(1 Lowest—5 Highest)
• **3**

**Fair Value**
• **50⅜**

**Risk**
• **Average**

**Earn./Div. Rank**
• **NR**

**Technical Eval.**
• **Bullish** since 6/95

**Rel. Strength Rank**
(1 Lowest—99 Highest)
• **81**

**Insider Activity**
• **Neutral**

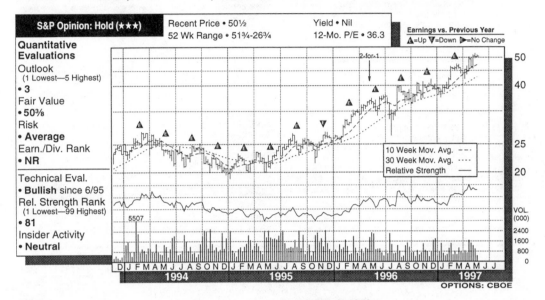

10 Week Mov. Avg. — – –
30 Week Mov. Avg. - - - -
Relative Strength ——

OPTIONS: CBOE

## Overview - 19-MAY-97

Sales should increase about 24% in FY 98 (Jan.), boosted by moderate same-store sales growth of about 5%, and by the planned opening of new stores. This follows the opening of 22 stores in FY 97. Gross margins should widen slightly, on the higher volume, partly offset by competitive pricing. With a growing store base, the company's expense ratios will be better leveraged. Operating income should increase more than 20%. Interest expense will be higher, on increased debt to fund the company's aggressive capital expenditure program. The company is plowing its strong cash flow and expanded borrowings into expansion. In the third quarter of FY 96, Kohl's brought the servicing of its credit card receivables in-house. This boosted earnings beginning in FY 97, and also should improve sales over time, as KSS aggressively markets its credit card and targets customers for promotions and special events.

## Valuation - 19-MAY-97

The shares of this well managed regional retailer appear fairly valued at recent levels. Over the past three years, Kohl's has continued to gain market share, with strong same-store sales gains, and to outperform most other family apparel retailers by a wide margin. The company's aggressive store opening program, particularly its entry into the Northeast, its low cost structure, and its conservative balance sheet continue to bode well for earnings gains over the next few years. The company's core earnings growth rate is in the range of 20% to 22%, and this appears to be already reflected in the stock price. Nevertheless, the shares are a worthwhile holding for long-term capital gains.

## Key Stock Statistics

| | | | |
| --- | --- | --- | --- |
| S&P EPS Est. 1998 | 1.70 | Tang. Bk. Value/Share | 6.27 |
| P/E on S&P Est. 1998 | 29.7 | Beta | NA |
| S&P EPS Est. 1999 | 2.05 | Shareholders | 4,500 |
| Dividend Rate/Share | Nil | Market cap. (B) | $ 3.7 |
| Shs. outstg. (M) | 74.0 | Inst. holdings | 73% |
| Avg. daily vol. (M) | 0.204 | | |

Value of $10,000 invested 5 years ago: NA

## Fiscal Year Ending Jan. 31

| | 1997 | 1996 | 1995 | 1994 | 1993 | 1992 |
| --- | --- | --- | --- | --- | --- | --- |
| **Revenues (Million $)** | | | | | | |
| 1Q | 468.6 | 368.4 | 308.0 | 250.3 | 212.0 | 264.0 |
| 2Q | 474.6 | 363.5 | 292.4 | 257.4 | 218.0 | 258.0 |
| 3Q | 598.0 | 486.8 | 389.5 | 341.0 | 285.0 | 237.0 |
| 4Q | 846.9 | 707.0 | 564.3 | 457.1 | 382.0 | 247.0 |
| Yr. | 2,388 | 1,926 | 1,554 | 1,306 | 1,097 | 1,006 |
| **Earnings Per Share ($)** | | | | | | |
| 1Q | 0.19 | 0.16 | 0.15 | 0.10 | 0.06 | 0.13 |
| 2Q | 0.20 | 0.15 | 0.13 | 0.09 | -0.10 | 0.16 |
| 3Q | 0.30 | 0.10 | 0.19 | 0.18 | 0.15 | -0.06 |
| 4Q | 0.70 | 0.57 | 0.46 | 0.39 | 0.32 | 0.08 |
| Yr. | 1.39 | 0.98 | 0.93 | 0.76 | 0.44 | 0.30 |

**Next earnings report expected: late May**

## Dividend Data

No cash dividends have been paid. The company has no current plans to pay dividends on its common stock and intends to retain all earnings for investment in its business.

This report is for information purposes and should not be considered a solicitation to buy or sell any security. Neither S&P nor any other party guarantee its accuracy or make warranties regarding results from its usage. Redistribution is prohibited without written permission. Copyright © 1997

A Division of The **McGraw-Hill** Companies

## Business Summary - 19-MAY-97

As of mid-March 1997, Kohl's was operating 150 family-oriented, specialty department stores, primarily in the Midwest. The stores feature quality, moderately priced national brand merchandise, including apparel, shoes, accessories, soft home products and housewares. Sales by merchandise category in recent fiscal years (Jan.) were:

|  | FY 97 | FY 96 |
|---|---|---|
| Apparel | 60.6% | 58.2% |
| Accessories/shoes | 19.1% | 19.2% |
| Soft home/housewares | 12.5% | 12.5% |
| Hardlines | 7.8% | 10.1% |

At February 1 1997, the company had 150 stores, located in Illinois (31), Wisconsin (28), Ohio (27), Michigan (14), Indiana (13), Minnesota (13), Kansas (5), Iowa (4), North Carolina (3), Missouri (3), Nebraska (2), Kentiucky (2), Pennsylvania (2), North Dakota (1), South Dakota (1) and West Virginia (1). Stores are designed to help customers shop without assistance, and feature simple layouts and in-store signs.

As a complement to its national brands, KSS offers private label merchandise under several names. It plans to increase private label sales to about 20%. The company has been phasing out its electronics business, which was to be totally eliminated in 1996.

The company planned to open about 30 stores in FY 98. Capital expenditures in FY 97 are projected at about $200 million. The company's store expansion emphasizes existing markets, where it can leverage advertising, purchasing, transportation and other regional expenses; and contiguous markets where it can extend regional facilities.

## Important Developments

**Apr. '97**—Kohl's said same-store sales rose 11.5% year to year in the five weeks ended April 5, 1997. Sales were strong in all markets, including the eight new stores in the Washington, DC, and Baltimore trade areas. The company plans to open a total of 30 new stores in FY 98, and also plans to open a distribution center in Winchester, VA, to support these stores. Seven stores were slated to open in the Philadelphia market in April. Operating income rose 22% in FY 97, driven by an 11.3% increase in same-store sales. Gross margins widened to 32.9% of sales, while SG&A expenses declined to 22.5% of sales. The company opened 22 new stores and relocated one in FY 97.

## Capitalization

**Long Term Debt:** $312,031,000 (2/1/97).

### Per Share Data ($)

| (Year Ended Jan. 31) | 1997 | 1996 | 1995 | 1994 | 1993 | 1992 | 1991 | 1990 | 1989 | 1988 |
|---|---|---|---|---|---|---|---|---|---|---|
| Tangible Bk. Val. | 6.28 | 4.74 | 3.60 | 2.89 | 2.05 | 1.08 | 0.39 | NA | NA | NA |
| Cash Flow | 1.98 | 1.45 | 1.30 | 1.08 | 0.70 | 0.63 | NA | NA | NA | NA |
| Earnings | 1.39 | 0.98 | 0.93 | 0.76 | 0.44 | 0.30 | 0.33 | NA | NA | NA |
| Dividends | Nil | Nil | Nil | Nil | Nil | Nil | NA | NA | NA | NA |
| Payout Ratio | Nil | Nil | Nil | Nil | Nil | Nil | NA | NA | NA | NA |
| Cal. Yrs. | 1996 | 1995 | 1994 | 1993 | 1992 | 1991 | 1990 | 1989 | 1988 | 1987 |
| Prices - High | 42 | 27⁵/₈ | 27⁵/₈ | 26¹/₈ | 16 | NA | NA | NA | NA | NA |
| - Low | 25³/₈ | 19 | 19⁵/₈ | 13¹/₈ | 6⁵/₈ | NA | NA | NA | NA | NA |
| P/E Ratio - High | 30 | 28 | 30 | 34 | 36 | NA | NA | NA | NA | NA |
| - Low | 18 | 19 | 21 | 17 | 15 | NA | NA | NA | NA | NA |

### Income Statement Analysis (Million $)

| | 1997 | 1996 | 1995 | 1994 | 1993 | 1992 | 1991 | 1990 | 1989 | 1988 |
|---|---|---|---|---|---|---|---|---|---|---|
| Revs. | 2,388 | 1,926 | 1,554 | 1,306 | 1,097 | 1,006 | 863 | NA | NA | NA |
| Oper. Inc. | 233 | 184 | 151 | 126 | 99 | 73.9 | 75.1 | NA | NA | NA |
| Depr. | 44.0 | 34.0 | 27.4 | 23.2 | 16.7 | 18.7 | 18.7 | NA | NA | NA |
| Int. Exp. | 17.9 | 13.5 | 7.4 | 6.7 | 14.7 | 20.2 | NA | NA | NA | NA |
| Pretax Inc. | 171 | 123 | 117 | 96.7 | 50.1 | 31.7 | NA | NA | NA | NA |
| Eff. Tax Rate | 40% | 41% | 42% | 42% | 43% | 45% | NA | NA | NA | NA |
| Net Inc. | 102 | 72.7 | 68.5 | 55.7 | 28.7 | 17.5 | 22.9 | NA | NA | NA |

### Balance Sheet & Other Fin. Data (Million $)

| | 1997 | 1996 | 1995 | 1994 | 1993 | 1992 | 1991 | 1990 | 1989 | 1988 |
|---|---|---|---|---|---|---|---|---|---|---|
| Cash | 8.9 | 2.8 | 30.4 | 8.5 | 4.2 | 0.9 | NA | NA | NA | NA |
| Curr. Assets | 465 | 300 | 286 | 202 | 211 | 179 | 465 | NA | NA | NA |
| Total Assets | 1,122 | 805 | 659 | 469 | 445 | 398 | NA | NA | NA | NA |
| Curr. Liab. | 236 | 155 | 172 | 115 | 106 | 139 | NA | NA | NA | NA |
| LT Debt | 312 | 188 | 109 | 52.0 | 95.0 | 89.0 | 108 | NA | NA | NA |
| Common Eqty. | 517 | 411 | 334 | 263 | 207 | 134 | 121 | NA | NA | NA |
| Total Cap. | 868 | 629 | 463 | 329 | 314 | 232 | NA | NA | NA | NA |
| Cap. Exp. | 223 | 132 | 108 | 58.8 | 46.3 | 27.5 | 11.3 | NA | NA | NA |
| Cash Flow | 146 | 107 | 95.9 | 78.9 | 45.4 | 36.2 | 41.6 | NA | NA | NA |
| Curr. Ratio | 2.0 | 1.9 | 1.7 | 1.8 | 2.0 | 1.3 | NA | NA | NA | NA |
| % LT Debt of Cap. | 35.9 | 29.8 | 23.5 | 15.7 | 30.3 | 38.5 | NA | NA | NA | NA |
| % Net Inc.of Revs. | 4.3 | 3.8 | 4.4 | 4.3 | 2.6 | 1.7 | 2.6 | NA | NA | NA |
| % Ret. on Assets | 10.6 | 9.9 | 12.1 | 12.2 | 6.1 | 4.0 | NA | NA | NA | NA |
| % Ret. on Equity | 22.1 | 19.5 | 22.9 | 23.7 | 26.5 | 24.6 | NA | NA | NA | NA |

Data as orig. reptd.; bef. results of disc. opers. and/or spec. items. Per share data adj. for stk. divs. as of ex-div. date. E-Estimated. NA-Not Available. NM-Not Meaningful. NR-Not Ranked.

**Office**—N54 W13600 Woodale Drive, Menomonee Falls, WI 53051. **Tel**—(414) 783-5800. **Chrmn & CEO**—W. S. Kellogg. **Pres**—J. H. Baker. **VP, CFO & Investor Contact**—Arlene Meier (414-783-1646). **VP & Secy**—J. F. Herma. **Dirs**—J. H. Baker, J. F. Herma, W. S. Kellogg, L. Montgomery, F. V. Sica, H. Simon, P. M. Sommerhauser, R. E. White. **Transfer Agent & Registrar**—Bank of New York, NYC. **Incorporated**—in Delaware in 1988; reincorporated in Wisconsin in 1993. **Empl**—21,200. **S&P Analyst:** Karen J. Sack, CFA

# Lowe's Companies

**1386D**

NYSE Symbol **LOW**

In S&P 500

**19-MAY-97**

**Industry:** Retail (Building Supplies)

**Summary:** This company retails building materials and supplies, lumber, hardware and appliances through more than 402 stores in 24 states.

---

**S&P Opinion: Accumulate (★★★★)**

| Recent Price • 39 | Yield • 0.6% |
|---|---|
| 52 Wk Range • 43½-28⅝ | 12-Mo. P/E • 22.4 |

**Quantitative Evaluations**

Outlook
(1 Lowest—5 Highest)
• **4⁻**

Fair Value
• **44¼**

Risk
• **Average**

Earn./Div. Rank
• **A-**

Technical Eval.
• **Bullish** since 5/95

Rel. Strength Rank
(1 Lowest—99 Highest)
• **66**

Insider Activity
• **Unfavorable**

**Earnings vs. Previous Year**
▲=Up ▼=Down ▶=No Change

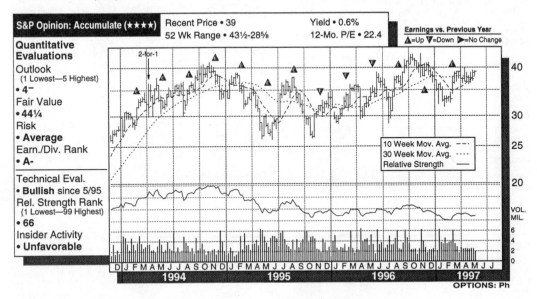

10 Week Mov. Avg. ---
30 Week Mov. Avg. ·····
Relative Strength —

D J F M A M J J A S O N D | J F M A M J J A S O N D | J F M A M J J A S O N D | J F M A M J J
1994 | 1995 | 1996 | 1997

OPTIONS: Ph

---

## Overview - 19-MAY-97

Improved consumer demand should boost same-store sales in FY 98 (Jan.) by about 6%, with total company sales up about 25%, benefiting from newer and larger stores that offer a broader selection of merchandise, with wider overall margins. SG&A expenses will increase as a percentage of sales, reflecting higher staffing and training necessary in larger stores. Depreciation charges will also increase, as the company opened 60 new units in FY 97, and continues to execute an aggressive capital expenditure program approximating $1 billion; 80% of capital spending is for new store expansion. Interest expense should rise, in part as a result of the increased capital expenditure program. Store expansion of 15% annually for the next five years, together with emphasis on larger, more productive stores, should put earnings back on a growth track. For the long-term, we remain optimistic that earnings will continue to advance, as LOW gains market share in the highly fragmented, $134 billion home improvement industry.

## Valuation - 19-MAY-97

The shares have rebounded from a selloff in February and March on concerns about higher interest rates as well as lower home sales and resales. But sales gains have remained healthy and we believe that should continue in coming periods, boosted by penetration into new markets, larger more productive units and by a favorable merchandise mix. An 18% rise in earnings per share is projected for FY 98, with a similar gain seen for FY 99. Consequently, we continue to recommend that the shares be accumulated for capital gains. The shares of this growth company warrant a premium multiple to that of the market.

## Key Stock Statistics

| | | | |
|---|---|---|---|
| S&P EPS Est. 1998 | 2.05 | Tang. Bk. Value/Share | 12.10 |
| P/E on S&P Est. 1998 | 19.0 | Beta | 0.83 |
| Dividend Rate/Share | 0.22 | Shareholders | 7,400 |
| Shs. outstg. (M) | 173.0 | Market cap. (B) | $ 6.7 |
| Avg. daily vol. (M) | 0.455 | Inst. holdings | 64% |

Value of $10,000 invested 5 years ago: $ 47,376

### Fiscal Year Ending Jan. 31

| | 1998 | 1997 | 1996 | 1995 | 1994 | 1993 |
|---|---|---|---|---|---|---|
| **Revenues (Million $)** | | | | | | |
| 1Q | 2,401 | 1,907 | 1,635 | 1,397 | 992.1 | 883.0 |
| 2Q | — | 2,459 | 1,978 | 1,647 | 1,242 | 1,062 |
| 3Q | — | 2,193 | 1,766 | 1,579 | 1,158 | 991.0 |
| 4Q | — | 2,042 | 1,697 | 1,487 | 1,146 | 910.0 |
| Yr. | — | 8,600 | 7,075 | 6,111 | 4,538 | 3,846 |
| **Earnings Per Share ($)** | | | | | | |
| 1Q | 0.41 | 0.29 | 0.37 | 0.35 | 0.20 | 0.16 |
| 2Q | — | 0.70 | 0.53 | 0.47 | 0.31 | 0.20 |
| 3Q | — | 0.43 | 0.27 | 0.34 | 0.22 | 0.13 |
| 4Q | — | 0.32 | 0.24 | 0.29 | 0.17 | 0.08 |
| Yr. | E2.05 | 1.74 | 1.41 | 1.44 | 0.89 | 0.58 |

**Next earnings report expected: mid August**

**Dividend Data** (Dividends have been paid since 1961.)

| Amount ($) | Date Decl. | Ex-Div. Date | Stock of Record | Payment Date |
|---|---|---|---|---|
| 0.050 | May. 31 | Jul. 15 | Jul. 17 | Jul. 31 '96 |
| 0.050 | Sep. 23 | Oct. 15 | Oct. 17 | Oct. 31 '96 |
| 0.055 | Dec. 06 | Jan. 15 | Jan. 17 | Jan. 31 '97 |
| 0.055 | Apr. 02 | Apr. 14 | Apr. 16 | Apr. 30 '97 |

---

This report is for information purposes and should not be considered a solicitation to buy or sell any security. Neither S&P nor any other party guarantee its accuracy or make warranties regarding results from its usage. Redistribution is prohibited without written permission. Copyright © 1997

*A Division of The McGraw·Hill Companies*

## Business Summary - 19-MAY-97

Lowe's Companies is a retail distributor of building materials, consumer durables and home center products for the do-it-yourself and home construction markets. At January 31, 1997, it was operating 402 retail stores in 24 states, principally in the South Atlantic and south central U.S.

Contributions to sales by product line in recent fiscal years (Jan. 31) were:

| | FY 97 | FY 96 |
|---|---|---|
| Structural lumber | 9% | 12% |
| Building materials | 21% | 22% |
| Home decoration | 6% | 5% |
| Kitchen, bath & laundry | 12% | 12% |
| Paint & sundries | 8% | 7% |
| Plumbing & electrical | 17% | 17% |
| Yard, patio & garden | 8% | 9% |
| Power tools & hardware | 12% | 10% |
| Outdoor hardlines | 7% | 6% |

At January 31, 1997, the company had total sales floor space of 30.4 million sq. ft., a 27% increase from the level a year earlier. The average sales floor size was 76,000 sq. ft., versus 66,000 sq. ft. a year earlier. The company has been increasing the size of its stores over the past three years. Large stores average about 86,500 sq. ft. These units represent 78.5% of the sales base, and accounted for 61% of sales in FY 97, and 53% of operating profits.

## Important Developments

**May '97**—Same-store sales rose 2% in the month of April; same-store sales at large stores rose 4%. Management said that same-unit sales in April were hurt by the unusually cool and wet weather, slowing sales of seasonal categories, such as outdoor power equipment and lawn and garden items. The company planned to open 60 to 65 new stores in 1997 with about 70% in new markets, the balance in relocations, which would encompass additional square footage. Capital expenditures for FY 98 are targeted at $1.2 billion. LOW's goal is to operate 600 stores by the year 2000.

## Capitalization

**Long Term Debt:** $788,637,000 (5/2/97).

## Per Share Data ($)

| (Year Ended Jan. 31) | 1997 | 1996 | 1995 | 1994 | 1993 | 1992 | 1991 | 1990 | 1989 | 1988 |
|---|---|---|---|---|---|---|---|---|---|---|
| Tangible Bk. Val. | 12.79 | 10.30 | 8.90 | 5.91 | 5.02 | 4.59 | 4.68 | 4.33 | 3.95 | 3.69 |
| Cash Flow | 2.92 | 2.34 | 2.15 | 1.44 | 1.05 | 0.44 | 0.82 | 0.82 | 0.73 | 0.60 |
| Earnings | 1.74 | 1.41 | 1.44 | 0.89 | 0.58 | 0.05 | 0.48 | 0.51 | 0.46 | 0.36 |
| Dividends | 0.21 | 0.19 | 0.17 | 0.32 | 0.15 | 0.14 | 0.13 | 0.12 | 0.11 | 0.11 |
| Payout Ratio | 12% | 13% | 12% | 36% | 25% | 305% | 27% | 24% | 25% | 30% |
| **Cal. Yrs.** | 1996 | 1995 | 1994 | 1993 | 1992 | 1991 | 1990 | 1989 | 1988 | 1987 |
| Prices - High | 43½ | 38⅞ | 41⅜ | 29⅞ | 12¾ | 9¼ | 12⅜ | 8 | 6⅛ | 8¼ |
|    - Low | 28⅝ | 26 | 26⅝ | 12 | 8 | 5¾ | 4⅝ | 5¼ | 4⅛ | 3⅞ |
| P/E Ratio - High | 25 | 28 | 29 | 34 | 22 | NM | 26 | 16 | 13 | 23 |
|    - Low | 16 | 18 | 18 | 13 | 14 | NM | 10 | 10 | 9 | 11 |

## Income Statement Analysis (Million $)

| | | | | | | | | | | |
|---|---|---|---|---|---|---|---|---|---|---|
| Revs. | 8,600 | 7,075 | 6,111 | 4,538 | 3,846 | 3,056 | 2,833 | 2,651 | 2,517 | 2,442 |
| Oper. Inc. | 701 | 540 | 481 | 297 | 211 | 151 | 169 | 174 | 168 | 159 |
| Depr. | 198 | 150 | 110 | 80.5 | 69.8 | 58.3 | 51.4 | 46.1 | 41.2 | 38.5 |
| Int. Exp. | 65.1 | 54.7 | 44.8 | 26.6 | 19.4 | 19.9 | 23.0 | 22.4 | 24.2 | 23.1 |
| Pretax Inc. | 454 | 352 | 344 | 198 | 126 | 5.0 | 100 | 109 | 106 | 91.0 |
| Eff. Tax Rate | 36% | 35% | 35% | 34% | 33% | NM | 29% | 31% | 35% | 38% |
| Net Inc. | 292 | 226 | 224 | 132 | 84.7 | 6.5 | 71.1 | 74.9 | 69.2 | 56.0 |

## Balance Sheet & Other Fin. Data (Million $)

| | | | | | | | | | | |
|---|---|---|---|---|---|---|---|---|---|---|
| Cash | 70.0 | 171 | 268 | 108 | 54.8 | 30.8 | 50.1 | 55.6 | 60.3 | 43.9 |
| Curr. Assets | 1,851 | 1,604 | 1,557 | 1,084 | 746 | 770 | 616 | 596 | 578 | 552 |
| Total Assets | 4,435 | 3,556 | 3,106 | 2,202 | 1,609 | 1,441 | 1,203 | 1,147 | 1,086 | 1,027 |
| Curr. Liab. | 1,349 | 950 | 946 | 681 | 500 | 589 | 338 | 308 | 286 | 232 |
| LT Debt | 767 | 866 | 681 | 592 | 314 | 114 | 159 | 168 | 190 | 186 |
| Common Eqty. | 2,217 | 1,657 | 1,420 | 874 | 733 | 669 | 683 | 646 | 587 | 582 |
| Total Cap. | 3,086 | 2,607 | 2,150 | 1,492 | 1,063 | 788 | 865 | 840 | 800 | 795 |
| Cap. Exp. | 677 | 520 | 414 | 337 | 243 | 140 | 91.0 | 92.0 | 82.0 | 102 |
| Cash Flow | 490 | 376 | 333 | 212 | 155 | 65.0 | 123 | 121 | 110 | 95.0 |
| Curr. Ratio | 1.4 | 1.7 | 1.6 | 1.6 | 1.5 | 1.3 | 1.8 | 1.9 | 2.0 | 2.4 |
| % LT Debt of Cap. | 24.9 | 33.3 | 31.7 | 39.7 | 29.5 | 14.4 | 18.4 | 20.0 | 23.8 | 23.4 |
| % Net Inc.of Revs. | 3.4 | 3.2 | 3.7 | 2.9 | 2.2 | 0.2 | 2.5 | 2.8 | 2.7 | 2.3 |
| % Ret. on Assets | 7.3 | 6.8 | 8.2 | 6.9 | 5.6 | 0.5 | 6.1 | 6.7 | 6.7 | 5.6 |
| % Ret. on Equity | 15.1 | 14.7 | 18.9 | 16.3 | 12.1 | 1.0 | 10.8 | 12.1 | 12.2 | 10.0 |

Data as orig. reptd.; bef. results of disc. opers. and/or spec. items. Per share data adj. for stk. divs. as of ex-div. date. E-Estimated. NA-Not Available. NM-Not Meaningful. NR-Not Ranked.

**Office**—State Highway 268 East (P.O. Box 1111), North Wilkesboro, NC 28656. **Tel**—(910) 651-4000. **Website**—http://www.lowes.com **Chrmn**—R. L. Strickland. **Pres & COO**—R. L. Tillman. **SVP & Secy**—W. C. Warden Jr. **SVP, CFO & Treas**—T. E. Whiddon. **Investor Contacts**—W. Cliff Oxford, Clarrissa S. Felts. **Dirs**—W. A. Andres, J. M. Belk, C. A. Farmer, P. Fulton, J. F. Halpin, L. G. Herring, R. B. Long, C. B. Malone, R. G. Schwartz, R. L. Strickland, R. L. Tillman. **Transfer Agent & Registrar**—Wachovia Bank of North Carolina, Winston-Salem. **Incorporated**—in North Carolina in 1952. **Empl**— 53,492. **S&P Analyst:** Karen J. Sack, CFA

# STANDARD &POOR'S
## STOCK REPORTS

# MBNA Corp.

# 1391Y

NYSE Symbol **KRB**

In S&P 500

**17-MAY-97**

**Industry:** Consumer Finance

**Summary:** The nation's second largest lender through bank credit cards and leading issuer of affinity cards, MBNA also provides retail deposit and financial transaction processing services.

| | |
|---|---|
| **S&P Opinion: Buy (★★★★)** | Recent Price • 31¼  Yield • 1.5% |
| | 52 Wk Range • 37⅞-16¾  12-Mo. P/E • 22.2 |

**Quantitative Evaluations**

**Outlook**
(1 Lowest—5 Highest)
• **5**

**Fair Value**
• **42¼**

**Risk**
• **Average**

**Earn./Div. Rank**
• **A-**

**Technical Eval.**
• **Bullish** since 2/95

**Rel. Strength Rank**
(1 Lowest—99 Highest)
• **38**

**Insider Activity**
• **Neutral**

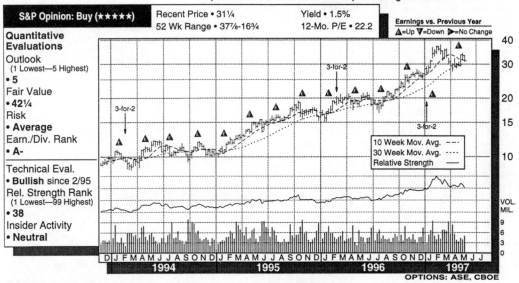

Earnings vs. Previous Year
▲=Up ▼=Down ▷=No Change

10 Week Mov. Avg. — - —
30 Week Mov. Avg. - - - -
Relative Strength ——

OPTIONS: ASE, CBOE

## Overview - 13-MAY-97

Industry trends favoring the growing use of credit cards and a rapidly expanding cardholder base should translate into solid earnings gains in 1997. MBNA's unique marketing strategy includes the targeting of individual membership organizations and developing co-branding relationships with commercial firms. Cardholders are thus encouraged to use the company's credit card over competing cards by showing support for endorsing firms or to receive various economic incentives for using the card. Aided by these factors, managed loans should increase better than 30% in 1997. Despite an expected rise in the level of delinquencies, partly reflecting a seasoning of receivables, MBNA's superior growth prospects and ability to increase market share and control credit costs should allow it to generate further strong earnings growth.

## Valuation - 13-MAY-97

After an early 1997 rise on the announcement that rival First USA was being acquired by Banc One Corp. at a healthy premium to market price, the shares were hit with pressure on news that another rival was experiencing credit quality problems. Fundamentally, the shares remain an excellent value, based on the company's projected growth rate. Delinquency levels, which remain the focus of much debate lately, have increased on weakness in the consumer credit sector but remain well below those of other credit card companies, reflecting the superior credit quality of MBNA's loan portfolio. Earnings should continue to be driven by a combination of exceptional credit card receivables growth, aided by successful marketing strategies and expanding market share, good control of credit costs, and greater operating efficiency. With earnings gains in excess of 20% expected in each of the next two years, we continue to recommend the shares for superior capital appreciation.

## Key Stock Statistics

| | | | |
|---|---|---|---|
| S&P EPS Est. 1997 | 1.65 | Tang. Bk. Value/Share | 4.46 |
| P/E on S&P Est. 1997 | 18.9 | Beta | 2.08 |
| S&P EPS Est. 1998 | 2.05 | Shareholders | 2,400 |
| Dividend Rate/Share | 0.48 | Market cap. (B) | $ 10.4 |
| Shs. outstg. (M) | 334.1 | Inst. holdings | 67% |
| Avg. daily vol. (M) | 0.808 | | |

Value of $10,000 invested 5 years ago: $ 68,025

## Fiscal Year Ending Dec. 31

| | 1998 | 1997 | 1996 | 1995 | 1994 | 1993 |
|---|---|---|---|---|---|---|
| **Revenues (Million $)** | | | | | | |
| 1Q | — | — | 719.9 | 536.4 | 389.7 | 307.4 |
| 2Q | — | — | 765.8 | 622.2 | 423.8 | 340.4 |
| 3Q | — | — | 824.2 | 689.7 | 492.8 | 359.3 |
| 4Q | — | — | 969.3 | 718.2 | 547.5 | 385.7 |
| Yr. | — | — | 3,279 | 2,565 | 1,853 | 1,393 |
| **Earnings Per Share ($)** | | | | | | |
| 1Q | — | 0.34 | 0.26 | 0.20 | 0.16 | 0.12 |
| 2Q | — | — | 0.29 | 0.23 | 0.17 | 0.14 |
| 3Q | — | — | 0.37 | 0.28 | 0.22 | 0.17 |
| 4Q | — | — | 0.41 | 0.32 | 0.24 | 0.19 |
| Yr. | E2.05 | E1.65 | 1.33 | 1.02 | 0.79 | 0.61 |

**Next earnings report expected: mid July**

**Dividend Data** (Dividends have been paid since 1991.)

| Amount ($) | Date Decl. | Ex-Div. Date | Stock of Record | Payment Date |
|---|---|---|---|---|
| 0.160 | Oct. 15 | Dec. 05 | Dec. 09 | Jan. 01 '97 |
| 3-for-2 | Oct. 15 | Jan. 02 | Dec. 16 | Dec. 31 '96 |
| 0.120 | Jan. 14 | Mar. 13 | Mar. 17 | Apr. 01 '97 |
| 0.120 | Apr. 21 | Jun. 12 | Jun. 16 | Jul. 01 '97 |

This report is for information purposes and should not be considered a solicitation to buy or sell any security. Neither S&P nor any other party guarantee its accuracy or make warranties regarding results from its usage. Redistribution is prohibited without written permission. Copyright © 1997

*A Division of The McGraw-Hill Companies*

## Business Summary - 13-MAY-97

MBNA Corp. is one of the world's largest lenders through bank credit cards, and is the leading issuer of affinity credit cards, marketed primarily through endorsements of membership associations and financial institutions. Credit cards issued to affinity group members often carry custom graphics and the name and logo of the endorsing group.

MBNA offers two general types of credit cards -- premium (gold) and standard -- issued under either the MasterCard or Visa name. The premium card is marketed to members of endorsing organizations, customers of endorsing financial institutions, and to MBNA's qualifying standard card customers. Premium card usage and average account balances are usually higher than those of standard card customers. The company uses the standard card for new customer acquisition and future premium account development.

The company also offers unsecured lines of credit and secured loans to individuals, including home equity loans and airplane loans, through its MBNA Consumer Services subsidiary, which is licensed in 42 states and the District of Columbia.

In addition, MBNA accepts deposits, primarily money market deposits and certificates of deposit, and offers credit insurance to its credit card customers. In 1996, it began offering property and casualty insurance, initially automobile insurance, and plans to offer life insurance in 1997.

Loan receivables at the end of 1996 were $10.1 billion, compared to $8.1 billion the year before. At 1996 year end, the reserve for loan losses, which is set aside for possible loan defaults, was $118.4 million (1.17% of loans receivable), up from $104.9 million (1.20%) a year earlier. The provision for loan losses, which is added to the reserve, amounted to $178.2 million in 1996, versus $138.2 million in 1995. Net credit losses, or the amount of loans actually written off as uncollectible, were $172.7 million in 1996 (1.98% of average loans), up from $134.7 million (1.91%) in 1995.

At December 31, 1996, total managed loans, which include securitized loans and loans held for securitization, amounted to $38.6 billion, a 45% increase over year-end 1995. Delinquency on total managed loans was 4.28% in 1996 (3.70% in 1995).

### Capitalization

**Long Term Debt:** $3,950,358,000 (12/96).
**Preferred Stock:** 12,000,000 shs. ($0.01 par).

### Per Share Data ($)

| (Year Ended Dec. 31) | 1996 | 1995 | 1994 | 1993 | 1992 | 1991 | 1990 | 1989 | 1988 | 1987 |
|---|---|---|---|---|---|---|---|---|---|---|
| Tangible Bk. Val. | 4.46 | 3.63 | 2.60 | 2.13 | 1.82 | 1.65 | NA | NA | NA | NA |
| Earnings | 1.33 | 1.03 | 0.79 | 0.61 | 0.51 | 0.44 | 0.39 | 0.31 | 0.27 | 0.23 |
| Dividends | 0.43 | 0.37 | 0.32 | 0.28 | 0.26 | 0.24 | NA | NA | NA | NA |
| Payout Ratio | 32% | 36% | 41% | 46% | 51% | 53% | NA | NA | NA | NA |
| Prices - High | 29⅛ | 19⅜ | 12⅛ | 11¼ | 7½ | 6 | NA | NA | NA | NA |
| - Low | 15⅛ | 10 | 8½ | 6⅜ | 5¼ | 3⅜ | NA | NA | NA | NA |
| P/E Ratio - High | 22 | 19 | 15 | 18 | 14 | 14 | NA | NA | NA | NA |
| - Low | 11 | 10 | 11 | 10 | 10 | 8 | NA | NA | NA | NA |

### Income Statement Analysis (Million $)

| | 1996 | 1995 | 1994 | 1993 | 1992 | 1991 | 1990 | 1989 | 1988 | 1987 |
|---|---|---|---|---|---|---|---|---|---|---|
| Net Int. Inc. | 640 | 544 | 532 | 474 | 358 | 240 | 164 | 117 | 150 | 172 |
| Tax Equiv. Adj. | 1.8 | 1.8 | 1.6 | 1.6 | 1.5 | 1.3 | Nil | Nil | Nil | Nil |
| Non Int. Inc. | 1,896 | 1,425 | 1,014 | 740 | 577 | 540 | 452 | 344 | 255 | 168 |
| Loan Loss Prov. | 178 | 138 | 108 | 99 | 97.5 | 86.7 | 58.0 | 43.3 | 63.3 | 65.9 |
| Exp./Op. Revs. | 62% | 63% | 64% | 64% | 60% | 59% | 58% | 56% | 50% | 43% |
| Pretax Inc. | 731 | 585 | 441 | 190 | 272 | 235 | 204 | 159 | 137 | NA |
| Eff. Tax Rate | 35% | 40% | 40% | NM | 37% | 36% | 37% | 34% | 34% | NA |
| Net Inc. | 474 | 353 | 267 | 208 | 173 | 149 | 129 | 104 | 90.0 | 75.0 |
| % Net Int. Marg. | 5.52 | 5.74 | 7.61 | 8.76 | 7.20 | 5.20 | 5.90 | 5.40 | 6.50 | NA |

### Balance Sheet & Other Fin. Data (Million $)

| | 1996 | 1995 | 1994 | 1993 | 1992 | 1991 | 1990 | 1989 | 1988 | 1987 |
|---|---|---|---|---|---|---|---|---|---|---|
| Earning Assets: | | | | | | | | | | |
| Money Mkt | 877 | 574 | 268 | 31.0 | 81.0 | 475 | 439 | 50.0 | NA | NA |
| Inv. Securities | 2,318 | 2,096 | 2,002 | 1,409 | 1,265 | 1,293 | 102 | 102 | NA | NA |
| Com'l Loans | Nil | Nil | Nil | Nil | Nil | Nil | Nil | Nil | Nil | Nil |
| Other Loans | 10,129 | 8,135 | 5,707 | 3,726 | 3,979 | 3,486 | 3,240 | 2,261 | 1,907 | 2,503 |
| Total Assets | 17,035 | 13,229 | 9,672 | 7,320 | 6,455 | 6,009 | 4,580 | 2,859 | 2,276 | 2,674 |
| Demand Deposits | 234 | 170 | 101 | 71.0 | 70.0 | 65.0 | 87.0 | 126 | NA | NA |
| Time Deposits | 9,918 | 8,439 | 6,531 | 5,171 | 4,498 | 5,029 | 4,115 | 1,617 | NA | NA |
| LT Debt | 3,950 | 2,658 | 1,564 | 780 | 471 | Nil | 0.6 | 27.4 | 48.8 | 53.4 |
| Common Eqty. | 1,704 | 1,265 | 920 | 769 | 661 | 592 | 219 | 262 | 209 | 183 |
| % Ret. on Assets | 3.1 | 3.1 | 3.2 | 3.2 | 3.0 | 2.8 | 3.9 | 4.1 | 3.5 | 3.0 |
| % Ret. on Equity | 32.0 | 35.5 | 32.7 | 30.0 | 28.6 | 37.0 | 49.0 | 37.2 | 38.3 | 49.0 |
| % Loan Loss Resv. | 1.5 | 2.2 | 1.8 | 2.6 | 2.5 | 2.8 | 3.0 | 3.6 | 3.9 | 2.2 |
| % Loans/Deposits | 74.3 | 94.5 | 86.1 | 71.1 | 87.1 | 68.4 | 77.1 | 129.7 | 125.3 | 203.1 |
| % Equity to Assets | 9.8 | 9.6 | 9.7 | 10.5 | 10.4 | 7.6 | 7.9 | 11.1 | 9.3 | 6.5 |

Data as orig. reptd.; bef. results of disc. opers. and/or spec. items. Per share data adj. for stk. divs. as of ex-div. date. E-Estimated. NA-Not Available. NM-Not Meaningful. NR-Not Ranked.

**Office**—400 Christiana Rd., Newark, DE 19713. **Tel**—(800) 362-6255; (302) 453-9930. **Chrmn & CEO**—A. Lerner. **Pres**—C. M. Cawley. **EVP-CFO & Treas**—M. S. Kaufman.**Investor Contact**—Brian D. Dalphon (302-432-1251). **Dirs**—J. H. Berick, C. M. Cawley, B. R. Civiletti, A. Lerner, R. D. Lerner, S. L. Markowitz, M. Rosenthal. **Transfer Agent & Registrar**—National City Bank, Cleveland. **Incorporated**—in Maryland in 1990. **Empl**—15,000. **S&P Analyst:** Stephen R. Biggar

# McAfee Associates, Inc.    4558P

Nasdaq Symbol **MCAF**

**22-MAY-97**

**Industry:** Computer (Software & Services)

**Summary:** McAfee develops, markets, distributes and supports network security and management software products.

| S&P Opinion: Accumulate (★★★★) | Recent Price • 60½ 52 Wk Range • 65½-23⅞ | Yield • Nil 12-Mo. P/E • 56.0 | Earnings vs. Previous Year ▲=Up ▼=Down ▷=No Change |

## Quantitative Evaluations

**Outlook** (1 Lowest—5 Highest)
• **NA**

**Fair Value**
• **NA**

**Risk**
• **High**

**Earn./Div. Rank**
• **NR**

---

**Technical Eval.**
• **Bullish** since 5/97

**Rel. Strength Rank** (1 Lowest—99 Highest)
• **95**

**Insider Activity**
• **NA**

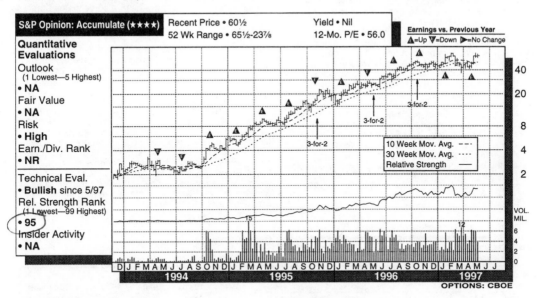

Legend: 10 Week Mov. Avg. – – –; 30 Week Mov. Avg. · · · ·; Relative Strength —

OPTIONS: CBOE

## Overview - 07-MAY-97

McAfee Associates provides anti-virus, network management, and help-desk support software. The company pioneered software distribution over the Internet and has grabbed 70% of unit volume shipments in anti-virus software. With a two year subscription licensing period, MCAF boasts approximately 90% recurring revenue. From its origins in virus detection, MCAF has developed and acquired technologies in network management and most recently help-desk software, with the acquisition of Vycor Corp. in March 1996. The company recently discovered UNIX and e-mail viruses and plans to offer protection from new ActiveX viruses. Revenues should continue to grow over 45% for the next two years. Gross margins are expected to narrow slightly due to a gradual shift in the sales mix away from products distributed over the Web. As a result, earnings should advance between 40-45% in 1997 and 1998.

## Valuation - 07-MAY-97

The shares jumped over 15% in late April as investors responded favorably to strong first quarter results that boasted a 117% rise in revenue. McAfee operates in three high-growth businesses and has gained solid market share in anti-virus software. In addition, network management software market share has grown considerably and the Vycor help-desk unit is winning large enterprise accounts. At current levels we feel that investors should add to positions, and we continue to give MCAF shares an accumulate rating. Based on our revised 1997 and 1998 earnings per share estimates of $1.50 and $2.05, respectively, the shares are trading at a discount to the company's long-term growth rate of 35-40%.

## Key Stock Statistics

| | | | |
|---|---|---|---|
| S&P EPS Est. 1997 | 1.50 | Tang. Bk. Value/Share | 3.05 |
| P/E on S&P Est. 1997 | 40.3 | Beta | NA |
| S&P EPS Est. 1998 | 2.05 | Shareholders | 300 |
| Dividend Rate/Share | Nil | Market cap. (B) | $ 3.1 |
| Shs. outstg. (M) | 48.7 | Inst. holdings | 100% |
| Avg. daily vol. (M) | 1.009 | | |

Value of $10,000 invested 5 years ago: NA

### Fiscal Year Ending Dec. 31

| | 1997 | 1996 | 1995 | 1994 | 1993 | 1992 |
|---|---|---|---|---|---|---|
| **Revenues (Million $)** | | | | | | |
| 1Q | 73.36 | 33.85 | 16.52 | 5.72 | 4.06 | 2.94 |
| 2Q | — | 40.77 | 18.57 | 8.30 | 4.34 | 3.39 |
| 3Q | — | 47.29 | 25.61 | 8.71 | 4.56 | 3.56 |
| 4Q | — | 59.22 | 29.36 | 10.17 | 4.95 | 3.79 |
| Yr. | — | 181.1 | 90.07 | 32.90 | 17.91 | 13.68 |
| **Earnings Per Share ($)** | | | | | | |
| 1Q | 0.37 | 0.02 | 0.07 | -0.07 | 0.04 | — |
| 2Q | E0.34 | 0.18 | 0.08 | -0.04 | 0.05 | — |
| 3Q | E0.31 | 0.24 | 0.01 | 0.06 | 0.05 | — |
| 4Q | E0.48 | 0.29 | 0.14 | 0.07 | 0.05 | — |
| Yr. | E1.50 | 0.73 | 0.30 | 0.03 | 0.18 | 0.17 |

**Next earnings report expected: late July**

### Dividend Data

| Amount ($) | Date Decl. | Ex-Div. Date | Stock of Record | Payment Date |
|---|---|---|---|---|
| 3-for-2 | Sep. 17 | Oct. 18 | Oct. 07 | Oct. 17 '96 |

This report is for information purposes and should not be considered a solicitation to buy or sell any security. Neither S&P nor any other party guarantee its accuracy or make warranties regarding results from its usage. Redistribution is prohibited without written permission. Copyright © 1997   *A Division of The McGraw-Hill Companies*

## Business Summary - 07-MAY-97

McAfee Associates (MCAF) has been one of the most effective users of the Internet as a distribution medium. Since its first day, McAfee has put its software on the Internet for free downloading. World Wide Web users can log on to the company's website and take whatever they want. After a trial period of 30 days, they are asked to pay for the software. With one of the top five most frequently visited websites on the Internet, McAfee has been able to command a hefty 70% market share for the anti-virus software. From this widespread installed base, the company has expanded its product offerings to network anti-virus software, local-area network (LAN) management tools, help desk software, and storage management software.

MCAF provides industry-leading network security products for anti-virus protection as well as client/server network management tools. VirusScan, the company's flagship product, scans for known and unknown viruses prior to installation of a PC. When the scan is completed, the program becomes memory resident and protects systems from further infection.

Moving beyond virus protection for the PC, MCAF offers numerous anti-virus protection software to detect viruses over networks: NetShield provides virus protection for network file servers, Webscan scans Web browsers and e-mail systems for viruses, Bootshield provides pre-boot protection from boot-sector viruses, and ROMShield checks computers' BIOS prior to booting up a system.

The company also offers network management tools which help network administrators manage and maintain LAN resources. Products include Saber LAN Workstation (SLW), a suite product that provides software metering, hardware and software inventory, printer management, and file auditing. MCAF also sells point products separately from SLW, such as SiteMeter, SaberTools, and SiteInventory.

In April 1996, MCAF acquired Vycor Corp., a maker of client-server help desk software. Vycor Enterprise is a suite of help desk tools offering problem management, resolution and prevention. The suite provides access to trouble ticketing and knowledge bases through telephony, e-mail and Web browsers.

During the first quarter of 1997, McAfee released the latest version of its flagship anti-virus program, VirusScan 3.0, as well as GroupScan 3.0 and GroupShield 3.0 for the groupware anti-virus market. In February 1997, McAfee discovered the first macro computer virus to specifically target users of Microsoft's popular Microsoft Mail (MS-Mail) e-mail software. The virus, which is called ShareFun, searches through a user's e-mail directory and automatically generates and transmits e-mail messages with virus-infected attachments. ShareFun also infects all subsequent Word documents that are opened by the user from within Word.

### Capitalization

**Long Term Debt:** None (3/97).

### Per Share Data ($)

| (Year Ended Dec. 31) | 1996 | 1995 | 1994 | 1993 | 1992 | 1991 | 1990 | 1989 | 1988 | 1987 |
|---|---|---|---|---|---|---|---|---|---|---|
| Tangible Bk. Val. | 3.05 | 1.31 | 0.50 | 0.49 | 0.27 | NA | NA | NA | NA | NA |
| Cash Flow | 0.85 | 0.36 | 0.06 | 0.19 | 0.17 | NA | NA | NA | NA | NA |
| Earnings | 0.73 | 0.30 | 0.03 | 0.18 | 0.17 | 0.09 | NA | NA | NA | NA |
| Dividends | Nil | Nil | Nil | Nil | Nil | Nil | NA | NA | NA | NA |
| Payout Ratio | Nil | Nil | Nil | Nil | Nil | Nil | NA | NA | NA | NA |
| Prices - High | 52$\frac{7}{8}$ | 23$\frac{1}{2}$ | 6 | 6 | 6$\frac{7}{8}$ | NA | NA | NA | NA | NA |
| - Low | 13$\frac{7}{8}$ | 4$\frac{3}{8}$ | 1$\frac{15}{16}$ | 1$\frac{5}{16}$ | 3$\frac{7}{8}$ | NA | NA | NA | NA | NA |
| P/E Ratio - High | 72 | 78 | 180 | 33 | 41 | NA | NA | NA | NA | NA |
| - Low | 19 | 15 | 58 | 7 | 23 | NA | NA | NA | NA | NA |

### Income Statement Analysis (Million $)

| | 1996 | 1995 | 1994 | 1993 | 1992 | 1991 | 1990 | 1989 | 1988 | 1987 |
|---|---|---|---|---|---|---|---|---|---|---|
| Revs. | 181 | 90.1 | 32.9 | 17.9 | 13.7 | NA | NA | NA | NA | NA |
| Oper. Inc. | 73.2 | 40.0 | 2.9 | 11.7 | 10.5 | NA | NA | NA | NA | NA |
| Depr. | 6.0 | 3.0 | 1.2 | 0.2 | 0.1 | NA | NA | NA | NA | NA |
| Int. Exp. | Nil | Nil | Nil | Nil | 4.5 | NA | NA | NA | NA | NA |
| Pretax Inc. | 70.7 | 26.0 | 2.3 | 12.2 | 6.1 | NA | NA | NA | NA | NA |
| Eff. Tax Rate | 45% | 43% | 40% | 40% | 19% | NA | NA | NA | NA | NA |
| Net Inc. | 39.0 | 14.9 | 1.4 | 7.3 | 11.1 | NA | NA | NA | NA | NA |

### Balance Sheet & Other Fin. Data (Million $)

| | 1996 | 1995 | 1994 | 1993 | 1992 | 1991 | 1990 | 1989 | 1988 | 1987 |
|---|---|---|---|---|---|---|---|---|---|---|
| Cash | 127 | 55.4 | 26.5 | 27.7 | NA | NA | NA | NA | NA | NA |
| Curr. Assets | 164 | 90.7 | 45.2 | 37.3 | NA | NA | NA | NA | NA | NA |
| Total Assets | 195 | 104 | 56.0 | 39.0 | 29.0 | NA | NA | NA | NA | NA |
| Curr. Liab. | 41.3 | 35.8 | 24.7 | 15.7 | NA | NA | NA | NA | NA | NA |
| LT Debt | Nil | Nil | Nil | Nil | Nil | NA | NA | NA | NA | NA |
| Common Eqty. | 150 | 63.5 | 23.0 | 18.3 | 10.3 | NA | NA | NA | NA | NA |
| Total Cap. | 150 | 63.5 | 23.0 | 18.3 | 10.3 | NA | NA | NA | NA | NA |
| Cap. Exp. | 7.2 | 1.6 | 0.7 | 0.5 | 0.2 | NA | NA | NA | NA | NA |
| Cash Flow | 45.0 | 17.9 | 2.6 | 7.5 | 11.2 | NA | NA | NA | NA | NA |
| Curr. Ratio | 3.9 | 2.5 | 1.8 | 2.4 | NA | NA | NA | NA | NA | NA |
| % LT Debt of Cap. | Nil | Nil | Nil | Nil | Nil | NA | NA | NA | NA | NA |
| % Net Inc.of Revs. | 21.5 | 16.6 | 4.2 | 40.8 | 80.9 | NA | NA | NA | NA | NA |
| % Ret. on Assets | 26.1 | 16.8 | 2.9 | 21.5 | 64.7 | NA | NA | NA | NA | NA |
| % Ret. on Equity | 36.6 | 30.3 | 6.7 | 51.1 | NM | NA | NA | NA | NA | NA |

Data as orig. reptd.; bef. results of disc. opers. and/or spec. items. Per share data adj. for stk. divs. as of ex-div. date. E-Estimated. NA-Not Available. NM-Not Meaningful. NR-Not Ranked.

**Office**—2710 Walsh Avenue, Santa Clara, CA 95051**Tel**—(408) 988-3822 **Website**—http://www.mcafee.com **Chrmn, Pres & CEO**—W. L. Larson. **VP-Fin & CFO**—P. Goyal. **Investor Contact**—R. T. Duryea. **VP-Secy**—R. J. Schwei. **Dirs**—J. Bolger, J. T. Chambers, L. G. Denend , V. Gemmell, E. L. Harper, W L . Larson. **Transfer Agent & Registrar**—Chemical Trust Company of California**Incorporated**—in Delaware.**Empl**— 0. S&P Analyst: Aydin Tuncer

# ✓Medtronic, Inc.

## 1466P

NYSE Symbol **MDT**

**In S&P 500**

**17-MAY-97**

**Industry:**
Health Care (Medical Products & Supplies)

**Summary:** The world's leading producer of implantable cardiac pacemakers, this company also makes implantable defibrillators, heart valves, and other cardiac and neurological products.

| S&P Opinion: Accumulate (★★★★) | Recent Price • 68 | Yield • 0.6% |
| --- | --- | --- |
| | 52 Wk Range • 71¾-47 | 12-Mo. P/E • 31.0 |

**Quantitative Evaluations**

**Outlook**
(1 Lowest—5 Highest)
• **2⁻**

**Fair Value**
• **65¾**

**Risk**
• **Average**

**Earn./Div. Rank**
• **A+**

**Technical Eval.**
• **Bullish** since 4/92

**Rel. Strength Rank**
(1 Lowest—99 Highest)
• **62**

**Insider Activity**
• **Unfavorable**

**Earnings vs. Previous Year**
▲=Up ▼=Down ▷=No Change

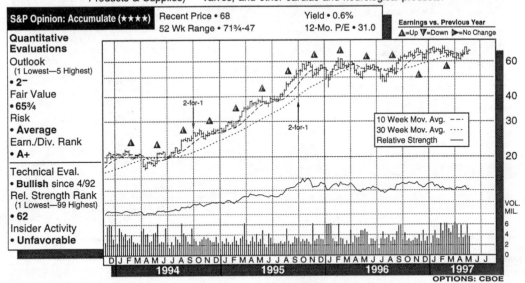

10 Week Mov. Avg. – – –
30 Week Mov. Avg. · · · ·
Relative Strength ——

2-for-1

2-for-1

VOL. MIL.

OPTIONS: CBOE

## Overview - 08-APR-97

Medtronic should produce another 20% or better gain in sales in FY 98 (Apr.), bolstered by continued strong demand for MDT's state-of-the-art pacemakers and other cardiac and neurological products. The pacing business should be spurred by gains in replacement unit sales and contributions from new state-of-the-art Thera and Kappa pacers. Strengthened by the new Jewel implantable defibrillator with Active Can technology, another robust advance is seen for tachyarrhythmia (rapid heart beating) product sales, although increasing competition in that market may temper the gain. New products such as the beStent and Wiktor coronary stents are spurring vascular product sales, while rapid medical acceptance in Europe of neurostimulation to treat Parkinson's disease is boosting neurological volume. Margins should widen on the higher volume, a better product mix and productivity enhancements.

## Valuation - 08-APR-97

The shares have held up well during the recent market turbulence, buoyed by strength in defensive medical issues and the company's continued robust sales and earnings growth. MDT holds about 50% of the world bradycardia pacing market, which is growing at 8% to 10% a year. Bolstered by its new Jewel family of implantable defibrillators, Medtronic also has about 45% of the tachyarrhythmia treatment market, which is growing 20%-25% annually. The development of innovative new medical products and strategic acquisitions have enabled MDT to increase its share of all markets it serves to 33% in fiscal 1996, up from 24% in fiscal 1991. Continued projected rapid earnings growth appears to justify the rich multiple enjoyed by the shares, which remain attractive for above-average long-term appreciation.

## Key Stock Statistics

| | | | |
| --- | --- | --- | --- |
| S&P EPS Est. 1997 | 2.22 | Tang. Bk. Value/Share | 5.62 |
| P/E on S&P Est. 1997 | 30.6 | Beta | 0.98 |
| S&P EPS Est. 1998 | 2.65 | Shareholders | 21,900 |
| Dividend Rate/Share | 0.38 | Market cap. (B) | $ 16.2 |
| Shs. outstg. (M) | 238.2 | Inst. holdings | 63% |
| Avg. daily vol. (M) | 0.834 | | |

Value of $10,000 invested 5 years ago: $ 29,856

## Fiscal Year Ending Apr. 30

| | 1998 | 1997 | 1996 | 1995 | 1994 | 1993 |
| --- | --- | --- | --- | --- | --- | --- |
| **Revenues (Million $)** | | | | | | |
| 1Q | — | 600.9 | 523.8 | 403.8 | 331.3 | 330.0 |
| 2Q | — | 598.2 | 518.5 | 408.1 | 332.1 | 332.0 |
| 3Q | — | 598.8 | 529.2 | 413.7 | 344.6 | 308.2 |
| 4Q | — | — | 596.1 | 516.7 | 393.0 | 358.3 |
| Yr. | — | — | 2,169 | 1,742 | 1,391 | 1,328 |
| **Earnings Per Share ($)** | | | | | | |
| 1Q | — | 0.53 | 0.43 | 0.28 | 0.23 | 0.19 |
| 2Q | — | 0.54 | 0.45 | 0.30 | 0.24 | 0.25 |
| 3Q | — | 0.54 | 0.47 | 0.31 | 0.25 | 0.20 |
| 4Q | — | E0.61 | 0.54 | 0.38 | 0.29 | 0.24 |
| Yr. | E2.65 | E2.22 | 1.88 | 1.27 | 1.01 | 0.89 |

**Next earnings report expected: late May**

**Dividend Data** (Dividends have been paid since 1977.)

| Amount ($) | Date Decl. | Ex-Div. Date | Stock of Record | Payment Date |
| --- | --- | --- | --- | --- |
| 0.095 | Jun. 27 | Jul. 02 | Jul. 05 | Aug. 02 '96 |
| 0.095 | Aug. 28 | Oct. 09 | Oct. 11 | Nov. 01 '96 |
| 0.095 | Nov. 21 | Jan. 08 | Jan. 10 | Jan. 31 '97 |
| 0.095 | Mar. 08 | Apr. 02 | Apr. 04 | Apr. 30 '97 |

This report is for information purposes and should not be considered a solicitation to buy or sell any security. Neither S&P nor any other party guarantee its accuracy or make warranties regarding results from its usage. Redistribution is prohibited without written permission. Copyright © 1997

*A Division of The McGraw-Hill Companies*

## Business Summary - 08-APR-97

Medtronic is the world's leading medical technology company, specializing in cardiac pacemakers and defibrillators. A broad line of other products such as angioplasty catheters, stents, heart valves, and neurological products are also offered. Medtronic was formed in 1949 by Earl Bakken and Palmer Hermundslie. Bakken invented the first battery-powered cardiac pacemaker in the late 1950s. Foreign operations provided 43% of sales and 40% of profits in FY 96. Sales by business segments in recent fiscal years were:

|  | FY 96 | FY 95 |
|---|---|---|
| Cardiac pacing products | 68% | 66% |
| Nonpacing cardiovascular items | 24% | 26% |
| Neurological and other products | 8% | 8% |

The company is the world's leading producer of implantable cardiac pacemakers, with about half of the $2.3 billion worldwide bradycardia (slow or irregular heart beating) pacing market. Cardiac pacing products consist of implantable pacemakers, leads and accessories. Pacemakers, which are sold under the Thera, Elite, Kappa and other names, include models that can be noninvasively programmed by a physician to adjust

sensing, electrical pulse intensity, duration, rate and other factors, as well as pacers that can sense in both the upper and lower chambers of the heart and produce appropriate impulses.

A full line of implantable defibrillators is sold under the Jewel name for the treatment of tachyarrhythmia (abnormally fast heart rhythms). These devices monitor the heart and, when a very rapid heart rhythm is detected, send either a series of electrical impulses or an electrical shock to return the heart to a normal rhythm. MDT has an estimated 45% share of this market, which is estimated at about $700 million worldwide.

Nonpacing cardiovascular products include vascular and cardiac surgical products. Vascular devices consist primarily of coronary angioplasty catheters, coronary stents and electrophysiological catheters. Cardiac surgery products include heart valves, cannulae, oxygenators and other blood management items.

Neurological and other products include implantable neurostimulation systems, external neurostimulation devices, a drug administration system, electrodes and cables and various related devices.

### Capitalization

**Long Term Liabilities:** $155,402,000 (1/31/97).

---

### Per Share Data ($)

| (Year Ended Apr. 30) | 1996 | 1995 | 1994 | 1993 | 1992 | 1991 | 1990 | 1989 | 1988 | 1987 |
|---|---|---|---|---|---|---|---|---|---|---|
| Tangible Bk. Val. | 5.62 | 5.78 | 4.53 | 3.64 | 3.35 | 2.87 | 2.49 | 2.21 | 1.86 | 1.52 |
| Cash Flow | 2.36 | 1.74 | 1.29 | 1.12 | 0.93 | 0.76 | 0.64 | 0.58 | 0.51 | 0.44 |
| Earnings | 1.88 | 1.27 | 1.01 | 0.89 | 0.68 | 0.56 | 0.51 | 0.46 | 0.39 | 0.33 |
| Dividends | 0.32 | 0.21 | 0.17 | 0.14 | 0.12 | 0.10 | 0.09 | 0.08 | 0.07 | 0.06 |
| Payout Ratio | 17% | 16% | 17% | 15% | 18% | 18% | 17% | 16% | 16% | 17% |
| Cal. Yrs. | 1995 | 1994 | 1993 | 1992 | 1991 | 1990 | 1989 | 1988 | 1987 | 1986 |
| Prices - High | 60 | 28 | 23⅞ | 26⅛ | 23⅝ | 11½ | 8⅞ | 6¼ | 6¾ | 5¾ |
|    - Low | 26¼ | 17¼ | 12⅞ | 15⅞ | 9⅝ | 7⅜ | 4⅞ | 4¼ | 4 | 2¾ |
| P/E Ratio - High | 32 | 22 | 24 | 29 | 35 | 20 | 18 | 14 | 17 | 18 |
|    - Low | 14 | 14 | 13 | 18 | 14 | 13 | 10 | 9 | 10 | 8 |

### Income Statement Analysis (Million $)

| | 1996 | 1995 | 1994 | 1993 | 1992 | 1991 | 1990 | 1989 | 1988 | 1987 |
|---|---|---|---|---|---|---|---|---|---|---|
| Revs. | 2,169 | 1,742 | 1,391 | 1,328 | 1,177 | 1,021 | 837 | 742 | 653 | 502 |
| Oper. Inc. | 759 | 543 | 396 | 332 | 305 | 243 | 195 | 174 | 155 | 132 |
| Depr. | 112 | 107 | 63.0 | 54.7 | 59.4 | 37.0 | 30.2 | 26.4 | 24.8 | 26.4 |
| Int. Exp. | 8.0 | 9.0 | 8.2 | 10.4 | 13.4 | 13.8 | 10.1 | 8.3 | 5.7 | 4.1 |
| Pretax Inc. | 668 | 442 | 347 | 313 | 243 | 196 | 160 | 150 | 131 | 109 |
| Eff. Tax Rate | 34% | 34% | 33% | 33% | 34% | 32% | 32% | 35% | 34% | 32% |
| Net Inc. | 438 | 294 | 232 | 212 | 162 | 133 | 109 | 97.0 | 87.0 | 74.0 |

### Balance Sheet & Other Fin. Data (Million $)

| | 1996 | 1995 | 1994 | 1993 | 1992 | 1991 | 1990 | 1989 | 1988 | 1987 |
|---|---|---|---|---|---|---|---|---|---|---|
| Cash | 461 | 324 | 181 | 156 | 110 | 113 | 52.0 | 51.0 | 79.0 | 114 |
| Curr. Assets | 1,343 | 1,104 | 846 | 775 | 696 | 612 | 479 | 421 | 421 | 366 |
| Total Assets | 2,503 | 1,947 | 1,623 | 1,286 | 1,163 | 1,024 | 856 | 760 | 641 | 560 |
| Curr. Liab. | 525 | 456 | 439 | 348 | 309 | 292 | 260 | 232 | 189 | 126 |
| LT Debt | 15.3 | 14.2 | 20.2 | 10.9 | 8.6 | 7.9 | 8.0 | 7.8 | 9.1 | 5.5 |
| Common Eqty. | 1,789 | 1,335 | 1,053 | 841 | 796 | 683 | 541 | 474 | 396 | 387 |
| Total Cap. | 1,850 | 1,385 | 1,090 | 857 | 823 | 706 | 566 | 495 | 425 | 410 |
| Cap. Exp. | 164 | 96.9 | 86.0 | 87.4 | 77.2 | 73.7 | 58.5 | 56.3 | 37.7 | 27.0 |
| Cash Flow | 549 | 401 | 295 | 266 | 221 | 170 | 139 | 124 | 111 | 100 |
| Curr. Ratio | 2.6 | 2.4 | 1.9 | 2.2 | 2.3 | 2.1 | 1.8 | 1.8 | 2.2 | 2.9 |
| % LT Debt of Cap. | 1.0 | 1.0 | 1.9 | 1.3 | 1.0 | 1.1 | 1.4 | 1.6 | 2.1 | 1.3 |
| % Net Inc.of Revs. | 20.1 | 16.9 | 16.7 | 15.9 | 13.7 | 13.1 | 13.0 | 13.1 | 13.2 | 14.7 |
| % Ret. on Assets | 19.7 | 16.5 | 15.9 | 17.5 | 14.8 | 13.6 | 13.4 | 13.9 | 14.8 | 13.7 |
| % Ret. on Equity | 28.0 | 24.7 | 24.5 | 26.2 | 21.9 | 20.9 | 21.3 | 22.4 | 22.7 | 20.3 |

Data as orig. reptd.; bef. results of disc. opers. and/or spec. items. Per share data adj. for stk. divs. as of ex-div. date. E-Estimated. NA-Not Available. NM-Not Meaningful. NR-Not Ranked.

**Office**—7000 Central Ave. N.E., Minneapolis, MN 55432. **Tel**—(612) 574-4000; (800) 328-2518. **Website**—http://www.medtronic. com **Chrmn & CEO**—W. W. George. **Vice Chrmn**—G. D. Nelson. **Pres & COO**—A. D. Collins, Jr. **SVP & Secy**—R. E. Lund. **SVP & CFO**—R. L. Ryan. **Investor Contact**—Christopher O'Connell (612-574-3038). **Dirs**—F. C. Blodgett, A. D. Collins, Jr., W. W. George, A. M. Gotto, Jr., B. P. Healy, T. E. Holloran, G. D. Nelson, R. L. Schall, J. W. Schuler, G. W. Simonson, G. M. Sprenger, R. A. Swalin. **Transfer Agent & Registrar**—Norwest Bank Minnesota, South St. Paul. **Incorporated**—in Minnesota in 1957. **Empl**— 8,896. **S&P Analyst:** H.B. Saftlas

# MGIC Investment

## 1400R

NYSE Symbol **MTG**

In S&P 500

**17-MAY-97**

**Industry:** Financial (Diversified)

**Summary:** Through its Mortgage Guaranty Insurance Corp. unit, this holding company is a leading U.S. provider of private mortgage insurance coverage.

| | |
|---|---|
| **S&P Opinion: Accumulate (★★★★)** | |

| Recent Price • 86⅞ | Yield • 0.2% |
|---|---|
| 52 Wk Range • 90⅝-53½ | 12-Mo. P/E • 19.1 |

**Quantitative Evaluations**

Outlook
(1 Lowest—5 Highest)
• **4+**

Fair Value
• **105**

Risk
• **Low**

Earn./Div. Rank
• **NR**

Technical Eval.
• **Bullish** since 9/94

Rel. Strength Rank
(1 Lowest—99 Highest)
• **86**

Insider Activity
• **Neutral**

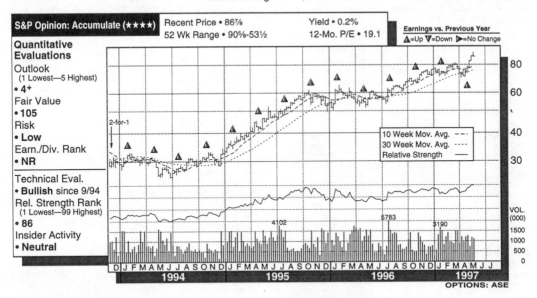

Earnings vs. Previous Year
▲=Up ▼=Down ▶=No Change

10 Week Mov. Avg. ---
30 Week Mov. Avg. ·····
Relative Strength —

2-for-1

VOL. (000)

1500
1000
500
0

D J F M A M J J A S O N D J F M A M J J A S O N D J F M A M J J A S O N D J F M A M J J
**1994** **1995** **1996** **1997**

OPTIONS: ASE

## Overview - 10-APR-97

Wisconsin-based MGIC Investment Corp., the largest mortgage insurer in the U.S., reported 24% year to year growth in earnings per share in 1997's first quarter, on a 17% rise in revenues. Net premiums earned and investment income were up 18% and 22%, respectively, while expenses advanced just 9.2%. New business volume should remain robust in the coming quarters, as home buyers move to minimize the impact of rising credit costs by locking in current interest rates. With favorable industry trends in place, we expect MGIC to achieve an approximate 20% increase in earnings in 1997, fueled by growth in insurance in force, investment portfolio gains, and improved efficiency and loss performance. The percentage of loans in default has edged up in recent quarters, rising to 1.97% at March 31, 1997, from 1.70% a year earlier. While defaults may trend higher over the course of 1997, the level should remain manageable, aided by the use of sophisticated credit scoring models.

## Valuation - 10-APR-97

MGIC's shares are down about 3%, year to date, closely following the decline in the broader market. Despite the recent weakness, we reiterate our accumulate recommendation as we believe the company is well positioned for a strong 1997. With earnings expected to advance around 20% this year, the shares remain attractive at 14X our 1997 earnings estimate of $5.20 a share. Favorable industry and economic trends should allow for the continued expansion of MGIC's insurance in force. Coupled with an improved risk profile and further operational efficiencies, this growth should allow for superior results over the remainder of the year.

## Key Stock Statistics

| | | | |
|---|---|---|---|
| S&P EPS Est. 1997 | 5.20 | Tang. Bk. Value/Share | 23.17 |
| P/E on S&P Est. 1997 | 16.7 | Beta | 1.51 |
| S&P EPS Est. 1998 | 6.10 | Shareholders | 400 |
| Dividend Rate/Share | 0.20 | Market cap. (B) | $ 5.1 |
| Shs. outstg. (M) | 59.0 | Inst. holdings | 90% |
| Avg. daily vol. (M) | 0.209 | | |

Value of $10,000 invested 5 years ago: $ 42,514

## Fiscal Year Ending Dec. 31

| | 1998 | 1997 | 1996 | 1995 | 1994 | 1993 |
|---|---|---|---|---|---|---|
| **Revenues (Million $)** | | | | | | |
| 1Q | — | 205.1 | 174.6 | 140.2 | 118.0 | 90.70 |
| 2Q | — | — | 182.3 | 148.6 | 123.0 | 98.05 |
| 3Q | — | — | 189.7 | 159.3 | 127.9 | 105.1 |
| 4Q | — | — | 199.1 | 169.8 | 133.4 | 109.7 |
| Yr. | — | — | 745.6 | 617.9 | 502.2 | 403.5 |

| | 1998 | 1997 | 1996 | 1995 | 1994 | 1993 |
|---|---|---|---|---|---|---|
| **Earnings Per Share ($)** | | | | | | |
| 1Q | — | 1.21 | 0.98 | 0.76 | 0.56 | 0.43 |
| 2Q | — | E1.26 | 1.05 | 0.84 | 0.65 | 0.54 |
| 3Q | — | E1.33 | 1.11 | 0.90 | 0.71 | 0.57 |
| 4Q | — | E1.40 | 1.19 | 0.99 | 0.78 | 0.61 |
| Yr. | E6.10 | E5.20 | 4.33 | 3.50 | 2.70 | 2.16 |

**Next earnings report expected: mid July**

**Dividend Data** (Dividends have been paid since 1991.)

| Amount ($) | Date Decl. | Ex-Div. Date | Stock of Record | Payment Date |
|---|---|---|---|---|
| 0.040 | Oct. 24 | Nov. 06 | Nov. 08 | Dec. 02 '96 |
| 0.040 | Jan. 23 | Feb. 05 | Feb. 07 | Mar. 03 '97 |
| 0.050 | May. 01 | May. 15 | May. 19 | Jun. 02 '97 |
| 2-for-1 | May. 01 | Jun. 03 | May. 19 | Jun. 02 '97 |

This report is for information purposes and should not be considered a solicitation to buy or sell any security. Neither S&P nor any other party guarantee its accuracy or make warranties regarding results from its usage. Redistribution is prohibited without written permission. Copyright © 1997

*A Division of The McGraw·Hill Companies*

### Business Summary - 10-APR-97

Since 1957, MGIC Investment Corp. has helped millions of Americans afford a new home by providing insurance to mortgage lenders on low down payment loans. As a leader in the private mortgage insurance (PMI) industry, MGIC is well positioned to take advantage of favorable market trends, such as growth in affordable housing programs and increased PMI coverage requirements by the Federal Home Loan Mortgage Corp. ("Freddie Mac") and the Federal National Mortgage Association ("Fannie Mae"). In recent years, the company has parlayed its customer-service orientation and credit quality focus into consistent, strong revenue and earnings growth. In addition to mortgage insurance, MGIC provides underwriting and contract services related to home mortgage lending.

Operating through Mortgage Guarantee Insurance Corp., MGIC Investment generates the vast majority of its revenues through premiums earned on mortgage insurance. Mortgage insurance expands home ownership opportunities by enabling buyers to purchase homes with less than a 20% down payment. In the event of a home owner default, PMI reduces, and in some cases eliminates, the loss to the insured institution. Typically, mortgage lenders require the borrowers to fund the insurance premiums. Furthermore, by improving the credit quality of the underlying loans, mortgage insurance facilitates the sale of low down payment mortgage loans in the secondary market, principally to Freddie Mac and Fannie Mae.

With its close ties to the housing market, the private mortgage insurance business can be highly cyclical. MGIC, however, has reported steady, consistent revenue and earnings growth in recent years. With rising home ownership rates and the inability of many first time buyers to produce 20% down payments, this trend is likely to continue.

Since MGIC pays the coverage percentage of the claim amount on defaults (generally 6% to 30%), adequate credit controls are imperative. Despite the recent upward trend in losses (the percentage of insured loans in default rose to 1.97% at March 31, 1997 versus 1.70% a year earlier), the company has demonstrated a sound risk management policy, characterized by a geographically diverse portfolio, sophisticated credit scoring models and aggressive loss mitigation efforts.

Through investments in technology, MGIC has been able to achieve economies of scale. Expenses as a percentage of revenues fell to 19% at the end of 1997's first quarter, from 21% a year earlier.

### Capitalization

**Long Term Debt:** None (3/97).

### Per Share Data ($)

| (Year Ended Dec. 31) | 1996 | 1995 | 1994 | 1993 | 1992 | 1991 | 1990 | 1989 | 1988 | 1987 |
|---|---|---|---|---|---|---|---|---|---|---|
| Tangible Bk. Val. | 23.17 | 19.13 | 14.34 | 12.22 | 10.17 | 8.50 | 6.89 | 5.73 | NA | NA |
| Oper. Earnings | NA | NA | NA | NA | NA | NA | NA | NA | NA | NA |
| Earnings | 4.33 | 3.50 | 2.70 | 2.16 | 1.74 | 1.34 | 1.12 | 0.52 | 0.28 | NA |
| Dividends | 0.16 | 0.16 | 0.16 | 0.15 | 0.14 | 0.03 | NA | NA | NA | NA |
| Payout Ratio | 4% | 5% | 6% | 7% | 8% | 3% | NA | NA | NA | NA |
| Prices - High | 77¾ | 62 | 34¼ | 35⅝ | 25¾ | 20⅞ | NA | NA | NA | NA |
| - Low | 50½ | 32¾ | 25 | 24¾ | 15¾ | 13⅝ | NA | NA | NA | NA |
| P/E Ratio - High | 18 | 18 | 13 | 17 | 15 | 16 | NA | NA | NA | NA |
| - Low | 12 | 9 | 9 | 11 | 9 | 10 | NA | NA | NA | NA |

### Income Statement Analysis (Million $)

| | 1996 | 1995 | 1994 | 1993 | 1992 | 1991 | 1990 | 1989 | 1988 | 1987 |
|---|---|---|---|---|---|---|---|---|---|---|
| Premium Inc. | 617 | 507 | 404 | 299 | 226 | 183 | 168 | 148 | 137 | 121 |
| Net Invest. Inc. | 105 | 87.5 | 75.2 | 64.7 | 58.3 | 52.5 | 47.5 | 43.7 | 32.4 | 32.8 |
| Oth. Revs. | 23.2 | 23.8 | 23.0 | 39.5 | 37.4 | 22.5 | 11.7 | 8.4 | 9.6 | NA |
| Total Revs. | 746 | 618 | 502 | 404 | 322 | 258 | 227 | 201 | 179 | NA |
| Pretax Inc. | 365 | 291 | 217 | 175 | 142 | 107 | 88.0 | 38.0 | 16.0 | -28.0 |
| Net Oper. Inc. | NA | NA | NA | NA | NA | NA | NA | NA | NA | NA |
| Net Inc. | 258 | 208 | 160 | 127 | 102 | 75.0 | 60.0 | 29.0 | 15.0 | NA |

### Balance Sheet & Other Fin. Data (Million $)

| | 1996 | 1995 | 1994 | 1993 | 1992 | 1991 | 1990 | 1989 | 1988 | 1987 |
|---|---|---|---|---|---|---|---|---|---|---|
| Cash & Equiv. | 37.2 | 38.9 | 27.8 | 26.8 | 23.0 | 21.6 | 16.0 | 14.5 | NA | NA |
| Premiums Due | Nil | Nil | NA | NA | 8.8 | 7.5 | 13.0 | NA | NA | NA |
| Invest. Assets: Bonds | 2,032 | 1,683 | 1,289 | 1,056 | 893 | 775 | 603 | 519 | NA | NA |
| Invest. Assets: Stocks | 4.0 | 3.8 | 3.6 | 3.4 | 3.1 | 1.3 | 1.3 | 11.2 | NA | NA |
| Invest. Assets: Loans | Nil | Nil | Nil | Nil | Nil | Nil | Nil | Nil | NA | NA |
| Invest. Assets: Total | 2,036 | 1,687 | 1,293 | 1,100 | 896 | 777 | 604 | 531 | 421 | 395 |
| Deferred Policy Costs | 32.0 | 38.0 | 42.9 | 45.8 | 42.1 | 37.7 | 30.3 | 24.3 | NA | NA |
| Total Assets | 2,222 | 1,875 | 1,476 | 1,343 | 1,023 | 894 | 712 | 649 | 553 | 527 |
| Debt | 35.4 | 35.8 | 36.1 | 36.5 | 36.7 | 37.0 | 37.2 | 37.4 | NA | NA |
| Common Eqty. | 1,366 | 1,121 | 838 | 712 | 592 | 492 | 366 | 308 | 268 | 253 |
| Prop. & Cas. Loss Ratio | 38.0 | 37.5 | 37.9 | 35.8 | 38.4 | 44.4 | 29.2 | 39.2 | 30.5 | 48.9 |
| Prop. & Cas. Expense Ratio | 21.6 | 24.6 | 28.1 | 25.7 | 24.6 | 24.0 | 32.4 | 34.6 | 28.1 | 28.6 |
| Prop. & Cas. Combined Ratio | 59.6 | 62.1 | 66.0 | 61.5 | 63.0 | 68.4 | 61.6 | 73.8 | 58.6 | 77.5 |
| % Return On Revs. | 34.6 | 41.1 | 31.9 | 31.5 | 31.8 | 29.1 | 26.6 | 14.2 | 8.3 | NA |
| % Ret. on Equity | 20.7 | 21.2 | 20.6 | 19.5 | 18.9 | 17.5 | 17.9 | 9.9 | 5.7 | NA |

Data as orig. reptd.; bef. results of disc. opers. and/or spec. items. Per share data adj. for stk. divs. as of ex-div. date. E-Estimated. NA-Not Available. NM-Not Meaningful. NR-Not Ranked.

**Office**—MGIC Plaza, 250 East Kilbourn Ave., Milwaukee, WI 53202. **Tel**—(414) 347-6480. **Website**—http://www.mgic.com **Pres & CEO**—W. H. Lacy. **EVP & CFO**—J. M. Lauer. **SVP & Secy**—J.H. Lane. **Dirs**—J. A. Abbott, M. K. Bush, K. E. Case, D. S. Engelman, J. D. Ericson, K. M. Jastrow II, W. H. Lacy, S. B. Lubar, W.A. McIntosh, L. M. Muna, W. J. Roper, P. J. Wallison, E. J. Zore. **Transfer Agent & Registrar**—Firstar Trust Co., Milwaukee. **Incorporated**—in Wisconsin in 1984. **Empl**— 1,026. **S&P Analyst:** Brendan McGovern

# STANDARD &POOR'S
## STOCK REPORTS

D/o **Merck & Co.**

**1476**

NYSE Symbol **MRK**

**In S&P 500**

**17-MAY-97**

**Industry:**
Health Care (Drugs -
Major Pharmaceuticals)

**Summary:** Merck is one of the world's largest prescription pharmaceuticals concerns. Its Medco unit is the leading U.S. pharmacy benefits management company.

| S&P Opinion: Accumulate (★★★★) | Recent Price • 91¼ | Yield • 1.8% |
| --- | --- | --- |
| | 52 Wk Range • 99⅞-58¼ | 12-Mo. P/E • 27.3 |

**Earnings vs. Previous Year**
▲=Up ▼=Down ▶=No Change

**Quantitative Evaluations**

**Outlook**
(1 Lowest—5 Highest)
• **2+**

**Fair Value**
• **84½**

**Risk**
• **Low**

**Earn./Div. Rank**
• **A+**

**Technical Eval.**
• **Bullish** since 6/96

**Rel. Strength Rank**
(1 Lowest—99 Highest)
• **59**

**Insider Activity**
• **Neutral**

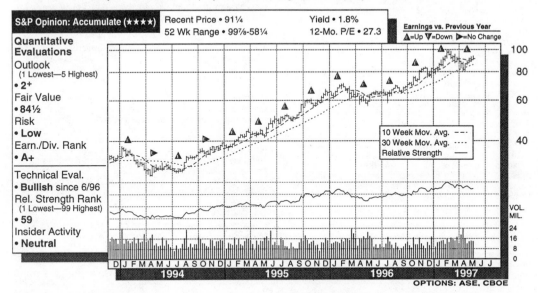

10 Week Mov. Avg. ---
30 Week Mov. Avg. ····
Relative Strength ——

VOL. MIL.

OPTIONS: ASE, CBOE

## Overview - 12-MAY-97

Fueled by strength in established lines and contributions from new drugs, another strong double-digit sales gain is indicated for 1997. Volume growth should be paced by robust gains in the new Cozaar/Hyzaar angiotensin II blocker anti-hypertensives, Proscar for enlarged prostates, Trusopt glaucoma treatment, and Zocor cholesterol lowering agent. Recent results from a Scandinavian study showed Zocor was able to save lives and prevent heart attacks in people with heart disease and high cholesterol. Good gains are also seen for new drugs such as Fosamax for osteoporosis, Crixivan for AIDS, and Varivax chicken pox vaccine. The Medco managed care unit should also chalk up strong growth, aided by continued expansion of the membership base. Margins should benefit from the greater volume and productivity improvements.

## Valuation - 12-MAY-97

Together with those of most other leading drug companies, the shares held up well in recent months, despite high volatility in the general market. Investors have been gratified by Merck's robust ongoing earnings growth, with first quarter EPS up 20%. Results benefited from a 23% rise in sales, cost controls and productivity improvements. These factors more than offset negative foreign exchange and the effects of inflation. Merck is expected to retain its premier status in the U.S. drug industry, aided by an unmatched broad-based portfolio of high-quality drugs in important therapeutic classes, a strong lineup of new products, and continuing benefits and synergies from Medco. Over the next two years, Merck plans to seek regulatory clearance for eight new drugs and 12 supplemental claims for existing products. The shares remain attractive for above-average capital appreciation.

## Key Stock Statistics

| | | | |
| --- | --- | --- | --- |
| S&P EPS Est. 1997 | 3.80 | Tang. Bk. Value/Share | 4.34 |
| P/E on S&P Est. 1997 | 24.0 | Beta | 1.46 |
| S&P EPS Est. 1998 | 4.35 | Shareholders | 247,300 |
| Dividend Rate/Share | 1.68 | Market cap. (B) | $110.4 |
| Shs. outstg. (M) | 1210.0 | Inst. holdings | 51% |
| Avg. daily vol. (M) | 2.632 | | |

Value of $10,000 invested 5 years ago: $ 18,636

### Fiscal Year Ending Dec. 31

| | 1998 | 1997 | 1996 | 1995 | 1994 | 1993 |
| --- | --- | --- | --- | --- | --- | --- |
| **Revenues (Million $)** | | | | | | |
| 1Q | — | 5,568 | 4,530 | 3,817 | 3,514 | 2,380 |
| 2Q | — | — | 4,909 | 4,136 | 3,792 | 2,574 |
| 3Q | — | — | 4,983 | 4,171 | 3,792 | 2,544 |
| 4Q | — | — | 5,406 | 4,557 | 3,872 | 3,001 |
| Yr. | — | — | 19,829 | 16,681 | 14,970 | 10,498 |
| **Earnings Per Share ($)** | | | | | | |
| 1Q | — | 0.84 | 0.70 | 0.61 | 0.54 | 0.54 |
| 2Q | — | E0.95 | 0.80 | 0.69 | 0.61 | 0.15 |
| 3Q | — | E0.99 | 0.83 | 0.70 | 0.62 | 0.62 |
| 4Q | — | E1.02 | 0.87 | 0.70 | 0.61 | 0.56 |
| Yr. | E4.35 | E3.80 | 3.20 | 2.70 | 2.38 | 1.87 |

**Next earnings report expected: mid July**

**Dividend Data** (Dividends have been paid since 1935.)

| Amount ($) | Date Decl. | Ex-Div. Date | Stock of Record | Payment Date |
| --- | --- | --- | --- | --- |
| 0.340 | May. 29 | Jun. 06 | Jun. 10 | Jul. 01 '96 |
| 0.400 | Jul. 23 | Sep. 04 | Sep. 06 | Oct. 01 '96 |
| 0.400 | Nov. 26 | Dec. 05 | Dec. 09 | Jan. 02 '97 |
| 0.420 | Feb. 25 | Mar. 05 | Mar. 07 | Apr. 01 '97 |

This report is for information purposes and should not be considered a solicitation to buy or sell any security. Neither S&P nor any other party guarantee its accuracy or make warranties regarding results from its usage. Redistribution is prohibited without written permission. Copyright © 1997 | A Division of The McGraw·Hill Companies

## Business Summary - 12-MAY-97

Merck is the premier U.S.-based pharmaceutical company, manufacturing and marketing a wide range of prescription drugs in many therapeutic classes both in the U.S. and abroad. Foreign business is important, with operations outside of North America representing 28% of sales and 22% of pretax income in 1996. The company was originally founded in 1887 as a U.S. branch of E. Merck of Germany and grew significantly in subsequent years through aggressive new drug development and acquisition programs.

The company is the undisputed leader in vast market for high-margin cardiovascular drugs, with five drugs generating aggregate sales of over $7.4 billion in 1996. Key products include cholesterol-lowering agents such as Zocor (sales of $2.8 billion) and Mevacor ($1.3 billion); and treatments for high blood pressure and congestive heart failure like Vasotec/Vaseretic ($2.5 billion) and Prinivil/Prinzide ($485 million). Merck has an estimated 40% share of the rapidly expanding worldwide cholesterol reduction market and about one third of the moderately growing hypertension-angina market. Cozaar/Hyzaar, the first of a new class of antihypertensives, is exhibiting vigorous growth aided by an improved side effect profile over other blood pressure agents.

Other drugs exhibiting notable strength include Fosamax for osteoporosis, whose sales are being helped by recent FDA approval to market the drug for the prevention of osteoporosis (a bone-thinning disease which affects postmenopausal women); and Crixivan, a protease inhibitor AIDS drug, which in combination of other agents has been able to decrease HIV in the bloodstream to undetectable levels. Other key drugs include Pepcid antiulcer agent and Proscar for enlarged prostates.

The huge success of Merck's drugs has enabled it support a $1.5 billion R&D program, which promises to spawn an ongoing stream of blockbuster drugs in the years ahead. Key products in late stage clinical trials include treatments for migraine, asthma, male pattern baldness, and angina. Merck recently discovered a new class of anti-infectives aimed at drug resistant bacteria which could revolutionize the antibiotics market.

Through a joint venture with Astra AB of Sweden, Merck sells Prilosec, the world's second largest anti-ulcer drug. Over-the-counter medications such as Pepcid AC and others are offered through a venture with Johnson & Johnson. Merck plans to combine its animal health business with those of Rhone-Poulenc. Merck-Medco Managed Care provides mail order drug and related services to nearly 50 million people.

## Capitalization

**Long Term Debt:** $1,155,900,000 (12/96).
**Minority Interest:** $2,310,200,000 (12/96).

### Per Share Data ($)

| (Year Ended Dec. 31) | 1996 | 1995 | 1994 | 1993 | 1992 | 1991 | 1990 | 1989 | 1988 | 1987 |
|---|---|---|---|---|---|---|---|---|---|---|
| Tangible Bk. Val. | 4.34 | 4.00 | 3.15 | 2.69 | 4.24 | 4.06 | 3.12 | 2.78 | 2.23 | 1.61 |
| Cash Flow | 3.80 | 3.24 | 2.92 | 2.20 | 2.37 | 2.04 | 1.72 | 1.43 | 1.18 | 0.90 |
| Earnings | 3.20 | 2.70 | 2.38 | 1.87 | 2.12 | 1.83 | 1.52 | 1.26 | 1.02 | 0.74 |
| Dividends | 1.48 | 1.28 | 1.16 | 1.06 | 0.96 | 0.79 | 0.67 | 0.57 | 0.46 | 0.30 |
| Payout Ratio | 46% | 47% | 49% | 57% | 45% | 43% | 44% | 45% | 45% | 40% |
| Prices - High | 84¼ | 67¼ | 39½ | 44⅛ | 56⅝ | 55¾ | 30⅜ | 27 | 19⅞ | 24⅞ |
|      - Low | 56½ | 36⅜ | 28⅛ | 28⅝ | 40½ | 27⅜ | 22⅜ | 18¾ | 16 | 13⅝ |
| P/E Ratio - High | 26 | 25 | 17 | 24 | 27 | 30 | 20 | 21 | 20 | 33 |
|      - Low | 18 | 13 | 12 | 15 | 19 | 15 | 15 | 15 | 16 | 18 |

### Income Statement Analysis (Million $)

| | 1996 | 1995 | 1994 | 1993 | 1992 | 1991 | 1990 | 1989 | 1988 | 1987 |
|---|---|---|---|---|---|---|---|---|---|---|
| Revs. | 19,829 | 16,681 | 14,970 | 10,498 | 9,663 | 8,603 | 7,672 | 6,550 | 5,939 | 5,061 |
| Oper. Inc. | 5,912 | 5,262 | 5,075 | 4,262 | 3,782 | 3,352 | 2,883 | 2,443 | 2,056 | 1,558 |
| Depr. | 731 | 667 | 670 | 377 | 290 | 243 | 231 | 206 | 189 | 189 |
| Int. Exp. | 139 | 99 | 124 | 84.7 | 72.7 | 68.7 | 69.8 | 53.2 | 76.5 | 56.4 |
| Pretax Inc. | 5,685 | 4,889 | 4,509 | 3,153 | 3,596 | 3,192 | 2,730 | 2,321 | 1,915 | 1,434 |
| Eff. Tax Rate | 29% | 30% | 32% | 30% | 31% | 33% | 34% | 34% | 35% | 35% |
| Net Inc. | 3,881 | 3,335 | 2,997 | 2,166 | 2,447 | 2,122 | 1,781 | 1,495 | 1,207 | 906 |

### Balance Sheet & Other Fin. Data (Million $)

| | 1996 | 1995 | 1994 | 1993 | 1992 | 1991 | 1990 | 1989 | 1988 | 1987 |
|---|---|---|---|---|---|---|---|---|---|---|
| Cash | 2,181 | 3,349 | 2,270 | 1,542 | 1,094 | 1,412 | 1,197 | 1,144 | 1,550 | 1,148 |
| Curr. Assets | 7,727 | 8,618 | 6,922 | 5,735 | 4,400 | 4,311 | 3,766 | 3,410 | 3,389 | 3,007 |
| Total Assets | 24,293 | 23,832 | 21,857 | 19,928 | 11,086 | 9,499 | 8,030 | 6,757 | 6,127 | 5,680 |
| Curr. Liab. | 4,829 | 5,690 | 5,449 | 5,896 | 3,617 | 2,814 | 2,827 | 1,907 | 1,909 | 2,209 |
| LT Debt | 1,156 | 1,373 | 1,146 | 1,121 | 496 | 494 | 124 | 118 | 143 | 167 |
| Common Eqty. | 11,971 | 11,736 | 11,139 | 10,022 | 5,003 | 4,916 | 3,834 | 3,521 | 2,856 | 2,117 |
| Total Cap. | 15,437 | 13,109 | 14,735 | 12,650 | 6,215 | 6,296 | 4,764 | 4,459 | 3,878 | 3,248 |
| Cap. Exp. | 1,197 | 1,006 | 1,009 | 1,013 | 1,067 | 1,042 | 671 | 433 | 373 | 254 |
| Cash Flow | 4,612 | 4,002 | 3,667 | 2,543 | 2,737 | 2,364 | 2,013 | 1,702 | 1,396 | 1,095 |
| Curr. Ratio | 1.6 | 1.5 | 1.3 | 1.0 | 1.2 | 1.5 | 1.3 | 1.8 | 1.8 | 1.4 |
| % LT Debt of Cap. | 7.5 | 10.5 | 7.8 | 8.9 | 8.0 | 7.8 | 2.6 | 2.6 | 3.7 | 5.2 |
| % Net Inc.of Revs. | 19.6 | 20.0 | 20.0 | 20.6 | 25.3 | 24.7 | 23.2 | 22.8 | 20.3 | 17.9 |
| % Ret. on Assets | 16.1 | 14.6 | 14.4 | 13.5 | 23.9 | 24.2 | 24.3 | 23.3 | 20.4 | 17.1 |
| % Ret. on Equity | 33.1 | 29.2 | 28.4 | 27.9 | 49.6 | 48.5 | 48.9 | 47.0 | 48.4 | 39.5 |

Data as orig. reptd.; bef. results of disc. opers. and/or spec. items. Per share data adj. for stk. divs. as of ex-div. date. E-Estimated. NA-Not Available. NM-Not Meaningful. NR-Not Ranked.

**Office**—One Merck Drive, P.O. Box 100, Whitehouse Station, NJ 08889. **Tel**—(908) 423-1000. **Website**—http://www.merck.com **Chrmn, Pres & CEO**—R. V. Gilmartin. **Secy**—C. A. Colbert. **VP & CFO**—J. C. Lewent. **Treas**—C. Dorsa. **Investor Contact**—Gary Lubin (908-423-6883). **Dirs**—H. B. Atwater, Jr., Sir Derek Birkin, L. A. Bossidy, W. G. Bowen, J. B. Cole, C. K. Davis, L. C. Elam, C. E. Exley, Jr., R. V. Gilmartin, W. N. Kelley, E. M. Scolnick, S. O. Thier, D. Weatherstone. **Transfer Agent & Registrar**—Norwest Bank Minnesota. **Incorporated**—in New Jersey in 1934. **Empl**—49,100. **S&P Analyst:** H. B. Saftlas

# STANDARD &POOR'S
## STOCK REPORTS

# Microsoft Corp.

# 4608M

Nasdaq Symbol **MSFT**

**In S&P 500**

**17-MAY-97**

**Industry:** Computer (Software & Services)

**Summary:** Microsoft develops and markets a diverse line of systems and applications microcomputer software, including the Windows 95 operating system for IBM and compatible PCs.

| S&P Opinion: Accumulate (★★★★) | Recent Price • 115⅜ | Yield • Nil |
| --- | --- | --- |
| | 52 Wk Range • 123½-53¾ | 12-Mo. P/E • 51.1 |

**Quantitative Evaluations**

**Outlook**
(1 Lowest—5 Highest)
• **3⁻**

**Fair Value**
• **119**

**Risk**
• **Low**

**Earn./Div. Rank**
• **B+**

**Technical Eval.**
• **Bullish** since 3/94

**Rel. Strength Rank**
(1 Lowest—99 Highest)
• **86**

**Insider Activity**
• **Neutral**

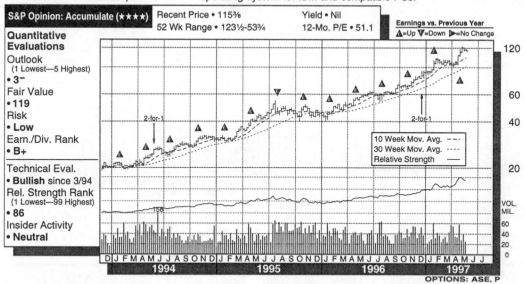

Earnings vs. Previous Year  ▲=Up ▼=Down ▶=No Change

10 Week Mov. Avg. ---
30 Week Mov. Avg. ····
Relative Strength —

OPTIONS: ASE, P

## Overview - 23-APR-97

Revenues should advance over 35% through the end of calendar 1997, reflecting continued strength in operating systems, desktop applications and enterprise software. Shipments of Windows 95, the newest release of the Windows operating system, should remain strong, aided by higher PC shipments. The company's Office suite of applications, which includes Word and Excel, is the dominant force in the business application market; it should continue to sell well, aided by the shipment of Office 97, an eagerly awaited upgrade. Enterprise software products, including Windows NT, are expected to continue gaining momentum. New offerings, including Internet solutions, and contributions from acquisitions, should also boost revenues. Margins are expected to widen, despite continued high R&D spending, benefiting from greater volume, a more favorable product mix, manufacturing efficiencies, and well controlled expenses. Earnings are expected to benefit from the increased sales and steady margins.

## Valuation - 23-APR-97

The shares have risen sharply since mid-1993, reflecting strong earnings gains powered by the company's dominant position in PC operating systems and leading position in PC business applications. Near term earnings drivers include strength of Windows 95, a strong upgrade cycle associated with shipment of Office 97, and robust growth of Windows NT. Together with its mainstay of PC operating systems and applications, new products, including enterprise and Internet solutions, should continue to aid the company's earnings. The stock, which sells at about 36 times our FY 98 earnings estimate, deserves its premium market valuation, in light of MSFT's strong competitive position and bright earnings prospects. The shares are expected to outperform the market in coming months.

## Key Stock Statistics

| | | | |
| --- | --- | --- | --- |
| S&P EPS Est. 1997 | 2.60 | Tang. Bk. Value/Share | 5.79 |
| P/E on S&P Est. 1997 | 44.4 | Beta | 1.47 |
| S&P EPS Est. 1998 | 2.90 | Shareholders | 37,900 |
| Dividend Rate/Share | Nil | Market cap. (B) | $138.9 |
| Shs. outstg. (M) | 1203.2 | Inst. holdings | 34% |
| Avg. daily vol. (M) | 8.697 | | |

Value of $10,000 invested 5 years ago: $ 62,258

### Fiscal Year Ending Jun. 30

| | 1998 | 1997 | 1996 | 1995 | 1994 | 1993 |
| --- | --- | --- | --- | --- | --- | --- |
| **Revenues (Million $)** | | | | | | |
| 1Q | — | 2,295 | 2,016 | 1,247 | 983.0 | 818.0 |
| 2Q | — | 2,680 | 2,195 | 1,482 | 1,129 | 938.0 |
| 3Q | — | 3,208 | 2,205 | 1,587 | 1,244 | 958.0 |
| 4Q | — | — | 2,255 | 1,621 | 1,293 | 1,039 |
| Yr. | — | — | 8,671 | 5,937 | 4,649 | 3,753 |
| **Earnings Per Share ($)** | | | | | | |
| 1Q | — | 0.47 | 0.39 | 0.25 | 0.20 | 0.17 |
| 2Q | — | 0.57 | 0.45 | 0.30 | 0.24 | 0.19 |
| 3Q | — | 0.79 | 0.44 | 0.32 | 0.21 | 0.20 |
| 4Q | — | E0.77 | 0.43 | 0.29 | 0.29 | 0.22 |
| Yr. | E2.90 | E2.60 | 1.71 | 1.16 | 0.94 | 0.79 |

**Next earnings report expected: late July**

### Dividend Data

| Amount ($) | Date Decl. | Ex-Div. Date | Stock of Record | Payment Date |
| --- | --- | --- | --- | --- |
| 2-for-1 | Nov. 12 | Dec. 09 | Nov. 22 | Dec. 06 '96 |

This report is for information purposes and should not be considered a solicitation to buy or sell any security. Neither S&P nor any other party guarantee its accuracy or make warranties regarding results from its usage. Redistribution is prohibited without written permission. Copyright © 1997   *A Division of The McGraw·Hill Companies*

## Business Summary - 23-APR-97

This dominant player in the PC software market, which rose to prominence on the popularity of its operating systems software, now rules the business applications software market and has its sights set on becoming the leading provider of software and services for the Internet. By virtue of its size, market positioning and financial strength, Microsoft (MSFT) is a formidable competitor in any market it targets. Earnings have grown at a 30% compounded annual rate over the four years through 1996, aided by a strong PC market in general, new product introductions and market share gains.

MSFT is best known for its operating systems software programs which, according to industry sources, run over 85% of the PCs currently in use. Its original DOS operating system helped IBM and compatible PCs achieve the dominance they enjoy today. DOS gave way to Windows, a graphical user interface program run in conjunction with DOS, which made using a PC easier than when running under DOS alone. A successor program, Windows 95, is MSFT's current flagship PC operating system, selling over 3 million copies a month, with sales closely tied to PC shipments. Windows NT, a network operating system providing network management and administration tools, security and operating stability, posted 100% growth in 1996 over 1995 levels and now ships about 165,000 units a month.

MSFT muscled its way into the business applications market in the early 1990s through a line-up of strong offerings combined with aggressive and innovative marketing and sales techniques. Its Office 97 suite, which includes the popular Word (word processing), Excel (spreadsheet) and PowerPoint (graphics) software programs, is now by far the number one selling application software package. The company is also devoting resources and forming alliances to offer interactive media, including children's titles, games and information products.

MSFT has rapidly repositioned itself as a major provider of software and services for the Internet. Its Explorer browser is a solid alternative to market leading Netscape's Navigator. In addition, MSFT's server and development tools for the Internet are being well received.

The company continues to spend heavily on research and development. Some $2 billion (about 20% of revenues) is expected to be spent in FY 97 (Jun.), of which about $400 million will be targeted directly at the Internet.

Powerful distribution channels, including strong relationships with original equipment manufacturers (OEMs, the makers of PCs), relationships with resellers, as well as guaranteed shelf space on retail stores all give MSFT an advantage over smaller, less well established rivals.

### Capitalization

**Long Term Debt:** None (3/97).

### Per Share Data ($)

| (Year Ended Jun. 30) | 1996 | 1995 | 1994 | 1993 | 1992 | 1991 | 1990 | 1989 | 1988 | 1987 |
|---|---|---|---|---|---|---|---|---|---|---|
| Tangible Bk. Val. | 5.79 | 4.54 | 3.83 | 2.88 | 1.98 | 1.27 | 0.88 | 0.55 | 0.38 | 0.25 |
| Cash Flow | 2.09 | 1.38 | 1.14 | 0.90 | 0.69 | 0.47 | 0.30 | 0.19 | 0.14 | 0.08 |
| Earnings | 1.71 | 1.16 | 0.94 | 0.79 | 0.60 | 0.41 | 0.26 | 0.17 | 0.12 | 0.07 |
| Dividends | Nil | Nil | Nil | Nil | Nil | Nil | Nil | Nil | Nil | Nil |
| Payout Ratio | Nil | Nil | Nil | Nil | Nil | Nil | Nil | Nil | Nil | Nil |
| Prices - High | 86⅛ | 54⅝ | 32⅝ | 24½ | 23¾ | 18⅝ | 9 | 5 | 3⅞ | 4⅜ |
|    - Low | 40 | 29⅛ | 19½ | 17⅝ | 16½ | 8⅛ | 4⅝ | 2½ | 2½ | 1⁵/₁₆ |
| P/E Ratio - High | 50 | 47 | 35 | 31 | 39 | 45 | 35 | 29 | 32 | 61 |
|    - Low | 23 | 25 | 21 | 22 | 27 | 20 | 18 | 15 | 20 | 18 |

### Income Statement Analysis (Million $)

| | 1996 | 1995 | 1994 | 1993 | 1992 | 1991 | 1990 | 1989 | 1988 | 1987 |
|---|---|---|---|---|---|---|---|---|---|---|
| Revs. | 8,671 | 5,937 | 4,649 | 3,753 | 2,759 | 1,843 | 1,183 | 804 | 591 | 346 |
| Oper. Inc. | 3,558 | 2,307 | 1,963 | 1,464 | 1,097 | 714 | 434 | 260 | 190 | 120 |
| Depr. | 480 | 269 | 237 | 138 | 101 | 67.0 | 46.0 | 25.0 | 17.0 | 8.0 |
| Int. Exp. | Nil | Nil | 2.0 | 1.0 | 2.0 | 4.5 | 3.6 | 2.3 | 1.5 | 0.8 |
| Pretax Inc. | 3,379 | 2,167 | 1,722 | 1,401 | 1,041 | 671 | 411 | 251 | 184 | 121 |
| Eff. Tax Rate | 35% | 33% | 33% | 32% | 32% | 31% | 32% | 32% | 33% | 41% |
| Net Inc. | 2,195 | 1,453 | 1,146 | 953 | 708 | 463 | 279 | 171 | 124 | 72.0 |

### Balance Sheet & Other Fin. Data (Million $)

| | 1996 | 1995 | 1994 | 1993 | 1992 | 1991 | 1990 | 1989 | 1988 | 1987 |
|---|---|---|---|---|---|---|---|---|---|---|
| Cash | 6,940 | 4,750 | 3,614 | 2,290 | 1,345 | 686 | 449 | 301 | 183 | 132 |
| Curr. Assets | 7,839 | 5,620 | 4,312 | 2,850 | 1,770 | 1,029 | 720 | 469 | 345 | 213 |
| Total Assets | 10,093 | 7,210 | 5,363 | 3,805 | 2,640 | 1,644 | 1,105 | 721 | 493 | 288 |
| Curr. Liab. | 2,425 | 1,347 | 913 | 563 | 447 | 293 | 187 | 159 | 118 | 47.0 |
| LT Debt | Nil | Nil | Nil | Nil | Nil | Nil | Nil | Nil | Nil | 2.0 |
| Common Eqty. | 6,908 | 5,333 | 4,450 | 3,242 | 2,193 | 1,351 | 919 | 562 | 375 | 239 |
| Total Cap. | 7,033 | 5,458 | 4,450 | 3,242 | 2,193 | 1,351 | 919 | 562 | 375 | 241 |
| Cap. Exp. | 494 | 495 | 278 | 239 | 318 | 275 | 159 | 92.0 | 72.0 | 58.0 |
| Cash Flow | 2,675 | 1,722 | 1,383 | 1,091 | 809 | 530 | 326 | 196 | 141 | 79.0 |
| Curr. Ratio | 3.2 | 4.2 | 4.7 | 5.1 | 4.0 | 3.5 | 3.9 | 3.0 | 2.9 | 4.6 |
| % LT Debt of Cap. | Nil | Nil | Nil | Nil | Nil | Nil | Nil | Nil | Nil | 0.8 |
| % Net Inc.of Revs. | 25.3 | 24.5 | 24.7 | 25.4 | 25.7 | 25.1 | 23.6 | 21.2 | 21.0 | 20.8 |
| % Ret. on Assets | 25.4 | 23.1 | 25.0 | 29.1 | 32.5 | 33.4 | 30.1 | 27.9 | 31.5 | 31.0 |
| % Ret. on Equity | 35.9 | 29.7 | 29.8 | 34.6 | 39.3 | 40.4 | 37.1 | 36.1 | 40.0 | 37.5 |

Data as orig. reptd.; bef. results of disc. opers. and/or spec. items. Per share data adj. for stk. divs. as of ex-div. date. E-Estimated. NA-Not Available. NM-Not Meaningful. NR-Not Ranked.

**Office**—One Microsoft Way, Redmond, WA 98052-6399. **Tel**—(206) 882-8080. **Website**—http://www.microsoft.com **Chrmn & CEO**—W. H. Gates III. **CFO**—M. W. Brown. **Secy**—W. H. Neukom. **Investor Contact**—Carla Lewis. **Dirs**—P. G. Allen, J. E. Barad, W. H. Gates III, R. Hackborn, D. F. Marquardt, R. D. O'Brien, W. G. Reed Jr., J. A. Shirley. **Transfer Agent**—ChaseMellon Shareholder Services, Ridgefield Park, NJ. **Incorporated**—in Washington in 1981; reincorporated in Delaware in 1986. **Empl**— 20,561. **S&P Analyst:** Peter C. Wood, CFA

**19-MAY-97**   Industry:
Financial (Diversified)

**Summary:** MM provides risk management services to clients seeking alternatives to traditional commercial insurance for certain risk exposure, especially workers' compensation.

| Quantitative Evaluations | | |
|---|---|---|
| Outlook (1 Lowest—5 Highest) | • **NA** | |
| Fair Value | • **NA** | |
| Risk | • **Average** | |
| Earn./Div. Rank | • **B+** | |
| Technical Eval. | • **Bearish** since 4/97 | |
| Rel. Strength Rank (1 Lowest—99 Highest) | • **64** | |
| Insider Activity | • **Neutral** | |

Recent Price • 37⅞   Yield • 0.9%
52 Wk Range • 40-26⅞   12-Mo. P/E • 19.0

Earnings vs. Previous Year
▲=Up ▼=Down ▶=No Change

10 Week Mov. Avg. ---
30 Week Mov. Avg. ·····
Relative Strength —

4-for-3

## Business Profile - 19-MAY-97

MM is a leader in the alternative insurance market, which is one of the fastest growing segments of the insurance industry. It includes self-insurance and captive insurance programs, representing about one-third of the commercial lines insurance market in the U.S. MM's income is principally derived from fees for the services it provides to clients; typically, it earns between 11% and 13% of a client's premium in fee income. Pretax profit margins on these fees are consistently in the 40%-to-45% range. In recent periods, the company has further diversified its product line to include, in addition to corporate risk management (its original business segment), program business (its fastest growing segment), financial services, and specialty brokerage for alternative risk transfer insurers and reinsurers.

## Operational Review - 19-MAY-97

For the three months ended March 31, 1997, total revenues advanced 29%, year to year, principally reflecting a 22% increase in fee income, 53% higher premiums earned, and a 15% rise in net investment income. Total expenses were up 39%, fueled by higher acquisition costs, losses and loss expenses incurred, and operating expenses. Pretax income rose 8.0%. Following taxes at 17.6%, versus 21.8%, and minority interests of $207,000 in the 1996 period, income from continuing operations climbed 16%, to $10,685,000 ($0.54 a share, on 3.0% more shares) from $9,182,000 ($0.48).

## Stock Performance - 16-MAY-97

In the past 30 trading days, MM's shares have increased 7%, compared to a 9% rise in the S&P 500. Average trading volume for the past five days was 37,180 shares, compared with the 40-day moving average of 48,892 shares.

## Key Stock Statistics

| | | | |
|---|---|---|---|
| Dividend Rate/Share | 0.36 | Shareholders | 400 |
| Shs. outstg. (M) | 18.6 | Market cap. (B) | $0.703 |
| Avg. daily vol. (M) | 0.033 | Inst. holdings | 75% |
| Tang. Bk. Value/Share | 10.22 | | |
| Beta | 0.31 | | |

Value of $10,000 invested 5 years ago: $ 22,550

### Fiscal Year Ending Dec. 31

| | 1997 | 1996 | 1995 | 1994 | 1993 | 1992 |
|---|---|---|---|---|---|---|
| **Revenues (Million $)** | | | | | | |
| 1Q | 47.19 | 36.69 | 28.77 | 29.53 | 26.01 | 17.68 |
| 2Q | — | 40.61 | 32.70 | 30.49 | 20.82 | 19.55 |
| 3Q | — | 32.78 | 34.78 | 33.61 | 31.38 | — |
| 4Q | — | 47.62 | 26.99 | 35.18 | 27.93 | 28.07 |
| Yr. | — | 157.7 | 123.2 | 128.7 | 106.1 | 91.36 |
| **Earnings Per Share ($)** | | | | | | |
| 1Q | 0.54 | 0.48 | 0.38 | 0.33 | 0.25 | 0.21 |
| 2Q | — | 0.47 | 0.43 | 0.32 | 0.27 | 0.22 |
| 3Q | — | 0.49 | 0.43 | 0.35 | 0.32 | 0.22 |
| 4Q | — | 0.49 | 0.40 | 0.35 | 0.32 | 0.23 |
| Yr. | — | 1.93 | 1.64 | 1.35 | 1.16 | 0.88 |

**Next earnings report expected: early August**

### Dividend Data (Dividends have been paid since 1991.)

| Amount ($) | Date Decl. | Ex-Div. Date | Stock of Record | Payment Date |
|---|---|---|---|---|
| 0.080 | Jul. 24 | Aug. 07 | Aug. 09 | Aug. 23 '96 |
| 0.090 | Oct. 22 | Nov. 06 | Nov. 08 | Nov. 22 '96 |
| 0.090 | Jan. 30 | Feb. 05 | Feb. 07 | Feb. 21 '97 |
| 0.090 | Apr. 22 | May. 07 | May. 09 | May. 23 '97 |

This report is for information purposes and should not be considered a solicitation to buy or sell any security. Neither S&P nor any other party guarantee its accuracy or make warranties regarding results from its usage. Redistribution is prohibited without written permission. Copyright © 1997

*A Division of The McGraw-Hill Companies*

## Business Summary - 19-MAY-97

Mutual Risk Management provides risk management services to clients seeking alternatives to traditional commercial insurance for certain risk exposures, especially workers' compensation. Risk management involves analyzing loss exposure and developing risk financing methods to reduce exposure. The use of loss financing methods in place of traditional insurance, known as the alternative market, involves client self-funding of a significant amount of loss exposure, transferring only unpredictable excess risk to insurers. In 1996, revenues rose 24% from those of the prior year, and were divided as follows:

|  | 1996 | 1995 |
|---|---|---|
| Fee income | 51% | 50% |
| Premiums earned | 36% | 38% |
| Net investment income | 14% | 13% |
| Realized capital losses | -1% | -1% |

MM's principal source of profits is fees received for services provided to clients in connection with its programs. The structure of MM's programs places most underwriting risk with the client. For regulatory and other reasons, however, the company is required to assume a limited amount of risk. It does not seek to earn income from underwriting risk, but from fees for services provided. Through its subsidiaries, MM provides risk management services in the U.S., Bermuda, Barbados, the Cayman Islands and Europe.

In connection with many programs, Legion Insurance Co., licensed in 49 states and the District of Columbia, issues an insurance policy to the client and reinsures the premium and liability related to the client's chosen retention. For most programs, Legion retains only the relatively small portion of the premium associated with its retention of a portion of the specific and aggregate excess risk, ceding the majority of premiums and risk to the clients' IPC (Insurance Profit Center) Program and the balance to unaffiliated excess reinsurers.

Subsidiaries include Park International Ltd., a wholesale insurance broker; MRM Hancock Ltd., a reinsurance broker; Captive Managers, which provide a full range of administrative and accounting services to unaffiliated captive insurers; The Worksafe Group, Inc., which operates a proprietary loss control system; IPC Companies, which are multiple-line insurance and reinsurance companies; and Commonwealth Risk Services, Inc., a marketing subsidiary. During 1996, MM acquired The Hemisphere Group Ltd., which provides administrative services to offshore mutual funds, Professional Underwriters Corp., and Legion Indemnity.

## Capitalization

**Long Term Debt:** $122,210,991 (12/96).

### Per Share Data ($)

| (Year Ended Dec. 31) | 1996 | 1995 | 1994 | 1993 | 1992 | 1991 | 1990 | 1989 | 1988 | 1987 |
|---|---|---|---|---|---|---|---|---|---|---|
| Tangible Bk. Val. | 10.22 | 8.91 | 6.85 | 6.46 | 5.30 | 3.90 | 2.51 | 1.73 | NA | NA |
| Oper. Earnings | 2.05 | 1.68 | 1.38 | 1.15 | 0.88 | 0.68 | NA | NA | NA | NA |
| Earnings | 1.93 | 1.64 | 1.35 | 1.16 | 0.88 | 0.69 | 0.45 | 0.31 | 0.22 | 0.42 |
| Dividends | 0.32 | 0.25 | 0.22 | 0.16 | 0.12 | 0.05 | Nil | Nil | Nil | Nil |
| Payout Ratio | 17% | 16% | 16% | 14% | 14% | 7% | Nil | Nil | Nil | Nil |
| Prices - High | 37¼ | 34⅜ | 22⅜ | 24⅝ | 20¼ | 17⅝ | NA | NA | NA | NA |
|   - Low | 26⅞ | 18⅝ | 15⅞ | 15⅞ | 12⅞ | 8½ | NA | NA | NA | NA |
| P/E Ratio - High | 19 | 21 | 17 | 21 | 23 | 26 | NA | NA | NA | NA |
|   - Low | 14 | 11 | 12 | 14 | 15 | 12 | NA | NA | NA | NA |

### Income Statement Analysis (Million $)

| | 1996 | 1995 | 1994 | 1993 | 1992 | 1991 | 1990 | 1989 | 1988 | 1987 |
|---|---|---|---|---|---|---|---|---|---|---|
| Premium Inc. | 56.4 | 48.2 | 68.2 | 55.2 | 50.4 | 24.4 | 17.5 | 13.4 | 12.6 | NA |
| Net Invest. Inc. | 22.5 | 16.1 | 11.4 | 9.5 | 9.2 | 6.6 | 3.5 | 2.6 | 2.3 | NA |
| Oth. Revs. | 79.1 | 58.9 | 49.0 | 41.4 | 31.7 | 23.3 | 18.1 | 13.2 | 9.3 | NA |
| Total Revs. | 158 | 123 | 129 | 106 | 91.4 | 54.3 | 39.1 | 29.2 | 24.2 | NA |
| Pretax Inc. | 45.6 | 39.3 | 32.3 | 27.2 | 21.7 | 15.6 | 8.2 | 5.6 | 4.0 | NA |
| Net Oper. Inc. | 39.2 | 30.6 | 24.5 | 20.5 | 15.4 | 10.0 | NA | NA | NA | NA |
| Net Inc. | 37.2 | 29.9 | 24.0 | 20.7 | 15.6 | 10.3 | 5.5 | 3.9 | 2.7 | NA |

### Balance Sheet & Other Fin. Data (Million $)

| | 1996 | 1995 | 1994 | 1993 | 1992 | 1991 | 1990 | 1989 | 1988 | 1987 |
|---|---|---|---|---|---|---|---|---|---|---|
| Cash & Equiv. | 57.2 | 83.1 | 48.0 | 32.4 | 51.7 | 24.8 | 25.5 | 13.7 | NA | NA |
| Premiums Due | 73.6 | 39.2 | 19.0 | 15.9 | 10.1 | 6.2 | 3.3 | 2.9 | NA | NA |
| Invest. Assets: Bonds | 400 | 352 | 235 | 205 | 148 | 120 | 65.0 | 41.0 | NA | NA |
| Invest. Assets: Stocks | Nil | Nil | Nil | Nil | Nil | Nil | Nil | Nil | NA | NA |
| Invest. Assets: Loans | Nil | Nil | Nil | Nil | 0.6 | 0.6 | 1.2 | 1.5 | NA | NA |
| Invest. Assets: Total | 400 | 352 | 235 | 205 | 149 | 120 | 66.0 | 43.0 | NA | NA |
| Deferred Policy Costs | 20.6 | 19.1 | 9.5 | 8.0 | 6.8 | 3.6 | 1.5 | 1.0 | NA | NA |
| Total Assets | 1,639 | 1,374 | 1,018 | 859 | 499 | 405 | 310 | 253 | NA | NA |
| Debt | 122 | 116 | 3.0 | 6.0 | 8.0 | 9.0 | 10.0 | 4.0 | NA | NA |
| Common Eqty. | 208 | 167 | 122 | 114 | 95.6 | 62.6 | 34.0 | 23.9 | NA | NA |
| Prop. & Cas. Loss Ratio | NA | NA | 56.4 | 73.0 | 84.4 | 93.4 | 99.2 | 95.4 | NA | NA |
| Prop. & Cas. Expense Ratio | NA | NA | 83.9 | 64.7 | 45.7 | 51.6 | 72.7 | 81.4 | NA | NA |
| Prop. & Cas. Combined Ratio | NA | NA | 140.3 | 137.7 | 130.1 | 145.0 | 171.9 | 176.8 | NA | NA |
| % Return On Revs. | 23.6 | 24.1 | 18.6 | 19.5 | 17.1 | 19.0 | 14.1 | 13.4 | 11.3 | NA |
| % Ret. on Equity | 19.9 | 20.3 | 20.2 | 19.8 | 19.6 | 20.9 | 18.0 | 16.5 | 13.2 | NA |

Data as orig. reptd.; bef. results of disc. opers. and/or spec. items. Per share data adj. for stk. divs. as of ex-div. date. E-Estimated. NA-Not Available. NM-Not Meaningful. NR-Not Ranked.

**Office**—44 Church St., P. O. Box HM 2064, Hamilton, Bermuda.**Tel**—(441) 295-5688. **Website**—http://www.mutrisk.com **Chrmn & CEO**—R. A. Mulderig. **Pres**—J. Kessock, Jr. **SVP, CFO & Investor Contact**—James C. Kelly. **Dirs**—R. E. Dailey, D. J. Doyle, A. E. Engel, A. W. Fulkerson, W. F. Galtney, Jr., J. Kessock, Jr., R. A. Mulderig, G. R. Partridge, B. H. Patrick, J. S. Rosenbloom, J. D. Sargent, R. G. Turner. **Transfer Agent & Registrar**—Boston EquiServe L.P., Canton, MA. **Incorporated**—in Bermuda in 1977. **Empl**— 433. **S&P Analyst:** Thomas C. Ferguson

# Newpark Resources

## 1670M

NYSE Symbol **NR**

**17-MAY-97**

**Industry:**
Oil & Gas (Drilling & Equipment)

**Summary:** NR provides integrated environmental and oilfield services to the oil and gas exploration and production industry in the Gulf Coast Area.

## Quantitative Evaluations

Recent Price • 47
52 Wk Range • 49½-31

Yield • Nil
12-Mo. P/E • 28.8

**Outlook**
(1 Lowest—5 Highest)
• **5**

**Fair Value**
• **74¼**

**Risk**
• **Average**

**Earn./Div. Rank**
• **B**

**Technical Eval.**
• **NA**

**Rel. Strength Rank**
(1 Lowest—99 Highest)
• **70**

**Insider Activity**
• **NA**

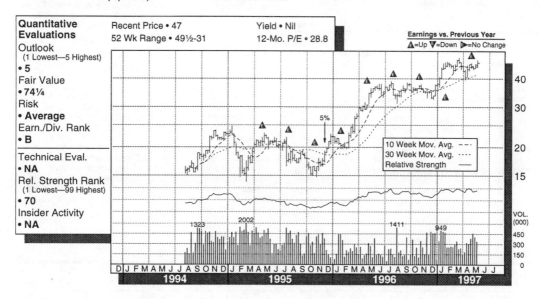

Earnings vs. Previous Year
▲=Up ▼=Down ▶=No Change

10 Week Mov. Avg. – – –
30 Week Mov. Avg. ·····
Relative Strength —

VOL. (000)

## Business Profile - 15-MAY-97

Newpark Resources, which provides environmental services primarily to the oil and natural gas exploration and production industry, is pursuing opportunities to transfer the technologies and methods it has developed in these areas to other markets. NR is developing a new market for mat rental in Algeria and preparing to take its patented waste processing and injection technology into new markets including the domestic industrial waste disposal business concentrated along the U.S. Gulf Coast. Meanwhile, NR has been making acquisitions. It recently acquired SBM Drilling Fluids Management, Inc., a full service drilling fluids company, in a pooling transaction valued at $26 million. Officers and directors own about 5% of NR shares. A two-for-one stock split is to be distributed on June 20, 1997.

## Operational Review - 15-MAY-97

Revenues for the first quarter of 1997 advanced 40%, year to year. Mat rental operations benefited from an improvement in the domestic energy drilling market that began in the 1996 fourth quarter. Nonhazardous oilfield waste operations were helped by an August 1996 acquisition and increased Gulf Coast drilling activity. Net income more than doubled to $7.0 million ($0.45 a share, on 33% more shares), from $3.3 million ($0.28).

## Stock Performance - 16-MAY-97

In the past 30 trading days, NR's shares have increased 15%, compared to a 9% rise in the S&P 500. Average trading volume for the past five days was 66,600 shares, compared with the 40-day moving average of 65,479 shares.

## Key Stock Statistics

| | | | |
|---|---|---|---|
| Dividend Rate/Share | Nil | Shareholders | 4,000 |
| Shs. outstg. (M) | 15.2 | Market cap. (B) | $0.713 |
| Avg. daily vol. (M) | 0.081 | Inst. holdings | 70% |
| Tang. Bk. Value/Share | 8.24 | | |
| Beta | 0.22 | | |

Value of $10,000 invested 5 years ago: $ 63,677

### Fiscal Year Ending Dec. 31

| | 1997 | 1996 | 1995 | 1994 | 1993 | 1992 |
|---|---|---|---|---|---|---|
| **Revenues (Million $)** | | | | | | |
| 1Q | 39.81 | 26.77 | 22.21 | 17.15 | 11.74 | -- |
| 2Q | — | 26.18 | 22.45 | 19.40 | 13.05 | -- |
| 3Q | — | 28.55 | 24.79 | 21.17 | 15.67 | -- |
| 4Q | — | 40.04 | 28.53 | 21.92 | 15.87 | -- |
| Yr. | — | 121.5 | 97.98 | 79.63 | 56.33 | 49.50 |
| **Earnings Per Share ($)** | | | | | | |
| 1Q | 0.45 | 0.30 | 0.24 | 0.17 | -- | -- |
| 2Q | — | 0.34 | 0.30 | 0.22 | -- | -- |
| 3Q | — | 0.28 | 0.26 | 0.23 | -- | -- |
| 4Q | — | 0.54 | 0.36 | 0.28 | -- | -- |
| Yr. | — | 1.46 | 1.16 | 0.90 | 0.49 | 0.43 |

**Next earnings report expected: late July**

### Dividend Data

| Amount ($) | Date Decl. | Ex-Div. Date | Stock of Record | Payment Date |
|---|---|---|---|---|
| 2-for-1 | — | Jun. 23 | May. 30 | Jun. 20 '97 |

This report is for information purposes and should not be considered a solicitation to buy or sell any security. Neither S&P nor any other party guarantee its accuracy or make warranties regarding results from its usage. Redistribution is prohibited without written permission. Copyright © 1997

*A Division of The McGraw-Hill Companies*

STANDARD
&POOR'S
STOCK REPORTS

**Newpark Resources, Inc.**

**1670M**
**17-MAY-97**

## Business Summary - 15-MAY-97

Newpark Resources, Inc. provides integrated environmental services to the oil and gas exploration and production industry in the Gulf Coast area, primarily in Louisiana and Texas. Revenue contributions by product line in recent years:

|  | 1996 | 1995 | 1994 |
|---|---|---|---|
| Offsite waste processing | 37% | 32% | 26% |
| Mat rental | 27% | 31% | 29% |
| Integrated services | 35% | 35% | 43% |
| Other | 1% | 2% | 2% |

Offsite waste processing involves the collection, processing and disposal of oilfield waste, primarily NOW (nonhazardous oilfield waste) and NORM (naturally occurring radioactive material). Newpark also treats NOW at the well site, remediates waste pits and other contaminated sites, and provides general oilfield services in connection with these waste-related services. In its NOW processing and disposal business, Newpark processes the majority of the NOW received at its facilities for injection into environmentally secure geologic formations deep underground and creates from the remainder a product that is used as intermediate daily cover material or as cell liner and construction material at municipal waste landfills.

Mat rental involves providing the oil and gas exploration and production industry with a patented interlocking mat system that provides temporary worksites in unstable soil conditions typically found along the Gulf Coast. Besides providing mats to the oil and gas exploration and production industry in Louisiana and Texas, mats are also provided to other types of customers such as builders of pipelines, electrical distribution systems, and highways in and through wetland environments in the coastal areas of the Southeastern states, particularly Florida and Georgia. In 1995, through a joint venture, NR began marketing its mat rental services in Venezuela.

Integrated services include site assessment and preparation; on-site management of oilfield waste; the construction, maintenance and removal of permanent production facilities; complete site remediation services upon completion of the drilling or production cycle; and general oilfield construction services. Integrated services are marketed both individually or in combination with the company's proprietary services,

In August 1996, NR acquired the marine-related nonhazardous oilfield waste collection operations of Campbell Wells Ltd. for about $70.5 million. In January 1997, NR acquired from a major oil company a property which Newpark plans to license as an industrial waste disposal facility. In April 1997, NR acquired an additional injection facility comprising two wells on 37 acres near its existing Big Hill, Texas, site.

## Capitalization

**Long Term Debt:** $34,612,000 (12/96).

### Per Share Data ($)

| (Year Ended Dec. 31) | 1996 | 1995 | 1994 | 1993 | 1992 | 1991 | 1990 | 1989 | 1988 | 1987 |
|---|---|---|---|---|---|---|---|---|---|---|
| Tangible Bk. Val. | 8.24 | 6.88 | 5.65 | 4.72 | 4.31 | NA | NA | NA | NA | NA |
| Cash Flow | 2.82 | 2.10 | 1.62 | 1.11 | 1.02 | NA | NA | NA | NA | NA |
| Earnings | 1.46 | 1.16 | 0.90 | 0.49 | 0.43 | 0.46 | 0.33 | NA | NA | NA |
| Dividends | Nil | Nil | Nil | Nil | Nil | Nil | Nil | NA | NA | NA |
| Payout Ratio | Nil | Nil | Nil | Nil | Nil | Nil | Nil | NA | NA | NA |
| Prices - High | 39 | 24¾ | 23¾ | 10¾ | 10¾ | NA | NA | NA | NA | NA |
| - Low | 19⅝ | 14 | 7⅞ | 7⅛ | 6⅜ | NA | NA | NA | NA | NA |
| P/E Ratio - High | 27 | 21 | 26 | 22 | 25 | NA | NA | NA | NA | NA |
| - Low | 13 | 12 | 9 | 14 | 15 | NA | NA | NA | NA | NA |

### Income Statement Analysis (Million $)

| | 1996 | 1995 | 1994 | 1993 | 1992 | 1991 | 1990 | 1989 | 1988 | 1987 |
|---|---|---|---|---|---|---|---|---|---|---|
| Revs. | 122 | 97.9 | 79.6 | 56.3 | 49.5 | 44.6 | 31.7 | NA | NA | NA |
| Oper. Inc. | 51.4 | 30.9 | 19.3 | 10.3 | 10.6 | NA | NA | NA | NA | NA |
| Depr. | 17.2 | 10.0 | 7.4 | 5.9 | 5.7 | NA | NA | NA | NA | NA |
| Int. Exp. | 3.8 | 3.7 | 2.7 | 1.3 | 0.9 | 1.6 | 1.4 | NA | NA | NA |
| Pretax Inc. | 28.3 | 17.0 | 9.3 | 3.1 | 4.1 | 3.1 | 1.3 | NA | NA | NA |
| Eff. Tax Rate | 35% | 28% | NM | NM | 1.20% | 2.40% | Nil | NA | NA | NA |
| Net Inc. | 18.5 | 12.2 | 9.4 | 4.8 | 4.0 | 3.0 | 1.3 | NA | NA | NA |

### Balance Sheet & Other Fin. Data (Million $)

| | 1996 | 1995 | 1994 | 1993 | 1992 | 1991 | 1990 | 1989 | 1988 | 1987 |
|---|---|---|---|---|---|---|---|---|---|---|
| Cash | 1.9 | 1.0 | 1.4 | 1.2 | NA | NA | NA | NA | NA | NA |
| Curr. Assets | 62.1 | 56.3 | 31.5 | 29.0 | NA | NA | NA | NA | NA | NA |
| Total Assets | 283 | 153 | 111 | 90.0 | 75.0 | 53.0 | 40.0 | NA | NA | NA |
| Curr. Liab. | 32.0 | 24.2 | 17.9 | 23.6 | NA | NA | NA | NA | NA | NA |
| LT Debt | 34.6 | 46.7 | 28.9 | 12.4 | 10.4 | 3.8 | 2.1 | NA | NA | NA |
| Common Eqty. | 203 | 77.5 | 63.7 | 53.4 | 45.7 | 40.2 | 7.2 | NA | NA | NA |
| Total Cap. | 238 | 124 | 93.0 | 66.0 | 56.0 | 44.0 | 9.0 | NA | NA | NA |
| Cap. Exp. | 43.7 | 24.0 | 23.1 | 9.7 | 13.0 | NA | NA | NA | NA | NA |
| Cash Flow | 35.6 | 22.2 | 16.8 | 10.7 | 9.7 | NA | NA | NA | NA | NA |
| Curr. Ratio | 1.9 | 2.3 | 1.8 | 1.2 | NA | NA | NA | NA | NA | NA |
| % LT Debt of Cap. | 14.5 | 37.6 | 31.2 | 18.9 | 18.5 | 8.6 | 23.6 | NA | NA | NA |
| % Net Inc.of Revs. | 15.2 | 12.5 | 11.8 | 8.5 | 8.3 | 6.7 | 3.9 | NA | NA | NA |
| % Ret. on Assets | 8.5 | 9.3 | 9.3 | 5.8 | 6.4 | 6.4 | NA | NA | NA | NA |
| % Ret. on Equity | 13.2 | 17.3 | 16.1 | 9.7 | 9.5 | 12.6 | NA | NA | NA | NA |

Data as orig. reptd.; bef. results of disc. opers. and/or spec. items. Per share data adj. for stk. divs. as of ex-div. date. E-Estimated. NA-Not Available. NM-Not Meaningful. NR-Not Ranked.

**Office**—3850 N. Causeway, Suite 1770, Metairie, LA 70002. **Tel**—(504) 838-8222. **Website**—http://www.newpark.com **Chrm & Pres**—J. D. Cole. **VP-CFO & Investor Contact**—Matthew W. Hardey. **Dirs**—D, Attar, W. T. Ballantine, J. D. Cole, W. W. Goodson, D. P. Hunt, A. J. Kaufman, J. H. Stone. **Transfer Agent & Registrar**—American Stock Transfer & Trust Co., NYC. **Incorporated**—in Nevada in 1932; reincorporated in Delaware in 1991. **Empl**— 600. **S&P Analyst:** N.J. DeVita

# STANDARD &POOR'S
STOCK REPORTS

# Norrell Corp.

**1686R**

NYSE Symbol **NRL**

In S&P SmallCap 600

**17-MAY-97**

**Industry:**
Services (Employment)

**Summary:** This company provides a broad range of temporary personnel and outsourcing services through a national network of company-owned and franchised locations.

## Quantitative Evaluations

**Outlook**
(1 Lowest—5 Highest)
• **NA**

**Fair Value**
• **NA**

**Risk**
• **Average**

**Earn./Div. Rank**
• **NR**

**Technical Eval.**
• **Bullish** since 5/97

**Rel. Strength Rank**
(1 Lowest—99 Highest)
• **87**

**Insider Activity**
• **Unfavorable**

Recent Price • 29⅜
52 Wk Range • 34½-20⅜

Yield • 0.5%
12-Mo. P/E • 27.5

10 Week Mov. Avg. – – –
30 Week Mov. Avg. ∙∙∙∙∙
Relative Strength ———

OPTIONS: Ph

## Business Profile - 15-MAR-97

Looking ahead to the next three quarters of FY 97 (Oct.), NRL plans to continue to execute its strategy of cross-selling to large account clients, and targeting selected acquisitions. The company's professional services division recently completed the acquisition of Comtex Information Systems, a provider of information technology consulting services with annual revenues of $43 million. In the first quarter of FY 97, professional service sales increased 188%, reflecting the Comtex acquisition and strong internal growth in excess of 45%. The company said the ongoing shift in revenue mix toward professional services indicates progress in its strategy to expand its faster-growing and higher-margin businesses.

## Operational Review - 15-MAR-97

Revenues in the three months ended January 26, 1997, rose 23%, year to year, reflecting a 188% increase in professional service sales, which outweighed smaller increases in staffing (14%) and outsourcing services (17%). Margins widened on a favorable shift in revenue mix and the leveraging of SG&A over higher volumes; operating income surged 51%. Following higher interest expense and non-cash charges associated with acquisitions, pretax income advanced 40%. After taxes at 38.0%, versus 38.5%, net income was up 41%, to $7,201,000 ($0.28, on 3.9% more shares), from $5,114,000 ($0.21, as adjusted for a 2-for-1 split in July 1996).

## Stock Performance - 16-MAY-97

In the past 30 trading days, NRL's shares have increased 20%, compared to a 9% rise in the S&P 500. Average trading volume for the past five days was 14,720 shares, compared with the 40-day moving average of 36,792 shares.

## Key Stock Statistics

| | | | |
|---|---|---|---|
| Dividend Rate/Share | 0.16 | Shareholders | 200 |
| Shs. outstg. (M) | 24.0 | Market cap. (B) | $0.705 |
| Avg. daily vol. (M) | 0.021 | Inst. holdings | 41% |
| Tang. Bk. Value/Share | 2.25 | | |
| Beta | NA | | |

Value of $10,000 invested 5 years ago: NA

### Fiscal Year Ending Oct. 31

| | 1997 | 1996 | 1995 | 1994 | 1993 | 1992 |
|---|---|---|---|---|---|---|
| **Revenues (Million $)** | | | | | | |
| 1Q | 281.2 | 229.3 | 186.1 | 154.0 | 123.0 | — |
| 2Q | — | 250.3 | 196.7 | 167.0 | 135.0 | — |
| 3Q | — | 255.3 | 202.2 | 173.0 | 144.0 | — |
| 4Q | — | 279.0 | 227.6 | 187.0 | 161.0 | — |
| Yr. | — | 1,014 | 812.6 | 681.0 | 562.0 | 399.2 |
| **Earnings Per Share ($)** | | | | | | |
| 1Q | 0.28 | 0.21 | 0.16 | -- | -- | — |
| 2Q | — | 0.25 | 0.17 | -- | -- | — |
| 3Q | — | 0.26 | 0.19 | -- | -- | — |
| 4Q | — | 0.28 | 0.19 | -- | -- | — |
| Yr. | — | 1.00 | 0.72 | 0.70 | 0.11 | — |

Next earnings report expected: **early June**

### Dividend Data (Dividends have been paid since 1994.)

| Amount ($) | Date Decl. | Ex-Div. Date | Stock of Record | Payment Date |
|---|---|---|---|---|
| 2-for-1 | Jun. 05 | Jul. 09 | Jun. 24 | Jul. 08 '96 |
| 0.035 | Sep. 10 | Sep. 18 | Sep. 20 | Oct. 01 '96 |
| 0.040 | Dec. 10 | Dec. 17 | Dec. 19 | Jan. 02 '97 |
| 0.040 | Mar. 07 | Mar. 13 | Mar. 17 | Apr. 01 '97 |

This report is for information purposes and should not be considered a solicitation to buy or sell any security. Neither S&P nor any other party guarantee its accuracy or make warranties regarding results from its usage. Redistribution is prohibited without written permission. Copyright © 1997

A Division of The **McGraw·Hill** Companies

## Business Summary - 15-MAR-97

Norrell Corp. is a leading provider of staffing, outsourcing and professional services through a network of 418 company-owned, franchise and outsourcing locations. NRL employs more than 8,000 associates, and in FY 97 (Oct.) will place over 220,000 people in both temporary and long-term assignments.

The company's overall business strategy is focused on: (i) providing a seamless "spectrum of services" to its clients including traditional temporary services, short-term and long-term staffing, value-added outsourcing solutions, and professional services; (ii) establishing itself as a recognized high quality service provider; and (iii) continuing to grow its existing base of business by developing new product offerings from existing services, expanding into additional skill classes, functional areas and technology, and entering into selected new markets. In 1996, the company: 1) expanded its capabilities in higher-growth, higher-margin services, such as teleservices and information technology services; 2) continued to re-engineer its service delivery process to enhance customer satisfaction; and 3) continued to focus on operational factors that increase efficiency and profitability.

As a national provider of temporary personnel and staffing services (73% of FY 96 sales), the company supplies its 18,000 clients with the services of individuals having a wide variety of office, light industrial and other skills, including secretarial, word processing, data entry, telemarketing, assembly, picking, packing and sorting, and shipping and receiving. In addition to providing temporary personnel and staffing services, the company provides its clients with outsourcing solutions (21% of FY 96 sales) in a similar range of office and business functions.

The professional services division (6% of FY 96 sales) recently completed the acquisition of Comtex Information Systems, a provider of information technology consulting services with annual revenues of $43 million. In the first quarter of FY 97, professional service sales increased 188%, reflecting the Comtex acquisition and strong internal growth in excess of 45%. NRL also offers professional services in the financial area including providing accounting, bookkeeping and other financial services. The company said the ongoing shift in revenue mix toward professional services indicates progress in its strategy to expand its faster-growing and higher margin businesses.

During FY 96, revenues generated from contracts with IBM and UPS accounted for 15.6% and 12.0%, respectively, of total revenues. No other client accounted for more than 10% of revenues in FY 96.

### Capitalization

**Long Term Debt:** $99,281,000 (1/97).
**Options:** To purchase 3,017,360 shs. at $3.05 to $32.00 ea. (10/95).

### Per Share Data ($)

| (Year Ended Oct. 31) | 1996 | 1995 | 1994 | 1993 | 1992 | 1991 | 1990 | 1989 | 1988 | 1987 |
|---|---|---|---|---|---|---|---|---|---|---|
| Tangible Bk. Val. | 2.25 | 2.55 | 2.15 | 0.82 | 0.15 | NA | NA | NA | NA | NA |
| Cash Flow | 1.25 | 0.91 | 0.93 | 0.43 | 0.46 | 0.18 | NA | NA | NA | NA |
| Earnings | 1.00 | 0.72 | 0.70 | 0.11 | 0.11 | -0.21 | 0.19 | NA | NA | NA |
| Dividends | 0.13 | 0.12 | 0.03 | Nil | Nil | Nil | Nil | NA | NA | NA |
| Payout Ratio | 14% | 17% | 4% | Nil | Nil | Nil | Nil | NA | NA | NA |
| Prices - High | 34½ | 17 | 9⅞ | NA | NA | NA | NA | NA | NA | NA |
|    - Low | 12⅝ | 9 | 7 | NA | NA | NA | NA | NA | NA | NA |
| P/E Ratio - High | 34 | 24 | 14 | NA | NA | NA | NA | NA | NA | NA |
|    - Low | 13 | 12 | 10 | NA | NA | NA | NA | NA | NA | NA |

### Income Statement Analysis (Million $)

| | 1996 | 1995 | 1994 | 1993 | 1992 | 1991 | 1990 | 1989 | 1988 | 1987 |
|---|---|---|---|---|---|---|---|---|---|---|
| Revs. | 1,014 | 813 | 681 | 562 | 399 | 351 | 375 | 374 | NA | NA |
| Oper. Inc. | 50.1 | 35.1 | 29.0 | 26.9 | 19.7 | 19.8 | NA | NA | NA | NA |
| Depr. | 6.3 | 4.4 | 5.3 | 7.6 | 7.9 | 8.3 | NA | NA | NA | NA |
| Int. Exp. | 1.2 | 0.2 | 1.8 | 3.7 | 4.5 | 6.2 | 6.5 | 7.3 | NA | NA |
| Pretax Inc. | 51.1 | 29.0 | 26.5 | 5.8 | 6.4 | -3.7 | 7.5 | 10.7 | NA | NA |
| Eff. Tax Rate | 39% | 42% | 43% | 45% | 55% | NM | 44% | 39% | NA | NA |
| Net Inc. | 25.3 | 16.8 | 15.1 | 3.2 | 2.9 | -4.4 | 4.2 | 6.5 | NA | NA |

### Balance Sheet & Other Fin. Data (Million $)

| | 1996 | 1995 | 1994 | 1993 | 1992 | 1991 | 1990 | 1989 | 1988 | 1987 |
|---|---|---|---|---|---|---|---|---|---|---|
| Cash | 8.9 | 5.1 | 7.4 | 3.7 | 3.9 | NA | NA | NA | NA | NA |
| Curr. Assets | 167 | 133 | 107 | 118 | 80.0 | 69.0 | 73.0 | 82.0 | NA | NA |
| Total Assets | 263 | 176 | 148 | 163 | 135 | 125 | 143 | 155 | NA | NA |
| Curr. Liab. | 103 | 79.8 | 62.1 | 88.4 | 53.9 | 47.2 | 42.1 | 51.2 | NA | NA |
| LT Debt | 23.3 | 2.1 | 0.4 | 19.2 | 27.7 | 45.3 | 60.9 | 59.3 | NA | NA |
| Common Eqty. | 98.0 | 70.2 | 65.1 | 42.1 | 43.2 | 24.8 | 33.9 | 36.1 | NA | NA |
| Total Cap. | 121 | 72.3 | 65.5 | 61.2 | 70.9 | 70.1 | 94.8 | 95.4 | NA | NA |
| Cap. Exp. | 7.4 | 5.8 | 2.0 | 3.1 | 1.2 | 1.6 | NA | NA | NA | NA |
| Cash Flow | 31.6 | 21.2 | 20.4 | 10.7 | 10.8 | 3.8 | NA | NA | NA | NA |
| Curr. Ratio | 1.6 | 1.7 | 1.7 | 1.3 | 1.5 | 1.5 | 1.7 | 1.6 | NA | NA |
| % LT Debt of Cap. | 19.2 | 2.8 | 0.6 | 31.3 | 39.1 | 64.6 | 64.2 | 62.1 | NA | NA |
| % Net Inc.of Revs. | 2.5 | 2.1 | 2.2 | 0.6 | 0.7 | NM | 1.1 | 1.7 | NA | NA |
| % Ret. on Assets | 11.4 | 10.4 | 9.7 | 2.1 | 2.2 | NM | 2.8 | 4.0 | NA | NA |
| % Ret. on Equity | 29.6 | 24.8 | 28.2 | 7.4 | 8.5 | NM | 11.9 | 16.3 | NA | NA |

Data as orig. reptd.; bef. results of disc. opers. and/or spec. items. Per share data adj. for stk. divs. as of ex-div. date. E-Estimated. NA-Not Available. NM-Not Meaningful. NR-Not Ranked.

**Office**—3535 Piedmont Rd. N.E., Atlanta, GA 30305. **Tel**—(404) 240-3000. **Website**—http://www.norrell.com **Chrmn**—G. W. Millner. **Pres & CEO**—C. D. Miller. **COO**—J.R. Riddle. **VP & CFO**—C. Kent Garner. **VP & Secy**—M. H. Hain. **Dirs**—L. J. Bryan, L. E. Burch III, K. Johnson-Street, D. A. McMahon, F. A. Metz Jr., C. D. Miller, G. W. Millner, N. C. Reynolds, C. E. Sanders, T. A. Vadnais. **Transfer Agent & Registrar**—First Union National Bank of North Carolina, Charlotte. **Incorporated**—in Georgia in 1965. **Empl**—8,000. **S&P Analyst:** Ronald M. Mushock

# Oracle Corporation

**4876T**

Nasdaq Symbol **ORCL**

In S&P 500

**17-MAY-97**

**Industry:** Computer (Software & Services)

**Summary:** Oracle supplies computer software products used for database management, applications development and decision support, as well as end-user and other applications.

**S&P Opinion: Buy (★★★★)**

| Recent Price • 44⅜ | Yield • Nil |
| --- | --- |
| 52 Wk Range • 51-32 | 12-Mo. P/E • 41.1 |

**Earnings vs. Previous Year**
▲=Up ▼=Down ▶=No Change

## Quantitative Evaluations

**Outlook** (1 Lowest—5 Highest)
• 5

**Fair Value**
• 57¼

**Risk**
• Average

**Earn./Div. Rank**
• B

**Technical Eval.**
• **Bearish** since 2/97

**Rel. Strength Rank** (1 Lowest—99 Highest)
• 85

**Insider Activity**
• **Neutral**

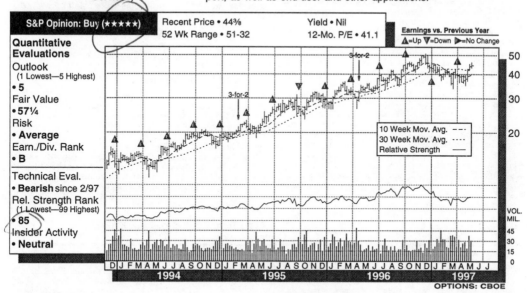

10 Week Mov. Avg. – – –
30 Week Mov. Avg. ·······
Relative Strength ——

OPTIONS: CBOE

## Overview - 18-MAR-97

Revenues should increase approximately 35% through FY 98 (May), reflecting strong demand for the company's relational database management system, robust sales of application products, continuing demand for services, and expansion of worldwide economies. Products for the UNIX and desktop environments (which account for about 90% of total revenues) should continue to grow rapidly. The availability of new products, including the expected June 1997 shipment of Oracle 8, a major upgrade to the company's flagship database program, bodes well. Margins are expected to be maintained in the FY 97 fourth quarter, as higher volume and expense controls are offset by a higher tax rate. However, margins should widen in FY 98, on a reduction of the tax rate along with continued volume efficiencies and cost controls. Comparisons in FY 98 should benefit from the greater revenues, wider margins, and absence of a nonrecurring acquisition charge of $0.04 a share in the FY 97 third quarter.

## Valuation - 18-MAR-97

Operating earnings should remain strong through FY 98. The database software segment is growing rapidly, as organizations cope with managing and utilizing the massive data stored on their computer systems. ORCL's leadership position bodes well for future results. The core database server business is strong, applications software revenues should grow rapidly, and there is a continuing need for additional services. The shares, which have fallen from their December 1996 highs, were recently trading at a P/E about equal to 75% of the projected growth rate over the next several years, based on calendar 1997 estimates. The strong earnings growth that we expect should help the stock outperform the market in coming months.

## Key Stock Statistics

| | | | |
| --- | --- | --- | --- |
| S&P EPS Est. 1997 | 1.20 | Tang. Bk. Value/Share | 2.85 |
| P/E on S&P Est. 1997 | 37.0 | Beta | 0.91 |
| S&P EPS Est. 1998 | 1.70 | Shareholders | 5,500 |
| Dividend Rate/Share | Nil | Market cap. (B) | $ 29.0 |
| Shs. outstg. (M) | 653.4 | Inst. holdings | 51% |
| Avg. daily vol. (M) | 6.028 | | |

Value of $10,000 invested 5 years ago: $ 137,715

### Fiscal Year Ending May 31

| | 1998 | 1997 | 1996 | 1995 | 1994 | 1993 |
| --- | --- | --- | --- | --- | --- | --- |
| **Revenues (Million $)** | | | | | | |
| 1Q | — | 1,052 | 771.8 | 556.5 | 398.0 | 307.0 |
| 2Q | — | 1,311 | 967.2 | 670.3 | 452.2 | 353.0 |
| 3Q | — | 1,373 | 1,020 | 722.3 | 482.8 | 370.0 |
| 4Q | — | — | 1,464 | 1,018 | 668.1 | 472.6 |
| Yr. | — | — | 4,223 | 2,967 | 2,001 | 1,503 |
| **Earnings Per Share ($)** | | | | | | |
| 1Q | — | 0.17 | 0.08 | 0.09 | 0.06 | 0.02 |
| 2Q | — | 0.27 | 0.20 | 0.14 | 0.09 | 0.05 |
| 3Q | — | 0.25 | 0.22 | 0.16 | 0.11 | 0.04 |
| 4Q | — | E0.51 | 0.40 | 0.27 | 0.17 | 0.10 |
| Yr. | E1.70 | E1.20 | 0.90 | 0.67 | 0.43 | 0.21 |

**Next earnings report expected: late June**

## Dividend Data

No cash dividends have been paid. A three-for-two stock split was effected in February 1995. A "poison pill" stock purchase rights plan was adopted in 1990.

This report is for information purposes and should not be considered a solicitation to buy or sell any security. Neither S&P nor any other party guarantee its accuracy or make warranties regarding results from its usage. Redistribution is prohibited without written permission. Copyright © 1997 | *A Division of The* **McGraw·Hill** *Companies*

## Business Summary - 08-OCT-96

Oracle Corporation develops, markets and supports computer software products used for database management, network communications, applications development and end-user applications. Its principal product is the ORACLE relational database management system (DBMS). The company offers its products, along with consulting, education, support and systems integration services, worldwide.

Database management systems software permits multiple users and applications to access data concurrently while protecting the data against user and program errors and against computer and network failures. Database management systems are used to support the data access and data management requirements of transaction processing and decision support systems. The ORACLE relational DBMS runs on a broad range of massively parallel, clustered, symmetrical multiprocessing, minicomputers, workstations and personal computers using the industry standard SQL language.

A variety of applications development products, sold as add-ons to the ORACLE relational DBMS, increase programmer productivity and allow non-programmers to design, develop and maintain their own programs. Access tools enable end users and decision support analysts to perform rapid querying, reporting and analysis of stored data.

The company also offers an integrated family of end-user financial applications, including general ledger, purchasing, payables, assets, receivables and revenue accounting programs, as well as manufacturing and human resource applications. These application products use the ORACLE relational DBMS and related development and decision support tools.

ORCL offers consulting, education and systems integration services to assist customers in the design and development of applications based on company products.

### Important Developments

**Mar. '97**—Total revenues in the third quarter of FY 97 (May) grew 35%, year to year; core database license revenues rose 32%, applications rose 61%, tools declined 9% and services advanced 41%.

**Mar. '97**—In the third quarter of FY 97. the company recorded a $36.8 million ($0.04 a share) charge for the writeoff of in-process research and development associated with its acqusition (for $81 million in cash) of the remaining shares of 13%-owned Datalogix, a vendor of process manufacturing applications.

### Capitalization

**Long Term Debt:** $300,950,000 (2/97).

### Per Share Data ($)

| (Year Ended May 31) | 1996 | 1995 | 1994 | 1993 | 1992 | 1991 | 1990 | 1989 | 1988 | 1987 |
|---|---|---|---|---|---|---|---|---|---|---|
| Tangible Bk. Val. | 2.85 | 1.87 | 1.15 | 0.82 | 0.69 | 0.56 | 0.66 | 0.40 | 0.25 | 0.16 |
| Cash Flow | 1.23 | 0.89 | 0.52 | 0.30 | 0.18 | 0.07 | 0.25 | 0.17 | 0.09 | 0.04 |
| Earnings | 0.90 | 0.67 | 0.43 | 0.22 | 0.10 | -0.02 | 0.19 | 0.14 | 0.07 | 0.03 |
| Dividends | Nil | Nil | Nil | Nil | Nil | Nil | Nil | Nil | Nil | Nil |
| Payout Ratio | Nil | Nil | Nil | Nil | Nil | Nil | Nil | Nil | Nil | Nil |
| Cal. Yrs. | 1995 | 1994 | 1993 | 1992 | 1991 | 1990 | 1989 | 1988 | 1987 | 1986 |
| Prices - High | 32½ | 20⅝ | 16¾ | 6⅜ | 3¾ | 6¼ | 5¾ | 2½ | 2⅛ | 13/16 |
| - Low | 17¾ | 11⅝ | 6 | 2⅝ | 1¼ | 1¹/₁₆ | 2¹/₁₆ | 1¼ | 9/16 | ⅜ |
| P/E Ratio - High | 36 | 31 | 39 | 30 | 39 | NM | 30 | 18 | 29 | 29 |
| - Low | 20 | 17 | 14 | 12 | 13 | NM | 11 | 9 | 8 | 13 |

### Income Statement Analysis (Million $)

| | | | | | | | | | | |
|---|---|---|---|---|---|---|---|---|---|---|
| Revs. | 4,223 | 2,967 | 2,001 | 1,503 | 1,178 | 1,028 | 971 | 584 | 282 | 131 |
| Oper. Inc. | 1,124 | 797 | 485 | 297 | 165 | 81.0 | 226 | 143 | 75.0 | 33.0 |
| Depr. | 220 | 148 | 65.2 | 56.2 | 50.9 | 54.5 | 35.9 | 19.7 | 10.6 | 4.6 |
| Int. Exp. | 6.6 | 7.0 | 6.9 | 9.0 | 18.6 | 24.0 | 12.1 | 4.3 | 1.5 | 1.2 |
| Pretax Inc. | 920 | 659 | 423 | 218 | 96.0 | -13.0 | 173 | 120 | 65.0 | 28.0 |
| Eff. Tax Rate | 34% | 33% | 33% | 35% | 36% | NM | 32% | 32% | 34% | 44% |
| Net Inc. | 603 | 442 | 284 | 142 | 62.0 | -12.0 | 117 | 82.0 | 43.0 | 16.0 |

### Balance Sheet & Other Fin. Data (Million $)

| | | | | | | | | | | |
|---|---|---|---|---|---|---|---|---|---|---|
| Cash | 841 | 586 | 465 | 358 | 177 | 101 | 50.0 | 49.0 | 49.0 | 38.0 |
| Curr. Assets | 2,284 | 1,617 | 1,076 | 842 | 641 | 586 | 569 | 337 | 192 | 109 |
| Total Assets | 3,357 | 2,425 | 1,595 | 1,184 | 956 | 858 | 787 | 460 | 250 | 144 |
| Curr. Liab. | 1,455 | 1,055 | 682 | 551 | 406 | 479 | 284 | 178 | 102 | 48.0 |
| LT Debt | 0.9 | 81.7 | 82.8 | 86.4 | 95.9 | 18.0 | 89.1 | 33.5 | 5.4 | 9.0 |
| Common Eqty. | 1,870 | 1,211 | 741 | 528 | 435 | 345 | 388 | 231 | 135 | 83.0 |
| Total Cap. | 1,880 | 1,321 | 862 | 623 | 541 | 369 | 499 | 276 | 147 | 95.0 |
| Cap. Exp. | 308 | 262 | 251 | 41.3 | 46.6 | 60.7 | 89.3 | 68.4 | 31.0 | 16.9 |
| Cash Flow | 823 | 589 | 349 | 198 | 112 | 42.0 | 153 | 101 | 54.0 | 20.0 |
| Curr. Ratio | 1.6 | 1.5 | 1.6 | 1.5 | 1.6 | 1.2 | 2.0 | 1.9 | 1.9 | 2.3 |
| % LT Debt of Cap. | 1.0 | 6.2 | 9.6 | 13.9 | 17.7 | 4.9 | 17.9 | 12.1 | 3.6 | 9.5 |
| % Net Inc.of Revs. | 14.3 | 14.9 | 14.2 | 9.4 | 5.2 | NM | 12.1 | 14.0 | 15.2 | 11.9 |
| % Ret. on Assets | 20.9 | 22.0 | 20.4 | 13.2 | 6.7 | NM | 18.6 | 22.6 | 21.5 | 15.1 |
| % Ret. on Equity | 39.1 | 45.2 | 44.6 | 29.2 | 15.6 | NM | 37.5 | 43.9 | 38.8 | 27.4 |

Data as orig. reptd.; bef. results of disc. opers. and/or spec. items. Per share data adj. for stk. divs. as of ex-div. date. E-Estimated. NA-Not Available. NM-Not Meaningful. NR-Not Ranked.

**Office**—500 Oracle Parkway, Redwood Shores, CA 94065. **Reincorporated**—in Delaware in 1987. **Tel**—(415) 506-7000. **E-mail**—investor@oracle.com **Website**—http://www.oracle.com **Chrmn, Pres & CEO**—L. J. Ellison. **EVP & CFO**—J. O. Henley. **SVP & Secy**—R. L. Ocampo, Jr. **Investor Contact**—Catherine Buan. **Dirs**—M. J. Boskin, L. J. Ellison, J. O. Henley, R. J. Lane, D. L. Lucas, D. W. Yocam. **Transfer Agent & Registrar**—Harris Trust & Savings Bank, Chicago. **Empl**— 28,844. **S&P Analyst:** Peter C. Wood, CFA

**17-MAY-97**

**Industry:**
Health Care (Managed Care)

**Summary:** Oxford Health operates managed healthcare plans in New York, New Jersey, Connecticut, Pennsylvania and New Hampshire.

**S&P Opinion: Accumulate (★★★★)**

| Recent Price • 63⅝ | Yield • Nil |
|---|---|
| 52 Wk Range • 68⅞-27⅝ | 12-Mo. P/E • 44.9 |

**Quantitative Evaluations**

Outlook
(1 Lowest—5 Highest)
• **5**

Fair Value
• **101**

Risk
• **Average**

Earn./Div. Rank
• **B**

Technical Eval.
• **Bullish** since 8/96

Rel. Strength Rank
(1 Lowest—99 Highest)
• **62**

Insider Activity
• **Unfavorable**

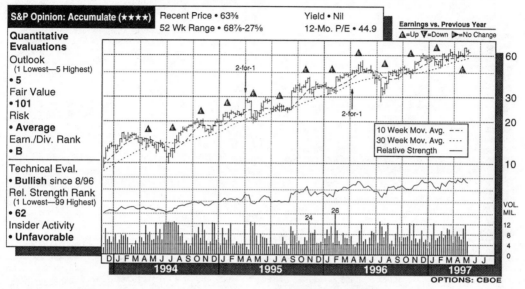

Earnings vs. Previous Year
▲=Up ▼=Down ▶=No Change

10 Week Mov. Avg. ---
30 Week Mov. Avg. ·····
Relative Strength —

OPTIONS: CBOE

## Overview - 17-MAR-97

Total revenues surpassed the $3 billion mark in 1996, reflecting another strong year for the Freedom point-of-service plan (334,700 members added since 1995 year-end) and growth in the "pure" HMO plan (80,300), along with gains in both the Medicare (57,900) and Medicaid (56,400) segments. For 1997, total revenues should approach $4.2 billion, as enrollment moves towards 2,000,000 and modest premium rate increases are implemented. With regard to margins, the full year medical loss ratio (MLR) is likely to approximate 80%, although the MLR will fluctuate during individual reporting periods because of seasonal factors. Administrative costs, which consumed about 15.5% of revenues in 1996, should settle at about 15% in 1997, providing an additional boost to EPS growth.

## Valuation - 17-MAR-97

We recently lowered our investment opinion to Hold from Strong Buy, primarily reflecting the belief that at a price of $66, the stock was fully priced at a P/E multiple to 38 times our 1997 EPS estimate of $1.75. In addition, we have concerns regarding the company's ongoing transition to a new computer and database system. While the conversion should provide greater efficiencies in the future, the transition process significantly disrupted the collections process in recent months, and the problem could be exacerbated by strong enrollment gains in the early portion of 1997 as the system comes under an increasing load. The issue also delayed the company's payments to network providers, but Oxford has agreed that it will now pay physician claims within 30 days. Over the long term, we remain bullish on the company's prospects and feel the stock will reward patient investors seeking exposure to the managed healthcare industry.

## Key Stock Statistics

| | | | |
|---|---|---|---|
| S&P EPS Est. 1997 | 1.85 | Tang. Bk. Value/Share | 7.73 |
| P/E on S&P Est. 1997 | 34.3 | Beta | 1.47 |
| S&P EPS Est. 1998 | 2.40 | Shareholders | 500 |
| Dividend Rate/Share | Nil | Market cap. (B) | $ 4.9 |
| Shs. outstg. (M) | 77.8 | Inst. holdings | 91% |
| Avg. daily vol. (M) | 1.686 | | |

Value of $10,000 invested 5 years ago: $ 235,813

## Fiscal Year Ending Dec. 31

| | 1998 | 1997 | 1996 | 1995 | 1994 | 1993 |
|---|---|---|---|---|---|---|
| **Revenues (Million $)** | | | | | | |
| 1Q | — | 987.3 | 658.1 | 331.1 | 125.5 | 57.10 |
| 2Q | — | — | 725.3 | 409.1 | 156.4 | 68.50 |
| 3Q | — | — | 811.3 | 480.2 | 199.6 | 85.80 |
| 4Q | — | — | 880.3 | 537.4 | 232.1 | 94.30 |
| Yr. | — | — | 3,075 | 1,765 | 713.6 | 305.8 |
| **Earnings Per Share ($)** | | | | | | |
| 1Q | — | 0.42 | 0.25 | 0.14 | 0.08 | 0.05 |
| 2Q | — | E0.43 | 0.28 | 0.15 | 0.09 | 0.05 |
| 3Q | — | E0.48 | 0.33 | 0.21 | 0.11 | 0.06 |
| 4Q | — | E0.52 | 0.38 | 0.21 | 0.13 | 0.07 |
| Yr. | E2.40 | E1.85 | 1.24 | 0.71 | 0.41 | 0.22 |

**Next earnings report expected: early August**

## Dividend Data

The company has never paid cash dividends on its common stock. A 2-for-1 stock split was effected in March 1995.

This report is for information purposes and should not be considered a solicitation to buy or sell any security. Neither S&P nor any other party guarantee its accuracy or make warranties regarding results from its usage. Redistribution is prohibited without written permission. Copyright © 1997

*A Division of The McGraw·Hill Companies*

STANDARD
&POOR'S
STOCK REPORTS

# Oxford Health Plans

## 4885K
### 17-MAY-97

## Business Summary - 20-FEB-97

Oxford Health Plans Inc. provides healthcare benefit plans in New York, New Jersey, Pennsylvania, Connecticut and New Hampshire. Products include point-of-service plans, traditional health maintenance organizations (HMOs), third-party administration of employer-funded benefit plans and dental plans.

The Freedom Plan (64% of total premiums earned in 1995) is a point-of-service managed care option that combines the benefits of Oxford's HMOs with those of conventional fee-for-service health insurance. The Freedom Plan gives members the option of either using Oxford's HMO plan or choosing unaffiliated physicians. Small to medium-size employers (10 to 1,500 employees) are targeted for the product. At 1996 year-end, Freedom Plan enrollment was 1,015,100, up from 680,400 a year-earlier.

Oxford's licensed HMOs (11%) offer plans in each of the states in which the company operates. About 650 employers currently offer Oxford's HMO programs, of which about 40% are located in New York. At December 31, 1996, commercial HMO membership was 192,300, versus 112,000 at the end of 1995.

The company's New York, New Jersey and Connecticut HMOs provide Medicare (14%) and Medicaid (10%) plans to eligible individuals. At the end of 1996, Medicare membership had surged to 125,000 from 67,100 a year earlier, while enrollment in the Medicaid plan rose to 162,000 from 105,600.

Oxford also offers health plans under which employers self-insure health care expenses and pays for health claims only as they are incurred. In return, OXHP earns fees to provide claims processing and health care cost containment services through its provider network and utilization management programs. Self-funded enrollment was 41,100 at December 31, 1996, down from 42,600 a year-earlier.

The company maintains a network of about 29,900 physicians in New York (13,800), New Jersey (6,300), Pennsylvania (6,300) and Connecticut (3,500). It also maintains a contractual network of over 1,200 dentists through which it offers two dental benefit plans.

Oxford is also developing a program under which it organizes private practice physicians into small medical groups in order to achieve the operating efficiencies and quality control of larger medical groups. By 1995 year-end, a total of 119 practice groups with 2,500 primary care doctors had been established, and Oxford was expecting to have over 190 practice groups organized by 1996 year-end.

### Important Developments

**Feb. '97**—Oxford said that, as of mid-February 1997, enrollment had reached 1,690,000, up by 155,000 members from the level at 1996 year-end, as it continued to attract new members from competing Blue Cross plans, indemnity (fee-for-service) insurance carriers, and other preferred provider organization health plans.

### Capitalization

**Long Term Obligations:** None (12/96).

### Per Share Data ($)

| (Year Ended Dec. 31) | 1996 | 1995 | 1994 | 1993 | 1992 | 1991 | 1990 | 1989 | 1988 | 1987 |
|---|---|---|---|---|---|---|---|---|---|---|
| Tangible Bk. Val. | 7.73 | 3.20 | 1.99 | 1.46 | 0.13 | NA | NA | NA | NA | NA |
| Cash Flow | 1.41 | 1.03 | 0.51 | 0.27 | 0.15 | NA | NA | NA | NA | NA |
| Earnings | 1.24 | 0.71 | 0.40 | 0.22 | 0.13 | 0.08 | 0.03 | NA | NA | NA |
| Dividends | Nil | Nil | Nil | Nil | Nil | Nil | Nil | NA | NA | NA |
| Payout Ratio | Nil | Nil | Nil | Nil | Nil | Nil | Nil | NA | NA | NA |
| Prices - High | 62¼ | 41⅞ | 20⅞ | 14 | NA | NA | NA | NA | NA | NA |
|     - Low | 27⅝ | 19¼ | 9⅞ | 4 | NA | NA | NA | NA | NA | NA |
| P/E Ratio - High | 50 | 59 | 52 | 62 | NA | NA | NA | NA | NA | NA |
|     - Low | 22 | 27 | 24 | 18 | NA | NA | NA | NA | NA | NA |

### Income Statement Analysis (Million $)

| | 1996 | 1995 | 1994 | 1993 | 1992 | 1991 | 1990 | 1989 | 1988 | 1987 |
|---|---|---|---|---|---|---|---|---|---|---|
| Revs. | 3,075 | 1,765 | 714 | 306 | 151 | NA | NA | NA | NA | NA |
| Oper. Inc. | 190 | 118 | 51.4 | 22.7 | 10.7 | NA | NA | NA | NA | NA |
| Depr. | 13.2 | 23.0 | 7.1 | 2.9 | 1.3 | NA | NA | NA | NA | NA |
| Int. Exp. | Nil | Nil | Nil | Nil | Nil | NA | NA | NA | NA | NA |
| Pretax Inc. | 172 | 91.4 | 49.5 | 26.1 | 13.8 | NA | NA | NA | NA | NA |
| Eff. Tax Rate | 42% | 43% | 44% | 43% | 42% | NA | NA | NA | NA | NA |
| Net Inc. | 100 | 52.4 | 27.9 | 14.9 | 8.0 | NA | NA | NA | NA | NA |

### Balance Sheet & Other Fin. Data (Million $)

| | 1996 | 1995 | 1994 | 1993 | 1992 | 1991 | 1990 | 1989 | 1988 | 1987 |
|---|---|---|---|---|---|---|---|---|---|---|
| Cash | 839 | 369 | 191 | 110 | NA | NA | NA | NA | NA | NA |
| Curr. Assets | 1,201 | 492 | 255 | 135 | NA | NA | NA | NA | NA | NA |
| Total Assets | 1,347 | 609 | 315 | 166 | 106 | NA | NA | NA | NA | NA |
| Curr. Liab. | 749 | 389 | 188 | 75.0 | NA | NA | NA | NA | NA | NA |
| LT Debt | Nil | Nil | Nil | Nil | Nil | NA | NA | NA | NA | NA |
| Common Eqty. | 598 | 220 | 127 | 91.0 | 66.0 | NA | NA | NA | NA | NA |
| Total Cap. | 598 | 220 | 127 | 91.0 | 66.0 | NA | NA | NA | NA | NA |
| Cap. Exp. | 48.3 | 83.9 | 30.8 | 11.7 | 2.9 | NA | NA | NA | NA | NA |
| Cash Flow | 113 | 75.4 | 35.0 | 17.8 | 9.3 | NA | NA | NA | NA | NA |
| Curr. Ratio | 1.6 | 1.3 | 1.4 | 1.8 | NA | NA | NA | NA | NA | NA |
| % LT Debt of Cap. | Nil | Nil | Nil | Nil | 0.3 | NA | NA | NA | NA | NA |
| % Net Inc.of Revs. | 3.2 | 3.0 | 3.9 | 4.9 | 5.3 | NA | NA | NA | NA | NA |
| % Ret. on Assets | 10.2 | 11.2 | 11.6 | 11.0 | 9.6 | NA | NA | NA | NA | NA |
| % Ret. on Equity | 24.4 | 29.7 | 25.6 | 19.0 | 14.5 | NA | NA | NA | NA | NA |

Data as orig. reptd.; bef. results of disc. opers. and/or spec. items. Per share data adj. for stk. divs. as of ex-div. date. E-Estimated. NA-Not Available. NM-Not Meaningful. NR-Not Ranked.

**Office**—800 Connecticut Ave., Norwalk, CT 06854. **Tel**—(203) 852-1442.**Chrmn & CEO**—S. F. Wiggins. **Pres & COO**—W. M. Sullivan.**CFO**—A. B. Cassidy. **VP & Contr**—B. R. Shanahan. **Dirs**—J. B. Adamson, R. B. Milligan Jr., F. F. Nazem, M. J. Radosevich, T. A. Scully, B. H. Safirstein, S. F. Wiggins. **Transfer Agent**—Fleet National Bank, Providence, RI. **Incorporated**—in Delaware in 1984. **Empl**— 4,000. **S&P Analyst:** Robert M. Gold.

**17-MAY-97**　Industry:
Computer (Software & Services)

**Summary:** This company is a leader in the mechanical design automation industry with its Pro/ENGINEER line of integrated software products.

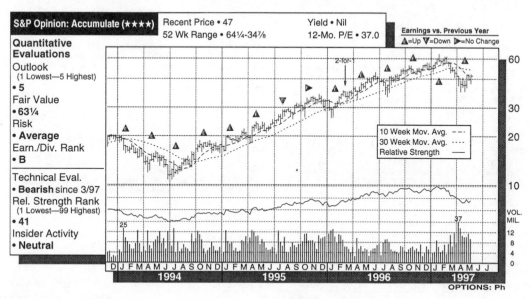

| S&P Opinion: Accumulate (★★★★) | Recent Price • 47 | Yield • Nil |
| | 52 Wk Range • 64¼-34⅞ | 12-Mo. P/E • 37.0 |

**Quantitative Evaluations**

Outlook
(1 Lowest—5 Highest)
• **5**

Fair Value
• **63¼**

Risk
• **Average**

Earn./Div. Rank
• **B**

Technical Eval.
• **Bearish** since 3/97

Rel. Strength Rank
(1 Lowest—99 Highest)
• **41**

Insider Activity
• **Neutral**

Earnings vs. Previous Year
▲=Up ▼=Down ▶=No Change

10 Week Mov. Avg. ----
30 Week Mov. Avg. ·······
Relative Strength ——

OPTIONS: Ph

## Overview - 15-APR-97

Revenues are expected to advance over 40% in FY 97 (Sep.), reflecting continued strong demand for Pro/ENGINEER mechanical design automation software and associated modules, and an ongoing need for services, as well as higher average selling prices. The company enjoys a high level of repeat business and continues to add new accounts, gaining market share at the expense of more established competitors. While reported international results are expected to be penalized by a strong U.S. dollar, margins should widen slightly, as volume efficiencies outweigh the costs of continued investments in R&D. EPS should benefit from anticipated higher revenues, modest margin expansion, and a lower tax rate, as well as a stock repurchase program. Strengthening of worldwide economies would also aid results. FY 97 comparisons should also benefit from the absence of a charge of $0.15 a share related to the acquisition of project modeling and management software technology.

## Valuation - 15-APR-97

While the overall market for mechanical design automation software is growing slowly, Parametric has enjoyed very rapid growth. Its Pro/ENGINEER product line is gaining market share, through the displacement of incumbent competitors, as well as through the addition of seats (software units) within its own list of customers. We expect continued market share gains, as the company invests in enhancing Pro/ENGINEER with additional features and performance capabilities, and strengthens its worldwide sales organization. The stock's premium valuation is deserved. In light of projected earnings gains, the shares are expected to outperform the market in coming months.

## Key Stock Statistics

| | | | |
|---|---|---|---|
| S&P EPS Est. 1997 | 1.65 | Tang. Bk. Value/Share | 4.02 |
| P/E on S&P Est. 1997 | 28.5 | Beta | 1.62 |
| S&P EPS Est. 1998 | 2.20 | Shareholders | 1,700 |
| Dividend Rate/Share | Nil | Market cap. (B) | $ 6.0 |
| Shs. outstg. (M) | 127.5 | Inst. holdings | 87% |
| Avg. daily vol. (M) | 2.026 | | |

Value of $10,000 invested 5 years ago: $ 62,406

### Fiscal Year Ending Sep. 30

| | 1998 | 1997 | 1996 | 1995 | 1994 | 1993 |
|---|---|---|---|---|---|---|
| **Revenues (Million $)** | | | | | | |
| 1Q | — | 183.5 | 125.4 | 72.02 | 53.52 | 32.50 |
| 2Q | — | 198.0 | 140.5 | 83.53 | 58.02 | 38.00 |
| 3Q | — | — | 157.1 | 97.02 | 63.62 | 43.52 |
| 4Q | — | — | 177.1 | 119.2 | 69.09 | 49.01 |
| Yr. | — | — | 600.1 | 394.3 | 244.3 | 163.1 |
| **Earnings Per Share ($)** | | | | | | |
| 1Q | — | 0.37 | 0.25 | 0.17 | 0.13 | 0.08 |
| 2Q | — | 0.39 | 0.28 | 0.19 | 0.13 | 0.08 |
| 3Q | — | E0.43 | 0.31 | 0.11 | 0.15 | 0.10 |
| 4Q | — | E0.46 | 0.20 | 0.16 | 0.16 | 0.11 |
| Yr. | E2.20 | E1.65 | 1.04 | 0.60 | 0.57 | 0.38 |

Next earnings report expected: mid July

### Dividend Data

No cash dividends have been paid. The shares were split two-for-one in February 1996, 1993 and 1992.

This report is for information purposes and should not be considered a solicitation to buy or sell any security. Neither S&P nor any other party guarantee its accuracy or make warranties regarding results from its usage. Redistribution is prohibited without written permission. Copyright © 1997

*A Division of The* **McGraw-Hill** *Companies*

## Business Summary - 15-APR-97

Parametric Technology Corporation develops, markets and supports a family of fully integrated software products for the automation of the mechanical design-through-manufacturing process, a complex, iterative process encompassing a broad spectrum of distinct engineering disciplines that is essential to the development of virtually all manufactured products, from consumer items to jet aircraft.

The company's mechanical design automation (MDA) products enable end-users to reduce the time-to-market and manufacturing costs for their products and, through the easy evaluation of multiple design alternatives, to improve product quality.

Parametric's product line consists of its core product, Pro/ENGINEER, and more than 70 related application modules. Pro/ENGINEER is a parametric, feature-driven solid modeling system used in the detailed design phase of the MDA cycle. Other modules include Pro/DESIGN, a conceptual design tool; Pro/DETAIL and Pro/DRAFT, which generate detailed manufacturing drawings; and Pro/ASSEMBLY, used to design and manage very complex assemblies. The company's practice has been to issue two major releases of its product line annually, with each generally including several new products. Parametric's ability to develop new products rapidly is facilitated by the modular structure of its software code. The company's products run on a wide range of workstations.

Marketing and sales efforts are focused primarily on electronic equipment, aerospace, automotive, consumer products and telecommunications companies, with sales made directly to strategic customers and indirectly through value-added resellers and original equipment manufacturers.

End-users of the company's products range from small companies to some of the world's largest manufacturing organizations.

In the fourth quarter of FY 96 (Sep.), Parametric recorded a $32,119,000 ($0.15 a share) charge to reflect the writeoff of in-process R&D, as well as other costs associated with the acquisition of acquired project modeling and management software technology from Greenshire License Co. In the fourth quarter of FY 95, the company recorded a charge of $10.4 million ($0.07 a share, as adjusted) to reflect costs associated with its acquisition of Rasna Corp. In the third quarter of FY 95, it recorded a $19.0 million ($0.10 a share, as adjusted) nonrecurring charge.

### Important Developments

**Apr. '97**—In the second quarter of FY 97, the company shipped 7,475 new seats (units) of software, bringing the total installed base to more than 85,990 seats. Repeat business from the existing customer base accounted for 73% of total revenue.

### Capitalization

**Long Term Debt:** None (3/97).

### Per Share Data ($)

| (Year Ended Sep. 30) | 1996 | 1995 | 1994 | 1993 | 1992 | 1991 | 1990 | 1989 | 1988 | 1987 |
|---|---|---|---|---|---|---|---|---|---|---|
| Tangible Bk. Val. | 4.02 | 2.97 | 2.13 | 1.35 | 0.76 | 0.43 | 0.30 | -0.06 | NA | NA |
| Cash Flow | 1.16 | 0.68 | 0.61 | 0.39 | 0.20 | 0.10 | 0.06 | 0.03 | NA | NA |
| Earnings | 1.04 | 0.60 | 0.57 | 0.38 | 0.19 | 0.09 | 0.06 | 0.02 | -0.02 | NA |
| Dividends | Nil | Nil | Nil | Nil | Nil | Nil | Nil | Nil | Nil | NA |
| Payout Ratio | Nil | Nil | Nil | Nil | Nil | Nil | Nil | Nil | Nil | NA |
| Prices - High | 56¾ | 36¼ | 20⅛ | 22⅜ | 14⅛ | 7⅝ | 2⅝ | 1¹³/₁₆ | NA | NA |
| - Low | 25⅞ | 16 | 10¾ | 11¼ | 6⅜ | 1⅞ | 1¼ | 1 | NA | NA |
| P/E Ratio - High | 55 | 60 | 35 | 60 | 76 | 81 | 48 | 98 | NM | NA |
| - Low | 25 | 27 | 19 | 30 | 34 | 20 | 23 | 72 | NM | NA |

### Income Statement Analysis (Million $)

| | 1996 | 1995 | 1994 | 1993 | 1992 | 1991 | 1990 | 1989 | 1988 | 1987 |
|---|---|---|---|---|---|---|---|---|---|---|
| Revs. | 600 | 394 | 244 | 163 | 86.7 | 44.7 | 25.5 | 11.0 | 3.3 | NA |
| Oper. Inc. | 222 | 128 | 107 | 68.8 | 32.3 | 15.1 | 8.0 | 2.7 | NA | NA |
| Depr. | 16.8 | 9.5 | 4.6 | 2.7 | 1.3 | 0.7 | 0.6 | 0.5 | NA | NA |
| Int. Exp. | Nil | NM | NA | NM | NM | 0.1 | 0.1 | 0.1 | 0.1 | NA |
| Pretax Inc. | 216 | 128 | 107 | 68.5 | 33.2 | 15.9 | 8.6 | 2.3 | -0.8 | NA |
| Eff. Tax Rate | 36% | 39% | 37% | 37% | 37% | 35% | 35% | 31% | Nil | NA |
| Net Inc. | 138 | 77.4 | 66.9 | 42.9 | 21.1 | 10.3 | 5.6 | 1.6 | -0.8 | NA |

### Balance Sheet & Other Fin. Data (Million $)

| | 1996 | 1995 | 1994 | 1993 | 1992 | 1991 | 1990 | 1989 | 1988 | 1987 |
|---|---|---|---|---|---|---|---|---|---|---|
| Cash | 434 | 308 | 207 | 123 | 73.5 | 34.5 | 24.6 | 3.3 | NA | NA |
| Curr. Assets | 562 | 400 | 271 | 165 | 99 | 48.7 | 33.1 | 6.8 | NA | NA |
| Total Assets | 659 | 454 | 287 | 177 | 107 | 51.0 | 35.0 | 8.0 | NA | NA |
| Curr. Liab. | 146 | 82.0 | 44.3 | 28.9 | 27.0 | 7.7 | 4.5 | 2.2 | NA | NA |
| LT Debt | Nil | NM | NA | NM | Nil | 0.0 | 0.2 | 0.6 | NA | NA |
| Common Eqty. | 512 | 371 | 242 | 147 | 78.7 | 42.0 | 28.8 | -0.9 | NA | NA |
| Total Cap. | 512 | 371 | 243 | 148 | 80.2 | 43.2 | 30.1 | 5.4 | NA | NA |
| Cap. Exp. | 29.7 | 12.9 | 9.1 | 7.4 | 3.6 | 0.8 | 0.5 | 0.1 | 0.3 | NA |
| Cash Flow | 155 | 86.9 | 71.5 | 45.6 | 22.4 | 11.0 | 6.2 | 1.8 | NA | NA |
| Curr. Ratio | 3.8 | 4.9 | 6.1 | 5.7 | 3.7 | 6.3 | 7.3 | 3.1 | NA | NA |
| % LT Debt of Cap. | NM | NM | NA | Nil | Nil | NM | 0.7 | 10.3 | NA | NA |
| % Net Inc.of Revs. | 23.0 | 19.6 | 27.4 | 26.3 | 24.3 | 23.1 | 22.0 | 14.5 | NM | NA |
| % Ret. on Assets | 24.8 | 20.4 | 28.4 | 29.7 | 26.2 | 23.9 | 13.3 | NA | NA | NA |
| % Ret. on Equity | 31.2 | 24.9 | 33.8 | 37.5 | 34.3 | 28.8 | NM | NA | NA | NA |

Data as orig. reptd.; bef. results of disc. opers. and/or spec. items. Per share data adj. for stk. divs. as of ex-div. date. E-Estimated. NA-Not Available. NM-Not Meaningful. NR-Not Ranked.

**Office**—128 Technology Drive, Waltham, MA 02154. **Tel**—(617) 398-5000. **Fax**—(617) 398-6000.**Chrmn & CEO**—S. C. Walske. **Pres & COO**—C. R. Harrison.**CFO**—E. Gillis. **SVP, Treas**—M. J. Gallagher. **VP & Investor Contact**—John W. Hudson. **Dirs**—R. N. Goldman, D. K. Grierson, C. R. Harrison, M. E. Porter, N. G. Posternak, S. C. Walske. **Transfer Agent & Registrar**—American Stock Transfer & Trust Co., NYC. **Incorporated**—in Massachusetts in 1985. **Empl**— 3,133. **S&P Analyst:** Peter C. Wood, CFA

# Paychex, Inc.

**4937**

Nasdaq Symbol **PAYX**

In S&P MidCap 400

**17-MAY-97**

**Industry:** Services (Data Processing)

**Summary:** This company mainly provides computerized payroll accounting services to small and medium-size firms nationwide.

**S&P Opinion: Accumulate (★★★★)**

| Recent Price • 50⅛ | Yield • 0.7% |
|---|---|
| 52 Wk Range • 63⅝-38¼ | 12-Mo. P/E • 51.7 |

## Quantitative Evaluations

**Outlook** (1 Lowest—5 Highest)
• **1⁻**

**Fair Value**
• **42**

**Risk**
• **Average**

**Earn./Div. Rank**
• **A-**

**Technical Eval.**
• **Bearish** since 1/97

**Rel. Strength Rank** (1 Lowest—99 Highest)
• **76**

**Insider Activity**
• **Neutral**

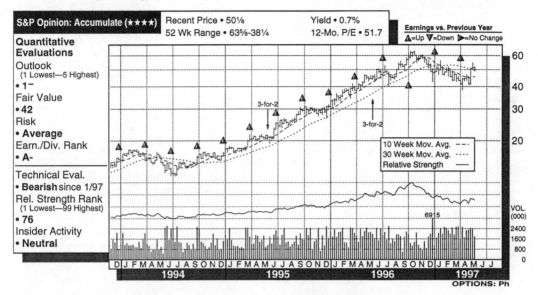

Earnings vs. Previous Year
▲=Up ▼=Down ▶=No Change

10 Week Mov. Avg. - - -
30 Week Mov. Avg. ·····
Relative Strength ——

VOL. (000)

OPTIONS: Ph

## Overview - 20-MAR-97

Operating revenues (as restated for the company's pooling of interests merger with National Business Solutions) are expected to increase over 25% in the final quarter of FY 97 (May) and in FY 98, reflecting strength across all major product areas, especially growth in the core payroll client base, further penetration of key add-on services, including Taxpay and Direct Deposit, and a more aggressive move into the human resources area. Margins should widen on the higher revenues, merger related synergies, the implementation of price increases and well controlled operating expenses. We expect net income to increase about 35% in FY 97 and almost 30% in FY 98. In October 1996, the company raised its quarterly dividend 50%, to $0.09 a share.

## Valuation - 20-MAR-97

The stock gained over 50% in 1996, aided by strong and consistent earnings gains. The company continues to benefit from a growing move toward outsourcing, as small businesses realize that it is often cost effective and more efficient for a company like PAYX to handle payroll and other routine processing services. Building on its successful core payroll operations, the company has moved into complementary areas, including the paying of taxes for customers, direct deposit, and employee benefit administrative services. We expect earnings to grow about 30% through FY 98 and foresee the potential of upside surprises to our earnings estimates. The shares trade at about 38 times earnings, or about a 25% premium to the company's growth rate, based on our calendar 1997 earnings estimate. However, this premium valuation is deserved and could widen further, as the company's future appears bright. We expect the shares to outperform the market in the months ahead.

## Key Stock Statistics

| | | | |
|---|---|---|---|
| S&P EPS Est. 1997 | 1.05 | Tang. Bk. Value/Share | 2.78 |
| P/E on S&P Est. 1997 | 47.7 | Beta | 0.90 |
| S&P EPS Est. 1998 | 1.35 | Shareholders | 3,700 |
| Dividend Rate/Share | 0.36 | Market cap. (B) | $ 3.6 |
| Shs. outstg. (M) | 72.3 | Inst. holdings | 53% |
| Avg. daily vol. (M) | 0.456 | | |

Value of $10,000 invested 5 years ago: $ 75,329

## Fiscal Year Ending May 31

| | 1998 | 1997 | 1996 | 1995 | 1994 | 1993 |
|---|---|---|---|---|---|---|
| **Revenues (Million $)** | | | | | | |
| 1Q | — | 166.0 | 76.18 | 62.92 | 53.33 | 45.30 |
| 2Q | — | 169.5 | 78.23 | 63.77 | 54.31 | 45.70 |
| 3Q | — | 195.6 | 84.94 | 68.64 | 57.57 | 48.60 |
| 4Q | — | — | 85.94 | 71.85 | 58.84 | 50.37 |
| Yr. | — | — | 325.3 | 267.2 | 224.1 | 190.0 |
| **Earnings Per Share ($)** | | | | | | |
| 1Q | — | 0.24 | 0.18 | 0.14 | 0.10 | 0.08 |
| 2Q | — | 0.25 | 0.19 | 0.15 | 0.11 | 0.08 |
| 3Q | — | 0.27 | 0.19 | 0.13 | 0.10 | 0.07 |
| 4Q | — | E0.29 | 0.21 | 0.15 | 0.11 | 0.08 |
| Yr. | E1.35 | E1.05 | 0.77 | 0.58 | 0.42 | 0.30 |

**Next earnings report expected: early July**

**Dividend Data** (Dividends have been paid since 1988.)

| Amount ($) | Date Decl. | Ex-Div. Date | Stock of Record | Payment Date |
|---|---|---|---|---|
| 0.090 | Oct. 03 | Oct. 24 | Oct. 28 | Nov. 25 '96 |
| 0.090 | Jan. 09 | Jan. 28 | Jan. 30 | Feb. 20 '97 |
| 0.090 | Apr. 10 | Apr. 29 | May. 01 | May. 22 '97 |
| 3-for-2 | Apr. 10 | May. 30 | May. 08 | May. 29 '97 |

This report is for information purposes and should not be considered a solicitation to buy or sell any security. Neither S&P nor any other party guarantee its accuracy or make warranties regarding results from its usage. Redistribution is prohibited without written permission. Copyright © 1997

*A Division of The McGraw·Hill Companies*

STANDARD
&POOR'S
STOCK REPORTS

# Paychex, Inc.

**4937**

17-MAY-97

## Business Summary - 20-MAR-97

Paychex, Inc. was formed in 1979 through the consolidation of 17 corporations providing computerized payroll accounting services nationwide. The company concentrates on small to medium-size firms. As of May 31, 1996, its 75 branch operating centers and 23 sales offices were furnishing services to about 234,000 clients. PAYX believes that it ranks as the second-largest U.S. payroll accounting services company.

Services include preparation of paychecks, earnings statements and internal accounting records. The company supplies clients with all required monthly, quarterly and annual payroll tax returns for federal, state and local governments. The computerized Paychex system utilizes proprietary software that is regularly updated to accommodate regulatory changes.

Taxpay is an extension of the company's payroll service. PAYX deposits payroll taxes and files returns for Taxpay clients, and assumes full responsibility for accurate and timely filings. Taxpay is used by over 55% of clients nationwide.

The company also provides enhanced payroll services, including an automatic salary deposit service (Direct Deposit) which electronically transmits the net payroll for client's employees to banks throughout the Federal Reserve System. In addition, a digital check signing and inserting service is offered.

PAYX does not have written contracts with clients, but 80% of businesses served in FY 94 (May) and FY 95 continued as clients in FY 96.

The company's Human Resources Services division provides employee management services and fringe benefit products including customized employee handbooks, management manuals, job descriptions and personnel forms as well as 401-K recordkeeping services, group health and disability insurance, workers' compensation and group life, and Section 125 Cafeteria Plans. The cafeteria plans allow employees to pay for certain fringe benefits with pretax dollars, with a resultant savings to the employer of Social Security taxes.

## Important Developments

**Mar. '97**—Revenues in the third quarter of FY 97 advanced 27%, year to year (as restated for the acquisiiton of National Business Solutions, Inc.), reflecting a 21% gain in payroll revenues (to 50% of total revenue) and a 34% increase in PEO/HRS revenues (50%). Operating income from payroll services rose 50%, to $25.9 million; operating income from the PEO/HRS segment increased 18%, to $900,000 (including $400,000 of start-up costs related to the March opening of six offices).

## Capitalization

**Long Term Debt:** None (2/97).

### Per Share Data ($)

| (Year Ended May 31) | 1996 | 1995 | 1994 | 1993 | 1992 | 1991 | 1990 | 1989 | 1988 | 1987 |
|---|---|---|---|---|---|---|---|---|---|---|
| Tangible Bk. Val. | 2.78 | 2.07 | 1.61 | 1.27 | 1.01 | 0.82 | 0.71 | 0.61 | 0.48 | 0.36 |
| Cash Flow | 0.97 | 0.75 | 0.58 | 0.45 | 0.35 | 0.27 | 0.24 | 0.23 | 0.18 | 0.13 |
| Earnings | 0.77 | 0.58 | 0.42 | 0.30 | 0.21 | 0.15 | 0.13 | 0.15 | 0.11 | 0.08 |
| Dividends | 0.22 | 0.15 | 0.10 | 0.07 | 0.05 | 0.04 | 0.03 | 0.02 | Nil | Nil |
| Payout Ratio | 28% | 25% | 23% | 22% | 22% | 26% | 23% | 12% | Nil | Nil |
| Cal. Yrs. | 1995 | 1994 | 1993 | 1992 | 1991 | 1990 | 1989 | 1988 | 1987 | 1986 |
| Prices - High | 33¼ | 18⅛ | 16¾ | 11⅞ | 6⅞ | 4 | 5⅜ | 4 | 4⅛ | 3⅜ |
|    - Low | 17⅛ | 12⅝ | 10 | 6⅜ | 2⅞ | 2⅜ | 3⅜ | 2⅞ | 2³/₁₆ | 1⅝ |
| P/E Ratio - High | 43 | 31 | 40 | 40 | 33 | 28 | 42 | 28 | 38 | 43 |
|    - Low | 22 | 22 | 24 | 21 | 14 | 16 | 26 | 20 | 21 | 21 |

### Income Statement Analysis (Million $)

| | 1996 | 1995 | 1994 | 1993 | 1992 | 1991 | 1990 | 1989 | 1988 | 1987 |
|---|---|---|---|---|---|---|---|---|---|---|
| Revs. | 325 | 267 | 224 | 190 | 161 | 137 | 120 | 101 | 79.0 | 64.0 |
| Oper. Inc. | 81.4 | 62.1 | 47.8 | 37.1 | 28.4 | 21.7 | 19.4 | 20.0 | 15.4 | 13.4 |
| Depr. | 13.9 | 11.0 | 11.0 | 10.4 | 9.6 | 8.4 | 7.3 | 5.9 | 4.7 | 3.3 |
| Int. Exp. | Nil | 0.2 | 0.1 | 0.1 | 0.1 | 0.2 | 0.2 | 0.2 | 0.2 | 0.2 |
| Pretax Inc. | 72.7 | 54.4 | 39.0 | 28.0 | 19.5 | 14.0 | 13.2 | 15.0 | 11.2 | 10.2 |
| Eff. Tax Rate | 28% | 28% | 28% | 29% | 30% | 32% | 35% | 37% | 38% | 50% |
| Net Inc. | 52.3 | 39.0 | 28.1 | 20.0 | 13.7 | 9.6 | 8.6 | 9.4 | 6.9 | 5.1 |

### Balance Sheet & Other Fin. Data (Million $)

| | 1996 | 1995 | 1994 | 1993 | 1992 | 1991 | 1990 | 1989 | 1988 | 1987 |
|---|---|---|---|---|---|---|---|---|---|---|
| Cash | 117 | 83.7 | 55.6 | 38.1 | 20.0 | 11.0 | 15.8 | 19.4 | 13.8 | 9.2 |
| Curr. Assets | 165 | 124 | 87.0 | 64.2 | 41.6 | 29.7 | 31.4 | 32.5 | 23.3 | 16.7 |
| Total Assets | 220 | 168 | 130 | 107 | 86.2 | 70.4 | 62.1 | 54.8 | 42.5 | 32.6 |
| Curr. Liab. | 28.1 | 26.7 | 19.0 | 17.8 | 13.7 | 10.5 | 10.2 | 9.5 | 6.0 | 4.7 |
| LT Debt | Nil | 0.5 | 0.7 | 1.2 | 1.6 | 2.0 | 1.6 | 2.1 | 2.8 | 2.4 |
| Common Eqty. | 191 | 140 | 109 | 85.2 | 67.4 | 54.5 | 47.2 | 40.2 | 31.5 | 24.0 |
| Total Cap. | 191 | 141 | 110 | 87.8 | 70.7 | 58.3 | 50.6 | 44.4 | 35.8 | 27.5 |
| Cap. Exp. | 17.0 | 12.3 | 11.6 | 8.7 | 13.5 | 17.4 | 15.4 | 9.1 | 8.1 | 5.4 |
| Cash Flow | 66.3 | 50.1 | 39.1 | 30.4 | 23.3 | 18.0 | 15.9 | 15.4 | 11.6 | 8.4 |
| Curr. Ratio | 5.9 | 4.7 | 4.6 | 3.6 | 3.0 | 2.8 | 3.1 | 3.4 | 3.9 | 3.6 |
| % LT Debt of Cap. | Nil | 0.4 | 0.7 | 1.4 | 2.3 | 3.5 | 3.3 | 4.8 | 7.7 | 8.6 |
| % Net Inc.of Revs. | 16.1 | 14.7 | 12.5 | 10.5 | 8.5 | 7.0 | 7.1 | 9.3 | 8.7 | 8.0 |
| % Ret. on Assets | 26.9 | 26.2 | 23.7 | 20.6 | 17.4 | 14.5 | 14.6 | 19.4 | 18.4 | 17.3 |
| % Ret. on Equity | 31.7 | 31.5 | 28.9 | 26.1 | 22.4 | 18.9 | 19.6 | 26.3 | 24.9 | 24.0 |

Data as orig. reptd.; bef. results of disc. opers. and/or spec. items. Per share data adj. for stk. divs. as of ex-div. date. E-Estimated. NA-Not Available. NM-Not Meaningful. NR-Not Ranked.

**Office**—911 Panorama Trail South, Rochester, NY 14625-0397. **Tel**—(716) 385-6666. **Chrmn, Pres & CEO**—B. T. Golisano. **CFO, Secy, Treas & Investor Contact**—G. Thomas Clark. **Dirs**—D. W. Brinckman, S. D. Brooks, G. T. Clark, B. T. Golisano, P. Horsley, G. M. Inman, H. P. Messina Jr., J. R. Sebo. **Transfer Agent**—American Stock Transfer & Trust Co., NYC.**Incorporated**—in Delaware in 1979. **Empl**—3,950. **S&P Analyst:** Peter C. Wood, CFA

**17-MAY-97**

**Industry:**
Manufacturing (Specialized)

**Summary:** PAXAR manufactures bar-code tag and labeling systems, as well as printed labels, woven labels and merchandise tags, for the apparel and textile industries.

| Quantitative Evaluations | |
|---|---|
| **Outlook** (1 Lowest—5 Highest) • **4** | |
| **Fair Value** • **22¾** | |
| **Risk** • **Average** | |
| **Earn./Div. Rank** • **B+** | |
| **Technical Eval.** • **Bullish** since 3/95 | |
| **Rel. Strength Rank** (1 Lowest—99 Highest) • **30** | |
| **Insider Activity** • **Unfavorable** | |

Recent Price • 18½
52 Wk Range • 21-12⅞

Yield • Nil
12-Mo. P/E • 22.6

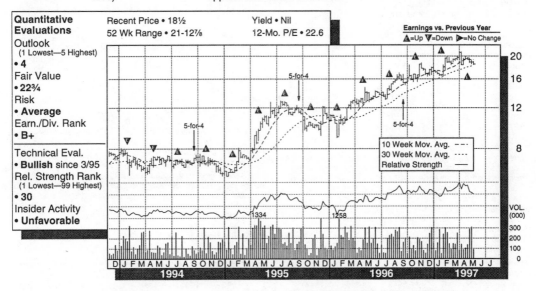

Earnings vs. Previous Year
▲=Up ▼=Down ▷=No Change

10 Week Mov. Avg. - - -
30 Week Mov. Avg. · · · ·
Relative Strength ——

1994    1995    1996    1997

## Business Profile - 12-MAY-97

The company attributes its strong growth in recent years to a strategy of focusing on apparel and textile customers. In June 1995, a new company formed by PAXAR and Odyssey Partners L.P. acquired Monarch Marking Systems and related operations from Pitney Bowes for $127 million in cash. Monarch is a manufacturer of bar code systems and supplies. In March 1997, the company bought out Odyssey's interest in Monarch, and it is now a wholly owned subsidiary of the company. Based on recent strength in sales and the completion of a restructuring at Monarch, managment is optimistic regarding results in 1997.

## Operational Review - 12-MAY-97

Revenues for the three months ended March 31, 1997, climbed 53%, year to year, reflecting the consolidation of Monarch, 17% higher international sales, an improved domestic apparel retail environment, and new product introductions. Gross margins widened on the higher volume and restructuring actions at Monarch, and following a 66% increase in SG&A expenses, operating profit advanced 64%. In the absence of equity income from an affiliate, and with a sharp jump in interest expense, pretax income gained 35%. After taxes at 29.7%, versus 28.0%, net income was up 31%, to $5,702,000 ($0.20 a share, on 2.6% more shares), from $4,343,000 ($0.15, as adjusted).

## Stock Performance - 16-MAY-97

In the past 30 trading days, PXR's shares have increased 0.68%, compared to a 9% rise in the S&P 500. Average trading volume for the past five days was 17,400 shares, compared with the 40-day moving average of 33,246 shares.

## Key Stock Statistics

| | | | |
|---|---|---|---|
| Dividend Rate/Share | Nil | Shareholders | 900 |
| Shs. outstg. (M) | 27.9 | Market cap. (B) | $0.517 |
| Avg. daily vol. (M) | 0.044 | Inst. holdings | 31% |
| Tang. Bk. Value/Share | 3.35 | | |
| Beta | 0.63 | | |

Value of $10,000 invested 5 years ago: $ 64,156

### Fiscal Year Ending Dec. 31

| | 1997 | 1996 | 1995 | 1994 | 1993 | 1992 |
|---|---|---|---|---|---|---|
| **Revenues (Million $)** | | | | | | |
| 1Q | 80.46 | 52.75 | 50.52 | 35.98 | 36.20 | 30.90 |
| 2Q | — | 57.55 | 52.90 | 42.46 | 36.34 | 36.20 |
| 3Q | — | 51.94 | 49.31 | 41.01 | 32.62 | 31.00 |
| 4Q | — | 57.58 | 48.71 | 47.16 | 33.69 | 34.50 |
| Yr. | — | 219.8 | 201.4 | 166.6 | 138.9 | 132.6 |
| **Earnings Per Share ($)** | | | | | | |
| 1Q | 0.20 | 0.15 | 0.14 | 0.08 | 0.10 | 0.09 |
| 2Q | — | 0.20 | 0.16 | 0.12 | 0.10 | 0.11 |
| 3Q | — | 0.19 | 0.13 | 0.10 | 0.08 | 0.05 |
| 4Q | — | 0.23 | 0.14 | 0.12 | 0.07 | 0.09 |
| Yr. | — | 0.77 | 0.56 | 0.42 | 0.35 | 0.33 |

**Next earnings report expected: late July**

### Dividend Data

| Amount ($) | Date Decl. | Ex-Div. Date | Stock of Record | Payment Date |
|---|---|---|---|---|
| 5-for-4 | Aug. 07 | Sep. 10 | Aug. 21 | Sep. 09 '96 |

This report is for information purposes and should not be considered a solicitation to buy or sell any security. Neither S&P nor any other party guarantee its accuracy or make warranties regarding results from its usage. Redistribution is prohibited without written permission. Copyright © 1997

*A Division of The* **McGraw·Hill** *Companies*

## Business Summary - 12-MAY-97

PAXAR Corporation is a fully integrated manufacturer and distributor of label systems, bar-code systems, labels, tags and related supplies and services for apparel manufacturers and retailers.

To broaden its product line and enhance its market position, the company has developed new products and completed several acquisitions since 1986. In 1994, it acquired Collitex and Astria, two related Italian companies engaged in the woven label business. It also purchased an 80% interest in Orvafin, an Italian company engaged in the production and distribution of inks and coated fabrics for labeling systems. In 1995, the company acquired a 49.5% interest in Monarch Marking Systems, a manufacturer of bar code systems and supplies; it purchased the remaining interest in March 1997. In January 1996, PAXAR purchased Brian Pulfrey, Ltd., a manufacturer of printed labels and tags in Nottingham, England.

The company's tag and label systems consist primarily of bar-code tag systems and hot-stamp label printers. These systems let customers print, cut and batch large volumes of tags and labels in their own plants. PAXAR's bar-code tag systems include personal computers, electronic bar-code printers, thermal ink, pre-printed tag stock and supporting software. Hot-stamp printing systems include hot-stamp printers, fabrics, inks and printing accessories, which are used by manufacturers for in-house printing of care labels and labels that carry brand logo, size and other information for the retail customer. Tag and label systems and supplies accounted for 50% and 54% of net sales in 1996 and 1995, respectively.

PAXAR also designs and produces finished tags and woven and printed labels in its manufacturing facilities in the U.S., England, Italy and Hong Kong, and ships them to domestic and international apparel manufacturers. Its labels are printed on a wide range of fabrics and other materials. Labels are often attached to garments early in the manufacturing process, and must withstand all production processes and remain legible through washing and dry cleaning by the consumer.

The company has more than 10,000 customers, including major retailers and apparel manufacturers such as Levi Strauss, Sears, J.C. Penney, The Limited, Liz Claiborne, Sara Lee, Land's End and L.L. Bean. In 1996, Levi Strauss accounted for 11% of total sales.

### Important Developments

**Apr. '97**—PAXAR redeemed all $100 million of Monarch's 12.5% senior notes due 2003. Redemption of the outstanding notes represented completion of the second stage of PXR's strategy to purchase Monarch, and allowed the company to replace this high-yield debt with lower-cost financing.

### Capitalization

**Long Term Debt:** $215,952,000 (3/97).

### Per Share Data ($)

| (Year Ended Dec. 31) | 1996 | 1995 | 1994 | 1993 | 1992 | 1991 | 1990 | 1989 | 1988 | 1987 |
|---|---|---|---|---|---|---|---|---|---|---|
| Tangible Bk. Val. | 3.62 | 2.86 | 2.33 | 2.30 | 1.94 | 1.14 | 0.99 | 0.91 | 0.71 | 0.70 |
| Cash Flow | 1.11 | 0.85 | 0.67 | 0.52 | 0.48 | 0.29 | 0.18 | 0.33 | 0.15 | 0.18 |
| Earnings | 0.77 | 0.56 | 0.42 | 0.34 | 0.33 | 0.16 | 0.05 | 0.19 | 0.05 | 0.10 |
| Dividends | Nil | Nil | Nil | Nil | Nil | Nil | Nil | Nil | Nil | Nil |
| Payout Ratio | Nil | Nil | Nil | Nil | Nil | Nil | Nil | Nil | Nil | Nil |
| Prices - High | 18¾ | 12⅞ | 8⅛ | 8⅜ | 9⅛ | 3 | 2 | 2½ | 2 | 1¹¹⁄₁₆ |
| - Low | 8⅞ | 6⅛ | 6⅛ | 5⅜ | 2⅞ | 1³⁄₁₆ | 1¹⁄₁₆ | 1¹⁄₁₆ | 1¹⁄₁₆ | ⁹⁄₁₆ |
| P/E Ratio - High | 24 | 23 | 19 | 24 | 28 | 19 | 36 | 13 | 36 | 17 |
| - Low | 12 | 11 | 14 | 16 | 9 | 7 | 20 | 6 | 20 | 6 |

### Income Statement Analysis (Million $)

| | 1996 | 1995 | 1994 | 1993 | 1992 | 1991 | 1990 | 1989 | 1988 | 1987 |
|---|---|---|---|---|---|---|---|---|---|---|
| Revs. | 220 | 201 | 167 | 139 | 133 | 88.9 | 72.9 | 73.8 | 56.2 | 42.7 |
| Oper. Inc. | 36.1 | 31.3 | 24.8 | 19.6 | 18.3 | 9.9 | 6.0 | 8.6 | 5.3 | 5.8 |
| Depr. | 9.7 | 8.1 | 6.8 | 4.7 | 3.6 | 2.8 | 2.7 | 2.3 | 1.8 | 1.3 |
| Int. Exp. | 1.4 | 1.6 | 0.9 | 0.8 | 0.5 | 1.1 | 1.5 | 1.9 | 1.5 | 0.8 |
| Pretax Inc. | 29.1 | 22.1 | 17.1 | 14.5 | 13.9 | 6.0 | 1.8 | 6.7 | 2.0 | 3.7 |
| Eff. Tax Rate | 25% | 29% | 32% | 35% | 40% | 42% | 36% | 38% | 43% | 43% |
| Net Inc. | 21.8 | 15.7 | 11.6 | 9.4 | 8.4 | 3.4 | 1.1 | 4.2 | 1.2 | 2.1 |

### Balance Sheet & Other Fin. Data (Million $)

| | 1996 | 1995 | 1994 | 1993 | 1992 | 1991 | 1990 | 1989 | 1988 | 1987 |
|---|---|---|---|---|---|---|---|---|---|---|
| Cash | 6.7 | 6.7 | 4.5 | 0.7 | 0.3 | 0.3 | 1.2 | 0.3 | 0.6 | 0.8 |
| Curr. Assets | 78.3 | 70.9 | 64.0 | 47.8 | 42.4 | 30.3 | 26.6 | 27.3 | 24.4 | 19.1 |
| Total Assets | 182 | 157 | 129 | 85.5 | 72.8 | 51.1 | 43.0 | 44.3 | 43.9 | 34.5 |
| Curr. Liab. | 28.9 | 24.3 | 25.0 | 17.6 | 14.1 | 13.1 | 9.1 | 10.2 | 6.7 | 8.1 |
| LT Debt | 19.9 | 23.1 | 13.8 | 0.7 | 2.1 | 10.2 | 10.9 | 13.0 | 21.3 | 10.2 |
| Common Eqty. | 120 | 95.2 | 77.9 | 62.5 | 52.8 | 25.0 | 20.8 | 19.2 | 15.1 | 14.8 |
| Total Cap. | 152 | 129 | 102 | 67.9 | 58.6 | 38.0 | 34.0 | 34.1 | 37.2 | 26.3 |
| Cap. Exp. | 13.8 | 12.3 | 11.2 | 12.6 | 8.5 | 6.6 | 3.2 | 1.5 | 2.6 | 2.5 |
| Cash Flow | 31.5 | 23.8 | 18.4 | 14.0 | 12.0 | 6.3 | 3.9 | 6.4 | 3.0 | 3.4 |
| Curr. Ratio | 2.7 | 2.9 | 2.6 | 2.7 | 3.0 | 2.3 | 2.9 | 2.7 | 3.6 | 2.4 |
| % LT Debt of Cap. | 13.1 | 17.9 | 13.5 | 1.1 | 3.6 | 27.0 | 32.1 | 38.0 | 57.2 | 38.8 |
| % Net Inc.of Revs. | 9.9 | 7.8 | 7.0 | 6.7 | 6.3 | 3.9 | 1.6 | 5.6 | 2.1 | 4.9 |
| % Ret. on Assets | 12.9 | 11.0 | 10.7 | 11.8 | 12.2 | 7.2 | 2.6 | 9.4 | 3.0 | 7.1 |
| % Ret. on Equity | 20.3 | 18.2 | 16.4 | 16.2 | 19.9 | 14.8 | 5.7 | 24.2 | 7.8 | 15.1 |

Data as orig. reptd.; bef. results of disc. opers. and/or spec. items. Per share data adj. for stk. divs. as of ex-div. date. E-Estimated. NA-Not Available. NM-Not Meaningful. NR-Not Ranked.

**Office**—105 Corporate Park Drive, White Plains, NY 10604-3814. **Tel**—(914) 697-6800. **Fax**—(914) 697-6893. **Website**—http://www.paxar.com **Chrmn & CEO**—A. Hershaft. **Pres & COO**—V. Hershaft. **VP, CFO, Secy & Investor Contact**—Jack R. Plaxe. **Dirs**—J. Becker, L. Benatar, A. Hershaft, V. Hershaft, R. G. Laidlaw, T. R. Loemker, D. E. McKinney, S. Merians, R. T. Puopolo. W. W. Williams. **Transfer Agent & Registrar**—ChaseMellon Shareholder Services, S. Hackensack, NJ. **Incorporated**—in New York in 1946. **Empl**— 2,095. **S&P Analyst:** Ted Groesbeck

# PeopleSoft, Inc.

**4961H**

Nasdaq Symbol **PSFT**

**17-MAY-97**

**Industry:**
Computer (Software & Services)

**Summary:** This growing software firm develops and sells a family of cross-industry, human resource management, financial, distribution and manufacturing applications.

**S&P Opinion: Hold (★★★)**

| | |
|---|---|
| Recent Price • 48½ | Yield • Nil |
| 52 Wk Range • 56¾-28¼ | 12-Mo. P/E • NM |

**Quantitative Evaluations**

Outlook
(1 Lowest—5 Highest)
• **NA**

Fair Value
• **NA**

Risk
• **Average**

Earn./Div. Rank
• **NR**

Technical Eval.
• **Bullish** since 9/96

Rel. Strength Rank
(1 Lowest—99 Highest)
• **91**

Insider Activity
• **Neutral**

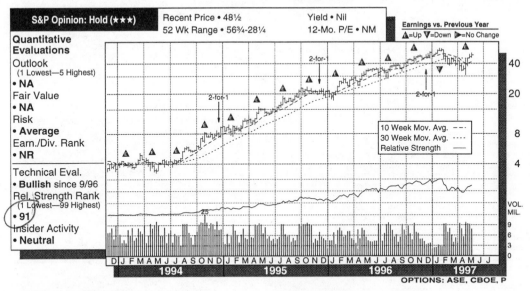

Earnings vs. Previous Year
△=Up ▽=Down ▷=No Change

10 Week Mov. Avg. -- -
30 Week Mov. Avg. ....
Relative Strength —

OPTIONS: ASE, CBOE, P

## Overview - 14-MAY-97

Revenues in 1997 are expected to continue their rapid ascent, rising well over 50% from those of 1996, driven by solid gains in the licensing of core software products, as well as even more rapid growth in the services business. In 1996, license revenue generated from the Peoplesoft HRMS product totaled $142.5 million (56% of total license fees), versus $87.8 million (64%) in 1995. Peoplesoft Financials, Distribution and Manufacturing license fees totaled $110.3 million (44%) and $50.0 million (36%) in 1996 and 1995, respectively. Revenue growth should be strong throughout the world. Margins are expected to widen, on volume related efficiencies, despite a less favorable revenue mix of services. Comparisons in 1997 will benefit from the absence of $0.16 of nonrecurring charges recorded in the 1996 fourth quarter.

## Valuation - 14-MAY-97

The shares of this major applications software vendor, which more than doubled in 1996, have retrenched along with the general market thus far in 1997, despite continued rapid sales and earnings growth. The company's flagship human resource management system continues to grow rapidly. Peoplesoft has extended its application products to include financial, distribution and, most recently, manufacturing applications; these products are also being well received. The company's software applications are well positioned, and revenue and earnings are expected to grow rapidly in 1997. The shares were recently trading at 57X our projection of 1997 EPS. The stock deserves a premium valuation, in light of the company's superior growth prospects. However, we believe that the shares are fairly valued, and expect the stock only to move in line with the market in coming months.

## Key Stock Statistics

| | | | |
|---|---|---|---|
| S&P EPS Est. 1997 | 0.70 | Tang. Bk. Value/Share | 2.35 |
| P/E on S&P Est. 1997 | 69.3 | Beta | NA |
| S&P EPS Est. 1998 | 1.05 | Shareholders | 1,300 |
| Dividend Rate/Share | Nil | Market cap. (B) | $ 5.3 |
| Shs. outstg. (M) | 108.5 | Inst. holdings | 63% |
| Avg. daily vol. (M) | 2.334 | | |

Value of $10,000 invested 5 years ago: NA

### Fiscal Year Ending Dec. 31

| | 1998 | 1997 | 1996 | 1995 | 1994 | 1993 |
|---|---|---|---|---|---|---|
| **Revenues (Million $)** | | | | | | |
| 1Q | — | 153.6 | 82.28 | 40.10 | 20.10 | 10.00 |
| 2Q | — | — | 102.7 | 51.30 | 24.90 | 13.30 |
| 3Q | — | — | 117.4 | 60.09 | 29.60 | 14.90 |
| 4Q | — | — | 147.7 | 76.02 | 38.30 | 20.00 |
| Yr. | — | — | 450.0 | 227.6 | 112.9 | 58.20 |
| **Earnings Per Share ($)** | | | | | | |
| 1Q | — | 0.14 | 0.08 | 0.04 | 0.02 | 0.01 |
| 2Q | — | E0.15 | 0.10 | 0.06 | 0.03 | 0.02 |
| 3Q | — | E0.18 | 0.11 | 0.07 | 0.03 | 0.02 |
| 4Q | — | E0.23 | 0.01 | 0.10 | 0.05 | 0.03 |
| Yr. | E1.05 | E0.70 | 0.30 | 0.27 | 0.14 | 0.08 |

**Next earnings report expected: late July**

### Dividend Data

| Amount ($) | Date Decl. | Ex-Div. Date | Stock of Record | Payment Date |
|---|---|---|---|---|
| 2-for-1 | Oct. 23 | Dec. 02 | Nov. 15 | Nov. 29 '96 |

This report is for information purposes and should not be considered a solicitation to buy or sell any security. Neither S&P nor any other party guarantee its accuracy or make warranties regarding results from its usage. Redistribution is prohibited without written permission. Copyright © 1997

*A Division of The McGraw-Hill Companies*

STANDARD
&POOR'S
STOCK REPORTS

**PeopleSoft, Inc.**

**4961H**
**17-MAY-97**

## Business Summary - 14-MAY-97

PeopleSoft, Inc. designs, develops, markets and supports a family of cross-industry, human resource management and financial system applications for use throughout large and medium-sized organizations. Its products operate on a wide range of hardware platforms, including IBM mainframes, UNIX-based minicomputers from Digital Equipment, Hewlett-Packard and others, and personal computers operating on local area networks. The company has designed its software products specifically for the client/server model of computing. Revenues in recent years were derived as follows:

|              | 1996 | 1995 | 1994 |
|--------------|------|------|------|
| License fees | 56%  | 59%  | 61%  |
| Services     | 44%  | 41%  | 39%  |

PeopleSoft Human Resource Management System (HRMS) products (which accounted for 55% and 62% of license revenues in 1996 and 1995, respectively) include the human resource module, which provides support for personnel administration, recruitment, position management, training and development, health and safety, skills inventory, career planning, affirmative action planning and EEO reporting; the benefits administration module, which provides the capabilities required to support daily benefits administration activities; the flexible spending account administration module for claims tracking and processing; the payroll module, which provides a full in-house payroll administration and production facility for payroll calculations, check printing, tax reporting and deduction and benefit calculations; and the payroll interface module, which provides an interface between HRMS data and third-party payroll systems.

The company's financial application product family (43% and 35%, respectively, in 1996 and 1995) includes the general ledger module; the receivables module; the payables module; and the asset management module. The company also offers distribution and manufacturing application products and application development and administration, analysis, reporting and workflow tools.

## Important Developments

**Apr. '97**—In the 1997 first quarter, contracting activity for software products and related bundled services totaled $145.6 million, versus $74.1 million in the 1996 interim.

**Feb. '97**—In the fourth quarter of 1996, the company recorded nonrecurring charges totaling $29.4 million ($0.16 a share), consisting of $26.5 million related to the acquisition of the PMI manufacturing software vendors and $2.9 million for the acquisition of Red Pepper Software.

## Capitalization

**Long Term Liabilities:** None (3/97).

### Per Share Data ($)

| (Year Ended Dec. 31) | 1996 | 1995 | 1994 | 1993 | 1992 | 1991 | 1990 | 1989 | 1988 | 1987 |
|---|---|---|---|---|---|---|---|---|---|---|
| Tangible Bk. Val. | 2.35 | 1.59 | 1.01 | 0.77 | 0.57 | 0.02 | NA | NA | NA | NA |
| Cash Flow | 0.52 | 0.37 | 0.21 | 0.10 | 0.07 | 0.03 | NA | NA | NA | NA |
| Earnings | 0.30 | 0.27 | 0.14 | 0.08 | 0.06 | 0.03 | NA | NA | NA | NA |
| Dividends | Nil | Nil | Nil | Nil | Nil | Nil | NA | NA | NA | NA |
| Payout Ratio | Nil | Nil | Nil | Nil | Nil | Nil | NA | NA | NA | NA |
| Prices - High | 52¼ | 23½ | 9⅞ | 5⅛ | 4 | NA | NA | NA | NA | NA |
|    - Low | 17⅛ | 7½ | 3¼ | 3 | 2⅞ | NA | NA | NA | NA | NA |
| P/E Ratio - High | NM | 87 | 71 | 61 | 67 | NA | NA | NA | NA | NA |
|     - Low | NM | 28 | 23 | 36 | 47 | NA | NA | NA | NA | NA |

### Income Statement Analysis (Million $)

| | 1996 | 1995 | 1994 | 1993 | 1992 | 1991 | 1990 | 1989 | 1988 | 1987 |
|---|---|---|---|---|---|---|---|---|---|---|
| Revs. | 450 | 228 | 113 | 58.2 | 31.6 | 17.1 | NA | NA | NA | NA |
| Oper. Inc. | 112 | 56.2 | 29.0 | 14.4 | 8.9 | 4.4 | NA | NA | NA | NA |
| Depr. | 26.7 | 11.3 | 7.3 | 1.9 | 0.8 | 0.4 | NA | NA | NA | NA |
| Int. Exp. | Nil | Nil | Nil | 0.0 | 0.1 | 0.1 | NA | NA | NA | NA |
| Pretax Inc. | 61.7 | 48.9 | 23.9 | 13.7 | 8.1 | 3.1 | NA | NA | NA | NA |
| Eff. Tax Rate | 42% | 40% | 39% | 39% | 40% | 38% | NA | NA | NA | NA |
| Net Inc. | 35.9 | 29.4 | 14.6 | 8.4 | 4.8 | 1.9 | NA | NA | NA | NA |

### Balance Sheet & Other Fin. Data (Million $)

| | 1996 | 1995 | 1994 | 1993 | 1992 | 1991 | 1990 | 1989 | 1988 | 1987 |
|---|---|---|---|---|---|---|---|---|---|---|
| Cash | 197 | 126 | 88.0 | 56.7 | 42.1 | 2.1 | NA | NA | NA | NA |
| Curr. Assets | 397 | 244 | 149 | 97.0 | 60.0 | 14.0 | NA | NA | NA | NA |
| Total Assets | 540 | 314 | 172 | 108 | 64.0 | 16.0 | NA | NA | NA | NA |
| Curr. Liab. | 287 | 156 | 78.0 | 35.4 | 15.7 | 8.2 | NA | NA | NA | NA |
| LT Debt | Nil | Nil | Nil | Nil | 0.3 | 0.4 | NA | NA | NA | NA |
| Common Eqty. | 253 | 157 | 93.3 | 72.1 | 47.7 | 1.3 | NA | NA | NA | NA |
| Total Cap. | 253 | 157 | 93.3 | 72.1 | 47.9 | 7.0 | NA | NA | NA | NA |
| Cap. Exp. | 18.3 | 53.2 | 18.2 | 5.8 | 2.1 | 1.2 | NA | NA | NA | NA |
| Cash Flow | 62.6 | 40.6 | 21.8 | 10.3 | 5.2 | 2.0 | NA | NA | NA | NA |
| Curr. Ratio | 1.4 | 1.6 | 1.9 | 2.7 | 3.8 | 1.7 | NA | NA | NA | NA |
| % LT Debt of Cap. | Nil | Nil | Nil | Nil | 0.5 | 5.7 | NA | NA | NA | NA |
| % Net Inc.of Revs. | 8.0 | 12.9 | 12.9 | 14.5 | 15.3 | 11.1 | NA | NA | NA | NA |
| % Ret. on Assets | 8.3 | 12.1 | 3.5 | 9.3 | 10.9 | NA | NA | NA | NA | NA |
| % Ret. on Equity | 17.3 | 21.1 | 17.6 | 13.4 | 17.6 | NA | NA | NA | NA | NA |

Data as orig. reptd.; bef. results of disc. opers. and/or spec. items. Per share data adj. for stk. divs. as of ex-div. date. E-Estimated. NA-Not Available. NM-Not Meaningful. NR-Not Ranked.

**Office**—4440 Rosewood Dr., Pleasanton, CA 94588. **Tel**—(510) 225-3000. **Website**—http://www.peoplesoft.com **Chrmn, Pres & CEO**—D. A. Duffield. **SVP-Fin, CFO, Secy & Investor Contact**—Ronald E. F. Codd. **Dirs**—A. G. Battle, E. F. Codd, A. W. Duffield, D. A. Duffield, G. J. Still, Jr., C. J. Yansouni. **Transfer Agent**—Boston EquiServe, Canton, MA. **Incorporated**—in Delaware in 1987. **Empl**— 2.867. **S&P Analyst:** Peter C. Wood, CFA

# STANDARD &POOR'S
STOCK REPORTS

# Pfizer Inc.

# 1810

NYSE Symbol **PFE**

**In S&P 500**

**17-MAY-97**

**Industry:**
Health Care (Drugs - Major Pharmaceuticals)

**Summary:** This leading global pharmaceutical company also has interests in hospital products, animal health items and consumer products.

**S&P Opinion: Buy (★★★★)**

| Recent Price • 100¾ | Yield • 1.4% |
|---|---|
| 52 Wk Range • 102½-65⅝ | 12-Mo. P/E • 32.4 |

## Quantitative Evaluations

**Outlook**
(1 Lowest—5 Highest)
• **2⁻**

**Fair Value**
• **94%**

**Risk**
• **Low**

**Earn./Div. Rank**
• **A-**

**Technical Eval.**
• **Bullish** since 7/94

**Rel. Strength Rank**
(1 Lowest—99 Highest)
• **83**

**Insider Activity**
• **NA**

**Earnings vs. Previous Year**
▲=Up ▼=Down ▶=No Change

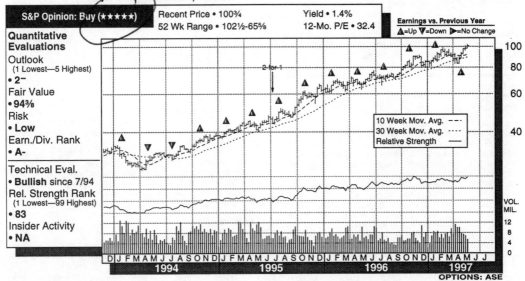

10 Week Mov. Avg. -----
30 Week Mov. Avg. ·······
Relative Strength ——

OPTIONS: ASE

## Overview - 13-MAY-97

Pfizer should again post strong double-digit earnings growth in 1997, fueled primarily by a strong lineup of new drugs. Key products exhibiting impressive gains include Norvasc and Cardura cardiovasculars (up 29% and 26%, respectively, in the first quarter of 1997), Zithromax anti-infective (up 65%), Zoloft antidepressant (up 24%), and Glucotrol XL treatment for diabetes (up 48%). Volume should also be augmented by new drugs such as Zyrtec low-sedating antihistamine, Aricept for Alzheimer's, and Lipitor cholesterol-lowering agent. Gains in these drugs should significantly outweigh declining sales in older lines such as Procardia XL cardiovascular, Glucotrol anti-diabetic, and Feldene antiarthritic. Gains are also seen for hospital products, consumer items and animal health products. Profitability should benefit the better volume, an improved product mix, and a lower tax rate.

## Valuation - 13-MAY-97

The shares have moved steadily higher over the past three years, buoyed by strength in pharmaceutical issues in general, and by Pfizer's impressive earnings gains. Earnings growth is being driven by a strong portfolio of new drugs that account for over two thirds of Pfizer's drug sales. Bolstered by expansion in its drug portfolio, PFE currently ranks sixth in the worldwide drug industry, up from 13th five years ago. The worldwide sales force has recently been increased about 17%, to about 11,000. During 1997, the company plans to file new drug applications for ziprasidone antipsychotic, Viagra for male erectile dysfunction, and dofetilide for cardiac arrhythmias. The R&D pipeline also includes promising treatments for migraine, cancer, diabetic neuropathy, fungal infections and other conditions. We continue to recommend purchase of the shares, which are being split two for one in June.

## Key Stock Statistics

| | | | |
|---|---|---|---|
| S&P EPS Est. 1997 | 3.50 | Tang. Bk. Value/Share | 8.03 |
| P/E on S&P Est. 1997 | 28.8 | Beta | 1.26 |
| S&P EPS Est. 1998 | 4.10 | Shareholders | 65,000 |
| Dividend Rate/Share | 1.36 | Market cap. (B) | $ 65.1 |
| Shs. outstg. (M) | 646.4 | Inst. holdings | 62% |
| Avg. daily vol. (M) | 1.339 | | |

Value of $10,000 invested 5 years ago: $ 26,664

## Fiscal Year Ending Dec. 31

| | 1998 | 1997 | 1996 | 1995 | 1994 | 1993 |
|---|---|---|---|---|---|---|
| **Revenues (Million $)** | | | | | | |
| 1Q | — | 3,002 | 2,682 | 2,338 | 1,983 | 2,338 |
| 2Q | — | — | 2,661 | 2,401 | 1,923 | 2,401 |
| 3Q | — | — | 2,803 | 2,539 | 2,075 | 1,873 |
| 4Q | — | — | 3,160 | 2,744 | 2,300 | 1,989 |
| Yr. | — | — | 11,306 | 10,021 | 8,281 | 7,478 |
| **Earnings Per Share ($)** | | | | | | |
| 1Q | — | 0.93 | 0.81 | 0.68 | 0.59 | 0.68 |
| 2Q | — | E0.72 | 0.61 | 0.49 | 0.42 | 0.49 |
| 3Q | — | E0.95 | 0.80 | 0.66 | 0.54 | -0.32 |
| 4Q | — | E0.90 | 0.77 | 0.64 | 0.54 | 0.45 |
| Yr. | E4.10 | E3.50 | 2.99 | 2.47 | 2.09 | 1.02 |

**Next earnings report expected: mid July**

## Dividend Data (Dividends have been paid since 1901.)

| Amount ($) | Date Decl. | Ex-Div. Date | Stock of Record | Payment Date |
|---|---|---|---|---|
| 0.300 | Oct. 24 | Nov. 06 | Nov. 08 | Dec. 12 '96 |
| 0.340 | Jan. 23 | Feb. 05 | Feb. 07 | Mar. 13 '97 |
| 0.340 | Apr. 24 | May. 07 | May. 09 | Jun. 12 '97 |
| 2-for-1 | Jan. 23 | Jul. 01 | Jun. 02 | Jun. 30 '97 |

This report is for information purposes and should not be considered a solicitation to buy or sell any security. Neither S&P nor any other party guarantee its accuracy or make warranties regarding results from its usage. Redistribution is prohibited without written permission. Copyright © 1997   *A Division of The McGraw·Hill Companies*

## Business Summary - 13-MAY-97

Pfizer (PFE) traces its history back to 1849, when it was founded by Charles Pfizer and Charles Erhart as a chemical products firm. Today, it is a leading global pharmaceutical firm, marketing a wide range of prescription drugs. It also holds important interests in hospital products, animal health items and consumer products. Overseas business is very significant, representing 47% of total sales and 39% of profits in 1996. Business segment contributions in 1996 were:

|  | Sales | Profits |
|---|---|---|
| Health care | 85% | 96% |
| Animal health | 11% | 3% |
| Consumer | 4% | 1% |

Prescription pharmaceuticals, accounting for 72% of total sales in 1996, are the chief engine of PFE's growth. The company's pharmaceuticals growth has significantly exceeded that of the overall industry in recent years, bolstered by an exceptionally strong portfolio of blockbuster drugs.

Principal cardiovascular drugs include Norvasc calcium channel blocker heart drug (sales of $1.8 billion in 1996). Other heart drugs include Procardia XL ($1.0 billion) and Cardura ($533 million). In early 1997, Pfizer and Warner-Lambert co-launched Lipitor, a promising new drug for reducing elevated levels of cholesterol and triglycerides. Infectious disease drugs consist of Diflu-

can antifungal ($910 million); Zithromax broad-spectrum quinolone antibiotic ($619 million); and Unasyn, Sulperazon and Vibramycin antibiotics. Other drugs include Zoloft anti-depressant ($1.3 billion), Glucotrol and Glucotrol XL for diabetes, Zyrtec/Reactine antihistamine, and Feldene anti-arthritic.

PFE plans to spend $2 billion on R&D in 1997, up from $1.7 billion in 1996. Key compounds in the pipeline include Trovan broad-spectrum quinolone antibiotic, ziprasidone antipsychotic, Viagra for male erectile dysfunction, dofetilide for cardiac arrhythmias, eletriptan for migraine, several cancer treatments, and other drugs for diabetic neuropathy, fungal infections and other ailments.

Hospital products (13% of sales) include Howmedica, a leading maker of reconstructive hip, knee and bone cement products and other implantable items; Schneider angioplasty catheters; and Valleylab electrosurgical and ultrasound surgical equipment.

The animal health product line (11%) includes feed additives, vaccines, antibiotics, antihelmintics and other veterinary products. Consumer products (4%) include Ben-Gay ointment, Visine eye drops, Desitin ointment, Pacquin hand cream, Plax dental rinse, Bain de Soleil skin care products and Barbasol shave creams.

### Capitalization

**Long Term Debt:** $687,000,000 (12/96).
**Minority Interest:** $50,000,000.

### Per Share Data ($)

| (Year Ended Dec. 31) | 1996 | 1995 | 1994 | 1993 | 1992 | 1991 | 1990 | 1989 | 1988 | 1987 |
|---|---|---|---|---|---|---|---|---|---|---|
| Tangible Bk. Val. | 8.57 | 6.69 | 6.88 | 6.02 | 7.26 | 7.63 | 7.71 | 6.86 | 6.50 | 5.54 |
| Cash Flow | 3.66 | 3.06 | 2.56 | 1.42 | 2.01 | 1.42 | 1.51 | 1.30 | 1.45 | 1.27 |
| Earnings | 2.99 | 2.47 | 2.09 | 1.02 | 1.63 | 1.07 | 1.20 | 1.01 | 1.17 | 1.02 |
| Dividends | 1.20 | 1.04 | 0.94 | 0.84 | 0.74 | 0.66 | 0.60 | 0.55 | 0.50 | 0.45 |
| Payout Ratio | 40% | 42% | 45% | 82% | 46% | 60% | 49% | 53% | 42% | 43% |
| Prices - High | 91¼ | 66⅞ | 39¾ | 37⅞ | 43½ | 43⅛ | 20½ | 19 | 15⅛ | 19¼ |
|     - Low | 60¼ | 37¼ | 26⅝ | 26¼ | 32⅝ | 18⅜ | 13⅝ | 13½ | 11⅞ | 10⅜ |
| P/E Ratio - High | 31 | 27 | 19 | 37 | 27 | 40 | 17 | 19 | 13 | 19 |
|     - Low | 20 | 15 | 13 | 26 | 20 | 17 | 11 | 13 | 10 | 10 |

### Income Statement Analysis (Million $)

|  | 1996 | 1995 | 1994 | 1993 | 1992 | 1991 | 1990 | 1989 | 1988 | 1987 |
|---|---|---|---|---|---|---|---|---|---|---|
| Revs. | 11,306 | 10,021 | 8,281 | 7,478 | 7,230 | 6,950 | 6,406 | 5,671 | 5,385 | 4,920 |
| Oper. Inc. | 3,444 | 2,527 | 2,248 | 1,906 | 1,686 | 1,471 | 1,254 | 1,153 | 1,189 | 1,103 |
| Depr. | 430 | 374 | 289 | 254 | 260 | 238 | 217 | 201 | 187 | 172 |
| Int. Exp. | 170 | 205 | 142 | 121 | 116 | 138 | 142 | 131 | 87.0 | 66.0 |
| Pretax Inc. | 2,804 | 2,299 | 1,862 | 851 | 1,535 | 944 | 1,103 | 917 | 1,104 | 1,011 |
| Eff. Tax Rate | 31% | 32% | 30% | 23% | 29% | 23% | 27% | 25% | 28% | 31% |
| Net Inc. | 1,929 | 1,554 | 1,298 | 658 | 1,094 | 722 | 801 | 681 | 791 | 690 |

### Balance Sheet & Other Fin. Data (Million $)

|  | 1996 | 1995 | 1994 | 1993 | 1992 | 1991 | 1990 | 1989 | 1988 | 1987 |
|---|---|---|---|---|---|---|---|---|---|---|
| Cash | 1,637 | 1,512 | 2,019 | 1,177 | 1,704 | 1,548 | 1,068 | 1,058 | 808 | 1,031 |
| Curr. Assets | 6,468 | 6,152 | 5,788 | 4,733 | 5,385 | 4,808 | 4,436 | 4,505 | 4,095 | 4,101 |
| Total Assets | 14,667 | 12,729 | 11,099 | 9,331 | 9,590 | 9,635 | 9,052 | 8,325 | 7,638 | 6,923 |
| Curr. Liab. | 5,640 | 5,187 | 4,826 | 3,444 | 3,217 | 3,421 | 3,117 | 2,912 | 2,344 | 1,957 |
| LT Debt | 687 | 833 | 604 | 571 | 571 | 397 | 193 | 191 | 227 | 249 |
| Common Eqty. | 6,954 | 5,507 | 4,324 | 3,865 | 4,719 | 5,026 | 5,092 | 4,536 | 4,301 | 3,882 |
| Total Cap. | 7,944 | 6,553 | 5,179 | 4,665 | 5,472 | 5,742 | 5,666 | 5,062 | 4,866 | 4,471 |
| Cap. Exp. | 774 | 696 | 672 | 634 | 674 | 594 | 548 | 457 | 344 | 258 |
| Cash Flow | 2,359 | 1,928 | 1,588 | 912 | 1,353 | 960 | 1,019 | 882 | 978 | 862 |
| Curr. Ratio | 1.1 | 1.2 | 1.2 | 1.4 | 1.7 | 1.4 | 1.4 | 1.5 | 1.7 | 2.1 |
| % LT Debt of Cap. | 8.6 | 12.7 | 11.7 | 12.2 | 10.4 | 6.9 | 3.4 | 3.8 | 4.7 | 5.6 |
| % Net Inc.of Revs. | 17.1 | 15.5 | 15.7 | 8.8 | 15.1 | 10.4 | 12.5 | 12.0 | 14.7 | 14.0 |
| % Ret. on Assets | 14.1 | 13.0 | 12.8 | 7.0 | 11.5 | 7.7 | 9.2 | 8.5 | 10.8 | 11.4 |
| % Ret. on Equity | 31.0 | 31.6 | 32.0 | 15.4 | 22.6 | 14.3 | 16.7 | 15.4 | 19.3 | 18.9 |

Data as orig. reptd.; bef. results of disc. opers. and/or spec. items. Per share data adj. for stk. divs. as of ex-div. date. E-Estimated. NA-Not Available. NM-Not Meaningful. NR-Not Ranked.

**Office**—235 E. 42nd St., New York, NY 10017. **Registrar**—Mellon Securities Trust Co., NYC. **Tel**—(212) 573-2323. **Website**—http://www.pfizer.com **Chrmn & CEO**—W. C. Steere, Jr. **EVP & CFO**—D. L. Shedlarz. **SVP & Secy**—C. L. Clemente. **Investor Contact**—J. R. Gardner. **Dirs**—M. S. Brown, M. A. Burns, W. D. Cornwell, G. B. Harvey, C. J. Horner, S. O. Ikenberry, H. P. Kamen, T. G. Labrecque, F. G. Rohatyn, R. J. Simmons, W. C. Steere, Jr., J.-P. Valles. **Transfer Agent**—Co. office. **Incorporated**—in Delaware in 1942. **Empl**— 46,500. **S&P Analyst:** H.B. Saftlas

# STANDARD &POOR'S
## STOCK REPORTS

# PhyCor, Inc.

**4984C**

Nasdaq Symbol **PHYC**

In **S&P SmallCap 600**

**17-MAY-97**

**Industry:** Health Care (Managed Care)

**Summary:** PhyCor acquires and operates multi-specialty medical clinics, and develops and manages independent practice associations (IPAs).

---

| S&P Opinion: Accumulate (★★★★) | Recent Price • 27¾ | Yield • Nil |
| --- | --- | --- |
| | 52 Wk Range • 41¾-22⅞ | 12-Mo. P/E • 42.0 |

**Quantitative Evaluations**

**Outlook** (1 Lowest—5 Highest)
• 5

**Fair Value**
• 44

**Risk**
• High

**Earn./Div. Rank**
• NR

**Technical Eval.**
• **Bearish** since 2/97

**Rel. Strength Rank** (1 Lowest—99 Highest)
• 36

**Insider Activity**
• Neutral

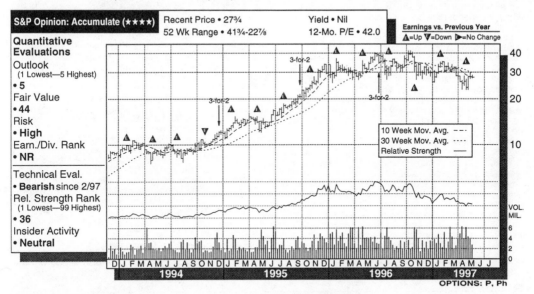

Earnings vs. Previous Year — ▲=Up ▼=Down ▶=No Change

10 Week Mov. Avg. - - -
30 Week Mov. Avg. · · · ·
Relative Strength ——

OPTIONS: P, Ph

---

## Overview - 13-MAY-97

Revenue growth in excess of 35% can be expected through 1998, aided by strong performance at existing sites and the inclusion of acquired clinics. On a "same-store" basis, we look for revenue growth in the 10-15% range going forward. Despite higher costs associated with the company's acquisitions, we expect to see operating costs expand at roughly the same pace as revenues, as efforts to lower clinic operating expenses offset higher staffing costs and rising capital outlays (including spending on information systems). Interest costs should decline as funds generated from a recent public stock offering are used to retire debt. Clinic acquisitions, which are expected to continue during 1997, are generally additive to the company's earnings from the outset.

## Valuation - 13-MAY-97

We maintain a bullish stance on the stock despite signs of slowing same-clinic revenue growth in recent quarters, as a full acquisition pipeline should help propel solid top-line and earnings momentum at least through 1997. Same-clinic revenues were expected to settle in the 12% to 14% range, and our expectations were realized in the first quarter of 1997 as revenues from existing sites rose 13.2%. Although the shares typically command a P/E multiple above the PPM group average, such a lofty level is warranted given the company's EPS growth record, proven ability to successfully integrate multi-specialty clinic acquisitions and highly-regarded management team. Earnings gains in excess of 30% are viewed as sustainable in the foreseeable future, and we look for EPS of $0.85 in 1997 and $1.10 in 1998. However, trading in the stock is likely to remain volatile as the current P/E (33 times our 1997 estimate) leaves no room for EPS shortfalls.

## Key Stock Statistics

| | | | |
| --- | --- | --- | --- |
| S&P EPS Est. 1997 | 0.85 | Tang. Bk. Value/Share | NM |
| P/E on S&P Est. 1997 | 32.6 | Beta | 1.07 |
| S&P EPS Est. 1998 | 1.10 | Shareholders | 13,700 |
| Dividend Rate/Share | Nil | Market cap. (B) | $ 1.8 |
| Shs. outstg. (M) | 63.3 | Inst. holdings | 73% |
| Avg. daily vol. (M) | 0.891 | | |

Value of $10,000 invested 5 years ago: NA

### Fiscal Year Ending Dec. 31

| | 1998 | 1997 | 1996 | 1995 | 1994 | 1993 |
| --- | --- | --- | --- | --- | --- | --- |
| **Revenues (Million $)** | | | | | | |
| 1Q | — | 250.6 | 162.5 | 92.76 | 49.77 | 39.90 |
| 2Q | — | — | 176.6 | 99.2 | 50.46 | 39.62 |
| 3Q | — | — | 196.4 | 114.0 | 63.18 | 41.81 |
| 4Q | — | — | 230.8 | 135.6 | 79.08 | 46.00 |
| Yr. | — | — | 766.3 | 441.6 | 242.5 | 167.4 |
| **Earnings Per Share ($)** | | | | | | |
| 1Q | — | 0.19 | 0.13 | 0.09 | 0.08 | 0.06 |
| 2Q | — | E0.20 | 0.14 | 0.09 | 0.09 | 0.06 |
| 3Q | — | E0.22 | 0.15 | 0.11 | 0.07 | 0.07 |
| 4Q | — | E0.24 | 0.18 | 0.12 | 0.08 | 0.08 |
| Yr. | E1.10 | E0.85 | 0.60 | 0.41 | 0.32 | 0.28 |

**Next earnings report expected: late July**

## Dividend Data

| Amount ($) | Date Decl. | Ex-Div. Date | Stock of Record | Payment Date |
| --- | --- | --- | --- | --- |
| 3-for-2 | May. 17 | Jun. 17 | May. 31 | Jun. 14 '96 |

---

This report is for information purposes and should not be considered a solicitation to buy or sell any security. Neither S&P nor any other party guarantee its accuracy or make warranties regarding results from its usage. Redistribution is prohibited without written permission. Copyright © 1997

*A Division of The McGraw·Hill Companies*

STANDARD
&POOR'S
STOCK REPORTS

# PhyCor, Inc.

**4984C**

17-MAY-97

## Business Summary - 13-MAY-97

PhyCor Inc. has capitalized on the evolving healthcare delivery system by leading the emerging physician practice management industry, where it seeks to acquire and operate multi-specialty medical clinics and develop independent practice associations (IPAs). By organizing previously unaffiliated physicians into professionally managed networks, the company allows these physicians to focus their attention on the provision of healthcare services, rather than on administrative duties, and these large networks have significant bargaining power when negotiating for large contracts with managed care entities. PHYC currently operates 47 clinics with over 3,200 physicians in 27 states, and manages IPAs with over 15,000 physicians in 23 markets. About 53% of its affiliated physicians are primary care providers.

A multi-specialty clinic provides a wide range of primary and specialty physician care through an organized physician group practice representing various medical specialties. The company targets for acquisition primary care-oriented clinics typically staffed by 25 to 200 physicians. Upon acquisition of a clinic's operating assets, PHYC negotiates a long-term agreement with the affiliated physician group under which it provides the equipment and facilities used in its medical practice, manages clinic operations, employs most of the non-physician personnel and receives a service fee.

PHYC also positions the clinics for participation in organized health care systems by establishing alliances with HMOs, insurers and hospitals, and by enhancing medical management systems.

PhyCor's clinics also offer ancillary services, which accounted for about 26% of gross clinic revenues in 1996. Most provide imaging services, including CAT scanning, mammography, nuclear medicine, ultrasound and X-ray. Many also have clinical laboratories and pharmacies. Ambulatory surgery units and rehabilitation services are in place or are being planned in most clinics, while several offer diabetes centers, weight management programs, renal dialysis and home infusion therapy.

PHYC's IPAs, which are networks of independent physicians, provide capitated medical services to about 375,000 members, including 69,000 Medicare beneficiaries. IPAs allow formerly unaffiliated doctors to assume and more effectively manage capitated risk. The combination of multi-specialty clinic management services and IPA management services lets the company offer its management services to virtually all types of physician organizations.

In 1996, net revenues earned by the physician groups and IPAs affiliated with the company were from private payor and insurance (35%), managed care (42%), Medicare (20%) and Medicaid (3%).

### Capitalization

**Long Term Debt:** $123,536,000 (12/96).

### Per Share Data ($)

| (Year Ended Dec. 31) | 1996 | 1995 | 1994 | 1993 | 1992 | 1991 | 1990 | 1989 | 1988 | 1987 |
|---|---|---|---|---|---|---|---|---|---|---|
| Tangible Bk. Val. | NM | 1.49 | 4.86 | 2.89 | 2.44 | 1.84 | NM | NA | NA | NA |
| Cash Flow | 1.25 | 0.81 | 0.66 | 0.51 | -0.39 | 0.25 | 0.21 | -0.11 | -0.21 | NA |
| Earnings | 0.60 | 0.41 | 0.28 | 0.28 | -0.57 | 0.05 | 0.00 | -0.23 | -0.22 | NA |
| Dividends | Nil | Nil | Nil | Nil | Nil | Nil | Nil | Nil | Nil | NA |
| Payout Ratio | Nil | Nil | Nil | Nil | Nil | Nil | Nil | Nil | Nil | NA |
| Prices - High | 41¾ | 34 | 12½ | 9⅛ | 5¼ | NA | NA | NA | NA | NA |
| - Low | 25½ | 10⅞ | 7½ | 4 | 2¼ | NA | NA | NA | NA | NA |
| P/E Ratio - High | 70 | 84 | 44 | 46 | NM | NA | NA | NA | NA | NA |
| - Low | 42 | 27 | 27 | 20 | NM | NA | NA | NA | NA | NA |

### Income Statement Analysis (Million $)

| | 1996 | 1995 | 1994 | 1993 | 1992 | 1991 | 1990 | 1989 | 1988 | 1987 |
|---|---|---|---|---|---|---|---|---|---|---|
| Revs. | 766 | 442 | 242 | 167 | 136 | 90.0 | 64.0 | 24.0 | 1.0 | NA |
| Oper. Inc. | 122 | 67.5 | 31.4 | 17.9 | 13.6 | 7.6 | 4.9 | 1.2 | -1.0 | NA |
| Depr. | 40.2 | 21.4 | 12.2 | 6.1 | 4.5 | 2.7 | 2.7 | 0.8 | 0.0 | NA |
| Int. Exp. | 16.0 | 5.2 | 4.0 | 3.9 | 4.5 | 3.8 | 3.0 | 2.2 | 0.0 | NA |
| Pretax Inc. | 59.2 | 35.8 | 16.5 | 8.2 | -13.3 | 1.3 | 0.2 | -1.6 | -0.9 | NA |
| Eff. Tax Rate | 39% | 39% | 29% | 13% | NM | 43% | 67% | Nil | Nil | NA |
| Net Inc. | 36.4 | 21.8 | 11.7 | 7.1 | -13.7 | 0.8 | 0.1 | -1.6 | -0.9 | NA |

### Balance Sheet & Other Fin. Data (Million $)

| | 1996 | 1995 | 1994 | 1993 | 1992 | 1991 | 1990 | 1989 | 1988 | 1987 |
|---|---|---|---|---|---|---|---|---|---|---|
| Cash | 30.5 | 18.8 | 6.5 | 3.2 | 9.1 | 2.6 | 3.6 | 2.1 | NA | NA |
| Curr. Assets | 383 | 218 | 145 | 77.5 | 69.4 | 39.6 | 33.5 | 13.4 | NA | NA |
| Total Assets | 1,119 | 644 | 351 | 171 | 141 | 93.0 | 79.0 | 34.0 | 5.0 | NA |
| Curr. Liab. | 170 | 106 | 64.3 | 30.5 | 33.5 | 17.7 | 15.5 | 6.0 | NA | NA |
| LT Debt | 409 | 127 | 84.9 | 66.8 | 51.2 | 49.3 | 38.9 | 20.0 | 1.3 | NA |
| Common Eqty. | 452 | 389 | 184 | 70.0 | 53.9 | 2.4 | 1.3 | NA | NA | NA |
| Total Cap. | 860 | 516 | 269 | 137 | 105 | 75.0 | 63.0 | 28.0 | 4.0 | NA |
| Cap. Exp. | 50.1 | 29.2 | 17.5 | 13.9 | 13.6 | 6.3 | 4.3 | 0.5 | 0.1 | NA |
| Cash Flow | 76.6 | 43.3 | 23.9 | 13.3 | -9.3 | 3.5 | 2.8 | -0.8 | -0.9 | NA |
| Curr. Ratio | 2.3 | 2.0 | 2.3 | 2.5 | 2.1 | 2.2 | 2.2 | 2.2 | NA | NA |
| % LT Debt of Cap. | 47.5 | 24.6 | 31.6 | 48.8 | 48.7 | 66.0 | 61.5 | 71.0 | 36.7 | NA |
| % Net Inc.of Revs. | 4.7 | 4.9 | 4.8 | 4.3 | NM | 0.8 | 0.1 | NM | NM | NA |
| % Ret. on Assets | 4.1 | 4.4 | 3.8 | 4.4 | NM | 0.9 | 1.0 | NM | NM | NA |
| % Ret. on Equity | 8.7 | 7.6 | 7.9 | 11.1 | NM | 41.4 | 3.6 | NM | NM | NA |

Data as orig. reptd.; bef. results of disc. opers. and/or spec. items. Per share data adj. for stk. divs. as of ex-div. date. E-Estimated. NA-Not Available. NM-Not Meaningful. NR-Not Ranked.

**Office**—30 Burton Hills Blvd., Suite 340, Nashville, TN 37215. **Tel**—(615) 665-9066. **Chrmn, Pres & CEO**—J. C. Hutts. **EVP & Secy**—T. S. Dent. **VP, Treas & CFO**—J. K. Crawford. **Dirs**—R. B. Ashworth, S. A. Brooks Jr., T. S. Dent, W. C. Dunn, C. S. Givens, J. A. Hill, J. C. Hutts, J. A. Moncrief, D. W. Reeves, R. D. Wright. **Transfer Agent**—First Union National Bank of North Carolina, Charlotte. **Incorporated**—in Tennessee in 1988. **Empl**— 15,000. **S&P Analyst:** Robert M. Gold

# Procter & Gamble   1868

NYSE Symbol **PG**

In S&P 500

**17-MAY-97**

**Industry:** Household Products (Nondurables)

**Summary:** This leading consumer products company markets household and personal care products in more than 140 countries.

---

| S&P Opinion: Buy (★★★★) | Recent Price • 130⅝ | Yield • 1.4% |
| --- | --- | --- |
| | 52 Wk Range • 135-82⅜ | 12-Mo. P/E • 27.4 |

**Earnings vs. Previous Year**
▲=Up ▼=Down ▶=No Change

**Quantitative Evaluations**

**Outlook** (1 Lowest—5 Highest)
• **2⁺**

**Fair Value**
• **121**

**Risk**
• **Low**

**Earn./Div. Rank**
• **A**

**Technical Eval.**
• **Bullish** since 4/97

**Rel. Strength Rank** (1 Lowest—99 Highest)
• **75**

**Insider Activity**
• **Unfavorable**

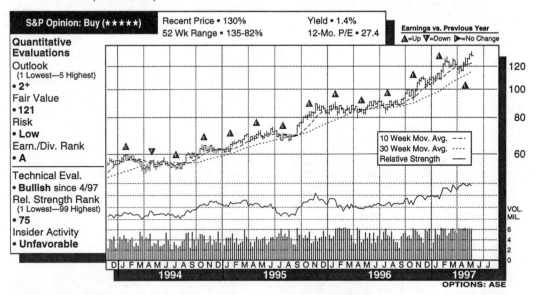

10 Week Mov. Avg. - - -
30 Week Mov. Avg. · · · · ·
Relative Strength ——

OPTIONS: ASE

---

## Overview - 28-APR-97

We expect sales to grow in the mid-to-upper single digit range for the foreseeable future, fueled by international volume growth, acquisitions, joint ventures, penetration into emerging growth markets, and new products. Despite pricing pressures in Europe where PG is introducing its everyday low price strategy, and higher marketing and advertising costs aimed at supporting new products and increasing or maintaining share, margins should widen on a lower overall cost structure. Lower raw material prices and more efficient distribution should also boost margins, as should an ongoing shift in the sales mix to higher-margin personal, beauty and health care products. In April, the company agreed to acquire Tambrands, Inc., the leading tampon producer in the U.S., for approximately $1.85 billion, allowing P&G to re-enter the worldwide tampon market with the number one Tampax brand. Over the next few years, earnings growth should outpace sales growth. Net profits are expected to rise about 12% to 14% annually.

## Valuation - 28-APR-97

Over the years, PG's shares have trended upward on steady, fairly predictable earnings growth. The shares are now trading at about 22 times our estimated earnings per share of $5.45 for FY 98. This price-earnings multiple is toward the high end of PG's historical annual price earnings multiple range. However, given PG's impressive track record, we recommend that the shares be purchased by risk-averse investors who are focused on a longer-term, buy-and-hold strategy and are looking for above-average appreciation potential. A history of annual dividend increases lends additional appeal to the stock, as does the company's increased penetration in fast-growing emerging growth markets. An aggressive share buyback program is a plus.

## Key Stock Statistics

| | | | |
| --- | --- | --- | --- |
| S&P EPS Est. 1997 | 4.85 | Tang. Bk. Value/Share | 8.10 |
| P/E on S&P Est. 1997 | 26.9 | Beta | 1.20 |
| S&P EPS Est. 1998 | 5.45 | Shareholders | 216,300 |
| Dividend Rate/Share | 1.80 | Market cap. (B) | $ 88.8 |
| Shs. outstg. (M) | 679.5 | Inst. holdings | 46% |
| Avg. daily vol. (M) | 1.364 | | |

Value of $10,000 invested 5 years ago: $ 30,808

### Fiscal Year Ending Jun. 30

| | 1998 | 1997 | 1996 | 1995 | 1994 | 1993 |
| --- | --- | --- | --- | --- | --- | --- |
| **Revenues (Million $)** | | | | | | |
| 1Q | — | 8,903 | 9,027 | 8,161 | 7,564 | 7,880 |
| 2Q | — | 9,142 | 9,090 | 8,467 | 7,788 | 7,840 |
| 3Q | — | 8,771 | 8,587 | 8,312 | 7,441 | 7,350 |
| 4Q | — | — | 8,580 | 8,494 | 7,503 | 7,365 |
| Yr. | — | — | 35,284 | 33,434 | 30,296 | 30,433 |
| **Earnings Per Share ($)** | | | | | | |
| 1Q | — | 1.39 | 1.27 | 1.12 | 0.95 | 0.57 |
| 2Q | — | 1.35 | 1.18 | 1.06 | 0.92 | 0.81 |
| 3Q | — | 1.26 | 1.07 | 0.88 | 0.66 | 0.73 |
| 4Q | — | E0.85 | 0.77 | 0.65 | 0.56 | -1.83 |
| Yr. | E5.45 | E4.85 | 4.29 | 3.71 | 3.09 | 0.25 |

**Next earnings report expected: early August**

**Dividend Data** (Dividends have been paid since 1891.)

| Amount ($) | Date Decl. | Ex-Div. Date | Stock of Record | Payment Date |
| --- | --- | --- | --- | --- |
| 0.450 | Jul. 10 | Jul. 17 | Jul. 19 | Aug. 15 '96 |
| 0.450 | Oct. 08 | Oct. 16 | Oct. 18 | Nov. 15 '96 |
| 0.450 | Jan. 14 | Jan. 22 | Jan. 24 | Feb. 14 '97 |
| 0.450 | Apr. 08 | Apr. 16 | Apr. 18 | May. 15 '97 |

---

This report is for information purposes and should not be considered a solicitation to buy or sell any security. Neither S&P nor any other party guarantee its accuracy or make warranties regarding results from its usage. Redistribution is prohibited without written permission. Copyright © 1997

*A Division of The McGraw·Hill Companies*

## Business Summary - 28-APR-97

Procter & Gamble markets a wide range of laundry, cleaning, paper, beauty care, health care, and food and beverage products in more than 140 countries around the world. In July 1991, it acquired Revlon Inc.'s worldwide Max Factor and Betrix lines of cosmetics and fragrances, and in FY 95 (Jun.) it acquired Giorgio of Beverly Hills from Avon and the European tissue business of Vereinigte Papierwerke Schickedanz AG. In early 1993, the company sold its commercial pulp business and exited the 100%-juice business. Contributions by business segment in FY 96 were:

| | Sales | Profits |
|---|---|---|
| Laundry/cleaning products | 31% | 37% |
| Beauty care products | 20% | 19% |
| Food & beverage products | 12% | 11% |
| Paper | 29% | 25% |
| Health care | 8% | 8% |

North America contributed 49% of sales and 65% of net income in FY 96; Europe, the Middle East and Africa, 34% and 22%; Asia, 11% and 7%; and Latin America, 6% and 6%.

Among the more popular laundry and cleaning brands are Ariel, Tide, Cascade, Dawn, Mr. Proper, and Downy. Net sales increased 4.4% in FY 96, year to year.

Beauty care products include Pantene, Vidal Sassoon, Secret, Safeguard, Olay, Cover Girl and Giorgio Beverly Hills.

Food and beverage products include Folgers, Jif, Sunny Delight, Pringles, Crisco and Duncan Hines.

Paper products include Bounty, Charmin, Always, Whisper, Pampers and Attends.

Health care products include Crest, Scope, Metamucil, Vicks and Aleve.

## Important Developments

Apr. '97—Commenting on results for its FY 97 (Jun.) third quarter, PG said the 18% year-to-year rise in share earnings reflected a 2% increase in worldwide sales, on 4% unit volume growth, and improved margins resulting from the higher volume and cost savings arising from restructuring efforts. Weaker currencies in Europe, Asia and Latin America caused the difference between the sales and volume growth rates.

Apr. '97—Procter & Gamble agreed to acquire Tambrands, Inc., and its market-leading tampon brand, Tampax, for approximately $1.85 billion in cash. The acquisition will allow P&G to re-enter the tampon category with an established brand. Subject to various approvals, the transaction is expected to be completed in the first quarter of FY 98.

## Capitalization

**Long Term Debt:** $4,283,000,000 (12/96).
**Preferred Stock:** $1,874,000,000.

### Per Share Data ($)

| (Year Ended Jun. 30) | 1996 | 1995 | 1994 | 1993 | 1992 | 1991 | 1990 | 1989 | 1988 | 1987 |
|---|---|---|---|---|---|---|---|---|---|---|
| Tangible Bk. Val. | 8.10 | 5.97 | 7.19 | 5.20 | 4.75 | 4.23 | 5.67 | 4.49 | 6.48 | 6.00 |
| Cash Flow | 6.27 | 5.53 | 4.75 | 1.92 | 3.97 | 3.39 | 3.36 | 2.81 | 2.42 | 1.31 |
| Earnings | 4.29 | 3.71 | 3.09 | 0.25 | 2.62 | 2.46 | 2.25 | 1.78 | 1.49 | 0.47 |
| Dividends | 1.60 | 1.40 | 1.32 | 1.10 | 1.02 | 0.98 | 0.88 | 0.75 | 0.69 | 0.68 |
| Payout Ratio | 37% | 38% | 43% | 449% | 39% | 39% | 39% | 41% | 46% | 144% |
| Prices - High | 111 | 89½ | 64⅝ | 58⅞ | 55¾ | 47¾ | 45⅝ | 35⅛ | 22 | 25⅞ |
| - Low | 79⅜ | 60⅝ | 51¼ | 45¼ | 45⅛ | 38 | 30⅞ | 21⅛ | 17⅝ | 15 |
| P/E Ratio - High | 26 | 24 | 21 | NM | 21 | 19 | 20 | 20 | 15 | 55 |
| - Low | 19 | 16 | 17 | NM | 17 | 15 | 14 | 12 | 12 | 32 |

### Income Statement Analysis (Million $)

| | | | | | | | | | | |
|---|---|---|---|---|---|---|---|---|---|---|
| Revs. | 35,284 | 33,434 | 30,296 | 30,433 | 29,362 | 27,026 | 24,081 | 21,398 | 19,336 | 17,000 |
| Oper. Inc. | 6,173 | 5,432 | 5,442 | 4,301 | 3,777 | 3,549 | 3,072 | 2,727 | 2,429 | 2,177 |
| Depr. | 1,358 | 1,253 | 1,134 | 1,140 | 910 | 847 | 770 | 688 | 633 | 565 |
| Int. Exp. | 484 | 488 | 482 | 577 | 535 | 412 | 445 | 398 | 332 | 361 |
| Pretax Inc. | 4,669 | 4,000 | 3,346 | 349 | 349 | 2,687 | 2,421 | 1,939 | 1,630 | 617 |
| Eff. Tax Rate | 35% | 34% | 34% | 23% | 35% | 34% | 34% | 38% | 37% | 47% |
| Net Inc. | 3,046 | 2,645 | 2,211 | 269 | 1,872 | 1,773 | 1,602 | 1,206 | 1,020 | 327 |

### Balance Sheet & Other Fin. Data (Million $)

| | | | | | | | | | | |
|---|---|---|---|---|---|---|---|---|---|---|
| Cash | 2,520 | 2,178 | 2,656 | 2,322 | 1,776 | 1,384 | 1,407 | 1,587 | 1,065 | 741 |
| Curr. Assets | 10,807 | 10,842 | 9,988 | 9,975 | 9,366 | 8,435 | 7,644 | 6,578 | 5,593 | 4,981 |
| Total Assets | 27,730 | 28,125 | 25,535 | 24,935 | 24,025 | 20,468 | 18,487 | 16,351 | 14,820 | 13,715 |
| Curr. Liab. | 7,825 | 8,648 | 8,040 | 8,287 | 7,642 | 6,733 | 5,417 | 4,656 | 4,224 | 3,458 |
| LT Debt | 4,670 | 5,161 | 4,980 | 5,174 | 5,223 | 4,111 | 3,588 | 3,698 | 2,462 | 2,524 |
| Common Eqty. | 9,836 | 8,676 | 8,677 | 7,308 | 7,085 | 5,741 | 6,518 | 5,215 | 6,337 | 5,740 |
| Total Cap. | 17,030 | 16,281 | 14,159 | 12,798 | 15,777 | 13,157 | 12,364 | 11,248 | 10,121 | 9,670 |
| Cap. Exp. | 2,179 | 2,146 | 1,841 | 1,911 | 1,911 | 1,979 | 1,300 | 1,029 | 1,018 | 990 |
| Cash Flow | 4,301 | 3,796 | 3,243 | 1,307 | 2,688 | 2,542 | 2,325 | 1,878 | 1,642 | 881 |
| Curr. Ratio | 1.4 | 1.3 | 1.2 | 1.2 | 1.2 | 1.3 | 1.4 | 1.4 | 1.3 | 1.4 |
| % LT Debt of Cap. | 27.4 | 31.7 | 35.2 | 40.4 | 33.1 | 31.2 | 29.0 | 32.9 | 24.3 | 26.1 |
| % Net Inc.of Revs. | 8.6 | 7.9 | 7.3 | 0.9 | 6.4 | 6.6 | 6.7 | 5.6 | 5.3 | 1.9 |
| % Ret. on Assets | 10.9 | 9.9 | 8.7 | 1.1 | 8.5 | 9.2 | 8.9 | 7.9 | 7.1 | 2.4 |
| % Ret. on Equity | 31.8 | 32.7 | 26.3 | 2.0 | 27.7 | 28.0 | 25.7 | 21.1 | 16.7 | 5.5 |

Data as orig. reptd.; bef. results of disc. opers. and/or spec. items. Per share data adj. for stk. divs. as of ex-div. date. E-Estimated. NA-Not Available. NM-Not Meaningful. NR-Not Ranked.

**Office**—1 Procter & Gamble Plaza, Cincinnati, OH 45202. **Registrar**—PNC Bank, Cincinnati, OH. **Tel**—(513) 983-1100. **Chrmn & CEO**—J. E. Pepper. **Pres & COO**—D. I. Jager. **SVP & CFO**—E. G. Nelson. **Secy**—T. L. Overbey. **Treas**—C. C. Daley, Jr. **Investor Contact**—G. A. Dowdell. **Dirs**—E. L. Artzt, N. R. Augustine, D. R. Beall, G. F. Brunner, R. B. Cheney, H. Einsmann, R. J. Ferris, J. T. Gorman, D. I. Jager, C. R. Lee, L. Martin, J. E. Pepper, J. C. Sawhill, J. F. Smith, Jr., R. Snyderman, R. D. Storey, M. v.N. Whitman. **Transfer Agent**—Co. itself. **Incorporated**—in Ohio in 1905. **Empl**— 103,000. **S&P Analyst:** Maureen C. Carini

# Respironics, Inc.  5082

NASDAQ Symbol **RESP**

**In S&P SmallCap 600**

**17-MAY-97**

**Industry:** Health Care (Medical Products & Supplies)

**Summary:** This company makes respiratory medical products for use in the home, hospitals and in emergency care situations.

| Quantitative Evaluations | |
|---|---|
| **Outlook** (1 Lowest—5 Highest) | **5** |
| **Fair Value** | **25⅛** |
| **Risk** | **High** |
| **Earn./Div. Rank** | **B** |
| **Technical Eval.** | **Bullish** since 3/97 |
| **Rel. Strength Rank** (1 Lowest—99 Highest) | **54** |
| **Insider Activity** | **Neutral** |

Recent Price • 19½
52 Wk Range • 25-13½
Yield • Nil
12-Mo. P/E • 20.3

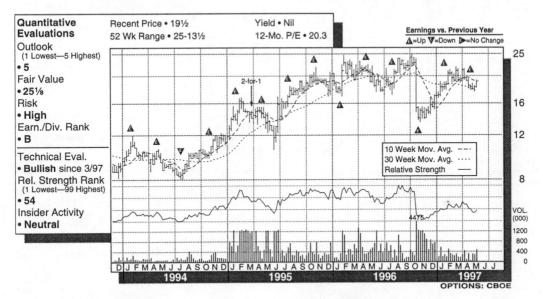

10 Week Mov. Avg. – – –
30 Week Mov. Avg. ·····
Relative Strength —

Earnings vs. Previous Year
▲=Up ▼=Down ▶=No Change

OPTIONS: CBOE

## Business Profile - 09-MAY-97

In April 1997, Respironics received FDA market approval for its new Quartet Clinical System to diagnose and treat obstructive sleep apnea. Sales have improved in recent quarters, aided by the introduction of new products and recent acquisitions. In 1996, Respironics increased its investment in R&D and introduced several new products, including the BiPAP S/T-D Ventilatory Support System and the Virtuoso Smart CPAP system. Sales to international markets have risen (accounting for almost 25% of FY 96 revenues) as the company seeks new regions for growth. The shares have rebounded from their October 1996 decline following the decision by a large customer (accounting for 16% of FY '96 sales) to purchase fewer sleep apnea and ventilator systems from Respironics.

## Operational Review - 09-MAY-97

Based on a brief report, net sales advanced 39% in the nine months ended March 31, 1997, year to year, reflecting continued growth in all product lines, greater shipments to international markets, and contributions from acquisitions. Results also benefited from the successful introduction of new products. Net income was up 37%, to $14.4 million ($0.71 a share, based on 13% more shares), from $10.5 million ($0.59).

## Stock Performance - 16-MAY-97

In the past 30 trading days, RESP's shares have declined 3%, compared to a 9% rise in the S&P 500. Average trading volume for the past five days was 91,420 shares, compared with the 40-day moving average of 54,410 shares.

## Key Stock Statistics

| | | | |
|---|---|---|---|
| Dividend Rate/Share | Nil | Shareholders | 1,400 |
| Shs. outstg. (M) | 19.7 | Market cap. (B) | $0.385 |
| Avg. daily vol. (M) | 0.053 | Inst. holdings | 49% |
| Tang. Bk. Value/Share | 6.85 | | |
| Beta | 0.24 | | |

Value of $10,000 invested 5 years ago: $ 30,291

### Fiscal Year Ending Jun. 30

| | 1997 | 1996 | 1995 | 1994 | 1993 | 1992 |
|---|---|---|---|---|---|---|
| **Revenues (Million $)** | | | | | | |
| 1Q | 34.11 | 26.68 | 21.67 | 18.23 | 15.20 | 9.80 |
| 2Q | 43.00 | 30.24 | 23.87 | 18.60 | 17.20 | 10.90 |
| 3Q | 47.81 | 32.65 | 25.60 | 19.31 | 17.92 | 13.00 |
| 4Q | — | 36.20 | 28.31 | 22.04 | 19.01 | 15.30 |
| Yr. | — | 125.8 | 99.4 | 78.17 | 69.29 | 49.00 |
| **Earnings Per Share ($)** | | | | | | |
| 1Q | 0.22 | 0.18 | 0.14 | 0.05 | 0.09 | 0.07 |
| 2Q | 0.24 | 0.20 | 0.15 | 0.12 | 0.10 | 0.07 |
| 3Q | 0.25 | 0.21 | 0.17 | 0.13 | 0.11 | 0.08 |
| 4Q | — | 0.24 | 0.20 | -0.03 | 0.13 | 0.10 |
| Yr. | — | 0.84 | 0.67 | 0.27 | 0.43 | 0.32 |

**Next earnings report expected: late July**

## Dividend Data

Cash dividends have never been paid. A two-for-one stock split was effected in March 1995.

This report is for information purposes and should not be considered a solicitation to buy or sell any security. Neither S&P nor any other party guarantee its accuracy or make warranties regarding results from its usage. Redistribution is prohibited without written permission. Copyright © 1997

*A Division of The McGraw·Hill Companies*

## Business Summary - 09-MAY-97

Respironics designs, produces and sells medical products which address a wide range of respiratory and pulmonary problems by assisting patient breathing. These products are used in home, hospital, and alternative care settings and in emergency medical situations.

RESP's principal product, the REMstar Choice Nasal CPAP system (retail price of $1,100 to $1,600), is designed to treat a sleeping disorder known as obstructive sleep apnea (the repeated cessation of breathing during sleep caused by anatomical disorders). The disorder is commonly found in obese individuals, and consumption of alcohol and tranquilizers can make the problem worse. The REMStar system consists of a small, portable air pressurization device, air pressure controls and a nasal mask worn by the patient at home during sleep, and uses a pulmonary procedure known as Continuous Positive Airway Pressure (CPAP). Sales of obstructive sleep apnea therapy products and related accessories and replacement parts accounted for 67% of net sales in fiscal 1996.

The company's primary ventilatory product is the BiPAP Ventilatory Support System (priced at $2,800 to $8,000), a low-pressure, electrically-driven flow generator with an electronic pressure control designed to augment patient ventilation by supplying pressurized air through a nasal mask. The Hospital BiPAP Ventilatory Support System (introduced in May 1992) includes accessories such as an airway pressure monitor, a detachable control panel, a disposable circuit and a mounting stand. Sales of ventilatory products and related accessories accounted for 27% of fiscal 1996 net sales.

Three types of face masks are provided by RESP: air-filled cushion anesthesia masks primarily for use during surgery; disposable resuscitation masks for use in emergency medical situations; and masks used with CPAP and BiPAP devices, including nasal sealing flap masks and two masks that were approved by the U.S. FDA in early 1996 (Monarch Mini Mask, GEL Mask). The company also makes single-use resuscitation products for use in emergency medicine.

In April 1997, RESP received FDA market approval for its new Quartet Clinical System to diagnose and treat obstructive sleep apnea.

In February 1997, the company acquired its exclusive German distributor of therapy systems and accessories used in the treatment of Obstructive Sleep Apnea and other respiratory disorders, with 1996 sales of $22 million, for about $10.25 million. Respironics said that this acquisition, combined with its 1996 purchase of European based LIFECARE International, a maker of portable ventilation products, demonstrates its effort to expand internationally.

### Capitalization

**Long Term Debt:** $9,257,212 (12/96).
**Minority Interest:** $631,895.

### Per Share Data ($)

| (Year Ended Jun. 30) | 1996 | 1995 | 1994 | 1993 | 1992 | 1991 | 1990 | 1989 | 1988 | 1987 |
|---|---|---|---|---|---|---|---|---|---|---|
| Tangible Bk. Val. | 6.85 | 3.38 | 2.71 | 2.41 | 1.95 | 1.61 | 0.77 | 0.62 | 0.52 | 0.26 |
| Cash Flow | 1.06 | 0.89 | 0.48 | 0.65 | 0.44 | 0.35 | 0.19 | 0.13 | 0.14 | 0.11 |
| Earnings | 0.84 | 0.67 | 0.28 | 0.43 | 0.32 | 0.26 | 0.15 | 0.10 | 0.12 | 0.10 |
| Dividends | Nil | Nil | Nil | Nil | Nil | Nil | Nil | Nil | Nil | Nil |
| Payout Ratio | Nil | Nil | Nil | Nil | Nil | Nil | Nil | Nil | Nil | Nil |
| Prices - High | 24¾ | 22¼ | 12¼ | 15½ | 15⅜ | 7¼ | 5⅜ | 2⅜ | 1⅞ | NA |
| - Low | 17 | 10½ | 8 | 7⅞ | 6¼ | 4¼ | 2⅛ | 1³⁄₁₆ | 1⁷⁄₁₆ | NA |
| P/E Ratio - High | 29 | 33 | 44 | 36 | 41 | 28 | 35 | 24 | 16 | NA |
| - Low | 20 | 16 | 29 | 19 | 20 | 17 | 14 | 12 | 15 | NA |

### Income Statement Analysis (Million $)

| | 1996 | 1995 | 1994 | 1993 | 1992 | 1991 | 1990 | 1989 | 1988 | 1987 |
|---|---|---|---|---|---|---|---|---|---|---|
| Revs. | 126 | 100 | 78.2 | 69.3 | 49.0 | 36.0 | 23.0 | 16.8 | 14.0 | 10.2 |
| Oper. Inc. | 27.8 | 21.4 | 17.0 | 14.6 | 9.7 | 6.8 | 3.3 | 1.8 | 1.9 | 1.7 |
| Depr. | 4.0 | 3.8 | 3.6 | 3.9 | 2.1 | 1.3 | 0.6 | 0.4 | 0.3 | 0.2 |
| Int. Exp. | 0.2 | 0.2 | 0.2 | 0.2 | 0.2 | 0.3 | 0.1 | 0.0 | 0.0 | 0.0 |
| Pretax Inc. | 25.2 | 18.5 | 6.8 | 11.1 | 8.1 | 5.6 | 3.0 | 1.7 | 1.7 | 1.5 |
| Eff. Tax Rate | 39% | 37% | 30% | 34% | 34% | 32% | 27% | 22% | 24% | 33% |
| Net Inc. | 15.3 | 11.7 | 4.7 | 7.4 | 5.4 | 3.8 | 2.2 | 1.3 | 1.3 | 1.0 |

### Balance Sheet & Other Fin. Data (Million $)

| | 1996 | 1995 | 1994 | 1993 | 1992 | 1991 | 1990 | 1989 | 1988 | 1987 |
|---|---|---|---|---|---|---|---|---|---|---|
| Cash | 65.3 | 16.1 | 12.4 | 14.6 | 10.2 | 11.3 | 2.2 | 2.4 | 3.0 | 0.9 |
| Curr. Assets | 116 | 52.9 | 40.2 | 36.4 | 27.8 | 21.9 | 11.7 | 8.1 | 7.9 | 3.7 |
| Total Assets | 144 | 78.0 | 58.9 | 54.6 | 43.5 | 36.1 | 19.8 | 9.9 | 9.2 | 4.5 |
| Curr. Liab. | 16.5 | 13.5 | 9.2 | 11.2 | 7.8 | 5.8 | 5.9 | 1.8 | 2.5 | 1.7 |
| LT Debt | 5.0 | 5.5 | 4.9 | 4.3 | 4.3 | 4.5 | 3.6 | Nil | 0.0 | 0.1 |
| Common Eqty. | 122 | 58.3 | 44.2 | 39.1 | 31.4 | 25.8 | 10.3 | 8.1 | 6.6 | 2.5 |
| Total Cap. | 127 | 64.6 | 49.7 | 43.4 | 35.7 | 30.3 | 13.9 | 8.1 | 6.7 | 2.7 |
| Cap. Exp. | 6.2 | 6.9 | 8.4 | 6.7 | 3.5 | 3.1 | 5.8 | 0.9 | 0.7 | 0.4 |
| Cash Flow | 19.3 | 15.5 | 8.3 | 11.2 | 7.5 | 5.1 | 2.7 | 1.7 | 1.6 | 1.2 |
| Curr. Ratio | 7.0 | 3.9 | 4.4 | 3.2 | 3.6 | 3.8 | 2.0 | 4.6 | 3.2 | 2.1 |
| % LT Debt of Cap. | 3.9 | 8.6 | 9.8 | 9.9 | 12.0 | 15.0 | 25.6 | Nil | 0.4 | 5.1 |
| % Net Inc.of Revs. | 0.1 | 11.7 | 6.1 | 10.7 | 11.0 | 10.5 | 9.4 | 7.8 | 9.4 | 10.1 |
| % Ret. on Assets | 13.8 | 17.0 | 8.3 | 15.0 | 13.4 | 12.6 | 14.4 | 13.6 | 17.7 | NA |
| % Ret. on Equity | 17.1 | 22.7 | 11.3 | 20.9 | 18.7 | 19.8 | 23.2 | 17.6 | 26.7 | NA |

Data as orig. reptd.; bef. results of disc. opers. and/or spec. items. Per share data adj. for stk. divs. as of ex-div. date. E-Estimated. NA-Not Available. NM-Not Meaningful. NR-Not Ranked.

**Office**—1001 Murry Ridge Dr., Murrysville, PA 15668. **Tel**—(412) 733-0200. **Website**—http://www.respironics.com **Chrmn**—G. E. McGinnis. **Pres & CEO**—D. S. Meteny. **VP & CFO**—D. J. Bevevino. **Treas**—J. C. Woll. **Secy & Investor Contact**—Dorita A. Pishko (412) 733-0209. **Dirs**—D. P. Barry, D. A. Cotter, J. H. Hardie, D. H. Jones, J. C. Lawyer, C. Littell, G. J. Magovern, G. E. McGinnis, D. S. Meteny, B. Shou-Chung Zau.**Transfer Agent & Registrar**—ChaseMellon Shareholder Services, Pittsburgh.**Incorporated**—in Pennsylvania in 1976; reincorporated in Delaware in 1984. **Empl**— 1,217. **S&P Analyst:**   Jennifer B. Kelly

# Robbins & Myers  5104
### Nasdaq Symbol ROBN

**17-MAY-97**

**Industry:** Electrical Equipment

**Summary:** Robbins & Myers makes industrial pumps, large glass-lined vessels and industrial mixing equipment.

| S&P Opinion: Buy (★★★★) | Recent Price • 30¼ | Yield • 0.7% |
|---|---|---|
| | 52 Wk Range • 31¼-19 | 12-Mo. P/E • 13.7 |

**Quantitative Evaluations**

Outlook (1 Lowest—5 Highest)
• **3⁻**

Fair Value
• **29⅜**

Risk
• **Average**

Earn./Div. Rank
• **B+**

Technical Eval.
• **Bullish** since 1/95

Rel. Strength Rank (1 Lowest—99 Highest)
• **86**

Insider Activity
• **Neutral**

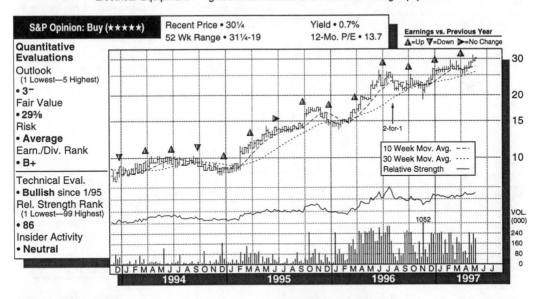

Earnings vs. Previous Year
▲=Up ▼=Down ▷=No Change

10 Week Mov. Avg. ———
30 Week Mov. Avg. ----
Relative Strength ———

2-for-1

1052

VOL. (000)

## Overview - 13-MAR-97

Robbins & Myers should continue to post solid earnings and revenue growth in FY 97 (Aug.), fueled by strong worldwide pharmaceutical and chemical industry demand for ROBN's glass-lined industrial vessels and mixing equipment, recent acquisitions, and high order backlogs. For the longer term, we expect revenue expansion to be aided by greater international penetration and higher sales of related products. Gross margins in 1997 may experience pressure, as a result of an increased proportion of sales of lower margin products, but pretax margins should widen, as cost savings from acquisitions are realized in product development and administrative areas. The Moyno unit is benefiting from strong demand from the oil service sector. With the economy continuing to grow somewhat faster than anticipated at the start of the year, the backlog remains strong. We anticipate that management will announce additional acquisitions over time.

## Valuation - 13-MAR-97

The shares have risen significantly since early 1996, reflecting healthy order backlogs, a strong earnings outlook, and good sales momentum, as ROBN has exceeded analyst earnings estimates. Despite the cyclical nature of the company's businesses, we believe that income will continue to grow, aided by ROBN's diversification into different areas through numerous acquisitions in recent years. The shares were recently trading at 13X our FY 97 EPS estimate of $2.10, and at 12X our FY 98 estimate of $2.30 (fully diluted), well below the market multiple. However, we believe that earnings of this growth cyclical will continue to expand at a rate in excess of that of the average company in the S&P 500.

## Key Stock Statistics

| | | | |
|---|---|---|---|
| S&P EPS Est. 1997 | 2.10 | Tang. Bk. Value/Share | NM |
| P/E on S&P Est. 1997 | 14.4 | Beta | 0.61 |
| S&P EPS Est. 1998 | 2.40 | Shareholders | 1,600 |
| Dividend Rate/Share | 0.20 | Market cap. (B) | $0.329 |
| Shs. outstg. (M) | 10.9 | Inst. holdings | 39% |
| Avg. daily vol. (M) | 0.042 | | |

Value of $10,000 invested 5 years ago: $ 36,837

### Fiscal Year Ending Aug. 31

| | 1998 | 1997 | 1996 | 1995 | 1994 | 1993 |
|---|---|---|---|---|---|---|
| **Revenues (Million $)** | | | | | | |
| 1Q | — | 93.82 | 81.21 | 68.63 | 21.90 | 21.40 |
| 2Q | — | 93.21 | 84.18 | 70.87 | 22.57 | 20.10 |
| 3Q | — | — | 89.88 | 79.97 | 25.02 | 22.71 |
| 4Q | — | — | 95.69 | 83.48 | 52.17 | 20.89 |
| Yr. | — | — | 351.0 | 303.0 | 121.7 | 85.06 |
| **Earnings Per Share ($)** | | | | | | |
| 1Q | — | 0.58 | 0.38 | 0.28 | 0.18 | 0.22 |
| 2Q | — | 0.56 | 0.39 | 0.29 | 0.21 | 0.19 |
| 3Q | — | — | 0.52 | 0.21 | 0.21 | 0.21 |
| 4Q | — | — | 0.55 | 0.33 | 0.01 | 0.03 |
| Yr. | E2.40 | E2.10 | 1.84 | 1.09 | 0.60 | 0.59 |

**Next earnings report expected: mid June**

### Dividend Data (Dividends have been paid since 1989.)

| Amount ($) | Date Decl. | Ex-Div. Date | Stock of Record | Payment Date |
|---|---|---|---|---|
| 2-for-1 | Jun. 26 | Aug. 01 | Jul. 12 | Jul. 31 '96 |
| 0.044 | Oct. 01 | Oct. 11 | Oct. 16 | Oct. 31 '96 |
| 0.050 | Dec. 11 | Jan. 09 | Jan. 13 | Jan. 31 '97 |
| 0.050 | Mar. 20 | Apr. 10 | Apr. 14 | Apr. 30 '97 |

This report is for information purposes and should not be considered a solicitation to buy or sell any security. Neither S&P nor any other party guarantee its accuracy or make warranties regarding results from its usage. Redistribution is prohibited without written permission. Copyright © 1997

A Division of The McGraw-Hill Companies

# Robbins & Myers, Inc.



**Business Summary - 13-MAR-97**

Several years ago, Robbins & Myers sold several diverse businesses, to focus solely on making industrial pumps. ROBN is now the world's largest producer of progressing cavity pumps for the oil & gas industry. Through a subsequent turnaround acquisition, ROBN has also become the world's largest producer of industrial glass-lined metal containers (called vessels), for large multinational drug companies and specialty chemical producers. In addition, the company manufactures industrial mixing equipment, also for drug makers and specialty chemical concerns. Gross, operating and net margins (after special items), in recent fiscal years (Aug.) were:

| | 1996 | 1995 | 1994 |
|---|---|---|---|
| Gross margins | 34% | 33% | 37% |
| Operating margins | 11% | 8.7% | 9.9% |
| Net margins | 5.6% | 4.3% | 5.2% |

About 35% of total revenues are derived from higher margin replacement part sales. ROBN obtains about 40% of revenues sales from overseas markets.

The Pfaudler unit produces ROBN's industrial vessels (40% of sales), which are used to hold highly corrosive chemicals. The Moyno Industrial Products and Moyno Oilfield Products units make ROBN's progressing cavity pumps (30% of sales). These pumps are used by oil drillers to lift oil to the surface. The Moyno Oilfield Products unit also makes a hydraulic motors, for use in directional drilling, a new drilling procedure. The company sees strong growth potential for its hydraulic motor; according to ROBN, oil producers are applying the new directional drilling procedure to its oil rigs. The Chemineer unit manufactures motor-driven industrial mixing equipment (20% of sales), used to mix industrial materials and chemicals. The Edlon unit (10% of sales), makes and applies Teflon (tm) and related coatings to materials used in the electronics industry.

Management primarily targets the oil & gas, pharmaceutical and specialty chemical markets. The oil & gas industry is ROBN's strongest growth market. ROBN sees continued strong growth opportunities in this segment, due to ongoing conversions of existing oil rigs to directional drilling applications, and expansion of global exploration and development. ROBN estimates a total of 1,700 drilling rigs, worldwide. Robbins sees growth in the pharmaceutical industry, reflecting anticipated need for pharmaceuticals from underdeveloped countries, and maturing populations in developed countries. The company finds the specialty chemical industry attractive because specialty chemical producers offer value-added chemicals, and thus are not vulnerable to price volatility as commodity chemical producers. Robbins believes growth in the specialty chemical industry is being driven by demand for improved pesticides, herbicides and fertilizers, and specialty chemical production expansion in emerging countries.

**Capitalization**

**Long Term Debt:** $83,961,000 (11/96).

| Per Share Data ($) (Year Ended Aug. 31) | 1996 | 1995 | 1994 | 1993 | 1992 | 1991 | 1990 | 1989 | 1988 | 1987 |
|---|---|---|---|---|---|---|---|---|---|---|
| Tangible Bk. Val. | -1.58 | -1.64 | -1.98 | 4.15 | 4.92 | 4.74 | 3.91 | 3.61 | 2.96 | 2.58 |
| Cash Flow | 3.09 | 2.33 | 1.02 | 0.85 | 0.99 | 2.12 | 0.96 | 0.87 | 0.80 | 0.13 |
| Earnings | 1.84 | 1.10 | 0.60 | 0.59 | 0.75 | 0.87 | 0.54 | 0.43 | 0.33 | -0.36 |
| Dividends | 0.17 | 0.15 | 0.15 | 0.12 | 0.09 | 0.07 | 0.05 | 0.01 | Nil | Nil |
| Payout Ratio | 9% | 14% | 25% | 20% | 13% | 8% | 9% | 3% | Nil | Nil |
| Prices - High | 26 1/2 | 17 1/2 | 10 1/4 | 10 3/4 | 10 | 10 3/4 | 6 | 4 5/8 | 3 7/8 | 3 1/8 |
| - Low | 13 5/8 | 8 1/2 | 8 1/4 | 7 3/4 | 6 1/2 | 4 5/8 | 3 7/8 | 3 3/8 | 1 3/4 | 1 9/16 |
| P/E Ratio - High | 14 | 16 | 17 | 18 | 13 | 12 | 11 | 11 | 12 | NM |
| - Low | 7 | 8 | 14 | 13 | 9 | 5 | 7 | 8 | 5 | NM |
| **Income Statement Analysis (Million $)** | | | | | | | | | | |
| Revs. | 351 | 303 | 122 | 85.0 | 76.0 | 79.0 | 109 | 106 | 98.0 | 92.0 |
| Oper. Inc. | 52.6 | 39.5 | 20.6 | 13.4 | 13.2 | 12.9 | 10.6 | 11.3 | 11.1 | 7.9 |
| Depr. | 13.9 | 12.4 | 4.3 | 2.8 | 2.4 | 2.0 | 4.3 | 4.3 | 4.6 | 4.7 |
| Int. Exp. | 7.1 | 7.3 | 1.5 | 0.1 | 0.1 | 0.1 | 0.1 | 0.7 | 1.2 | 1.4 |
| Pretax Inc. | 32.4 | 19.0 | 10.6 | 9.8 | 9.8 | 9.7 | 6.0 | 4.4 | 3.4 | -3.7 |
| Eff. Tax Rate | 37% | 38% | 40% | 37% | 20% | 11% | 10% | 4.90% | 7.40% | NM |
| Net Inc. | 20.3 | 11.8 | 6.4 | 6.2 | 7.9 | 8.7 | 5.4 | 4.2 | 3.1 | -3.5 |
| **Balance Sheet & Other Fin. Data (Million $)** | | | | | | | | | | |
| Cash | 7.1 | 10.2 | 16.1 | 24.5 | 24.1 | 31.4 | 6.6 | 2.4 | 1.3 | 0.8 |
| Curr. Assets | 114 | 110 | 104 | 48.3 | 46.0 | 51.0 | 36.0 | 33.0 | 29.0 | 29.0 |
| Total Assets | 300 | 270 | 258 | 85.0 | 74.0 | 69.0 | 66.0 | 60.0 | 54.0 | 57.0 |
| Curr. Liab. | 76.4 | 77.7 | 58.5 | 15.0 | 11.7 | 14.7 | 14.6 | 15.5 | 18.7 | 18.8 |
| LT Debt | 72.2 | 61.8 | 80.3 | Nil | 0.9 | 0.9 | 1.0 | 1.1 | 0.5 | 7.2 |
| Common Eqty. | 91.4 | 70.0 | 57.0 | 52.3 | 56.3 | 49.2 | 44.6 | 39.6 | 31.5 | 28.4 |
| Total Cap. | 164 | 132 | 137 | 52.3 | 57.0 | 50.0 | 46.0 | 41.0 | 32.0 | 36.0 |
| Cap. Exp. | 16.5 | 10.1 | 11.4 | 5.3 | 12.4 | 4.2 | 5.4 | 5.8 | 3.8 | 6.8 |
| Cash Flow | 34.2 | 24.2 | 10.7 | 9.0 | 10.3 | 10.6 | 9.7 | 8.4 | 7.7 | 1.3 |
| Curr. Ratio | 1.5 | 1.4 | 1.8 | 3.2 | 3.9 | 3.5 | 2.5 | 2.1 | 1.5 | 1.5 |
| % LT Debt of Cap. | 44.1 | 47.0 | 58.5 | Nil | 1.6 | 1.8 | 2.3 | 2.8 | 1.5 | 20.2 |
| % Net Inc.of Revs. | 5.8 | 3.9 | 5.2 | 7.3 | 10.4 | 11.0 | 5.0 | 4.0 | 3.2 | NM |
| % Ret. on Assets | 7.1 | 4.5 | 3.7 | 7.8 | 10.9 | 12.8 | 8.7 | 7.2 | 5.6 | NM |
| % Ret. on Equity | 25.2 | 18.7 | 11.6 | 11.4 | 14.8 | 18.4 | 12.9 | 11.5 | 10.4 | NM |

Data as orig. reptd.; bef. results of disc. opers. and/or spec. items. Per share data adj. for stk. divs. as of ex-div. date. E-Estimated. NA-Not Available. NM-Not Meaningful. NR-Not Ranked.

**Office**—1400 Kettering Tower, Dayton, OH 45423. **Tel**—(513) 222-2610. **Chrmn**—M. H. Murch IV. **Pres & CEO**—D. W. Duval. **VP & CFO**—G. M. Walker. **Secy & Treas.**—S. R. Ley. **Investor Contact**—Hugh E. Becker (513-225-3335). **Dirs**—D. W. Duval, R. J. Kegerreis, T. P. Loftis, W. D. Manning, Jr., M. H. Murch IV, J. F. Tatar, J. N. Taylor, Jr. **Transfer Agent & Registrar**—KeyCorp Shareholder Services, Cleveland. **Incorporated**—in Ohio in 1928. **Empl**— 2,460. **S&P Analyst:** Robert Natale, C.F.A., Robert Friedman

# Robert Half International    1940

NYSE Symbol **RHI**

In S&P MidCap 400

**17-MAY-97**

**Industry:**
Services (Employment)

**Summary:** This company is the world's largest specialized provider of temporary and permanent personnel in the fields of accounting and finance.

| Quantitative Evaluations | | |
|---|---|---|
| **Outlook** (1 Lowest—5 Highest) • **4⁻** | Recent Price • 42 | Yield • Nil |
| **Fair Value** • **44** | 52 Wk Range • 44¾-24⅛ | 12-Mo. P/E • 38.2 |

**Outlook**
(1 Lowest—5 Highest)
• **4⁻**

**Fair Value**
• **44**

**Risk**
• **Average**

**Earn./Div. Rank**
• **B**

**Technical Eval.**
• **Bullish** since 10/92

**Rel. Strength Rank**
(1 Lowest—99 Highest)
• **80**

**Insider Activity**
• **NA**

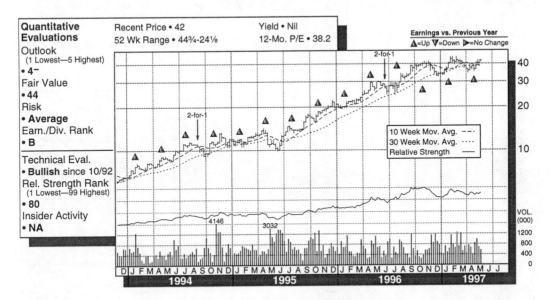

Earnings vs. Previous Year
▲=Up ▼=Down ▶=No Change

2-for-1

10 Week Mov. Avg. ---
30 Week Mov. Avg. ·····
Relative Strength —

VOL. (000)

1994    1995    1996    1997

## Business Profile - 14-MAY-97

Robert Half's sales, earnings and cash flow have risen rapidly over the past five years, driven by strong demand for the company's services, which it believes is the result of an increased acceptance of the use of professional staffing services. RHI believes that its ability to adjust billing and wage rates according to underlying market conditions has allowed it to buck the industry trend toward narrower gross margins. The company's gross margin in the first quarter of 1997 was 39.5%, up from 39.1% in the same period last year. The employment services industry should continue to benefit from favorable economic conditions in the U.S.

## Operational Review - 14-MAY-97

Revenues in the three months ended March 31, 1997, rose 44%, year to year, attributed to greater demand for all staffing services. Margins widened, reflecting well-controlled direct costs of services; operating income grew 49%. Following much greater interest income, stemming from an increase in cash and equivalents and a decrease in outstanding indebtedness, net income was up 50%, to $19,920,000 ($0.32 a share, on 3.8% more shares), from $13,239,000 ($0.22).

## Stock Performance - 16-MAY-97

In the past 30 trading days, RHI's shares have increased 17%, compared to a 9% rise in the S&P 500. Average trading volume for the past five days was 109,700 shares, compared with the 40-day moving average of 133,438 shares.

## Key Stock Statistics

| | | | |
|---|---|---|---|
| Dividend Rate/Share | Nil | Shareholders | 1,600 |
| Shs. outstg. (M) | 60.0 | Market cap. (B) | $ 2.5 |
| Avg. daily vol. (M) | 0.151 | Inst. holdings | 68% |
| Tang. Bk. Value/Share | 2.24 | | |
| Beta | 0.79 | | |

Value of $10,000 invested 5 years ago: $ 149,333

### Fiscal Year Ending Dec. 31

| | 1997 | 1996 | 1995 | 1994 | 1993 | 1992 |
|---|---|---|---|---|---|---|
| **Revenues (Million $)** | | | | | | |
| 1Q | 283.0 | 196.2 | 49.67 | 99.9 | 69.57 | 52.70 |
| 2Q | — | 210.6 | 148.6 | 106.5 | 72.45 | 53.40 |
| 3Q | — | 232.9 | 159.3 | 114.9 | 77.06 | 55.10 |
| 4Q | — | 258.8 | 175.9 | 125.0 | 87.09 | 59.03 |
| Yr. | — | 898.6 | 628.5 | 446.3 | 306.2 | 220.2 |
| **Earnings Per Share ($)** | | | | | | |
| 1Q | 0.32 | 0.22 | 0.15 | 0.10 | 0.05 | 0.02 |
| 2Q | — | 0.23 | 0.16 | 0.11 | 0.06 | 0.02 |
| 3Q | — | 0.26 | 0.17 | 0.12 | 0.06 | 0.03 |
| 4Q | — | 0.29 | 0.19 | 0.13 | 0.07 | 0.03 |
| Yr. | — | 1.00 | 0.68 | 0.46 | 0.23 | 0.09 |

**Next earnings report expected: late July**

### Dividend Data

| Amount ($) | Date Decl. | Ex-Div. Date | Stock of Record | Payment Date |
|---|---|---|---|---|
| 2-for-1 | — | Jun. 10 | May. 17 | Jun. 07 '96 |

This report is for information purposes and should not be considered a solicitation to buy or sell any security. Neither S&P nor any other party guarantee its accuracy or make warranties regarding results from its usage. Redistribution is prohibited without written permission. Copyright © 1997

*A Division of The McGraw·Hill Companies*

## Business Summary - 14-MAY-97

Robert Half International Inc. is the world's largest specialized provider of temporary and permanent personnel in the fields of accounting and finance. It operates more than 200 offices in 37 states and five foreign countries, under the names Accountemps, Robert Half, OfficeTeam, RHI Consulting and The Affiliates. Foreign operations accounted for approximately 10% of total revenues in 1996.

The Accountemps temporary services division offers customers a means to manage uneven or peak work loads for accounting, tax and finance personnel caused by predictable events such as vacations, taking inventories, tax work, month-end activities and special projects, as well as unpredictable events, including illnesses and emergencies. Businesses increasingly view the use of temporary employees as a means of controlling personnel costs and converting such costs from fixed to variable. The temporary workers are employees of, and compensated by, Accountemps.

The company's Robert Half division specializes in placing accounting, financial, tax and banking personnel. Fees are paid by the employer and are generally a percentage of the new employee's annual salary. No fee for permanent placement services is charged to employment candidates.

OfficeTeam, which commenced operations in 1991, places temporary and permanent office and administrative personnel, ranging from word processors to office managers.

Since 1994, RHI Consulting has provided information technology contract consultants in areas ranging from multiple platform systems integration to end-user support, including specialists in programming, networking, systems integration, database design and help desk support.

In 1992, RHI acquired The Affiliates, a small operation that places temporary and permanent employees in paralegal, legal administrative and legal secretary positions.

The company markets its services to clients, as well as employment candidates. Local marketing and recruiting is generally conducted by each office or related group of offices through yellow pages advertisements, classified advertisements and radio. National advertising conducted by RHI consists primarily of print advertisements in national newspapers, magazines and trade journals.

The temporary staffing services industry is highly competitive and highly fragmented, with more than 15,000 firms competing throughout the world. The industry is affected by the economic environment, and benefits from the current scenario of low unemployment, low inflation and moderate economic growth.

### Capitalization

**Notes Payable:** $3,719,000 (3/97).

### Per Share Data ($)

| (Year Ended Dec. 31) | 1996 | 1995 | 1994 | 1993 | 1992 | 1991 | 1990 | 1989 | 1988 | 1987 |
|---|---|---|---|---|---|---|---|---|---|---|
| Tangible Bk. Val. | 2.24 | 1.26 | 0.43 | -0.35 | -1.12 | -1.22 | -1.45 | -1.47 | -1.35 | -1.00 |
| Cash Flow | 1.19 | 0.82 | 0.59 | 0.36 | 0.22 | 0.22 | 0.33 | 0.40 | 0.33 | 0.21 |
| Earnings | 1.00 | 0.68 | 0.46 | 0.23 | 0.09 | 0.09 | 0.19 | 0.29 | 0.25 | 0.16 |
| Dividends | Nil | Nil | Nil | Nil | Nil | Nil | Nil | Nil | Nil | 0.01 |
| Payout Ratio | Nil | Nil | Nil | Nil | Nil | Nil | Nil | Nil | Nil | 8% |
| Prices - High | 41½ | 22⅜ | 13⅜ | 7½ | 3⅝ | 3⅛ | 4⅝ | 5 | 5⅞ | 4⅞ |
| - Low | 19½ | 9⅞ | 6⅜ | 3⅛ | 2⅝ | 1¾ | 2¹/₁₆ | 4 | 3⅛ | 1¹³/₁₆ |
| P/E Ratio - High | 41 | 33 | 29 | 32 | 39 | 36 | 23 | 17 | 23 | 31 |
| - Low | 19 | 14 | 14 | 14 | 28 | 20 | 11 | 14 | 12 | 11 |

### Income Statement Analysis (Million $)

| | 1996 | 1995 | 1994 | 1993 | 1992 | 1991 | 1990 | 1989 | 1988 | 1987 |
|---|---|---|---|---|---|---|---|---|---|---|
| Revs. | 899 | 629 | 446 | 306 | 220 | 209 | 249 | 235 | 182 | 106 |
| Oper. Inc. | 113 | 77.0 | 54.0 | 32.2 | 18.6 | 21.1 | 30.9 | 35.5 | 28.5 | 15.1 |
| Depr. | 11.9 | 8.3 | 7.3 | 6.6 | 6.4 | 6.4 | 6.0 | 5.2 | 3.7 | 2.2 |
| Int. Exp. | 0.7 | 0.8 | 1.6 | 4.0 | 4.3 | 6.6 | NA | 7.6 | 6.4 | 3.5 |
| Pretax Inc. | 104 | 69.1 | 45.2 | 21.6 | 7.9 | 8.0 | 14.9 | 23.6 | 20.1 | 13.5 |
| Eff. Tax Rate | 41% | 42% | 42% | 46% | 45% | 49% | 41% | 43% | 40% | 46% |
| Net Inc. | 61.1 | 40.3 | 26.1 | 11.7 | 4.4 | 4.1 | 8.9 | 13.5 | 12.0 | 7.3 |

### Balance Sheet & Other Fin. Data (Million $)

| | 1996 | 1995 | 1994 | 1993 | 1992 | 1991 | 1990 | 1989 | 1988 | 1987 |
|---|---|---|---|---|---|---|---|---|---|---|
| Cash | 80.2 | 41.3 | 2.6 | 1.8 | 0.6 | 0.8 | 1.2 | 3.1 | 35.8 | 36.7 |
| Curr. Assets | 218 | 134 | 67.7 | 47.5 | 32.3 | 31.4 | 37.8 | 42.0 | 63.4 | 56.5 |
| Total Assets | 416 | 301 | 228 | 205 | 182 | 179 | 188 | 184 | 195 | 156 |
| Curr. Liab. | 86.6 | 55.9 | 29.6 | 22.2 | 14.7 | 19.5 | 18.7 | 17.8 | 31.3 | 18.6 |
| LT Debt | 5.1 | 1.5 | 3.1 | 32.3 | 61.0 | 61.6 | 80.8 | 89.0 | 88.5 | 80.7 |
| Common Eqty. | 308 | 228 | 177 | 134 | 91.0 | 84.4 | 77.3 | 68.7 | 61.7 | 48.1 |
| Total Cap. | 329 | 245 | 198 | 182 | 167 | 159 | 170 | 167 | 160 | 134 |
| Cap. Exp. | 18.0 | 8.4 | 4.8 | 2.3 | 1.1 | 0.8 | 3.3 | 3.9 | 1.7 | NM |
| Cash Flow | 73.0 | 48.6 | 33.4 | 18.4 | 10.8 | 10.5 | 14.9 | 18.7 | 15.7 | 9.5 |
| Curr. Ratio | 2.5 | 2.4 | 2.3 | 2.1 | 2.2 | 1.6 | 2.0 | 2.4 | 2.0 | 3.0 |
| % LT Debt of Cap. | 1.6 | 0.6 | 1.6 | 17.7 | 36.5 | 38.6 | 47.6 | 53.4 | 55.5 | 60.4 |
| % Net Inc.of Revs. | 6.8 | 6.4 | 5.9 | 3.8 | 2.0 | 1.9 | 3.6 | 5.7 | 6.6 | 6.9 |
| % Ret. on Assets | 17.1 | 15.2 | 11.8 | 5.7 | 2.4 | 2.2 | 4.8 | 7.2 | 6.8 | 4.9 |
| % Ret. on Equity | 22.8 | 19.9 | 16.5 | 9.9 | 4.9 | 4.9 | 12.2 | 21.0 | 21.8 | 14.4 |

Data as orig. reptd.; bef. results of disc. opers. and/or spec. items. Per share data adj. for stk. divs. as of ex-div. date. E-Estimated. NA-Not Available. NM-Not Meaningful. NR-Not Ranked.

**Office**—2884 Sand Hill Rd., Suite 200, Menlo Park, CA 94025. **Tel**—(415) 234-6000. **Chrmn, Pres & CEO**—H. M. Messmer, Jr. **SVP, CFO & Treas**—M. K. Waddell. **VP & Secy**—S. Karel. **Dirs**—A. S. Berwick, Jr., F. P. Furth, E. W. Gibbons, H. M. Messmer Jr., F. A. Richman, T. J. Ryan, J. S. Schaub. **Transfer Agent & Registrar**—Chemical Trust Co. of California, SF. **Incorporated**—in Delaware in 1980. **Empl**— 2,900. **S&P Analyst:** Stephen J. Tekirian

# STANDARD &POOR'S
STOCK REPORTS

# Schering-Plough

## 1985J

NYSE Symbol **SGP**

In S&P 500

**17-MAY-97**

**Industry:**
Health Care (Drugs - Major Pharmaceuticals)

**Summary:** This company is a leading producer of prescription and OTC pharmaceuticals and has important interests in sun care, animal health and foot care products.

| S&P Opinion: Accumulate (★★★★) | | |
|---|---|---|
| Recent Price • 86½ | Yield • 1.8% | |
| 52 Wk Range • 88¼-53⅞ | 12-Mo. P/E • 25.1 | |

**Quantitative Evaluations**

**Outlook**
(1 Lowest—5 Highest)
• **3**

**Fair Value**
• **82¾**

**Risk**
• **Low**

**Earn./Div. Rank**
• **A+**

**Technical Eval.**
• **Bullish** since 5/96

**Rel. Strength Rank**
(1 Lowest—99 Highest)
• **87**

**Insider Activity**
• **Neutral**

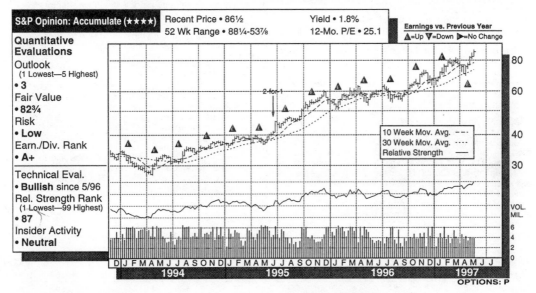

Earnings vs. Previous Year
▲=Up ▼=Down ▷=No Change

10 Week Mov. Avg. ---
30 Week Mov. Avg. ······
Relative Strength —

2-for-1

1994 1995 1996 1997

OPTIONS: P

## Overview - 15-MAY-97

Sales should post another healthy gain in 1997. Despite ongoing generic erosion in the Proventil anti-asthma line, volume should benefit from continued strong gains in Claritin and Claritin-D nonsedating antihistamine agents (sales rose 49% in the first quarter of 1997), Intron A anticancer and anti-infective agent (up 19%) and cardiovascular drugs (up 14%). Sales of Claritin should benefit from a planned entry in Japan (pending regulatory approval), while new indications should boost Intron A volume. New products such as Cedax antibiotic, Nasonex allergy drug and Fareston breast cancer treatment should also augment sales. Modest gains are forecast for the company's dermatological products, animal health items and consumer products. Margins should be well maintained, on improved volume and cost efficiencies.

## Valuation - 15-MAY-97

The shares appreciated with the rest of the drug group in recent months, buoyed by strong earnings momentum and investor preference for recession-resistant drug stocks. Near term results should continue to benefit from growth in Claritin, the No. 1 worldwide antihistamine; Intron A, an important antiviral/anticancer agent; and Vancenase, an inhaled steroid for allergies. New drugs such as Cedax, Nasonex and Fareston should also boost sales. The company's mix of popular prescription drugs and OTC medications, its highly productive R&D program and strict controls on operating costs should provide the basis for continued strong earnings growth in the years ahead. The R&D pipeline includes new treatments for allergies, asthma, cancer, infections and heart disease. The shares, which are being split two for one in June, are attractive for above-average long-term total return.

## Key Stock Statistics

| | | | |
|---|---|---|---|
| S&P EPS Est. 1997 | 3.80 | Tang. Bk. Value/Share | 6.28 |
| P/E on S&P Est. 1997 | 22.8 | Beta | 1.20 |
| S&P EPS Est. 1998 | 4.30 | Shareholders | 35,000 |
| Dividend Rate/Share | 1.52 | Market cap. (B) | $ 31.6 |
| Shs. outstg. (M) | 365.9 | Inst. holdings | 60% |
| Avg. daily vol. (M) | 0.743 | | |

Value of $10,000 invested 5 years ago: $ 29,752

### Fiscal Year Ending Dec. 31

| | 1998 | 1997 | 1996 | 1995 | 1994 | 1993 |
|---|---|---|---|---|---|---|
| **Revenues (Million $)** | | | | | | |
| 1Q | — | 1,568 | 1,383 | 1,224 | 1,162 | 1,090 |
| 2Q | — | — | 1,477 | 1,333 | 1,190 | 1,123 |
| 3Q | — | — | 1,382 | 1,257 | 1,126 | 1,062 |
| 4Q | — | — | 1,414 | 1,291 | 1,180 | 1,066 |
| Yr. | — | — | 5,656 | 5,104 | 4,657 | 4,341 |
| **Earnings Per Share ($)** | | | | | | |
| 1Q | — | 1.03 | 0.89 | 0.77 | 0.65 | 0.57 |
| 2Q | — | E1.00 | 0.86 | 0.74 | 0.63 | 0.54 |
| 3Q | — | E0.90 | 0.79 | 0.68 | 0.59 | 0.51 |
| 4Q | — | E0.87 | 0.76 | 0.66 | 0.54 | 0.49 |
| Yr. | E4.30 | E3.80 | 3.30 | 2.85 | 2.41 | 2.11 |

**Next earnings report expected: late July**

**Dividend Data** (Dividends have been paid since 1952.)

| Amount ($) | Date Decl. | Ex-Div. Date | Stock of Record | Payment Date |
|---|---|---|---|---|
| 0.330 | Oct. 22 | Oct. 30 | Nov. 01 | Nov. 26 '96 |
| 0.330 | Jan. 28 | Feb. 05 | Feb. 07 | Feb. 28 '97 |
| 0.380 | Apr. 22 | Apr. 30 | May. 02 | May. 27 '97 |
| 2-for-1 | Apr. 22 | Jun. 04 | May. 02 | Jun. 03 '97 |

This report is for information purposes and should not be considered a solicitation to buy or sell any security. Neither S&P nor any other party guarantee its accuracy or make warranties regarding results from its usage. Redistribution is prohibited without written permission. Copyright © 1997

A Division of The McGraw-Hill Companies

## Business Summary - 15-MAY-97

Schering-Plough is a leading maker of niche-oriented prescription pharmaceuticals. Interests are also held in animal health products, over-the-counter (OTC) medications, and consumer products. The company traces its history to Ernst Schering, a Berlin chemist who founded the company in 1864. International operations accounted for 42% of sales and 30% of profits in 1996. Schering is also a leader in biotechnology, with strong positions in genomics and gene therapy. Contributions by business segment in 1996 were:

|  | Sales | Profits |
|---|---|---|
| Pharmaceutical products | 89% | 92% |
| Health care products | 11% | 8% |

Respiratory/allergy drugs are Schering's largest product category, accounting for about 37% of total 1996 sales. SGP is the U.S. leader in allergy/respiratory products, as well as a principal factor in these markets overseas. The lead products are Claritin nonsedating antihistamine and Claritin D combination decongestant, the world's largest selling antihistamines with 1996 sales of $1.2 billion. Claritin has over 40% of the U.S. market. Other allergy/respiratory drugs include Proventil, Theo-Dur, and Uni-Dur asthma treatments; and Vancenase allergy nasal products and Vanceril asthma inhaler.

Anti-infectives and anticancer products (20% of 1996 sales) consist of Intron-A, the leading alpha interferon marketed for several anticancer and antiviral indications; Eulexin, a treatment for prostatic cancer; Cedax, a third-generation cephalosporin antibiotic; Leucomax, a granulocyte macrophage colony stimulating factor; Netromycin, an aminoglycoside antibiotic; and Ethyol, a cytoprotective agent.

Dermatological products (10%) include high-potency steroids such as Diprolene and Diprosone; Elocon, a topical steroid cream and ointment; and Lotrisone, a topical antifungal and anti-inflammatory cream. Cardiovasculars (9%) consist of Imdur, an oral nitrate; Nitro-Dur, a transdermal nitroglycerin patch for angina pectoris; Normodyne, an anti-hypertensive; and K-Dur, a potassium supplement. Other products (13%) include Losec anti-ulcer drug (marketed overseas), Fibre Trim diet aid products, animal health items and other drugs.

Health care products encompass OTC medicines (4%) such as Afrin nasal spray, Chlor-Trimeton allergy tablets, Coricidin and Drixoral cold medications, Correctal laxative and Gyne-Lotrimin for vaginal yeast infections; foot care items (5%) sold under Dr. Scholl's and other names; and Coppertone and other sun care products (2%).

### Capitalization

**Long Term Debt:** $46,000,000 (3/97).

### Per Share Data ($)

| (Year Ended Dec. 31) | 1996 | 1995 | 1994 | 1993 | 1992 | 1991 | 1990 | 1989 | 1988 | 1987 |
|---|---|---|---|---|---|---|---|---|---|---|
| Tangible Bk. Val. | 5.64 | 4.46 | 3.78 | 3.61 | 3.53 | 2.86 | 4.31 | 3.94 | 3.30 | 2.95 |
| Cash Flow | 3.77 | 3.27 | 2.82 | 2.44 | 2.10 | 1.77 | 1.49 | 1.27 | 1.08 | 0.88 |
| Earnings | 3.30 | 2.85 | 2.41 | 2.11 | 1.80 | 1.51 | 1.25 | 1.05 | 0.87 | 0.68 |
| Dividends | 1.28 | 1.16 | 0.99 | 0.87 | 0.75 | 0.63 | 0.53 | 0.44 | 0.35 | 0.26 |
| Payout Ratio | 39% | 41% | 41% | 41% | 42% | 40% | 42% | 43% | 40% | 36% |
| Prices - High | 73⅛ | 60¾ | 38 | 35½ | 35⅛ | 33⅝ | 25⅜ | 21½ | 14⅞ | 13⅞ |
| - Low | 50½ | 35½ | 27¼ | 25⅞ | 25 | 20⅜ | 18½ | 13⅞ | 11⅜ | 7⅞ |
| P/E Ratio - High | 22 | 21 | 16 | 17 | 19 | 22 | 20 | 21 | 17 | 20 |
| - Low | 15 | 12 | 11 | 12 | 14 | 14 | 15 | 13 | 13 | 11 |

### Income Statement Analysis (Million $)

| | 1996 | 1995 | 1994 | 1993 | 1992 | 1991 | 1990 | 1989 | 1988 | 1987 |
|---|---|---|---|---|---|---|---|---|---|---|
| Revs. | 5,656 | 5,104 | 4,657 | 4,341 | 4,056 | 3,616 | 3,323 | 3,158 | 2,969 | 2,699 |
| Oper. Inc. | 1,820 | 1,609 | 1,407 | 1,234 | 1,124 | 1,003 | 832 | 767 | 684 | 590 |
| Depr. | 173 | 157 | 158 | 127 | 120 | 115 | 109 | 99 | 95.0 | 90.0 |
| Int. Exp. | 56.0 | 69.0 | 68.0 | 61.0 | 71.0 | 77.0 | 89.0 | 100 | 124 | 92.0 |
| Pretax Inc. | 1,606 | 1,395 | 1,213 | 1,078 | 954 | 861 | 769 | 646 | 534 | 455 |
| Eff. Tax Rate | 25% | 25% | 24% | 24% | 25% | 25% | 27% | 27% | 27% | 31% |
| Net Inc. | 1,213 | 1,053 | 922 | 825 | 720 | 646 | 565 | 471 | 390 | 316 |

### Balance Sheet & Other Fin. Data (Million $)

| | 1996 | 1995 | 1994 | 1993 | 1992 | 1991 | 1990 | 1989 | 1988 | 1987 |
|---|---|---|---|---|---|---|---|---|---|---|
| Cash | 536 | 322 | 161 | 429 | 529 | 927 | 920 | 935 | 808 | 786 |
| Curr. Assets | 2,365 | 1,956 | 1,739 | 1,901 | 2,013 | 2,102 | 2,000 | 2,047 | 1,914 | 1,784 |
| Total Assets | 5,398 | 4,665 | 4,326 | 4,317 | 4,157 | 4,013 | 4,103 | 3,614 | 3,426 | 3,180 |
| Curr. Liab. | 2,599 | 2,362 | 2,029 | 2,132 | 1,969 | 1,528 | 1,530 | 1,214 | 1,336 | 1,333 |
| LT Debt | 47.0 | 87.0 | 186 | 182 | 184 | 754 | 183 | 186 | 190 | 190 |
| Common Eqty. | 2,060 | 1,623 | 1,574 | 1,582 | 1,597 | 1,346 | 2,081 | 1,955 | 1,677 | 1,443 |
| Total Cap. | 2,374 | 1,965 | 2,006 | 1,940 | 1,980 | 2,286 | 2,436 | 2,271 | 1,988 | 1,746 |
| Cap. Exp. | 325 | 294 | 272 | 365 | 403 | 339 | 243 | 186 | 156 | 118 |
| Cash Flow | 1,386 | 1,210 | 1,080 | 952 | 840 | 760 | 674 | 571 | 485 | 406 |
| Curr. Ratio | 0.9 | 0.8 | 0.9 | 0.9 | 1.0 | 1.4 | 1.3 | 1.7 | 1.4 | 1.3 |
| % LT Debt of Cap. | 2.0 | 4.4 | 9.3 | 9.4 | 9.3 | 33.0 | 7.5 | 8.2 | 9.5 | 10.9 |
| % Net Inc.of Revs. | 21.5 | 20.6 | 19.8 | 19.0 | 17.8 | 17.9 | 17.0 | 14.9 | 13.1 | 11.7 |
| % Ret. on Assets | 24.1 | 23.4 | 21.8 | 19.8 | 17.7 | 16.7 | 14.8 | 13.4 | 11.8 | 10.5 |
| % Ret. on Equity | 65.9 | 65.9 | 59.6 | 52.7 | 49.2 | 39.9 | 28.3 | 25.9 | 24.9 | 22.3 |

Data as orig. reptd.; bef. results of disc. opers. and/or spec. items. Per share data adj. for stk. divs. as of ex-div. date. E-Estimated. NA-Not Available. NM-Not Meaningful. NR-Not Ranked.

**Office**—One Giralda Farms, Madison, NJ 07940-1000. **Tel**—(201) 822-7000. **Fax**—(201) 822-7048. **Website**—http://www.sch-plough.com **Chrmn**—R. P. Luciano. **Pres & CEO**—R. J. Kogan. **Sr VP & Investor Contact**—Geraldine U. Foster. **VP & Secy**—W. J. Silbey. **VP-Fin**—J. L. Wyszomierski. **VP-Treas**—E. K. Moore. **Dirs**—H. W. Becherer, H. A. D'Andrade, D. C. Garfield, R. E. Herzlinger, R. J. Kogan, R. P. Luciano, H. B. Morley, C. E. Mundy, Jr., R. de J. Osborne, P. F. Russo, W. A. Schreyer, R. F. W. van Oordt, R. J. Ventres, J. Wood. **Transfer Agent & Registrar**—Bank of New York, NYC. **Incorporated**—in New Jersey in 1970. **Empl**— 20,600. **S&P Analyst:** H. B. Saftlas

# SCI Systems

**1959**

NYSE Symbol **SCI**

In S&P SmallCap 600

**17-MAY-97**

**Industry:**
Electrical Equipment

**Summary:** SCI is one of the world's largest electronics contract manufacturers, with the greatest surface mount technology production capacity in the merchant market.

| S&P Opinion: Accumulate (★★★★) | Recent Price • 57¼ | Yield • Nil |
| --- | --- | --- |
| | 52 Wk Range • 63½-30 | 12-Mo. P/E • 16.5 |

**Quantitative Evaluations**

**Outlook**
(1 Lowest—5 Highest)
• **4**

**Fair Value**
• **69⅛**

**Risk**
• **High**

**Earn./Div. Rank**
• **B+**

**Technical Eval.**
• **NA**

**Rel. Strength Rank**
(1 Lowest—99 Highest)
• **64**

**Insider Activity**
• **Neutral**

**Earnings vs. Previous Year**
▲=Up ▼=Down ▶=No Change

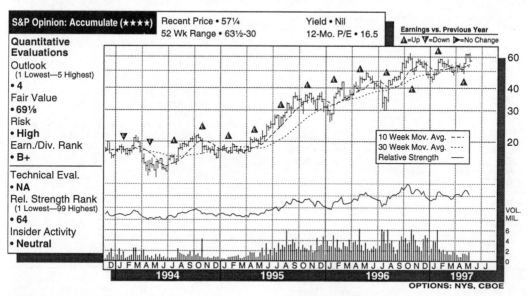

10 Week Mov. Avg. ---
30 Week Mov. Avg. ·····
Relative Strength —

OPTIONS: NYS, CBOE

## Overview - 01-MAY-97

This major electronics contract manufacturer designs and builds printed circuit boards and has benefited from the trend in the computer industry to outsource production of those items. This was demonstrated by SCI's 1994 purchase of Hewlett-Packard's Grenoble, France, surface mount center and the acquisition of a modern 360,000-sq.-ft. facility in Fountain, CO, from Apple Computer during the fourth quarter of FY 96 (Jun.). Also during FY 96, SCI built two facilities, and it is currently building a plant in Penang, Malaysia, and expanding its Irvine, Scotland, facility. The company also has plans for two more projects in FY 98. The trend in outsourcing is expected to continue as it provides OEMs with solutions to the problems of rapid change in manufacturing technologies, new product proliferation, short product life cycles, intense cost pressures and heightened user reliability and quality expectations.

## Valuation - 01-MAY-97

Revenues in FY 97's first nine months increased 32%, as higher volumes, especially in finished product assembly, outweighed lower average selling prices. Net income rose 43%, and primary EPS of $2.66 compared favorably against $1.88. We forecast revenue growth amounting to 20% over the next two fiscal years, and net income should climb at a slightly faster rate, reflecting margin improvement. The company's return on equity has been steadily improving, rising to 21% in FY 97's third quarter from 16% a year earlier. We see continued earnings growth for the company and have raised our primary EPS estimate for the full fiscal year to $3.60 from $3.55 and expect $4.10 in FY 98. The stock trading at about 16 times our new estimate appears quite attractive and warrants accumulation.

## Key Stock Statistics

| | | | |
| --- | --- | --- | --- |
| S&P EPS Est. 1997 | 3.60 | Tang. Bk. Value/Share | 15.96 |
| P/E on S&P Est. 1997 | 15.9 | Beta | 2.28 |
| S&P EPS Est. 1998 | 4.10 | Shareholders | 2,100 |
| Dividend Rate/Share | Nil | Market cap. (B) | $ 1.7 |
| Shs. outstg. (M) | 29.8 | Inst. holdings | 80% |
| Avg. daily vol. (M) | 0.285 | | |

Value of $10,000 invested 5 years ago: $ 88,076

### Fiscal Year Ending Jun. 30

| | 1998 | 1997 | 1996 | 1995 | 1994 | 1993 |
| --- | --- | --- | --- | --- | --- | --- |
| **Revenues (Million $)** | | | | | | |
| 1Q | — | 1,420 | 876.6 | 618.4 | 421.0 | 350.0 |
| 2Q | — | 1,482 | 1,204 | 621.5 | 422.9 | 451.0 |
| 3Q | — | 1,320 | 1,113 | 591.5 | 424.1 | 455.6 |
| 4Q | — | — | 1,352 | 842.3 | 584.5 | 441.4 |
| Yr. | — | — | 4,545 | 2,674 | 1,852 | 1,697 |
| **Earnings Per Share ($)** | | | | | | |
| 1Q | — | 0.83 | 0.51 | 0.36 | 0.33 | 0.20 |
| 2Q | — | 0.97 | 0.74 | 0.37 | 0.33 | 0.34 |
| 3Q | — | 0.86 | 0.63 | 0.39 | 0.02 | 0.34 |
| 4Q | — | E0.94 | 0.81 | 0.48 | 0.40 | 0.31 |
| Yr. | E4.10 | E3.60 | 2.69 | 1.63 | 1.08 | 1.09 |

**Next earnings report expected: early August**

## Dividend Data

A loan agreement limits cash payments. A three-for-two stock split was effected in 1987.

This report is for information purposes and should not be considered a solicitation to buy or sell any security. Neither S&P nor any other party guarantee its accuracy or make warranties regarding results from its usage. Redistribution is prohibited without written permission. Copyright © 1997

*A Division of The McGraw-Hill Companies*

## Business Summary - 01-MAY-97

Founded as Space Craft Inc. in 1961 to provide electronic systems to the U.S. Government, SCI Systems adopted a more down-to-earth approach in the mid-1970s by targeting the commercial sector. Today, SCI manufactures electronic products for the computer, aerospace, defense, telecommunications, medical and entertainment industries. Although SCI derives a majority of its revenues from hardware manufacturing and maintains a broad technology base, it is primarily a vertically integrated engineering and manufacturing services provider. The company is expected to post over $5 billion in revenue in FY 97 (Jun.), a tremendous leap from the FY 87 total of $553 million.

SCI operates through two divisions: Commercial and Government.

The Commercial division is the leading international supplier of full-service contract manufacturing for the electronics industry. A steady shift to outsourcing is continuing, as original equipment manufacturers seek solutions to the problems of rapid change in manufacturing technologies, new product proliferation, short product life cycles, intense cost pressures and heightened user reliability and quality expectations. SCI makes printed circuit boards using pin-in-hole (PIH) and surface mount technology (SMT). SMT is the production technique of growing preference, offering smaller size, lower cost and higher reliability. The company operates 155 automated SMT assembly lines in eight countries,

making it one of the largest SMT producers in the world and the leader in the merchant market.

The Government division provides a wide range of high-performance systems and subsystems for use by the U.S. and foreign governments and by the defense and aerospace industries. The division designs and manufactures electronic and electromechanical systems and subsystems for launch vehicle, satellite, aircraft and surface applications, with emphasis on instrumentation, voice and data communications and computers. During 1996, production of voice and communication control systems continued in support of the F-15, F-16, F-18 and AV-8 aircraft, as well as the government's global positioning system user equipment. Contract manufacturing has recently been expanded in missile electronics, transportation products and ruggedized portable computer assemblies.

Hewlett-Packard accounted for 47% of net sales in FY 96 and the company's 10 largest customers contributed over 70% of revenues. U.S. export and foreign sales totaled 35% of net sales in FY 96, down from 44% in FY 95.

Backlog at the end of March 1997 amounted to $2.81 billion, up 15% from $2.45 billion a year earlier.

### Capitalization

**Long Term Debt:** $442,352,000 (12/96), incl. $281,863,000 of 5% sub. notes conv. into com. at $48.75 a sh.

## Per Share Data ($)

| (Year Ended Jun. 30) | 1996 | 1995 | 1994 | 1993 | 1992 | 1991 | 1990 | 1989 | 1988 | 1987 |
|---|---|---|---|---|---|---|---|---|---|---|
| Tangible Bk. Val. | 15.96 | 12.64 | 11.02 | 9.98 | 8.62 | 8.26 | 7.93 | 7.85 | 6.97 | 6.04 |
| Cash Flow | 4.71 | 3.42 | 2.84 | 2.45 | 2.00 | 1.89 | 1.74 | 2.23 | 1.86 | 1.36 |
| Earnings | 2.69 | 1.63 | 1.08 | 1.09 | 0.18 | 0.16 | 0.11 | 1.00 | 0.91 | 0.77 |
| Dividends | Nil | Nil | Nil | Nil | Nil | Nil | Nil | Nil | Nil | Nil |
| Payout Ratio | Nil | Nil | Nil | Nil | Nil | Nil | Nil | Nil | Nil | Nil |
| Prices - High | 63 | 38 | 22¼ | 23⅜ | 18½ | 10⅛ | 13⅛ | 16 | 15¼ | 23⅛ |
|    - Low | 25¾ | 17 | 12⅝ | 14⅜ | 6½ | 5⅞ | 5¼ | 7⅝ | 10⅝ | 11⅛ |
| P/E Ratio - High | 23 | 23 | 21 | 21 | NM | 63 | NM | 16 | 17 | 30 |
|    - Low | 10 | 10 | 12 | 13 | NM | 37 | NM | 8 | 12 | 14 |

## Income Statement Analysis (Million $)

| | 1996 | 1995 | 1994 | 1993 | 1992 | 1991 | 1990 | 1989 | 1988 | 1987 |
|---|---|---|---|---|---|---|---|---|---|---|
| Revs. | 4,545 | 2,674 | 1,852 | 1,697 | 1,045 | 1,129 | 1,179 | 987 | 774 | 553 |
| Oper. Inc. | 221 | 141 | 119 | 95.0 | 52.3 | 70.5 | 60.6 | 67.2 | 58.1 | 38.7 |
| Depr. | 61.0 | 49.8 | 48.6 | 40.9 | 38.2 | 36.2 | 34.0 | 25.6 | 19.9 | 12.3 |
| Int. Exp. | 26.0 | 18.4 | 15.4 | 16.8 | 15.5 | 22.4 | 27.1 | 18.5 | 13.7 | 12.0 |
| Pretax Inc. | 136 | 75.7 | 46.9 | 37.4 | 1.0 | 2.4 | 2.3 | 25.2 | 26.7 | 20.0 |
| Eff. Tax Rate | 40% | 40% | 36% | 29% | NM | NM | Nil | 17% | 29% | 20% |
| Net Inc. | 81.0 | 45.2 | 29.9 | 26.6 | 3.8 | 3.5 | 2.3 | 20.9 | 19.0 | 16.0 |

## Balance Sheet & Other Fin. Data (Million $)

| | 1996 | 1995 | 1994 | 1993 | 1992 | 1991 | 1990 | 1989 | 1988 | 1987 |
|---|---|---|---|---|---|---|---|---|---|---|
| Cash | 46.5 | 10.0 | 36.0 | 16.0 | 39.0 | 26.0 | 28.0 | 32.0 | 16.0 | 119 |
| Curr. Assets | 1,004 | 745 | 721 | 580 | 449 | 382 | 451 | 487 | 374 | 352 |
| Total Assets | 1,283 | 981 | 920 | 780 | 613 | 551 | 630 | 624 | 485 | 436 |
| Curr. Liab. | 455 | 465 | 326 | 244 | 194 | 128 | 135 | 171 | 122 | 119 |
| LT Debt | 339 | 156 | 278 | 249 | 219 | 234 | 318 | 278 | 210 | 181 |
| Common Eqty. | 472 | 350 | 305 | 278 | 192 | 186 | 176 | 170 | 152 | 133 |
| Total Cap. | 816 | 507 | 584 | 531 | 415 | 423 | 495 | 453 | 363 | 317 |
| Cap. Exp. | 110 | 80.3 | 46.5 | 84.1 | 29.8 | 30.3 | 62.7 | 50.7 | 42.8 | 29.6 |
| Cash Flow | 142 | 95.1 | 78.6 | 67.4 | 42.0 | 39.7 | 36.4 | 46.5 | 38.8 | 28.3 |
| Curr. Ratio | 2.2 | 1.6 | 2.2 | 2.4 | 2.3 | 3.0 | 3.3 | 2.8 | 3.1 | 3.0 |
| % LT Debt of Cap. | 41.6 | 30.9 | 47.7 | 46.9 | 52.8 | 55.2 | 64.3 | 61.5 | 57.7 | 57.1 |
| % Net Inc.of Revs. | 1.8 | 1.7 | 1.6 | 1.6 | 0.4 | 0.3 | 0.2 | 2.1 | 2.5 | 2.9 |
| % Ret. on Assets | 3.6 | 4.8 | 3.5 | 3.4 | 0.7 | 0.6 | 0.4 | 3.8 | 4.1 | 4.5 |
| % Ret. on Equity | 9.8 | 3.8 | 10.2 | 10.1 | 2.0 | 1.9 | 1.3 | 13.0 | 13.3 | 12.9 |

Data as orig. reptd.; bef. results of disc. opers. and/or spec. items. Per share data adj. for stk. divs. as of ex-div. date. E-Estimated. NA-Not Available. NM-Not Meaningful. NR-Not Ranked.

**Office**—2101 W. Clinton Ave., Huntsville, AL 35805. **Tel**—(302) 998-0592. **Chrmn & CEO**—O. B. King. **Pres & COO**—A. E. Sapp Jr. **Secy**—M. M. Sullivan. **Dirs**—H. H. Callaway, W. E. Fruhan Jr., O. B. King, J. C. Moquin, A. E. Sapp Jr., W. Shortridge, G. R. Tod, J. M. Ward. **Transfer Agent & Registrar**—ChaseMellon Shareholder Services. **Incorporated**—in Delaware in 1961. **Empl**— 15,524. **S&P Analyst:**  Ted Groesbeck

**17-MAY-97**

**Industry:**
Computers (Peripherals)

**Summary:** Seagate is a leading maker of rigid magnetic disk drives for a wide range of computers from PCs to supercomputers. It also makes disk drive parts and other storage products.

| S&P Opinion: Buy (★★★★) | Recent Price • 48½ | Yield • Nil |
| | 52 Wk Range • 56¼-18⅛ | 12-Mo. P/E • 16.1 |

**Quantitative Evaluations**

**Outlook**
(1 Lowest—5 Highest)
• **4⁻**

**Fair Value**
• **58¾**

**Risk**
• **High**

**Earn./Div. Rank**
• **B**

**Technical Eval.**
• **Bearish** since 12/96

**Rel. Strength Rank**
(1 Lowest—99 Highest)
• **59**

**Insider Activity**
• **Neutral**

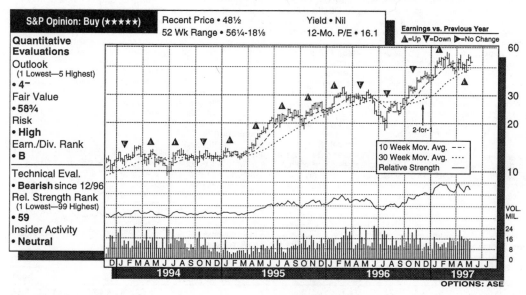

Earnings vs. Previous Year
▲=Up ▼=Down ▶=No Change

10 Week Mov. Avg. – – –
30 Week Mov. Avg. ·······
Relative Strength ——

2-for-1

VOL. MIL.

OPTIONS: ASE

## Overview - 09-APR-97

Sales should rise about 20% in the fourth quarter of FY 97 and for all of FY 98, reflecting a higher level of unit shipments, aided by strong demand in general for disk drives and strong product positioning in the desktop and high performance drive market, aided by new products. Seagate is well positioned at the high end of the disk drive market, and should benefit from a move to higher capacity drives, stemming from the greater storage requirements of enhanced graphics, video, sound and computer networks. Margins should widen, on volume efficiencies, manufacturing cost reductions, moderated price declines, and a more favorable disk drive product mix, as well as increased contributions from software offerings. Per share earnings comparisons should also benefit from the absence of $1.14 (as adjusted) in charges recorded in the third quarter and $0.10 (adjusted) in charges recorded in the fourth quarter of FY 96.

## Valuation - 09-APR-97

The shares of this highly regarded storage vendor have rebounded sharply from their mid-1996 lows, on solid financial results and underlying expansion of the storage market. The introduction of new products as well as strong demand and moderated price competition should drive revenue and earnings growth through FY 98 (Jun.). SEG remains well positioned, particularly in the high capacity/high performance (and higher margin) segment of the market. Strong relationships with major OEMs, together with a proven ability to manage product cycles, bode well for continued operating success. The shares, which trade at about 13 times our estimated FY 98 earnings, are expected to outperform the market in coming months.

## Key Stock Statistics

| | | | |
|---|---|---|---|
| S&P EPS Est. 1997 | 3.60 | Tang. Bk. Value/Share | 10.27 |
| P/E on S&P Est. 1997 | 13.5 | Beta | 2.08 |
| S&P EPS Est. 1998 | 4.30 | Shareholders | 6,000 |
| Dividend Rate/Share | Nil | Market cap. (B) | $ 12.0 |
| Shs. outstg. (M) | 247.2 | Inst. holdings | 82% |
| Avg. daily vol. (M) | 2.989 | | |

Value of $10,000 invested 5 years ago: $ 106,301

### Fiscal Year Ending Jun. 30

| | 1998 | 1997 | 1996 | 1995 | 1994 | 1993 |
|---|---|---|---|---|---|---|
| **Revenues (Million $)** | | | | | | |
| 1Q | — | 2,061 | 2,141 | 933.2 | 773.9 | 742.6 |
| 2Q | — | 2,400 | 2,340 | 1,130 | 815.9 | 776.7 |
| 3Q | — | 2,502 | 2,093 | 1,185 | 909.3 | 754.1 |
| 4Q | — | — | 2,015 | 1,292 | 1,001 | 770.2 |
| Yr. | — | — | 8,588 | 4,540 | 3,500 | 3,044 |
| **Earnings Per Share ($)** | | | | | | |
| 1Q | — | 0.59 | 0.61 | 0.15 | 0.25 | 0.43 |
| 2Q | — | 0.91 | 0.74 | 0.54 | 0.29 | 0.46 |
| 3Q | — | 1.01 | -0.79 | 0.49 | 0.46 | 0.28 |
| 4Q | — | E1.09 | 0.46 | 0.60 | 0.54 | 0.24 |
| Yr. | E4.30 | E3.60 | 1.03 | 1.76 | 1.54 | 1.40 |

**Next earnings report expected: mid July**

### Dividend Data

| Amount ($) | Date Decl. | Ex-Div. Date | Stock of Record | Payment Date |
|---|---|---|---|---|
| 2-for-1 | Oct. 24 | Nov. 27 | Nov. 11 | Nov. 26 '96 |

This report is for information purposes and should not be considered a solicitation to buy or sell any security. Neither S&P nor any other party guarantee its accuracy or make warranties regarding results from its usage. Redistribution is prohibited without written permission. Copyright © 1997

*A Division of The McGraw·Hill Companies*

## Business Summary - 09-APR-97

None other than the current chairman of the NYSE called Seagate Technology a "blue chip" company last fall. While Seagate is not normally associated with "chips" (disk drives are its strong suit), the compliment from the Big Board's boss is testimony to SEG's market leading positions in revenues, profits, gross margin, operating margin, research and development, and capital investment.

The largest independent provider of mass storage products for computers and related equipment, Seagate's core business is in disk drives. Seagate is the most diversified of the disk drive vendors, offering more than 50 drive models with form factors (a measure of the disk size accommodated) of 2.5, 3.5 and 5.25 inches, and capacities ranging from 540 megabytes to 23 gigabytes. Products are differentiated by form factor and on a price/performance basis.

The company pursues a strategy of vertical integration, meaning it makes many of the component parts for its drives itself. Seagate is a major designer and manufacturer of major disk drive components, including thin film and magnetoresistive recording heads, head stack assemblies, media and motors.

Pricing has always been an issue in the disk drive industry. Prices for the same capacity class of disk drives trend only one way -- down. However, higher unit sales owing to industry consolidation, strong demand and increased manufacturing capability, combined with an improving product mix of higher capacity drives and continued manufacturing cost reductions, have benefitted Seagate's earnings in recent periods.

In addition to its core disk drive business, SEG continues to broaden its strategy to more fully address the markets for the storage, retrieval and management of data. Seagate offers a complete line of mini-cartridge and DAT tape drive products used primarily for system backup purposes. Through its fast growing Seagate Software unit, SEG also provides storage management and information management software solutions. Also, Seagate sells flash memory products.

The company has strong relationships with its customers, primarily major original equipment manufacturers (OEMs), and has proven itself able to manage the industry's increasingly short product cycles.

Capital expenditures, seen at around $850 million in FY 97, are expected to exceed $1 billion in FY 98.

Non-recurring charges in FY 96 (Jun.) were as follows: $42.4 million ($0.10 a share; as adjusted ) in the fourth quarter; and $314.1 million ($1.14; adjusted) in the third quarter. Non-recurring charges in FY 95 were: $15.0 million ($0.11 a share; adjusted) in the fourth quarter; $12.8 million ($0.10; adjusted) in the third quarter; and $43.0 million ($0.31; adjusted) in the first quarter. The charges were taken mainly for asset writedowns and restructuring costs related to acquisitions.

## Capitalization

**Long Term Debt:** $701,916 (3/97).

### Per Share Data ($)

| (Year Ended Jun. 30) | 1996 | 1995 | 1994 | 1993 | 1992 | 1991 | 1990 | 1989 | 1988 | 1987 |
|---|---|---|---|---|---|---|---|---|---|---|
| Tangible Bk. Val. | 10.27 | 9.40 | 9.12 | 7.67 | 6.31 | 5.88 | 5.32 | 4.43 | 4.44 | 3.68 |
| Cash Flow | 3.04 | 3.03 | 2.48 | 2.51 | 1.68 | 1.52 | 1.92 | 0.77 | 1.27 | 1.68 |
| Earnings | 1.03 | 1.76 | 1.54 | 1.40 | 0.46 | 0.47 | 0.96 | 0.00 | 0.77 | 1.40 |
| Dividends | Nil | Nil | Nil | Nil | Nil | Nil | Nil | Nil | Nil | Nil |
| Payout Ratio | Nil | Nil | Nil | Nil | Nil | Nil | Nil | Nil | Nil | Nil |
| Prices - High | 42¾ | 27⅜ | 14⅜ | 12⅝ | 11¼ | 10 | 9⅞ | 8⅛ | 11¾ | 22⅞ |
|    - Low | 18⅛ | 11⅞ | 9⅜ | 6⅝ | 4½ | 3⅝ | 2⅞ | 4¼ | 3¼ | 4⅞ |
| P/E Ratio - High | 42 | 16 | 9 | 9 | 24 | 21 | 10 | NM | 15 | 16 |
|    - Low | 18 | 7 | 6 | 5 | 10 | 8 | 3 | NM | 4 | 3 |

### Income Statement Analysis (Million $)

| | 1996 | 1995 | 1994 | 1993 | 1992 | 1991 | 1990 | 1989 | 1988 | 1987 |
|---|---|---|---|---|---|---|---|---|---|---|
| Revs. | 8,588 | 4,540 | 3,500 | 3,044 | 2,875 | 2,677 | 2,413 | 1,372 | 1,266 | 958 |
| Oper. Inc. | 1,044 | 630 | 449 | 439 | 309 | 256 | 297 | 91.0 | 151 | 208 |
| Depr. | 417 | 187 | 138 | 155 | 169 | 138 | 118 | 78.0 | 50.0 | 28.0 |
| Int. Exp. | 55.8 | 33.0 | 26.3 | 23.5 | 34.0 | 42.5 | 48.7 | 24.1 | 21.9 | 5.1 |
| Pretax Inc. | 331 | 409 | 322 | 271 | 85.0 | 82.0 | 150 | NM | 99 | 186 |
| Eff. Tax Rate | 36% | 37% | 30% | 28% | 26% | 23% | 22% | 26% | 22% | 25% |
| Net Inc. | 213 | 260 | 225 | 195 | 63.0 | 63.0 | 117 | NM | 77.0 | 140 |

### Balance Sheet & Other Fin. Data (Million $)

| | 1996 | 1995 | 1994 | 1993 | 1992 | 1991 | 1990 | 1989 | 1988 | 1987 |
|---|---|---|---|---|---|---|---|---|---|---|
| Cash | 1,174 | 1,247 | 1,334 | 629 | 504 | 252 | 263 | 190 | 93.0 | 396 |
| Curr. Assets | 3,399 | 2,445 | 2,246 | 1,471 | 1,259 | 1,184 | 1,139 | 652 | 685 | 647 |
| Total Assets | 5,240 | 3,361 | 2,878 | 2,031 | 1,817 | 1,880 | 1,851 | 1,077 | 1,094 | 814 |
| Curr. Liab. | 1,438 | 910 | 703 | 544 | 502 | 591 | 550 | 265 | 288 | 109 |
| LT Debt | 798 | 540 | 549 | 281 | 321 | 393 | 510 | 305 | 304 | 302 |
| Common Eqty. | 2,466 | 1,542 | 1,328 | 1,045 | 862 | 766 | 675 | 442 | 436 | 354 |
| Total Cap. | 3,616 | 2,326 | 2,097 | 1,450 | 1,280 | 1,254 | 1,269 | 812 | 806 | 705 |
| Cap. Exp. | 907 | 353 | 198 | 174 | 82.0 | 99 | 58.0 | 63.0 | 208 | 65.0 |
| Cash Flow | 630 | 447 | 363 | 350 | 232 | 201 | 235 | 78.0 | 128 | 167 |
| Curr. Ratio | 2.4 | 2.7 | 3.2 | 2.7 | 2.5 | 2.0 | 2.1 | 2.5 | 2.4 | 6.0 |
| % LT Debt of Cap. | 22.1 | 23.2 | 26.2 | 19.4 | 25.0 | 31.4 | 40.2 | 37.6 | 37.8 | 42.8 |
| % Net Inc.of Revs. | 2.5 | 5.7 | 6.4 | 6.4 | 2.2 | 2.3 | 4.9 | NM | 6.1 | 14.6 |
| % Ret. on Assets | 4.2 | 8.4 | 8.9 | 10.2 | 3.3 | 3.3 | 7.3 | NM | 8.0 | 24.8 |
| % Ret. on Equity | 9.7 | 18.2 | 18.4 | 20.5 | 7.6 | 8.6 | 19.0 | 0.1 | 19.4 | 49.4 |

Data as orig. reptd.; bef. results of disc. opers. and/or spec. items. Per share data adj. for stk. divs. as of ex-div. date. E-Estimated. NA-Not Available. NM-Not Meaningful. NR-Not Ranked.

**Office**—920 Disc Drive, Scotts Valley, CA 95066. **Tel**—(408) 438-6550. **Website**—http://www.seagate.com **Chrmn, Pres, CEO & COO**—A. F. Shugart. **SVP-Fin, CFO & Secy**—D. L. Waite. **Investor Contact**—Deborah Peterson. **Dirs**—G. B. Filler, K. E. Haughton, R. A. Kleist, L. Perlman, A. F. Shugart, T. P. Stafford, L. L. Wilkening. **Transfer Agent & Registrar**—Harris Trust Co of California. **Incorporated**—in California in 1978; reincorporated in Delaware in 1986. **Empl**— 101,000. **S&P Analyst:** Peter C. Wood, CFA

# Solectron Corp.

**2052R**

NYSE Symbol **SLR**

In S&P MidCap 400

**17-MAY-97**

**Industry:** Electrical Equipment

**Summary:** This company provides customized, integrated manufacturing services to OEMs in the electronics industry, including the assembly of printed circuit boards.

| S&P Opinion: Accumulate (★★★★) | Recent Price • 59 | Yield • Nil |
| --- | --- | --- |
| | 52 Wk Range • 62⅝-29 | 12-Mo. P/E • 25.2 |

**Quantitative Evaluations**

Outlook
(1 Lowest—5 Highest)
• **4⁻**

Fair Value
• **75⅛**

Risk
• **Average**

Earn./Div. Rank
• **B+**

Technical Eval.
• **Bullish** since 9/96

Rel. Strength Rank
(1 Lowest—99 Highest)
• **79**

Insider Activity
• **Neutral**

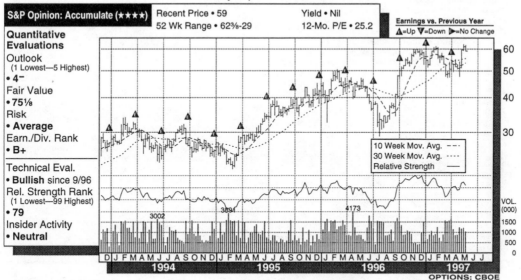

**Earnings vs. Previous Year**
▲=Up ▼=Down ▶=No Change

10 Week Mov. Avg. ---
30 Week Mov. Avg. ·····
Relative Strength —

OPTIONS: CBOE

## Overview - 18-MAR-97

This contract manufacturer of computer components is benefiting from the spread of outsourcing in the design, manufacture and distribution of computer hardware. This trend is expected to continue for some time and is emerging in Europe. OEMs realize significant advantages from this solution, including reduced time to market, reduced capital investment, which results in more efficient asset utilization, improved inventory management and purchasing power and faster access to new and changing technologies. SLR's strategy is to provide technically advanced, quality products, seek manufacturing partnerships, provide higher margin turnkey operations, and diversify its geographic operations. In executing this strategy, the company purchased the custom manufacturing operations of Texas Instruments, Fine Pitch Technology, and Force Computers in 1996.

## Valuation - 18-MAR-97

Revenues rose 31% year to year in the second quarter of FY 97 (Aug.), reflecting the acquisition of Force Computers, which added about $30 million, strong growth in printed circuit boards and increases in the network and telecom businesses. However, results were pinched by weakness in the systems and test segments, a cancelled order, and a product delay caused by a slight component shortage due to an imbalance between product lead time and the company's ordering cycle. Gross margins widened due to the inclusion of Force Computers, but operating costs surged to 5.5% of revenues, up from a 4.0% run rate. Net income in the quarter advanced 36% to a record $37.6 million ($0.65 a share), which was in line with our expectations. We are revising downward our FY 97 EPS estimate to $2.60 from $2.70, reflecting dilution from the Force acquisition, but we still view the stock as attractive at 19X current EPS estimates.

## Key Stock Statistics

| | | | | |
| --- | --- | --- | --- | --- |
| S&P EPS Est. 1997 | 2.60 | Tang. Bk. Value/Share | 13.34 |
| P/E on S&P Est. 1997 | 22.7 | Beta | 1.92 |
| S&P EPS Est. 1998 | 3.50 | Shareholders | 1,200 |
| Dividend Rate/Share | Nil | Market cap. (B) | $ 3.2 |
| Shs. outstg. (M) | 54.4 | Inst. holdings | 83% |
| Avg. daily vol. (M) | 0.228 | | |

Value of $10,000 invested 5 years ago: $ 67,913

### Fiscal Year Ending Aug. 31

| | 1998 | 1997 | 1996 | 1995 | 1994 | 1993 |
| --- | --- | --- | --- | --- | --- | --- |
| **Revenues (Million $)** | | | | | | |
| 1Q | — | 807.7 | 690.6 | 506.7 | 321.8 | 136.5 |
| 2Q | — | 858.7 | 657.2 | 471.3 | 327.2 | 187.4 |
| 3Q | — | — | 680.5 | 516.9 | 365.1 | 241.9 |
| 4Q | — | — | 788.8 | 570.7 | 442.6 | 270.5 |
| Yr. | — | — | 2,817 | 2,066 | 1,457 | 836.3 |
| **Earnings Per Share ($)** | | | | | | |
| 1Q | — | 0.58 | 0.54 | 0.43 | 0.28 | 0.12 |
| 2Q | — | 0.65 | 0.54 | 0.43 | 0.29 | 0.19 |
| 3Q | — | E0.67 | 0.53 | 0.48 | 0.35 | 0.21 |
| 4Q | — | E0.70 | 0.59 | 0.48 | 0.39 | 0.27 |
| Yr. | E3.50 | E2.60 | 2.19 | 1.82 | 1.32 | 0.80 |

**Next earnings report expected: mid June**

## Dividend Data

No cash dividends have been paid. The shares were split two for one in 1993 and in 1992.

This report is for information purposes and should not be considered a solicitation to buy or sell any security. Neither S&P nor any other party guarantee its accuracy or make warranties regarding results from its usage. Redistribution is prohibited without written permission. Copyright © 1997

*A Division of The McGraw-Hill Companies*

## Business Summary - 18-MAR-97

Solectron provides customized, integrated manufacturing services to original equipment manufacturers (OEMs) in the electronics industry, mainly sophisticated electronic assembly and turnkey manufacturing. Electronic assembly involves the manufacture of complex printed circuit boards using surface mount (SMT) and pin-through-hole (PTH) interconnection technologies and the testing and assembly of electronic systems and subsystems. In addition to assembly, turnkey manufacturing services include procurement and materials management, and consultation on board design and manufacturability. Other services include flexible cable assembly, refurbishment, disk duplication and packaging, remanufacturing and testing.

In FY 96 (Aug.), Hewlett Packard (HWP) accounted for 11% of total sales, and SLR's 10 largest customers contributed 64% of revenues, which compared with over 70% in the past two fiscal years. Sales made outside of the U.S. accounted for approximately 30%, down from 38% a year earlier.

To achieve excellence in manufacturing, Solectron combines computer-aided manufacturing and testing with just-in-time manufacturing, total quality control, statistical process control and continuous flow manufacturing. The company has expanded its manufacturing capacity over the past few years and now has operations on three continents. In the U.S., operations are carried out in Milpitas, Mountainview, San Jose, and Santa Ana, CA; Charlotte, NC; Austin, TX; Everett, WA; and through a recently opened facility in Westboro, MA. The Charlotte facility was acquired from IBM in 1992, Everett from HWP in 1993, Austin from Texas Instruments, and the California facilities, excluding Milpitas, as part of the Fine Pitch acquisition in March 1996. Also, capacity was added at SLR's Milpitas and Charlotte facilities in early FY 96. In Europe, operations began with the 1992 acquisition of IBM's PTH electronic card assembly operations in Bordeaux, France. In 1993, Solectron acquired the manufacturing facilities of Philips Electronics in Dunfermline, Scotland. Elsewhere in Europe, the company now has operations in Boebligen, Germany, pursuant to the November 1995 purchase of HWP's printed circuit assembly operations, and in Munich through the acquisition of Force Computers. In Asia, SLR established a manufacturing facility in Penang, Malaysia, in 1991 and a significant expansion was completed there in FY 94. Also, the company has new found presence in Sweden, Belgium and Israel with the purchase of Force Computers in November 1996, and opened a wholly owned subsidiary located in Suzhou, China, in December 1996.

## Capitalization

**Long Term Debt:** $389,015,000 (2/97), incl. cap. lease obligs.

| Per Share Data ($) (Year Ended Aug. 31) | 1996 | 1995 | 1994 | 1993 | 1992 | 1991 | 1990 | 1989 | 1988 | 1987 |
|---|---|---|---|---|---|---|---|---|---|---|
| Tangible Bk. Val. | 13.34 | 10.85 | 8.01 | 6.42 | 3.16 | 1.86 | 1.48 | 1.15 | 1.02 | 0.82 |
| Cash Flow | 3.81 | 3.22 | 2.40 | 1.49 | 0.82 | 0.71 | 0.58 | 0.40 | 0.32 | NA |
| Earnings | 2.19 | 1.82 | 1.32 | 0.80 | 0.44 | 0.35 | 0.32 | 0.24 | 0.17 | 0.08 |
| Dividends | Nil | Nil | Nil | Nil | Nil | Nil | Nil | Nil | Nil | Nil |
| Payout Ratio | Nil | Nil | Nil | Nil | Nil | Nil | Nil | Nil | Nil | Nil |
| Prices - High | 60 1/8 | 45 1/8 | 34 | 29 3/4 | 18 3/4 | 9 1/8 | 4 3/8 | 1 7/8 | NA | NA |
| - Low | 29 | 22 1/8 | 23 3/8 | 16 1/2 | 8 1/8 | 2 3/16 | 1 3/4 | 1 1/2 | NA | NA |
| P/E Ratio - High | 27 | 25 | 26 | 37 | 42 | 26 | 14 | 8 | NA | NA |
| - Low | 13 | 12 | 18 | 21 | 18 | 6 | 5 | 6 | NA | NA |
| **Income Statement Analysis (Million $)** | | | | | | | | | | |
| Revs. | 2,817 | 2,066 | 1,457 | 836 | 407 | 265 | 205 | 130 | 93.0 | 60.0 |
| Oper. Inc. | 260 | 185 | 134 | 79.5 | 39.9 | 27.2 | 20.1 | 11.7 | 8.2 | 5.4 |
| Depr. | 84.8 | 61.4 | 45.7 | 26.4 | 12.7 | 9.3 | 6.3 | 3.2 | 2.8 | 2.3 |
| Int. Exp. | 15.7 | 9.5 | 10.7 | 10.6 | 5.4 | 2.2 | 1.2 | 1.0 | 0.8 | 0.4 |
| Pretax Inc. | 173 | 120 | 84.2 | 48.6 | 24.1 | 16.4 | 13.3 | 7.6 | 5.0 | 3.0 |
| Eff. Tax Rate | 34% | 34% | 34% | 37% | 40% | 44% | 44% | 44% | 40% | 50% |
| Net Inc. | 114 | 79.5 | 55.5 | 30.6 | 14.5 | 9.2 | 7.4 | 4.3 | 3.0 | 1.5 |
| **Balance Sheet & Other Fin. Data (Million $)** | | | | | | | | | | |
| Cash | 229 | 149 | 162 | 170 | 154 | 8.0 | 15.0 | 4.0 | 2.0 | NA |
| Curr. Assets | 1,145 | 726 | 602 | 469 | 271 | 107 | 68.0 | 45.0 | 38.0 | NA |
| Total Assets | 1,452 | 941 | 766 | 603 | 309 | 135 | 89.0 | 61.0 | 48.0 | 32.0 |
| Curr. Liab. | 358 | 371 | 293 | 204 | 72.1 | 71.7 | 39.5 | 30.1 | 24.3 | NA |
| LT Debt | 387 | 30.0 | 141 | 137 | 131 | 12.0 | 13.0 | 9.0 | 5.0 | 3.0 |
| Common Eqty. | 701 | 538 | 331 | 261 | 104 | 47.0 | 36.0 | 19.0 | 17.0 | 14.0 |
| Total Cap. | 1,087 | 568 | 471 | 398 | 235 | 60.0 | 49.0 | 29.0 | 22.0 | 16.0 |
| Cap. Exp. | 115 | 114 | 59.0 | 68.3 | 16.7 | 10.0 | 4.9 | 1.9 | 1.1 | 0.5 |
| Cash Flow | 199 | 141 | 101 | 57.0 | 27.2 | 18.6 | 13.7 | 7.5 | 5.8 | 3.8 |
| Curr. Ratio | 3.2 | 2.0 | 2.1 | 2.3 | 3.8 | 1.5 | 1.7 | 1.5 | 1.6 | NA |
| % LT Debt of Cap. | 35.6 | 5.3 | 29.8 | 34.4 | 55.7 | 20.9 | 26.1 | 32.7 | 22.6 | 15.9 |
| % Net Inc.of Revs. | 4.1 | 3.9 | 3.8 | 3.7 | 3.6 | 3.5 | 3.6 | 3.3 | 3.2 | 2.5 |
| % Ret. on Assets | 9.5 | 9.4 | 8.1 | 6.2 | 6.0 | 8.2 | 9.9 | 7.9 | 7.5 | 5.6 |
| % Ret. on Equity | 18.4 | 18.4 | 18.6 | 15.7 | 17.5 | 22.2 | 26.9 | 23.5 | 19.4 | 11.5 |

Data as orig. reptd.; bef. results of disc. opers. and/or spec. items. Per share data adj. for stk. divs. as of ex-div. date. E-Estimated. NA-Not Available. NM-Not Meaningful. NR-Not Ranked.

**Office**—777 Gibraltar Dr., Milpitas, CA 95035. **Tel**—(408) 957-8500. **Website**—http://www.oakridge.com/Solectron **Chrmn, Pres & CEO**—K. Nishimura. **SVP, CFO, Secy & Investor Contact**—Susan S. Wang. **Dirs**—W. H. Chen, R. A. D'Amore, C. A. Dickinson, H. Fridrich, K. E. Haughton, P. R. Low, K. Nishimura, W. F. Sanders, O. Yamada. **Transfer Agent & Registrar**—Boston EquiServe LP Shareholder Svcs., Canton, MA. **Incorporated**—in California in 1977. **Empl**— 12,999. **S&P Analyst:** Ted Groesbeck

# Staples, Inc.

**5316K**

Nasdaq Symbol **SPLS**

In S&P MidCap 400

**19-MAY-97**

**Industry:** Retail (Specialty)

**Summary:** This leading operator of office products superstores recently agreed to merge with Office Depot, Inc.

| | | |
|---|---|---|
| **S&P Opinion: Buy (★★★★)** | Recent Price • 22¼ | Yield • Nil |
| | 52 Wk Range • 26⅜-14⅜ | 12-Mo. P/E • 34.8 |

**Quantitative Evaluations**

Outlook (1 Lowest—5 Highest)
• **3⁻**

Fair Value
• **20%**

Risk
• **Average**

Earn./Div. Rank
• **B**

Technical Eval.
• **Bullish** since 1/97

Rel. Strength Rank (1 Lowest—99 Highest)
• **83**

Insider Activity
• **NA**

**Earnings vs. Previous Year**
▲=Up ▼=Down ▶=No Change

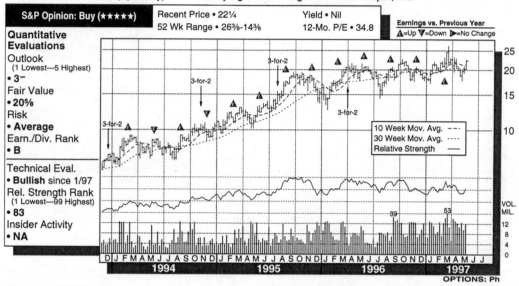

10 Week Mov. Avg. – – –
30 Week Mov. Avg. · · · ·
Relative Strength —

OPTIONS: Ph

## Overview - 19-MAY-97

Revenues in FY 98 (Jan.) for SPLS as presently constituted are expected to rise over 25% from those of FY 97, reflecting the opening of new stores, the full-year benefit of 114 net new stores added in FY 97, comparable-store sales growth of around 10%, and further strong gains in the delivery and contract stationer segments. If the planned merger with Office Depot is approved, SPLS expects to open about 120 new stores in FY 98, close about 40 stores, and sell 63 stores to OfficeMax. Profitability should improve, reflecting the leveraging of store payroll and fixed store operating expenses over a larger sales base and smaller increases in pre-opening expenses, which should outweigh a less favorable revenue mix. Long-term prospects are enhanced by the strong growth seen for the small business and home office markets. The acquisition of Office Depot is expected to be accretive to earnings. Our EPS estimate for FY 98 includes $0.07 in one-time costs related to the proposed merger.

## Valuation - 19-MAY-97

Although the FTC has twice voted against the Staples/Office Depot merger, we are maintaining our buy opinion on SPLS as we like the pre-merger Staples based on its strong fundamentals while the proposed merger will diversify the company's geographic reach and better position it for the long term. The combined company is expected to benefit from new store openings and the fast-growing small business and home office markets, which should result in strong top-line growth over the next few years. We also expect EPS gains to exceed sales increases, as the merger is likely to result in significant purchasing and marketing efficiencies. Although the stock is trading at a rich multiple based on our FY 98 estimate for the pre-merger Staples, the premium valuation is justified as we believe EPS can grow about 30% annually for several years.

## Key Stock Statistics

| | | | |
|---|---|---|---|
| S&P EPS Est. 1998 | 0.80 | Tang. Bk. Value/Share | 4.19 |
| P/E on S&P Est. 1998 | 27.8 | Beta | 1.54 |
| Dividend Rate/Share | Nil | Shareholders | 9,100 |
| Shs. outstg. (M) | 162.3 | Market cap. (B) | $ 3.6 |
| Avg. daily vol. (M) | 2.405 | Inst. holdings | 89% |

Value of $10,000 invested 5 years ago: $ 39,872

## Fiscal Year Ending Jan. 31

| | 1998 | 1997 | 1996 | 1995 | 1994 | 1993 |
|---|---|---|---|---|---|---|
| **Revenues (Million $)** | | | | | | |
| 1Q | 1,155 | 916.8 | 668.8 | 398.0 | 251.0 | 187.4 |
| 2Q | — | 808.1 | 605.0 | 385.8 | 241.3 | 192.9 |
| 3Q | — | 1,079 | 818.8 | 552.1 | 301.1 | 240.4 |
| 4Q | — | 1,164 | 975.5 | 664.7 | 328.4 | 262.5 |
| Yr. | — | 3,968 | 3,068 | 2,000 | 1,122 | 883.1 |

| | | | | | | |
|---|---|---|---|---|---|---|
| **Earnings Per Share ($)** | | | | | | |
| 1Q | 0.05 | 0.08 | 0.05 | 0.02 | 0.02 | 0.01 |
| 2Q | E0.13 | 0.09 | 0.06 | 0.02 | -0.04 | -0.01 |
| 3Q | E0.26 | 0.19 | 0.13 | 0.08 | 0.11 | 0.05 |
| 4Q | E0.36 | 0.28 | 0.21 | 0.14 | 0.11 | 0.08 |
| Yr. | E0.80 | 0.64 | 0.46 | 0.28 | 0.21 | 0.15 |

**Next earnings report expected: mid August**

## Dividend Data

No cash dividends have been paid, and Staples does not expect to pay any in the foreseeable future. A shareholder rights plan was adopted in February 1994. 3-for-2 stock splits were effected in December 1993, October 1994 and July 1995.

This report is for information purposes and should not be considered a solicitation to buy or sell any security. Neither S&P nor any other party guarantee its accuracy or make warranties regarding results from its usage. Redistribution is prohibited without written permission. Copyright © 1997 | A Division of The *McGraw-Hill* Companies

## Business Summary - 19-MAY-97

Staples, Inc., is a leading office supplies distributor with a total of 599 high-volume office superstores in over 100 markets across the U.S. and Canada as of May 15, 1997. In September 1996, SPLS agreed to merge with Office Depot, Inc. (NYSE: ODP). Sales by major product category in recent fiscal years (Jan.) were:

|  | FY 97 | FY 96 |
|---|---|---|
| Office supplies, services & other supplies | 46.4% | 52.4% |
| Equipment & business machines | 22.7% | 19.6% |
| Computers & related products | 21.6% | 19.8% |
| Office furniture | 9.3% | 8.2% |

Stores operate under the names Staples--The Office Superstore, Staples Express, Business Depot and Bureau en Gros. The prototype superstore has approximately 23,000 sq. ft. of sales area, carries over 8,000 stock items and generally is located in a suburban area. Express stores average 9,000 sq. ft., stock about 5,600 items and are located in downtown business areas. Items are priced at discounts ranging from 30% to 70% below manufacturer suggested list prices. SPLS opened 115 stores and closed one store in FY 97. It also has a mail order delivery operation and a contract stationer business, and it is a joint venture partner in retail and mail order operations in the U.K. and Germany.

Staples targets what it considers the four major end-user groups in the office product market: consumers and home offices; small businesses (fewer than 50 office workers); medium-size businesses (more than 50); and large businesses (more than 1,000).

### Important Developments

**Apr. '97**—The FTC voted a second time to block the proposed merger between Staples and Office Depot (NYSE: ODP), claiming that the combination would substantially reduce competition in markets served by both companies. SPLS and ODP agreed to vigorously contest the ruling, and are scheduled to appear in Federal Court in late May for a Preliminary Injunction hearing, and anticipate a decision in mid to late June. Earlier, in March 1997, the two companies agreed in principle to sell 63 stores to OfficeMax (NYSE: OMX) for $108.75 million in an attempt to convince the FTC to allow the merger. Previously, in September 1996, Staples and ODP signed a definitive agreement to merge, with stockholders of ODP to receive 1.14 shares of SPLS for each ODP share. ODP operates 572 superstores and had 1996 revenues of $6.1 billion.

### Capitalization

**Long Term Debt:** $391,342,000 (2/1/97); incl. $300 mil. of 4.5% debs. due 2000, conv. into com. at $22 a sh.

**Options:** To buy 20,397,713 shs. (2/1/97).

### Per Share Data ($)

| (Year Ended Jan. 31) | 1997 | 1996 | 1995 | 1994 | 1993 | 1992 | 1991 | 1990 | 1989 | 1988 |
|---|---|---|---|---|---|---|---|---|---|---|
| Tangible Bk. Val. | 4.19 | 3.35 | 1.93 | 2.09 | 1.82 | 1.23 | 0.70 | 0.81 | 0.81 | NA |
| Cash Flow | 0.97 | 0.72 | 0.49 | 0.38 | 0.29 | 0.21 | 0.10 | 0.08 | Nil | NA |
| Earnings | 0.64 | 0.46 | 0.28 | 0.21 | 0.15 | 0.09 | 0.05 | 0.06 | -0.03 | -0.16 |
| Dividends | Nil | Nil | Nil | Nil | Nil | Nil | Nil | Nil | Nil | Nil |
| Payout Ratio | Nil | Nil | Nil | Nil | Nil | Nil | Nil | Nil | Nil | Nil |
| Cal. Yrs. | 1996 | 1995 | 1994 | 1993 | 1992 | 1991 | 1990 | 1989 | 1988 | 1987 |
| Prices - High | 22⅝ | 19⅜ | 11 | 8¼ | 8⅛ | 6⅛ | 3½ | 3⅜ | NA | NA |
|    - Low | 12⅝ | 9½ | 6½ | 4⅝ | 5 | 1⅞ | 1¾ | 1¹⁵/₁₆ | NA | NA |
| P/E Ratio - High | 35 | 41 | 39 | 39 | 55 | 64 | 72 | 58 | NA | NA |
|    - Low | 20 | 20 | 23 | 22 | 33 | 20 | 36 | 32 | NA | NA |

### Income Statement Analysis (Million $)

| | 1997 | 1996 | 1995 | 1994 | 1993 | 1992 | 1991 | 1990 | 1989 | 1988 |
|---|---|---|---|---|---|---|---|---|---|---|
| Revs. | 3,968 | 3,068 | 2,000 | 1,122 | 883 | 547 | 299 | 182 | 120 | 40.0 |
| Oper. Inc. | 260 | 191 | 110 | 67.7 | 48.8 | 27.5 | 12.0 | 5.3 | -0.1 | -7.9 |
| Depr. | 56.0 | 43.6 | 28.7 | 19.9 | 15.5 | 9.1 | 4.0 | 1.3 | 1.9 | 0.6 |
| Int. Exp. | 20.1 | 19.9 | 8.4 | 7.1 | 5.1 | 6.3 | 3.9 | 0.6 | 0.8 | 0.2 |
| Pretax Inc. | 173 | 120 | 63.9 | 40.4 | 27.7 | 12.9 | 5.6 | 6.3 | -1.8 | -7.7 |
| Eff. Tax Rate | 39% | 39% | 38% | 37% | 42% | 39% | 35% | 32% | NM | NM |
| Net Inc. | 106 | 73.7 | 39.9 | 25.4 | 16.1 | 7.9 | 3.7 | 4.3 | -1.9 | -7.7 |

### Balance Sheet & Other Fin. Data (Million $)

| | 1997 | 1996 | 1995 | 1994 | 1993 | 1992 | 1991 | 1990 | 1989 | 1988 |
|---|---|---|---|---|---|---|---|---|---|---|
| Cash | 106 | 111 | 71.0 | 112 | 111 | 52.4 | 58.9 | 16.2 | 1.5 | 8.6 |
| Curr. Assets | 1,151 | 926 | 640 | 374 | 346 | 177 | 138 | 52.0 | 64.0 | 26.0 |
| Total Assets | 1,788 | 1,403 | 1,008 | 581 | 494 | 286 | 204 | 84.0 | 82.0 | 41.0 |
| Curr. Liab. | 603 | 422 | 350 | 159 | 116 | 54.4 | 53.1 | 16.5 | 19.1 | 14.2 |
| LT Debt | 391 | 344 | 249 | 122 | 120 | 80.9 | 79.2 | 4.0 | 4.0 | 5.5 |
| Common Eqty. | 762 | 611 | 385 | 282 | 247 | 145 | 69.0 | 63.0 | 58.0 | 21.0 |
| Total Cap. | 1,153 | 955 | 634 | 405 | 367 | 226 | 148 | 67.0 | 62.0 | 27.0 |
| Cap. Exp. | 200 | 116 | 64.7 | 52.1 | 27.5 | 29.5 | 21.9 | 12.0 | 4.9 | 11.7 |
| Cash Flow | 162 | 117 | 68.6 | 45.2 | 31.6 | 17.0 | 7.7 | 5.6 | Nil | NA |
| Curr. Ratio | 1.9 | 2.2 | 1.8 | 2.4 | 3.0 | 3.2 | 2.6 | 3.2 | 3.3 | 1.8 |
| % LT Debt of Cap. | 33.9 | 36.0 | 39.3 | 30.2 | 32.6 | 35.9 | 53.5 | 5.9 | 6.4 | 20.8 |
| % Net Inc.of Revs. | 2.7 | 2.4 | 2.0 | 2.3 | 1.8 | 1.5 | 1.2 | 2.3 | NM | NM |
| % Ret. on Assets | 6.7 | 6.1 | 4.7 | 4.7 | 3.7 | 3.0 | 2.5 | 5.1 | NM | NM |
| % Ret. on Equity | 15.5 | 14.8 | 11.1 | 9.5 | 7.4 | 6.9 | 5.5 | 7.0 | NM | NM |

Data as orig. reptd.; bef. results of disc. opers. and/or spec. items. Per share data adj. for stk. divs. as of ex-div. date. E-Estimated. NA-Not Available. NM-Not Meaningful. NR-Not Ranked.

**Office**—One Research Dr., Westborough, MA 01581. **Tel**—(508) 370-8500. **Website**—http://www.staples.com **Chrmn & CEO**—T. G. Stemberg. **Pres & COO**—M. Hanaka. **EVP & CFO**—J. J. Mahoney. **SVP & Treas**—R. K. Mayerson. **VP & Secy**—P. M. Schwarzenbach. **Investor Contact**—S. J. Levenson. **Dirs**—M. E. Burton, M. E. Hanaka, W. L. Heisey, L. Kahn, J. L. Moody Jr., R. T. Moriarty, R. C. Nakasone, W. M. Romney, T. G. Stemberg, M. Trust, P. F. Walsh. **Transfer Agent**—First National Bank of Boston. **Incorporated**—in Delaware in 1985. **Empl**— 24,994. **S&P Analyst:** Michael V. Pizzi

**17-MAY-97**  **Industry:** Computers (Hardware)

**Summary:** Sun makes high-performance workstations for engineering, scientific and technical markets, and also sells servers and operating system software.

| S&P Opinion: Accumulate (★★★★) | Recent Price • 32⅛ | Yield • Nil |
| --- | --- | --- |
| | 52 Wk Range • 35⅛-22 | 12-Mo. P/E • 19.4 |

**Quantitative Evaluations**

Outlook
(1 Lowest—5 Highest)
• **4+**

Fair Value
• **37¾**

Risk
• **Average**

Earn./Div. Rank
• **B**

Technical Eval.
• **Bullish** since 4/97

Rel. Strength Rank
(1 Lowest—99 Highest)
• **81**

Insider Activity
• **Neutral**

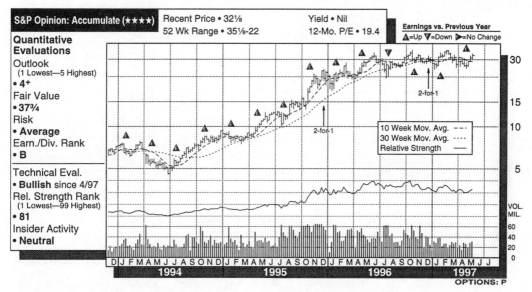

Earnings vs. Previous Year ▲=Up ▼=Down ▶=No Change

10 Week Mov. Avg. ---
30 Week Mov. Avg. ····
Relative Strength ——

OPTIONS: P

## Overview - 28-APR-97

Revenues are forecast to grow 20% in FY 97 (Jun.), benefiting from a new and more powerful product line-up, growing contributions from Internet-related products, and Sun's continued success in penetrating new commercial markets with client-server solutions. Sun has been benefiting from demand for its new workstation and high-end server products based on its UltraSPARC processor technology, and production of its new Starfire high-end server is expected to ramp up sharply in the fourth quarter. Gross margins have been in a strong uptrend, aided by strong sales of more richly configured servers, but are likely to remain flat as SUNW takes aggressive pricing actions in certain key markets. Expense growth should remain brisk, reflecting continued efforts to build up the commercial enterprise infrastructure, enhanced R&D initiatives, and investments to increase Sun's visibility. EPS comparisons should remain favorable, helped by additional share buybacks. Sun's goal is to achieve compound earnings growth of 15% over any three-year period.

## Valuation - 28-APR-97

The shares remain attractive. Sun is well positioned to capitalize on strong growth opportunities in commercial client-server and Internet/intranet markets. It has aggressively launched new products that target these markets, as exhibited by the recent introduction of the Ultra Enterprise servers and JAVA line of microprocessors. These efforts should prove to be additive to both revenues and gross margins, and should fuel EPS growth of 15% to 20% over the next several years. In light of this favorable situation, and based on their current valuation, the shares, which were split two for one in December 1996, should be accumulated for their above-average appreciation potential.

## Key Stock Statistics

| | | | |
| --- | --- | --- | --- |
| S&P EPS Est. 1997 | 1.82 | Tang. Bk. Value/Share | 6.06 |
| P/E on S&P Est. 1997 | 17.7 | Beta | 0.81 |
| S&P EPS Est. 1998 | 2.15 | Shareholders | 3,800 |
| Dividend Rate/Share | Nil | Market cap. (B) | $ 11.8 |
| Shs. outstg. (M) | 368.1 | Inst. holdings | 55% |
| Avg. daily vol. (M) | 5.128 | | |

Value of $10,000 invested 5 years ago: $ 45,286

### Fiscal Year Ending Jun. 30

| | 1998 | 1997 | 1996 | 1995 | 1994 | 1993 |
| --- | --- | --- | --- | --- | --- | --- |
| **Revenues (Million $)** | | | | | | |
| 1Q | — | 1,859 | 1,485 | 1,273 | 960.5 | 856.0 |
| 2Q | — | 2,082 | 1,751 | 1,475 | 1,131 | 1,051 |
| 3Q | — | 2,115 | 1,840 | 1,505 | 1,196 | 1,141 |
| 4Q | — | — | 2,018 | 1,648 | 1,403 | 1,261 |
| Yr. | — | — | 7,095 | 5,902 | 4,690 | 4,309 |
| **Earnings Per Share ($)** | | | | | | |
| 1Q | — | 0.32 | 0.21 | 0.10 | 0.04 | 0.01 |
| 2Q | — | 0.46 | 0.32 | 0.21 | 0.11 | 0.06 |
| 3Q | — | 0.58 | 0.36 | 0.27 | 0.15 | 0.12 |
| 4Q | — | E0.55 | 0.31 | 0.32 | 0.21 | 0.18 |
| Yr. | E2.15 | E1.82 | 1.21 | 0.90 | 0.51 | 0.37 |

Next earnings report expected: mid July

### Dividend Data

| Amount ($) | Date Decl. | Ex-Div. Date | Stock of Record | Payment Date |
| --- | --- | --- | --- | --- |
| 2-for-1 | Aug. 08 | Dec. 11 | Nov. 18 | Dec. 10 '96 |

This report is for information purposes and should not be considered a solicitation to buy or sell any security. Neither S&P nor any other party guarantee its accuracy or make warranties regarding results from its usage. Redistribution is prohibited without written permission. Copyright © 1997

A Division of The **McGraw·Hill** Companies

## Business Summary - 28-APR-97

Sun Microsystems is a leading supplier of networked computing products including workstations, servers, software, microprocessors and a full range of services and support. Computer systems are used mainly for commercial and technical applications. Net revenues by geographic area in recent fiscal years (Jun.):

|  | FY 96 | FY 95 | FY 94 |
|---|---|---|---|
| U.S. | 49% | 49% | 49% |
| Europe | 27% | 26% | 26% |
| Rest of World | 24% | 25% | 25% |

The UNIX operating system is the foundation for Sun's open systems approach, which utilizes and licenses its own SPARC (Scalable Processor ARChitecture) microprocessor. In late 1995 and early 1996, Sun unveiled a line of workstations and servers based on its new UltraSPARC processor technology.

Sun's workstations range from low cost X-terminals to high performance color graphics systems. Current desktops include the low-end SPARCstation 4 and SPARCstation 5, the high-performance SPARCstation 20 series and the new family of Ultra workstations. The company's servers can be used for file sharing, enabling users to access data distributed across multiple storage devices and networks, or as compute resources, to distribute compute-intensive applications across multiple processors. Servers include the low end SPARCstation 5 for small workgroups and a line of Ultra Enterprise Servers for mid-range and high-end. The company's Netra servers provide preconfigured solutions for Internet and Intranet publishing.

Software offerings include Solaris, an open client-server UNIX system software environment offered on SPARC and Intel platforms and Solstice, a software suite that manages large heterogenous networks.

In FY 96, Sun formed JavaSoft to develop, market and support Java, an object-oriented programming language. The Java programming language has attracted tremendous interest in the software development industry because of its portability; software created in Java can run on any type of system, including PCs, workstations and World Wide Web browsers. It is especially attractive as a tool for designing software for distribution over the Internet, because any one can access and use it.

R&D expenses amounted to 10% of revenues in FY 96, versus 9.5% in FY 95.

In July 1996, Sun acquired Lighthouse Design, Ltd., a leading provider of object-based developer and productivity tools. It also purchased the SPARC/Solaris related assets of Cray Research from Silicon Graphics, including Cray's high-end server business, for an undisclosed amount. In April 1996, the company purchased Integrated Micro Products (IMP), a U.K.-based supplier of fault tolerant computing products for the telecommunications industry, for $96.1 million.

### Capitalization

**Long Term Liabilities:** $107,266,000 (03/97).

| Per Share Data ($) (Year Ended Jun. 30) | 1996 | 1995 | 1994 | 1993 | 1992 | 1991 | 1990 | 1989 | 1988 | 1987 |
|---|---|---|---|---|---|---|---|---|---|---|
| Tangible Bk. Val. | 6.06 | 5.39 | 4.34 | 4.02 | 3.71 | 3.15 | 2.50 | 1.97 | 1.28 | 0.90 |
| Cash Flow | 1.93 | 1.52 | 1.15 | 0.93 | 0.96 | 1.00 | 0.78 | 0.48 | 0.38 | 0.23 |
| Earnings | 1.21 | 0.90 | 0.51 | 0.37 | 0.43 | 0.46 | 0.30 | 0.19 | 0.22 | 0.14 |
| Dividends | Nil | Nil | Nil | Nil | Nil | Nil | Nil | Nil | Nil | Nil |
| Payout Ratio | Nil | Nil | Nil | Nil | Nil | Nil | Nil | Nil | Nil | Nil |
| Prices - High | 35⅛ | 20 | 9⅜ | 10¼ | 9 | 9⅝ | 9⅜ | 5¾ | 5⅛ | 5¾ |
|     - Low | 18 | 7½ | 4⅝ | 5¼ | 5⅝ | 5¼ | 3¾ | 3⅜ | 3¼ | 2¾ |
| P/E Ratio - High | 29 | 22 | 19 | 28 | 21 | 21 | 31 | 30 | 23 | 41 |
|     - Low | 15 | 8 | 9 | 14 | 13 | 11 | 12 | 18 | 15 | 20 |

### Income Statement Analysis (Million $)

| | 1996 | 1995 | 1994 | 1993 | 1992 | 1991 | 1990 | 1989 | 1988 | 1987 |
|---|---|---|---|---|---|---|---|---|---|---|
| Revs. | 7,095 | 5,902 | 4,690 | 4,309 | 3,589 | 3,221 | 2,466 | 1,765 | 1,052 | 538 |
| Oper. Inc. | 1,017 | 741 | 526 | 473 | 477 | 516 | 361 | 191 | 162 | 93.0 |
| Depr. | 284 | 241 | 248 | 232 | 215 | 221 | 184 | 103 | 51.0 | 25.0 |
| Int. Exp. | 9.1 | 17.8 | 21.8 | 34.9 | 45.2 | 49.4 | 37.4 | 14.3 | 12.4 | 6.1 |
| Pretax Inc. | 709 | 523 | 283 | 224 | 255 | 284 | 154 | 78.0 | 111 | 69.0 |
| Eff. Tax Rate | 33% | 32% | 31% | 30% | 32% | 33% | 28% | 22% | 40% | 48% |
| Net Inc. | 476 | 356 | 196 | 157 | 173 | 190 | 111 | 61.0 | 66.0 | 36.0 |

### Balance Sheet & Other Fin. Data (Million $)

| | 1996 | 1995 | 1994 | 1993 | 1992 | 1991 | 1990 | 1989 | 1988 | 1987 |
|---|---|---|---|---|---|---|---|---|---|---|
| Cash | 990 | 1,228 | 883 | 1,139 | 1,220 | 834 | 394 | 54.0 | 128 | 216 |
| Curr. Assets | 3,034 | 2,934 | 2,305 | 2,272 | 2,148 | 1,801 | 1,297 | 880 | 532 | 397 |
| Total Assets | 3,801 | 3,545 | 2,898 | 2,768 | 2,672 | 2,326 | 1,779 | 1,269 | 757 | 524 |
| Curr. Liab. | 1,489 | 1,331 | 1,148 | 947 | 839 | 713 | 493 | 463 | 260 | 155 |
| LT Debt | 60.2 | 91.0 | 116 | 154 | 313 | 351 | 359 | 143 | 125 | 127 |
| Common Eqty. | 2,251 | 2,123 | 1,628 | 1,643 | 1,485 | 1,213 | 927 | 662 | 370 | 241 |
| Total Cap. | 2,312 | 2,214 | 1,745 | 1,797 | 1,798 | 1,564 | 1,286 | 805 | 495 | 368 |
| Cap. Exp. | 296 | 242 | 213 | 196 | 186 | 192 | 213 | 205 | 117 | 76.0 |
| Cash Flow | 760 | 596 | 444 | 389 | 389 | 411 | 295 | 164 | 117 | 61.0 |
| Curr. Ratio | 2.0 | 2.2 | 2.0 | 2.4 | 2.6 | 2.5 | 2.6 | 1.9 | 2.1 | 2.6 |
| % LT Debt of Cap. | 2.6 | 4.1 | 6.7 | 8.6 | 17.4 | 22.5 | 27.9 | 17.7 | 25.2 | 34.6 |
| % Net Inc.of Revs. | 6.7 | 6.0 | 4.2 | 3.6 | 4.8 | 5.9 | 4.5 | 3.4 | 6.3 | 6.8 |
| % Ret. on Assets | 13.0 | 11.0 | 7.2 | 5.7 | 6.8 | 9.1 | 7.3 | 5.7 | 10.1 | 9.7 |
| % Ret. on Equity | 21.8 | 18.9 | 12.5 | 9.9 | 12.6 | 17.5 | 13.4 | 11.2 | 21.1 | 19.3 |

Data as orig. reptd.; bef. results of disc. opers. and/or spec. items. Per share data adj. for stk. divs. as of ex-div. date. E-Estimated. NA-Not Available. NM-Not Meaningful. NR-Not Ranked.

**Office**—2550 Garcia Ave., Mountain View, CA 94043-1100. **Tel**—(415) 960-1300. **Chrmn & CEO**—S. G. McNealy. **VP & CFO**—M. Lehman. **VP & Secy**—M. H. Morris. **Investor Contact**—M. Paisley. **Dirs**—L. J. Doerr, J. Estrin, R. J. Fisher, W. R. Hearst III, R. L. Long, S. G. McNealy, M. K. Oshman, A. M. Spence. **Transfer Agent & Registrar**—Bank of Boston. **Incorporated**—in California in 1982. **Empl**— 20,739. **S&P Analyst:** Megan Graham Hackett

# STANDARD &POOR'S
STOCK REPORTS

# SunAmerica Inc.

**2161T**

NYSE Symbol **SAI**

In S&P MidCap 400

**17-MAY-97**  Industry: Financial (Diversified)

**Summary:** SAI specializes in selling tax-deferred, long-term savings products for the pre-retirement market.

| S&P Opinion: Accumulate (★★★★) | Recent Price • 44¾ | Yield • 0.9% |
|---|---|---|
| | 52 Wk Range • 51-26⅛ | 12-Mo. P/E • 20.3 |

**Quantitative Evaluations**

Outlook (1 Lowest—5 Highest)
• **3⁻**

Fair Value
• **46¼**

Risk
• **Average**

Earn./Div. Rank
• **A**

Technical Eval.
• **Bullish** since 2/95

Rel. Strength Rank (1 Lowest—99 Highest)
• **62**

Insider Activity
• **Favorable**

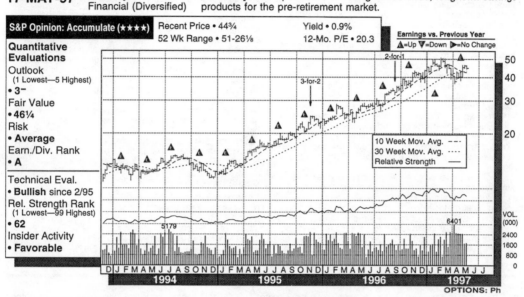

Earnings vs. Previous Year  ▲=Up ▼=Down ▶=No Change

- 10 Week Mov. Avg. ---
- 30 Week Mov. Avg. ····
- Relative Strength —

OPTIONS: Ph

## Overview - 13-MAY-97

Earnings have benefited from the company's continued focus on retirement savings products, geared toward an aging population. EPS in the second quarter of FY 97 (Sep.) rose 29% year to year, to $0.62, from $0.48. Return on equity was at 21% (an all-time high), and operating earnings were up 34% to $0.67 per share, ahead of analyst expectations, and well above the $0.50 of a year earlier. The earnings growth for the quarter was driven by 19% higher variable annuity sales (up 44% for the first half), boosted by acquisitions, a favorable interest rate environment, and increased demand for the flexibility offered by company products. SAI's share of the variable annuity market has doubled in the last two years. SAI has also benefited from greater marketing efforts, and an expanding captive distribution network, which now stands at 7,100. Its ability to sell both variable and fixed annuities, in addition to a diverse mix of innovative retirement savings products, offers potential for growth, even in the face of unfavorable market conditions.

## Valuation - 13-MAY-97

Although the shares more than doubled since the beginning of 1996, they have exhibited some volatility lately, despite SAI's staying ahead of recent earnings estimates. However, with its wide range of retirement savings products, strong distribution network, and an aggressive marketing campaign, SunAmerica continues to be in an enviable position to service the retirement planning needs of baby boomers. Earnings should continue to grow in 1997 and 1998. Given the company's potential for significant long-term growth, especially after the acquisition of John Alden's annuity business, and its expanding sales force, the shares remain attractive at around 17X our FY 97 operating EPS estimate (revised upward to $2.59 from $2.39, to reflect recent acquisitions).

## Key Stock Statistics

| | | | |
|---|---|---|---|
| S&P EPS Est. 1997 | 2.59 | Tang. Bk. Value/Share | 10.66 |
| P/E on S&P Est. 1997 | 17.3 | Beta | 1.74 |
| S&P EPS Est. 1998 | 2.95 | Shareholders | 2,200 |
| Dividend Rate/Share | 0.40 | Market cap. (B) | $ 5.4 |
| Shs. outstg. (M) | 119.9 | Inst. holdings | 69% |
| Avg. daily vol. (M) | 0.435 | | |

Value of $10,000 invested 5 years ago: $ 71,311

### Fiscal Year Ending Sep. 30

| | 1998 | 1997 | 1996 | 1995 | 1994 | 1993 |
|---|---|---|---|---|---|---|
| **Revenues (Million $)** | | | | | | |
| 1Q | — | 431.3 | 303.8 | 155.0 | 228.6 | 210.8 |
| 2Q | — | 459.2 | 342.9 | 259.3 | 222.3 | 214.9 |
| 3Q | — | — | 404.7 | 279.7 | 225.8 | 225.5 |
| 4Q | — | — | 422.9 | 254.9 | 232.2 | 233.1 |
| Yr. | — | — | 1,475 | 1,064 | 905.8 | 884.2 |
| **Earnings Per Share ($)** | | | | | | |
| 1Q | — | 0.58 | 0.47 | 0.33 | 0.28 | 0.21 |
| 2Q | — | 0.62 | 0.48 | 0.34 | 0.29 | 0.22 |
| 3Q | — | E0.67 | 0.49 | 0.35 | 0.30 | 0.23 |
| 4Q | — | E0.67 | 0.51 | 0.40 | 0.32 | 0.25 |
| Yr. | E2.95 | E2.59 | 1.95 | 1.42 | 1.20 | 0.92 |

Next earnings report expected: late July

### Dividend Data (Dividends have been paid since 1962.)

| Amount ($) | Date Decl. | Ex-Div. Date | Stock of Record | Payment Date |
|---|---|---|---|---|
| 2-for-1 | Aug. 02 | Sep. 03 | Aug. 21 | Aug. 30 '96 |
| 0.100 | Nov. 08 | Nov. 14 | Nov. 18 | Nov. 25 '96 |
| 0.100 | Feb. 14 | Feb. 20 | Feb. 24 | Mar. 03 '97 |
| 0.100 | May. 02 | May. 08 | May. 12 | May. 16 '97 |

This report is for information purposes and should not be considered a solicitation to buy or sell any security. Neither S&P nor any other party guarantee its accuracy or make warranties regarding results from its usage. Redistribution is prohibited without written permission. Copyright © 1997

A Division of The McGraw-Hill Companies

## Business Summary - 13-MAY-97

With the fifth largest securities sales force in the U.S. (Merrill Lynch, Smith Barney, Dean Witter, and PaineWebber are in the top four spots), SunAmerica is in a strong position to sell tax-deferred, long-term savings products and investments to the expanding pre-retirement market. Its registered representatives are dedicated solely to selling its life insurance products (and related investments), while competitors' sales forces are not so exclusive, and since over half of all annuity sales are made by banks and brokers, any distribution advantage is a plus. SAI also sells its products through a broad spectrum of other financial service distribution channels, including registered representatives of unaffiliated broker-dealers, independent general insurance agents and financial institutions. In addition, SAI's SunAmerica Asset Management had over $2 billion of assets under management at the end of FY 96 (Sep.).

Much of SunAmerica's recent success is due to its innovative and diverse product line of variable annuities, which are increasingly popular with aging baby boomers looking for a tax-deferred means of building up their assets. Products can be structured in a variety of ways, and allow the investor to capture more stock market-oriented (or bond, money market, or guaranteed fixed rate) returns than other retirement products availa-

ble. The company's flagship product, Polaris, has had phenomenal growth, rising from 25th place two years ago, to fifth place among all variable annuity products in the U.S.

SunAmerica continues to augment its internal growth, through the acquisition of annuity reserves, as well as small broker-dealers. During FY 96, SunAmerica purchased a total of $4.7 billion of annuity reserves, with the largest being $3.1 billion from Ford Life Insurance Co. In the first quarter of 1997, SAI completed its purchase of the annuity business of John Alden Financial Corp., which has about $5 billion of annuity reserves. SAI's prior investment in its operating systems has enabled efficient assimilation of the new businesses by significantly lowering the unit cost of processing.

Currently SAI's captive (working exclusively for SunAmerica) sales force is at 7,100; SAI's goal is to have 10,000 representatives by the year 2000.

## Capitalization

**Preferred Stock:** $335,869,000 (3/97).

**Nontransferable Class B Stock:** 10,848,000 shs. ($1 par); 10 votes per sh.; div. at 90% of com.; conv. sh.-for-sh. into com.; E. Broad holds 79%.

**Trust Preferred Securities:** $547,631,000 (3/97).

**Long Term Debt:** $1,004,585,000 (3/97).

### Per Share Data ($)

| (Year Ended Sep. 30) | 1996 | 1995 | 1994 | 1993 | 1992 | 1991 | 1990 | 1989 | 1988 | 1987 |
|---|---|---|---|---|---|---|---|---|---|---|
| Tangible Bk. Val. | 11.12 | 7.76 | 5.46 | 6.05 | 4.49 | 3.72 | 2.96 | 3.61 | 3.97 | 3.68 |
| Earnings | 1.95 | 1.42 | 1.19 | 0.92 | 0.60 | 0.44 | 0.34 | 0.27 | 0.25 | 0.65 |
| Dividends | 0.30 | 0.20 | 0.13 | 0.07 | 0.07 | 0.07 | 0.06 | 0.04 | 0.11 | 0.08 |
| Payout Ratio | 15% | 14% | 11% | 7% | 10% | 15% | 17% | 16% | 44% | 13% |
| Prices - High | 46¼ | 24⅞ | 15⅜ | 15½ | 9¼ | 6⅝ | 4 | 5¼ | 5⅜ | 6⅜ |
|    - Low | 22⅛ | 12 | 11⅛ | 8½ | 5⅛ | 1�۹⁄16 | 1¹⁄16 | 2⅛ | 3½ | 3 |
| P/E Ratio - High | 24 | 16 | 13 | 17 | 15 | 15 | 12 | 20 | 21 | 10 |
|    - Low | 11 | 18 | 9 | 9 | 8 | 4 | 3 | 8 | 14 | 5 |

### Income Statement Analysis (Million $)

| | 1996 | 1995 | 1994 | 1993 | 1992 | 1991 | 1990 | 1989 | 1988 | 1987 |
|---|---|---|---|---|---|---|---|---|---|---|
| Premium Inc. | 105 | 84.6 | 79.5 | 67.5 | 57.7 | 48.5 | 34.7 | 31.2 | 73.1 | 102 |
| Invest. Inc. | 1,254 | 906 | 758 | 754 | 763 | 741 | 671 | 490 | 431 | 324 |
| Oth. Revs. | 107 | 76.4 | 86.9 | 83.7 | 71.8 | 71.1 | 146 | 60.8 | 64.2 | 184 |
| Total Revs. | 1,466 | 1,067 | 903 | 884 | 837 | 815 | 818 | 551 | 496 | 508 |
| Int. Exp. | 741 | 539 | 464 | 491 | 544 | 579 | 538 | 380 | 341 | 255 |
| Exp./Op. Revs. | 74% | 74% | 73% | 79% | 87% | 92% | 93% | 92% | 104% | 92% |
| Pretax Inc. | 392 | 280 | 240 | 184 | 107 | 68.0 | 55.5 | 43.2 | -19.4 | 41.3 |
| Eff. Tax Rate | 30% | 31% | 31% | 31% | 32% | 38% | 40% | 40% | NM | 41% |
| Net Inc. | 274 | 194 | 165 | 127 | 72.2 | 42.1 | 33.4 | 26.1 | -20.4 | 24.6 |

### Balance Sheet & Other Fin. Data (Million $)

| | 1996 | 1995 | 1994 | 1993 | 1992 | 1991 | 1990 | 1989 | 1988 | 1987 |
|---|---|---|---|---|---|---|---|---|---|---|
| Receivables | Nil | Nil | 0.1 | 0.1 | 0.1 | 113 | 112 | 92.4 | 97.2 | NA |
| Cash & Invest. | 16,199 | 10,809 | 9,280 | 10,312 | 9,422 | 7,583 | 7,275 | 5,887 | 5,690 | 3,938 |
| Loans | Nil | Nil | Nil | Nil | Nil | Nil | Nil | Nil | Nil | Nil |
| Total Assets | 23,727 | 16,844 | 14,656 | 15,214 | 13,398 | 11,001 | 10,079 | 7,020 | 6,610 | 4,911 |
| Capitalization: | | | | | | | | | | |
| Debt | 573 | 525 | 501 | 508 | 434 | 455 | 532 | 459 | 742 | 541 |
| Equity | 1,276 | 891 | 587 | 631 | 463 | 385 | 319 | 365 | 156 | NA |
| Total | 2,234 | 1,738 | 1,463 | 1,618 | 1,164 | 905 | 916 | 889 | 912 | NA |
| Price Times Bk. Val.: High | 3.6 | 3.0 | 2.8 | 2.6 | 2.1 | 1.8 | 1.4 | 1.4 | 1.3 | 1.7 |
| Price Times Bk. Val.: Low | 2.0 | 1.5 | 2.0 | 1.4 | 1.1 | 0.4 | 0.4 | 0.6 | 0.9 | 0.8 |
| % Return On Revs. | 18.7 | 18.1 | 18.3 | 14.4 | 8.6 | 5.2 | 4.1 | 4.8 | NM | 4.8 |
| % Ret. on Assets | 1.4 | 1.2 | 1.1 | 0.9 | 0.6 | 0.4 | 0.4 | 0.4 | NM | 0.6 |
| % Ret. on Equity | 25.3 | 26.0 | 16.9 | 19.7 | 15.2 | 11.9 | 9.8 | 10.0 | NM | NA |
| Loans/Equity | Nil | Nil | Nil | Nil | Nil | Nil | Nil | Nil | Nil | Nil |

Data as orig. reptd.; bef. results of disc. opers. and/or spec. items. Per share data adj. for stk. divs. as of ex-div. date. E-Estimated. NA-Not Available. NM-Not Meaningful. NR-Not Ranked.

**Office**—1 SunAmerica Center, Century City, Los Angeles, CA 90067-6022. **Tel**—(310) 772-6000. **Chrmn, Pres & CEO**—E. Broad. **VP & Treas**—S. H. Richland. **VP & Secy**—S. L. Harris. **Investor Contact**—Karel Carnohan (310-772-6535).**Dirs**—W. F. Aldinger, R. J. Arnault, E. Broad, K. Hastie-Williams, D. O. Maxwell, B. Munitz, L. Pollack, C. E. Reichardt, R. D. Rohr, S. C. Sigoloff, H. M. Williams. **Transfer Agent & Registrar**—First Interstate Bank, LA. **Incorporated**—in Maryland in 1961. **Empl**— 1,600. **S&P Analyst**: E. Fitzpatrick

# Price (T. Rowe) Associates    5027T

Nasdaq Symbol **TROW**

**In S&P MidCap 400**

**17-MAY-97**

**Industry:** Investment Management

**Summary:** This company operates one of the largest no-load mutual fund complexes in the U.S.

| | |
|---|---|
| **S&P Opinion: Accumulate (★★★★)** | Recent Price • 48⅝    Yield • 1.1%<br>52 Wk Range • 54¼-22¾    12-Mo. P/E • 30.6 |

**Earnings vs. Previous Year**
▲=Up ▼=Down ▶=No Change

**Quantitative Evaluations**

**Outlook**
(1 Lowest—5 Highest)
• **2**

**Fair Value**
• **46½**

**Risk**
• **Average**

**Earn./Div. Rank**
• **A-**

**Technical Eval.**
• **Bullish** since 4/97

**Rel. Strength Rank**
(1 Lowest—99 Highest)
• **91**

**Insider Activity**
• **Neutral**

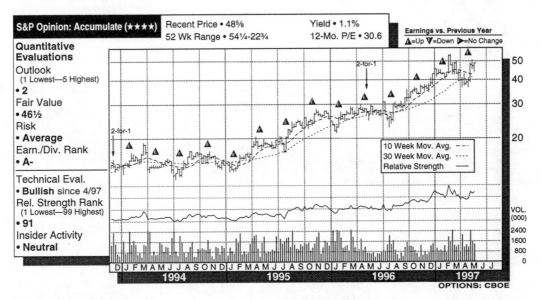

10 Week Mov. Avg. – – –
30 Week Mov. Avg. · · · ·
Relative Strength ——

OPTIONS: CBOE

## Overview - 06-MAY-97

Assets under management, the driver of earnings, are expected to benefit from an estimated $6.5 billion in net fund sales in 1997, somewhat below the $8.6 billion of inflows recorded for 1996. Stock funds, which carry relatively high fees, are experiencing strong sales, benefiting from TROW's name recognition, favorable investment performance, and increased retirement savings on the part of the baby boomer generation. Bond fund sales have been more sluggish. Under a scenario of modestly higher interest rates in 1997, debt funds are likely to experience only small net inflows. As a partial offset, some 85% of TROW's clients reinvest dividends and interest. Investment income could be helped by rising financial markets, although the outlook, as always, is uncertain. Stable profit margins are anticipated.

## Valuation - 06-MAY-97

The shares carry an accumulate recommendation. TROW is looking more like a long-term takeover candidate. Its longtime President and CEO retired recently, and numerous commercial banks would love to own the company because of its relatively stable fee income, favorable growth prospects, broad array of fund offerings, and leading presence in the 401(k) market. Because it is a premier franchise, a takeover price could be in the neighborhood of $55 a share, based on the average of several approaches. In addition, the company should experience solid earnings growth in 1997, largely due to continued gains in assets under management, primarily stock mutual funds. Finally, the company's profit margins are extremely wide compared to industrial concerns, due to the attractive economics of the asset management business.

## Key Stock Statistics

| | | | |
|---|---|---|---|
| S&P EPS Est. 1997 | 1.90 | Tang. Bk. Value/Share | 5.92 |
| P/E on S&P Est. 1997 | 25.6 | Beta | 1.66 |
| Dividend Rate/Share | 0.52 | Shareholders | 2,600 |
| Shs. outstg. (M) | 57.6 | Market cap. (B) | $ 2.8 |
| Avg. daily vol. (M) | 0.331 | Inst. holdings | 47% |

Value of $10,000 invested 5 years ago: $ 46,593

### Fiscal Year Ending Dec. 31

| | 1997 | 1996 | 1995 | 1994 | 1993 | 1992 |
|---|---|---|---|---|---|---|
| **Revenues (Million $)** | | | | | | |
| 1Q | 168.0 | 132.4 | 97.85 | 91.93 | 68.72 | 58.55 |
| 2Q | — | 143.7 | 104.8 | 92.47 | 72.68 | 59.01 |
| 3Q | — | 150.1 | 113.2 | 96.94 | 78.77 | 62.19 |
| 4Q | — | 159.8 | 123.4 | 101.0 | 89.88 | 65.37 |
| Yr. | — | 586.1 | 439.3 | 382.4 | 310.0 | 245.1 |
| **Earnings Per Share ($)** | | | | | | |
| 1Q | 0.45 | 0.33 | 0.25 | 0.22 | 0.17 | 0.12 |
| 2Q | E0.47 | 0.40 | 0.30 | 0.24 | 0.19 | 0.14 |
| 3Q | E0.48 | 0.42 | 0.35 | 0.26 | 0.19 | 0.17 |
| 4Q | E0.50 | 0.44 | 0.35 | 0.26 | 0.24 | 0.16 |
| Yr. | E1.90 | 1.59 | 1.25 | 1.00 | 0.80 | 0.60 |

**Next earnings report expected: late July**

**Dividend Data** (Dividends have been paid since 1986.)

| Amount ($) | Date Decl. | Ex-Div. Date | Stock of Record | Payment Date |
|---|---|---|---|---|
| 0.105 | Jun. 06 | Jun. 20 | Jun. 24 | Jul. 08 '96 |
| 0.105 | Sep. 16 | Sep. 25 | Sep. 27 | Oct. 11 '96 |
| 0.130 | Dec. 19 | Dec. 26 | Dec. 30 | Jan. 14 '97 |
| 0.130 | Mar. 07 | Mar. 19 | Mar. 21 | Apr. 07 '97 |

This report is for information purposes and should not be considered a solicitation to buy or sell any security. Neither S&P nor any other party guarantee its accuracy or make warranties regarding results from its usage. Redistribution is prohibited without written permission. Copyright © 1997

*A Division of The McGraw-Hill Companies*

## Business Summary - 06-MAY-97

T. Rowe Price Associates is investment adviser to the T. Rowe Price family of no-load mutual funds, and is one of the largest publicly-held mutual fund complexes in the U.S. The company is the successor to an investment counseling business formed in 1937 by the late T. Rowe Price. Assets under management at December 31, 1996, totaled $99.4 billion (of which $48.6 billion was related to retirement savings), up from $75.4 billion ($37.3 billion) a year earlier, and were divided:

|  | 1996 | 1995 |
|---|---|---|
| Stocks | 68% | 61% |
| Bonds | 17% | 22% |
| Money market | 9% | 10% |
| GICs & real estate | 6% | 7% |

Mutual funds are pooled investments representing the savings of numerous individuals that are invested in stocks, bonds and other assets managed by a portfolio manager in the hope of either outperforming a market average or meeting a similar goal. No-load funds are sold without a sales commission. The mutual fund industry is defined by the Investment Company Act of 1940 and is primarily regulated by the SEC.

Stock funds invest in the equity securities of companies listed on the New York Stock Exchange or American Stock Exchange or which trade on the Nasdaq market or a foreign exchange such as those found in Europe, the Far East and Latin America. Bond funds invest in various debt instruments such as U.S. Government obligations, corporate debentures, mortgage-related securities issued by the Fannie Mae and similar issues. TROW's relatively diverse mix of assets confers the advantage of helping to attract and retain investors who may wish to switch between funds as part of their asset allocation strategy. TROW also manages private accounts for individuals and institutions. Some 29% of assets under management are invested in international securities, a large part of which are managed by a 50%-owned unit, Rowe Price-Fleming International.

Revenues are obtained primarily from fees for managing various portfolios. A typical schedule would be as follows: a blended or average fee of 0.60% of assets under management for a domestic equity fund, 0.75% for an international or global fund, 0.50% for a corporate bond fund, and 0.40% for a money market fund. Other revenues are obtained from billing the funds for transfer agent and record keeping functions, investment income and gains, and assorted services such as discount brokerage.

About one-half of the company's total assets under management represent retirement savings: IRAs for individuals, Keoghs for the self-employed, and others.

## Capitalization

**Debt:** None (12/96).

**Minority Interest:** $38,168,000.

### Per Share Data ($)

| (Year Ended Dec. 31) | 1996 | 1995 | 1994 | 1993 | 1992 | 1991 | 1990 | 1989 | 1988 | 1987 |
|---|---|---|---|---|---|---|---|---|---|---|
| Tangible Bk. Val. | 5.92 | 4.68 | 3.65 | 3.35 | 2.52 | 2.27 | 1.92 | 1.73 | 1.35 | 1.01 |
| Cash Flow | NA | NA | NA | NA | NA | NA | NA | NA | NA | NA |
| Earnings | 1.59 | 1.25 | 1.00 | 0.80 | 0.60 | 0.51 | 0.36 | 0.50 | 0.45 | 0.33 |
| Dividends | 0.45 | 0.35 | 0.28 | 0.22 | 0.19 | 0.17 | 0.15 | 0.12 | 0.08 | 0.06 |
| Payout Ratio | 28% | 28% | 28% | 28% | 32% | 33% | 43% | 23% | 17% | 16% |
| Prices - High | 45⅝ | 28⅜ | 19⅛ | 16½ | 12½ | 11½ | 7⅞ | 7⅜ | 4½ | 6⅜ |
| - Low | 21⅜ | 13½ | 12⅜ | 10⅛ | 8¼ | 4¾ | 3⅝ | 4¼ | 2½ | 2³⁄₁₆ |
| P/E Ratio - High | 29 | 23 | 19 | 21 | 21 | 23 | 22 | 15 | 10 | 19 |
| - Low | 13 | 11 | 12 | 13 | 14 | 9 | 10 | 9 | 5 | 7 |

### Income Statement Analysis (Million $)

| | 1996 | 1995 | 1994 | 1993 | 1992 | 1991 | 1990 | 1989 | 1988 | 1987 |
|---|---|---|---|---|---|---|---|---|---|---|
| Commissions | 569 | 426 | 376 | 302 | 238 | 196 | 166 | 151 | 137 | 128 |
| Int. Inc. | 17.0 | 12.8 | 6.6 | 8.0 | 7.0 | 9.0 | 4.1 | 8.4 | 5.3 | 4.6 |
| Total Revs. | 586 | 439 | 382 | 310 | 245 | 205 | 170 | 160 | 142 | 132 |
| Int. Exp. | Nil | Nil | NA | NA | 1.7 | 1.7 | 0.3 | 0.4 | 0.2 | 0.2 |
| Pretax Inc. | 187 | 144 | 121 | 91.0 | 63.6 | 53.5 | 37.7 | 49.0 | 45.4 | 37.9 |
| Eff. Tax Rate | 39% | 38% | 38% | 39% | 37% | 38% | 39% | 36% | 39% | 44% |
| Net Inc. | 99 | 76.5 | 61.2 | 48.9 | 35.8 | 30.4 | 20.9 | 29.7 | 26.6 | 19.9 |

### Balance Sheet & Other Fin. Data (Million $)

| | 1996 | 1995 | 1994 | 1993 | 1992 | 1991 | 1990 | 1989 | 1988 | 1987 |
|---|---|---|---|---|---|---|---|---|---|---|
| Total Assets | 479 | 365 | 297 | 263 | 206 | 180 | 162 | 128 | 105 | 79.0 |
| Cash Items | 115 | 81.4 | 60.0 | 46.2 | 34.0 | 26.9 | 10.2 | 40.0 | 26.6 | 21.9 |
| Receivables | 73.2 | 55.8 | 46.7 | 43.1 | 30.1 | 29.6 | 22.2 | 24.4 | 20.2 | 17.7 |
| Secs. Owned | 143 | 122 | 93.0 | 97.1 | 66.3 | 68.3 | 75.8 | 36.0 | 30.7 | 13.8 |
| Sec. Borrowed | Nil | Nil | Nil | Nil | Nil | Nil | Nil | Nil | Nil | Nil |
| Due Brokers & Cust. | 73.1 | 56.1 | 17.7 | 15.1 | 12.9 | 12.7 | 10.2 | 11.0 | 8.0 | 7.3 |
| Other Liabs. | 21.9 | 13.4 | 49.9 | 39.4 | 25.8 | 18.4 | 17.0 | 12.6 | 15.1 | 12.1 |
| Capitalization: | | | | | | | | | | |
| Debt | Nil | Nil | 13.4 | 12.9 | 13.2 | 16.0 | 22.4 | 2.6 | 3.0 | 1.6 |
| Equity | 346 | 274 | 216 | 196 | 154 | 133 | 112 | 101 | 79.0 | 58.0 |
| Total | 384 | 296 | 245 | 218 | 167 | 148 | 134 | 104 | 82.0 | 60.0 |
| % Return On Revs. | 16.8 | 17.4 | 16.0 | 15.8 | 14.6 | 14.8 | 12.3 | 18.6 | 18.7 | 15.0 |
| % Ret. on Assets | 23.3 | 23.1 | 21.8 | 20.9 | 18.6 | 17.8 | 14.5 | 25.5 | 28.9 | 28.0 |
| % Ret. on Equity | 31.8 | 31.2 | 29.7 | 27.9 | 25.0 | 24.9 | 19.6 | 32.8 | 38.8 | 40.1 |

Data as orig. reptd.; bef. results of disc. opers. and/or spec. items. Per share data adj. for stk. divs. as of ex-div. date. E-Estimated. NA-Not Available. NM-Not Meaningful. NR-Not Ranked.

**Office**—100 E. Pratt St., Baltimore, MD 21202. **Tel**—(410) 345-2000. **Chrmn & Pres**—G. A. Roche. **CFO & Secy**—A. M. Younger, Jr. **Investor Contact**—Steven Norwitz. **Dirs**—G. J. Collins, J. E. Halbkat, Jr., H. H. Hopkins, J. A. C. Kennedy, J. J. Laporte, R. L. Menschel, W. T. Reynolds, J. S. Riepe, G. A. Roche, B. C. Rogers, J. W. Rosenblum, R. L. Strickland, M. D. Testa, P. C. Walsh, A. M. Whittemore. **Transfer Agent & Registrar**—Norwest Bank Minnesota. **Incorporated**—in Maryland in 1947. **Empl**— 2,650. **S&P Analyst:** Paul L. Huberman, CFA

**17-MAY-97**

**Industry:**
Electrical Equipment

**Summary:** This company makes electrical components, electrical contacts and assemblies, thermostatic and clad metal products, and mechanical scales.

## Quantitative Evaluations

**Outlook**
(1 Lowest—5 Highest)
• **4**‾

**Fair Value**
• **27⅞**

**Risk**
• **Average**

**Earn./Div. Rank**
• **B+**

**Technical Eval.**
• **Bullish** since 4/97

**Rel. Strength Rank**
(1 Lowest—99 Highest)
• **84**

**Insider Activity**
• **Favorable**

| Recent Price • 23 | Yield • 0.9% |
| 52 Wk Range • 25-12½ | 12-Mo. P/E • 17.0 |

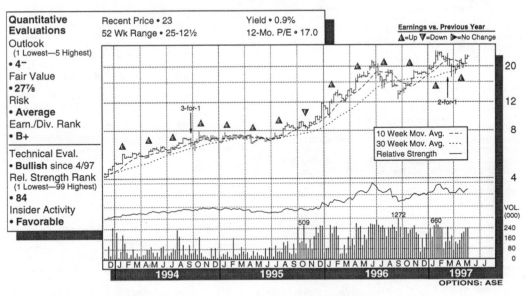

Earnings vs. Previous Year
▲=Up ▼=Down ▶=No Change

10 Week Mov. Avg. ---
30 Week Mov. Avg. ....
Relative Strength —

OPTIONS: ASE

## Business Profile - 14-MAY-97

This maker of electronic components (52% of 1996 sales), metallurgical product (37%) and test and measurement products (12%) has expanded through internal growth and acquisitions. In 1996, Technitrol (TNL) acquired a majority interest in Netwave Technologies, Inc., formed in 1996 to acquire the assets of the wireless local area network business formerly conducted by Xircom, Inc. It also acquired Doduco GmbH, a maker of precious metal contacts, bimetal products and certain contact prodcut modules, with operations in Germany and Spain. Earlier, in 1995, the company acquired Pulse Engineering, Inc., a designer, maker and seller of electronic components and modules.

## Operational Review - 14-MAY-97

Net sales rose 68% in the three months ended March 31, 1997, year to year, reflecting increased metallurgical product sales due to the 1996 acquisition of Doduco and continued growth in electronic component sales. Margins narrowed on greater costs; operating income was up 39%. After taxes at 35.3%, versus 36.5%, income from continuing operations advanced 41%, to $6.6 million ($0.40 a share), from $4.6 million ($0.29). Results exclude gains from discontinue operations of $281,000 ($0.02 per share), versus $830,000 ($0.05).

## Stock Performance - 16-MAY-97

In the past 30 trading days, TNL's shares have increased 20%, compared to a 9% rise in the S&P 500. Average trading volume for the past five days was 48,720 shares, compared with the 40-day moving average of 34,874 shares.

## Key Stock Statistics

| | | | |
|---|---|---|---|
| Dividend Rate/Share | 0.21 | Shareholders | 700 |
| Shs. outstg. (M) | 16.1 | Market cap. (B) | $0.370 |
| Avg. daily vol. (M) | 0.045 | Inst. holdings | 37% |
| Tang. Bk. Value/Share | 5.97 | | |
| Beta | 1.44 | | |

Value of $10,000 invested 5 years ago: $ 57,558

### Fiscal Year Ending Dec. 31

| | 1997 | 1996 | 1995 | 1994 | 1993 | 1992 |
|---|---|---|---|---|---|---|
| **Revenues (Million $)** | | | | | | |
| 1Q | 92.81 | 62.85 | 40.04 | 34.96 | 26.10 | 24.00 |
| 2Q | — | 68.03 | 39.39 | 37.82 | 25.30 | 25.70 |
| 3Q | — | 59.05 | 35.94 | 36.59 | 25.31 | 26.60 |
| 4Q | — | 84.14 | 61.03 | 37.08 | 23.74 | 22.30 |
| Yr. | — | 274.1 | 176.4 | 146.4 | 100.5 | 98.60 |
| **Earnings Per Share ($)** | | | | | | |
| 1Q | 0.40 | 0.34 | 0.14 | 0.11 | 0.05 | 0.07 |
| 2Q | — | 0.32 | 0.17 | 0.15 | 0.07 | 0.06 |
| 3Q | — | 0.26 | 0.14 | 0.15 | 0.08 | 0.06 |
| 4Q | — | 0.34 | 0.24 | 0.16 | 0.08 | 0.05 |
| Yr. | — | 1.27 | 0.71 | 0.57 | 0.28 | 0.24 |

**Next earnings report expected: mid July**

**Dividend Data** (Dividends have been paid since 1975.)

| Amount ($) | Date Decl. | Ex-Div. Date | Stock of Record | Payment Date |
|---|---|---|---|---|
| 0.100 | Sep. 19 | Oct. 09 | Oct. 11 | Oct. 25 '96 |
| 0.100 | Nov. 18 | Jan. 08 | Jan. 10 | Jan. 24 '97 |
| 2-for-1 | Jan. 23 | Mar. 03 | Feb. 07 | Feb. 28 '97 |
| 0.052 | Mar. 20 | Apr. 09 | Apr. 11 | Apr. 25 '97 |

This report is for information purposes and should not be considered a solicitation to buy or sell any security. Neither S&P nor any other party guarantee its accuracy or make warranties regarding results from its usage. Redistribution is prohibited without written permission. Copyright © 1997

*A Division of The McGraw·Hill Companies*

## Business Summary - 14-MAY-97

This maker of electronic components (52% of 1996 sales), metallurgical product (37%) and test and measurement products (12%) has expanded through internal growth and acquisitions. In 1996, Technitrol (TNL) acquired a majority interest in Netwave Technologies, Inc., formed in 1996 to acquire the assets of the wireless local area network business formerly conducted by Xircom, Inc. It also acquired Doduco GmbH, a maker of precious metal contacts, bimetal products and certain contact prodcut modules, with operations in Germany and Spain. Earlier, in 1995, the company acquired Pulse Engineering, Inc., a designer, maker and seller of electronic components and modules.

The electronic components business includes Pulse Engineering and Netwave Technologies, which provide a broad array of magnetics-based components, miniature chip inductors, modules and wireless network products for use primarily in local area network (LAN) and telecommunication products.

The metallurgical products business includes the operations of Advanced Matallurgy, Inc. (AMI), Doduco GmbH and Chace Precision Metals, Inc., which make electrical contacts (used in circuit protection), assemblies (used in high-voltage circuit breakers), thermostatic metals (bonded metal laminates that convert a change in temperature to a mechanical action) and clad metals (laminates of two or more metals bonded together for nonthermostatic applications).

In April 1997, Technitrol agreed to sell its test and measurement products business to Ametek Inc., for $34 million in cash. Products included electronic force measurement products (such as hand-held digital force gauges) and materials testing systems (to determine the strength of materials such as packaging). The sale, which remains subject to U.S. regulatory approvals, is expected to be reported as a discontinued operation in the 1997 first quarter results. Assets related to production of document counters and dispensers, the smallest segment of this business, were sold in March 1996 for about $3.7 million.

In November 1996, trading in the company's shares moved to the New York Stock Exchange from the American Stock Exchange.

### Capitalization

**Long Term Debt:** $35,125,000 (3/97).
**Minority Interest:** $7,000.

### Per Share Data ($)

| (Year Ended Dec. 31) | 1996 | 1995 | 1994 | 1993 | 1992 | 1991 | 1990 | 1989 | 1988 | 1987 |
|---|---|---|---|---|---|---|---|---|---|---|
| Tangible Bk. Val. | 5.62 | 4.71 | 3.80 | 3.37 | 3.24 | 3.23 | 3.18 | 2.96 | 2.48 | 2.12 |
| Cash Flow | 1.84 | 1.23 | 1.02 | 0.69 | 0.65 | 0.56 | 0.70 | 0.94 | 0.68 | 0.52 |
| Earnings | 1.27 | 0.71 | 0.57 | 0.28 | 0.24 | 0.23 | 0.39 | 0.64 | 0.49 | 0.43 |
| Dividends | 0.20 | 0.19 | 0.47 | 0.19 | 0.19 | 0.19 | 0.19 | 0.15 | 0.12 | 0.07 |
| Payout Ratio | 16% | 27% | 81% | 67% | 79% | 80% | 48% | 23% | 25% | 16% |
| Prices - High | 21⅞ | 11⅞ | 8 | 5⅛ | 5½ | 5 | 6⅞ | 7⅛ | 5 | 5 |
| - Low | 9⅝ | 6⅝ | 5 | 3¾ | 3⅜ | 4 | 3⅜ | 4⅞ | 3⅜ | 2¼ |
| P/E Ratio - High | 17 | 17 | 14 | 18 | 23 | 21 | 18 | 11 | 10 | 12 |
| - Low | 8 | 9 | 9 | 14 | 14 | 17 | 9 | 8 | 7 | 5 |

### Income Statement Analysis (Million $)

| | 1996 | 1995 | 1994 | 1993 | 1992 | 1991 | 1990 | 1989 | 1988 | 1987 |
|---|---|---|---|---|---|---|---|---|---|---|
| Revs. | 274 | 176 | 146 | 100 | 99 | 81.2 | 83.6 | 91.9 | 68.9 | 43.3 |
| Oper. Inc. | 39.1 | 21.7 | 17.8 | 10.3 | 9.7 | 8.6 | 11.2 | 15.1 | 11.6 | 9.9 |
| Depr. | 9.1 | 6.2 | 5.3 | 4.9 | 4.9 | 3.9 | 3.7 | 3.5 | 2.2 | 1.1 |
| Int. Exp. | 1.2 | 1.4 | 1.1 | 0.4 | 0.7 | 0.6 | 0.8 | 1.5 | 1.1 | 0.1 |
| Pretax Inc. | 31.0 | 14.5 | 11.4 | 5.2 | 4.3 | 4.7 | 7.6 | 10.6 | 9.0 | 9.3 |
| Eff. Tax Rate | 34% | 36% | 39% | 35% | 35% | 41% | 39% | 28% | 37% | 45% |
| Net Inc. | 20.4 | 9.3 | 6.9 | 3.4 | 2.8 | 2.8 | 4.6 | 7.6 | 5.7 | 5.1 |

### Balance Sheet & Other Fin. Data (Million $)

| | 1996 | 1995 | 1994 | 1993 | 1992 | 1991 | 1990 | 1989 | 1988 | 1987 |
|---|---|---|---|---|---|---|---|---|---|---|
| Cash | 43.5 | 13.9 | 8.7 | 7.7 | 2.7 | 6.7 | 13.9 | 7.3 | 8.6 | 12.4 |
| Curr. Assets | 143 | 82.6 | 54.0 | 37.2 | 33.4 | 34.8 | 35.3 | 34.6 | 34.9 | 25.2 |
| Total Assets | 218 | 145 | 84.8 | 58.6 | 55.7 | 52.5 | 51.6 | 52.5 | 53.8 | 30.7 |
| Curr. Liab. | 67.8 | 39.3 | 23.9 | 13.1 | 10.2 | 11.6 | 9.0 | 9.9 | 10.2 | 4.0 |
| LT Debt | 39.7 | 15.1 | 15.1 | 5.1 | 6.9 | 6.4 | 5.0 | 7.3 | 14.1 | 1.3 |
| Common Eqty. | 104 | 84.7 | 45.8 | 40.3 | 38.7 | 38.3 | 37.4 | 35.0 | 29.0 | 24.6 |
| Total Cap. | 143 | 100 | 60.9 | 45.4 | 45.5 | 40.9 | 42.6 | 42.6 | 43.7 | 26.7 |
| Cap. Exp. | 11.7 | 5.9 | 4.4 | 2.7 | 8.9 | 4.6 | 2.7 | 2.7 | 15.7 | 0.9 |
| Cash Flow | 29.6 | 15.9 | 12.2 | 8.3 | 7.7 | 6.6 | 8.3 | 11.0 | 7.9 | 6.3 |
| Curr. Ratio | 2.1 | 2.1 | 2.3 | 2.8 | 3.3 | 3.0 | 3.9 | 3.5 | 3.4 | 6.3 |
| % LT Debt of Cap. | 27.7 | 15.1 | 24.8 | 11.3 | 15.1 | 6.4 | 11.7 | 17.1 | 32.4 | 4.8 |
| % Net Inc.of Revs. | 7.5 | 5.3 | 4.7 | 3.3 | 2.9 | 3.4 | 5.5 | 8.2 | 8.2 | 11.9 |
| % Ret. on Assets | 11.2 | 8.1 | 9.7 | 5.9 | 5.2 | 5.3 | 8.9 | 14.2 | 13.4 | 18.5 |
| % Ret. on Equity | 21.7 | 20.7 | 16.1 | 8.5 | 7.3 | 7.3 | 12.8 | 23.5 | 21.1 | 22.8 |

Data as orig. reptd.; bef. results of disc. opers. and/or spec. items. Per share data adj. for stk. divs. as of ex-div. date. E-Estimated. NA-Not Available. NM-Not Meaningful. NR-Not Ranked.

**Office**—1210 Northbrook Dr., Suite 385, Trevose, PA 19053. **Tel**—(215) 355-2900. **Chrmn**—J. M. Papada III. **Pres & CEO**—T. J. Flakoll. **Treas**—D. D. Littles. **Dirs**—S. E. Basara, J. E. Burrows Jr., T. J. Flakoll, J. B. Harrison, R. E. Hock, G. Humes, E. M. Mazze, J. M. Papada III. **Transfer Agent & Registrar**—Registrar & Transfer Co., Cranford, NJ. **Incorporated**—in Pennsylvania in 1947. **Empl**—9,300. **S&P Analyst:** J.B.K.

# STANDARD &POOR'S
STOCK REPORTS

# Tellabs, Inc.

**5376R**

Nasdaq Symbol **TLAB**

In S&P 500

**17-MAY-97**

**Industry:** Communications Equipment

**Summary:** This company designs, makes, markets and services voice and data equipment used in public and private communications networks worldwide.

| S&P Opinion: Hold (★★★) | Recent Price • 45¼ | Yield • Nil |
| --- | --- | --- |
| | 52 Wk Range • 48½-24½ | 12-Mo. P/E • 55.9 |

**Quantitative Evaluations**

Outlook
(1 Lowest—5 Highest)
• **4⁻**

Fair Value
• **52½**

Risk
• **Average**

Earn./Div. Rank
• **B**

Technical Eval.
• **Bullish** since 10/92

Rel. Strength Rank
(1 Lowest—99 Highest)
• **87**

Insider Activity
• **Favorable**

**Earnings vs. Previous Year**
▲=Up ▼=Down ▶=No Change

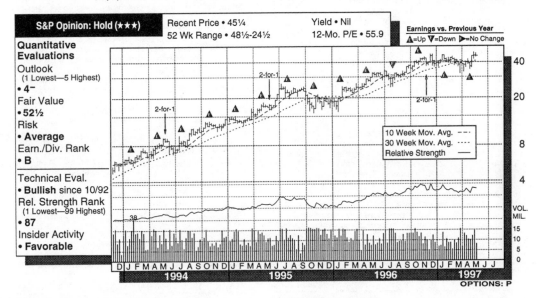

10 Week Mov. Avg. ———
30 Week Mov. Avg. - - - -
Relative Strength ———

**OPTIONS: P**

## Overview - 23-APR-97

Revenues are expected to continue to grow around 40% in 1997, reflecting higher sales of SONET-based TITAN digital cross-connect and Martis DXX systems. While sales of the company's CABLESPAN telephony system have not ramped up as quickly as expected, results showed signs of improvement in the first quarter of 1997. TLAB reported a 44% increase in sales, with a 61% jump in sales of TITAN 5500 systems and a 65% climb in sales of Martis DXX systems. Results benefited from the effects of deregulation and competition in the U.S., and from the company's continued expansion into newly developing international markets. The company is ramping up research and development expenditures for wireless local loop, ATM, and cable telephony products. Gross margins are expected to remain stable in 1997 at about 60%, while R&D expenses should be about 13% of sales. Longer term, the company's goal is to reach annual revenue of $2 billion by the year 2000.

## Valuation - 23-APR-97

The shares, split 2-for-1 in November 1996, reacted very favorably to the announcement of strong first quarter earnings, which were above analyst expectations. We are optimistic about continued growth for TITAN and Martis in 1997, especially with expanding international opportunities for Martis. In addition, the acquisition of Steinbrecher Corp. creates new opportunities in the wireless markets of newly industrialized nations. However, despite this positive outlook, we currently view the shares as fully valued, trading at about 28X our revised 1997 EPS estimate of 1.35. Results for the first quarter of 1997 included a $0.07 per share gain from the sale of stock.

## Key Stock Statistics

| | | | |
| --- | --- | --- | --- |
| S&P EPS Est. 1997 | 1.35 | Tang. Bk. Value/Share | 2.93 |
| P/E on S&P Est. 1997 | 33.5 | Beta | 1.40 |
| S&P EPS Est. 1998 | 1.60 | Shareholders | 3,000 |
| Dividend Rate/Share | Nil | Market cap. (B) | $ 8.1 |
| Shs. outstg. (M) | 179.7 | Inst. holdings | 69% |
| Avg. daily vol. (M) | 2.228 | | |

Value of $10,000 invested 5 years ago: $ 251,098

**Fiscal Year Ending Dec. 31**

| | 1998 | 1997 | 1996 | 1995 | 1994 | 1993 |
| --- | --- | --- | --- | --- | --- | --- |
| **Revenues (Million $)** | | | | | | |
| 1Q | — | 247.1 | 172.3 | 142.2 | 99.5 | 64.70 |
| 2Q | — | — | 189.5 | 159.9 | 123.0 | 71.50 |
| 3Q | — | — | 234.3 | 151.8 | 123.0 | 77.10 |
| 4Q | — | — | 272.9 | 181.3 | 148.6 | 107.2 |
| Yr. | — | — | 869.0 | 635.2 | 494.2 | 320.5 |
| **Earnings Per Share ($)** | | | | | | |
| 1Q | — | 0.34 | 0.17 | 0.13 | 0.06 | 0.03 |
| 2Q | — | E0.28 | -0.10 | 0.15 | 0.09 | 0.03 |
| 3Q | — | E0.34 | 0.25 | 0.15 | 0.10 | 0.03 |
| 4Q | — | E0.39 | 0.32 | 0.21 | 0.15 | 0.08 |
| Yr. | E1.60 | E1.35 | 0.64 | 0.63 | 0.40 | 0.17 |

**Next earnings report expected: mid July**

**Dividend Data**

| Amount ($) | Date Decl. | Ex-Div. Date | Stock of Record | Payment Date |
| --- | --- | --- | --- | --- |
| 2-for-1 | Oct. 24 | Nov. 18 | Oct. 31 | Nov. 15 '96 |

This report is for information purposes and should not be considered a solicitation to buy or sell any security. Neither S&P nor any other party guarantee its accuracy or make warranties regarding results from its usage. Redistribution is prohibited without written permission. Copyright © 1997 | A Division of The McGraw-Hill Companies

## Business Summary - 23-APR-97

Tellabs, Inc. designs, manufactures and markets voice and data transport and network access systems that are used worldwide by telephone companies, long distance carriers, alternate service providers, cellular and other wireless service providers, cable operators, government agencies, utilities, and business end users. Its products include digital cross-connect systems, managed digital networks and network access products.

Network access products (15% of sales in 1996) include digital signal processing (DSP) products, special service products and local access products such as echo cancellers and T-coders; special service products (SSP) such as voice frequency products; and local access products such as high bit digital subscriber line (HDSL) products and the CABLESPAN system.

Managed digital networks (28%) include the Martis DXX multiplexer, statistical multiplexers, packet switches, T1 multiplexers and network management systems. These products are used to combine voice, data and video applications for transmission over T1, FT1, E1, Nx56 and Nx64 facilities. The products provide for more efficient utilization of the bandwidth and access to dedicated servers.

Digital cross-connect systems (57%) include the company's TITAN 5500 series, which consists of software intensive digital cross-connect systems and network management platforms. These systems are typically used to build the wideband and broadband transmission infrastructure of telecommunication service providers.

In April 1996, TLAB acquired Steinbrecher Corp., which formed the basis for the new Wireless Systems division. This business unit is developing products for two target markets -- the wireless local loop and wideband base stations. Wireless local loop technology uses radio technology to provide residential and small business customers with telephony service, providing an economical alternative to the installation of wireline infrastructure. Wideband microcell base stations provide wireless coverage in harder to cover areas such as inside buildings and congested areas such as airports and downtown locations.

Products are sold through the company's direct sales organization and selected distributors to Bell Operating Companies (28% of total sales in 1996), independent telephone companies (7%), interexchange carriers (18%), and others (14%). International sales accounted for 30% of the total in 1996.

### Important Developments

Feb. '97—TLAB acquired Trelcom Oy of Espo, Finland, for approximately $3 million. Trelcom specializes in digital subscriber line (DSL) technology, application specific integrated circuit (ASIC) development, and digital signal processing for high-bit rate digital subscriber line (HDSL) modems. Trelcom had sales of almost $1.5 million in FY 96.

### Capitalization

**Long Term Debt:** $4,115,000 (3/97).

## Per Share Data ($)

| (Year Ended Dec. 31) | 1996 | 1995 | 1994 | 1993 | 1992 | 1991 | 1990 | 1989 | 1988 | 1987 |
|---|---|---|---|---|---|---|---|---|---|---|
| Tangible Bk. Val. | 2.93 | 2.18 | 1.42 | 0.93 | 1.01 | 0.90 | 0.85 | 0.79 | 0.74 | 0.67 |
| Cash Flow | 0.82 | 0.76 | 0.51 | 0.24 | 0.15 | 0.09 | 0.11 | 0.10 | 0.13 | 0.09 |
| Earnings | 0.64 | 0.63 | 0.40 | 0.17 | 0.10 | 0.05 | 0.06 | 0.05 | 0.09 | 0.07 |
| Dividends | Nil | Nil | Nil | Nil | Nil | Nil | Nil | Nil | Nil | Nil |
| Payout Ratio | Nil | Nil | Nil | Nil | Nil | Nil | Nil | Nil | Nil | Nil |
| Prices - High | 46¾ | 26⅜ | 14 | 6¾ | 2³⁄₁₆ | 1¹³⁄₁₆ | 1¼ | 1¼ | 1⁵⁄₁₆ | 1⅝ |
| - Low | 15¼ | 11¾ | 5½ | 1⁹⁄₁₆ | 1⁵⁄₁₆ | 1 | 1¹⁄₁₆ | 1¹⁄₁₆ | 1⁵⁄₁₆ | 1³⁄₁₆ |
| P/E Ratio - High | 73 | 42 | 35 | 39 | 22 | 43 | 24 | 26 | 15 | 23 |
| - Low | 24 | 19 | 14 | 9 | 13 | 24 | 13 | 15 | 11 | 12 |

## Income Statement Analysis (Million $)

| | 1996 | 1995 | 1994 | 1993 | 1992 | 1991 | 1990 | 1989 | 1988 | 1987 |
|---|---|---|---|---|---|---|---|---|---|---|
| Revs. | 869 | 635 | 494 | 320 | 259 | 213 | 211 | 181 | 155 | 136 |
| Oper. Inc. | 276 | 180 | 119 | 43.0 | 25.0 | 14.0 | 17.0 | 19.0 | 20.0 | 18.0 |
| Depr. | 32.6 | 24.0 | 19.5 | 10.7 | 8.6 | 8.4 | 8.3 | 8.2 | 5.5 | 4.4 |
| Int. Exp. | 1.2 | 0.1 | 1.8 | 0.5 | 0.1 | 0.4 | 0.9 | 0.5 | 0.3 | 0.4 |
| Pretax Inc. | 175 | 163 | 97.8 | 35.8 | 19.2 | 7.0 | 10.7 | 9.3 | 17.6 | 16.7 |
| Eff. Tax Rate | 33% | 29% | 26% | 15% | 12% | 5.60% | 25% | 25% | 23% | 34% |
| Net Inc. | 118 | 116 | 72.4 | 30.5 | 16.9 | 6.6 | 8.1 | 7.1 | 13.5 | 10.7 |

## Balance Sheet & Other Fin. Data (Million $)

| | 1996 | 1995 | 1994 | 1993 | 1992 | 1991 | 1990 | 1989 | 1988 | 1987 |
|---|---|---|---|---|---|---|---|---|---|---|
| Cash | 90.4 | 162 | 74.7 | 45.6 | 49.4 | 44.3 | 38.5 | 42.4 | 44.8 | 52.3 |
| Curr. Assets | 475 | 366 | 221 | 176 | 144 | 128 | 111 | 106 | 97.0 | 94.0 |
| Total Assets | 744 | 552 | 390 | 329 | 211 | 186 | 172 | 158 | 141 | 131 |
| Curr. Liab. | 132 | 99 | 82.0 | 112 | 35.0 | 32.0 | 32.0 | 27.0 | 19.0 | 17.0 |
| LT Debt | 2.8 | 2.8 | 2.8 | 2.8 | 3.8 | 4.0 | 4.2 | 4.4 | 4.4 | 4.9 |
| Common Eqty. | 591 | 433 | 293 | 207 | 167 | 145 | 130 | 120 | 112 | 104 |
| Total Cap. | 601 | 447 | 297 | 210 | 174 | 154 | 139 | 131 | 122 | 114 |
| Cap. Exp. | 64.8 | 35.0 | 23.0 | 40.1 | 18.8 | 7.2 | 13.9 | 15.4 | 10.9 | 8.8 |
| Cash Flow | 151 | 139 | 91.9 | 41.2 | 25.5 | 15.0 | 16.4 | 15.3 | 18.9 | 15.1 |
| Curr. Ratio | 5.6 | 3.7 | 2.7 | 1.6 | 4.1 | 4.0 | 3.4 | 3.9 | 5.2 | 5.6 |
| % LT Debt of Cap. | 0.5 | 1.0 | 1.0 | 1.4 | 2.2 | 2.6 | 3.0 | 3.3 | 3.6 | 4.3 |
| % Net Inc.of Revs. | 13.6 | 18.3 | 14.6 | 9.5 | 6.5 | 3.1 | 3.8 | 3.9 | 8.7 | 7.9 |
| % Ret. on Assets | 18.2 | 24.5 | 20.1 | 11.1 | 8.4 | 3.6 | 4.9 | 4.7 | 10.1 | 8.7 |
| % Ret. on Equity | 23.0 | 32.0 | 29.0 | 16.0 | 10.6 | 4.7 | 6.4 | 6.1 | 12.7 | 10.9 |

Data as orig. reptd.; bef. results of disc. opers. and/or spec. items. Per share data adj. for stk. divs. as of ex-div. date. E-Estimated. NA-Not Available. NM-Not Meaningful. NR-Not Ranked.

**Office**—4951 Indiana Ave., Lisle, IL 60532. **Tel**—(630) 378-8800. **Website**—www.tellabs.com**Pres & CEO**—M. J. Birck.**EVP, CFO, Treas & Investor Contact**—Peter A. Guglielmi (630-378-6111).**VP & Secy**—C. C. Gavin.**Dirs**—M. J. Birck, J. D. Foulkes, P. A. Guglielmi, B. J. Jackman, F. A. Krehbiel, S.P. Marshall, W. F. Souders, J. H. Suwinski.**Transfer Agent**—Harris Trust & Savings Bank, Chicago. **Incorporated**—in Delaware in 1992.**Empl**— 3,418. **S&P Analyst:** Aydin Tuncer

# The Money Store     4643

Nasdaq Symbol **MONE**

**17-MAY-97**

**Industry:** Consumer Finance

**Summary:** With a network more than 225 branch offices in all 50 states, this financial services company originates, sells and services consumer and commercial loans.

**S&P Opinion: Accumulate (★★★★)**

| | |
|---|---|
| Recent Price • 24 | Yield • 0.6% |
| 52 Wk Range • 32½-16⅜ | 12-Mo. P/E • 15.2 |

**Quantitative Evaluations**

**Outlook** (1 Lowest—5 Highest)
• **4⁻**

**Fair Value**
• **29¼**

**Risk**
• **High**

**Earn./Div. Rank**
• **NR**

**Technical Eval.**
• **Bearish** since 3/97

**Rel. Strength Rank** (1 Lowest—99 Highest)
• **57**

**Insider Activity**
• **Neutral**

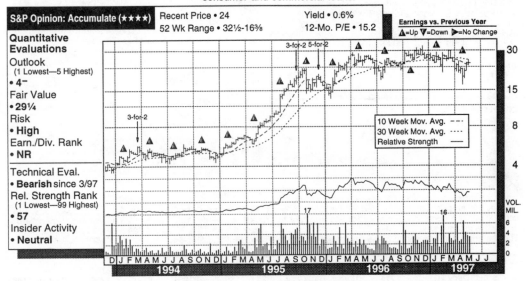

Earnings vs. Previous Year
▲=Up ▼=Down ▶=No Change

10 Week Mov. Avg. ----
30 Week Mov. Avg. ····
Relative Strength ——

## Overview - 28-APR-97

EPS advanced 52%, year to year, in the first quarter of 1997, reflecting the continued rapid growth of loan originations in all of MONE's product areas. An active television advertiser, the company has successfully leveraged its franchise recognition to become a market leader in home equity, small business and student lending. We expect loan originations to grow more than 30% in coming periods, paced by new product offerings in the home equity segment, coupled with a push into auto finance. In the home equity (67% of serviced portfolio in 1997's first quarter) and auto (4.6%) markets, MONE targets "sub-prime" borrowers who cannot get credit elsewhere. Given the rising levels of consumer bankruptcies and the maturation of the current economic expansion, maintaining credit quality is a critical issue for The Money Store. In the first quarter, home equity and auto delinquency rates trended higher, to 6.59% and 3.43% of the serviced portfolio, respectively. We expect these delinquencies to continue to rise over the course of 1997, but to remain within manageable levels.

## Valuation - 28-APR-97

Fears that rising interest rates will slow the rate of loan originations and cause delinquencies to drift still higher have prompted investors to trim MONE's market capitalization by approximately 42% from its 52-week high. We expect loan origination growth to continue at a rapid clip, as overextended borrowers seek to consolidate debts and reduce monthly payments through home equity loans. We remain cautious about rising consumer delinquencies, but with the shares trading at a steep discount to MONE's expected EPS growth rate, credit concerns appear to be fully discounted in the stock price. We continue to recommend accumulation of the shares for superior capital appreciation.

## Key Stock Statistics

| | | | |
|---|---|---|---|
| S&P EPS Est. 1997 | 1.85 | Tang. Bk. Value/Share | 7.59 |
| P/E on S&P Est. 1997 | 13.0 | Beta | 1.88 |
| S&P EPS Est. 1998 | 2.20 | Shareholders | 200 |
| Dividend Rate/Share | 0.14 | Market cap. (B) | $ 1.4 |
| Shs. outstg. (M) | 57.8 | Inst. holdings | 66% |
| Avg. daily vol. (M) | 1.084 | | |

Value of $10,000 invested 5 years ago: $ 96,118

### Fiscal Year Ending Dec. 31

| | 1998 | 1997 | 1996 | 1995 | 1994 | 1993 |
|---|---|---|---|---|---|---|
| **Revenues (Million $)** | | | | | | |
| 1Q | — | 190.5 | 154.8 | 91.80 | 69.30 | 44.20 |
| 2Q | — | — | 178.4 | 112.7 | 77.30 | 46.10 |
| 3Q | — | — | 202.2 | 145.3 | 84.70 | 55.00 |
| 4Q | — | — | 243.4 | 160.9 | 99.1 | 74.50 |
| Yr. | — | — | 778.7 | 510.6 | 330.5 | 219.8 |
| **Earnings Per Share ($)** | | | | | | |
| 1Q | — | 0.41 | 0.27 | 0.14 | 0.11 | 0.09 |
| 2Q | — | E0.43 | 0.32 | 0.21 | 0.14 | 0.10 |
| 3Q | — | E0.47 | 0.38 | 0.26 | 0.16 | 0.13 |
| 4Q | — | E0.54 | 0.49 | 0.34 | 0.20 | 0.16 |
| Yr. | E2.20 | E1.85 | 1.44 | 0.95 | 0.62 | 0.48 |

**Next earnings report expected: late July**

### Dividend Data (Dividends have been paid since 1992.)

| Amount ($) | Date Decl. | Ex-Div. Date | Stock of Record | Payment Date |
|---|---|---|---|---|
| 0.025 | Jul. 24 | Aug. 13 | Aug. 15 | Sep. 01 '96 |
| 0.030 | Oct. 23 | Nov. 13 | Nov. 15 | Dec. 01 '96 |
| 0.030 | Jan. 22 | Feb. 12 | Feb. 15 | Mar. 01 '97 |
| 0.035 | Apr. 23 | May. 13 | May. 15 | Jun. 01 '97 |

This report is for information purposes and should not be considered a solicitation to buy or sell any security. Neither S&P nor any other party guarantee its accuracy or make warranties regarding results from its usage. Redistribution is prohibited without written permission. Copyright © 1997   *A Division of The McGraw-Hill Companies*

## Business Summary - 28-APR-97

The Money Store is a financial services company that originates, sells and services certain types of consumer and commercial loans. The company specializes in home equity loans, loans guaranteed in part by the U.S. Small Business Administration (SBA) and government-guaranteed student loans. At year-end 1996, MONE operated out of 217 locations and was doing business in all 50 states, Washington, DC, and Puerto Rico.

In the past three years, loans originated or serviced by the company (in millions) were as follows:

|  | 1996 | 1995 | 1994 |
|---|---|---|---|
| Loans originated or purchased | $5,700 | $3,823 | $2,779 |
| Home equity loans | 68% | 75% | 72% |
| SBA loans | 18% | 12% | 15% |
| Student loans | 10% | 10% | 13% |
| Auto loans | 4% | 3% | --- |
| Serviced loans | $12,200 | $8,621 | $5,898 |

Substantially all loans originated and purchased by MONE are sold to institutional investors. This increases liquidity, reduces the need to access capital markets and reduces certain risks associated with interest rate fluctuations. The company generally retains the right to service the loans it sells.

The majority of home equity loans originated by the company are to borrowers owning a single-family detached home who typically need funds for education, home improvements or debt consolidation. It currently operates 81 home equity loan origination offices in 36 states and Washington, DC, and intends to enter, gradually, but more rapidly than in the past, all remaining major geographic markets in the U.S.

MONE was the largest U.S. SBA lender in each of the past 13 years. The focus of its SBA lending activities is to originate owner-user commercial real estate mortgage loans under the SBA guidelines.

In January 1995, the company established an auto finance division, offering loans for new and used automobiles, primarily in the sub-prime market. The division has 26 branch offices in 21 states.

## Important Developments

**Apr. '97**—In the 1997 first quarter, delinquencies were 6.59% of home equity loans serviced (5.95% at year-end 1996), 6.47% of commercial loans serviced (5.89%) and 3.43% of auto loans serviced (3.03%).

## Capitalization

**$1.72 Mandatory Conv. Pfd. Stk.:** 4,600,000 shs. (no par); ea. conv. into 0.833 of a com. sh. until mandatory conversion 12/1/99 into 0.833 to 1.000 of a com. sh.

**Notes Payable:** $1,316,962,000 (3/97).

### Per Share Data ($)

| (Year Ended Dec. 31) | 1996 | 1995 | 1994 | 1993 | 1992 | 1991 | 1990 | 1989 | 1988 | 1987 |
|---|---|---|---|---|---|---|---|---|---|---|
| Tangible Bk. Val. | 7.59 | 4.70 | 3.82 | 3.25 | 2.79 | 2.46 | 2.06 | 2.00 | 1.43 | 1.11 |
| Cash Flow | 1.71 | 1.12 | 0.73 | 0.54 | 0.38 | 0.38 | 0.29 | 0.50 | NA | NA |
| Earnings | 1.44 | 0.95 | 0.62 | 0.48 | 0.34 | 0.33 | 0.25 | 0.45 | 0.30 | 0.41 |
| Dividends | 0.10 | 0.07 | 0.05 | 0.04 | 0.01 | Nil | 0.01 | Nil | Nil | Nil |
| Payout Ratio | 7% | 7% | 8% | 8% | 3% | Nil | 4% | Nil | Nil | Nil |
| Prices - High | 32½ | 22⅛ | 5⅞ | 4⅞ | 4 | 3⅝ | NA | NA | NA | NA |
| - Low | 13 | 4¾ | 4⅛ | 2¾ | 1¹³⁄₁₆ | 2³⁄₁₆ | NA | NA | NA | NA |
| P/E Ratio - High | 23 | 23 | 10 | 10 | 12 | 11 | NA | NA | NA | NA |
| - Low | 9 | 5 | 7 | 6 | 5 | 7 | NA | NA | NA | NA |

### Income Statement Analysis (Million $)

| | 1996 | 1995 | 1994 | 1993 | 1992 | 1991 | 1990 | 1989 | 1988 | 1987 |
|---|---|---|---|---|---|---|---|---|---|---|
| Loan Fees | 234 | 157 | 68.1 | 58.2 | 60.9 | 57.4 | 55.2 | 39.4 | NA | NA |
| Int. Inc. | 545 | 354 | 260 | 160 | 95.0 | 81.0 | 65.0 | 68.0 | NA | NA |
| Total Revs. | 779 | 511 | 330 | 220 | 157 | 140 | 122 | 110 | 82.0 | 65.0 |
| Int. Exp. | 124 | 94.0 | 43.1 | 29.2 | 31.5 | 36.4 | 39.1 | 26.9 | 17.2 | 11.5 |
| Exp./Op. Revs. | 81% | 84% | 84% | 82% | 84% | 87% | 89% | 77% | 79% | 75% |
| Pretax Inc. | 145 | 83.0 | 53.0 | 40.6 | 25.6 | 18.9 | 13.7 | 25.5 | 16.8 | 16.4 |
| Eff. Tax Rate | 41% | 41% | 41% | 46% | 41% | 40% | 41% | 41% | 40% | 42% |
| Net Inc. | 85.7 | 48.7 | 31.3 | 21.8 | 15.2 | 11.4 | 8.1 | 15.1 | 10.1 | 13.5 |

### Balance Sheet & Other Fin. Data (Million $)

| | 1996 | 1995 | 1994 | 1993 | 1992 | 1991 | 1990 | 1989 | 1988 | 1987 |
|---|---|---|---|---|---|---|---|---|---|---|
| Net Prop. | 73.5 | 33.8 | 22.5 | 10.5 | 6.6 | 5.9 | 5.2 | 5.0 | NA | NA |
| Cash & Secs. | 322 | 179 | 161 | 87.0 | 75.0 | 46.0 | 32.0 | 40.0 | NA | NA |
| Loans | 1,406 | 1,045 | 637 | 571 | 349 | 402 | 384 | 319 | 265 | 184 |
| Total Assets | 2,612 | 1,792 | 1,165 | 910 | 612 | 602 | 557 | 478 | 377 | 274 |
| Capitalization: | | | | | | | | | | |
| Debt | 1,321 | 1,100 | 700 | 543 | 339 | 366 | 394 | 323 | 264 | 182 |
| Equity | 438 | 241 | 194 | 165 | 126 | 111 | 63.7 | 61.9 | 44.3 | 34.2 |
| Total | 1,904 | 1,341 | 894 | 708 | 465 | 477 | 458 | 385 | 308 | 217 |
| Price Times Bk. Val.: High | 4.3 | 4.7 | 1.6 | 1.5 | 1.4 | 1.5 | NA | NA | NA | NA |
| Price Times Bk. Val.: Low | 1.7 | 1.0 | 1.1 | 0.8 | 0.7 | 0.9 | NA | NA | NA | NA |
| Cash Flow | 101 | 57.2 | 36.8 | 24.7 | 17.1 | 13.1 | 9.5 | 16.5 | NA | NA |
| % Return On Revs. | 11.0 | 9.6 | 9.5 | 9.9 | 9.7 | 8.1 | 6.6 | 13.7 | 12.4 | 20.8 |
| % Ret. on Assets | 3.9 | 3.3 | 3.0 | 2.9 | 2.5 | 2.0 | 1.6 | 3.5 | 3.1 | 5.5 |
| % Ret. on Equity | 25.2 | 22.4 | 17.4 | 15.0 | 12.8 | 13.0 | 12.9 | 28.4 | 25.7 | 49.1 |

Data as orig. reptd.; bef. results of disc. opers. and/or spec. items. Per share data adj. for stk. divs. as of ex-div. date. E-Estimated. NA-Not Available. NM-Not Meaningful. NR-Not Ranked.

**Office**—2840 Morris Ave., Union, NJ 07083. **Tel**—(908) 686-2000. **Website**—http://www.themoneystore.com **Chrmn**—A. Turtletaub. **Pres & CEO**—M. Turtletaub. **Exec VP, CFO & Secy**—M. Dear. **Exec VP**—A. R. Medici. **Treas**—H. Puglisi. **Sr VP & Investor Contact**—Michael H. Benoff (916) 554-8010. **Dirs**—M. Dear, A. R. Medici, H. Puglisi, A. C. Schwartz Jr., A. Turtletaub, M. Turtletaub, A. L. Watson. **Transfer Agent & Registrar**—Registrar & Transfer Co., Cranford, NJ. **Incorporated**—in New Jersey in 1974. **Empl**—2,560. **S&P Analyst:** Brendan McGovern

# STANDARD &POOR'S
STOCK REPORTS

# Thermo Electron

## 2222

NYSE Symbol **TMO**

In S&P 500

**17-MAY-97**

**Industry:**
Manufacturing (Diversified)

**Summary:** This maker of analytical instruments, biomedical equipment, cogeneration systems and process equipment has sold minority interests in several publicly traded subsidiaries.

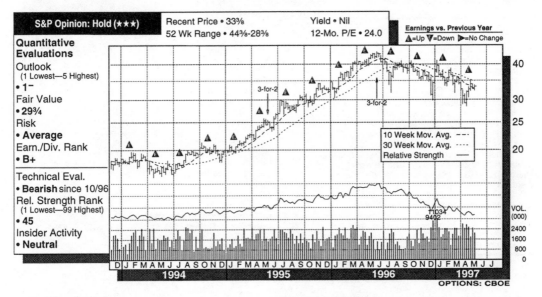

| S&P Opinion: Hold (★★★) | Recent Price • 33⅜ | Yield • Nil |
|---|---|---|
| | 52 Wk Range • 44⅜-28⅜ | 12-Mo. P/E • 24.0 |

**Quantitative Evaluations**

**Outlook**
(1 Lowest—5 Highest)
• **1⁻**

**Fair Value**
• **29¾**

**Risk**
• **Average**

**Earn./Div. Rank**
• **B+**

**Technical Eval.**
• **Bearish** since 10/96

**Rel. Strength Rank**
(1 Lowest—99 Highest)
• **45**

**Insider Activity**
• **Neutral**

Earnings vs. Previous Year
▲=Up ▼=Down ▶=No Change

10 Week Mov. Avg. – – –
30 Week Mov. Avg. ⋯⋯
Relative Strength ——

OPTIONS: CBOE

---

## Overview - 07-APR-97

In 1996, TMO continued to focus on its current strategy of acquiring complementary businesses, while spinning out other operations into separate subsidiaries. After a 29% increase in 1996, revenues are expected to advance another 20% in 1997, as TMO focuses on improving the operations of new businesses. With the successful integration of the Fisons businesses and the acquisition of already profitable Life Sciences, the company expects Thermo Instrument to generate over half of its 1997 revenues. Despite reduced federal spending, Thermo TerraTech and ThermoTrex are expected to show improvement, but high costs will continue to restrict Thermo Power. Although the company does not expect to record restructuring charges in 1997, it anticipates sharply lower gains from the issuance of stock in subsidiaries. Overall, we expect earnings to grow 15% to 18% in 1997.

## Valuation - 07-APR-97

We are maintaining our hold recommendation on the shares. The company has been successfully growing through acquisitions; however, its ability to generate sustainable internal growth remains to be seen. Although the ThermoLase hair removal business has sparked public interest, margins at this subsidiary will remain under pressure as it continues to expand. Overall, the company believes that it can improve operating results by transforming low-margin acquisitions into more profitable ones. With growth from acquisitions expected to slow in 1997, TMO must improve operating margins at least 30% from 1996 levels to meet its goals. Although the shares were recently trading near their 52-week low, we see them as fairly valued, at about 19X our 1997 EPS estimate of $1.60.

## Key Stock Statistics

| | | | |
|---|---|---|---|
| S&P EPS Est. 1997 | 1.60 | Tang. Bk. Value/Share | 4.48 |
| P/E on S&P Est. 1997 | 20.9 | Beta | 0.78 |
| Dividend Rate/Share | Nil | Shareholders | 9,200 |
| Shs. outstg. (M) | 149.9 | Market cap. (B) | $ 5.0 |
| Avg. daily vol. (M) | 0.538 | Inst. holdings | 62% |

Value of $10,000 invested 5 years ago: $ 24,162

### Fiscal Year Ending Dec. 31

| | 1997 | 1996 | 1995 | 1994 | 1993 | 1992 |
|---|---|---|---|---|---|---|
| **Revenues (Million $)** | | | | | | |
| 1Q | 763.5 | 652.4 | 478.5 | 350.5 | 292.8 | 204.4 |
| 2Q | — | 745.8 | 528.7 | 395.0 | 300.5 | 210.1 |
| 3Q | — | 740.0 | 570.4 | 406.5 | 318.4 | 242.9 |
| 4Q | — | 794.4 | 629.8 | 433.5 | 338.1 | 291.6 |
| Yr. | — | 2,933 | 2,207 | 1,585 | 1,250 | 949.0 |
| **Earnings Per Share ($)** | | | | | | |
| 1Q | 0.35 | 0.31 | 0.25 | 0.21 | 0.17 | 0.14 |
| 2Q | E0.38 | 0.32 | 0.26 | 0.22 | 0.19 | 0.15 |
| 3Q | E0.41 | 0.36 | 0.30 | 0.25 | 0.20 | 0.17 |
| 4Q | E0.44 | 0.36 | 0.31 | 0.25 | 0.21 | 0.20 |
| Yr. | E1.60 | 1.35 | 1.11 | 0.93 | 0.78 | 0.67 |

**Next earnings report expected: early August**

### Dividend Data (Dividends have been paid since 1996.)

| Amount ($) | Date Decl. | Ex-Div. Date | Stock of Record | Payment Date |
|---|---|---|---|---|
| 3-for-2 | Mar. 13 | Jun. 06 | May. 22 | Jun. 05 '96 |

---

This report is for information purposes and should not be considered a solicitation to buy or sell any security. Neither S&P nor any other party guarantee its accuracy or make warranties regarding results from its usage. Redistribution is prohibited without written permission. Copyright © 1997

A Division of The McGraw-Hill Companies

## Business Summary - 07-APR-97

Thermo Electron Corporation has developed businesses from existing technologies and through acquisitions. It has sold minority positions in subsidiaries capable of long-term growth. Segment contributions in 1996 were:

|                           | Sales | Profits |
|---------------------------|-------|---------|
| Instruments               | 41.1% | 50.4%   |
| Alternative-energy Systems| 11.5% | 13.8%   |
| Advanced Technologies     | 12.8% | 10.2%   |
| Process Equipment         | 9.8%  | 13.2%   |
| Biomedical Products       | 15.5% | 6.0%    |
| Environmental Services    | 9.3%  | 6.4%    |

Thermo Instrument Systems Inc. (82% owned) makes instruments to detect and measure air pollution, nuclear radioactivity and toxic substances. In August 1995, it spun off 73%-owned ThermoSpectra Corp. to focus on promising technologies. Thermo Power (64%) develops and makes packaged cogeneration and cooling systems. Thermo Fibertek (84%) makes processing machinery for the paper-making and recycling industries. Thermo TerraTech (81%) produces thermal processing systems to treat primary metals and metal parts, and, with TMO, owns 68% of Thermo Remediation, which remediates petroleum-contaminated soils.

Thermedics Inc. (55%) makes biomedical products and instruments used to detect explosives and narcotics. It owns, together with TMO, 54% of Thermo Cardiosystems, a producer of ventricular-assist devices, and 51%

of Thermo Voltek, a maker of high-voltage equipment. Thermotrex (51%) does research in electro-optical and advanced laser systems, thermodynamics and parallel and signal processing. It owns 64% of ThermoLase, which has developed a long-term hair removal system. Thermo Ecotek (82%), spun off in February 1995, operates alternative energy power systems.

Wholly owned Coleman Research Corp. provides systems integration, systems engineering, and analytical services to government and commercial customers.

### Important Developments

**Mar. '97**—Thermo Instrument (THI) acquired Life Sciences International PLC (LSI) in a transaction valued at about $395 million. THI believes that LSI is a good strategic fit that will significantly expand its manufacturing and marketing base in Europe and Asia, and will open up the clinical laboratory equipment and bio-analytical instrumentation markets. Separately, Thermedics, Inc. completed an IPO of Thermedics Detection, Inc. (TDX) through a rights offering. TDX manufactures quality assurance products for industrial applications and explosives detection.

### Capitalization

**Minority Interest:** $684,050,000.
**Long Term Obligs.:** $1,550,342,000 (12/96), incl. $369,997,000 of sr. conv. obligs. and $1,009,470,000 of subord. conv. obligs.

### Per Share Data ($)

| (Year Ended Dec. 31) | 1996 | 1995 | 1994 | 1993 | 1992 | 1991 | 1990 | 1989 | 1988 | 1987 |
|---|---|---|---|---|---|---|---|---|---|---|
| Tangible Bk. Val. | 4.21 | 3.59 | 8.63 | 7.96 | 6.07 | 5.52 | 4.34 | 2.33 | 2.06 | 2.02 |
| Cash Flow | 2.16 | 1.79 | 1.50 | 1.21 | 1.00 | 0.87 | 0.76 | 0.61 | 0.51 | 0.45 |
| Earnings | 1.35 | 1.11 | 0.93 | 0.78 | 0.67 | 0.58 | 0.49 | 0.40 | 0.34 | 0.30 |
| Dividends | Nil | Nil | Nil | Nil | Nil | Nil | Nil | Nil | Nil | Nil |
| Payout Ratio | Nil | Nil | Nil | Nil | Nil | Nil | Nil | Nil | Nil | Nil |
| Prices - High | 44⅜ | 34⅝ | 21¼ | 19¼ | 14⅛ | 13⅞ | 10½ | 11¼ | 6⅛ | 8½ |
|    - Low | 29¾ | 19½ | 16 | 13⅞ | 11⅛ | 7⅝ | 6½ | 5⅝ | 3¾ | 3 |
| P/E Ratio - High | 33 | 31 | 23 | 25 | 21 | 24 | 21 | 28 | 18 | 29 |
|    - Low | 22 | 18 | 17 | 18 | 17 | 13 | 13 | 14 | 11 | 10 |

### Income Statement Analysis (Million $)

| | 1996 | 1995 | 1994 | 1993 | 1992 | 1991 | 1990 | 1989 | 1988 | 1987 |
|---|---|---|---|---|---|---|---|---|---|---|
| Revs. | 2,933 | 2,207 | 1,585 | 1,247 | 947 | 805 | 708 | 579 | 501 | 383 |
| Oper. Inc. | 399 | 332 | 242 | 163 | 95.5 | 65.3 | 56.9 | 32.6 | 30.0 | 22.1 |
| Depr. | 115 | 84.9 | 62.3 | 42.4 | 29.2 | 23.4 | 18.8 | 12.7 | 9.9 | 9.2 |
| Int. Exp. | 96.7 | 76.9 | 61.7 | 40.0 | 31.4 | 18.3 | 13.9 | 11.6 | 10.2 | 7.7 |
| Pretax Inc. | 375 | 299 | 204 | 131 | 102 | 79.0 | 58.0 | 37.0 | 29.0 | 25.0 |
| Eff. Tax Rate | 37% | 33% | 34% | 26% | 27% | 31% | 30% | 26% | 25% | 19% |
| Net Inc. | 191 | 140 | 103 | 76.6 | 60.6 | 47.1 | 33.9 | 24.6 | 20.1 | 18.1 |

### Balance Sheet & Other Fin. Data (Million $)

| | 1996 | 1995 | 1994 | 1993 | 1992 | 1991 | 1990 | 1989 | 1988 | 1987 |
|---|---|---|---|---|---|---|---|---|---|---|
| Cash | 1,846 | 462 | 998 | 700 | 369 | 422 | 178 | 210 | 136 | 144 |
| Curr. Assets | 3,132 | 22,021 | 1,683 | 1,245 | 830 | 763 | 494 | 416 | 331 | 296 |
| Total Assets | 5,141 | 3,745 | 3,020 | 2,474 | 1,818 | 1,199 | 898 | 624 | 490 | 426 |
| Curr. Liab. | 913 | 715 | 537 | 416 | 326 | 297 | 254 | 153 | 123 | 95.0 |
| LT Debt | 1,550 | 1,116 | 1,050 | 790 | 694 | 255 | 210 | 172 | 148 | 132 |
| Common Eqty. | 1,754 | 1,299 | 990 | 859 | 553 | 481 | 307 | 211 | 182 | 162 |
| Total Cap. | 4,065 | 2,947 | 2,426 | 1,989 | 1,451 | 869 | 614 | 450 | 357 | 320 |
| Cap. Exp. | 125 | 63.0 | 60.0 | 60.0 | 193 | 33.0 | 24.0 | 20.0 | 24.0 | 14.0 |
| Cash Flow | 306 | 225 | 166 | 119 | 89.8 | 70.4 | 52.6 | 37.3 | 30.0 | 27.3 |
| Curr. Ratio | 3.4 | 2.8 | 3.1 | 3.0 | 2.5 | 2.6 | 1.9 | 2.7 | 2.7 | 3.1 |
| % LT Debt of Cap. | 38.1 | 37.9 | 43.3 | 39.7 | 47.8 | 29.4 | 34.2 | 38.2 | 41.6 | 41.2 |
| % Net Inc.of Revs. | 6.5 | 6.3 | 6.5 | 6.1 | 6.4 | 5.8 | 4.8 | 4.2 | 4.0 | 4.7 |
| % Ret. on Assets | 4.3 | 4.1 | 3.7 | 3.3 | 3.9 | 4.1 | 4.2 | 4.3 | 4.4 | 5.0 |
| % Ret. on Equity | 12.5 | 12.0 | 10.9 | 10.1 | 11.5 | 10.9 | 12.3 | 12.3 | 11.7 | 11.9 |

Data as orig. reptd.; bef. results of disc. opers. and/or spec. items. Per share data adj. for stk. divs. as of ex-div. date. E-Estimated. NA-Not Available. NM-Not Meaningful. NR-Not Ranked.

**Office**—81 Wyman St., P.O. Box 9046, Waltham, MA 02254-9046. **Tel**—(617) 622-1000. **Website**—http://www.thermo.com **Chrmn, Pres & CEO**—G. N. Hatsopoulos. **CFO & Investor Contact**—John N. Hatsopoulos (617-622-1111). **VP-Fin**—P. F. Kelleher. **Secy**—Sandra L. Lambert. **Dirs**—J. M. Albertine, P. O. Crisp, E. P. Gyftopoulos, G. N. Hatsopoulos, F. Jungers, R. A. McCabe, F. E. Morris, D. E. Noble, H. S. Olayan, R. D. Wellington. **Transfer Agent & Registrar**—Bank of Boston. **Incorporated**—in Delaware in 1956; reincorporated in 1960. **Empl**— 17,760. **S&P Analyst:** Eric Hunter

# Travelers Group Inc.    2254A

NYSE Symbol **TRV**

In S&P 500

**19-MAY-97**

**Industry:** Insurance (Multi-Line)

**Summary:** This holding company offers investment services through Smith Barney Inc., consumer finance services, and an array of life and property-casualty insurance through the Travelers.

| S&P Opinion: Accumulate (★★★★) | | |
|---|---|---|
| Recent Price • 55¼ | Yield • 1.1% | |
| 52 Wk Range • 58⅜-29⅛ | 12-Mo. P/E • 15.0 | |

**Quantitative Evaluations**

**Outlook**
(1 Lowest—5 Highest)
• **3**

**Fair Value**
• **56¾**

**Risk**
• **Average**

**Earn./Div. Rank**
• **A**

**Technical Eval.**
• **Bullish** since 1/95

**Rel. Strength Rank**
(1 Lowest—99 Highest)
• **74**

**Insider Activity**
• **Favorable**

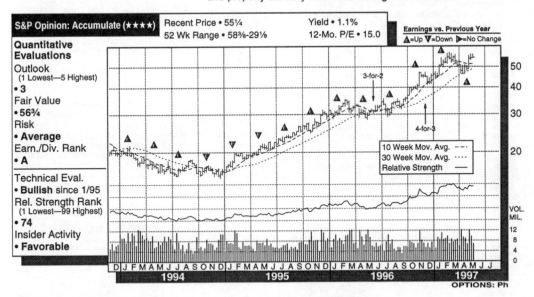

Earnings vs. Previous Year
▲=Up ▼=Down ▷=No Change

10 Week Mov. Avg. – – –
30 Week Mov. Avg. ·····
Relative Strength —

VOL. MIL.

OPTIONS: Ph

## Overview - 19-MAY-97

The forecast for higher earnings in 1997 and beyond is predicated on continued profit growth at Smith Barney. Results here in 1995 and 1996 were driven by robust investment market activity. Year to year comparisons in 1997 could become difficult if investor activity cools, although Smith Barney's emphasis on increasing its base of fee income could limit the decline. Cost cuts and productivity gains at Travelers Property Casualty Corp. will help offset a competitive premium pricing environment. TRV's decision to use most of the proceeds from the sale of its interest in MetraHealth to bolster the capital base of its life insurance unit enhances that division's competitive stance. Consumer finance earnings may continue to come under pressure from somewhat higher loan delinquencies in the first half of 1997, but overall the level of delinquencies is manageable. Stock repurchases, including the 17.3 million shares (adjusted for the November 1996 four-for-three stock split) reacquired during 1996, have aided per-share comparisons.

## Valuation - 19-MAY-97

After rising steadily during 1995 and early 1996 amid a favorable interest rate environment for most financial issues, the shares plateaued in mid-1996 amid concerns over the direction of interest rates and over eroding consumer credit quality. Once these fears subsided, the shares resumed their upward climb, but then weakened somewhat in April amid renewed interest rate fears. We used this near term weakness as an opportunity to upgrade our opinion to accumulate. Trading at about 12 times our 1998 operating earnings estimate (excluding realized investment gains) of $4.50 a share, the shares have additional upside potential.

## Key Stock Statistics

| | | | |
|---|---|---|---|
| S&P EPS Est. 1997 | 3.80 | Tang. Bk. Value/Share | 14.90 |
| P/E on S&P Est. 1997 | 14.5 | Beta | 2.10 |
| S&P EPS Est. 1998 | 4.50 | Shareholders | 55,100 |
| Dividend Rate/Share | 0.60 | Market cap. (B) | $ 35.4 |
| Shs. outstg. (M) | 641.4 | Inst. holdings | 67% |
| Avg. daily vol. (M) | 1.770 | | |

Value of $10,000 invested 5 years ago: NA

### Fiscal Year Ending Dec. 31

| | 1997 | 1996 | 1995 | 1994 | 1993 | 1992 |
|---|---|---|---|---|---|---|
| **Revenues (Million $)** | | | | | | |
| 1Q | 5,928 | 4,515 | 3,960 | 4,769 | 1,302 | — |
| 2Q | — | 5,426 | 4,172 | 4,601 | 1,284 | — |
| 3Q | — | 5,622 | 4,290 | 4,714 | 2,016 | — |
| 4Q | — | 5,782 | 4,161 | 4,381 | 2,195 | 1,269 |
| Yr. | — | 21,345 | 16,583 | 18,465 | 6,797 | 5,125 |
| **Earnings Per Share ($)** | | | | | | |
| 1Q | 0.96 | 0.77 | 0.45 | 0.49 | 0.45 | 0.49 |
| 2Q | — | 0.88 | 0.56 | 0.46 | 0.38 | 0.34 |
| 3Q | — | 0.84 | 0.68 | 0.49 | 0.51 | 0.36 |
| 4Q | — | 0.97 | 0.74 | 0.50 | 0.60 | 0.48 |
| Yr. | E3.80 | 3.45 | 2.43 | 1.93 | 1.94 | 1.67 |

**Next earnings report expected: mid July**

**Dividend Data** (Dividends have been paid since 1986.)

| Amount ($) | Date Decl. | Ex-Div. Date | Stock of Record | Payment Date |
|---|---|---|---|---|
| 0.150 | Oct. 23 | Oct. 31 | Nov. 04 | Nov. 22 '96 |
| 4-for-3 | Oct. 23 | Nov. 25 | Nov. 04 | Nov. 22 '96 |
| 0.150 | Jan. 22 | Jan. 30 | Feb. 03 | Feb. 21 '97 |
| 0.150 | Apr. 23 | May. 01 | May. 05 | May. 23 '97 |

This report is for information purposes and should not be considered a solicitation to buy or sell any security. Neither S&P nor any other party guarantee its accuracy or make warranties regarding results from its usage. Redistribution is prohibited without written permission. Copyright © 1997

A Division of The McGraw-Hill Companies

## Business Summary - 19-MAY-97

Travelers Group Inc. (formerly Travelers Inc. and, before that, Primerica Corp.) is a diversified financial services holding company. On December 31, 1993, TRV acquired the 73% of Travelers Corp. it did not already own for stock worth about $3.5 billion. Contributions to revenues in recent years:

|                                    | 1996 | 1995 |
|------------------------------------|------|------|
| Investment services                | 37%  | 41%  |
| Life insurance services            | 18%  | 23%  |
| Property-casualty insurance services | 38%  | 28%  |
| Consumer finance & other           | 7%   | 8%   |

Investment services consist of Smith Barney Inc., an investment banking and securities brokerage firm. TRV sold its 99% interest in RCM Capital Management in mid-1996. Assets under management (including those in the life and annuity units) at December 31, 1996, were $133.3 billion.

Insurance services include life, accident and health, property and casualty, and auto service contract insurance. Travelers Life and Annuities and Primerica Financial Services and its affiliates underwrite individual life insurance and market annuities and mutual funds. At year-end 1996, life insurance in force totaled $410 billion.

Consumer finance services include real estate-secured loans, personal loans, credit cards and other personal loans. Net consumer finance receivables were $8.1 billion at year-end 1996.

In April 1996, TRV acquired the domestic property-casualty operations of Aetna Life and Casualty Corp. for $4.0 billion and launched Travelers Property Casualty Corp. (TAP). Following an April 1996 initial public offering of common stock in the new company, TAP is approximately 82% owned by Travelers Group. TAP is the fourth largest U.S. property-casualty company, selling an array of personal and commercial lines coverage. TRV expects TAP will result in at least $300 million in annual pretax savings by the end of 1997.

## Important Developments

**Jan. '97**—TRV's operating income rose 37% in 1996, to $2.2 billion ($3.35 a share) from $1.6 billion ($2.44 a share) in 1995. The growth was driven by 48% higher earnings at Smith Barney (thanks to strength in the securities markets); and by a 68% surge in property-casualty insurance profits (due to the April 1996 acquisition of Aetna Inc's. p-c business and the subsequent formation of TAP). Life insurance profits rose 23%, but consumer finance earnings were off 9.7% due to higher loan losses.

## Capitalization

**Long Term Debt:** $10,276,000,000 (9/96).
**Preferred Stock:** $675,000,000.

### Per Share Data ($)

| (Year Ended Dec. 31) | 1996 | 1995 | 1994 | 1993 | 1992 | 1991 | 1990 | 1989 | 1988 | 1987 |
|---|---|---|---|---|---|---|---|---|---|---|
| Tangible Bk. Val. | 14.90 | 12.25 | 9.22 | 9.73 | 5.74 | 4.31 | 3.20 | 2.80 | 2.25 | 3.83 |
| Earnings | 3.50 | 2.43 | 1.93 | 1.94 | 1.67 | 1.07 | 0.82 | 0.72 | 0.90 | 0.50 |
| Dividends | 0.45 | 0.40 | 0.29 | 0.24 | 0.18 | 0.11 | 0.09 | 0.07 | 0.07 | 0.06 |
| Payout Ratio | 13% | 16% | 15% | 13% | 11% | 10% | 11% | 10% | 7% | 12% |
| Prices - High | 47½ | 32 | 21⅝ | 24¾ | 12½ | 10 | 9½ | 7½ | 7¼ | 8⅝ |
| - Low | 28¼ | 16¼ | 15¼ | 12⅛ | 8⅞ | 5½ | 4¼ | 5⅛ | 5⅛ | 4¼ |
| P/E Ratio - High | 14 | 11 | 11 | 13 | 7 | 9 | 12 | 10 | 8 | 17 |
| - Low | 8 | 7 | 8 | 6 | 5 | 5 | 5 | 7 | 6 | 9 |

### Income Statement Analysis (Million $)

| | 1996 | 1995 | 1994 | 1993 | 1992 | 1991 | 1990 | 1989 | 1988 | 1987 |
|---|---|---|---|---|---|---|---|---|---|---|
| Premium Inc. | 7,633 | 4,977 | 7,590 | 1,480 | 1,694 | 1,783 | 1,922 | 1,816 | 307 | 335 |
| Invest. Inc. | 5,549 | 4,355 | 3,637 | 718 | 605 | 688 | 839 | 873 | 82.0 | 88.0 |
| Oth. Revs. | 8,163 | 7,251 | 7,238 | 4,599 | 2,826 | 4,138 | 3,433 | 3,007 | 614 | 490 |
| Total Revs. | 21,345 | 16,583 | 18,465 | 6,797 | 5,125 | 6,608 | 6,194 | 5,695 | 1,004 | 912 |
| Int. Exp. | 2,259 | 1,956 | 1,284 | 707 | 674 | 876 | 1,027 | 1,001 | 244 | 199 |
| Exp./Op. Revs. | 86% | 85% | 90% | 78% | 81% | 89% | 91% | 91% | 76% | 85% |
| Pretax Inc. | 3,398 | 2,521 | 2,149 | 1,523 | 1,188 | 791 | 602 | 513 | 238 | 141 |
| Eff. Tax Rate | 31% | 35% | 38% | 36% | 36% | 36% | 36% | 35% | 32% | 28% |
| Net Inc. | 2,300 | 1,628 | 1,326 | 951 | 756 | 479 | 373 | 289 | 162 | 102 |

### Balance Sheet & Other Fin. Data (Million $)

| | 1996 | 1995 | 1994 | 1993 | 1992 | 1991 | 1990 | 1989 | 1988 | 1987 |
|---|---|---|---|---|---|---|---|---|---|---|
| Receivables | 12,174 | 10,123 | 12,256 | 10,477 | 3,220 | 3,263 | Nil | Nil | Nil | NA |
| Cash & Invest. | 56,745 | 42,831 | 40,347 | 43,725 | 3,618 | 3,696 | 3,522 | 3,511 | 3,377 | 870 |
| Loans | 5,722 | 5,936 | 6,746 | 6,216 | 5,655 | 6,772 | 8,301 | 7,348 | 5,282 | 2,903 |
| Total Assets | 151,067 | 114,475 | 115,297 | 101,360 | 23,397 | 21,561 | 19,689 | 17,955 | 14,435 | 4,306 |
| Capitalization: | | | | | | | | | | |
| Debt | 12,884 | 10,658 | 9,555 | 9,526 | 6,584 | 8,044 | 7,022 | 6,276 | 6,357 | 3,024 |
| Equity | 12,460 | 10,910 | 7,840 | 8,526 | 3,929 | 3,280 | 2,859 | 2,603 | 1,947 | 646 |
| Total | 25,294 | 21,568 | 18,333 | 18,052 | 10,813 | 11,323 | 9,881 | 8,878 | 8,514 | 3,670 |
| Price Times Bk. Val.: High | 3.2 | 2.6 | 2.3 | 2.5 | 2.1 | 2.3 | 3.0 | 2.7 | 3.2 | 2.3 |
| Price Times Bk. Val.: Low | 1.9 | 1.3 | 1.6 | 1.2 | 1.5 | 1.3 | 1.3 | 1.8 | 2.3 | 1.1 |
| % Return On Revs. | 10.8 | 9.8 | 7.2 | 14.0 | 14.8 | 7.2 | 6.0 | 5.1 | 16.1 | 11.1 |
| % Ret. on Assets | 1.7 | 1.4 | 1.2 | 1.5 | 3.4 | 2.3 | 2.0 | 1.8 | 1.7 | 2.2 |
| % Ret. on Equity | 18.9 | 16.4 | 15.2 | 15.5 | 20.8 | 15.6 | 13.7 | 12.7 | 12.5 | 12.7 |
| Loans/Equity | 50.0 | 54.4 | 0.8 | 1.0 | 1.6 | 1.8 | 2.9 | 2.8 | 3.2 | 3.4 |

Data as orig. reptd.; bef. results of disc opers. and/or spec. items. Per share data adj. for stk. divs. as of ex-div. date. E-Estimated. NA-Not Available. NM-Not Meaningful. NR-Not Ranked.

**Offices**—388 Greenwich St., New York, NY. 10013.**Tel**—(212) 816-8000. **Chrmn & CEO**—S. I. Weill. **Vice Chrmn**—J. B. Lane, R. I. Lipp, J. J. Plumeri. **Pres & COO**—J. Dimon.**VP-CFO**—H. G. Miller.**VP-Secy**—C. O. Prince III. **Treas**—J. T. Fadden.**Investor Contact**—Bill Pike (212) 816-8874.**Dirs**—C. M. Armstrong, K. J. Bialkin, E. H. Budd, J. A. Califano Jr., D. D. Danforth, R. F. Daniell, J. Dimon, L. B. Disharoon, G. R. Ford, A. D. Jordan, R. I. Lipp, D. C. Mecum, A. E. Pearson, F. J. Tasco, L. J. Wachner, S. I. Weill, J. R.— Wright Jr., A. Zankel. **Transfer Agent & Registrar**—First National Bank of Boston. **Incorporated**—in Delaware in 1968.**Empl**— 47,600. **S&P Analyst:** Catherine A. Seifert

# STANDARD &POOR'S
STOCK REPORTS

# Tribune Co.

**2255L**

NYSE Symbol **TRB**

In S&P 500

**14-MAY-97**

**Industry:** Publishing (Newspapers)

**Summary:** Tribune is a leading information, entertainment and education company, with interests including newspaper publishing and radio and TV broadcasting.

| S&P Opinion: Accumulate (★★★★) | Recent Price • 43⅛ | Yield • 1.5% |
|---|---|---|
| | 52 Wk Range • 44½-31⅝ | 12-Mo. P/E • 18.9 |

**Earnings vs. Previous Year**
▲=Up ▼=Down ▶=No Change

**Quantitative Evaluations**

**Outlook** (1 Lowest—5 Highest)
• **3⁺**

**Fair Value**
• **45¼**

**Risk**
• **Low**

**Earn./Div. Rank**
• **B+**

**Technical Eval.**
• **Bearish** since 2/97

**Rel. Strength Rank** (1 Lowest—99 Highest)
• **72**

**Insider Activity**
• **Favorable**

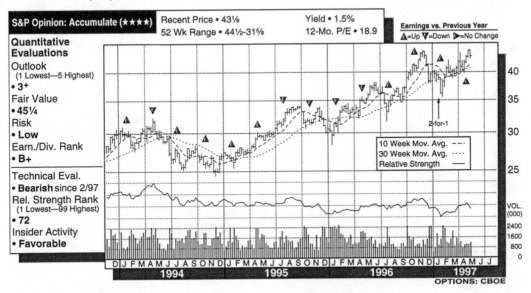

10 Week Mov. Avg. – – –
30 Week Mov. Avg. ·······
Relative Strength —

2-for-1

VOL. (000)

OPTIONS: CBOE

## Overview - 16-MAY-97

A sharp rise in consolidated revenues in 1997 will largely reflect the February 1997 acquisition of Renaissance Communications. A moderate increase in consolidated revenues from continuing publishing, broadcasting and entertainment operations is also seen for 1997. Operating margins will receive a strong boost from much lower newsprint costs on average. Profitability will also be aided by improved business conditions, cost controls and other factors, but capital spending will rise to about $135 million from $93.3 million in 1996. Despite expected continued startup and acquisition costs, education group operating profits should continue to grow. TRB expects the Renaissance acquisition to dilute earnings by roughly 10% in 1997. Equity earnings should improve, boosted by contributions from SoftKey and 33%-owned Qwest Broadcasting.

## Valuation - 16-MAY-97

The shares, at about 17X the $2.50 EPS we are projecting for 1997, are attractive for capital appreciation, based on the company's long-term record for building asset value and a positive long-term earnings outlook. A strategic partnership with SoftKey International is a major plus, opening the way for TRB to take greater advantage of opportunities in ohline multimedia than it could on a standalone basis. A healthy long-term outlook for advertising-supported media is another favorable factor. The acquisition of Renaissance Communications' six TV stations boosts TRB to the second largest television group in audience reach, with positive implications for revenue growth and profitability, notwithstanding initial dilution. TRB's low-risk commitment of its TV stations to the WB network provides a means to boost profitability and asset values. The stock's attractiveness is augmented by rising dividend income.

## Key Stock Statistics

| | | | |
|---|---|---|---|
| S&P EPS Est. 1997 | 2.50 | Tang. Bk. Value/Share | NM |
| P/E on S&P Est. 1997 | 17.3 | Beta | 0.66 |
| S&P EPS Est. 1998 | 2.95 | Shareholders | 5,200 |
| Dividend Rate/Share | 0.64 | Market cap. (B) | $ 5.4 |
| Shs. outstg. (M) | 122.7 | Inst. holdings | 40% |
| Avg. daily vol. (M) | 0.222 | | |

Value of $10,000 invested 5 years ago: $ 23,050

## Fiscal Year Ending Dec. 31

| | 1997 | 1996 | 1995 | 1994 | 1993 | 1992 |
|---|---|---|---|---|---|---|
| **Revenues (Million $)** | | | | | | |
| 1Q | 593.9 | 537.1 | 521.4 | 482.8 | 521.4 | 471.0 |
| 2Q | — | 641.9 | 577.2 | 573.8 | 577.2 | 557.0 |
| 3Q | — | 618.3 | 552.2 | 513.3 | 552.2 | 527.0 |
| 4Q | — | 608.3 | 593.8 | 591.1 | 513.8 | 553.0 |
| Yr. | — | 2,406 | 2,245 | 2,155 | 1,953 | 2,109 |
| **Earnings Per Share ($)** | | | | | | |
| 1Q | 0.49 | 0.37 | 0.44 | 0.26 | 0.44 | 0.08 |
| 2Q | E0.70 | 0.65 | 0.52 | 0.60 | 0.52 | 0.32 |
| 3Q | E0.60 | 0.50 | 0.31 | 0.32 | 0.31 | 0.23 |
| 4Q | E0.71 | 0.63 | 0.47 | 0.48 | 0.40 | 0.29 |
| Yr. | E2.50 | 2.15 | 1.75 | 1.66 | 1.28 | 0.91 |

**Next earnings report expected: mid July**

**Dividend Data** (Dividends have been paid since 1902.)

| Amount ($) | Date Decl. | Ex-Div. Date | Stock of Record | Payment Date |
|---|---|---|---|---|
| 0.300 | Oct. 22 | Nov. 26 | Nov. 29 | Dec. 12 '96 |
| 2-for-1 | Dec. 18 | Jan. 16 | Dec. 27 | Jan. 15 '97 |
| 0.160 | Feb. 18 | Feb. 27 | Mar. 03 | Mar. 13 '97 |
| 0.160 | May. 12 | May. 28 | May. 30 | Jun. 12 '97 |

This report is for information purposes and should not be considered a solicitation to buy or sell any security. Neither S&P nor any other party guarantee its accuracy or make warranties regarding results from its usage. Redistribution is prohibited without written permission. Copyright © 1997

A Division of The McGraw·Hill Companies

## Business Summary - 16-MAY-97

Tribune Company is a leading information, entertainment and education company with businesses in 12 of the nation's largest markets. Through newspapers, broadcasting, education and new media, the company reaches some 75% of U.S. households daily. One would expect stodginess from a company that has been around for over 150 years, but not Tribune Company. In recent years the company has aggressively expanded its size and scope, and significantly changed its business mix. Most recently, in February 1997, TRB acquired Renaissance Communications Corp., owner of six TV stations, for $1.13 billion in cash. During 1996, the company sold off its substantial interests in newsprint producer, QUNO Corp., acquired several education companies, and merged its Compton's unit into Softkey International.

TRB is the nation's second largest TV group broadcaster, whose 16 TV stations reach 33.4% of television households in the U.S. TV stations are located in New York City, Los Angeles, Chicago, Philadelphia, Dallas, Atlanta, Houston, Miami, Denver, Sacramento, Indianapolis, San Diego, Hartford, New Orleans, Harrisburg and Boston. Twelve stations are affiliated with The WB Network, in which TRB owns a minority interest, and the remaining four are Fox affiliates. TRB owns five radio stations: WGN-AM, Chicago; WQCD-FM, New York;

and KVOD-FM, KOSI-FM & KEZW-AM, Denver. The company has minority interests in Qwest Broadcasting LLC, and the TV Food Network. Tribune Entertainment develops, produces and syndicates first-run television programming, including such well-known programs as "The Geraldo Rivera Show" and "Soul Train." The company owns the Chicago Cubs Baseball team.

Tribune Publishing includes four daily newspapers: The Chicago Tribune, The Fort Lauderdale Sun-Sentinel, The Orlando Sentinel and the Newport News, VA, Daily Press.

The educational publishing division, formed in 1993, has grown rapidly to become the nation's leading publisher of supplemental education and core curriculum materials, and is a leader in providing multimedia products and services for the school and consumer markets. TRB has a 16% equity interest in SoftKey International, one of the world's largest publishers and distributors of multimedia software. TRB has a number of equity interests in emerging media businesses with emphasis on interactive services and Internet businesses. These include America Online, CheckFree Corporation, Open Market Inc., Digital City, Excite, Inc., The Learning Company, StarSight Telecast and others.

## Capitalization

**Long Term Debt:** $1,010,827,000 (12/96).

### Per Share Data ($)

| (Year Ended Dec. 31) | 1996 | 1995 | 1994 | 1993 | 1992 | 1991 | 1990 | 1989 | 1988 | 1987 |
|---|---|---|---|---|---|---|---|---|---|---|
| Tangible Bk. Val. | -1.62 | 0.53 | NM | NM | NM | NM | NM | NM | 1.17 | 0.44 |
| Cash Flow | 4.04 | 3.08 | 2.70 | 2.05 | 1.98 | 1.89 | 0.32 | 2.33 | 2.16 | 1.58 |
| Earnings | 2.15 | 1.75 | 1.66 | 1.28 | 0.91 | 0.97 | -0.61 | 1.58 | 1.39 | 0.90 |
| Dividends | 0.60 | 0.56 | 0.52 | 0.48 | 0.48 | 0.48 | 0.48 | 0.44 | 0.38 | 0.35 |
| Payout Ratio | 28% | 32% | 31% | 38% | 53% | 50% | NM | 26% | 27% | 38% |
| Prices - High | 44⅛ | 34½ | 32¼ | 30⅝ | 25⅜ | 24¼ | 24⅛ | 31⅝ | 21½ | 24⅞ |
|    - Low | 28⅜ | 25⅜ | 24½ | 24 | 19⅜ | 16⅝ | 15⅝ | 18¼ | 16⅞ | 14⅜ |
| P/E Ratio - High | 21 | 20 | 19 | 24 | 28 | 25 | NM | 20 | 15 | 28 |
|    - Low | 13 | 14 | 15 | 19 | 21 | 17 | NM | 11 | 12 | 16 |

### Income Statement Analysis (Million $)

| | 1996 | 1995 | 1994 | 1993 | 1992 | 1991 | 1990 | 1989 | 1988 | 1987 |
|---|---|---|---|---|---|---|---|---|---|---|
| Revs. | 2,406 | 2,245 | 2,155 | 1,953 | 2,096 | 2,035 | 2,353 | 2,455 | 2,335 | 2,160 |
| Oper. Inc. | 633 | 526 | 512 | 459 | 411 | 406 | 362 | 551 | 535 | 410 |
| Depr. | 143 | 121 | 115 | 103 | 140 | 119 | 124 | 108 | 117 | 107 |
| Int. Exp. | 47.8 | 21.8 | 20.6 | 25.8 | 52.7 | 65.1 | 62.3 | 61.5 | 67.6 | 56.6 |
| Pretax Inc. | 474 | 413 | 429 | 332 | 233 | 242 | -94.0 | 411 | 378 | 270 |
| Eff. Tax Rate | 40% | 41% | 44% | 43% | 41% | 41% | NM | 41% | 44% | 48% |
| Net Inc. | 283 | 245 | 242 | 189 | 137 | 142 | -64.0 | 242 | 210 | 142 |

### Balance Sheet & Other Fin. Data (Million $)

| | 1996 | 1995 | 1994 | 1993 | 1992 | 1991 | 1990 | 1989 | 1988 | 1987 |
|---|---|---|---|---|---|---|---|---|---|---|
| Cash | 274 | 22.9 | 21.8 | 18.5 | 16.8 | 17.0 | 13.6 | 27.7 | 15.1 | 34.7 |
| Curr. Assets | 887 | 546 | 544 | 491 | 574 | 589 | 618 | 657 | 646 | 609 |
| Total Assets | 3,701 | 3,288 | 2,786 | 2,536 | 2,752 | 2,795 | 2,826 | 3,051 | 2,942 | 2,758 |
| Curr. Liab. | 673 | 557 | 530 | 505 | 680 | 599 | 616 | 631 | 625 | 645 |
| LT Debt | 980 | 757 | 411 | 511 | 741 | 898 | 999 | 881 | 650 | 552 |
| Common Eqty. | 1,227 | 1,056 | 1,262 | 1,040 | 871 | 504 | 415 | 728 | 1,188 | 1,095 |
| Total Cap. | 2,397 | 2,361 | 1,894 | 1,695 | 1,720 | 1,920 | 1,962 | 2,194 | 2,045 | 1,818 |
| Cap. Exp. | 93.3 | 118 | 92.0 | 76.0 | 130 | 94.0 | 149 | 243 | 231 | 194 |
| Cash Flow | 496 | 399 | 339 | 273 | 258 | 244 | 43.0 | 338 | 327 | 249 |
| Curr. Ratio | 1.3 | 1.0 | 1.0 | 1.0 | 0.8 | 1.0 | 1.0 | 1.0 | 1.0 | 0.9 |
| % LT Debt of Cap. | 40.9 | 32.1 | 21.7 | 30.1 | 43.1 | 46.8 | 50.9 | 40.1 | 31.8 | 30.3 |
| % Net Inc.of Revs. | 11.8 | 11.0 | 11.2 | 9.7 | 6.5 | 7.0 | NM | 9.9 | 9.0 | 6.6 |
| % Ret. on Assets | 8.1 | 8.1 | 9.1 | 7.0 | 4.9 | 5.0 | NM | 8.4 | 7.5 | 5.4 |
| % Ret. on Equity | 23.2 | 18.4 | 19.5 | 17.6 | 13.9 | 27.1 | NM | 25.3 | 18.6 | 13.1 |

Data as orig. reptd.; bef. results of disc. opers. and/or spec. items. Per share data adj. for stk. divs. as of ex-div. date. E-Estimated. NA-Not Available. NM-Not Meaningful. NR-Not Ranked.

**Office**—435 N. Michigan Ave., Chicago, IL 60611. **Tel**—(312) 222-9100. **Website**—http://www.tribune.com **Chrmn, Pres & CEO**—J. W. Madigan. **Sr VP & CFO**—D. C. Grenesko. **VP & Secy**—C. H. Kenney. **VP & Treas**—D. J. Granat. **VP & Investor Contact**—Ruthellyn Musil (312) 222-3787. **Dirs**— J. C. Dowdle, D. E. Hernandez, R. E. LaBlanc, J. W. Madigan, N. H. Maynard, A. J. McKenna, K. Miller, J. J. O'Connor, D. H. Rumsfeld, D. S. Taft, A. R. Weber. **Transfer Agent & Registrar**—First Chicago Trust Co. of New York, Jersey City, NJ. **Incorporated**—in Illinois in 1861; reincorporated in Delaware in 1968. **Empl**— 10,500. **S&P Analyst:** William H. Donald

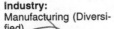

# Tyco International Ltd.          2262F

NYSE Symbol **TYC**

**In S&P 500**

**17-MAY-97**

**Industry:** Manufacturing (Diversified)

**Summary:** This leading manufacturer of fire protection systems also makes disposable medical products, flow control products, electrical and electronic components and packaging materials.

**S&P Opinion: Buy (★★★★)**

| Recent Price • 63¾ | Yield • 0.3% |
|---|---|
| 52 Wk Range • 65⅜-35½ | 12-Mo. P/E • 26.5 |

**Quantitative Evaluations**

**Outlook**
(1 Lowest—5 Highest)
• **3⁻**

**Fair Value**
• **62¾**

**Risk**
• **Low**

**Earn./Div. Rank**
• **B+**

**Technical Eval.**
• **Bullish** since 12/94

**Rel. Strength Rank**
(1 Lowest—99 Highest)
• **78**

**Insider Activity**
• **NA**

**Earnings vs. Previous Year**
▲=Up ▼=Down ▶=No Change

10 Week Mov. Avg. ---
30 Week Mov. Avg. ······
Relative Strength —

OPTIONS: Ph

## Overview - 30-APR-97

Solid sales growth should continue through FY 98 (Jun.), with gains expected in all operating segments. Sales should be driven by a strong internal growth agenda, a program of complementary acquisitions, and favorable global economies. Operating margins are likely to be flat, as a better sales mix, efficiencies derived through TYC's extensive capital investment program, and reduced overhead costs are offset by narrower margins typical of newly acquired units before full integration. Particular gains are likely in the fire and safety services area, where TYC should be aided by a continuing shift in service mix toward more profitable service and inspection and retrofit jobs; and the flow control segment, which should be boosted by recent acquisitions. The pending acquisitions of ADT Ltd. and AT&T's submarine systems business are not included in our estimates, but TYC's strategy is to acquire only companies that are immediately accretive to earnings; the ADT merger is seen adding about $0.30 to FY 98 EPS, while the AT&T unit should add $0.10 (if both are completed by FY 97 year-end, as TYC expects).

## Valuation - 30-APR-97

The shares have been in an uptrend since late 1994, driven by Tyco's favorable earnings reports and prospects, and investor excitement about TYC's savvy acquisition program. Given our enthusiasm for TYC's operating strategy and business sectors, we expect solid profit growth to continue through FY 98, and anticipate continued appreciation for the stock. The shares should also get a boost from the likely conclusion of the pending acquisitions of ADT Ltd. and the submarine systems business of AT&T, which appear to be natural fits with certain Tyco businesses, although Western Resources, a previously rebuffed hostile bidder for ADT, has taken legal action to stop the ADT transaction.

## Key Stock Statistics

| | | | |
|---|---|---|---|
| S&P EPS Est. 1997 | 2.55 | Tang. Bk. Value/Share | 4.61 |
| P/E on S&P Est. 1997 | 25.0 | Beta | 0.98 |
| S&P EPS Est. 1998 | 3.05 | Shareholders | 7,700 |
| Dividend Rate/Share | 0.20 | Market cap. (B) | $ 10.6 |
| Shs. outstg. (M) | 166.7 | Inst. holdings | 78% |
| Avg. daily vol. (M) | 0.698 | | |

Value of $10,000 invested 5 years ago: $ 38,439

### Fiscal Year Ending Jun. 30

| | 1998 | 1997 | 1996 | 1995 | 1994 | 1993 |
|---|---|---|---|---|---|---|
| **Revenues (Million $)** | | | | | | |
| 1Q | — | 1,479 | 1,216 | 1,054 | 790.0 | 809.0 |
| 2Q | — | 1,613 | 1,244 | 1,098 | 802.9 | 765.2 |
| 3Q | — | 1,654 | 1,258 | 1,135 | 809.9 | 744.2 |
| 4Q | — | — | 1,372 | 1,248 | 860.1 | 796.4 |
| Yr. | — | — | 5,090 | 4,535 | 3,263 | 3,115 |
| **Earnings Per Share ($)** | | | | | | |
| 1Q | — | 0.54 | 0.43 | 0.36 | 0.30 | 0.26 |
| 2Q | — | 0.58 | 0.46 | 0.17 | 0.32 | 0.29 |
| 3Q | — | 0.67 | 0.52 | 0.43 | 0.35 | 0.29 |
| 4Q | — | E0.76 | 0.62 | 0.47 | 0.38 | -0.05 |
| Yr. | E3.05 | E2.55 | 2.03 | 1.43 | 1.35 | 0.79 |

**Next earnings report expected: late July**

### Dividend Data (Dividends have been paid since 1975.)

| Amount ($) | Date Decl. | Ex-Div. Date | Stock of Record | Payment Date |
|---|---|---|---|---|
| 0.050 | Jun. 13 | Jul. 02 | Jul. 05 | Aug. 01 '96 |
| 0.050 | Sep. 12 | Oct. 02 | Oct. 04 | Nov. 01 '96 |
| 0.050 | Dec. 12 | Dec. 30 | Jan. 02 | Feb. 03 '97 |
| 0.050 | Mar. 13 | Apr. 01 | Apr. 03 | May. 01 '97 |

This report is for information purposes and should not be considered a solicitation to buy or sell any security. Neither S&P nor any other party guarantee its accuracy or make warranties regarding results from its usage. Redistribution is prohibited without written permission. Copyright © 1997

*A Division of The* **McGraw-Hill** *Companies*

STANDARD
&POOR'S
STOCK REPORTS

# Tyco International Ltd.

## 2262F
### 17-MAY-97

## Business Summary - 30-APR-97

Tyco International Ltd. (formerly Tyco Laboratories) is the world's largest manufacturer and installer of fire protection systems, and a leading producer of disposable medical products, packaging materials, flow control products and electrical and electronic components. Industry segment contributions in FY 96 (Jun.) were:

|  | Sales | Pretax Profits |
|---|---|---|
| Fire & safety services | 39% | 21% |
| Flow control products | 23% | 18% |
| Electrical & electronic components | 9% | 14% |
| Disposable & specialty products | 29% | 47% |

Operations outside North America accounted for 28% of sales and 11% of operating income in FY 96.

The company is the world's largest fire protection contractor. It designs, fabricates, installs and services automatic sprinkler, fire alarm and detection and fire suppression systems in buildings and other installations.

Flow control products consist of pipe, fittings, valves, meters and related products, which are used to transport, control and measure the flow of liquids and gases.

The electrical and electronic components segment makes underwater communications cable, cable assemblies, printed circuit boards, electrical conduit and related components. It also assembles backplanes for the electronics industry.

The disposable and specialty products segment produces medical supplies, adhesive products and tapes, disposable medical products, laminated and coated products, extrusion coated polyester yarns and woven fabrics, polyethylene film and film products, and specialty packaging materials and garment hangers. Disposable medical products operations were significantly expanded by the October 1994 acquisition of Kendall International (for $1.4 billion in stock).

## Important Developments

**Apr. '97**—Tyco agreed to acquire AT&T's submarine systems business (annual revenues of $1 billion), which makes, installs and maintains undersea fiber optic telecommunication cable systems, for $850 million.

**Mar. '97**—TYC reached an agreement to merge with ADT Ltd. through a complex stock swap valued at $5.6 billion. ADT is a leading installer and servicer of electronic security systems, with annual revenues of about $1.7 billion. Although TYC will effectively acquire ADT, the agreement is structured for legal purposes as a reverse merger, with ADT taking over TYC and renaming itself Tyco, to preserve ADT's reduced tax rate as an offshore company. Under the agreement, TYC shareholders would receive one share of the combined company for each share held, while ADT holders would receive 0.48133 of a share for each ADT share. The transaction would be taxable for TYC holders.

**Feb. '97**—TYC sold publicly 10 million common shares at $57.75 each.

## Capitalization

**Long Term Debt:** $893,665,000 (12/96).

### Per Share Data ($)

| (Year Ended Jun. 30) | 1996 | 1995 | 1994 | 1993 | 1992 | 1991 | 1990 | 1989 | 1988 | 1987 |
|---|---|---|---|---|---|---|---|---|---|---|
| Tangible Bk. Val. | 4.61 | 4.15 | 2.32 | 0.94 | 1.22 | 0.49 | 2.91 | 1.49 | 2.80 | 3.04 |
| Cash Flow | 2.57 | 2.32 | 2.07 | 1.48 | 1.74 | 1.99 | NA | 1.98 | 1.67 | 1.45 |
| Earnings | 2.03 | 1.43 | 1.35 | 0.79 | 1.03 | 1.29 | 1.45 | 1.15 | 0.96 | 0.63 |
| Dividends | 0.20 | 0.20 | 0.25 | 0.15 | 0.22 | 0.17 | 0.15 | 0.17 | 0.12 | 0.10 |
| Payout Ratio | 10% | 14% | 19% | 19% | 22% | 14% | 11% | 15% | 12% | 16% |
| Prices - High | 56 | 35⅝ | 27⅝ | 25⅞ | 21¼ | 26⅛ | 32⅞ | 26⅞ | 19¼ | 14⅛ |
|     - Low | 32⅜ | 23¼ | 21½ | 18¾ | 15⅜ | 4 | 18⅜ | 16⅛ | 10½ | 7⅞ |
| P/E Ratio - High | 28 | 18 | 20 | 33 | 21 | 20 | 23 | 23 | 20 | 22 |
|     - Low | 16 | 11 | 16 | 24 | 15 | 11 | 13 | 14 | 11 | 12 |

### Income Statement Analysis (Million $)

|  | 1996 | 1995 | 1994 | 1993 | 1992 | 1991 | 1990 | 1989 | 1988 | 1987 |
|---|---|---|---|---|---|---|---|---|---|---|
| Revs. | 5,090 | 4,535 | 3,263 | 3,115 | 3,066 | 3,108 | 2,103 | 1,971 | 1,575 | 1,062 |
| Oper. Inc. | 666 | 618 | 312 | 282 | 261 | 328 | 287 | 234 | 168 | 116 |
| Depr. | 83.0 | 133 | 66.2 | 63.1 | 66.5 | 64.8 | 43.7 | 40.6 | 33.2 | 28.8 |
| Int. Exp. | 62.0 | 63.0 | 45.0 | 50.5 | 63.3 | 73.9 | 41.3 | 45.0 | 25.8 | 11.3 |
| Pretax Inc. | 524 | 385 | 201 | 129 | 131 | 189 | 202 | 146 | 105 | 77.0 |
| Eff. Tax Rate | 41% | 44% | 38% | 44% | 28% | 38% | 41% | 38% | 37% | 43% |
| Net Inc. | 310 | 217 | 125 | 72.0 | 95.0 | 117 | 119 | 91.0 | 66.0 | 44.0 |

### Balance Sheet & Other Fin. Data (Million $)

|  | 1996 | 1995 | 1994 | 1993 | 1992 | 1991 | 1990 | 1989 | 1988 | 1987 |
|---|---|---|---|---|---|---|---|---|---|---|
| Cash | 69.4 | 66.0 | 6.2 | 32.9 | 32.1 | 22.7 | 15.8 | 9.9 | 7.4 | 3.7 |
| Curr. Assets | 1,696 | 1,452 | 1,048 | 1,133 | 1,107 | 1,098 | 732 | 728 | 605 | 399 |
| Total Assets | 3,954 | 3,381 | 2,416 | 2,459 | 2,452 | 2,393 | 1,417 | 1,399 | 941 | 594 |
| Curr. Liab. | 1,292 | 1,085 | 811 | 869 | 833 | 855 | 513 | 436 | 302 | 205 |
| LT Debt | 512 | 506 | 413 | 562 | 535 | 609 | 270 | 445 | 324 | 138 |
| Common Eqty. | 1,938 | 1,635 | 1,079 | 920 | 1,041 | 905 | 607 | 491 | 293 | 235 |
| Total Cap. | 2,469 | 2,151 | 1,506 | 1,490 | 1,602 | 1,538 | 904 | 963 | 640 | 390 |
| Cap. Exp. | 123 | 119 | 73.0 | 80.0 | 68.0 | 67.0 | 55.0 | 121 | 110 | 45.0 |
| Cash Flow | 393 | 350 | 191 | 135 | 162 | 182 | NA | NA | 132 | 100 |
| Curr. Ratio | 1.3 | 1.3 | 1.3 | 1.3 | 1.3 | 1.3 | 1.4 | 1.7 | 2.0 | 1.9 |
| % LT Debt of Cap. | 20.7 | 23.5 | 27.4 | 37.7 | 33.4 | 39.6 | 29.8 | 46.2 | 50.7 | 35.5 |
| % Net Inc.of Revs. | 6.1 | 4.8 | 3.8 | 2.3 | 3.1 | 3.8 | 5.7 | 4.6 | 4.2 | 4.2 |
| % Ret. on Assets | 8.5 | 6.6 | 5.1 | 3.0 | 3.9 | NA | 8.5 | 7.3 | 8.7 | 7.4 |
| % Ret. on Equity | 17.4 | 14.4 | 12.5 | 7.4 | 9.8 | NA | 21.7 | 21.9 | 25.3 | 19.8 |

Data as orig. reptd.; bef. results of disc. opers. and/or spec. items. Per share data adj. for stk. divs. as of ex-div. date. E-Estimated. NA-Not Available. NM-Not Meaningful. NR-Not Ranked.

**Office**—One Tyco Park, Exeter, NH 03833. **Tel**—(603) 778-9700. **Website**—http://www.tycoint.com **Chrmn, Pres & CEO**—L. D. Kozlowski. **VP & CFO**—M. H. Swartz. **Secy**—J. M. Berman. **SVP & Investor Contact**—David P. Brownell. **Dirs**—J. M. Berman, R. S. Bodman, J. F. Fort, S. W. Foss, R. A. Gilleland, P. M. Hampton, L. D. Kozlowski, F. E. Walsh, Jr. **Transfer Agent & Registrar**—ChaseMellon Shareholder Services, Ridgefield Park, NJ. **Incorporated**—in Massachusetts in 1962. **Empl**— 40,000. **S&P Analyst:** Michael W. Jaffe

# Vesta Insurance Group

## 2390R

NYSE Symbol **VTA**

**17-MAY-97**

**Industry:** Insurance (Property-Casualty)

**Summary:** Vesta is the holding company for a group of property and casualty insurance companies that offer reinsurance and primary insurance for personal and commercial risks.

## Quantitative Evaluations

**Outlook** (1 Lowest—5 Highest)
- **NA**

**Fair Value**
- **NA**

**Risk**
- **Average**

**Earn./Div. Rank**
- **NR**

**Technical Eval.**
- **Bullish** since 11/96

**Rel. Strength Rank** (1 Lowest—99 Highest)
- **84**

**Insider Activity**
- **Neutral**

| Recent Price • 42⅜ | Yield • 0.4% |
|---|---|
| 52 Wk Range • 46-24½ | 12-Mo. P/E • 15.2 |

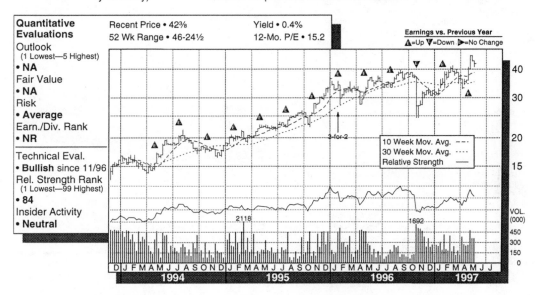

Earnings vs. Previous Year
▲=Up ▼=Down ▶=No Change

10 Week Mov. Avg. - - -
30 Week Mov. Avg. ·····
Relative Strength ——

VOL. (000)

## Business Profile - 12-MAY-97

Torchmark holds about 27% of the shares of this former subsidiary, a holding company for a property and casualty group that offers treaty reinsurance and primary insurance. On April 24, 1997, the company agreed to acquire the operating subsidiaries of Anthem Casualty Insurance Group, Inc., a Shelby, Ohio-based insurance holding company, for $238.8 million in cash. Anthem's operating subsidiaries are regional property/casualty insurers with approximately $275 million in annualized premium and GAAP equity of some $214 million.

## Operational Review - 12-MAY-97

Based on a brief report, net premiums earned in the three months ended March 31, 1997, declined 13%, year to year, reflecting the absence of the whole account quota share entered into in the third quarter of 1996. Total revenues slid 12%. Vesta's GAAP combined ratio was 86.7%, versus 90.9% a year earlier, as lower underwriting expense ratios more than offset higher loss and loss expense ratios. Net income climbed 20%, to $12.6 million ($0.68 a share), from $10.5 million ($0.56).

## Stock Performance - 16-MAY-97

In the past 30 trading days, VTA's shares have increased 28%, compared to a 9% rise in the S&P 500. Average trading volume for the past five days was 70,760 shares, compared with the 40-day moving average of 68,005 shares.

## Key Stock Statistics

| | | | |
|---|---|---|---|
| Dividend Rate/Share | 0.15 | Shareholders | 100 |
| Shs. outstg. (M) | 18.6 | Market cap. (B) | $0.787 |
| Avg. daily vol. (M) | 0.083 | Inst. holdings | 85% |
| Tang. Bk. Value/Share | 16.73 | | |
| Beta | NA | | |

Value of $10,000 invested 5 years ago: NA

### Fiscal Year Ending Dec. 31

| | 1997 | 1996 | 1995 | 1994 | 1993 | 1992 |
|---|---|---|---|---|---|---|
| **Revenues (Million $)** | | | | | | |
| 1Q | 132.1 | 150.1 | 79.80 | 59.80 | — | — |
| 2Q | — | 173.2 | 82.77 | 61.30 | — | — |
| 3Q | — | 94.51 | 130.5 | 74.55 | — | — |
| 4Q | — | 117.4 | 107.2 | 76.70 | — | — |
| Yr. | — | 535.3 | 400.3 | 272.4 | 153.1 | 106.8 |
| **Earnings Per Share ($)** | | | | | | |
| 1Q | 0.68 | 0.56 | 0.41 | 0.34 | 0.17 | -- |
| 2Q | — | 0.80 | 0.62 | 0.43 | 0.26 | -- |
| 3Q | — | 0.71 | 0.84 | 0.43 | 0.26 | — |
| 4Q | — | 0.60 | 0.40 | 0.35 | 0.21 | — |
| Yr. | — | 2.66 | 2.27 | 1.55 | 0.91 | 0.67 |

**Next earnings report expected: late July**

**Dividend Data** (Dividends have been paid since 1994.)

| Amount ($) | Date Decl. | Ex-Div. Date | Stock of Record | Payment Date |
|---|---|---|---|---|
| 0.038 | May. 21 | Jul. 11 | Jul. 15 | Aug. 01 '96 |
| 0.038 | Jul. 23 | Sep. 11 | Sep. 15 | Oct. 01 '96 |
| 0.038 | Nov. 01 | Jan. 13 | Jan. 15 | Jan. 31 '97 |
| 0.038 | Mar. 10 | Apr. 11 | Apr. 15 | Apr. 30 '97 |

This report is for information purposes and should not be considered a solicitation to buy or sell any security. Neither S&P nor any other party guarantee its accuracy or make warranties regarding results from its usage. Redistribution is prohibited without written permission. Copyright © 1997

*A Division of The McGraw-Hill Companies*

STANDARD
&POOR'S
STOCK REPORTS

# Vesta Insurance Group, Inc.

## 2390R
### 17-MAY-97

## Business Summary - 12-MAY-97

Vesta Insurance Group is an insurance holding company, formed in 1993, that owns all of the property and casualty insurance companies constituting the Vesta Group, including Vesta Fire Insurance Corp., its principal subsidiary. It offers treaty reinsurance and primary insurance on selected personal and commercial risks. In both reinsurance and primary insurance operations, the company focuses primarily on property coverages. Gross premiums written in 1996 totaled $769.6 million: 80% reinsurance and 20% primary insurance.

The company provides treaty reinsurance, principally through reinsurance intermediaries, primarily to small and medium-sized regional insurance companies located mainly in the Southwest, Midwest and Northeast. Vesta derived 90% of gross reinsurance premiums written in 1996 from the reinsurance of personal and commercial property risks. Principal lines of business reinsured include homeowner and commercial property coverages, non-standard automobile insurance, and collateral protection insurance.

Primary insurance includes homeowner insurance products, specialty commercial transportation products, commercial business coverages, and certain financial services products designed to protect the interests of financial institutions in real and personal property collateral. Primary insurance products are distributed through independent agents, except for certain personal lines products, which are distributed through a unit of Torchmark Corp., and financial services products.

Vesta focuses primarily on property coverages in all of its lines of business, while adjusting the mix and volume of its writings and retentions to respond to changes in market prices and to manage risk exposures. The company has used a substantial portion of additional capital to increase sales of property catastrophe reinsurance, the pricing of which has improved in recent years, and to increase writings of homeowners insurance.

In June 1995, the company acquired Hawaiian Insurance & Guaranty Co., Ltd. (HIG) for $35 million in cash. HIG, with about $65 million of total assets, writes personal lines of business in Hawaii, focusing on homeowners insurance.

In November 1996, Vesta announced a stock repurchase program of up to 2,000,000 of its common shares in the open market or in privately negotiated transactions. As of December 31, 1996, the company had repurchased a total of 375,000 shares under the program for an aggregate purchase price of $10.2 million.

## Capitalization

**Long Term Debt:** $98,268,000 (9/96).

### Per Share Data ($)

| (Year Ended Dec. 31) | 1996 | 1995 | 1994 | 1993 | 1992 | 1991 | 1990 | 1989 | 1988 | 1987 |
|---|---|---|---|---|---|---|---|---|---|---|
| Tangible Bk. Val. | 16.79 | 14.51 | 12.41 | 11.13 | 10.83 | NA | NA | NA | NA | NA |
| Oper. Earnings | NA | NA | NA | NA | NA | NA | NA | NA | NA | NA |
| Earnings | 2.66 | 2.27 | 1.55 | 0.91 | 0.67 | 0.54 | 0.44 | 0.42 | 0.45 | NA |
| Dividends | 0.15 | 0.13 | 0.10 | Nil | NA | NA | NA | NA | NA | NA |
| Payout Ratio | 6% | 6% | 6% | Nil | NA | NA | NA | NA | NA | NA |
| Prices - High | 39¾ | 37 | 21¾ | 16¾ | NA | NA | NA | NA | NA | NA |
| - Low | 24½ | 18⅜ | 13⅞ | 13⅛ | NA | NA | NA | NA | NA | NA |
| P/E Ratio - High | 15 | 16 | 14 | 18 | NA | NA | NA | NA | NA | NA |
| - Low | 9 | 8 | 9 | 14 | NA | NA | NA | NA | NA | NA |

### Income Statement Analysis (Million $)

| | 1996 | 1995 | 1994 | 1993 | 1992 | 1991 | 1990 | 1989 | 1988 | 1987 |
|---|---|---|---|---|---|---|---|---|---|---|
| Premium Inc. | 512 | 382 | 260 | 144 | 98.4 | 60.7 | 56.6 | 60.6 | 58.4 | NA |
| Net Invest. Inc. | 23.0 | 18.0 | 13.0 | 8.9 | 7.4 | 7.9 | 8.2 | 7.8 | 7.0 | NA |
| Oth. Revs. | 0.2 | 0.5 | 0.6 | 0.4 | 1.1 | 1.3 | 0.4 | 0.3 | 1.0 | NA |
| Total Revs. | 535 | 400 | 272 | 153 | 107 | 70.0 | 65.0 | 69.0 | 66.0 | NA |
| Pretax Inc. | 75.2 | 63.8 | 42.1 | 19.5 | 12.1 | 9.7 | 8.3 | 7.7 | 7.5 | NA |
| Net Oper. Inc. | NA | NA | NA | NA | NA | NA | NA | NA | NA | NA |
| Net Inc. | 50.2 | 42.7 | 29.2 | 12.9 | 8.3 | 6.7 | 5.5 | 5.3 | 5.5 | NA |

### Balance Sheet & Other Fin. Data (Million $)

| | 1996 | 1995 | 1994 | 1993 | 1992 | 1991 | 1990 | 1989 | 1988 | 1987 |
|---|---|---|---|---|---|---|---|---|---|---|
| Cash & Equiv. | 10.0 | 12.4 | 25.5 | 7.0 | NA | NA | NA | NA | NA | NA |
| Premiums Due | 259 | 185 | 69.4 | 44.6 | 103 | NA | NA | NA | NA | NA |
| Invest. Assets: Bonds | 415 | 412 | 277 | 244 | NA | NA | NA | NA | NA | NA |
| Invest. Assets: Stocks | 8.3 | 3.2 | 2.0 | 2.1 | NA | NA | NA | NA | NA | NA |
| Invest. Assets: Loans | Nil | Nil | Nil | Nil | NA | NA | NA | NA | NA | NA |
| Invest. Assets: Total | 423 | 416 | 279 | 247 | 243 | NA | NA | NA | NA | NA |
| Deferred Policy Costs | 75.5 | 67.8 | 32.8 | 27.6 | 27.0 | NA | NA | NA | NA | NA |
| Total Assets | 1,014 | 818 | 510 | 406 | 403 | NA | NA | NA | NA | NA |
| Debt | 98.3 | 98.2 | 28.0 | 28.0 | 28.0 | NA | NA | NA | NA | NA |
| Common Eqty. | 319 | 281 | 234 | 209 | 203 | NA | NA | NA | NA | NA |
| Prop. & Cas. Loss Ratio | 57.9 | 57.2 | 54.0 | 51.7 | 52.6 | 51.4 | 51.2 | 55.0 | 51.7 | NA |
| Prop. & Cas. Expense Ratio | 31.8 | 33.4 | 35.4 | 40.1 | 45.0 | 46.6 | 48.1 | 44.1 | 46.4 | NA |
| Prop. & Cas. Combined Ratio | 89.7 | 90.6 | 89.4 | 98.1 | 97.6 | 98.0 | 99.3 | 99.1 | 98.1 | NA |
| % Return On Revs. | 9.4 | 10.7 | 10.7 | 8.5 | 7.7 | 9.6 | 8.4 | 7.6 | 8.3 | NA |
| % Ret. on Equity | 16.8 | 16.6 | 13.2 | 6.3 | NA | NA | NA | NA | NA | NA |

Data as orig. reptd.; bef. results of disc. opers. and/or spec. items. Per share data adj. for stk. divs. as of ex-div. date. Bal. Sheet data in 1992 is as of Sep. 30, 1993, pro forma. P-c ratios are as reported by co. E-Estimated. NA-Not Available. NM-Not Meaningful. NR-Not Ranked.

**Office**—3760 River Run Drive, Birmingham, AL 35243. **Tel**—(205) 970-7000. **Chrmn**—R. K. Richey. **Pres & CEO**—R. Y. Huffman. **SVP & Treas &**—Stephen P. Leonard. **VP, CFO & Investor Contact**—B. R. Meredith. **Dirs**—W. M. Beale Jr., E. A. Camp III, R. A. Hershbarger, R. Y. Huffman, C. F. Palmer, J. W. Palmer, R. K. Richey, N. L. Rosenthal, K. A. Tucker. **Transfer Agent & Registrar**—First Chicago Trust Co. of New York, Jersey City, NJ. **Incorporated**—in Delaware in 1993. **Empl**—220. **S&P Analyst:** M.C.C.

# Viking Office Products  5557

Nasdaq Symbol **VKNG**

In S&P MidCap 400

**17-MAY-97**  Industry:
Retail (Specialty)

**Summary:** This company sells a wide variety of office products to small and medium-size businesses through direct marketing catalogs and programs.

| S&P Opinion: Accumulate (★★★★) | Recent Price • 16⅝ | Yield • Nil |
| --- | --- | --- |
| | 52 Wk Range • 34-13½ | 12-Mo. P/E • 20.5 |

**Quantitative Evaluations**

Outlook
(1 Lowest—5 Highest)
• **4⁻**

Fair Value
• **18⅛**

Risk
• **Average**

Earn./Div. Rank
• **NR**

Technical Eval.
• **Bearish** since 1/97

Rel. Strength Rank
(1 Lowest—99 Highest)
• **12**

Insider Activity
• **Neutral**

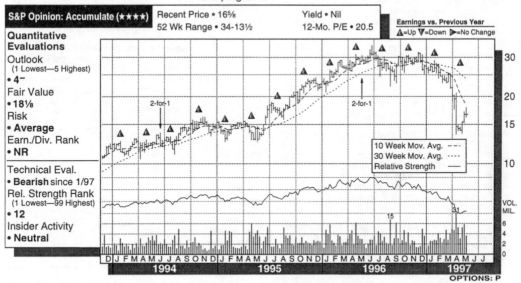

Earnings vs. Previous Year
▲=Up ▼=Down ▶=No Change

10 Week Mov. Avg. − − −
30 Week Mov. Avg. ......
Relative Strength ——

OPTIONS: P

## Overview - 30-APR-97

Revenues are expected to rise about 20% to 25% in FY 98 (Jun.), reflecting a larger customer base, aided by more catalogs mailed, an increase in the average revenue per customer, and the company's expansion efforts in the European market. Viking has built its reputation on providing high-quality service, which has enabled it to achieve a high level of repeat customers. Growth in the U.S. slowed in FY 97, reflecting lower paper prices, but paper comparisons will be more favorable as FY 98 progresses. Margins will likely remain under pressure in the near-term, due to start-up costs for new countries, unfavorable currency translation effects and the weaker paper pricing. Long-term prospects are favorable, reflecting further expansion opportunities in Europe and strong growth seen for the small and medium-size business markets.

## Valuation - 30-APR-97

The shares plunged in early April 1997 following VKNG's announcement that its FY 97 (Jun.) third quarter revenues rose by a weaker than expected 15%, year to year, due to slower growth in the United Kingdom and France, a stronger dollar, and sharply lower paper prices. As a result, we cut our EPS estimates for FY 97 and FY 98 to $0.82 and $1.00, respectively, from $0.90 and $1.15. However, Viking's fundamentals remain solid, and we believe the company can achieve EPS growth of over 20% in FY 98, helped by strong gains seen for the European market, especially in Germany, which has reached profitability. The shares are trading at a below average P/E multiple following the recent weakness in the stock, and we recommend accumulating the shares based on the above average earnings growth expected over the next few years. The company's significant presence in Europe is a long-term plus, as the U.S. market is becoming more competitive.

## Key Stock Statistics

| | | | |
| --- | --- | --- | --- |
| S&P EPS Est. 1997 | 0.82 | Tang. Bk. Value/Share | 2.97 |
| P/E on S&P Est. 1997 | 20.3 | Beta | 0.49 |
| S&P EPS Est. 1998 | 1.00 | Shareholders | 1,100 |
| Dividend Rate/Share | Nil | Market cap. (B) | $ 1.4 |
| Shs. outstg. (M) | 83.8 | Inst. holdings | 81% |
| Avg. daily vol. (M) | 0.865 | | |

Value of $10,000 invested 5 years ago: $ 38,550

### Fiscal Year Ending Jun. 30

| | 1998 | 1997 | 1996 | 1995 | 1994 | 1993 |
| --- | --- | --- | --- | --- | --- | --- |
| **Revenues (Million $)** | | | | | | |
| 1Q | — | 290.5 | 230.0 | 182.4 | 129.8 | 109.2 |
| 2Q | — | 316.5 | 250.4 | 189.2 | 133.1 | 106.3 |
| 3Q | — | 353.1 | 306.8 | 232.1 | 162.6 | 125.0 |
| 4Q | — | — | 268.5 | 208.2 | 139.5 | 109.1 |
| Yr. | — | — | 1,056 | 811.9 | 565.1 | 449.7 |
| **Earnings Per Share ($)** | | | | | | |
| 1Q | — | 0.19 | 0.15 | 0.12 | 0.08 | 0.04 |
| 2Q | — | 0.19 | 0.15 | 0.11 | 0.08 | 0.03 |
| 3Q | — | 0.24 | 0.21 | 0.17 | 0.13 | 0.08 |
| 4Q | — | E0.20 | 0.19 | 0.14 | 0.09 | 0.07 |
| Yr. | E1.00 | E0.82 | 0.70 | 0.54 | 0.38 | 0.21 |

Next earnings report expected: mid August

### Dividend Data

| Amount ($) | Date Decl. | Ex-Div. Date | Stock of Record | Payment Date |
| --- | --- | --- | --- | --- |
| 2-for-1 | Apr. 11 | May. 16 | May. 01 | May. 15 '96 |

This report is for information purposes and should not be considered a solicitation to buy or sell any security. Neither S&P nor any other party guarantee its accuracy or make warranties regarding results from its usage. Redistribution is prohibited without written permission. Copyright © 1997

A Division of The McGraw-Hill Companies

## Business Summary - 30-APR-97

Viking Office Products, Inc. sells office products to small and medium-size businesses through the use of direct marketing catalogs and database marketing programs. The company is one of the largest direct marketers of office products to small and medium-size businesses. Sales contributions by product group in recent fiscal years (Jun.) were:

|  | FY 96 | FY 95 | FY 94 |
|---|---|---|---|
| General office supplies & machines | 75% | 73% | 74% |
| Computer supplies | 17% | 16% | 15% |
| Business furniture | 8% | 11% | 11% |

Business in Europe and Australia accounted for 59% of total revenues in FY 96, versus 56% in FY 95.

During FY 96, the company mailed about 155.2 million catalogs (including 81.3 million to existing customers), up from 140.7 million (74.1 million) in FY 95. Viking had 1.9 million active customers (those who made at least one purchase during the past 12 months) in FY 96, compared with 1.2 million the year before.

Viking operates 10 distribution centers in the U.S., nine centers in Europe, and two centers in Australia. VKNG plans to open one additional center in Europe in calendar 1997.

Target customers are businesses with fewer than 100 office employees. The traditional source of office products for these businesses has been small retail dealers that purchase products from wholesalers in limited quantities for resale at or near manufacturers' list prices. In recent years, small and medium-size businesses have increased their purchases of office products from alternative distribution channels such as office product superstores, direct marketing companies, mass merchandisers and warehouse clubs. The entry of superstores into the office products market has raised customer price awareness and has resulted in increased price competition.

Viking offers a selection of more than 10,000 office products, including general office supplies, computer supplies, paper products, office furniture, selected business machines, janitorial and safety supplies and presentation supplies. Company strategy emphasizes frequent mailings of a variety of full-color catalogs, customer service, prompt order fulfillment and discounted prices. Viking believes that the majority of its sales is made in a range of 30% to 50% below manufacturers' suggested list prices.

### Important Developments

**Apr. '97**—The company reported that its revenues in the third quarter of FY 97 increased by a slower than anticipated 15%, year to year. The weaker growth was attributed to fewer billing days, slower growth in the United Kingdom and France, a stronger translated dollar, and paper pricing that was about 30% lower than a year earlier.

### Capitalization

**Long Term Debt:** None (3/97).

| Per Share Data ($) (Year Ended Jun. 30) | 1996 | 1995 | 1994 | 1993 | 1992 | 1991 | 1990 | 1989 | 1988 | 1987 |
|---|---|---|---|---|---|---|---|---|---|---|
| Tangible Bk. Val. | 2.97 | 2.19 | 1.48 | 1.02 | 0.79 | 0.29 | 0.18 | -0.42 | NA | NA |
| Cash Flow | 0.86 | 0.63 | 0.44 | 0.26 | 0.21 | 0.15 | 0.16 | 0.13 | NA | NA |
| Earnings | 0.70 | 0.54 | 0.38 | 0.21 | 0.17 | 0.11 | 0.11 | 0.09 | NA | NA |
| Dividends | Nil | Nil | Nil | Nil | Nil | Nil | Nil | Nil | NA | NA |
| Payout Ratio | Nil | Nil | Nil | Nil | Nil | Nil | Nil | Nil | NA | NA |
| Prices - High | 34 | 18⅞ | 13¾ | 12⅜ | 7¼ | 4⅜ | 1⅞ | NA | NA | NA |
|    - Low | 20⅞ | 12½ | 10½ | 5⅜ | 3¾ | 1⅛ | 1⅛ | NA | NA | NA |
| P/E Ratio - High | 49 | 35 | 36 | 58 | 43 | 39 | 16 | NA | NA | NA |
|    - Low | 30 | 23 | 28 | 25 | 22 | 10 | 10 | NA | NA | NA |

### Income Statement Analysis (Million $)

| | 1996 | 1995 | 1994 | 1993 | 1992 | 1991 | 1990 | 1989 | 1988 | 1987 |
|---|---|---|---|---|---|---|---|---|---|---|
| Revs. | 1,056 | 812 | 565 | 450 | 320 | 226 | 158 | 132 | 105 | 81.0 |
| Oper. Inc. | 95.6 | 72.6 | 52.7 | 33.0 | 24.1 | 17.7 | 16.2 | 14.5 | 11.1 | 7.2 |
| Depr. | 13.7 | 8.1 | 5.0 | 3.7 | 3.2 | 2.6 | 2.3 | 2.1 | 1.0 | 0.8 |
| Int. Exp. | 0.3 | 0.2 | 0.2 | 0.2 | 0.7 | 2.1 | 4.4 | 5.7 | Nil | Nil |
| Pretax Inc. | 89.6 | 72.3 | 52.1 | 32.1 | 22.4 | 13.5 | 10.7 | 7.7 | 11.3 | 7.4 |
| Eff. Tax Rate | 33% | 36% | 39% | 47% | 43% | 42% | 43% | 44% | 36% | 50% |
| Net Inc. | 60.5 | 46.1 | 31.8 | 17.2 | 12.8 | 7.8 | 6.1 | 4.3 | 7.2 | 3.7 |

### Balance Sheet & Other Fin. Data (Million $)

| | 1996 | 1995 | 1994 | 1993 | 1992 | 1991 | 1990 | 1989 | 1988 | 1987 |
|---|---|---|---|---|---|---|---|---|---|---|
| Cash | 44.8 | 47.4 | 48.5 | 30.9 | 12.5 | 0.8 | 1.0 | 0.1 | NA | NA |
| Curr. Assets | 269 | 227 | 172 | 120 | 88.6 | 51.6 | 35.3 | 26.5 | NA | NA |
| Total Assets | 400 | 308 | 227 | 165 | 136 | 96.0 | 78.0 | 71.0 | NA | NA |
| Curr. Liab. | 122 | 99 | 76.7 | 51.4 | 39.1 | 26.1 | 15.1 | 21.1 | NA | NA |
| LT Debt | Nil | Nil | Nil | Nil | Nil | 13.0 | 13.0 | 28.7 | NA | NA |
| Common Eqty. | 275 | 209 | 150 | 113 | 95.1 | 55.0 | 47.9 | 19.0 | NA | NA |
| Total Cap. | 278 | 209 | 151 | 114 | 96.6 | 69.8 | 62.8 | 49.6 | NA | NA |
| Cap. Exp. | 61.6 | 31.3 | 16.1 | 2.8 | 6.4 | 4.2 | 1.6 | 2.3 | 1.0 | 1.7 |
| Cash Flow | 74.2 | 54.2 | 36.8 | 20.8 | 16.0 | 10.4 | 8.4 | 6.2 | NA | NA |
| Curr. Ratio | 2.2 | 2.3 | 2.2 | 2.3 | 2.3 | 2.0 | 2.3 | 1.3 | NA | NA |
| % LT Debt of Cap. | Nil | Nil | Nil | Nil | Nil | 18.6 | 20.7 | 57.9 | NA | NA |
| % Net Inc.of Revs. | 5.7 | 5.7 | 5.6 | 3.8 | 4.0 | 3.4 | 3.9 | 3.3 | 6.9 | 4.6 |
| % Ret. on Assets | 17.1 | 17.2 | 16.0 | 11.4 | 10.5 | 8.8 | 6.7 | NA | NA | NA |
| % Ret. on Equity | 22.9 | 25.7 | 23.9 | 16.5 | 16.4 | 14.8 | 16.1 | NA | NA | NA |

Data as orig. reptd.; bef. results of disc. opers. and/or spec. items. Per share data adj. for stk. divs. as of ex-div. date. E-Estimated. NA-Not Available. NM-Not Meaningful. NR-Not Ranked.

**Office**—879 W. 190th St., 10th Floor, Los Angeles, CA 90248. **Tel**—(310) 225-4500. **Chrmn & CEO**—I. Helford. **Pres & COO**—M. B. Nelson. **EVP, CFO & Investor Contact**—F. R. Jarc. **Secy**—Charlotte Wiethoff. **Dirs**—L. A. Ault III, N. R. Austrian, C. P. Durkin Jr., I. Helford, J. D. Manley, B. Nelson.**Transfer Agent & Registrar**—American Stock Transfer & Trust Co., NYC. **Incorporated**—in California in 1960. **Empl**— 2,826. **S&P Analyst:** Michael V. Pizzi

# Vitalink Pharmacy Services    2398E

NYSE Symbol **VTK**

**17-MAY-97**

**Industry:**
Health Care (Specialized Services)

**Summary:** VTK provides medication, consulting and infusion therapy services to nursing facilities and their patients.

| Quantitative Evaluations | |
|---|---|
| **Outlook** (1 Lowest—5 Highest) | • **5** |
| **Fair Value** | • **31⅛** |
| **Risk** | • **Low** |
| **Earn./Div. Rank** | • **NR** |
| **Technical Eval.** | • **NA** |
| **Rel. Strength Rank** (1 Lowest—99 Highest) | • **25** |
| **Insider Activity** | • **Neutral** |

Recent Price • 18⅞
52 Wk Range • 25-16¼
Yield • Nil
12-Mo. P/E • 17.3

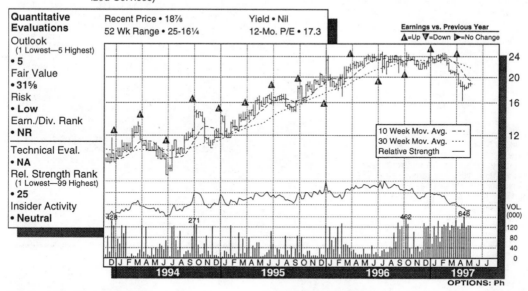

Earnings vs. Previous Year
▲=Up ▼=Down ▶=No Change

10 Week Mov. Avg. - - -
30 Week Mov. Avg. ....
Relative Strength —

OPTIONS: Ph

## Business Profile - 13-MAY-97

In April 1997, Vitalink Pharmacy Services said that about 5,000 new beds have been added since its February 1997 merger with TeamCare. The merger made VTK the second largest, publicly traded institutional pharmacy company, with annual revenues of about $420 million. As of April 1, Vitalink was serving 172,000 beds, up sharply from 54,300 in December 1996. In addition, the company has increased its product and service offerings as a result of the merger. VTK is now offering expanded clinical programs, such as wound care services and a disease state management wellness program. Separately, and also in April, Manor Care, Inc., which already owned about 45% of Vitalink's outstanding common shares. announced its intention to purchase up to 1.5 million additional VTK shares at $20 each. Trading in Vitalink shares shifted to the NYSE from the Nasdaq Stock Market in February 1997.

## Operational Review - 13-MAY-97

Net revenues for the first nine months of FY 97 (May) advanced 49%, year to year, aided by the February 1997 acquisition of TeamCare. Reduced gross margins, TeamCare's historically higher operating expenses as a percentage revenues, and amortization for one month of goodwill related to the TeamCare merger trimmed the gain in operating profit to 28%. After other income and tax items, net income was up 23%, to $0.82 a share on 8.3% more shares, from $0.72.

## Stock Performance - 16-MAY-97

In the past 30 trading days, VTK's shares have declined 0.66%, compared to a 9% rise in the S&P 500. Average trading volume for the past five days was 35,100 shares, compared with the 40-day moving average of 54,618 shares.

## Key Stock Statistics

| | | | |
|---|---|---|---|
| Dividend Rate/Share | Nil | Shareholders | 100 |
| Shs. outstg. (M) | 25.6 | Market cap. (B) | $0.483 |
| Avg. daily vol. (M) | 0.056 | Inst. holdings | 11% |
| Tang. Bk. Value/Share | 3.94 | | |
| Beta | 0.90 | | |

Value of $10,000 invested 5 years ago: NA

### Fiscal Year Ending May 31

| | 1997 | 1996 | 1995 | 1994 | 1993 | 1992 |
|---|---|---|---|---|---|---|
| **Revenues (Million $)** | | | | | | |
| 1Q | 39.37 | 31.82 | 26.91 | 22.36 | 12.30 | 8.70 |
| 2Q | 43.35 | 34.00 | 27.45 | 24.44 | 13.80 | 9.50 |
| 3Q | 69.77 | 36.50 | 28.79 | 25.32 | 19.20 | 10.40 |
| 4Q | — | 38.80 | 29.11 | 26.46 | 20.39 | 11.50 |
| Yr. | — | 141.1 | 112.3 | 98.57 | 65.71 | 40.20 |
| **Earnings Per Share ($)** | | | | | | |
| 1Q | 0.27 | 0.23 | 0.19 | 0.14 | 0.12 | 0.11 |
| 2Q | 0.28 | 0.24 | 0.20 | 0.17 | 0.12 | 0.12 |
| 3Q | 0.27 | 0.25 | 0.22 | 0.17 | 0.14 | 0.12 |
| 4Q | — | 0.27 | 0.22 | 0.18 | 0.15 | 0.11 |
| Yr. | — | 0.99 | 0.84 | 0.66 | 0.53 | 0.46 |

**Next earnings report expected: late June**

### Dividend Data

No dividends have been paid. The company does not expect to pay cash dividends in the foreseeable future, as it plans to retain earnings to finance operations and expansion.

This report is for information purposes and should not be considered a solicitation to buy or sell any security. Neither S&P nor any other party guarantee its accuracy or make warranties regarding results from its usage. Redistribution is prohibited without written permission. Copyright © 1997

A Division of The McGraw·Hill Companies

STANDARD
&POOR'S
STOCK REPORTS

# Vitalink Pharmacy Services, Inc.

## 2398E
### 17-MAY-97

## Business Summary - 13-MAY-97

Vitalink Pharmacy Services operates institutional pharmacies that specialize in pharmaceutical dispensing of individual medications, pharmacy consulting (drug regimen review for potential medication interaction, as well as regulatory compliance with medication and administration guidelines) and infusion therapy products and services.

Until recently, the company was an 82%-owned subsidiary of Manor Care, Inc., the third largest U.S. provider of long-term care services (in terms of number of beds). Vitalink has grown rapidly and profitably by entering new markets with clusters of Manor Care facilities and assuming service to those nursing facilities. About 48% of FY 96 (May) sales were made to Manor Care and its patients.

As of December 1996, Vitalink was servicing 54,300 beds through 23 institutional pharmacies and four regional infusion pharmacies. The company services each market in which it operates through a hub pharmacy or a satellite pharmacy. A market consists of nursing facilities within a 150-mile radius. Vitalink's growth strategy includes continued penetration of existing markets, expansion into additional markets in which there is a sufficient base of Manor Care beds to support a pharmacy, infusion therapy revenue generation created by targeting specific nursing facilities and home healthcare

agencies and acquisitions of pharmacies in existing or new markets.

The company's infusion therapy services include: preparing the product (nutrient, antibiotic, chemotherapy or other drugs or fluids), delivering the product and training others in administering the therapy (via tube, catheter or intravenously).

In July 1996, Vitalink acquired Medisco Pharmacies Inc., a provider of pharmacy and infusion services and medical supplies, for $5,291,000 in cash, $2,510,000 in assumed debt and future payments totaling $1,150,000. Medisco had revenues of $10 million for the 12 months ended June 30, 1996.

On February 13, 1997, Vitalink's common shares were listed on the New York Stock Exchange. Previously, the shares traded on the Nasdaq Stock Market.

In February 1997, Vitalink acquired GranCare, Inc.'s pharmacy subsidiary, TeamCare, for 11.6 million common shares, the redemption of $98 million of 9.375% senior subordinated notes, and assumption of $10 million of debt. The acquisition made VTK the second largest, publicly traded institutional pharmacy company, serving about 167,000 beds through 56 pharmacy locations with annual revenues of about $420 million.

### Capitalization

**Long Term Debt:** $105,832,000 (2/97).

### Per Share Data ($)

| (Year Ended May 31) | 1996 | 1995 | 1994 | 1993 | 1992 | 1991 | 1990 | 1989 | 1988 | 1987 |
|---|---|---|---|---|---|---|---|---|---|---|
| Tangible Bk. Val. | 3.94 | 3.16 | 2.40 | 2.25 | 3.14 | 2.84 | NA | NA | NA | NA |
| Cash Flow | 1.30 | 1.11 | 0.90 | 0.65 | 0.50 | 0.35 | NA | NA | NA | NA |
| Earnings | 0.99 | 0.84 | 0.66 | 0.53 | 0.46 | 0.31 | NA | NA | NA | NA |
| Dividends | Nil | Nil | Nil | Nil | Nil | Nil | NA | NA | NA | NA |
| Payout Ratio | Nil | Nil | Nil | Nil | Nil | Nil | NA | NA | NA | NA |
| Cal. Yrs. | 1995 | 1994 | 1993 | 1992 | 1991 | 1990 | 1989 | 1988 | 1987 | 1986 |
| Prices - High | 25⅜ | 15½ | 13¼ | 18 | NA | NA | NA | NA | NA | NA |
|   - Low | 11¾ | 8½ | 7½ | 10¼ | NA | NA | NA | NA | NA | NA |
| P/E Ratio - High | 26 | 18 | 20 | 34 | NA | NA | NA | NA | NA | NA |
|   - Low | 12 | 10 | 11 | 19 | NA | NA | NA | NA | NA | NA |

### Income Statement Analysis (Million $)

| | 1996 | 1995 | 1994 | 1993 | 1992 | 1991 | 1990 | 1989 | 1988 | 1987 |
|---|---|---|---|---|---|---|---|---|---|---|
| Revs. | 141 | 112 | 99 | 65.7 | 40.2 | 27.3 | 18.4 | 11.5 | 8.6 | 8.4 |
| Oper. Inc. | 27.0 | 22.0 | 18.0 | 13.0 | 9.2 | 6.2 | 4.2 | 2.0 | 1.5 | 2.0 |
| Depr. | 4.4 | 3.8 | 3.4 | 1.7 | 0.6 | 0.4 | 0.2 | 0.2 | 0.1 | 0.1 |
| Int. Exp. | 0.1 | 0.1 | 0.2 | 0.0 | 0.4 | Nil | Nil | Nil | Nil | Nil |
| Pretax Inc. | 23.3 | 19.6 | 15.5 | 12.2 | 9.0 | 6.2 | 4.3 | 2.0 | 1.5 | 2.0 |
| Eff. Tax Rate | 40% | 40% | 41% | 40% | 39% | 39% | 39% | 39% | 40% | 50% |
| Net Inc. | 13.9 | 11.7 | 9.2 | 7.3 | 5.5 | 3.8 | 2.7 | 1.3 | 0.9 | 1.0 |

### Balance Sheet & Other Fin. Data (Million $)

| | 1996 | 1995 | 1994 | 1993 | 1992 | 1991 | 1990 | 1989 | 1988 | 1987 |
|---|---|---|---|---|---|---|---|---|---|---|
| Cash | 0.9 | 0.2 | 0.6 | 0.4 | 0.3 | 0.1 | 0.1 | NA | NA | NA |
| Curr. Assets | 30.0 | 21.7 | 20.4 | 14.4 | 6.7 | 4.8 | 3.5 | NA | NA | NA |
| Total Assets | 96.0 | 80.7 | 69.6 | 57.4 | 47.0 | 14.0 | 10.1 | 7.0 | 5.3 | 4.3 |
| Curr. Liab. | 7.0 | 6.5 | 6.3 | 4.4 | 2.9 | 1.5 | 1.3 | NA | NA | NA |
| LT Debt | 2.6 | 1.8 | Nil | Nil | Nil | Nil | Nil | Nil | Nil | Nil |
| Common Eqty. | 86.3 | 72.3 | 60.7 | 51.5 | 44.2 | 12.5 | 8.8 | 6.1 | 4.9 | 3.9 |
| Total Cap. | 88.9 | 74.1 | 60.7 | 51.5 | 44.2 | 12.5 | 8.8 | 6.1 | 4.9 | 3.9 |
| Cap. Exp. | 3.5 | 2.2 | 1.6 | 1.5 | 1.4 | 1.2 | 0.7 | 0.3 | NA | NA |
| Cash Flow | 18.2 | 15.4 | 12.6 | 9.0 | 6.1 | 4.2 | 2.9 | 1.4 | 1.0 | 1.1 |
| Curr. Ratio | 4.3 | 3.3 | 3.2 | 3.2 | 2.3 | 3.3 | 2.7 | NA | NA | NA |
| % LT Debt of Cap. | 2.9 | 2.4 | Nil | Nil | Nil | Nil | Nil | Nil | Nil | Nil |
| % Net Inc.of Revs. | 9.8 | 10.4 | 9.3 | 11.2 | 13.7 | 13.8 | 14.5 | 10.8 | 10.8 | 11.7 |
| % Ret. on Assets | 15.7 | 15.6 | 13.8 | 14.1 | 17.2 | 31.4 | 31.1 | 20.4 | 19.3 | 22.8 |
| % Ret. on Equity | 17.5 | 17.5 | 16.4 | 15.3 | 18.5 | 35.4 | 35.9 | 22.7 | 21.1 | 25.0 |

Data as orig. reptd.; bef. results of disc. opers. and/or spec. items. Per share data adj. for stk. divs. as of ex-div. date. E-Estimated. NA-Not Available. NM-Not Meaningful. NR-Not Ranked.

**Office**—1250 E. Diehl Rd., Suite 208, Naperville, IL 60563. **Tel**—(708) 505-1320. **Chrmn & CEO**—D. C. Tomasso. **Vice Chrmn**—S. Bainum Jr. **Pres & COO**—D. L. DeNardo. **VP-Fin, CFO & Investor Contact**—Scott T. Macomber. **VP-Secy**—R. W. Horner, III, . **Dirs**—S. Bainum Jr., H. Blumenkrantz, J. R. Buckley, D. L. DeNardo, A. K. Gupta, J. A. MacCutcheon, J. H. Rempe, D. C. Tomasso, M. Wilensky. **Transfer Agent & Registrar**—ChaseMellon Shareholder Services, NYC. **Incorporated**—in Delaware in 1967. **Empl**— 945. **S&P Analyst:** N. J. DeVita

**17-MAY-97**

**Industry:**
Health Care (Drugs - Generic & Other)

**Summary:** Watson manufactures and sells off-patent medications and develops advanced drug delivery systems designed primarily to enhance the therapeutic benefits of pharmaceutical compounds.

## Quantitative Evaluations

**Outlook**
(1 Lowest—5 Highest)
• **5**

**Fair Value**
• **44⅜**

**Risk**
• **Average**

**Earn./Div. Rank**
• **NR**

**Technical Eval.**
• **Bearish** since 3/97

**Rel. Strength Rank**
(1 Lowest—99 Highest)
• **24**

**Insider Activity**
• **Neutral**

Recent Price • 35¼
52 Wk Range • 46⅛-26

Yield • Nil
12-Mo. P/E • 19.2

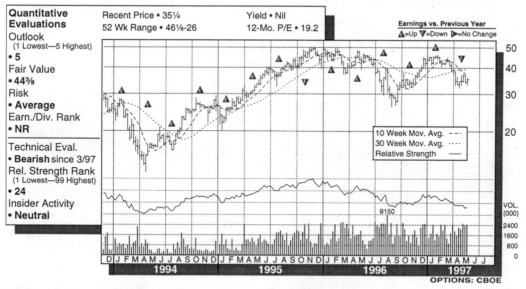

Earnings vs. Previous Year
▲=Up ▼=Down ▶=No Change

10 Week Mov. Avg.
30 Week Mov. Avg.
Relative Strength

VOL. (000)

OPTIONS: CBOE

## Business Profile - 13-MAY-97

Fueled by the company's pipeline of generic products and an aggressive expansion program, Watson's earnings have grown dramatically in recent years. In February 1997, WATS completed the purchase of Oclassen Pharmaceuticals, a specialty pharmaceutical company focused on the dermatology market, and in April 1997, it acquired Royce Laboratories. FDA product approvals in the first quarter of 1997 included NORCO for the relief of moderate to severe pain and Condylox Gel for the treatment of genital and perianal warts. Watson received its first NDA product approval, for Microzide (for mild to moderate hypertension), in December 1996.

## Operational Review - 13-MAY-97

Revenues in the three months ended March 31, 1997, advanced 14%, year to year, due to strong demand for core products and the initiation of sales for proprietary products Microzide and NORCO. Margins widened, reflecting a more favorable product mix and well controlled costs. Following an $8.9 million charge in the current period for costs related to the Oclassen acquisition, operating income fell 16%, to $16,636,000, from $19,764,000. After taxes at 40.0%, versus 28.8%, net income decreased 23%, to $14,546,000 ($0.35 a share), from $18,908,000 ($0.46, as restated). Excluding merger related expenses, net income in the first quarter of 1997 was $21,882,000 ($0.53).

## Stock Performance - 16-MAY-97

In the past 30 trading days, WATS's shares have increased 2%, compared to a 9% rise in the S&P 500. Average trading volume for the past five days was 548,580 shares, compared with the 40-day moving average of 488,749 shares.

## Key Stock Statistics

| | | | |
|---|---|---|---|
| Dividend Rate/Share | Nil | Shareholders | 1,900 |
| Shs. outstg. (M) | 43.2 | Market cap. (B) | $ 1.5 |
| Avg. daily vol. (M) | 0.529 | Inst. holdings | 56% |
| Tang. Bk. Value/Share | 10.39 | | |
| Beta | NA | | |

Value of $10,000 invested 5 years ago: NA

### Fiscal Year Ending Dec. 31

| | 1997 | 1996 | 1995 | 1994 | 1993 | 1992 |
|---|---|---|---|---|---|---|
| **Revenues (Million $)** | | | | | | |
| 1Q | 61.11 | 45.54 | 34.13 | 19.32 | 14.70 | 7.60 |
| 2Q | — | 47.61 | 36.99 | 21.03 | 16.34 | 7.70 |
| 3Q | — | 48.87 | 38.52 | 22.50 | 18.03 | 7.50 |
| 4Q | — | 52.10 | 43.30 | 24.21 | 18.45 | 11.90 |
| Yr. | — | 194.1 | 152.9 | 87.06 | 67.55 | 34.70 |
| **Earnings Per Share ($)** | | | | | | |
| 1Q | 0.35 | 0.45 | 0.33 | 0.23 | 0.15 | 0.04 |
| 2Q | — | 0.48 | 0.36 | 0.25 | 0.18 | 0.03 |
| 3Q | — | 0.50 | 0.14 | 0.27 | 0.19 | 0.05 |
| 4Q | — | 0.52 | 0.45 | 0.30 | 0.21 | 0.14 |
| Yr. | — | 1.95 | 1.29 | 1.05 | 0.74 | 0.26 |

Next earnings report expected: late July

## Dividend Data

No cash dividends have been paid, and none are anticipated in the foreseeable future.

This report is for information purposes and should not be considered a solicitation to buy or sell any security. Neither S&P nor any other party guarantee its accuracy or make warranties regarding results from its usage. Redistribution is prohibited without written permission. Copyright © 1997

*A Division of The McGraw·Hill Companies*

## Business Summary - 13-MAY-97

Watson Pharmaceuticals manufactures and sells off-patent (generic) pharmaceuticals and develops advanced drug delivery systems designed primarily to enhance the therapeutic benefits of pharmaceutical compounds.

The company pursues a balanced strategy of generating revenue through its long-established off-patent pharmaceutical business, to support the development of off-patent and proprietary products. The company targets difficult-to-produce niche off-patent pharmaceuticals to minimize competition with traditional commodity-oriented generic drug companies. For 1995 and 1996, sales of off-patent products accounted for approximately 86% of total revenues. Watson regularly reviews potential opportunities to acquire or invest in technologies, products or product rights and businesses compatible with its existing business.

The company currently manufactures and markets 29 off-patent products in 77 dosage strengths, and two branded products, Microzide and Norco. As of February 28, 1997, Watson had eight abbreviated new drug applications (ANDAs) representing six drugs pending before the FDA and several ethical drugs under development. Therapeutic products include anti-depressants, tranquilizers, anti-hypertensives, diuretics, oral contraceptives, anti-inflammatories and analgesics, as well as hormone replacement, asthma, anti-spasmodic and anti-diarrheal drugs. WATS has also developed proprietary drug delivery systems for various routes of administration, including transmucosal, oral, vaginal and transdermal, permitting defined adjustment of release rates.

Watson has made substantial investments in pharmaceutical joint ventures and plans to continue this type of investment in the future. The company owns a 50% interest in the outstanding common stock of Somerset Pharmaceuticals, which manufactures and markets the product Eldepryl for the treatment of Parkinson's disease. In 1989, the company and Rhone-Poulenc Rorer formed a partnership to develop and market Dilacor XR, used for the treatment of hypertension and angina. Royalty income from sales of Dilacor XR accounted for 14% of total revenues in 1995 and 1996.

Wholly-owned Oclassen Pharmaceuticals Inc. develops specialty prescription pharmaceuticals to prevent and treat skin diseases, and markets these products to dermatologists. Currently marketed products include Condylox Topical Solution for the treatment of external genital warts, Monodox for the treatment of acne, Cinobac for the treatment of urinary tract infections, and the topical steroids Cormax and Cordran, for the treatment of skin inflammation.

Recently acquired Royce Laboratories Inc. is an off-patent pharmaceutical company with approximately $23 million in sales for 1996. The acquisition of Royce provides Watson with an expanded product offering and a rich product development pipeline.

## Capitalization

**Long Term Liabs.:** $24,281,000 (3/97).

### Per Share Data ($)

| (Year Ended Dec. 31) | 1996 | 1995 | 1994 | 1993 | 1992 | 1991 | 1990 | 1989 | 1988 | 1987 |
|---|---|---|---|---|---|---|---|---|---|---|
| Tangible Bk. Val. | 10.39 | 7.95 | 6.50 | 5.41 | 2.97 | 1.24 | 0.97 | 0.81 | NA | NA |
| Cash Flow | 2.11 | 1.43 | 1.22 | 0.87 | 0.38 | 0.21 | 0.17 | NA | NA | NA |
| Earnings | 1.95 | 1.29 | 1.05 | 0.74 | 0.26 | 0.12 | 0.09 | 0.10 | 0.02 | NA |
| Dividends | Nil | Nil | Nil | Nil | Nil | Nil | Nil | Nil | Nil | NA |
| Payout Ratio | Nil | Nil | Nil | Nil | Nil | Nil | Nil | Nil | Nil | NA |
| Prices - High | 49½ | 50½ | 29½ | 38½ | NA | NA | NA | NA | NA | NA |
| - Low | 26 | 20 | 12¾ | 12 | NA | NA | NA | NA | NA | NA |
| P/E Ratio - High | 25 | 39 | 28 | 52 | NA | NA | NA | NA | NA | NA |
| - Low | 13 | 16 | 12 | 16 | NA | NA | NA | NA | NA | NA |

### Income Statement Analysis (Million $)

| | 1996 | 1995 | 1994 | 1993 | 1992 | 1991 | 1990 | 1989 | 1988 | 1987 |
|---|---|---|---|---|---|---|---|---|---|---|
| Revs. | 194 | 153 | 87.1 | 67.5 | 34.7 | 29.5 | 23.4 | 20.9 | 13.2 | NA |
| Oper. Inc. | 89.0 | 57.6 | 31.9 | 21.9 | 8.0 | 4.4 | 3.2 | NA | NA | NA |
| Depr. | 6.3 | 5.2 | 3.0 | 2.2 | 1.6 | 1.3 | 1.0 | NA | NA | NA |
| Int. Exp. | Nil | Nil | 0.5 | 0.4 | 0.4 | 0.4 | 0.6 | 0.6 | 0.4 | NA |
| Pretax Inc. | 109 | 72.8 | 30.0 | 20.1 | 6.0 | 2.9 | 1.8 | 1.8 | 0.4 | NA |
| Eff. Tax Rate | 33% | 34% | 38% | 39% | 40% | 46% | 31% | 29% | 42% | NA |
| Net Inc. | 73.3 | 47.9 | 18.7 | 12.2 | 3.6 | 1.6 | 1.2 | 1.3 | 0.3 | NA |

### Balance Sheet & Other Fin. Data (Million $)

| | 1996 | 1995 | 1994 | 1993 | 1992 | 1991 | 1990 | 1989 | 1988 | 1987 |
|---|---|---|---|---|---|---|---|---|---|---|
| Cash | 211 | 122 | 56.5 | 56.4 | 0.2 | 1.4 | 0.5 | 0.7 | 0.4 | NA |
| Curr. Assets | 280 | 198 | 87.1 | 78.7 | 16.0 | 12.5 | NA | NA | NA | NA |
| Total Assets | 420 | 322 | 130 | 105 | 31.2 | 23.9 | 18.9 | 18.4 | 14.8 | NA |
| Curr. Liab. | 21.4 | 29.0 | 12.0 | 10.1 | 7.4 | 5.2 | NA | NA | NA | NA |
| LT Debt | 2.9 | 3.6 | 5.1 | 12.1 | 4.0 | 2.7 | 3.0 | 2.9 | 2.4 | NA |
| Common Eqty. | 383 | 289 | 111 | 91.2 | 19.8 | 16.0 | 11.8 | 9.4 | 8.1 | NA |
| Total Cap. | 398 | 293 | 118 | 105 | 23.8 | 18.7 | 14.8 | 12.4 | 10.5 | NA |
| Cap. Exp. | 10.2 | 22.5 | 20.0 | 12.8 | 5.6 | 3.8 | 2.0 | NA | NA | NA |
| Cash Flow | 79.5 | 53.1 | 21.7 | 14.4 | 5.2 | 2.8 | 2.3 | NA | NA | NA |
| Curr. Ratio | 13.1 | 6.8 | 7.2 | 7.8 | 2.1 | 2.4 | NA | NA | NA | NA |
| % LT Debt of Cap. | 0.1 | 1.2 | 4.3 | 11.6 | 16.8 | 14.6 | 20.5 | 23.7 | 22.5 | NA |
| % Net Inc.of Revs. | 37.8 | 31.3 | 21.5 | 18.1 | 10.4 | 5.3 | 5.2 | 6.0 | 2.0 | NA |
| % Ret. on Assets | 19.8 | 16.4 | 15.9 | 18.0 | 12.8 | 7.3 | 6.5 | 7.5 | 2.6 | NA |
| % Ret. on Equity | 21.8 | 18.7 | 18.5 | 22.0 | 20.4 | 11.2 | 11.1 | 14.7 | 3.2 | NA |

Data as orig. reptd.; bef. results of disc. opers. and/or spec. items. Per share data adj. for stk. divs. as of ex-div. date. E-Estimated. NA-Not Available. NM-Not Meaningful. NR-Not Ranked.

**Office**—311 Bonnie Circle, Corona, CA 91720. **Tel**—(909) 270-1400. **Chrmn & CEO**—A. Y. Chao. **Pres**—M. Sharoky. **CFO**—C. Abad. **Secy**—M. J. Feldman. **Dirs**—A. Y. Chao, M. Fedida, M. J. Feldman, A. F. Hummel, A. D. Keith, M. Sharoky, R. R. Taylor. **Transfer Agent & Registrar**—ChaseMellon Shareholder Services, Los Angeles. **Incorporated**—in Nevada in 1985. **Empl**— 621. **S&P Analyst:** Richard Joy

# STANDARD &POOR'S
STOCK REPORTS

# Xilinx, Inc.

## 5672L

Nasdaq Symbol **XLNX**

**In S&P MidCap 400**

**17-MAY-97**

**Industry:**
Electronics (Semiconductors)

**Summary:** Xilinx is the world's leading supplier of programmable logic and related development system software.

| S&P Opinion: Hold (★★★) | | |
|---|---|---|
| Recent Price • 53¼ | Yield • Nil | |
| 52 Wk Range • 58½-24½ | 12-Mo. P/E • 38.3 | |

**Quantitative Evaluations**

**Outlook**
(1 Lowest—5 Highest)
• **3⁻**

**Fair Value**
• **57½**

**Risk**
• **High**

**Earn./Div. Rank**
• **B+**

**Technical Eval.**
• **Bullish** since 8/96

**Rel. Strength Rank**
(1 Lowest—99 Highest)
• **84**

**Insider Activity**
• **Neutral**

**Earnings vs. Previous Year**
▲=Up ▼=Down ▶=No Change

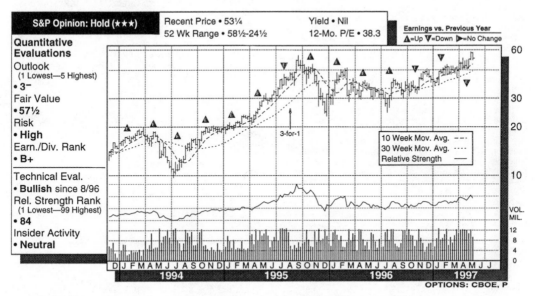

10 Week Mov. Avg. – – –
30 Week Mov. Avg. · · · ·
Relative Strength ——

3-for-1

VOL. MIL.

OPTIONS: CBOE, P

## Overview - 14-MAY-97

Due to the surprising strength of the company's most recent earnings, we have raised our revenue and EPS estimates for FY 98 (Mar.). Revenues are expected to advance approximately 25% to 30%, with growth returning to historical norms, as the industry-wide inventory correction that restricted results in FY 97 has been completed. Gains will accelerate in the second half of the year, led by the company's flagship XC 4000 line of programmable integrated circuits. We are encouraged by the record number of software seats sold in the fourth quarter of FY 97. XLNX's software is used to program the company's chips. The high-level of software purchases alleviates recent fears that XLNX would continue to lose market share to Altera Corp. Despite recent price cuts, gross margins should remain in the 60% to 62% range; XLNX is basically passing production cost savings to customers. Well controlled SG&A expenses will also aid profitability. Overall, we see EPS advancing to $1.80 in FY 98.

## Valuation - 14-MAY-97

Despite our higher EPS estimate, we don't recommend investors add to their positions at this time. The shares are trading at over 30X our FY 98 estimate, representing the high-end of the company's historical P/E range. We believe that the strong earnings gains expected in FY 98 are already reflected in the price of the stock. Xilinx remains a good holding for long-term investors seeking above average capital gains, and willing to tolerate volatile price swings. The company will benefit from strong demand for field programmable gate arrays (FPGAs) and complex programmable logic devices (CPLDs), which are expected to grow 25% to 30% annually.

## Key Stock Statistics

| | | | |
|---|---|---|---|
| S&P EPS Est. 1998 | 1.80 | Tang. Bk. Value/Share | 6.30 |
| P/E on S&P Est. 1998 | 29.6 | Beta | 1.95 |
| Dividend Rate/Share | Nil | Shareholders | 700 |
| Shs. outstg. (M) | 73.0 | Market cap. (B) | $ 3.9 |
| Avg. daily vol. (M) | 2.220 | Inst. holdings | 77% |

Value of $10,000 invested 5 years ago: $ 61,442

### Fiscal Year Ending Mar. 31

| | 1998 | 1997 | 1996 | 1995 | 1994 | 1993 |
|---|---|---|---|---|---|---|
| **Revenues (Million $)** | | | | | | |
| 1Q | — | 150.2 | 125.8 | 75.15 | 54.43 | 39.00 |
| 2Q | — | 130.6 | 141.2 | 79.51 | 60.07 | 42.50 |
| 3Q | — | 135.6 | 144.1 | 91.28 | 66.50 | 46.20 |
| 4Q | — | 151.8 | 149.7 | 109.2 | 75.44 | 50.20 |
| Yr. | — | 568.1 | 560.8 | 355.1 | 256.5 | 178.0 |
| **Earnings Per Share ($)** | | | | | | |
| 1Q | E0.41 | 0.41 | 0.07 | 0.16 | 0.12 | 0.08 |
| 2Q | E0.42 | 0.27 | 0.37 | 0.16 | 0.13 | 0.09 |
| 3Q | E0.46 | 0.33 | 0.41 | 0.21 | 0.15 | 0.10 |
| 4Q | E0.51 | 0.38 | 0.43 | 0.26 | 0.17 | 0.11 |
| Yr. | E1.80 | 1.39 | 1.28 | 0.80 | 0.57 | 0.38 |

**Next earnings report expected: mid July**

## Dividend Data

No cash dividends have been paid, and Xilinx does not expect to pay any in the foreseeable future. A three-for-one stock split was effected in August 1995.

This report is for information purposes and should not be considered a solicitation to buy or sell any security. Neither S&P nor any other party guarantee its accuracy or make warranties regarding results from its usage. Redistribution is prohibited without written permission. Copyright © 1997

*A Division of The* **McGraw·Hill** *Companies*

STANDARD
&POOR'S
STOCK REPORTS

# Xilinx, Inc.

# 5672L
17-MAY-97

## Business Summary - 14-MAY-97

Xilinx, Inc. is the leading supplier of field programmable gate arrays (FPGAs) and related development system software. Xilinx products are standard integrated circuits that are programmed by Xilinx customers to perform desired logic operations. These products provide high levels of integration and significant time and cost savings for electronic equipment manufacturers in the computer peripherals, telecommunications, industrial control and instrumentation and military markets.

FPGAs accounted for 97% and 96% of total revenues in FY 96 (Mar.) and FY 95, respectively. Development and system software sales made up the remaining revenues. Non-U.S. revenues were 35% of total revenues in FY 96, up from 31% in FY 95.

The company's FPGAs are proprietary integrated circuits designed by Xilinx; they provide a unique combination of the high logic density usually associated with custom gate arrays, the time-to-market advantages of programmable logic and the availability of a standard product. The company offers several families of FPGAs, ranging from 500 to 28,000 usable gates. The new XC4000EX family will offer densities up to 125,000 usable gates.

To implement the FPGA solution, system designers use proprietary Xilinx development system software, together with industry standard CAE software, to develop FPGA applications. At the end of FY 96, Xilinx had shipped approximately 26,700 development systems, as compared to 21,000 at the end of FY 95. The company's product line was expanded in April 1995 with the $35 million acquisition of NeoCAD, a private concern offering FPGA software design tools for programmable electronic technologies.

Xilinx is actively pursuing a strategy of broadening the markets it serves through the enhancement of software development tools, the introduction of architectures offering new functionality, and the reduction of semiconductor prices through continuous advancements in the manufacturing process.

## Important Developments

**Apr. '97**—In reporting results for the fourth quarter of FY 97, XLNX stated that while backlog was increasing, it is still dependent on orders received and shipped in the same quarter to achieve revenue growth. Furthermore, XLNX said FY 98 will see the return of the traditional seasonality in the business, with a relatively weak second quarter, and strong third and fourth quarters.

## Capitalization

**Long Term Debt:** $250,000,000 of conv. sub. debs. (3/97).

### Per Share Data ($)

| (Year Ended Mar. 31) | 1997 | 1996 | 1995 | 1994 | 1993 | 1992 | 1991 | 1990 | 1989 | 1988 |
|---|---|---|---|---|---|---|---|---|---|---|
| Tangible Bk. Val. | NA | 5.12 | 3.47 | 2.52 | 1.83 | 1.58 | 1.23 | 0.00 | NA | NA |
| Cash Flow | NA | 1.57 | 0.97 | 0.72 | 0.51 | 0.37 | 0.28 | 0.13 | 0.08 | -0.02 |
| Earnings | 1.39 | 1.28 | 0.80 | 0.57 | 0.38 | 0.30 | 0.23 | 0.11 | 0.06 | -0.03 |
| Dividends | Nil | Nil | Nil | Nil | Nil | Nil | Nil | Nil | Nil | Nil |
| Payout Ratio | Nil | Nil | Nil | Nil | Nil | Nil | Nil | Nil | Nil | Nil |
| Cal. Yrs. | 1996 | 1995 | 1994 | 1993 | 1992 | 1991 | 1990 | 1989 | 1988 | 1987 |
| Prices - High | 46½ | 55½ | 20⅝ | 18⅛ | 10⅜ | 10⅞ | 5⅝ | NA | NA | NA |
| - Low | 24½ | 18⅛ | 9⅝ | 7⅞ | 4⅞ | 4⅛ | 3⅛ | NA | NA | NA |
| P/E Ratio - High | 33 | 43 | 26 | 32 | 27 | 37 | 24 | NA | NA | NA |
| - Low | 18 | 14 | 12 | 14 | 13 | 14 | 14 | NA | NA | NA |

### Income Statement Analysis (Million $)

| | 1997 | 1996 | 1995 | 1994 | 1993 | 1992 | 1991 | 1990 | 1989 | 1988 |
|---|---|---|---|---|---|---|---|---|---|---|
| Revs. | NA | 561 | 355 | 256 | 178 | 136 | 98.0 | 50.0 | 30.0 | 14.0 |
| Oper. Inc. | NA | 208 | 107 | 76.0 | 50.2 | 39.2 | 25.8 | 10.2 | 5.7 | -1.1 |
| Depr. | NA | 22.5 | 12.2 | 10.8 | 8.6 | 5.6 | 3.1 | 1.4 | 1.2 | 0.9 |
| Int. Exp. | NA | 5.6 | 10.3 | 0.5 | 0.7 | 0.6 | 0.6 | 0.3 | 0.3 | 0.2 |
| Pretax Inc. | NA | 171 | 94.8 | 67.4 | 43.6 | 33.8 | 25.7 | 9.4 | 4.9 | -1.7 |
| Eff. Tax Rate | NA | 41% | 38% | 39% | 38% | 37% | 38% | 35% | 40% | Nil |
| Net Inc. | NA | 102 | 59.3 | 41.3 | 27.2 | 21.3 | 15.9 | 6.1 | 2.9 | -1.7 |

### Balance Sheet & Other Fin. Data (Million $)

| | 1997 | 1996 | 1995 | 1994 | 1993 | 1992 | 1991 | 1990 | 1989 | 1988 |
|---|---|---|---|---|---|---|---|---|---|---|
| Cash | NA | 378 | 123 | 116 | 84.8 | 81.3 | 71.8 | 13.1 | 9.5 | NA |
| Curr. Assets | NA | 539 | 256 | 194 | 137 | 121 | 100 | 29.0 | 20.0 | NA |
| Total Assets | NA | 721 | 321 | 226 | 163 | 147 | 112 | 35.0 | 23.0 | 12.0 |
| Curr. Liab. | NA | 103 | 76.1 | 51.1 | 35.7 | 33.0 | 24.6 | 9.8 | 7.3 | NA |
| LT Debt | NA | 250 | 0.9 | 2.2 | 3.9 | 5.0 | 3.8 | 2.0 | 1.7 | 1.3 |
| Common Eqty. | NA | 368 | 244 | 173 | 123 | 109 | 83.0 | 23.0 | 14.0 | 6.0 |
| Total Cap. | NA | 618 | 245 | 175 | 127 | 114 | 87.0 | 25.0 | 16.0 | 7.0 |
| Cap. Exp. | NA | 60.5 | 26.2 | 12.3 | 9.8 | 7.2 | 4.1 | 2.0 | 0.5 | 0.1 |
| Cash Flow | NA | 124 | 71.5 | 52.1 | 35.9 | 26.8 | 19.1 | 7.5 | 4.1 | -0.8 |
| Curr. Ratio | NA | 5.2 | 3.4 | 3.8 | 3.8 | 3.7 | 4.1 | 3.0 | 2.7 | NA |
| % LT Debt of Cap. | NA | 40.4 | 0.4 | 1.3 | 3.1 | 4.4 | 4.4 | 8.0 | 10.7 | 17.5 |
| % Net Inc.of Revs. | NA | 18.1 | 16.7 | 16.0 | 15.3 | 15.7 | 16.3 | 12.2 | 9.6 | NM |
| % Ret. on Assets | NA | 19.5 | 21.5 | 21.0 | 17.6 | 16.4 | 10.8 | 21.2 | 16.9 | NM |
| % Ret. on Equity | NA | 33.1 | 28.2 | 27.0 | 23.5 | 22.0 | 30.1 | 33.2 | 29.2 | NM |

Data as orig. reptd.; bef. results of disc. opers. and/or spec. items. Per share data adj. for stk. divs. as of ex-div. date. E-Estimated. NA-Not Available. NM-Not Meaningful. NR-Not Ranked.

**Office**—2100 Logic Dr., San Jose, CA 95124. **Tel**—(408) 559-7778. **Fax**—(408) 559-7114. **Website**—http://www.xilinx.com **Chrmn**—B. V. Vonderschmitt. **CEO**—W. P. Roelandts. **SVP-Fin & CFO**—G. M. Steel. **Secy**—R. C. Hinckley. **Investor Contact**—Maria Quillard (408-879-4988). **Dirs**—J. L. Doyle, P. T. Gianos, W. G. Howard Jr., W. P. Roelandts, B. V. Vonderschmitt. **Transfer Agent & Registrar**—First National Bank of Boston. **Incorporated**—in Delaware in 1990. **Empl**— 1,201. **S&P Analyst:** Stephen T. Madonna, CFA

# Zebra Technologies

## 5683K

NASDAQ Symbol **ZBRA**

In S&P SmallCap 600

**17-MAY-97**

**Industry:**
Manufacturing (Specialized)

**Summary:** Zebra Technologies is an international provider of demand label printers and supplies for users of automatic identification and data collection systems.

| Quantitative Evaluations | |
|---|---|
| **Outlook** (1 Lowest—5 Highest) | • **4** |
| **Fair Value** | • **32¾** |
| **Risk** | • **High** |
| **Earn./Div. Rank** | • **NR** |
| **Technical Eval.** | • **Bearish** since 4/97 |
| **Rel. Strength Rank** (1 Lowest—99 Highest) | • **94** |
| **Insider Activity** | • **NA** |

Recent Price • 28¼
52 Wk Range • 32¾-15

Yield • Nil
12-Mo. P/E • 19.8

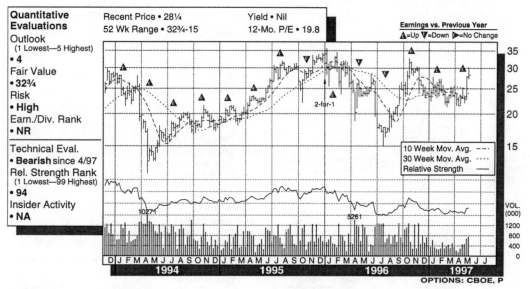

**Earnings vs. Previous Year**
▲=Up ▼=Down ▶=No Change

10 Week Mov. Avg. ---
30 Week Mov. Avg. ····
Relative Strength ——

OPTIONS: CBOE, P

## Business Profile - 12-MAY-97

ZBRA has benefited from escalating demand for bar-code and on-demand labeling applications in the non-retail sector of the world economy. The company seeks to offer customers the most advanced technology in bar-code labeling, and it announced a significant number of product introductions and enhancements in 1996 and continued in 1997's first quarter with the introduction of the A100 printer. Zebra recently announced the formation of the Personal Printer division, a new business unit that focuses on the design, development, manufacture and distribution of low-cost, desktop bar-code printers. In October 1996, the company agreed to merge with Eltron International, a manufacturer of low-cost bar-code laser printers. However, in November, the two companies called off the merger, citing inability to reach mutually agreeable terms.

## Operational Review - 12-MAY-97

Revenues for the three months ended March 31, 1997, rose 11%, year to year, reflecting continued demand for the company's products and new product introductions. Gross margins widened on a more favorable product mix, and with lower operating expenses, the absence of a writeoff related to acquired in-process technology, and a large increase in investment income, net income surged to $11,234,000 ($0.46 a share), from $5,249,000 ($0.22).

## Stock Performance - 16-MAY-97

In the past 30 trading days, ZBRA's shares have increased 24%, compared to a 9% rise in the S&P 500. Average trading volume for the past five days was 147,600 shares, compared with the 40-day moving average of 84,005 shares.

## Key Stock Statistics

| | | | |
|---|---|---|---|
| Dividend Rate/Share | Nil | Shareholders | 600 |
| Shs. outstg. (M) | 24.2 | Market cap. (B) | $0.685 |
| Avg. daily vol. (M) | 0.115 | Inst. holdings | 53% |
| Tang. Bk. Value/Share | 5.79 | | |
| Beta | 0.92 | | |

Value of $10,000 invested 5 years ago: $ 33,731

### Fiscal Year Ending Dec. 31

| | 1997 | 1996 | 1995 | 1994 | 1993 | 1992 |
|---|---|---|---|---|---|---|
| **Revenues (Million $)** | | | | | | |
| 1Q | 42.42 | 38.35 | 34.39 | 21.98 | 19.00 | 13.20 |
| 2Q | — | 40.49 | 35.49 | 25.89 | 21.64 | 14.90 |
| 3Q | — | 43.76 | 37.48 | 28.25 | 23.07 | 14.60 |
| 4Q | — | 47.12 | 41.23 | 30.99 | 23.74 | 15.97 |
| Yr. | — | 169.7 | 148.6 | 107.1 | 87.46 | 58.71 |
| **Earnings Per Share ($)** | | | | | | |
| 1Q | 0.46 | 0.22 | 0.27 | 0.17 | 0.15 | 0.09 |
| 2Q | — | 0.26 | 0.29 | 0.21 | 0.18 | 0.13 |
| 3Q | — | 0.36 | 0.04 | 0.24 | 0.22 | 0.13 |
| 4Q | — | 0.36 | 0.33 | 0.25 | 0.22 | 0.14 |
| Yr. | — | 1.19 | 0.94 | 0.87 | 0.76 | 0.50 |

Next earnings report expected: mid July

## Dividend Data

No cash dividends have been paid. A two-for-one stock split was effected in December 1995.

This report is for information purposes and should not be considered a solicitation to buy or sell any security. Neither S&P nor any other party guarantee its accuracy or make warranties regarding results from its usage. Redistribution is prohibited without written permission. Copyright © 1997 | A Division of The McGraw-Hill Companies

STANDARD
&POOR'S
STOCK REPORTS

# Zebra Technologies Corporation

**5683K**

**17-MAY-97**

## Business Summary - 12-MAY-97

Zebra Technologies Corp. designs, manufactures, sells and supports a broad line of computerized label/ticket printing systems and related specialty supplies. It provides bar-code labeling solutions, primarily to manufacturing customers and also to service and governmental entities worldwide, for use in automatic identification and data collection systems.

Products consist of a broad line of computerized demand bar-code label printers, specialty bar-code labeling/ticketing material (including a variety of adhesives), ink ribbons and PC-based bar-code software. Products are integrated to provide automatic identification labeling solutions for manufacturing, business and industrial applications. Sales of label printing systems provided 72% of revenues in 1996, up from 70% in 1994.

The company manufactures 10 thermal transfer/direct thermal label printing systems, which range in list price from $595 to $7,495. Hundreds of optional configurations can be selected as necessary to meet particular customer needs. As of early 1997, more than 225,000 Zebra bar-code printing systems had been installed at about 22,000 user sites worldwide.

All Zebra printing systems operate using Zebra Programming Language (ZPL), a proprietary printer driver language that was designed by the company and is compatible with virtually all computer operating systems, including UNIX, MS/DOS and Windows. Certain independent software vendors have written label preparation programs with ZPL drivers specifically for Zebra printers. ZPL's label format program can be run on a personal computer with ordinary word processing programs, making it adaptable to PC-based systems.

Zebra also sells related supplies, which include label/ticketing label stock, custom labels and tags, and thermal transfer ribbons. Sales of supplies accounted for about 23% of net sales in 1996, down from 24% in 1995.

Products are sold in the U.S and internationally through multiple distribution channels, including distributors, value-added resellers, original equipment manufacturers and directly through a national account program. Sales to international customers accounted for 44% of revenues in each of the past two years.

In July 1995, the company acquired Vertical Technologies, a software development firm that provides PC-based bar-code labeling, scanning and tracking software for small and medium-size businesses.

### Important Developments

**Mar. '97**—Zebra introduced the Barcode Anything A100 Label Printer, a low cost desktop label design and printing solution for small and medium-sized businesses designed for on-demand printing of product, asset, shipping and mailing labels.

### Capitalization

**Long Term Liabilities:** $2,211,000 (12/96).
**Cl. A Com. Stock:** 16,924,973 shs. ($0.01 par).
**Cl. B Com. Stock:** 7,315,404 shs. ($0.01 par); 10 votes. ea.

### Per Share Data ($)

| (Year Ended Dec. 31) | 1996 | 1995 | 1994 | 1993 | 1992 | 1991 | 1990 | 1989 | 1988 | 1987 |
|---|---|---|---|---|---|---|---|---|---|---|
| Tangible Bk. Val. | 5.79 | 4.47 | 3.41 | 2.53 | 1.76 | 1.28 | 0.59 | NA | NA | NA |
| Cash Flow | 1.35 | 1.03 | 0.93 | 0.80 | 0.53 | 0.50 | 0.53 | NA | NA | NA |
| Earnings | 1.19 | 0.94 | 0.88 | 0.76 | 0.50 | 0.48 | 0.51 | NA | NA | NA |
| Dividends | Nil | Nil | Nil | Nil | Nil | Nil | Nil | NA | NA | NA |
| Payout Ratio | Nil | Nil | Nil | Nil | Nil | Nil | Nil | NA | NA | NA |
| Prices - High | 35¾ | 35¼ | 28⅝ | 30⅜ | 12⅜ | 9½ | NA | NA | NA | NA |
| - Low | 15 | 18 | 11¾ | 10⅛ | 7¼ | 7¼ | NA | NA | NA | NA |
| P/E Ratio - High | 30 | 37 | 33 | 40 | 25 | 20 | NA | NA | NA | NA |
| - Low | 13 | 19 | 13 | 13 | 15 | 15 | NA | NA | NA | NA |

### Income Statement Analysis (Million $)

| | 1996 | 1995 | 1994 | 1993 | 1992 | 1991 | 1990 | 1989 | 1988 | 1987 |
|---|---|---|---|---|---|---|---|---|---|---|
| Revs. | 170 | 149 | 107 | 87.5 | 58.7 | 45.6 | 38.0 | NA | NA | NA |
| Oper. Inc. | 43.5 | 40.8 | 31.7 | 25.9 | 16.2 | 13.2 | 10.9 | NA | NA | NA |
| Depr. | 3.8 | 2.2 | 1.4 | 1.0 | 0.8 | 0.5 | 0.4 | NA | NA | NA |
| Int. Exp. | 0.1 | 0.1 | 0.3 | 0.2 | 0.2 | 0.1 | 0.0 | NA | NA | NA |
| Pretax Inc. | 44.6 | 38.0 | 32.9 | 28.5 | 17.8 | 13.3 | 10.7 | NA | NA | NA |
| Eff. Tax Rate | 35% | 41% | 36% | 36% | 34% | 19% | 1.60% | NA | NA | NA |
| Net Inc. | 28.9 | 22.6 | 21.1 | 18.3 | 11.8 | 10.8 | 10.5 | NA | NA | NA |

### Balance Sheet & Other Fin. Data (Million $)

| | 1996 | 1995 | 1994 | 1993 | 1992 | 1991 | 1990 | 1989 | 1988 | 1987 |
|---|---|---|---|---|---|---|---|---|---|---|
| Cash | 94.5 | 71.9 | 54.2 | 41.5 | 33.7 | 31.2 | 1.0 | NA | NA | NA |
| Curr. Assets | 149 | 119 | 88.7 | 71.5 | 51.4 | 46.8 | 14.2 | NA | NA | NA |
| Total Assets | 163 | 131 | 95.0 | 76.7 | 54.8 | 48.9 | 16.2 | NA | NA | NA |
| Curr. Liab. | 20.2 | 19.0 | 12.4 | 15.5 | 12.0 | 17.1 | 3.8 | NA | NA | NA |
| LT Debt | 2.2 | 2.2 | 0.2 | 0.3 | 0.3 | 0.4 | 0.4 | NA | NA | NA |
| Common Eqty. | 140 | 108 | 82.0 | 60.6 | 42.2 | 30.7 | 11.9 | NA | NA | NA |
| Total Cap. | 143 | 112 | 82.3 | 60.9 | 42.7 | 31.7 | 12.4 | NA | NA | NA |
| Cap. Exp. | 6.0 | 4.3 | 2.1 | 2.5 | 2.2 | 0.7 | 1.0 | NA | NA | NA |
| Cash Flow | 32.8 | 24.8 | 22.5 | 19.3 | 12.7 | 11.3 | 10.9 | NA | NA | NA |
| Curr. Ratio | 7.4 | 6.3 | 7.1 | 4.6 | 4.3 | 2.7 | 3.7 | NA | NA | NA |
| % LT Debt of Cap. | 1.5 | 2.0 | 0.3 | 0.5 | 0.8 | 1.3 | 3.6 | NA | NA | NA |
| % Net Inc.of Revs. | 17.0 | 15.2 | 19.7 | 20.9 | 20.2 | 23.8 | 27.7 | NA | NA | NA |
| % Ret. on Assets | 19.6 | 20.0 | 24.5 | 27.7 | 22.8 | 31.9 | NA | NA | NA | NA |
| % Ret. on Equity | 23.3 | 23.7 | 29.5 | 35.5 | 32.5 | 48.5 | NA | NA | NA | NA |

Data as orig. reptd.; bef. results of disc. opers. and/or spec. items. Per share data adj. for stk. divs. as of ex-div. date. E-Estimated. NA-Not Available. NM-Not Meaningful. NR-Not Ranked.

**Office**—333 Corporate Woods Pkwy., Vernon Hills, IL 60061.**Reincorporated**—in Delaware in 1991. **Tel**—(847) 634-6700. **Fax**—(847) 634-1830. **Website**—http://www.zebra.com **Chrmn & CEO**—E. L. Kaplan. **Pres**—J. K. Clements. **SVP & Secy**—G. Cless. **CFO, Treas & Investor Contact**—Charles R. Whitchurch. **Dirs**—G. Cless, E. L. Kaplan, C. Knowles, D. R. Riley, M. A. Smith. **Transfer Agent & Registrar**—Harris Trust & Savings Bank, Chicago. **Empl**—627. **S&P Analyst:** Ted Groesbeck

To purchase the latest version of any report in this book, for delivery by fax or mail, call:

S&P Reports On-Demand at 1-800-292-0808


To purchase a report from the Internet, visit:

http://www.stockinfo.standardpoor.com.

RODN
ORCL
MCAF
HMA
GE
BEN
DO
CA
CPQ
BTGC
Duke Power